VICTORIA
THE SEDUCTRESS

TO ANNA

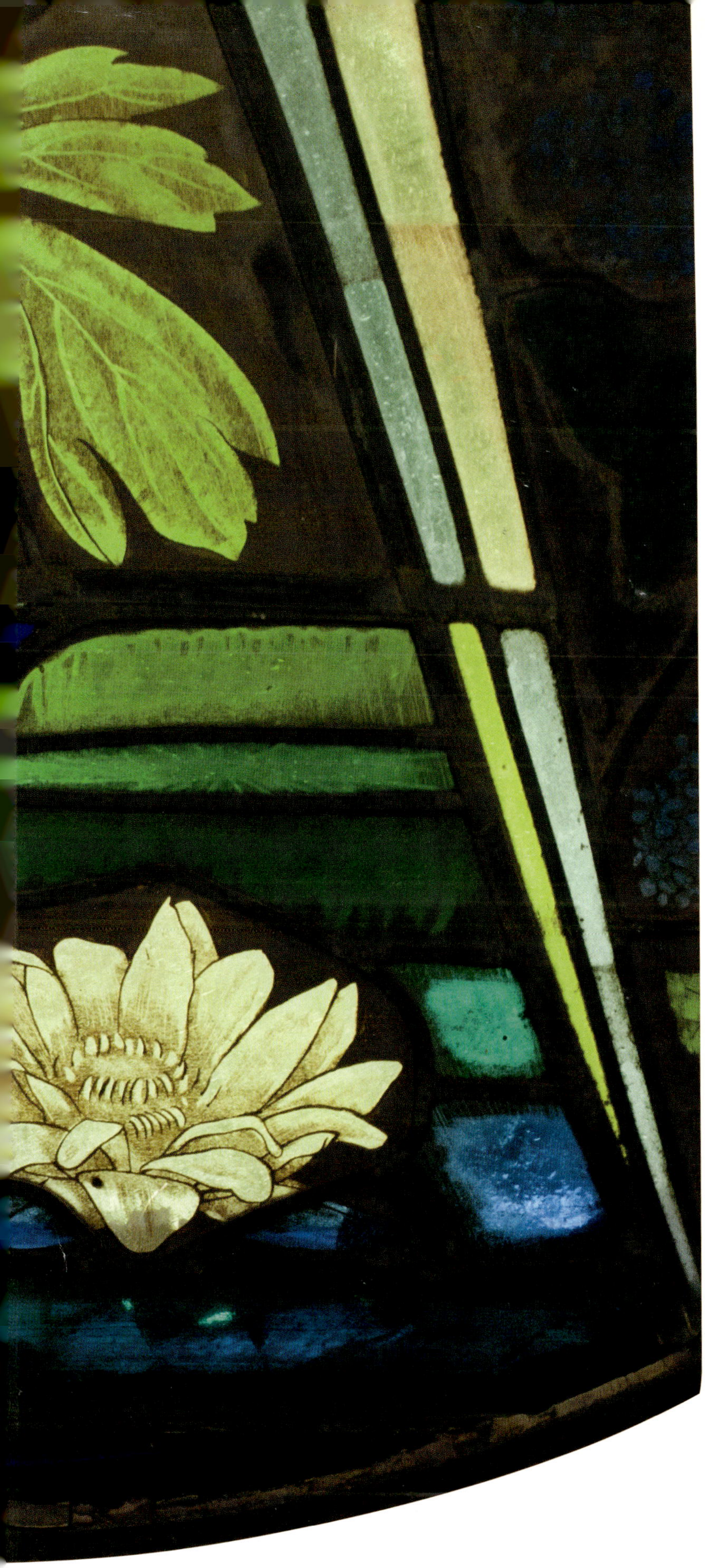

VICTORIA
THE SEDUCTRESS

*A Cultural and Natural History
of the World's Greatest Water Lily*

Tomasz Aniśko

Victoria featured in a stained glass window in a
mausoleum at Villa Taranto in Verbania, Italy.
TOMASZ ANIŚKO / LONGWOOD GARDENS

CONTENTS

Acknowledgments 6

Foreword 9

Chapter 1: ENLIGHTENED BOHEMIAN 11

Chapter 2: EL SABIO, OR THE WISE MAN 27

Chapter 3: NATURALISTE-VOYAGEUR 45

Chapter 4: THE ROMANTIC 57

Chapter 5: SURVEYOR OF EL DORADO 75

Chapter 6: PAPER WARRIOR 91

Chapter 7: KNIGHTED GARDENER 107

Chapter 8: RULE, BRITANNIA! 125

Chapter 9: WORLD CONQUEST 143

Chapter 10: TRUE AMERICAN 169

Chapter 11: TRANSCONTINENTAL 181

Chapter 12: THE BIRTH OF THE HYBRID 201

Chapter 13: LIFE IN CAPTIVITY 221

Chapter 14: THE ORIGIN 243

Chapter 15: A CREATURE OF CONTRADICTIONS 265

Chapter 16: SIZE MATTERS 287

Chapter 17: NIGHTFALL FEVER 313

Chapter 18: QUEEN'S DOMINION 329

Chapter 19: PALACES AND POOLS 355

Chapter 20: INSPIRED ARTS 389

Chapter 21: NYMPHS, GODDESSES, AND THE AMAZONS 415

Chapter 22: PEOPLE'S CHOICE 431

References 454

Index of People and Places 462

Victoria House at the National Botanical Garden of Belgium in Meise.

PAUL BORREMANS / COLLECTION OF THE NATIONAL BOTANIC GARDEN OF BELGIUM

ACKNOWLEDGMENTS

Research for this book began in 2005 with an expedition to Guyana and ended six years later with a trip to the lowlands of Bolivia. This long journey has taken me to places in South America where the giant water lilies were first discovered by European explorers of the nineteenth century: Thaddaeus Haenke in Bolivia, Aimé Bonpland and Alcide d'Orbigny in Argentina, Eduard Pöppig in Brazil, and Robert Schomburgk in Guyana. Visits to gardens, libraries, archives, and herbaria in the United States and across Europe allowed me to travel back in time and provided much of the historical material used in this book. During this thrilling adventure, I have met, corresponded with, and been helped by hundreds of most generous individuals, many of whom I believe have been seduced by the wondrous nymph. Without their support, guidance, and encouragement, this book never could have happened. To all of them, I owe a huge debt of gratitude.

In particular, I would like to thank Elena Arnautova (Komarov Botanical Garden, St. Petersburg), Cécile Aupic (National Museum of Natural History, Paris), Stuart Band (Chatsworth), Manuel Belgrano (Darwinion Institute of Botany, San Isidro), Fiona Bradley (Royal Botanic Gardens, Kew), Vincent Callebaut (Paris), Pascale Chesselet (National Museum of Natural History, Paris), Andrew Colligan (Missouri Botanical Garden, St. Louis), Andreas Daehnick (McKee Botanical Garden, Vero Beach), Denis Diagre (National Botanic Garden of Belgium, Meise), Olga Elina (Moscow), Bruno Erny (Botanical Garden of the University of Basel), Grace Fernandez (Tower Grove Park, St. Louis), Paula Fernandez de los Muros (Fairchild Tropical Botanic Garden, Coral Gables), Liz Fetchin (Phipps Conservatory and Botanical Gardens, Pittsburgh), Martin Freiberg (Botanical Garden of the University of Leipzig), Stephen Forbes (Botanic Gardens of Adelaide), Céline Froissart (Botanical Garden of the University of Strasbourg), Roberta Gallina (Villa Taranto Botanical Garden, Pallanza), Maria Gandolfo (Cornell University, Ithaca), Piotr Gawlak (Adam Mickewicz University Botanical Garden, Poznań), Gustavo Giberti (Juan A. Domínguez Pharmacological Museum, Buenos Aires), Don Goodman (Kanapaha Botanical Gardens, Gainesville), Edwin Harvey (Corrientes), Yvette Harvey (Royal Botanic Gardens, Kew), Reinout Havinga (Amsterdam Botanical Garden), Dirk Herkert (Wilhelma, Stuttgart), Oliver Hermann (Botanical Garden and Botanical Museum, Berlin-Dahlem), Stephen Hirt

Author and Patrick Nutt in Guyana in 2005.
Tomasz Aniśko / Longwood Gardens

(San Francisco), Matthias Hoffmann (Botanical Garden of Martin Luther University of Halle-Wittenberg), Pierre Ibisch (University of Applied Sciences, Eberswalde), John Wayne Jackson (Scottsdale), Otsuka Junichi (Kakegawa Kachoen), Leo Junikka (Botanical Garden and Herbarium of the University of Helsinki), Tony Kanellos (Botanic Gardens of Adelaide), Nura Abdul Karim (Singapore Botanic Gardens), Kit and Ben Knotts (Cocoa Beach), Hein Kramer (Amsterdam), Atsushi Kuyama (Sakuya Konohana Kan, Osaka), Gunvor Larsson (Bergius Botanic Garden, Stockholm), Lei Liang (American Academy, Rome), Wolfram Lobin (Botanical Garden of the University of Bonn), Jim Luteyn (New York Botanical Garden), Elena Lyakh (Central Siberian Botanical Garden, Novosibirsk), David Mabberley (Royal Botanic Gardens, Sydney), Carlos Magdalena (Royal Botanic Gardens, Kew), Robert Meade (United States Geological Service, Denver), Steve Messam (North Stainmore), Crina Mocan (Cluj-Napoca Botanical Garden), Jorge Monteverde (Buenos Aires), Scott Mori (New York Botanical Garden), Yara Mostazo Fernández (Royal Botanical Garden, Madrid), María Múlgura (Darwinion Institute of Botany, San Isidro), Diane Naylor (Chatsworth), Juan José Neiff (Center for Applied Coastal Ecology, Corrientes), Mark Nesbitt (Royal Botanic Gardens, Kew), Cindy Newlander (Denver Botanic Gardens), Peter Otto (University of Leipzig), Walter Pagels (San Diego), Won Soon Park (Yeomiji Botanical Garden), Artem Parshin (Moscow State University Botanical Garden), Sarah Phillips (Royal Botanic Gardens, Kew), Richard Piacentini (Phipps Conservatory and Botanical Gardens, Pittsburgh), Margie Radebaugh (Phipps Conservatory and Botanical Gardens, Pittsburgh), Markus Radscheit (Botanical Garden of the University of Bonn), Tonchi Ribero (Santa Cruz), Aurélie Roux (National Museum of Natural History, Paris), Pilar San Pio (Royal Botanical Garden, Madrid), Mio Sato (Kakegawa Kachoen), Laura Schoch (Phipps Conservatory and Botanical Gardens, Pittsburgh), Charmaine Scott (Wellington Botanic Garden), Jonathan Singer (New York), Thomas Ster (Botanical Garden of Graz), František Šuman (Děčín Castle), Roberto Tacchetto (Padua Botanical Garden), Marc Teissier (Les Cedres, Saint-Jean-Cap-Ferrat), Frédéric Tournay (Botanical Garden of the University of Strasbourg), Arthur Tucker (Delaware State University), Gerda van Uffelen (Leiden Botanical Garden), Roberto Vasquez (Santa Cruz), Alessandra Vinciguerra (La Mortella, Forio d'Ischia), Art Vogel (Leiden Botanical Garden), David Wakely (San Francisco), Jim Wehtje (Rochester), Stephen Wolf (Missouri Botanical Garden, St. Louis), Patricia Wuillemin (Bern), and Fernando Zuloaga (Darwinion Institute of Botany, San Isidro).

I also thank Longwood Gardens' staff, students, and volunteers, who contributed innumerable hours assisting me in creating this book. My special appreciation goes to Renata Abaumann, Kristina Aguilar, Larry Albee, Erica Anderson, Yoko Arakawa, Venice Bayrd, Morris Brooks, Kitty Byk, Emily Coggin, Marnie Conley, Daniela Freitag, Roberta Frey, Barbara Green, Gillian Hayward, Paul Hopkinson, Razvan Ionescu, Timothy Jennings, Christine Klepacz, Adam Koppeser, Sharon Loving, John Luttrell, Ger Meeuwissen, Kathleen Morgan, Patrick Nutt, Mary Jane Pahls, Colvin Randall, Sandy Reber, Paul B. Redman, Edward Somers, Dave Thompson, Rose Torelli, Inger Wallin, Carol Warfel, Irene Woodward, and Lezhong Wang.

Note on the Names of *Victoria*

To spare the reader the confusing inconsistency in how the scientific names of the giant lily have been typographically presented in historical sources with respect to the use of italics and the capitalization of specific epithets, I took the liberty to convert them to a style that reflects the current practice of italicizing the names and writing specific epithets with the initial lowercase. Therefore, the reader will find Victoria regia, Victoria amazonica, *and* Victoria cruziana *throughout this book, regardless of the style used in the referenced or quoted sources. I hope I will be forgiven this small infraction.*

FOREWORD

It is with much pleasure that we at Longwood Gardens share with you the story of one of our most popular and spectacular plants: *Victoria*. Written by Tomasz Aniśko, curator and plant explorer, the book details the story of *Victoria,* who remains as scientifically and aesthetically interesting today as when she was first discovered in the early nineteenth century. The great size and fierceness of her leaves and her curious sexuality present a compelling story of many "firsts" that has important ties to our gardens' history and to our city of Philadelphia, Pennsylvania.

The beginning of our story starts in 1798, when two Quaker brothers, Samuel and Joshua Peirce, developed an arboretum on their farm in Chester County. While European explorers were scouting South America, searching for *Victoria*, Samuel and Joshua were searching Pennsylvania and neighboring states for new trees to plant on the grounds of what would be Peirce's Park. This arboretum, located just thirty miles west of Philadelphia, was considered the finest collection of trees in nineteenth-century America. It was also the nucleus of what would become Longwood Gardens, one of the world's premier gardens.

By 1851, as *Victoria*'s popularity was spreading through the British Isles and Europe, Philadelphia became the first place in America where *Victoria* flowered. This was a crowning achievement for Caleb Cope, the president of the Pennsylvania Horticultural Society. By the early twentieth century, Longwood founder Pierre S. du Pont had begun creating new gardens around Peirce's Park, expanding the collections to include beautiful plants from all corners of the world. Many were imported, like Cope's first *Victoria*, from Europe.

Director Paul B. Redman in 2012.
Daniel Traub

This century-and-a-half-long legacy of exploring the world for novel plant subjects reached a climax in 1957, when the gardens opened a new aquatic display and showcased our first flowering *Victoria*. This historic event led to the first successful crossing of two species of giant lilies, *Victoria amazonica* and *Victoria cruziana*, just three years later—the first such triumph in America.

Today, hundreds of guests gather around our waterlily pools each day during the summer to see the story of *Victoria* come to life. It is our hope that this book not only documents *Victoria*'s past, but that it also inspires future generations to share in the fascination with this true queen of the plant world.

Paul B. Redman
Director, Longwood Gardens

The image of *Victoria* flower that opens Jonathan Singer's five-volume folio set titled *Botanica Magnifica*.
Jonathan Singer

First-night flower and a leaf section of *Victoria amazonica* reconstructed by Walter Fitch from specimens collected in Bolivia by Thomas Bridges and published in *Curtis's Botanical Magazine* in January 1847.
LONGWOOD GARDENS LIBRARY AND ARCHIVES

chapter 1

ENLIGHTENED BOHEMIAN

ON THE GENTLE SLOPES OF STÓG IZERSKI, one of the peaks in the Izera Mountains on the border between Poland and the Czech Republic, a number of springs feed streams that coalesce into the Izera River. The Izera first meanders through the grassy plateau below Stóg Izerski and then takes a southerly course toward Prague. Along the way it passes the base of a narrow sandstone cliff converted in the early fifteenth century into a rock castle named Vranov. As a fortress perched on and cut into the rock face, Vranov had many defensive advantages, but it offered little in the way of comfort to the inhabitants, who eventually abandoned it for an easier life down in the valley. The castle fell into neglect and eventually ruin. It probably would have remained as such if the ideas of Romanticism did not sweep forcefully through Europe at the turn of the nineteenth century, transforming crumbling ruins of all sorts into loci of spiritual and artistic inspiration.

When František Zachariáš Römisch, a wealthy Bohemian merchant, bought Vranov in 1802, he saw in it an epitome of the romantic landscape waiting to be revealed and appreciated. And what Römisch did not find in Vranov, he added to it: memorable inscriptions on the rocks, sarcophagi and monuments of heroic figures, busts of emperors and poets, and, to top it all, a neogothic summerhouse overlooking the Izera River.

Römisch spent more than twenty years improving Vranov and renamed his creation the Pantheon. A visitor to this romantic sanctuary can wander through the landscape and discover mementos of geniuses of the past. While most of the immortalized names are recognizable from the pages of history books, one monument is more enigmatic. On the left bank of the Izera stands a simple pedestal crowned with a stone globe. On the globe a single name is chiseled—"Henke." What great deeds, one may ask, did this individual accomplish to deserve a place in Römisch's Pantheon?

THADDAEUS HAENKE OF CHŘIBSKÁ

Römisch's "Henke," whose name is usually written as Haenke, died in South America when Römisch was building Vranov's Pantheon. He was born Thaddaeus (Tadeáš) Peregrinus Xaverius Haenke in 1761 in the small town of Chřibská (German Kreibitz), some 80 km (50 miles) northwest of Vranov. Haenke's family enjoyed a modestly prominent position in Chřibská: His father was a town judge and a cantor, and his mother came from a local stock of wealthy butchers. Although Chřibská was tucked away in the periphery of Bohemia—at that time a province of the Austro-Hungarian Empire—its centuries-old glass-making traditions connected it through a network of trade routes to other parts of Europe. Thus, the citizens of Chřibská had a heightened awareness of far-away places. This awareness was blamed for their longing to venture out into the bigger world, in days when travel was still a rare experience (Kühnel 1960).

In Chřibská, the spacious corner house where Thaddaeus Haenke was born and spent his childhood serves today as a museum.
TOMASZ ANIŚKO / LONGWOOD GARDENS

From his earliest years, Thaddaeus was surrounded by music and learned to sing and play the organ. At the age of eleven, he entered the Jesuit seminary of St. Wenceslaus in Prague to study Latin and music, with the intention of becoming a cantor, like his father. However, in 1773, Pope Clement XIV suppressed Jesuits across most of Europe, and the seminary closed. Soon after, a bout of pneumonia ended Haenke's singing career, and he gave up his musical studies altogether, turning to science and philosophy instead. He later entered the Charles University in Prague as a medical student. Here, Haenke's religious convictions and social views were confronted by the grand ideas of the Enlightenment, and he was gradually admitted into the circles of Bohemian scholars and free thinkers. There, he came under the tutelage of Joseph Gottfried Mikan, professor of medicine, botany, and chemistry. Mikan took Haenke into his house as an assistant and assigned him the responsibility of tending the university botanic garden (Stearn 1973). During that time, he became enchanted by the idea of collecting and studying plants in the wild. Soon Haenke was recognized with a medal awarded by the Royal Bohemian Society of Science for his study of the plants of Krkonoše (German Riesengebirge), a mountain range east of the Izera Mountains. Botanizing and hiking in the mountains also sparked his interest in observing and documenting local cultures. This later became a hallmark of Haenke's investigations (Kühnel 1960).

A simple monument to Thaddaeus Haenke is immersed in lush vegetation blanketing the banks of the Izera River, a telling reference to Haenke's travels on the rivers of South America.
Tomasz Aniśko / Longwood Gardens

In 1786, Haenke moved to Vienna to continue his studies in medicine and botany. He soon became acquainted with Nicolaus Joseph von Jacquin, a renowned professor of botany at the University of Vienna. Jacquin was famed for his explorations in the West Indies and Central America. He took the young Bohemian under his wing, opened his private library, and, through the tales of botanical wonders of the New World tropics, ignited Haenke's insatiable desire for learning about exotic flora.

Increasingly preoccupied with botanical subjects, Haenke delayed completion of his medical studies. His parents became alarmed that the prospect of their son becoming a country doctor was slipping away (Kühnel 1960). And they were right: Thaddaeus had bigger dreams by then. In his view, medicine was only a means to a more ambitious scientific career as a naturalist, an attitude characteristic of a true son of the Enlightenment.

AN EXTRAORDINARY EXPEDITION

In those days, the only way to earn the rank of a reputable naturalist in the eyes of the European scientific establishment was to embark, like Jacquin, on an expedition to the corners of Earth still awaiting discovery or exploration. Haenke did not have to wait long for such a life-changing opportunity. Three years into his studies in Vienna, his mentor Jacquin recommended him for perhaps the most ambitious and comprehensive scientific expedition to South America yet undertaken. The expedition was being organized on behalf of the Spanish government.

ENLIGHTENED BOHEMIAN   13

Thaddaeus Haenke portrait by
Vinzenz Raimond Grüner.
ÖSTERREICHISCHE NATIONALBIBLIOTHEK

Haenke's participation hinged on securing permission and financial backing from his own sovereign, Emperor Joseph II. A despotic Austrian monarch near the end of his rule and life, Joseph II enthusiastically patronized arts and science in accordance with his views on enlightened absolutism. Joseph II granted his consent and support on the condition that Haenke would return to Austria after the expedition. Without hesitation, the young Bohemian gave up the comforts and thrills of his Viennese life for the prospect of adventures and discoveries awaiting him in the Americas.

With the help of the Austrian ambassador in Madrid, Haenke's name was passed to Alessandro Malaspina, who was then assembling a crew of two hundred men to journey to the west coasts of South and North America then on to islands in the Pacific. The expedition's goal was not to discover new lands but to explore and thoroughly survey those already in the Spanish dominion (Ossenbach 2005). Haenke, then twenty-eight years old, was the youngest of the three botanists chosen for the expedition. The two others were Antonio Pineda, a Spaniard born in Guatemala, and Louis Née, a Frenchman working in the Royal Botanical Garden in Madrid (Ossenbach 2005). To Haenke's advantage, however, his training in chemistry and mineralogy was viewed as an important asset for the expedition, and his Bohemian scientific heritage (for centuries, Europe's premier glassmakers) was highly esteemed.

Malaspina himself was an Italian nobleman serving as an officer in the Spanish navy. In 1786–1788, he had circumnavigated the globe on behalf of the Royal Philippines Company. During that commercial venture, Malaspina conceived the idea of a scientific expedition to explore the American coast and Pacific islands. Back in Spain, he proposed the idea to the government in Madrid. Like his Austrian counterpart,

Carlos III, Spain's aging and ailing king, was a proponent of enlightened absolutism and a promoter of science. Carlos III approved the project shortly before his death that same year. Ironically, neither monarch who set Haenke on a course of botanical discoveries would live to see the fruits of his labor.

The expedition was well founded and superbly equipped. Two identical corvettes, *Descubierta* and *Atrevida*, were specially built and launched in April 1789. Malaspina commanded *Descubierta*, while José de Bustamante, a Spanish naval officer and explorer, helmed *Atrevida*.

REVOLUTION, SHIPWRECK, AND ICE-LOCKED ISLANDS

On June 26, 1789, Haenke departed Vienna for the Spanish port of Cádiz on the Atlantic coast, where Malaspina's crew was to assemble. Stopping first in Paris, Haenke had planned to purchase scientific instruments needed for the expedition, but he arrived mere days before the storming of the Bastille on July 14. Delayed by the turmoil that engulfed Paris, Haenke didn't reach Cádiz until July 31. Malaspina's corvettes had already sailed (Parodi 1964).

Historical accounts differ as to just how late Haenke was, from a few hours to a couple of days, but this adversity did not deter him. Boarding the first available merchant ship bound for South America, Haenke hoped to catch up with Malaspina in Montevideo. After a three-month voyage, however, the ship capsized in Río de la Plata on its approach to Montevideo on November 23. Haenke made it to the shore, but all of his possessions and scientific instruments were lost, save for a copy of Carl Linnaeus's book *Species Plantarum* and the credentials issued by the Spanish government (Parodi 1964).

If this calamity were not enough, Haenke had missed Malaspina again. The two Spanish corvettes had departed for Islas Malvinas (today's Falkland Islands) a week earlier. From there, Malaspina had set a course around Cape Horn to the western shore of South America. Haenke's next opportunity to join the expedition would be in Chile, but he had to take a land route to cross the Pampas plain and the Andes mountains—the first botanist ever to do so.

In Montevideo, Haenke recuperated from both the ship's wreck and a short illness that followed. There, he collected and dispatched to Cadiz a box filled with some eight hundred botanical specimens. In late December, he crossed the river to Buenos Aires, then the capital of the Spanish viceroyalty of Río de la Plata. Nicolás de Arredondo, the Spanish viceroy, warmly received Haenke, supplying money and equipment for the long journey to the western side of the continent (Parodi 1964). Haenke left Buenos Aires alone in late February 1790 at the height of the austral summer. After a grueling trek through hostile territory, he reached Santiago de Chile on April 2, carrying some fourteen hundred species of plants. To his relief, Malaspina was there, too.

Together, Malaspina and Haenke traveled from Santiago to the port of Valparaíso, where the corvettes were waiting. After a nine-month chase around half the globe, Haenke finally boarded *Descubierta*, which would become his home for the next three years. Malaspina assigned Haenke to Pineda, who was in charge of natural history collections. When the expedition resumed explorations, Haenke's long years of tedious

Thaddaeus Haenke, letter to Nicolaus von Jacquin, 1790:

Few people will have been able to arrive so near the sky and breathe the pure air of these heights that I have breathed through the space of various days during my applied observations. Alone as on similar trips, my health was in imminent danger under the weight of innumerable scarcities; perhaps even my life, if that beneficent spirit hadn't been watching over me so while [I was] on horrible precipices, in storms, in the sinking of the ship and under hordes of murderous Indians. The pay for my pains? Only a rich and beneficent collection of plants, those that from the external aspect seem to be engendered from another planet and bore the stamp of singularity and the grandness of their place of origin.

Parodi 1964, translated by Kathleen Morgan

A severely damaged portrait of Thaddaeus Haenke is stored in the archives of the Casa de la Cultura in Cochabamba.
GOBIERNO AUTÓNOMO MUNICIPAL DE COCHABAMBA, CASA DE LA CULTURA

studies in Prague and Vienna paid off. Haenke exhibited skills in many subjects beyond botany, including physics, geology, mineralogy, and chemistry, as well as anthropology and linguistics, proving himself to be a valuable addition to Malaspina's party. Even his medical training came in handy as he often assisted the expedition's surgeon. And when he discovered a clavichord in *Descubierta*'s salon, he delighted his shipmates with onboard performances of Haydn and Mozart (Parodi 1964).

The expedition plan called for a northerly course to Alaska, exploring coastal areas along the way. While the corvettes dropped the anchor in Callao, Haenke undertook an excursion to the Andean valleys of Peru. In June 1790, he reached the sources of Marañón and Huallaga, two tributaries to the Amazon basin. By following both rivers to the place they became navigable, Haenke was inspired to later propose establishing trade routes linking Peru with the Atlantic Ocean by way of the Amazon's tributaries.

In Alaska in 1791, the expedition searched for the legendary Northwest Passage between the Pacific and the Atlantic. Malaspina decided to try the Yakutat Bay, which was rumored to afford entrance to the passage. Upon discovering that the bay ended in a narrow inlet blocked by ice, he named it Puerto del Desengano or Disenchantment Bay, hinting at how his crew must have felt after their futile attempt. Curiously, Malaspina also chose this occasion to honor Haenke by naming a small ice-locked island in the middle of Disenchantment Bay after him.

The corvettes then headed south, stopping in Monterey, at that time the capital of Spanish Upper California. It is believed during that stop Haenke discovered coastal redwood (*Sequoia sempervirens*) and collected its seeds, which were later taken to Spain (Gicklhorn-Wien 1966). Upon reaching Acapulco in Mexico, Malaspina's ships turned west and set a course for Guam, the Philippines, and then south to New Zealand and Australia. There, Malaspina changed his mind about returning to Europe through the Indian Ocean and instead chose an easterly route across the South Pacific.

A SECOND CROSS-CONTINENTAL TREK

Back in Peru in July 1793, Malaspina decided that Haenke should traverse the South American continent again, collecting specimens and making observations before reuniting with the expedition at Buenos Aires or Montevideo. On September 3, Haenke left Lima and headed for the Andes. He followed the southerly route to La Paz in today's Bolivia. Failing to reach Buenos Aires or Montevideo, Haenke sent a letter to

Malaspina explaining that the scope of research he was conducting and the vastness of the territory he desired to explore made it impossible for him to arrive in time. He promised to return to Spain the following year (Kühnel 1960).

After five long years, Malaspina returned to Spain in September 1794. However, instead of basking in the glory of being a great explorer, he fell victim to the intrigues at the Spanish court. In 1796, he was jailed in the San Antón Castle in La Coruña. The Spanish government impounded all the documents and collections brought back from the expedition. This delayed publication of a full account of the expedition until almost a century later. After seven years of incarceration, Malaspina would finally be freed thanks to Napoleon's intervention. Exiled from Spain, Malaspina would return to his home in Tuscany, settle in the small town of Pontremoli, and die a few years later.

Meanwhile, Haenke could not keep the promise he made to Malaspina. It took him not one but three years to complete his investigations in the mountain regions of present-day Peru and Bolivia. One of the most remarkable plants the Bohemian botanist discovered during that time was *titanca*, an enormous herb of the bromeliad family, now called *Puya raimondii*. He found the plant near Sorata in today's Bolivia (Gicklhorn-Wien 1966). Standing roughly 12 m (39 feet) tall at the time of flowering, this vegetable wonder is considered the world's tallest herbaceous plant. A true naturalist, Haenke also broadened the scope of his inquiries to include collecting birds and animals, mapping navigable river routes, studying thermal springs, and even improving methods of extracting silver and mercury.

When Haenke arrived in the city of Cochabamba (Bolivia) in 1796, he had little desire to return to Europe. Malaspina was in jail, Haenke's expedition collections were locked up, his Viennese benefactor,

Plaza Colón in Cochabamba, Bolivia. Thaddaeus Haenke arrived here in 1796.

TOMASZ ANIŚKO / LONGWOOD GARDENS

ENLIGHTENED BOHEMIAN 17

Joseph II, had been replaced by a young reactionary, Emperor Francis II, and Austria was suffering repeated defeats by Napoleon's army. The century of the Enlightenment in Europe was coming to an end. In contrast, Cochabamba—the city of eternal spring thanks to its year-round mild climate—offered Haenke a respite after seven years of arduous exploration and a quiet time to examine and study his collections. In letters to his mother in Chřibská, Haenke praised the beauty of his adopted country: "Europe would de-populate itself if its citizens had clear notions of the happiness, the beauty, the affluence and the undisrupted, happy richness of these lands" (Kühnel 1960, translated by Daniela Freitag).

A NEW LIFE IN THE NEW WORLD

The Spanish viceroy in Buenos Aires allowed Haenke to retain the assignment and the salary of a royal naturalist and encouraged him to continue his studies and expeditions. Since printing was severely restricted in the Spanish colonies at that time, little of Haenke's work was published during his life. When not preoccupied with scientific pursuits or writing reports for the viceroy, the Bohemian, now in his mid-thirties, enjoyed Andean life to the fullest. A romantic relationship with his housekeeper gave him a son. Profits from his involvement in silver mining operations and a local medical practice allowed Haenke to purchase an estate some 150 km (93 miles) north of Cochabamba—Santa Cruz de Helicona—and to send money regularly to his mother in Chřibská. Haenke's musical talents were admired and appreciated by Cochabamba elites and opened the doors of the city's best homes. Driven by the ideals of the Enlightenment, Haenke seized every opportunity to advance the progress and the economy of the region: He promoted a small pox vaccination, cultivated medicinal plants and silkworms, improved the glass-making and saltpeter industries, and even started a botanical garden (Gicklhorn-Wien 1966).

In early 1800, Haenke was asked to survey the territory east of Santa Cruz de la Sierra in the foothills of the Andes. The town was being set up as a seat of a new provincial government. Since the area had been inflamed for some time by fighting among the various Indian tribes living there, the governor of Cochabamba assigned a military escort to Haenke's party. Perhaps it would be more accurate to describe this venture as a military expedition to subdue the rebellious indigenous tribes with a Bohemian botanist assigned as a naturalist. Whatever the intent for the expedition, Haenke's letters show his compassion for the natives and his opposition to the brutal exploitation of fellow human beings. Despite the circumstances, Haenke got along well with the local tribes, who in turn saw in him a miracle-working medicine man. He was moved by the trust, affection, and appreciation with which the Indians received his medical treatments (Kühnel 1960).

The expedition first headed east to the Brazilian border and then turned north to reach the province of Moxos in early 1801. Haenke had traversed the province seven years earlier on his way to Cochabamba (Kühnel 1960). In Moxos, he teamed with a Franciscan missionary named Father Luis de La Cueva (also written Lacueva), who was living among Yuracaré Indians settled along the rivers Chapare and Mamoré, tributaries

---

Thaddaeus Haenke, letter to his mother, 1800:

I left Cochabamba on 20 February with the intendant of this province in order to go to war with him against some thousand Indians; I do hope, however, that this war will come to an end soon. I am, thank heavens, healthy and refreshed, and I find myself now in a new land, again, of savage Indians and barbarians: however, they are a very good people who hurt no one, and who, moreover, take very good care of me. I had, in my youth, a special longing to be a missionary, now providence has so destined me as to have an opportunity every day to teach the savages not only in religion but also in several useful sciences and arts and this brings me their affection and love and esteem. . . . God willing the peace will come soon as I will then prepare to come to Spain, not before, however: as we now live here in these beautiful and peaceful countries endlessly better than in Europe.

Kühnel 1960, translated by Daniela Freitag

of the mighty Amazon. La Cueva had spent many years studying and recording the language of the Yuracaré and offered assistance and guidance to Haenke's party.

On one of his forays down the Mamoré, Haenke entered a marshy canal connected to the river. There, the Bohemian explorer unexpectedly came face-to-face with a plant that made an impression on him like no other before: a water lily of gigantic proportions. At that moment, the botanist who likely thought that he had seen it all—from the Pampas in the south to Alaska in the north, from the world's tallest trees in California to the world's tallest herbs in the Andes—was struck with awe. There is no record that Haenke himself published this discovery or gave a name to this plant. In fact, if it had not been for his Franciscan companion, no one would know what happened on that memorable day in 1801.

Some thirty years later, another botanist, a Frenchman named Alcide d'Orbigny, would travel through the Moxos territory, where he would also meet Father La Cueva. The Franciscan missionary would

During yearly floods, the Mamoré River, meandering through the province of Moxos, refills countless channels and ponds strung along its course.

TOMASZ ANIŚKO / LONGWOOD GARDENS

ENLIGHTENED BOHEMIAN 19

tell d'Orbigny that the sight of the enormous water lily had caused Haenke, "transported by admiration," to drop to his knees and praise the "author of so magnificent a creation." La Cueva's report would make Haenke the first in a long line of naturalists to be seduced by this aquatic marvel.

Haenke set up a camp near the site of the wondrous lily and reluctantly left a few days later "with much regret." Nothing is known from La Cueva about any specimens or drawings that Haenke might have prepared on site, but among Haenke's manuscripts, which are stored in the archives of the Royal Botanical Garden in Madrid, there are sketches of a flower and a leaf unmistakably recognizable as the giant lily and most likely executed at that time. From La Cueva's account, it was Haenke's spontaneous outburst of piety and religious devotion that made the most lasting impression on the missionary.

REVOLUTIONARY MISFORTUNES

Back in Cochabamba, Haenke enjoyed relative prosperity and security. He was dedicated to the studies of natural history until the forces set in motion by the French Revolution caught up with him in South America. While Napoleon was inflicting mortal blows to the Spanish colonial rule, the independence movement in South America was gaining strength. Soon the entire continent was ablaze with wars of liberation. Upper Peru, as Bolivia was known then, declared independence in 1809, but it would take sixteen years of struggle before it established itself as a republic.

Caught in the middle of this historical storm, Haenke sympathized with the independence movement. His relationship with Baltasar Hidalgo de Cisneros, the Spanish viceroy in Buenos Aires, became strained. On January 25, 1810, Cisneros sent a letter informing the governor of Cochabamba that Haenke's assignment as a naturalist had been terminated and that he should return to Spain immediately. Haenke responded with a request to delay his return for a year so he might finish important work, citing the discovery of rich deposits of saltpeter on the coast of Tarapacá (in today's Chile) a year earlier. He also claimed to be in precarious health resulting from an injury he suffered after falling off a horse (Parodi 1964). Cisneros denied his request, but a few weeks later, the viceroy himself was removed from his post in Buenos Aires when the May Revolution swept through that city, paving the way for the independence of Argentina and other Spanish colonies.

For the Bohemian botanist, Argentine independence meant Haenke would no longer receive a steady salary from the Spanish government. His sole sources of income were now profits from his estate, where he had cultivated land and built a small silver mine, and his medical practice. As the political and economic situation in Upper Peru deteriorated, the stalemate between royalist and independence forces brought the country to the brink of chaos. For the first time in two decades, Haenke contemplated returning to Europe. Watching the revolution unfold before his eyes filled him with pessimism. Blaming the Spanish rulers for subjugating the population of the colonies,

The giant water lilies inhabiting the backwaters of the Mamoré River in Bolivia were encountered by Thaddaeus Haenke in 1801.
TOMASZ ANIŚKO / LONGWOOD GARDENS

Alcide d'Orbigny, 1840:

While crossing the center of the American continent, I arrived in the midst of the Guarayo natives and ... met Father Lacueva, a Spanish missionary good and learned, who tried to convert them to Christianity. For the traveler who had been for a year with indigenous peoples, it was a joy to find a being with whom I could converse and be understood. I felt therefore a real pleasure to interview this venerable elder who, for not less than thirty years, had not ceased to live among savages. In one of these conversations that recalled joys unknown to me for a long time, he cited for me an anecdote of which the interest struck me vividly. Sent by the Spanish government to study the vegetation of Peru, the famous botanist Haenke, whose works unhappily have now been lost, found himself with a native in a pirogue on the river Mamoré, one of the greater tributaries of the Amazon. They discovered in a marsh near the bank a plant so beautiful and extraordinary that Haenke, transported by admiration upon seeing it, fell upon his knees, addressing the author of so magnificent a creation the homages of recognition that his astonishment and his deep emotion required. He stopped there, even camped there; and finally took his leave with much regret.

d'Orbigny 1840, translated by John Luttrell

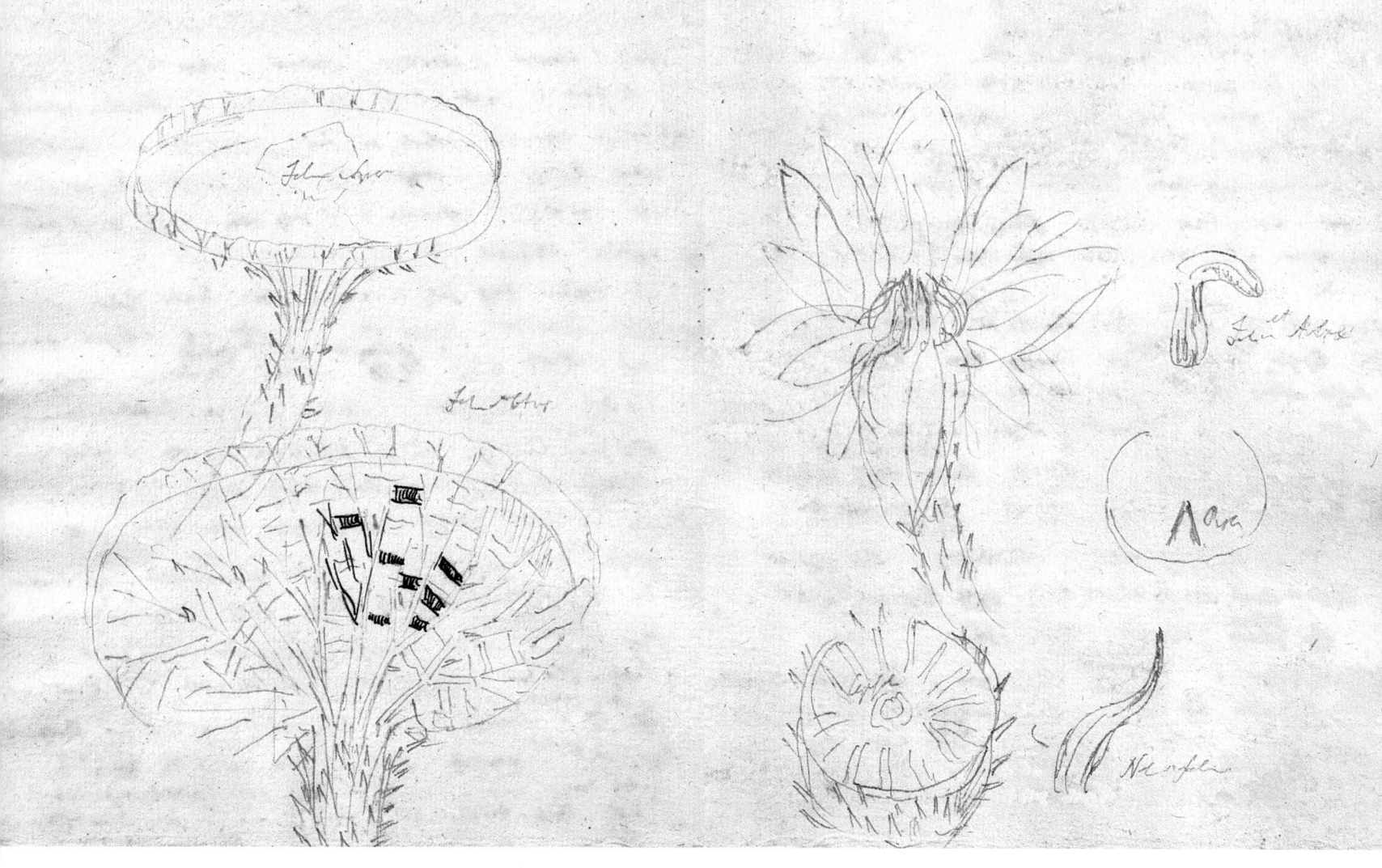

Undated sketches by Thaddaeus Haenke of the giant water lily, which the Bohemian discovered in Moxos in 1801.
Archivo del Real Jardín Botánico, CSIC, Madrid

he felt wedged between "barbaric conquerors" and "tyrannical avengers," neither of whom could guarantee peace and prosperity (Kühnel 1960, translated by Daniela Freitag). His situation became increasingly precarious: The supporters of independence viewed him a foreigner and a Spanish government official, while the royalists branded him a suspicious associate of the discredited Malaspina.

Leaving South America, however, was far harder than getting there. For starters, Haenke had no passport and no official dismissal documents that would allow him to return to Europe legally. In addition, now approaching his fifties, he was leery of starting over in a Europe torn apart by the Napoleonic wars. The many hardships he had endured over the years had taken a heavy toll on his health. Haenke was no longer the same relentless twenty-eight-year-old who had departed from Vienna to conquer the world. He felt trapped. With no apparent options, the Bohemian retreated to his mountain estate and concentrated on preparing a treatise on the natural history of the area. He was unable to send it to Europe for publication, however, because Cochabamba was constantly besieged by warring parties. Even his letters stopped arriving in Chřibská in 1811, an ominous sign of the dark veil being drawn over his life.

About five years later, Haenke died suddenly under mysterious circumstances. Although his death certificate, kept in the archives in Cochabamba, is dated November 4, 1816 (Frontaura Argandoña 1971), chroniclers disagree as to whether he died in 1816 or 1817, and several speculative versions of the events have been described (Kühnel 1960, Parodi 1964, Stearn 1973, Ossenbach 2005, Beidleman 2006). One account states that he was poisoned while in prison during the revolutionary turmoil. Another says that Haenke's maid mistakenly gave him a poisonous potion instead of a medicine while he lay ill at his home at Santa Cruz de Helicona. Less dramatic versions speak of Haenke dying of fever or a heart attack either at his home or en route to Cochabamba to seek medical treatment.

Even after his death, misfortunes followed. Buried at the Franciscan monastery in Cochabamba, Haenke rested in peace until 1937, when construction work required the cemetery to be relocated to another monastery in Tarata, 35 km (22 miles) south of Cochabamba. Apparently this work was carried out in a somewhat haphazard manner, so today the exact location of Haenke's final resting place remains a mystery. All of his possessions, including his estate, Santa Cruz de Helicona, were confiscated by the Spanish government; his papers were taken to Lima, the seat of the viceroy of Peru. Some were then forwarded to Cádiz, but many were never seen again.

HAENKE'S HISTORICAL FIRSTS

Thaddaeus Haenke was the first botanist to systematically explore the interior of South America, beginning with his solo trek across the Pampas and the Andes in 1790. Prior to his arrival, exploration was primarily limited to coastal areas or along the main rivers of that continent. He was the first botanist to discover three of the world's largest plants: coastal redwoods of California, *titanca* of the Andes, and the giant water lily of Mamoré. Ironically, none of these plants bears Haenke's name or was given a scientific appellation by him. The revolutionary upheaval of his time and the isolation from the centers of scientific thought in Europe may explain this paradox, but it also illuminates a novel trait in Haenke's research. While his collections counted in the thousands, he showed little interest in claiming priority for discovering these plants. His career evolved from being a cataloger of the natural world, concerned mainly with finding and describing new species, to a naturalist working tirelessly to explore plants that might offer some benefit to humanity—be it through medical, agricultural, or industrial use, such as sources of fiber, timber, resin, rubber, or dyes.

Haenke may be regarded as a pioneer of research that today forms the core of economic botany. Guided by the idealism of the Enlightenment, the *zeitgeist* of his generation, he exemplified a new breed of missionaries, those who instead of religious prophecies carried science and progress around the world (Kühnel 1960). Haenke stands tall in history as the embodiment of an eighteenth century humanist who abhorred war and violence, desired to help people in need, confronted authority and injustice, and strove untiringly for truth and knowledge.

A commemorative plaque was placed on the façade of Thaddaeus Haenke's home in Chřibská in 1885.

TOMASZ ANIŚKO / LONGWOOD GARDENS

ENLIGHTENED BOHEMIAN

At the time of Haenke's death, Römisch's Pantheon was well under way. Although most of his writings never reached European printing houses and receded into obscurity, Bohemians took great pride in their choirboy from Chřibská. Although many of his collections were lost, scattered, or hidden in the dusty archives of Madrid, seven boxes holding some fifteen thousand botanical specimens from the Malaspina expedition ended up in the National Museum in Prague in 1821. Perhaps it was this occasion that inspired Römisch to erect a monument on a bank of the Izera to honor the great explorer and to keep his memory alive among his compatriots. Circumstances prevented Thaddaeus Haenke from returning to his home in Bohemia, but the giant water lily he discovered along Mamoré in 1801 did arrive there a half century later. In 1852, the first flower of the South American nymph opened in the conservatories of the Děčín Castle, only 25 km (16 miles) down the road from Chřibská.

The first *Victoria* to flower in Bohemia was grown in the greenhouses occupying terraces below the Děčín Castle, only 25 km (16 miles) from Chřibská, Thaddaeus Haenke's hometown.
STATE REGIONAL ARCHIVES LITOMĚŘICE, BRANCH DĚČÍN

Franciscan monastery in Tarata where Thaddaeus Haenke's remains were relocated from Cochabamba in 1937.
TOMASZ ANIŚKO / LONGWOOD GARDENS

ENLIGHTENED BOHEMIAN

chapter 2

EL SABIO, OR THE WISE MAN

A YEAR BEFORE THADDAEUS HAENKE ENCOUNTERED *Victoria amazonica* in Bolivia, two other explorers were scouting the northern fringes of the lily's domain. In the summer of 1799, the Spanish corvette *Pizarro* arrived in the port of Cumuná (in today's Venezuela) with French botanist Aimé Bonpland and Prussian explorer Alexander von Humboldt on board. It was only the capricious nature of fortune that prevented them from becoming the first naturalists to find the great water lily.

Aimé Jacques Alexandre Goujaud-Bonpland was born on August 28, 1773, in the village of Saint-Maurice near La Rochelle, France. His father, Simon-Jacques Goujaud-Bonpland, was a distinguished physician and chief surgeon of La Charité Hospital in La Rochelle. His mother, Marguerite-Olive de la Coste, was the daughter of a sea captain. His father added Bonpland to his last name, probably to distinguish it from other branches of the Goujaud family. Later, Aimé adopted it as his last name.

Bonpland's early education was in local schools, but in 1791, at the age of eighteen, he was sent to Paris with his brother Michel Simon to study medicine. There, he also developed a keen interest in natural history, chiefly botany, and trained under renowned botanists such as Antoine Laurent de Jussieu and René Louiche Desfontaines. Both men were professors

Victoria cruziana at Longwood Gardens, oil on linen, a 2011 painting by Patricia Wuillemin.
PATRICIA WUILLEMIN

Aimé Bonpland, painted by R. Fugimay after Carlos Enrique Pellegrini, 1837.
MUSEO DE FARMACOBOTÁNICA "JUAN A. DOMÍNGUEZ," FACULTAD DE FARMACIA Y BIOQUÍMICA, UNIVERSIDAD DE BUENOS AIRES

at the National Museum of Natural History and members of the Academy of Sciences in Paris.

After finishing his medical training, Bonpland became a surgeon in the French navy at the port of Toulon, combining "the medical strain on his father's side and the naval one on his mother's" (Sarton 1943). When his tour of duty ended in 1795, he returned to Paris to continue his medical studies and to cultivate his interest in natural history. By the time he turned twenty-three, he felt torn between the two disciplines of botany and medicine.

In the spring of 1798, a chance meeting helped redirect Bonpland's life work. Bonpland was staying in the Hôtel Boston, the same hotel where Baron Alexander von Humboldt, a young Prussian aristocrat, rented an apartment. Humboldt later explained that their fortuitous meeting occurred "in the simplest manner in the world." Bonpland and Humboldt had seen each other occasionally in the concierge's lodge. "You know that when giving up the key of one's apartments on going out," Humboldt recalled, "one generally exchanges a few friendly words with the porter's wife. While so doing I often encountered a young man with a botanist's satchel over his arm; this was Bonpland; and in this manner we made acquaintance" (Bruhns 1873).

Two years earlier, Humboldt had inherited a large fortune. The bequest had enabled him to quit his career as a mining inspector and pursue his interests in scientific exploration. He soon began planning a grand expedition in natural history. Humboldt had just arrived in Paris—Europe's intellectual and scientific capital of that era—to consult with French naturalists and purchase scientific instruments. When the two young men met, Bonpland was without reliable means of support, while Humboldt had considerable financial resources. Despite the obvious social class differences, Humboldt saw in Bonpland a kindred spirit. The two forged a lifelong friendship.

Although Humboldt had been practicing botany, he considered Bonpland his superior in the field. Together, they began planning a joint expedition to Spanish America.

A GRAND ADVENTURE

In order to explore the viceroyalties of New Granada, Peru, and New Spain, Humboldt and Bonpland first needed permission from Carlos IV, king of Spain. These regions of the New World were officially closed to foreigners. With help from Baron Philippe von Forell, the Saxon ambassador to the Spanish court, Humboldt was able to convince the sympathetic officials in Madrid to authorize an exploratory mission into their colonial territories. By June 1799, the expedition was under way. Ironically, as their corvette left the Spanish port of La Coruña, Bonpland and Humboldt passed the island fortress of San Antón Castle, where Alessandro Malaspina, Haenke's commander, fretted in a state prison.

Aimé Bonpland (right) and Alexander von Humboldt in South America painted by Eduard Ender.
AKADEMIE DER WISSENSCHAFTEN, BERLIN / AKG-IMAGES

Five years later, Bonpland and Humboldt returned triumphantly to Europe. They had traveled nearly 15,000 km (9,000 miles) through Central and South America, gathering an enormous amount of data in botany, zoology, paleontology, geography, geology, meteorology, astronomy, and anthropology—information that would revolutionize nineteenth-century science. Bonpland had collected more than six thousand specimens of plants, including forty-five hundred new species. Their scientific achievements were unmatched, which led others to describe their expedition as the "second discovery of America" (Krapovickas 2008).

One plant Bonpland and Humboldt never saw, however, was the giant water lily. They were close. In May 1800, they reached San Carlos de Rio Negro (in modern-day Venezuela), where the Casiquiare Canal connects the Amazon Basin with the Orinoco River near the Brazilian border. They considered descending Rio Negro to the Amazon and continuing as far as the Brazilian coast. But they were warned that, as foreigners carrying surveying instruments, they might be viewed with mistrust and arrested by Portuguese

Aimé Bonpland (left) and Alexander von Humboldt along the Orinoco in New Granada engraved by Otto Roth after H. Lademann, 1870.

BILDARCHIV PREUSSISCHER KULTURBESITZ / ART RESOURCE, NEW YORK

authorities on suspicion of spying. According to Humboldt (1995), the Portuguese could not conceive how a sensible man could exhaust himself "measuring lands that did not belong to him." So Humboldt and Bonpland turned back toward Orinoco and missed an opportunity to be the first explorers to find the wonder nymph, a full year before Haenke's discovery along Río Mamoré.

Humboldt and Bonpland concluded their expedition in the spring of 1804. Before returning to France, Humboldt and Bonpland sailed to Philadelphia. Their ship was held up in the Delaware River due to quarantine regulations, though. Distressed, Humboldt wrote a letter to Philadelphia botanist Zaccheus Collins, begging him to "to deliver us from these vexations" (Humboldt 1804). Collins interceded, and a few days later, Humboldt and Bonpland were allowed to disembark. In Philadelphia, they conversed with American naturalists and later traveled to Washington, D.C., to share their discoveries with President Thomas Jefferson and Secretary of State James Madison. Humboldt and Bonpland had concluded their expedition in Central and South America just as Meriwether Lewis and William Clark were beginning their exploration of the North American West.

Back in Europe, the lives of Bonpland and Humboldt took very different turns. The expedition and the publications that followed established Humboldt as one of the titans of science—on par with Carl Linnaeus and Charles Darwin but with even broader interests that encompassed nearly all the branches of science. Bonpland fared less well. He did obtain a yearly pension from the French government in acknowledgment for the herbarium he presented to the Jardin des Plantes at the National Museum of Natural History in Paris. In 1808, he also became the botanist at Malmaison, Empress Joséphine's famous country château outside of Paris. Bonpland's friendship with Empress Joséphine had begun when he presented her with some rare seeds from his American voyage. She planted them in the Malmaison conservatories, and Bonpland had visited her there regularly. When Étienne Pierre Ventenat, the *intendant* of the garden, died a couple of years later, Joséphine asked Bonpland to succeed him.

Bonpland's years in Joséphine's service were happy ones. "Next to herborizing there was nothing he loved more than horticulture," remarked George Sarton, Harvard University science historian. "It was not enough for him to find plants, determine and collect them; he must see them grow and if possible to breed them. Moreover, practical occupation suited him better than purely intellectual or bookish ones from which he instinctively shrank" (Sarton 1943). Bonpland's personal life also took a new direction when he married Adeline, one of Joséphine's companions at Malmaison. But his contentment was short-lived. In 1810, Joséphine divorced Napoleon.

Alexander von Humboldt, letter to Carl Willdenow, 1801:

I am extremely satisfied with my traveling companion Alexandre [sic] Bonpland. He is a worthy pupil of Jussieu's, Desfontaines' and particularly of eccentric old Richard's (probably the best botanist in Paris). He is very active and diligent. He arranges himself readily with foreign customs and people, speaks Spanish very well, is very plucky and courageous. He possesses splendid qualities for a traveling naturalist. He has dried the plants—including more than 12,000 duplicates—on his own.

Lack 2009

Riachuelo, a tributary of Paraná, where Aimé Bonpland collected *Victoria cruziana* in 1821.
TOMASZ ANIŚKO / LONGWOOD GARDENS

Aimé Bonpland, letter to Robert Gore, 1850:

In the year 1820 I found, near the town of Corrientes, and not far from the forks of the Paraná and the river Paraguay, a magnificent aquatic plant, known to the natives by the name of maíz de agua; *I described it, and placed it in the genus* Nymphaea. *After leaving Paraguay, I again turned my attention to the [*maíz de agua*]: I have observed it in many of the rivers which join the Paraná, and in the Chaco, which I visited frequently, I found this vegetable growing very abundantly, overspreading the lakes with green; and more recently I have seen this new species of* Nymphaea *(which I described for the first time in 1820) in the river Mirivan [Miriñay]. This small stream, which rises from the great lake Ybera [Iberá], traverses the province of Corrientes, and mingles its water with those of the Uruguay. From those numerous localities the [*maíz de agua*] may be easily procured and propagated; and this useful and beautiful plant may become very common, particularly if the inhabitants take much interest in its cultivation.*

Hooker 1851

She was allowed to keep Malmaison, but four years later she died suddenly of pneumonia. After her death, the ownership of Malmaison passed to her son from her first marriage, Eugène de Beauharnais. Rather than remain in his service, Bonpland decided to return to South America.

JOURNEY TO ARGENTINA

The opportunity to go to Argentina arose when Bernardino Rivadavia, an envoy of the young Argentine republic and later its first president, invited Bonpland to Buenos Aires. Bonpland accepted the invitation, and in November 1816, he sailed from Le Havre with Adeline and her daughter from a previous marriage, Emma. Bonpland did not realize that he would never see France again.

In Buenos Aires, Bonpland settled into a routine of practicing medicine, collecting plants, and teaching natural history. He failed, however, to obtain the professional recognition or financial rewards he expected. Frustrated by this lack of success, he decided to make a radical change. In October 1820, Bonpland departed Buenos Aires, leaving behind—some say abandoning—his wife and stepdaughter. First, he journeyed north to Corrientes, a provincial capital near the confluence of the Paraná and Paraguay rivers. In May 1821, he traveled east to the province of Misiones to start a new venture: a plantation of *yerba maté* (*Ilex paraguariensis*) in Santa Ana, a ruined Jesuit mission on the river Paraná that had been deserted more than a half century earlier.

Bonpland had not, however, given up pursuing botanical discoveries. In March 1821, while exploring the Riachuelo River, a tributary of the Paraná near Corrientes, he found and collected a giant lily. The lily was locally known as *maíz de agua*.

Bonpland had first heard of this plant in Buenos Aires three years earlier when someone had brought him seeds—which he recorded provisionally as *Nelumbium* in his field diary—that had been collected near Santa Fe along Paraná, some 400 km (250 miles) upriver from the capital (Bell 2010). Now he had come face-to-face with the vegetable colossus. Regrettably, a dramatic turn of events a few months later would prevent Bonpland from sharing his discovery with his correspondents in Paris.

Aimé Bonpland's plant-hunting grounds at the confluence of the Riachuelo and Paraná near Corrientes.
Edwin E. Harvey

IMPRISONMENT AND CIVIL WAR

Bonpland's activities in Santa Ana had attracted the attention of his neighbor to the north: Paraguay's much feared consul, José Gaspar Rodriguez de Francia. Francia viewed Bonpland's success with *yerba maté* as interfering with his own attempts to monopolize the production of this highly profitable crop. In addition, Paraguay was claiming Misiones as part of its territory at that time, and Francia suspected Bonpland of being a French spy.

Ruins of a Jesuit misson in Santa Ana in Misiones where Aimé Bonpland established a plantation of *yerba maté,* or *Ilex paraguariensis,* in 1820.
Tomasz Aniśko / Longwood Gardens

El Sabio, or the Wise Man 33

Aimé Bonpland at São Borja, Brazil, around 1845. Portrait drawn by Alfred Demersay and lithographed by Achille Deveria.
Musée de la Ville de Paris / Musée Carnavalet, Paris / Giraudon / The Bridgeman Art Library

Alcide d'Orbigny, 1840:

I ... heard from an intimate friend of M. Bonpland, the companion and fellow-labourer of the famous Humboldt, that M. Bonpland having accidentally explored, eight years previous to my visit, (of course not in company with Humboldt, for it was long after their united travels,) a place near the little river called Riochuelo [sic], he saw from a distance this superb plant, and had well nigh precipitated himself off the raft into the river, in his desire to secure specimens; and that M. Bonpland could speak of little else for a whole month.

Hooker 1851

On December 8, 1821, Francia sent soldiers across the Paraná to destroy the plantation. Bonpland was kidnapped, taken to Paraguay, and then eventually banished to El Cerrito, located between Santa Rosa and Santa María. In El Cerrito, he was allowed to set up a small farm and to continue practicing medicine, but his movements were severely restricted: He was forbidden to leave Paraguay.

Humboldt and other friends in Europe worked tirelessly to obtain Bonpland's release, making diplomatic efforts through the French and English governments. But it was to no avail. In May 1829, Francia suddenly expelled Bonpland from El Cerrito and directed him to live in Itapúa (today's Encarnación) on the right bank of the Paraná.

A year later, authorities in Corrientes sent troops to Misiones to establish Argentinean control over this long-disputed territory along the Paraná's left bank. In February 1831, Bonpland, now fifty-seven years old, was finally allowed to leave Paraguay. He crossed the Paraná and traveled south to the Brazilian side of the Uruguay River near São Borja. There, he organized a new *estancia* and began to rebuild his life. He once more took up the life of a plantation owner, cultivating a wide variety of crops, distilling alcohol, producing liquors, operating carpentry and blacksmith's shops, and practicing medicine.

El Recreo, Aimé Bonpland's *estancia* on the banks of the Uruguay near Santa Ana in Corrientes, as seen by a German traveler, Robert Avé-Lallemant, who visited it in 1858.
LIBRARY OF THE ARNOLD ARBORETUM, HARVARD UNIVERSITY

Aimé Bonpland's 1821 sketch of *Victoria* fruit collected along the Riachuelo that accompanied entry number 543 in his field diary.
MUSÉUM NATIONAL D'HISTOIRE NATURELLE, PARIS

Aimé Bonpland:

I have left in Paraguay a well-established farm business; I cultivated cotton, sugar cane, peanuts, five varieties of manioc, several varieties of sweet potato, yerba maté, vineyards, oranges and several varieties of genus Citrus, *guava, etc. I have also left a distillery, a wood mill, a blacksmith shop and a four-room hospital, that was always full of sick people. To all this, I must add four hundred cows, ox, mules and horses to do the work on the farm.*

Krapovickas 2008, translated by Irene Woodward

EL SABIO, OR THE WISE MAN

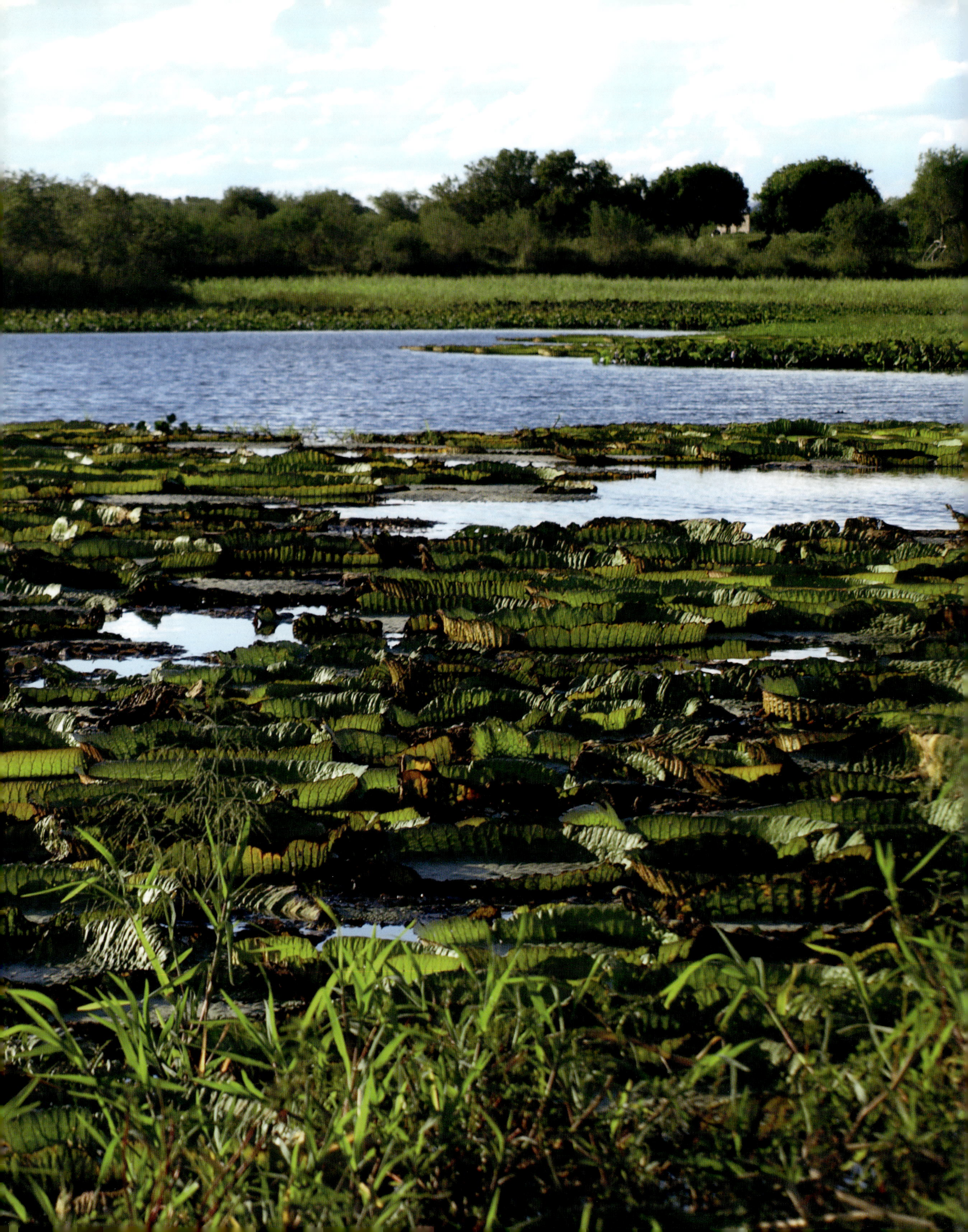

A daguerreotype image of Aimé Bonpland from the 1850s inscribed "taken in Paraguay."
ARCHIVES OF THE GRAY HERBARIUM, HARVARD UNIVERSITY

Aimé Bonpland:

What compensation could I find in the noise and bustle of Paris? Should I labour in some garret there for any bookseller who might undertake to print my books? Should I live there debarred from all other consolation save that of watching from time to time a rose blooming at my window? I should have to lose that which is to me of all things most precious, the society of my beloved plants, which have been my companions through life.

Bruhns 1873

Aimé Bonpland, letter to Robert Gore, 1850:

In 1835, at the request of Mons. Mirbel, Professor of Horticulture in the Jardin des Plantes at Paris, I sent him some seeds of this plant, as well as an exact and full description of the method of propagating it at Paris and in the colony of Algeria; unfortunately, however, since that time communication has become rare and difficult, and I have heard nothing of the package, which likewise contained many other useful objects.... In May, 1849, when at Río Pardo, on the banks of the Yucay [Jacuí], I was agreeably surprised to see all the ladies equipped with fans with correct miniature drawings of the Nymphaea, which I described twenty-nine years before. The sight of these fans caused me great pleasure, and was the source of much reflection, reminding me of the parcel I had sent to M. Mirbel. I remained in uncertainty of its fate till September of the same year, when being in Monte Video [Montevideo], and glancing at the Penny Magazine, I saw a plate of the [maíz de agua] on a larger scale, and more exact than that on the fans at Río Pardo. Thus, in short, I was relieved from any doubt as to whether I had made the plant known in Europe.

Hooker 1851

The news of Bonpland's release was widely celebrated across Europe. He received numerous awards and honorary degrees, including the Legion of Honor from France and the Order of the Red Eagle from Berlin. In addition, Germany's Imperial Leopold-Charles Academy for Natural Science renamed their official botanical journal *Bonplandia*.

Bonpland, however, did not enjoy his prosperity in São Borja for long. In 1838, a civil war that was consuming the Brazilian province of Rio Grande do Sul forced him from his plantation. He moved to the Argentinean side of the river Uruguay, leased 9,000 hectares (22,000 acres) from the province of Corrientes, and established another *estancia* in Santa Ana (today's Bonpland), south of Restauración (today's Paso de los Libres). In 1843, the hostilities ceased in Rio Grande do Sul, and seventy-year-old Bonpland returned to São Borja. Ten years later, in 1853, he relocated permanently to Santa Ana in Argentina.

In the years that followed, Bonpland abandoned thoughts of returning to Europe. He married an Indian woman, fathered three children, and became wholly absorbed by the problems of his adopted

Victoria cruziana near Corrientes.
TOMASZ ANIŚKO / LONGWOOD GARDENS

El Recreo, Aimé Bonpland's last *estancia*, photographed in 2008.
TOMASZ ANIŚKO / LONGWOOD GARDENS

> **Aimé Bonpland, letter to Charles-François de Mirbel, 1838:**
>
> *From the first days of May, 1837, I had fulfilled your wishes about the [maíz de agua], but an urgent cause obligated me to leave this city to travel to São Borja; and upon my return to Corrientes after some time, I am able to satisfy your request at last. Please forgive, I pray you, this delay and know that I did everything possible to furnish you the means to study and to publicize, with great exactitude, a plant that I discovered back in 1820; and which has justifiably held your attention. M. d'Orbigny, who visited this country, has of necessity seen and described the [maíz de agua] and made such a magnificent drawing of this plant, that I was truly embarrassed to send you eight pages almost covered with very badly traced lines. I am determined to send this to you, first because you have shown me your wish to have the parts that bear fruit; and perhaps also in the hope that something useful will be the result of my work, compared with that of M. d'Orbigny.... The eight pages of bad drawings that accompany the descriptions included here are enclosed in a tube of rust-proofed iron and placed in one of three boxes that I am sending to the Museum. The four jars are contained in a special little box.*
>
> Hamy 1906, translated by John Luttrell

country. In 1857, the eighty-four-year-old Bonpland contemplated taking his entire herbarium and manuscript collection to Paris. He wrote Humboldt in July, "My visit to France will be but of short duration; for I shall wish to return to my home at St. Anna, where I lead a life as happy as it is peaceful. There I trust I shall die, and my grave will be shadowed by the numerous trees that I have planted" (Bruhns 1873). Bonpland eventually decided against a trip to France. Instead, he deposited his herbarium collection in a provincial museum in Corrientes, which he had helped to create a few years earlier.

MAÍZ DE AGUA

After his release from captivity in Paraguay, Bonpland had regularly sent duplicates of his seed collections to Paris. It was not until 1835, however, that he had managed to ship seeds of the giant water lily known to Spanish settlers as *maíz de agua* (so called because it bears fruit with seeds that can be substituted for grains of maize to make a flour of superior whiteness).

In the first known attempt to introduce this plant in Europe, Bonpland sent seeds to Professor Charles-François Brisseau de Mirbel, head of the Jardin des Plantes in Paris.

Juan Bonpland, a great-great-grandson of Aimé Bonpland, sitting in 2008 at the base of one of the *Ceiba* trees planted by *El Sabio* at El Recreo.
TOMASZ ANIŚKO / LONGWOOD GARDENS

Aimé Bonpland, letter to Charles-François de Mirbel, 1850:

I was pleased to get some lovely fruits, well ripened, from the [maíz de agua] in the first days of June. Last year I had promised some seeds of this plant to M. Gore, chargé d'affaires of Her Britannic Majesty, because I had seen an engraving of my old plant from Corrientes in the Penny Magazine. *As I don't think it right to send some of these seeds only to England, today I'm ... send[ing] you some of these precious seeds. I still do not know the fate of the shipment I sent you from Corrientes in 1833 or 1835, but above all I fear we have been beaten by the English, who however even today have not seen all parts of this plant, especially the fruit.... The seeds that I send you are very fresh; they were taken from the waters of the Mirime [probably Río Miriñay near Santa Ana] at the beginning of last month.... I send also a few seeds ... to M. Vilmorin. I like to think that by his diligence we will imitate the Germans and the English, and that France will be seen to figure in the recognition of this plant, of which the form and the size of the leaves are truly surprising.*

Hamy 1906, translated by John Luttrell

EL SABIO, OR THE WISE MAN 39

Aimé Bonpland's field notes describing the 1850 collection of *Victoria regina* number 2491.
LONGWOOD GARDENS LIBRARY AND ARCHIVES

Aimé Bonpland, 1857:

In the early afternoon we took a trip down the river with the commander of El Bissón *and the English consul until we arrived at a stream situated south east of Asunción and an hour distant from that city. The trip had for me two objectives: the first of them was to observe the* maíz de agua *(Victoria regina), and the other one to find novel plants. When the mouth of the stream was reached… I had the agreeable surprise of seeing the large [expanse] of the* Victoria regina, *in which a great number of its leaves reached the size of two Spanish* varas *[1.67 m, 6 feet] in diameter. The flowers were generally much larger than I had observed and had a most beautiful [aspect]. The leaves in particular had a texture that seemed to me thinner, weaker, and of a less vivid green [color] than those of the* maíz de agua *of Corrientes. The collections that I have gathered impose upon me the obligation to study anew the* Regia regina *of Corrientes and to clarify whether the* maíz de agua *of Paraguay isn't dealing with a distinct species, similar to the* Regia regia *found in English Guyana and carried to Europe.*

Roqué and Romañach 2006,
translated by Kathleen Morgan

He also included a complete description of the plant with instructions on how to grow and care for it. Unfortunately, Mirbel's efforts to germinate the seeds were not successful (Wagner 1956). He wrote Bonpland requesting detailed illustrations, but it would be three years before Bonpland could comply.

For years afterward, Bonpland was unaware of the fate of the seeds he sent to France in 1835. On an 1849 visit to the Brazilian city of Rio Pardo, however, he saw ladies carrying imported hand fans decorated with representations of the giant lily. He also discovered similar illustrations in the British *Penny Magazine* and the *Illustrated London News* that detailed Joseph Paxton's success growing *Victoria* at Chatsworth in England. *Maíz de agua* had indeed reached Europe.

Prompted perhaps by the news of Paxton's success, Bonpland collected additional samples of *Victoria*. In May 1850, he pressed another herbarium specimen, number 2491 in his collection—this time labeling it *Victoria regina*. In June, he gathered an

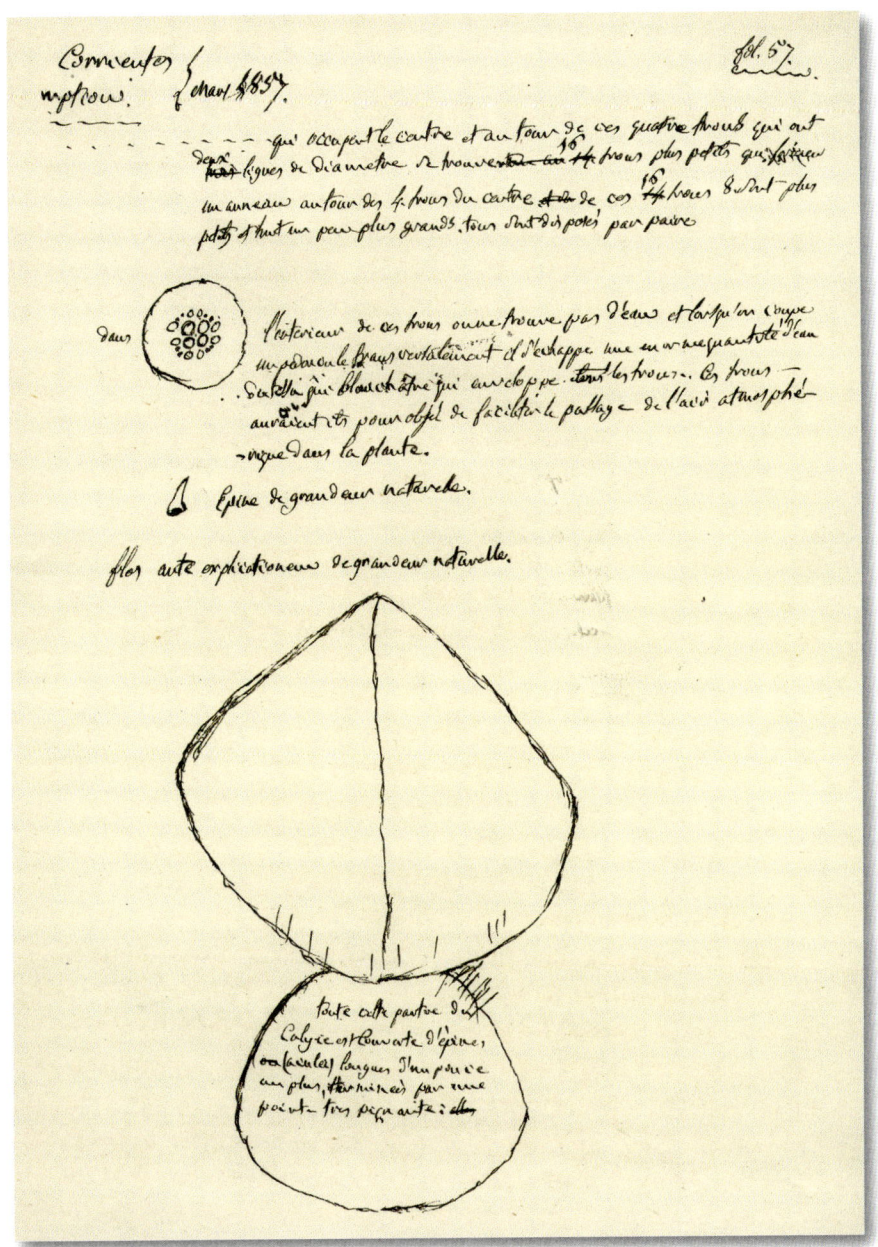

Aimé Bonpland's drawings accompanying his 1857 collection of *Victoria regina* number 2859 from the Paraguay River near Asunción.
LONGWOOD GARDENS LIBRARY AND ARCHIVES

Juan Pujol, address to the provincial council, 1856:

Here he [Bonpland] cultivates the land with the great care, intelligence and perseverance of a young man, and with no other purpose than to leave, when his days are done, a veritable botanical garden in the province. He has already succeeded in gathering there more than five thousand plants divided among more than a hundred kinds, which has encouraged the people of the Uruguayan coast to such extent that numerous gardens and vineyards can be found now in these areas that were so much against any form of culture previously. This well deserving Sabio, from whom the province will benefit so much, finds himself in poverty and does not have the means to purchase the piece of land that would allow him to settle definitely in the province.

Krapovickas 1970, translated by Irene Woodward

ample amount of seeds and forwarded them to Mirbel in Paris. He also sent seeds to Philippe-André de Vilmorin, founder of the renowned French arboretum Les Barres, and to Robert Gore, Britain's chargé d'affaires in Montevideo.

In 1857, seventeen years after the Paraguayan ruler Francia's death, Bonpland returned to Paraguay for the first time since his imprisonment. In a letter to Humboldt, he explained: "I am not afraid of saying that in the course of your immortal voyage we have not discovered a single place offering us as beautiful a flora, a site as varied and enchanting, as the neighborhood of Asunción. . . . For years it has been exceptional for me to find plants which I had not yet studied, yet in Asunción more than half were unknown to me. I am all afire with the desire to return to Paraguay" (Sarton 1943).

While in Asunción, the capital of Paraguay, the eighty-four-year-old Bonpland busied himself collecting plants. In a stream not far from the city, he found another site with *Victoria*. There, he pressed herbarium specimen number 2859, the

Robert Avé-Lallemant, 1859:

I dismounted amid the violent barking of four great dogs, and upon loudly clapping my hands there came forward a pleasing-looking young girl... [who] asked me in Spanish what I wanted. I gave her a letter to Bonpland, which she carried into one of the buildings that was meant to pass for a house, but returned shortly to conduct me into the other hut, which served as drawing-room and strangers' apartment.... I had not waited long when the eccentric old man, whose very existence we had begun to doubt, appeared before me. His eighty-five years had not impaired the erectness of his form, but his genial blue eyes beamed from a countenance deeply furrowed, and his voice betrayed the weakness of infirmity. His thin figure was clad in a shirt and trousers of white flannel, while on his stockingless feet he wore wooden slippers. He held out his hand to me in friendly greeting, and as I grasped it I felt the feverish heat that seemed to be consuming him. The whole scene in the midst of this desert region... without one of the attractions of civilized life, impressed me with an indescribable feeling of melancholy.

Bruhns 1873

last *maíz de agua* he would collect. Bonpland was probably unaware that French explorer Alcide d'Orbigny had named this plant *Victoria cruziana* or that it was different from "*Victoria Regina* of the English." He did notice certain dissimilarities between the *maíz de agua* plants in Paraguay and those he observed near Corrientes but never had an opportunity to compare them to the Amazonian ones. Bonpland maintained that *maíz de agua* belonged to *Nymphaea*, although he later admitted it probably deserved its own rank as a genus. In his later years, he sometimes wrote of *maíz de agua* as "*Regia regina*" or "*Regina regia*."

EL SABIO

As Argentina's first resident naturalist, Bonpland became widely known as *El Sabio*, or the Wise Man. In November 1856, the governor of Corrientes, Juan Pujol, obtained approval from the provincial council to grant *El Sabio* Bonpland the piece of land in Santa Ana on which he lived "as proof of the province's gratitude for the important services by Dr. Bonpland to the country during difficult times" (Krapovickas 1970, translated by Irene Woodward).

Less than eighteen months later, in April 1858, German physician Robert Avé-Lallemant, who was traveling in southern Brazil, visited Santa Ana. Prompted by

An ossuary of Aimé Bonpland in Paso de los Libres cemetery.
TOMASZ ANIŚKO / LONGWOOD GARDENS

In 2008, on the 150th anniversary of Aimé Bonpland's death, Argentina's postal service issued a commemorative stamp showing *El Sabio* from the 1837 portrait by Carlos Pellegrini against the backdrop of a leaf of yerba maté (*Ilex paraguariensis*).
LONGWOOD GARDENS LIBRARY AND ARCHIVES

rumors of Bonpland's death, Avé-Lallemant was anxious to see the illustrious botanist in order to provide a report of him to Humboldt in Berlin. He sailed down the river Uruguay to Restauración, and then rode on horseback through Santa Ana to Bonpland's *estancia*, El Recreo. He found the eighty-five-year-old botanist visibly on the decline but still able to converse. "Not many of those who had been so lucky to meet the great Alexander von Humboldt in Berlin," wrote Avé-Lallemant, "traveled as far as Uruguay to visit old Bonpland. It had been an internal necessity for me, a holy duty. . . . And who knows, I may have been the last envoy of European ancestry, European science, who had traveled many miles for the sole purpose of giving old Bonpland respect, love, and sincere friendship for himself and in the name of science" (Avé-Lallemant 1859, translated by Christine Klepacz).

Bonpland died less than a month after Avé-Lallemant's visit, on May 11, 1858. His remains were buried in the cemetery in Restauración, sadly deprived of the shade of the beloved trees he had planted at El Recreo and mentioned in his last letter to Humboldt. The news of Bonpland's death reached Humboldt in Berlin in August. Humboldt himself died almost exactly a year after his colleague, on May 6, 1859.

Robert Avé-Lallemant, 1859:

On my visiting him the next morning I found him very feeble; he had slept badly, and his wasted hands were burning with fever. I begged that he would allow me to nurse him, and assist him in the arrangement of any of his affairs, or conduct him to his friends at Uruguayana; but he declined all offers of assistance. Hopeless as his condition appeared, he would not entertain the thought of death; he seemed to think that as he had been accustomed to put off work all through life, so death might be postponed even at the last. With a cheerful air he invited me to visit him again in the course of "a few years"; cattle would then be grazing in the fields, the garden in beautiful order, and his dwelling completed and fitted up with all necessary furniture. . . . I begged him to give me his autograph as a remembrance, and he wrote upon the back of an old letter: "Aimé Bonpland." "That is badly written," he remarked, and wrote his name a second time, but even less successfully. "Ah," he exclaimed, "I have no longer the power to write"; and it seemed to me as if a tear stole down his cheek. Probably this was the last time that he ever wrote his name.

Bruhns 1873

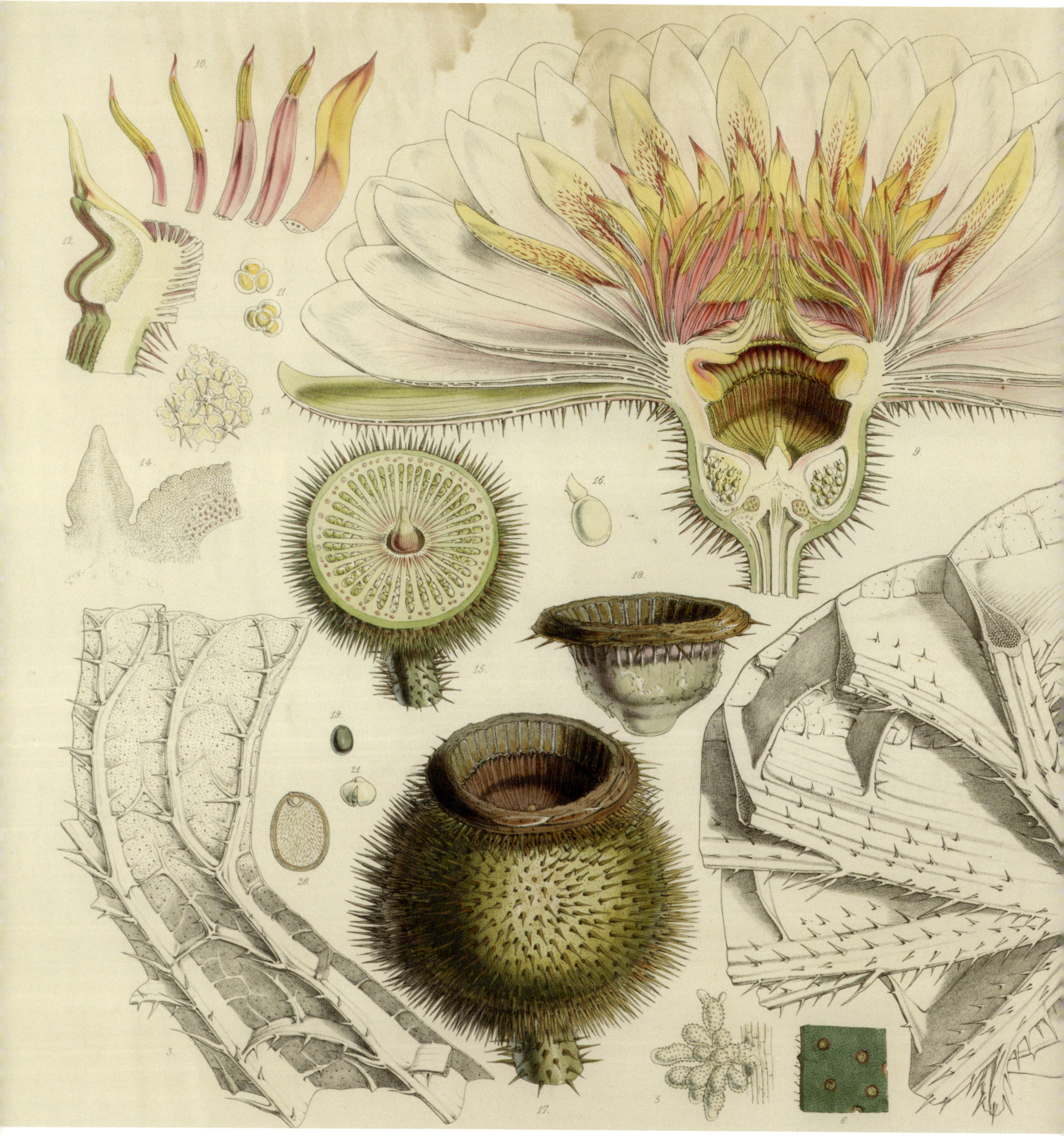

10.
12.
11.
13.
14.
9.
16.
15.
18.
19.
21.
20.
3.
17.
5.
6.

chapter 3

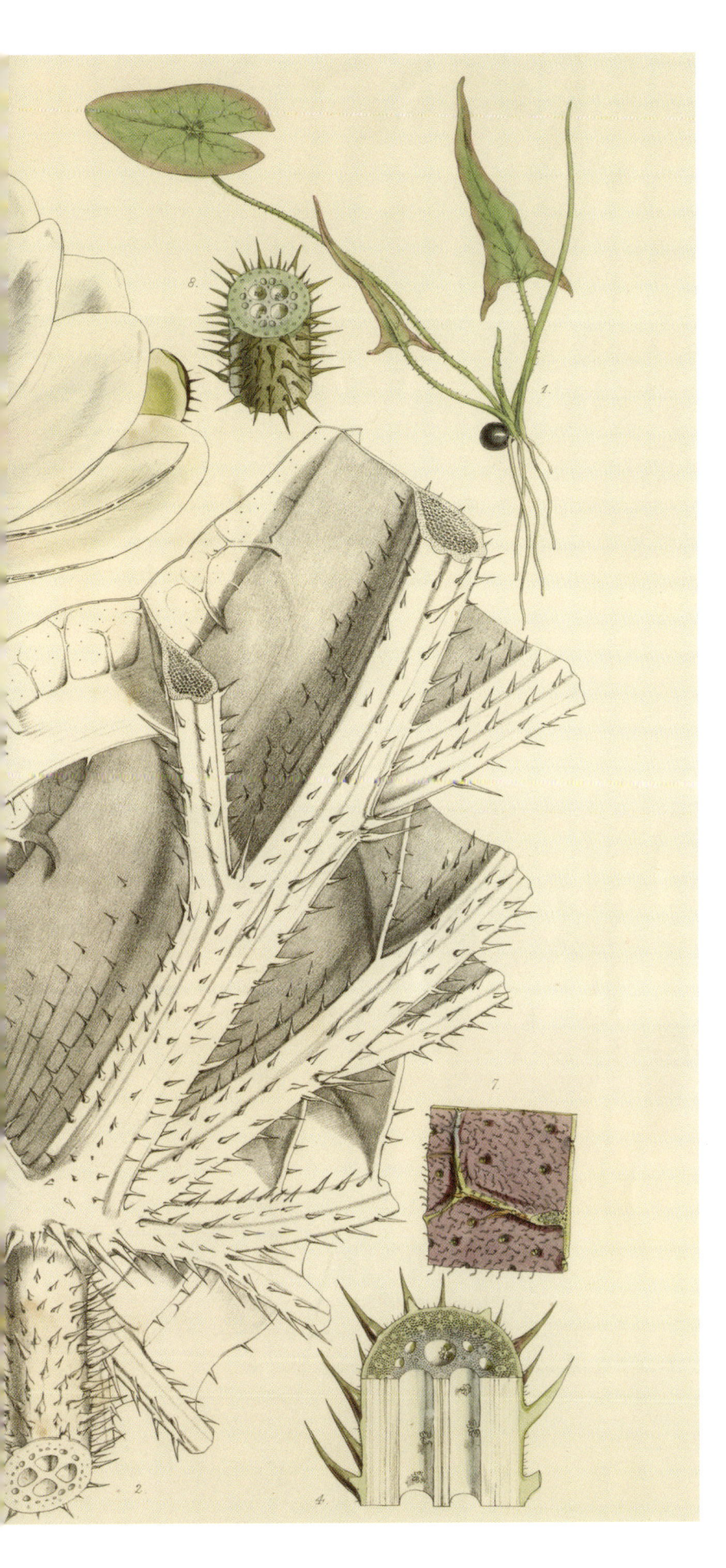

NATURALISTE-VOYAGEUR

LOCATED ON THE COAST OF THE BAY OF BISCAY, the French port city of La Rochelle was home to Aimé Bonpland in the late 1700s. It was also the place where the early scientific interests of France's next great naturalist—Alcide d'Orbigny—were cultivated.

In 1815, thirteen-year-old Alcide and his family moved to the small village of Esnandes outside La Rochelle. There, Aimé Bonpland briefly befriended the d'Orbignys before departing for South America in 1816. In those days, Esnandes was considered a rather unremarkable village, but it overlooked an immense shallow bay, and at low tide the sea receded several miles, providing an ideal site for culturing mussels and oysters, the sole industry there.

In 1820, d'Orbigny's family relocated to La Rochelle. At that time, it was one of France's most important ports. La Rochelle also had strong maritime traditions and had built its prosperity on grand sea voyages and exploration of the New World.

Encouraged by his father, Charles, a navy physician and avid amateur naturalist, young Alcide became fascinated by the marine life in La Rochelle. He prepared hundreds of drawings of the microscopic aquatic invertebrates he and his father discovered along the shore. In a letter to a friend, Charles d'Orbigny prized Alcide's help: "I have observed so much in my

Details of flower and leaf structure of *Victoria amazonica* growing in Syon House in London drawn by Walter Fitch for William Hooker's 1851 book *Victoria Regia*.
THE MCLEAN LIBRARY, THE PENNSYLVANIA HORTICULTURAL SOCIETY

Esnandes, a small village outside La Rochelle, where Alcide d'Orbigny spent several of his teenage years, is known for a shallow bay used for centuries for culturing mussels and oysters.
LONGWOOD GARDENS LIBRARY AND ARCHIVES

life that I can hardly see at all, and I am often obliged to borrow his eyes" (Heron-Allen 1917). He also used his son's "piercing and trained sight" to locate minute sea creatures on the bay's beaches and rocks, many that turned out to be previously unknown to science.

These frequent excursions helped refine Alcide's skills of observation and discovery as well as his talent for recording what he found. They also laid the groundwork for Alcide d'Orbigny's career as one of the foremost explorers of the nineteenth century—"second only to Humboldt," according to Charles Darwin (1945).

D'Orbigny continued his studies in Paris. There, he became a disciple of two influential professors at the National Museum of Natural History: geologist Louis Cordier and zoologist Georges Cuvier. With

The harbor of La Rochelle, where Alcide d'Orbigny's family relocated from nearby Esnandes in 1820.
LONGWOOD GARDENS LIBRARY AND ARCHIVES

46 VICTORIA: THE SEDUCTRESS

The National Museum of Natural History in Paris appointed young Alcide d'Orbigny *naturaliste-voyageur* and instructed him to embark on an expedition to South America.

Print Collection, Miriam and Ira D. Wallach Division of Art, Prints and Photographs, The New York Public Library, Astor, Lenox and Tilden Foundations

their support, twenty-three-year-old d'Orbigny was appointed *naturaliste-voyageur* by the museum in 1826 and sent on a scientific expedition to South America.

In preparation for the trip, d'Orbigny received special training at the museum on collecting and preserving plant and animal specimens as well as mineral samples. He received advice from many Parisian naturalists, and he even met with the great Alexander von Humboldt. Humboldt gave the young *naturaliste-voyageur* a barometer—a rare instrument in those days—and letters of introduction to his contacts in South America.

As d'Orbigny carefully planned his expedition, he realized that the funding provided by the museum fell short of what he needed. René Desfontaines, professor of botany at the museum, warned the aspiring explorer, "Do not start on so modest a sum, you will assuredly die of hunger" (Heron-Allen 1917). Seeking additional help, d'Orbigny approached the Duc de Rivoli of La-Ferté St. Aubin. The duke was notorious for his avarice, but he was also known to "loosen his purse-strings when he foresaw a real advantage to science" (Heron-Allen 1917). Impressed by d'Orbigny's plans, de Rivoli granted him additional funds.

DISCOVERING THE MARVELOUS IRUPÉ

On July 31, 1826, d'Orbigny set sail from the French port of Brest, arriving in Rio de Janeiro some two months later. From there, he continued south to Montevideo, where he was thrown in jail on a bogus pretense—a common fate among scientists exploring South America in those turbulent times. The French consul intervened, aided by a considerable bribe, and d'Orbigny was released and allowed to cross Río de la Plata to Buenos Aires.

In early 1827, the young naturalist took a journey up the Paraná River to the city of Corrientes. This would become his home base for a year while he systematically explored surrounding regions. Despite the fact that he was so close to where Bonpland was kept captive across the Paraná in Paraguay, d'Orbigny was unable to connect with his illustrious compatriot. Also, although *Victoria* was common to the region of Corrientes, d'Orbigny did not see the plant until nearly the end of his yearlong stay.

In February 1828, d'Orbigny planned his final excursion out of Corrientes. He rented a small boat and sent it upriver with orders to wait for him in Iribicuá near Itatí. Meanwhile, he traveled on land, exploring the banks of the Paraná. Upon reaching Iribicuá, accompanied only by two Guarani Indians, he began navigation down the Paraná on March 3, 1828. They soon arrived near the confluence of Paraná and San José Creek, one of its tributaries. There, in the marshes along the southern shores of the creek, d'Orbigny noticed from afar that a large expanse of water was covered by immense floating leaves. The Guaranis called the leaves *irupé*, literally water platters, because of their similarity to the large plates or lids of baskets used in that area.

D'Orbigny marveled at the beauty of the plant. He also recognized the nymph's affinity to Nymphaeaceae, the water lily family, and estimated that the size of the San José population of *irupé* was more than a square kilometer (half a square mile). Among the countless huge and curiously margined leaves there were superb pink and white flowers scenting the air with delicious fragrance. It was a grand scene of immense scale yet of "most magnificent harmony" (d'Orbigny 1840, translated by John Luttrell). D'Orbigny admired what he called the *colosse des végétaux* for a long while before collecting samples of leaves, flowers, and fruit.

When he arrived back in Corrientes, d'Orbigny drew *irupé* and showed the illustrations to his friends. He learned that the seeds of the plant were ground like corn (maize) into a pure white flour prized by local bakers for fancy pastries and cakes. For this reason, local Spaniards called the plant *maíz de agua,* or corn of the water. D'Orbigny also heard how Bonpland had discovered the same plant in Riachuelo seven years earlier, in 1821, and how the famed explorer had reacted to it with the same euphoria. D'Orbigny dried his pressed specimens and preserved others in alcohol. He sent them along with his drawings to the National Museum of Natural History in Paris.

From Corrientes, d'Orbigny returned to Buenos Aires and then traveled south to Patagonia, where he explored until September 1829. Later that year, he boarded a ship in Montevideo that took him around Cape Horn to the Pacific coast of South America.

Alcide d'Orbigny, 1840:

For eight months previously, on the frontier of Paraguay, I had explored all parts of the province of Corrientes when, at the beginning of 1827 [sic], descending the Paraná, in order to record its course, I found myself in a frail pirogue on this majestic river which, at three hundred leagues from the Plata, is still more than a league in breadth. Everything there is grandiose, everything is imposing; and, alone with two Guarani Indians, I lapsed into silence at the admiration which these sites, so beautiful and wild, inspired in me. Nevertheless, without doing justice to this superb natural setting, so greatly did this so enormous a mass of water seem to demand it, I desired a vegetation that would rival it, and I searched for it in vain! Shortly afterwards, at the place called Arroyo de San José, *the immense marshes of the southern shore began to expand the extent of the waters and, always alert, I began to notice in the distance a green and floating surface. Questioning my Guaranis, I learned from them that we were approaching the plant that they call* yrupé *(from* y, *water; and* rupé, *large platter or lid of a basket, literally translated: water platter); and an instant afterward I discovered this rich vegetation, of which the superlative reports surpassed my hopes, offering me a composition of the most magnificent harmony.*

d'Orbigny 1840, translated by John Luttrell

While collecting around Corrientes in 1828, Alcide d'Orbigny came upon a large expanse of water covered by immense leaves of *irupé*. Today, aerial photographs show thriving populations of *Victoria cruziana* in the same general area.

EDWIN E. HARVEY

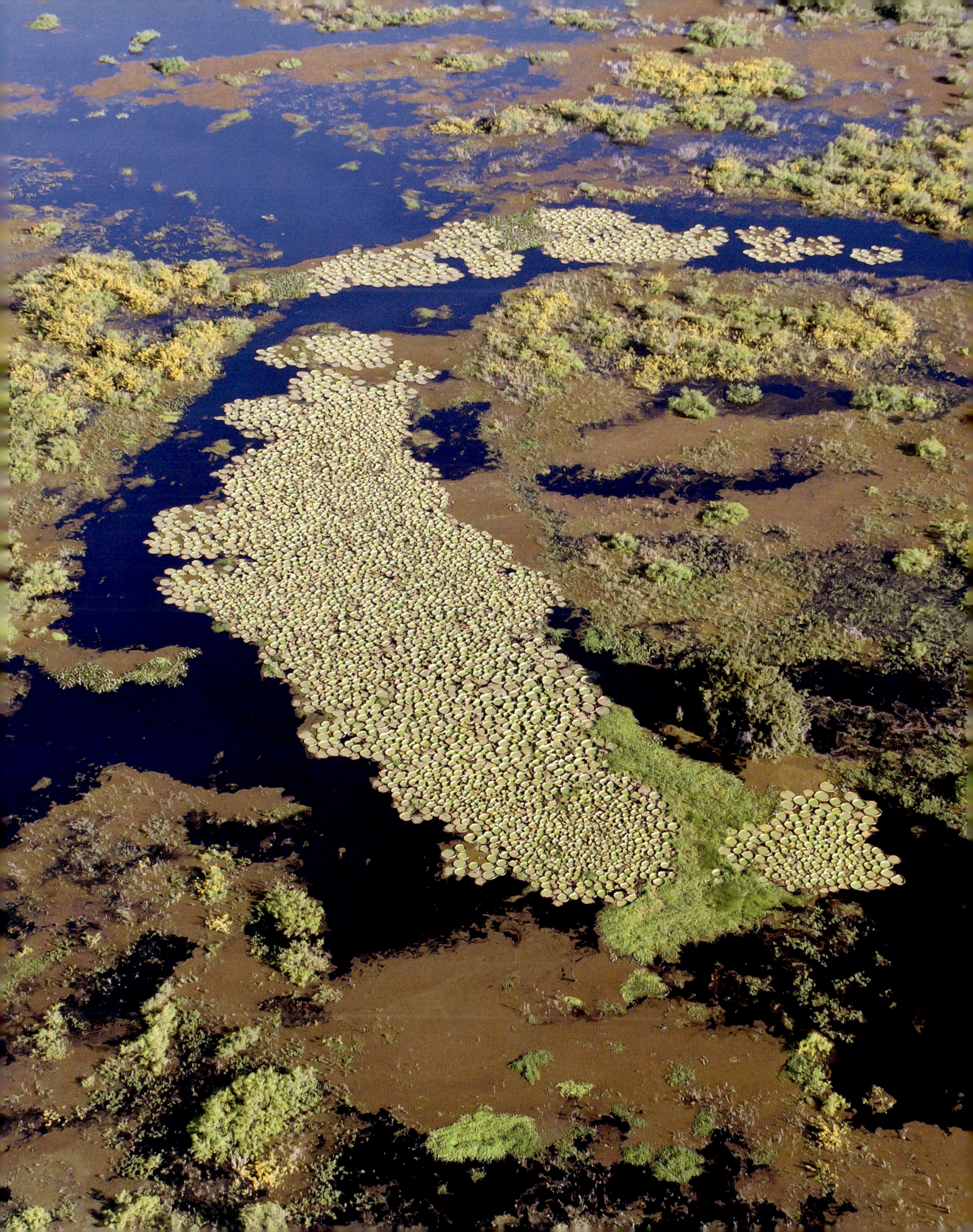

In Europe, *Victoria*'s native environment was envisioned to be a sanctuary of untouched primeval vegetation—wild, virgin, and full of drama, as illustrated in this nineteenth-century German plate. Alcide d'Orbigny, too, described the habitat of the *colosse des végétaux* as imposing.
AUTHOR'S COLLECTION

D'Orbigny stayed on the west side of the Andes until May 1830, when he crossed the mighty cordilleras to reach La Paz in Bolivia. While there, he was introduced to General Andrés de Santa Cruz, with whom he developed a lasting friendship. Santa Cruz was half-Spaniard, half-Indian and had recently been appointed president of the young republic. He commissioned the French explorer to inventory Bolivia's natural riches and survey new transportation routes to neighboring countries that would improve cross-border trade. Santa Cruz not only financed these Bolivian expeditions, but he also granted d'Orbigny citizenship as a token of gratitude for his service.

D'Orbigny wandered in Bolivia for the next three years. In June 1833, he reversed his trek across the Andes and concluded his historic South America journey. In September 1833, he departed for France from Valparaíso, Chile.

A SECOND LILY

During his time in Bolivia, d'Orbigny met an elderly Franciscan missionary named Father Luis de La Cueva. La Cueva had spent many years among the Yurakaré Indians, attempting to convert them to Christianity. At the same time, he had diligently studied their native language. After several months of traveling in the company of Indians, d'Orbigny rejoiced at the opportunity to converse with another emissary from distant Europe.

Despite their age difference, the two enjoyed sharing their experiences and observations. La Cueva recalled an event thirty years earlier when he had accompanied Bohemian botanist Thaddaeus Haenke down the Mamoré River through the province of Moxos in the Bolivian lowlands. One day, in a swamp that stretched along the shores of the river, Haenke's party had found a giant water lily. La Cueva's description of the plant sounded similar to the *irupé* d'Orbigny had discovered in the San José Creek near Corrientes.

Alcide d'Orbigny, 1835:

*The plant seems to belong to the family Nymphaeaceae, and is certainly allied to the nuphar, but its dimensions are gigantic.... The foliage is smooth above and furrowed below with numberless regular compartments, formed by the projecting, thick, hollow nerves, the air in which keeps the leaf upon the surface of the water. Leaf-stalks, flower-stalks, and ribs of the leaves, are alike cellular and covered with long prickles. Amid this expanse of foliage rise the broad flowers, upwards of a foot [30 cm] across, and either white, pink, or purple; always double, and diffusing a delicious odour. The fruit, which succeeds these flowers, is spherical, and half the size, when ripe, of the human head, full of roundish farinaceous seeds, which give to the plant the name of water-maize (*maíz de agua*), for the Spaniards collect the seeds, roast, and eat them. I was never weary of admiring the Colossus of the Vegetable Kingdom, and reluctantly pursued my way the same evening to Corrientes, after collecting specimens of the flowers, fruits, and seeds.*

Hooker 1847

50 VICTORIA: THE SEDUCTRESS

One of two wrinkled leaves of *Victoria cruziana* sent by Alcide d'Orbigny from Corrientes. They are thought to be the oldest herbarium specimens of the giant lily in existence.
MUSÉUM NATIONAL D'HISTOIRE NATURELLE, PARIS

Alcide d'Orbigny named his discovery *Victoria cruziana* after his Bolivian friend and patron, General Andrés de Santa Cruz, shown here in an 1836 portrait by José Gil de Castro.
Museo Nacional de Arquelogia, Antropologia e Historia del Peru

Alcide d'Orbigny, 1840:

A few months after my encounter with Father La Cueva, navigating numerous waterways of the province of Moxos . . . I was going up the Río de Madeiras towards the sources of the Mamoré; when, between the confluence of the Apéré and the Tijamuchi rivers . . . having always in mind my conversation with the good missionary, I finally espied upon the west bank, in an immense lake of stagnant water communicating with the river, I espied, as I say, the extraordinary plant that Haenke discovered; and, according to the description I had known before, belonging to the same genus as the maíz de agua *of Corrientes. Delighted to see these places witnessing to the exaltation of the German botanist, I felt a joy all the more vivid to encounter this vegetal giant, that it was easy for me to recognize from the underside of the leaves and by the purple sepals that the species before me differed specifically from the first. Following the example of Haenke, I camped in there and gathered a generous harvest of leaves and flowers; but, exposed relentlessly to the broiling sun of these inundated plains of the torrid zone and to the torrential rains that I endured before my arrival in an inhabited place, I was unable to conserve this second species; and was therefore deprived of carrying it back to Europe.*

d'Orbigny 1840, translated by John Luttrell

In March 1832, a few months after his encounter with La Cueva, d'Orbigny was traveling through the province of Moxos, where Haenke had made his discovery. D'Orbigny's party was navigating upriver from the Madeira to the sources of the Mamoré. Between the confluences of the Apéré and the Tijamuchi (tributaries of the Mamoré), d'Orbigny spotted Haenke's extraordinary lily within a vast expanse of stagnant water. Although the plant had obvious similarities to the *maíz de agua* of Corrientes, it had certain key differences. For instance, the leaves of Haenke's lily were purple underneath, while those d'Orbigny had found previously were green. This prompted the French explorer to think that he was seeing a different species.

Just as Haenke had done three decades earlier, d'Orbigny set up camp on the riverbank and collected leaves and flowers to prepare herbarium specimens. However, the primitive camp conditions, frequent torrential downpours, and delicate nature of the water lily tissue—which even under the best of circumstances is notoriously difficult to press and dry—made it impossible for d'Orbigny to preserve these specimens. Thus, he was deprived of the satisfaction of bringing them to Europe. He also had no way of knowing that, at the same time, German botanist Eduard Pöppig was racing to reach the mouth of the Amazon so he could return to Berlin and display his specimens and drawings of *mururú*, the giant water lily he had discovered near Ega. Later that year (1832), Pöppig would publish his findings, along with the lily's first scientific name of *Euryale amazonica*.

In 1833, after seven years of exploring Brazil, Uruguay, Argentina, Paraguay, Chile, Bolivia, and Peru, d'Orbigny returned to Paris with an astonishing collection: more than ten thousand specimens of plants, mammals, birds, reptiles, amphibians, fishes, and invertebrates. He immediately began organizing the collections, but cataloging and publishing the results of the expedition took twice as long as the expedition itself. His account, a veritable *opus magnum* titled *Voyage dans l'Amérique Méridionale* (1835–47), filled nearly five thousand pages in seven folio volumes and two atlases. *Voyage* is unquestionably one of the great monuments of science in the nineteenth century. Paleontology formed the core of d'Orbigny's scientific pursuits, and he soon was recognized as one of the field's pioneers and foremost authorities. His accomplishments eventually earned him the post of professor at the prestigious National Museum of Natural History in Paris.

In the first volume of *Voyage,* which appeared in 1835, d'Orbigny recalled his 1828 encounter with *irupé* in the San José Creek, but he did not assign a scientific appellation to it. Acknowledging that both Haenke and Bonpland preceded him in discovering the giant water lily, d'Orbigny left the task of classifying and naming the plant to Adolphe-Théodore Brongniart, a botanist at the museum. Based on collected specimens and drawings, Brongniart confirmed that the Corrientes plant constituted a novel species.

Alcide d'Orbigny's Herculean works in many fields of natural history earned him the honor of having his name engraved on the frieze decorating the Great Gallery of Evolution in the National Museum of Natural History in Paris.
TOMASZ ANIŚKO / LONGWOOD GARDENS

He intended to include its name and description in a future volume of d'Orbigny's *Voyage* dedicated to botany.

THE BRITISH CLAIM

Due to an unexpected turn of events in the fall of 1837, however, the name that d'Orbigny or Brongniart intended to christen the South American water lily was never revealed. At one of the meetings of the Academy of Sciences in Paris, a small pamphlet authored by English botanist John Lindley was presented. In it, Lindley, who had printed only twenty-five copies of the pamphlet, announced the discovery of a giant water lily in British Guiana. He named it *Victoria regia* to honor Queen Victoria, who had ascended the British throne earlier that year.

D'Orbigny instantly recognized the plant he'd found in the Mamoré five years earlier. He was offended—not only by Lindley's brazen disregard for the credit that he thought was rightfully his, but also by the choice of such a "pompous" name. When naming new species, d'Orbigny often recognized those who contributed to his discovery. "It is on this account," he wrote, "that I have with pleasure introduced into science, as an ineffaceable testimony of my gratitude, the names of many modest scientists whose persevering and indefatigable researches have so powerfully contributed to guaranteeing the results of my own" (Heron-Allen 1917).

A bust of Alcide d'Orbigny, along with other great French naturalists, can be seen outside the Gallery of Paleontology and Comparative Anatomy of the National Museum of Natural History in Paris.
TOMASZ ANIŚKO / LONGWOOD GARDENS

In an article in *L'Echo du Monde Savant,* D'Orbigny hastened to claim priority in the giant water lily's discovery. But predictably, his protests were met with a harsh response that was "more than heartrendingly biting" (Planchon and Van Houtte 1850–51, translated by John Luttrell). Botanists on the other side of the English Channel felt compelled to defend their claim to the plant honoring their young monarch. The outcry alarmed d'Orbigny. He feared that the lengthy preparation of descriptions of plants for the botanical volumes of *Voyage* would permit the English to forestall his effort to publish the scientific name of *irupé* from Corrientes. Thus, d'Orbigny announced it on the pages of the *Annales de Sciences Naturelles Botanique* in 1840. Instead of naming it after a "modest scientist," however, he chose to honor his Bolivian friend, President Santa Cruz, who had been recently deposed.

The name *Victoria cruziana* effectively married, intentionally or not, the regal ruler of the British Empire with a Mestizo leader of the Bolivian revolution. Was this d'Orbigny's nuanced way of getting even with the English botanists and poking fun at their pretentious name? We may never know. But the irony contained in the name was enough to make the botanists of Her Britannic Majesty adamantly deny the existence of another species of *Victoria* for many years. In fact, the English translation of d'Orbigny's 1840 paper omitted the paragraph expressing his grievances, calling it "a little expression of vexation that a botanist belonging to another country should have the privilege of first laying a scientific description of this gorgeous plant before the world." They replaced the paragraph with a statement falsely attributed to d'Orbigny, recognizing that "the honour of naming the original and first-found plant has been forestalled by Dr. Lindley, who calls it *Victoria regia*" (Hooker 1847). This Anglo-French sparring over the scientific name "marked by personal bitterness and national defensiveness" (Planchon and Van Houtte 1850–51, translated by John Luttrell) was viewed with embarrassment by other botanists, most of whom chose to remain silent on the subject.

A TITAN OF SCIENTIFIC STUDY

D'Orbigny did not dwell on the "veritable affront" from his English peers. He was accustomed to frequent dissensions and disputes with scholars of his time. Such disputes were "inevitable to the career of so bold and obstinate an innovator" (Heron-Allen 1917). As a titan of scientific study, d'Orbigny had vast interests encompassing all branches of natural history. Often blazing new trails through uncharted scientific fields, he lived a life strewn with as many scientific triumphs as disappointments. When championing the cause of paleontology, he was opposed by geologists, zoologists, and botanists alike, who sought to retain their authority over fossilized records. When his *Voyage* was completed in 1847, it contained the names and descriptions of several thousand new species of plants and animals he had discovered. Although *irupé* was not among them, he was indisputably the first naturalist, perhaps the first man, to find the South American lily in both the Paraná and the Amazon river systems and to realize that they represented distinct species.

On June 30, 1857, d'Orbigny died in the small town of Pierrefitte-sur-Seine outside Paris. He left an estate of more than one hundred thousand specimens of plants and animals housed at the National Museum of Natural History. These, along with his voluminous publications, are a telling testimony to his immense scientific productivity. D'Orbigny was envied and often denounced by his contemporaries. But a century and a half later, scientists have a much better understanding and appreciation of the legacy of the French explorer. In the words of one scientist, "We are greatly indebted to Alcide d'Orbigny the man, to d'Orbigny the great naturalist traveler, and to d'Orbigny the humanist" (Vénec-Peyré 2004). Likewise, gardeners are grateful to the French *naturaliste-voyageur* for giving them another *Victoria*.

Alcide d'Orbigny, 1840:

Upon returning to France in 1834, I spoke of my beautiful plants to Mr. Adolphe Brongniart and showed him my drawings. He had already recognized by my samples, conserved at the Museum, that this was a new form that ought to be described in the botanical portion of my travels, the publication of which began in January 1835. In the course of this same year I indicated summarily, in my historical narrative, my discovery of the species of Corrientes, without giving it a botanical name. In addition I received a veritable affront when, in 1837, I saw presented at the Academy of Sciences my plant from the province of Moxos under the pompous name Victoria regia, *given it by Mr. Lindley. I rushed to claim the priority of discovery of this genus, and inserted an article in* L'Echo du Monde Savant, *revisiting that which I had published in 1835.... However, my claim having caught the attention of the English; and knowing that strong promises were made by them to obtain even yet the advantage over France in the naming of the second species, I did not want to delay any longer in making it known; and, fearing that important commitments of Mr. Brongniart prevented him from publishing it promptly, I believed I should give it a name, leaving it to my savant collaborator to describe in detail its botanical characteristics. The species of the genus* Victoria *that I encountered at Corrientes, and that I have named* Victoria cruziana, *dedicating it to General Santa Cruz, to whom I owe in large measure the success of my voyage in Bolivia, differs from* Victoria regia *by its leaves being green on both sides and not green above and red underneath; by its green, and not red, sepals; by its broad ovary of greenish hue while it is narrower and reddish yellow in the other [species]; and lastly by its uniformly pink or white flower, while it is violet in the middle and white around the margin in* Victoria regia.

d'Orbigny 1840, translated by John Luttrell

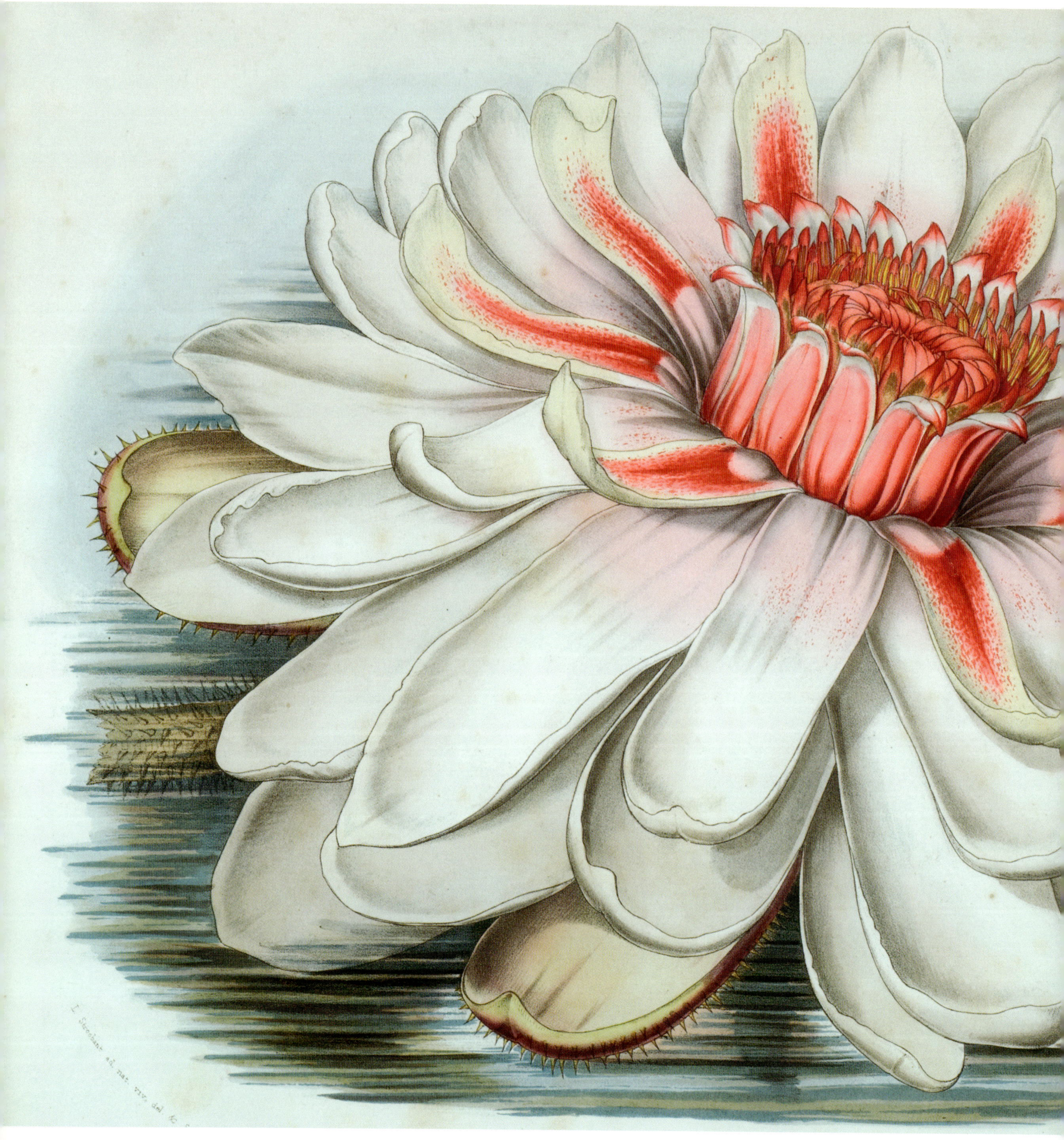
ad nat. viv. del.

chapter 4

THE ROMANTIC

Around the same time that Aimé Bonpland and Alexander von Humboldt were in Paris, planning their grand expedition to the tropics, and Thaddaeus Haenke was enjoying his best years in Cochabamba, a merchant named Christian Gottfried Pöppig and his wife, Carolina Amalia, welcomed their first son in Plauen, Saxony. Eduard Friedrich was born on July 16, 1798, into relative prosperity. Thanks to Carolina's rich dowry, Christian Pöppig was a partner at Plauen's biggest cotton printing manufacturer, a thriving industry at that time. Unfortunately, just two years after Eduard's birth, fierce competition from factories in England forced Pöppig's business into bankruptcy. Christian was crushed and succumbed to excessive drinking. His marriage ended in a divorce. Carolina moved back with her parents in Leipzig—Saxony's "little Paris" of Goethe's *Faust*—taking Eduard and his sister, Emilia Augusta, who was one year younger.

When he was only twelve, Eduard's mother died, and his uncle, Pastor Friedrich Gottlob Schirmer, became his guardian. While Emilia stayed home with Schirmer's family, Eduard was sent to St. Augustin School in Grimma, outside Leipzig, one of Saxony's premier institutions, famous for preparing future elites for government service. There, Eduard received a thorough humanistic education and developed his own expressive

Second-night flower of *Victoria amazonica*, a lithograph from Jules Planchon and Louis Van Houtte's book *La Victoria Regia*.
LONGWOOD GARDENS LIBRARY AND ARCHIVES

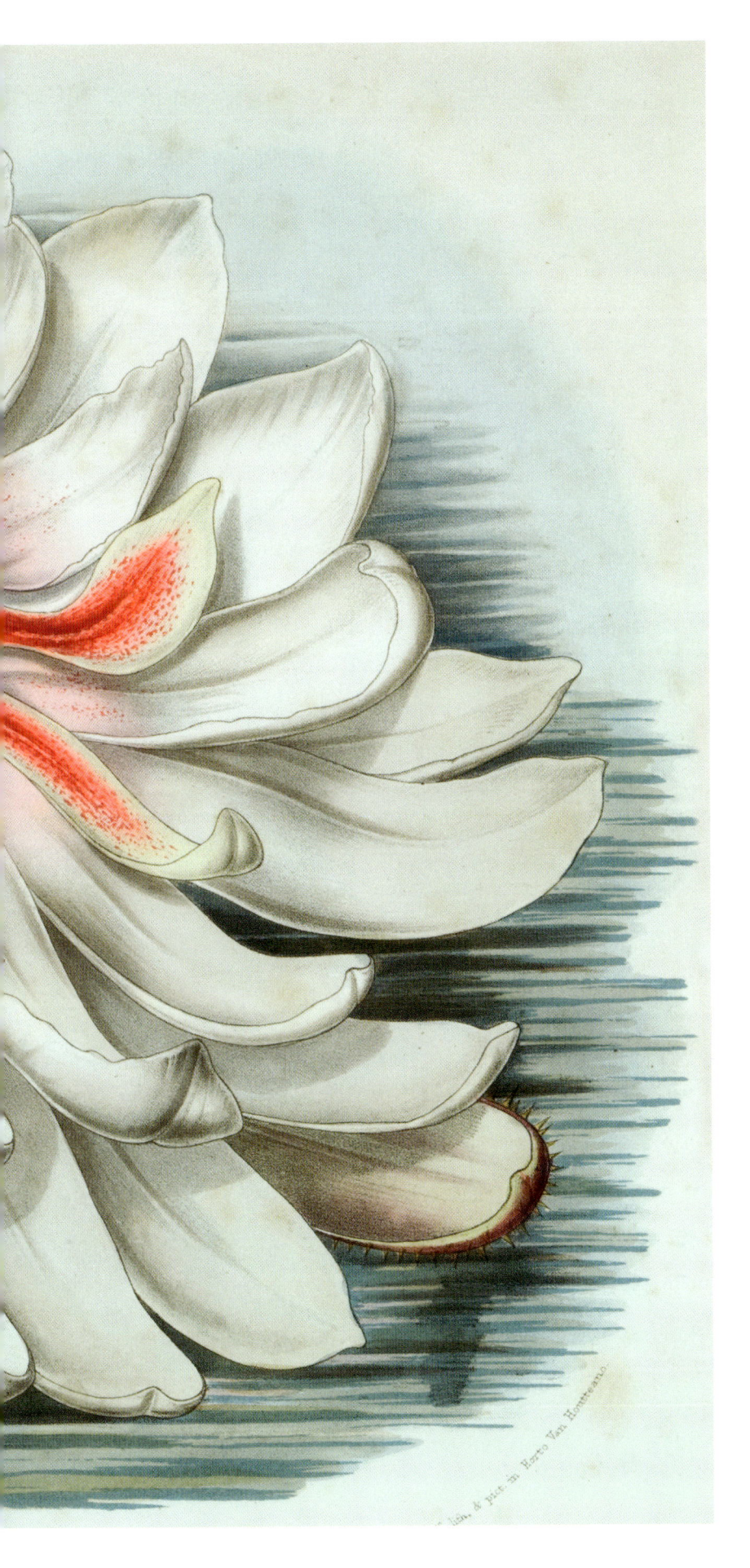

Eduard Pöppig, educated in Grimma and Leipzig, showed exceptional talent for nature writing during his early botanical peregrinations through central Europe.
HUNT INSTITUTE FOR BOTANICAL DOCUMENTATION

writing style, which would be highly praised in later years. St. Augustin and Grimma attracted many writers and artists in those days. One of them, Johann Gottfried Seume, was an intrepid adventurer famed for his travel writing. Seume immensely impressed young Pöppig and perhaps incited his own desire to travel.

AN APPETITE FOR ADVENTURE

After graduating from St. Augustin in 1815, Pöppig entered Leipzig University. But instead of continuing his studies in humanities, he chose to pursue degrees in medicine and natural history. Christian Friedrich Schwägrichen, professor of botany at the university and director of the botanical garden, became Pöppig's mentor. Over the next several years, Pöppig's studies in botany and zoology led him to undertake field excursions, collecting specimens across central Europe. Pöppig traveled from the Rhine River in Germany and southern France in the west, through the mountains of Switzerland and Austria, to the plains of Hungary in the east. His diaries from these early trips reveal his early gifts for writing and keen observation.

The journeys across Europe undoubtedly whetted Pöppig's appetite for an expedition on a scale of those undertaken by Haenke and Bonpland. However, in contrast to Haenke's expedition, which was financed by the Spanish government, or Bonpland's, which was funded with Baron von Humboldt's family fortune, Pöppig had to find another way to raise support. He hoped to earn money by practicing medicine during his trip, but he soon realized that most of his funding would come from the sales of his collections. Facilitated by a circle of friends and colleagues, especially those in the Society of Natural Science in Leipzig, Pöppig solicited subscribers throughout Germany who might purchase, preferably in advance, sets of various natural history objects he would collect on his trip. Within a few weeks of graduation, and with his plan and some funding in place, the young Saxon was ready to begin his great voyage.

In early May 1822, Pöppig sailed from Hamburg, becoming—like Haenke and Bonpland before him—another twenty-something medical doctor turned botanist who had given up the comforts of European life for the thrill and dangers of South American exploration. He landed in Havana, Cuba, at the end of June. Pöppig's plan was to find a job as a doctor on a local plantation, where he might settle in and dedicate his spare time to a thorough exploration of the surrounding area. After a week in Havana, Pöppig left for Matanzas on the island's northern coast. He then turned inland, finding work as a doctor on a coffee plantation in exchange for room and board. The following year, he traveled to the southern coast, collecting plants, insects, and birds. He hoped that these specimens would raise additional funding for his exploration of South America.

Unfortunately, Pöppig was met with one disappointment after another. His collections of Cuban bird pelts arrived in Europe in unsalable condition, partially eaten by insects. His manuscript on the vegetation of Cuba was lost in transit to Germany. To add to his misery, he often thought he had identified a new species, only to learn later that Bonpland and Humboldt had discovered it some twenty years earlier. Pöppig soon realized that his plan—to collect and then sell specimens to patrons in Germany—was not progressing fast enough for him to secure adequate funding for a long journey through South America. From Cuba, he wrote to Gustav Kunze, a Leipzig botanist who was helping to distribute Pöppig's collections to subscribers. He implored Kunze to obtain for him an advance yearly stipend for the next three years, whether from a state institution or from wealthy sponsors with interests in natural history. In return, Pöppig would offer prospective sponsors everything he would collect, with the provision that, in case of his premature death during the expedition, any unused funds would be reimbursed. For himself, he reserved only the right to describe and catalogue plants and insects.

In the spring of 1824, Pöppig left Cuba for the United States, opting to await letters from Germany there. Arriving first in Baltimore, the Saxon explorer headed to Pennsylvania. He spent the summer and fall collecting botanical specimens in the Allegheny Mountains and in the valley of the Susquehanna River. In June, he was invited to Philadelphia to present a paper on Cuban ground hutias to the members of the Academy of Natural Sciences. By winter, Pöppig had settled in McConnellsburg, a small town in

Eduard Pöppig, letter to Gustav Kunze, 1823:

It is nearly impossible to find anything botanically new in Cuba, perhaps in all of West Indies. All the effort and sweat, the danger of getting killed or of succumbing to the climate, result in very little reward. Eagerly one examines specimens brought home after a jolting midnight ride through deserted, deathly, pathless forests; happily one finds that the plants are unknown to Willdenow, Swartz or Persoon, only to find them clearly described in Römer and Schultes. And the plant that cost me such effort and gave me such initial pleasure is sure to be known to Humboldt. I gathered Oreodoxa regia, *cutting down the tree by the sweat of my brow (which the wealthy Humboldt surely did not have to do) and danced a victory jig when I found no match in Persoon. And then—Humboldt's work; and farewell my new discovery, adieu sketch and description! I have given up all hope of finding enough new plants for a planned edition on* Flora Cubensis, *I have perhaps forty to fifty. It would be embarrassing to return from such a great distance with such puny results, better write nothing at all. People in Europe think that if one just sets foot on the ground here one will crush half a dozen* Novae Species!

Urban 1896, translated by Kitty Byk

southern Pennsylvania on the main road leading from Philadelphia to the great North American west. While there, he prepared and shipped some twelve thousand specimens of his Cuban and Pennsylvanian collections to Germany, which his friends in Leipzig later distributed to subscribers. He also established connections with the scientific societies in Philadelphia and Baltimore and began writing for a German-language paper printed in Philadelphia.

A year passed, but the letters and funds he expected from Germany never arrived. With his financial resources quickly dwindling, Pöppig was forced to sell his scientific instruments and work as an estate manager in Philadelphia. His new job responsibilities precluded leaving the city for lengthy excursions. Instead, he devoted his free hours to the study of science.

SOUTH AMERICA AT LAST

It was not until September 1826 that Pöppig finally received letters of credit. "Imagine, Dear Friend," he wrote to one of his Leipzig benefactors, "at the end of March, I will botanize Chile! Isn't that a thought that outweighs everything else that daily life has to offer?" (Müller 1998, translated by Daniela Freitag).

To find a vessel bound for South America, Pöppig proceeded to Baltimore—the main departure port for ships carrying ammunition and supplies to South American colonies fighting for their independence. After six weeks in Baltimore (and four years since he'd left Germany), Pöppig boarded a ship on November 26, 1826, bound for Chile and his long-dreamed-of expedition.

On March 15, 1827, after a 110-day passage, Pöppig arrived in Valparaíso, Chile's main seaport. Although he was eager to begin his explorations, he had to wait out the approaching Southern Hemisphere winter in and around Valparaíso.

In early 1828, Pöppig set out to cross the Andes and visit the city of Mendoza in Argentina. While he was crossing one of the mountain streams, however, the Saxon explorer almost lost his life when his mules were overtaken and carried away by rapid waters. Clinging to rocks, Pöppig somehow managed to haul himself to safety, but his mules drowned and his equipment and supplies were lost. Disheartened, the botanist was forced to return to Valparaíso.

Pöppig spent his second Chilean winter in Talcahuano, a coastal town some 500 km (310 miles) south of Valparaíso, making occasional excursions into the surrounding countryside. The arrival of spring sent him inland into the Andean river valleys of Laja and Bíobío. In the summer, he headed to the village of Antuco, the area's easternmost inhabited place. On his arrival, however, he found Antuco in chaos, with violent infighting among local Indian tribes. Despite the dangers and severe restrictions on his movements, Pöppig gathered an impressive collection of botanical and zoological specimens, which he later dispatched to Leipzig.

When replacements for his lost equipment arrived in May 1829, Pöppig was ready to leave Chile. Two weeks later, he sailed to Callao in Peru. Prospects for collecting a bounty of natural history objects on the dry Peruvian coast were bleak, so Pöppig began

---

Eduard Pöppig, 1836:

It was very rarely that I made an excursion on horseback; experience soon proved that this was not a good mode, for many smaller plants were overlooked, and it is necessary to refrain from turning aside through almost impenetrable but inviting ravines, and on the brink of dangerous precipices. The naturalist who has once settled should never ride unless he wants to visit a distant point, and the intervening country is known to him. When he has arrived there, he may entrust his beast to anybody and proceed on foot.

Pöppig 1836b

Eduard Pöppig, 1836:

To whatever side you turn your eyes about Pampayaco, you see only a wilderness of thickly wooded mountains, where civilized man has never established himself, or has appeared only as a transitory passenger, leaving no trace behind. The soul of the observer is filled with a feeling of melancholy by the fact, that in the tropical countries the works of man disappear more completely and more rapidly than in any other habitable part of the globe, while Nature alone, vindicating her rights, flourishes unchanged in eternal youth and vigor. History speaks of colonies that once flourished in those mountains; but, did not scarcely perceptible traces in the forest indicate that trodden paths formerly connected the houses which have disappeared, we should be inclined to doubt the fact.

Pöppig 1836b

Eduard Pöppig commenced his journey down the entire length of the Amazon, launching three rafts on the Huallaga, an Amazon tributary, in May 1830. It took him a year to reach the lowlands of Peruvian Amazonia, where the rivers carrying a load of sediments from the Andes slow down and begin to meander.
Layne Kennedy / Corbis

preparing to journey over the Andes to Huánuco on the mountains' botanically rich eastern slopes and, from there, to the fabled Amazon. The plethora of plant and animal life in the forests of Huánuco, around Pampayaco, Cuchero, and Cassapi, finally fulfilled the Saxon naturalist's purpose in exploring South America.

Soon after he arrived in Huánuco, Pöppig suffered a serious setback. Shortly before Christmas Day 1829, he ventured into the forest on a collecting excursion that nearly ended his life. While cutting down a flowering tree from which he intended to prepare a pressed specimen, Pöppig suddenly felt a sharp burning pain in his leg. He realized that he had been bitten by a venomous snake and immediately rushed back to his house in Pampayaco. Fortunately, a local Creole was on hand to help him. Since there were no medical instruments, his skin was pierced with a packing needle and cut away in a circular direction with a knife to the muscles. After a copious amount of blood flow, the wound was cauterized with a heated gold

Eduard Pöppig, 1836:

A fortnight elapsed before I was able, with the assistance of an Indian, to leave my bed, and, stretched on the skin of an ounce before the door of my hut, again to enjoy the pure air and a more cheerful prospect. It was a lovely mild morning; several trees of the most beautiful kinds had blossomed during my imprisonment, and now looked invitingly from the neighboring wood. The gay butterflies sported familiarly around, and the voices of the birds sounded cheerfully from the crowns of the trees. As if desirous to reconcile her faithful disciple, and to make him forget what he had suffered, Nature appeared in her most festive dress.

Pöppig 1836b

The Romantic

Eduard Pöppig, 1836:

[T]o procure the wood for the raft, we rowed up the Huallaga twice.... We found enough trunks of the cork-like light Ochroma *[balsa] and we let those tree trunks float downriver to the village. [There] they were collected and stripped of the bark, weighed in the water and placed alongside each other. Across them, we fastened six hard beams with non-tearing vines, the air roots of* tamshi *(Carludovica sp.), a very strange parasitical growth, and, after only a day's hard work, we looked at the more or less finished raft. Pieces of a very hard wood were hammered into the whole length of the soft balsa trunks, crossing each other and connected into supports.... On top of those rested a plateau made of reed, high enough to be unreachable by regular waves, and covered with a double roof of* Heliconia *leaves—a room sufficient for the load and the separate sleeping places of the owner and his companions.... The size and careful construction of the finished, not ungraceful, raft won the admiration of the Indians. Without a doubt, the raft was the safest means of transportation under the circumstances; even though it was difficult to maneuver and slow, it was thus not subject to the danger of capsizing, and endlessly more comfortable than the smaller and narrower boats the natives use for long voyages.*

Pöppig 1836a, translated by Daniela Freitag

Upon the Marañón and Ucayali joining their waters, the Amazon—called Solimões by the Brazilians before its confluence with Rio Negro—carried Eduard Pöppig's party through a sublime and seemingly boundless landscape.
TOMASZ ANIŚKO / LONGWOOD GARDENS

coin. Soon his pain increased and frequent fainting fits ensued. When he briefly regained consciousness, Pöppig prepared to die. He wrote a few lines of farewell to his friends in Peru and Germany. As his condition worsened, the Creole attendant left him alone, lying insensible in bed. Later that night, Pöppig woke up perspiring profusely with a burning fever and severe pain in the wounded leg—the first indications of his recovery. A few more days of agony followed, but two weeks later, Pöppig was able to leave his bed.

The effects of the snakebite and its cure, combined with great privations and hardships, weakened Pöppig. For several months, he suffered from intermittent fever and was forced to extend his stay in Pampayaco. His journey down the Amazon was delayed until May 1830.

DOWN THE AMAZON

Pöppig would be only the third European to travel the entire length of the great river, from its source in the Andes, across the Brazilian plain, to its end at the Atlantic. Spanish conquistador Francisco de Orellana had survived the trip in 1542. Two centuries later, French geographer Charles Marie de La Condamine had repeated de Orellana's amazing achievement. Now, Pöppig hoped to follow them both.

With three rafts built of balsa wood, Pöppig began his journey on the Huallaga, an Amazon tributary. His first stop was Tocache, an abandoned mission, where he stayed several months in the company of his Indian servant and a dog. At his next stop in Juanjuí, Pöppig was detained by a local prefect on suspicion of spying. Released after a couple of months, he reached the village of Yurimaguas in early December, where he set up a base to explore the surrounding forests. In July 1831, Pöppig recruited a fresh crew, built a new and larger raft, and resumed his trip down the Huallaga toward its confluence with the Marañón.

Ega, known today as Tefé, situated on high ground above a lake at the confluence of the river Tefé and the Amazon, became Eduard Pöppig's base between September 1831 and March 1832.
Tomasz Aniśko / Longwood Gardens

Eduard Pöppig, 1836:

On the evening of September 3rd we tied up to a large sandbank, hoping that the observations leading us to believe that we were near the mouth of the Tefé were correct, but there was no way we could be sure of this in this lonely and completely unknown region. About midnight we noticed the gleam of a distant fire, appearing like a hope-bringing Pharos and despite darkness and fatigue we crossed the wide waters and found a camp of startled Indians, and were told that indeed we were only slightly below the mouth of the Tefé. Before daylight one of the natives went with a brief note asking for assistance to the commandant Bernardino Cauper in Ega, a learned Portuguese of great kindness. On the next day (September 4th) a large boat appeared and after transferring our possessions we left our raft to its fate and soon were traveling on the southern arm of the many branched stream, and then, surrounded by masses of caimans, followed the dark brown waters of the Tefé to its source in a pretty lake, which the inviting Ega overlooked from the hillside.

Hochstetter 1852, translated by Kitty Byk

On August 6, Pöppig's party reached the Marañón. Several days later, they arrived at the point where the river joins with the Ucayali and becomes the Amazon. The river carried the raft through a flat, monotonous landscape. Pöppig, however, was engaged by its sheer vastness, exalting the landscape as a nature of endless riches, where "the force of life expresses itself with such vigor that the traveler, far from experiencing the boredom of the voyage, continues the trip with increasing interest and every morning with new happiness greets the wilderness that is resting in holy quiet" (Pöppig 1836a, translated by Daniela Freitag).

As the trip continued, Pöppig and his crew rarely spent a night on the banks of the river. Instead, they stayed on islands in the middle, where they would be safe from animals and able to fish and replenish their provisions. Firewood on the islands was easily available thanks to the abundance of beached tree trunks that were washed downstream by floodwaters. On August 13, Pöppig's raft passed Iquitos, at that time a small village of twelve families. A week later, the Amazon carried them across the border into Brazil.

THE ROMANTIC

Pöppig faced many difficulties in Brazil due to the spreading insurgency against Pedro I, Brazil's first emperor. Many towns and villages along the Amazon had been ransacked and parts of their population were forced to flee and hide in the forests. The political unrest complicated both Pöppig's travels on the river and his collecting activities on shore. He was often forced to stay in places where he had not intended or to pass quickly through areas he would have preferred to explore.

In early September, Pöppig expected to reach the town of Ega (today's Tefé) at the confluence of the Amazon and the river Tefé. Unfortunately, the labyrinth of countless *igaripés* (side canals) and islands in the Amazon proved to be difficult to navigate with the cumbersome raft. In addition, Pöppig was worried that because Ega was not situated on the main stream of the Amazon but on the high shore of an adjacent lake formed at the mouth of the Tefé, they might pass by it unknowingly. After much searching, they finally encountered a group of local Indians, and Pöppig learned that they had already missed the Tefé and Ega. Since paddling upriver was not feasible, he sent a messenger to Ega requesting help. To his relief, the next day a large boat was dispatched to transport his collection and equipment to town. Meanwhile, the raft that had served Pöppig so well was abandoned.

In Ega, he moved into a house with an impressive view of the lake as well as comforts the Saxon botanist had not experienced in a long time. He immediately set out to systematically explore the surrounding areas. Ega offered many opportunities for excursions—particularly along the various arms of the lake, which turned into navigable channels when the water level rose high enough and flowed into the middle of the forest. Despite rumors of giant water snakes and innumerable caimans, Pöppig explored these streams in a frail boat accompanied only by his servant and his dog, To him, the greater danger came from the sudden storms that whipped up huge waves on the lake and threatened to capsize his boat. All hardships, however, were mitigated by the beauty and richness of the vegetation, which continually changed with the level of the lake between the seasons.

After the first couple of months of intense collecting, Pöppig's results became rather sparse. Increasingly, he sensed he was losing precious time, but difficulties in making travel arrangements, compounded by worrisome news about killings and robberies along the river, kept him in Ega. Even there, the unending rain, epidemic sickness among the local people, shortage of food, and, most of all, extensive flooding curtailed the explorer's activities. Travel was possible solely by boat. And the gathering of plants could only be done in deeply flooded wooded areas or in the few areas of high ground that were not under water.

It was during an excursion to one of the river's islands that the Saxon naturalist would make his most memorable discovery. The day began with yet another mishap: While Pöppig and his crew were preoccupied with collecting specimens on the island, their boat floated away. They found themselves

---

Eduard Pöppig, 1836:

My own boat distinguished itself through its lightness and ability to sail fast though only large enough to accommodate the owner, the Peruvian servant, and the faithful dog. Oftentimes we were absent for many days and, to the wonder of the natives, ventured forth into distant channels, that no one likes to travel, as they are said to be infested with giant snakes and where countless caimans of fearless courage surround the boat, the stare of their horrifying light-green eyes seeming to promise the death and destruction of the crew. Worse even than those reptiles, who are wrongly said to be harmless on land, are the storms, that, as harbingers of thunderstorms, begin with such force and speed that the wider waters are in an uproar within minutes and the waves roll up the flat shores of the lake like on the ocean beaches. With great effort does one prevent the boat from capsizing and it might be necessary to jump overboard to support the lighter boat during the thunderstorm, which luckily goes by fast, by holding on to the edges with one's hands while swimming with one's feet. Being soaked like this, however, is never threatening, as rain and river water are always very warm and the temperature of the air is so high that the thin cotton clothing which consists only of two parts dries very fast.

Pöppig 1836a, translated by Daniela Freitag

stranded in the middle of the river with nothing but a bush knife. After spending a long night sleeping in a tree, they managed to assemble a small, crude raft from wood found on the island. Crossing the river, they reached a plantation, where, fortunately, they were able to borrow a boat.

THE GLORIOUS EURYALE

This accidental detour took them through one of the countless *igaripés* opposite the confluence of the Tefé with the Amazon. Here, they came upon a large area covered by an enormous water lily, "the most magnificent plant of its tribe" in Pöppig's words (Hooker 1851). He likened the giant lily, known locally as *mururú*, to the Gorgon plant, an Asian species of similar proportions known by its scientific name *Euryale*. He recognized it as a new species, however, and added the epithet *amazonica*. The circumstances and the plant's larger-than-life scale made it impossible to prepare a dry herbarium specimen. Instead, Pöppig preserved parts of the flowers and leaves in alcohol and drew detailed life-size illustrations to take back with him to Leipzig.

To reach the areas away from the main stream of the Amazon, Eduard Pöppig traveled in a small canoe through a maze of channels, or *igaripés*, nameless but still large enough to vie with the major European rivers he knew.
TOMASZ ANIŚKO / LONGWOOD GARDENS

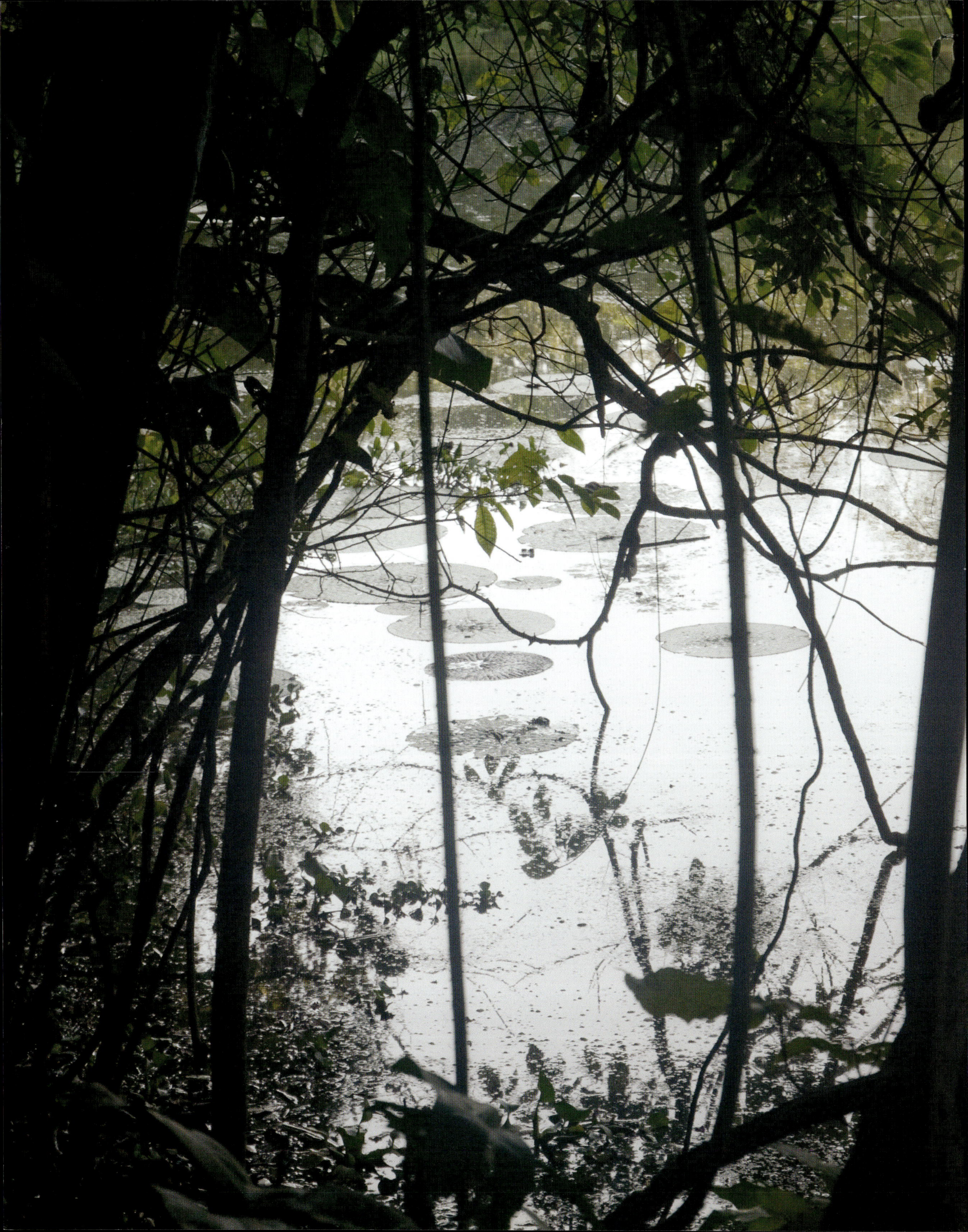

In early 1832, the worsening political situation, the fear of anarchist assaults, and the flight of much of Ega's population made Pöppig eager to leave town and reach the Atlantic coast as quickly as possible. Faced with a possible attack, the remaining residents formed a militia. "So it happened," wrote Pöppig, "that even the peaceful botanist had to report for patrols and nightly watches; a role all the more unhappily assumed as the original goal of the journey was relatively close; and it seemed that after so many efforts and after covering such a long distance the enjoyment of quiet and the absence of danger would have been well deserved" (Pöppig 1836a, translated by Daniela Freitag).

On February 12, he made his first attempt to depart Ega. Pöppig had to turn back, though, after the government issued orders prohibiting all travel on the river. A month later, he was given another chance to leave on a boat that was delivering a cargo of local products to Pará (today's Belém). Pöppig was permitted to rent a cabin and to load fourteen heavy crates filled with his priceless collections.

Unlike the previous legs of his expedition down the Amazon, the goal of this voyage was to escape Ega and to reach Pará before civil war broke out. Pöppig added only a few specimens to his collections, since the shores of the river were fairly monotonous and the speed at which his party traveled was not conducive to thorough exploration. To stay clear of marauding bands of insurgents, they navigated muddy side channels that were plagued by mosquitoes. Along the way, they found towns deserted, authorities scattered, and residents terrified by possible attacks. In two weeks, they reached Santarém, which was still under government control but succumbing to the fear of anarchy. Below Santarém, the situation became even more desperate due to their lack of food. "While I felt," wrote Pöppig, "for the first time in my yearlong travels, so exhausted that my mind was defeated by my body's weakness, fever and colic gripped the few remaining Indians, who alone were capable of maneuvering the clumsy vessel to Pará through a labyrinth of narrow canals" (Pöppig 1836a, translated by Daniela Freitag).

Pöppig's boat reached Pará on Easter morning 1832. The city, however, was not without its own troubles. The explorer had to wait for three months before he could board a ship bound for Antwerp. He spent that time in the little fishing village of Colares near the Atlantic coast. There, he was forced to part with his most devoted travel companion. "Soon after my arrival in Colares," he wrote, "some painful hours were caused by the death of my faithful dog Pastor, who had courageously accompanied me for five years, from Valparaíso to the coast of Brazil, through the storms of the ocean and the hurricanes of snow-covered mountains; had been always a cheerful and welcome companion on blooming hills and in dark forests; had faithfully shared joy and fatigue, abundance and poverty; and now, at the end of the journey, sunk under the effects of the last sufferings. Bitter tears fell upon the grave, which

Eduard Pöppig, 1836:

Only during the last months of the year is the biggest part of the land around Ega water-free. Wide planes of sand stretch between the hollowed out lakeshores, where the tall trees grow, and the clear surface of the lake and the streams that remain majestic even in times of lessened width. Countless islands, overgrown with willows, Hermesia, *young* Cecropia *and tree-like grasses, appear greening above the surface and the plants use this time of lower waters to spread and to attach themselves, and thus they protect the ground that carries them against the fate of being washed away by the next flood. Banks of fast-drying mud rise above the quickly receding rivers, and serve myriads of seagulls and* Rhynchops *building their nests, flat ditches from which the traveler, despite the mothers' cries, takes the not unpalatable, colorfully dotted eggs. The floor of the forests, sunken for quite some time beneath the aqueous veil and impregnated with new life, develops a multitude of little plants under the influence of the air and the rays of the sun, and half of the trees of the forest flower during this time—the spring in these parts.*

Pöppig 1836a, translated by Daniela Freitag

Victoria amazonica in the Mimiraúa Reserve near Tefé, Brazil.
Tomasz Aniśko / Longwood Gardens

The giant water lilies discovered by Eduard Pöppig in 1832, although no longer called *mururú* by the local residents, still inhabit the backwaters of the Amazon, like these oxbow lakes in the Mamiraúa Reserve, opposite the confluence of the Tefé with the Amazon.
Tomasz Aniśko / Longwood Gardens

Eduard Pöppig, 1832:

While exploring an island in the Solimões [the Amazon] our boat, only poorly secured, drifted off. . . . All our food, fire making supplies, tools, and fishing gear were in the boat, and we were left with only one bush knife. Unhappily rain began falling at dusk and continued all night and we spent the night in the broad branches of a tree. The next day . . . we laboriously constructed a small raft, using Cecropia, *guada reeds and tree fibers. With difficulty we crossed two arms of the river and the mouth of the Tefé and reached a small government-owned cotton plantation, where we were we were provided with a boat. For all these miseries, however, we were amply rewarded by the discovery of a truly magnificent plant. A large area of still waters near an island was covered with floating* Nymphaea-*like plants of giant size. It is a new species of the plant (according to De Candolle) reported in the East Indies. The flowers were more than a hand's spread in diameter, the outer petals white as snow, the inner ones a wonderful violet-purple. It seems to be by far the largest and most colorful of all water lilies.*

I knew that specimens would only survive if preserved in alcohol, so I had to be satisfied with saving only fragments of leaves and flowers, but I made detailed, life-size drawings of the flower.

Pöppig 1832, translated by Kitty Byk

an orange-tree overshadowed, and which received the faithful animal, to whom, after the lapse of years, the emotion and gratitude of his former master here erect a perishable monument" (Pöppig 1836b).

After a voyage of ten years, Pöppig, now age thirty-four, sailed from Pará on August 7, 1832. He would never set eyes on South America again. "Solemn were the moments of my parting from America," he recorded with his characteristically romantic flair. "The land of wonders, which, as it had many years before received the novice on the shores of the West Indies, in the full splendor of the tropical morning, now dismissed him in friendly repose, in the evening twilight. The unclouded sun sunk with accelerated rapidity in the horizon, and his last beams fell on the distant lines of the primeval forest, which here covers the flat coast of Brazil even to the sea. Night at length drew over all 'her slow and gradual veil,' the continent had vanished, and reminiscences alone remained as the fairest fruits of past enjoyment" (Pöppig 1836b).

Pöppig returned to Leipzig in October 1832. His collections had been arriving for several years, and his reputation as an accomplished explorer had preceded him. The following month, his description of *Euryale amazonica*, the giant water lily of the Amazon, was published in Germany, where it was received as one of the "most outstanding botanical finds" (Kühnel 1960, translated by Daniela Freitag).

But the water lily was only one of seventeen thousand plant specimens, representing about four thousand species, Pöppig collected in America. In the eyes of his peers, it was "an astonishing harvest for a lone collector in extremely primitive circumstances" (Stafleu 1969). Hundreds of his specimens of American fauna would later serve as the foundation of a zoological museum in Leipzig. Within the year,

THE ROMANTIC

Eduard Pöppig, 1836:

Our voyage amidst this Archipelago was excessively tedious, for the few Indians were so enfeebled by want and illness, that they were unable to row the vessel, and much time was lost in waiting for the ebb, or from the necessity of concealing ourselves when we approached some suspicious place.... Amidst these hardships we had advanced but slowly, and were scarcely able, on the 22d of April, to see the opposite shores of the basin.... We soon entered into branches of the stream, between islands where the vegetation appeared more pleasing. Nothing yet indicated the vicinity of a great commercial city, for the majestic forests rose from the mirror of the stream with the same virgin beauty and stillness as in the distant and uninhabited shores of the Peruvian Marañón. Morning at length dawned. The report of a cannon rolled over the surface of the water, others succeeded at regular intervals, and the melodious sound of many bells was added, and announced to us the long-wished-for secure asylum of Pará, and the morning of Easter Sunday. The light mist sunk into the water, and the beams of the rapidly rising sun illuminated the long rows of houses of the well-built city. Some ships of war and numerous merchantmen formed the foreground of the beautiful picture; and the flags of my native Europe, as if to welcome her son on his escape from so many dangers, slowly unfolded their gay colors in the morning breeze.

Pöppig 1836b

Eduard Pöppig likened the giant water lily to *Nymphaea* but recognized her close affinity to an Asian counterpart, the Gorgon plant, and named her *Euryale amazonica*.
LONGWOOD GARDENS LIBRARY AND ARCHIVES

70 VICTORIA: THE SEDUCTRESS

Back in Germany, Eduard Pöppig dedicated many years to describing and cataloging his immense South American collections.
HUNT INSTITUTE FOR BOTANICAL DOCUMENTATION

Pöppig was appointed a professor at the University of Leipzig. Soon afterward, he married Isidora Hasse, the daughter of a history professor at the university.

PÖPPIG'S UNENDURING LEGACY

Although widely admired for his skill in natural history writing—considered equal to or even greater than that of Humboldt—Pöppig never received the recognition or the fame of the great Prussian explorer. History suggests there are several reasons: His contemporaries described Pöppig as a loner, who early in his life retreated into the close circle of his family and a few friends. Did his solitary character come naturally to him? Or was it nurtured by the isolation he endured in South America? For many years, Pöppig's tedious work describing and evaluating his immense American collections kept him away from the

Notizen aus dem Gebiete der Natur- und Heilkunde.

Nro. 757. (Nro. 9. des XXXV. Bandes.) **November 1832.**

Gedruckt bei Lossius in Erfurt. In Commission bei dem Königl. Preußischen Gränz-Postamte zu Erfurt, der Königl. Sächs. Zeitungs-Expedition zu Leipzig, dem G. H. F. Thurn u. Taxischen Postamte zu Weimar und bei dem G. H. S. pr. Landes-Industrie-Comptoir. Preis eines ganzen Bandes, von 24 Bogen, 2 Rthlr. oder 3 Fl. 36 Kr., des einzelnen Stückes 3 ggl.

Naturkunde.

Doctor Pöppig's naturhistorische Reiseberichte *).
(Vergl. Notizen Bd. XX. S. 145., Bd. XXIII. S. 273 und S. 293., Bd. XXV. S. 1., Bd. XXVII. S. 209. und Bd. XXXI. S. 33. S. 305. S. 323. und Beil. zu Nro. 681., Bd. XXXII. S. 1. S. 145. S. 225. Bd. XXXIII. S. 17. S. 97. S. 145. Bd. XXXIV. S. 17. Bd. XXXV. S. 81. S. 96. 112.)

Amazonenstrom unterhalb Montalegre, Ende März 1832.

In diesen Provinzen Brasilien's hört die Möglichkeit, mittelst gemietheter Indier Flußreisen zu machen, auf, denn die Weißen und Mestizen haben seit den Unordnungen der letzten Jahre, es sich angelegen seyn lassen, die Ueberreste der seit etwa 40 Jahren unbeschützten und vernachlässigten (gezähmten) Indier der Dörfer zu vertreiben oder auszurotten. Man muß also geduldig auf Gelegenheiten warten, die überdieß weder wohlfeil noch bequem sind, und außerdem fast immer es nöthig machen, in einem engen Fahrzeuge mit Menschen zu leben, die für Nichts, wo die weiße Bevölkerung des Amazonenstromes allein aus deportirten Verbrechern bestand, hier ein passenderes Vaterland gefunden haben würden, als jetzt, wo, zum Troste der Fremden, wenigstens die Zahl der Nichtswürdigen nicht die überwiegende ist. — Diese Schwierigkeit des Fortkommens, und noch mehr das Eintreffen höchst unwillkommner Neuigkeiten über die Morde und Räubereien unterhalb Rio negro, verzögerten meine Abreise von Ega, selbst dann noch, als die immer geringer werdende Ausbeute empfindlich an den Verlust der kostbaren Zeit mahnte, und zur Verlegung des Aufenthaltes nach einem andern Orte aufforderte. Das unaufhörliche Regenwetter, ein allgemeiner Zustand von Krankheiten epidemischer Art (Wechselfieber, Catarrhe und Ruhren), denen sehr wenige der Einwohner entgingen, Mangel an Lebensmitteln, und vor allen die gränzenlosen Ueberschwemmungen dieses Jahres, verhinderten von den letzten Wochen des Januars an alle einträgliche Thätigkeit, oder erschwerten sie wenigstens in einem sehr hohen Grade. Alle Excursionen mußten von nun an im Kahne gemacht werden, und was irgend das Herbarium dieses Monats aufzuweisen hat, ist, mit kaum nennenswerthen Ausnahmen, nicht auf festem Boden stehend, sondern im Kahne, durch Eindringen in die Klafter hoch überschwemmten Wälder gesammelt worden. Nur in weiterer Entfernung von dem Ufer blieben die etwas erhöhteren Ländereien (terra firme) unüberschwemmt, und bildeten den Zufluchtsort der wenigen Landthiere, besonders der Schlangen, die ungesammelt bleiben mußten, weil in Ega weder ein kleines Faß, noch irgend ein anderes passendes Gefäß aufzutreiben war. Die Amphibien sind wenig oder nicht von denen von Maynas verschieden, nur eine kleine Runzelschlange ausgenommen, welche jedoch ebenfalls schon in den Termitenhaufen Cuba's gesammelt worden war. Zu bemerken ist übrigens, daß die in den Anden von Huanuco mit dem Namen Flamon oder Jergon belegte Schlange, über deren Giftigkeit ich in Cuchero sehr unangenehme Erfahrungen machte, (ihre Beschreibung wurde in einem der Berichte von Pampayaco gegeben) mit der großen Geraraca der Brasilier identisch ist. Da diese, als überall sehr verbreitet, den vielen europäischen Reisenden nicht entgangen seyn kann, so hört der Zweifel über die Species auf, und zugleich erhellt, daß die Angabe der Peruaner, sie wohne nur in den Cinchonenwäldern, ungegründet sey. Sie ändert in hellerer oder dunklerer Färbung häufig ab, etwa so wie die nordamericanische Klapperschlange, ohne deßhalb als Art verschieden zu seyn. Neben Aussaugung und Cauterisirung der Wunde bleibt innerliche und äußerliche Anwendung des Guaco (Mikania) immer das sicherste Mittel. Mit ihm habe ich in Ega drei Personen geheilt. So gemein diese Pflanze auch ist, so kannte sie doch Niemand, denn nur erst vor kurzer Zeit war das Gerücht über ihre Wirksamkeit von Peru hierher erschollen; ich ließ es mir daher angelegen seyn, sie in eine Menge von Gärten zu verpflanzen, und den Gebrauch zu lehren. Einen ähnlichen Dienst durch Belehrung über die Heilkräfte einiger Pflanzen, sollen die bairischen Naturforscher den Einwohnern erzeigt haben. Obgleich die Erscheinung reisender Naturforscher in Brasilien viel weniger auffällt, als in Peru, so erinnert man sich doch noch lebhaft des D. Martius und D. Spix, und erzählt viel von ihrer, hier etwas unbegreiflich erschienenen, Liebe zu allen Arten von „bichinhos" — wörtlich übersetzt, — kleinem Ungeziefer. Bei einen Abendspaziergange in der trocknen Capoeira-Waldung nahe an dem Flecken, in der Absicht, etwas Eßbares zu schießen, an dem es eben gebrach, traf ich sehr unvorhergesehen auf eine Onze, oder wie man in Peru unrichtiger sagt, einen Tiger. Er fiel auf den ersten Schuß todt zu Boden, indem die Entfernung kaum acht oder neun Schritte betrug. Gefährliches hat diese Jagd eben nicht, wenn man seines Gewehres gewiß ist, und das kalte Blut nicht verliert, denn die Onze greift nicht geradezu an; ausgenommen, es wäre ein weibliches Thier, von seinen Jungen begleitet. Es ist merkwürdig, die Onze zu beobachten, wenn sie sich unbemerkt glaubt; ihre Listen, um entweder ungesehen zu entkommen, oder heimlich bis an den Menschen heranzuschleichen, sind von der auffallendsten Art. Um sie zu schießen, geht man mit ihr in paralleler Richtung, bis man freieren Boden findet; wendet man sich dann gerade auf sie, so setzt sie sich hin, mit dem Schwanze spielend, aber sichtbar auf den Angriff sich vorbereitend. Man hat dann immer Gelegenheit, ein paar Kugeln in die Flinte laufen zu lassen, und sich des Zieles mit großer Ruhe zu versichern. Daß dieses Thier, obwohl schwer verwundet, gegen den Rauch des Schusses springe, ist eine Fabel; in Maynas, wo man es nur mit einer Lanze verfolgt, sagt man allgemein, daß eine oder zwei tiefe Wunden auch den größten Tiger feig machen, und dem Angreifenden Zeit verschaffen, den tödtlichen Stoß zu versetzen. Der zweite Theil der Aufgabe, das Thier nach Hause zu bringen, war schwieriger als der erstere, es muß mehr als 5 Arroben

---

*) Dieß ist nun der letzte dieser Reiseberichte, den die Notizen liefern. Hr. Dr. Pöppig ist zu Ende des vorigen Monats glücklich nach Deutschland zurückgekommen, und, nachdem er zu meiner Freude ein paar Tage in Weimar verweilt, in Leipzig eingetroffen. F.

spotlight. Meanwhile, interest in his grand expedition slowly faded. In addition, during Pöppig's later years, his administrative responsibilities at the university, zoological museum, herbarium, and botanical garden in Leipzig prevented him from completing many ambitious projects. He was unable to utilize his collections and observations from South America, which might have brought him the scholarly acclaim that Humboldt received.

In the end, this relentless naturalist, who overcame so many hardships in both North and South America and managed to emerge unscathed from the most improbable situations, succumbed to a debilitating illness. Constant pain lessened his ability to work, increasingly isolated him, and eventually led to his death on September 4, 1868.

Upon his return from South America, Eduard Pöppig became a professor at the University of Leipzig.
Universitätsarchiv Leipzig

Today, nothing remains of Pöppig's collections of the Amazonian water lily. The specimens he collected near Ega were destroyed when the Allied Forces bombed Leipzig during World War II. His drawings of *Euryale amazonica,* which ended up in a herbarium in Königsberg (today's Kaliningrad) in East Prussia, likely perished during the fierce fighting between the German and Soviet armies in 1945. Even the house he lived in and his gravestone in a Leipzig cemetery vanished in one of the air raids. While the explorer escaped the horrors of the civil war that engulfed Brazil in 1832, his collections, assembled so laboriously, fell victim to the destructive forces of warfare a century later.

Eduard Pöppig's report in the November 1832 issue of *Notizen aus dem Gebiete der Natur- und Heilkunde* contained the first published scientific name and description of the giant Amazonian lily.
The Academy of Natural Sciences, Ewell Sale Stewart Library and the Albert M. Greenfield Digital Imaging Center for Collections

The Romantic

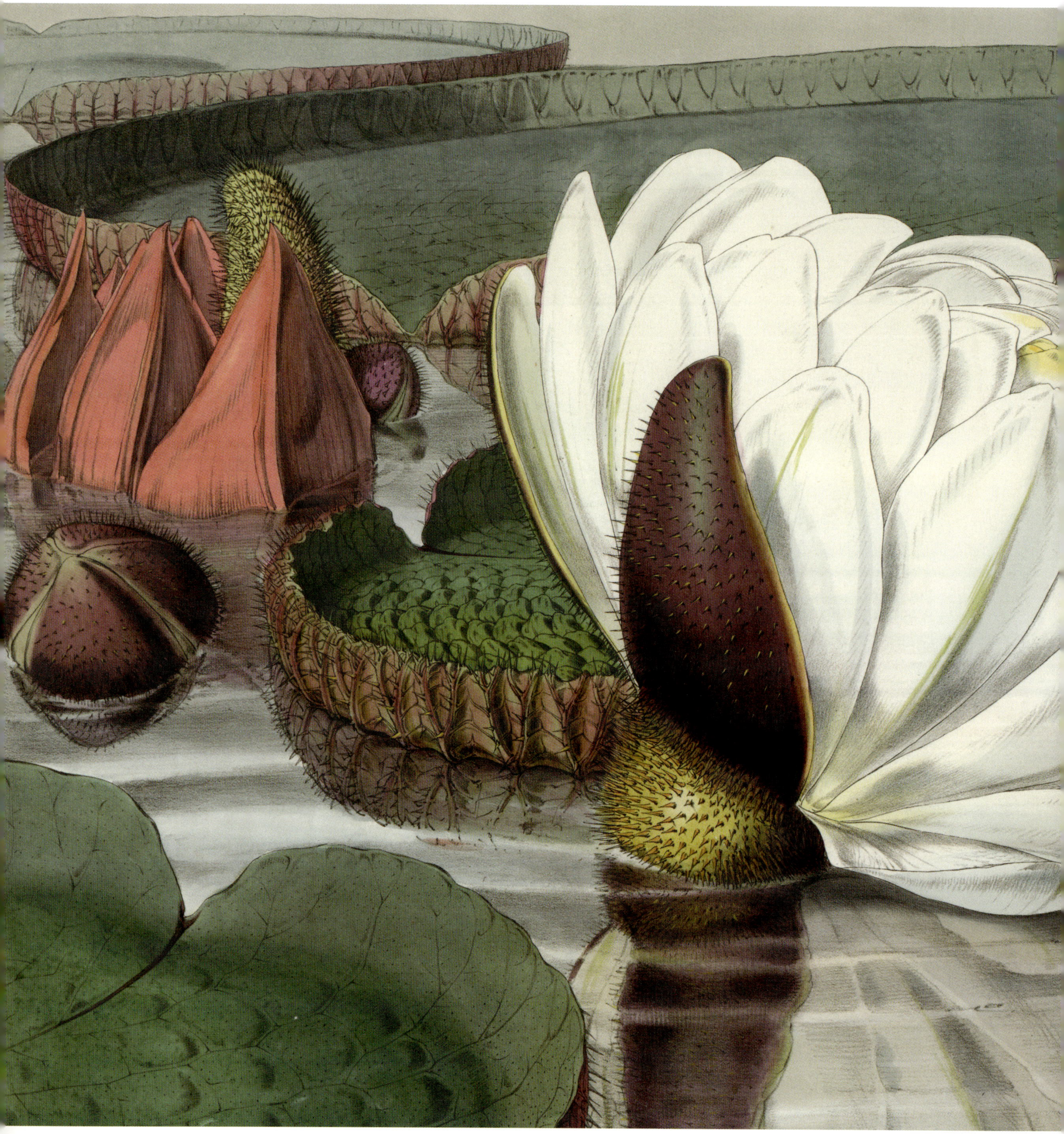

chapter 5

SURVEYOR OF EL DORADO

In 1832, when Eduard Pöppig was on his way home to Leipzig after a decade exploring the Americas, another young Saxon was desperately trying to anchor himself in the New World. Stranded in the West Indies, Robert Hermann Schomburgk had already suffered several setbacks since leaving Germany four years earlier.

In 1828, then twenty-four-year-old Schomburgk had boarded a ship to supervise transport of a cargo of Saxon Merino sheep to Virginia in the United States. Apparently, speculation on the value of the sheep didn't go as well as Schomburgk had hoped, because he soon entered the tobacco trade in Richmond. This venture, however, also failed, so the young entrepreneur decided to try his luck in the West Indies.

In 1829, Schomburgk sailed from New York to St. Thomas, which was then a Danish possession in the Virgin Islands. He established another new business there. A year later, fire destroyed Schomburgk's ledgers, library, and other possessions, and he decided that perhaps the merchant's life was not for him. Instead, he turned his attention to his first calling: natural history and exploration.

Schomburgk grew up in the small town of Freyburg on Unstrut River in Saxony, a region known for its vineyards that is often called the "Tuscany of the North." Schomburgk showed a prodigious inclination for the natural sciences from an early

First-night flower of *Victoria amazonica*, Walter Fitch's lithograph from William Hooker's 1851 book *Victoria Regia*.
The McLean Library, The Pennsylvania Horticultural Society

age. His father, a Lutheran minister, first taught him botany and nurtured his interest in the natural world. At fourteen, Robert was sent to nearby Naumberg to serve as an apprentice to a local merchant. Five years later, he moved to Leipzig to work for his uncle Heinrich. Perhaps recognizing Robert's fondness for science, Heinrich encouraged his nephew's studies in botany and natural history.

During his studies, Schomburgk took botanical excursions to other parts of Germany, which may have awakened his desire for travel and exploration. In Leipzig, he studied under Christian Schwäringen, who had mentored Pöppig before his grand expedition. But unlike Pöppig, Schomburgk never completed his courses. In 1828, a year after his mother died, the budding naturalist decided to abandon his botanical studies and pursue a mercantile career in the New World.

Schomburgk tried several business ventures in America, but they all failed. Disillusioned, he made the daring decision to transform himself from a failed merchant into an intrepid explorer. He started by writing letters to the Linnaean Society in London in 1830, offering to collect specimens for its members in exchange for underwriting his American explorations. He even included samples of a hundred plants from St. John in the Danish Virgin Islands to demonstrate his skill and ability. To Schomburgk's disappointment, he never received a reply.

In 1831, serendipity led him to Anegada in the nearby British Virgin Islands, where he viewed the wrecks of three ships carrying slaves to the West India colonies. These tragic but frequent events were caused by the low contours of the island, strong currents, abundant coral reefs, and, in Schomburgk's mind, inaccurate nautical charts of the archipelago. Convinced that more accurate maps would be valuable to the colonial rulers, Schomburgk first sought advice from the Danish commander at St. Thomas and then spent the next three months surveying the coastline of treacherous Anegada Island.

The following year, in 1832, Schomburgk sent his maps and reports to the Admiralty and the Royal Geographical Society in London. This time, he received a response from the Society's secretary, former naval captain Alexander Maconochie. Captain Maconochie expressed a favorable opinion of Schomburgk's work in Anegada, and a few months later, Schomburgk got word that his maps were to be published. However, his proposal to dedicate the maps to British ruler King William IV was deemed inappropriate and therefore rejected.

That year, just as Pöppig departed from the Brazilian port of Pará (today's Belém), carrying with him specimens, drawings, and descriptions of a giant water lily, his fellow Saxon was on the brink of becoming South America's next great explorer. Regular correspondence between Schomburgk and Maconochie ensued as the two discussed plans for future expeditions. Months passed, and many letters crossed the Atlantic before Schomburgk was informed in late 1834 that the council of the Royal Geographical Society had agreed to engage his services to explore Guiana. Moreover, the British government had granted him financial backing and patronage for the endeavor.

Even though there were four other European explorers who found *Victoria* before Robert Schomburgk, his name became most widely associated with the discovery of the South American water lily, shown here in a painting propped up behind Schomburgk.
HUNT INSTITUTE FOR BOTANICAL DOCUMENTATION

Schomburgk was thrilled and eager to begin. However, he was delayed by the parliamentary elections in Britain in early 1835. It was not until August of that year that Schomburgk stepped off a ship in Georgetown, capital of British Guiana, and set foot on the South American continent.

The upper reaches of many Guiana rivers have dangerous cataracts, which forced Schomburgk to abandon his plans to ascend the Essequibo in 1835.
TOMASZ ANIŚKO / LONGWOOD GARDENS

IN THE LAND OF WATERS

Guiana (today's Guyana), or "land of waters" in the local Indian dialect, was then a fairly recent addition to the British Empire. In the sixteenth century, early Spanish conquistadors had believed the region to be the site of the mythical El Dorado, prompting many explorers, including Sir Walter Raleigh, to search in vain for the "Lost City of Gold." In the seventeenth century, the Dutch had established the coastal colonies of Essequibo, Berbice, and Demerara, named after the three rivers around which these settlements grew. During the Napoleonic era, possession of these colonies changed hands several times between the Dutch, French, and British. But after the fall of Napoleon, Great Britain gained control over the three colonies, unifying them as British Guiana in 1831.

Although Guiana was not as precious as the conquistadors' imagined El Dorado, it was nevertheless the only piece of South America under British control. It also provided a source of lucrative profits from the colony's sugarcane plantations. Local settlements and plantations were limited, however, to a narrow strip of coastal lands, and the interior of the country, still predominantly inhabited by the Indians, remained unexplored. The outer boundaries of the new colony were also undefined. These boundaries were essential to making territorial claims against those of its neighbors, especially Venezuela to the west and Brazil to the south. It was this mythical region—which had stimulated the imagination of European travelers since the discovery of America—that Schomburgk entered in the summer of 1835.

Schomburgk's first expedition, which began in September 1835, attempted to follow Essequibo, Guiana's largest river, to its source. After only a couple of months, though, the explorers were blocked by impassable cataracts in the upper reaches of the river and had to turn back. Trying to lessen the disappointment of his patrons in London, Schomburgk named the 4-m (13-foot) waterfall that stymied the expedition's progress "King William IV Falls." Members of the Royal Geographical Society were hardly impressed and advocated suspension of his funding. The governor of the colony, however, James Carmichael Smyth, pledged his support and directed Schomburgk to carry on his work.

Schomburgk's next assignment was to survey the Corentyne, the easternmost river forming the border between British Guiana and Dutch-controlled Surinam. With the abolition of slavery in the British colonies in 1834, runaway slaves from Surinam had begun crossing the Corentyne into Guiana, causing great concern among the authorities in Georgetown. Eagerly, Schomburgk launched his expedition in September 1836. Again, a series of cataracts prevented his party from reaching the river's source. Fearing that this second fiasco might end his deployment in Guiana, Schomburgk decided to ascend the nearby Berbice River, east of Corentyne, in the Guiana territory. The Berbice was a smaller, marshy river with a meandering course. Clearly, it would not lead as far into the interior as either the Essequibo or the Corentyne, but at least it gave Schomburgk another chance to gather observations that might be favorably received in London.

An 1851 artist's interpretation of the scene showing Schomburgk's discovery of the "vegetable wonder" in the Berbice. The highly exaggerated flower was modeled on Schomburgk's 1837 drawing. The waterfall in the background references Christmas Falls even though the discovery took place a week after Schomburgk scaled the cataracts.
LONGWOOD GARDENS LIBRARY AND ARCHIVES

78 VICTORIA: THE SEDUCTRESS

An 1870 view of the Berbice River. Water lily pads were used to define the scene and anchor this dramatic landscape in Guiana.
LONGWOOD GARDENS LIBRARY AND ARCHIVES

When he reached New Amsterdam, a town at the mouth of the Berbice, Schomburgk informed the governor of the circumstances that had led to his return from the Corentyne. He asked for permission to travel up the river Berbice, arguing that "the season was too far advanced to undertake anything of import" (Rivière 2006). In addition to a crew of Indians operating several boats, Schomburgk's party included woodcutter Lewis Cameron, ornithologist William Vieth, and Charles Reiss, of whom little is known. With the governor's consent, they departed New Amsterdam on November 25.

By Christmas, the expedition reached a new series of formidable cataracts, which they named "Christmas Falls." This time, Schomburgk was determined to scale the obstacles, despite "the horrible stories of mountain spirits, gigantic snakes and thousands of kaymans [*sic*]" that, according to his Indian crew, awaited them above the cataracts (Rivière 2006).

Instead of mountain spirits, however, Schomburgk found something else. The discovery would not only save his Berbice expedition, it would change his life.

THE NYMPHAEA VICTORIA

On January 1, 1837, a week after they had surmounted the falls, Schomburgk's party entered a stretch of the Berbice where the river widened considerably into a placid lake. His mood that day was not particularly upbeat. "The entrance of the new year," Schomburgk confessed in his diary, "was . . . well calculated to enhance the feeling of disappointment, that we should at that advanced period be within so short a distance from the coast: a succession of adverse circumstances had almost taken place since we undertook the Corentyne expedition, difficulties beset us from the onset, and though I battled most resolutely to overcome them, and was determined to advance as long as there was any

Robert Schomburgk, letter to the Botanical Society of London, 1837:

It was on the 1st of January this year, while contending with the difficulties nature opposed in different forms to our progress up the river Berbice (in British Guiana), that we arrived at a point where the river expanded and formed a currentless basin. Some object on the southern extremity of this basin attracted my attention. It was impossible to form any idea what it could be, and animating the crew to increase the rate of their paddling, shortly afterwards we were opposite the object which had raised my curiosity. A vegetable wonder! All calamities were forgotten, I felt as a botanist, and felt myself rewarded. A gigantic leaf, from five to six feet [1.5 to 1.8 m] in diameter; salver shaped, with a broad rim of light green above, and a vivid crimson below, resting upon water. Quite in character with the wonderful leaf, was the luxuriant flower, consisting of many hundred petals, passing in alternate tints from pure white to rose and pink. The smooth water was covered with them, and I rowed from one to the other, and observed always something new to admire.

Gray 1837

SURVEYOR OF EL DORADO 79

Herbarium specimen of the giant water lily Robert Schomburgk collected in Berbice in 1837.
ROYAL BOTANIC GARDENS, KEW

80 VICTORIA: THE SEDUCTRESS

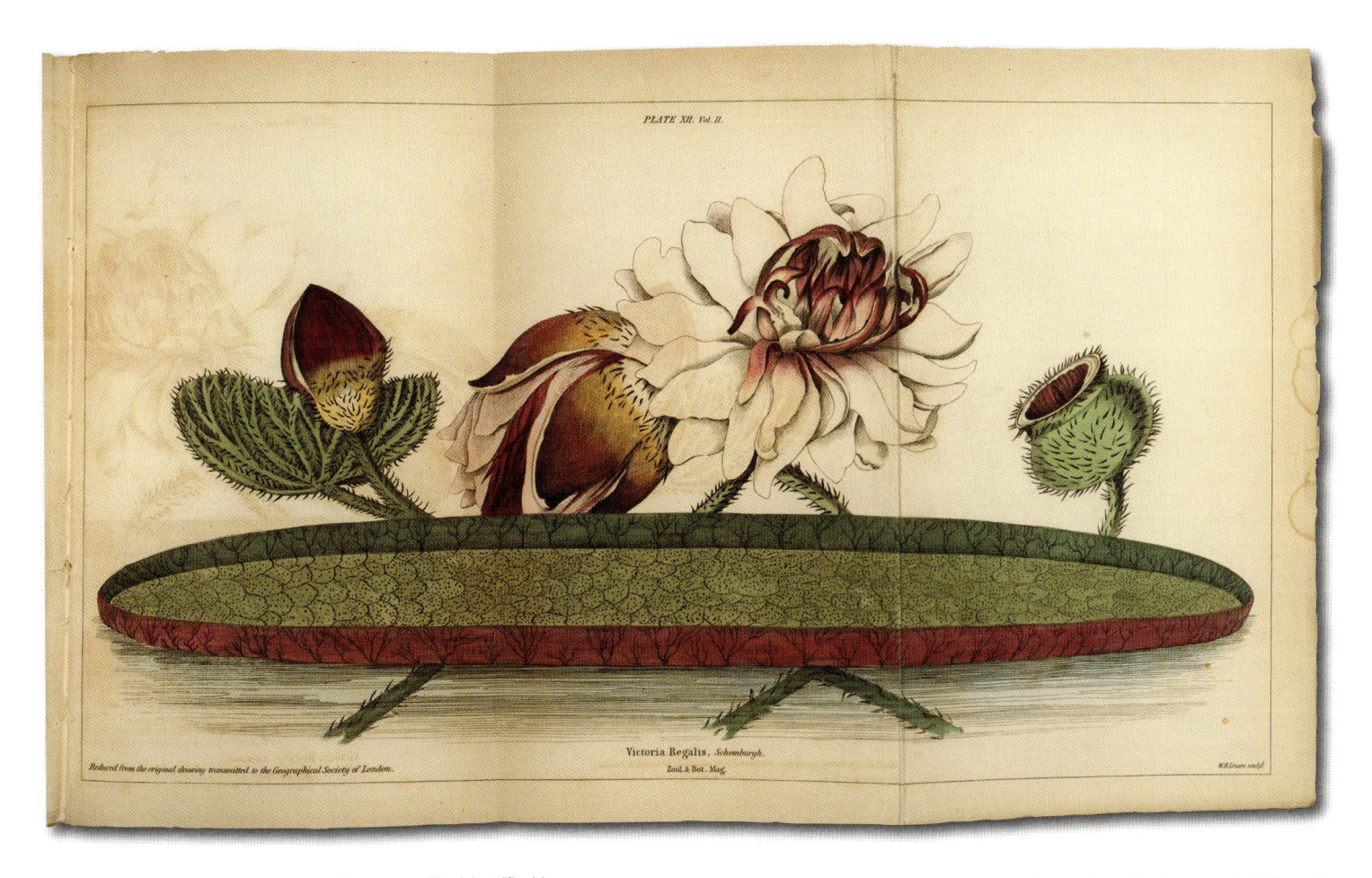

The earliest color illustration of the giant water lily, identified here erroneously as *Victoria regalis*, was published in 1838 in the *Magazine of Zoology and Botany*. It was prepared from Robert Schomburgk's drawings, which caused a stir among botanists in the United Kingdom and delighted the young Queen Victoria enough to permit naming the aquatic nymph after Her Royal Highness.

THE ACADEMY OF NATURAL SCIENCES, EWELL SALE STEWART LIBRARY

Robert Schomburgk, diary of an ascent of the River Berbice, 1837:

The crowd of feelings which oppressed my heart at my return, were very different from those with which we set out. On casting back an eye to the events which had occurred since the bow of my corial was turned in the contrary direction and we were gradually passing the precincts of the little town, much had happened since to depress my spirits, a succession of adverse circumstances assailed me during the whole Expedition and though I battled resolutely against their influence, they undermined my intentions and caused the failure of my plans; the opportunity was well calculated to bring them in renewed colours before my memory, to which the sad catastrophe that now prevented one of our number to return, added a chill, harsh enough to produce despondency, and yet at that moment I could say in my own heart: "I have done my duty!"

Rivière 2006

possibility of making progress, and famine did not threaten us, I could not feel but doubly the mortification on the first day of the year" (Rivière 2006).

While he was struggling with his depressing thoughts, Schomburgk spotted an unfamiliar shape on the opposite end of the lake. He urged his boatmen to paddle more vigorously, and soon they came face-to-face with a giant water lily—"a vegetable wonder" covering the surface of the lake and decorated with "luxuriant" flowers. All hardships forgotten, "I felt as a botanist, and felt myself rewarded," Schomburgk wrote. Enchanted with the surreal sight and the sweet perfume given off by the flowers, he directed the boat from one plant to the next, finding "something new to admire" every time (Gray 1837).

After his encounter with the colossal lily, Schomburgk continued the expedition for another month or so but was unable to reach the river's source. Still, he assembled a rather impressive collection

Robert Schomburgk's water lily, upon being granted the name of the royal patron, acquired the status of a symbol of the British colony, which continues to endure even in today's independent Guyana.
LONGWOOD GARDENS LIBRARY AND ARCHIVES

of artifacts, observations, and measurements describing the interior of Guiana. This included some eight thousand specimens of plants belonging to about four hundred species. Luckily for Schomburgk, among them was what he believed to be a newly discovered species of water lily. This single find would, in only a few months' time, influence Schomburgk's future as an explorer in ways he could never have imagined.

On their return, however, tragedy struck. On February 12, while his party was descending one of the Christmas cataracts, Charles Reiss drowned. Schomburgk was shaken by the loss of his twenty-two-year-old companion. "It became now my painful duty," Schomburgk wrote, "to make arrangements for his interment and the following morning was determined upon, to bring him to his last home." Schomburgk selected "a romantic spot," where Reiss's body, wrapped in a hammock in the absence of material from which to build a coffin, was laid and covered with "a pile of tufty stones," under which he rested "to await his maker's call" (Rivière 2006).

Upon reaching New Amsterdam on March 31, Schomburgk organized his collections and notes and sent a report with letters to his correspondents in London. His prospects of continuing to explore on behalf of the Royal Geographical Society were, at the moment, uncertain. Members of the Society who had heard news of Schomburgk's failure to reach the source of the Corentyne reviewed all of his correspondence and reports. They recommended immediately suspending his services until the results of Schomburgk's Berbice expedition were known.

In a letter written on May 11, Schomburgk announced the discovery of what he believed to be a new species of *Nymphaea* water lily. This letter, in which Schomburgk gave "a narrative full of interest and of life," was received at the office of the Royal Geographical Society in London on July 18. Three days later, two sets of drawings arrived as well. The drawings, "painted in situ with more artistic exaggeration than rigorous precision," caused "a sensation among the English cognoscenti" (Planchon and Van Houtte 1850–51, translated by John Luttrell).

FIT FOR A PRINCESS, MADE FOR A QUEEN

Schomburgk was eager to honor the sovereign, so it was understandable that he would choose the name of the royal patron for his greatest find. However, it would have been out of the question to name an aquatic nymph, which had chaste white flowers that turned blush pink upon being impregnated, after the seventy-one-year-old King William IV. Instead, Schomburgk proposed the name *Nymphaea Victoria* to recognize the princess whom he believed to be the royal patron of the Botanical Society (Rivière 2006).

Robert Schomburgk's published map of British Guiana was not only decorated with the image of *Victoria*, but it also identified the location of her discovery in the Berbice above Christmas Falls, making the plant a landmark.
DAVID RUMSEY MAP COLLECTION

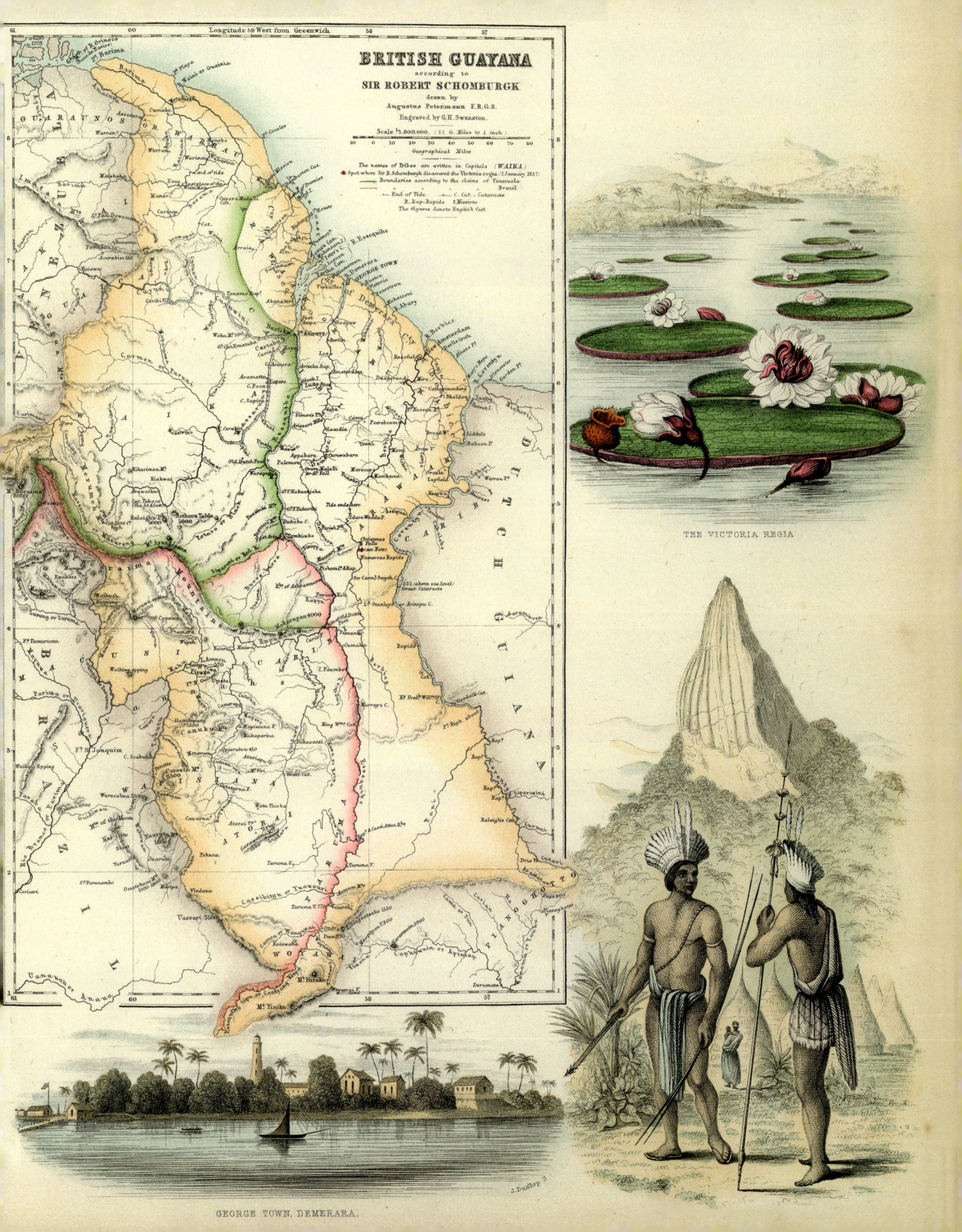

BRITISH GUAYANA
according to
SIR ROBERT SCHOMBURGK
drawn by
Augustus Petermann, F.R.G.S.
Engraved by G.H. Swanston

THE VICTORIA REGIA

GEORGE TOWN, DEMERARA.

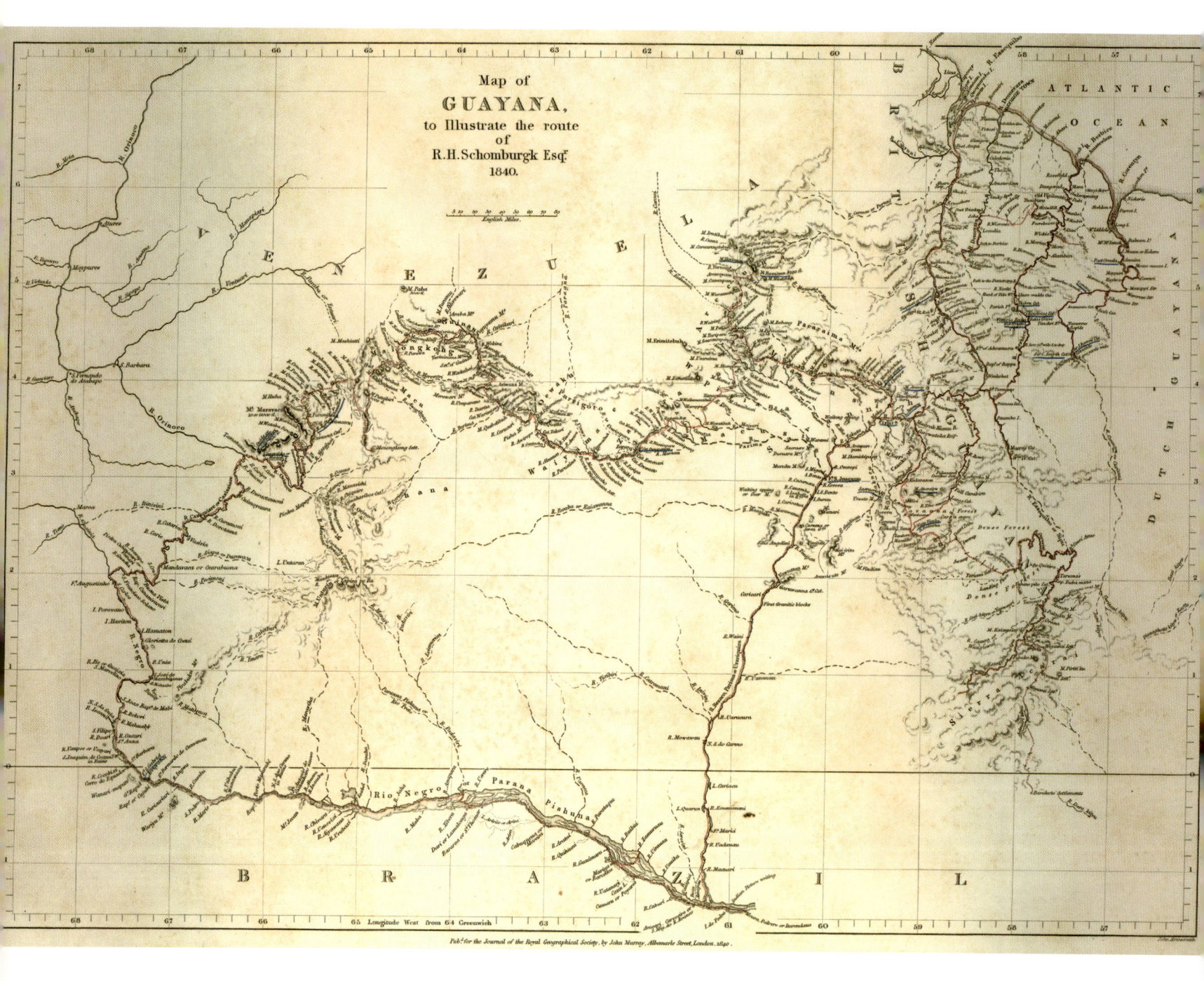

Robert Schomburgk's journey took him through the Brazilian and Venezuelan territories to Esmeralda on the Orinoco. His route followed the course of the rivers and linked the Orinoco with Rio Negro via Casiquiare Canal and Rio Essequibo with Rio Branco by way of Rupununi and Tacutu.
Rare Books and Manuscripts Collection, Temple University Libraries

In the meantime, on June 20, 1837, King William IV died. Since his many extramarital children were all considered illegitimate, the throne of the United Kingdom passed to William's eighteen-year-old niece, Alexandrina Victoria, who dropped her first name to become Queen Victoria. By the time Schomburgk's letter arrived in London, the old king had died and the young princess sat upon the throne.

Dedicating his greatest and most spectacular discovery to Victoria turned out to be the best choice the aspiring explorer could have made. When she learned about Schomburgk's discovery, Queen Victoria commanded to have the drawings of the Guiana lily delivered to the palace "for inspection" (Lindley and Paxton 1850–51). Three days later, a letter was sent from the royal palace to the Geographical Society "signifying Her Majesty's pleasure, that the name of *Victoria regia* should be affixed to the flower" (Lindley and Paxton 1850–51). Some years later, Schomburgk remarked that "a better name could not be chosen for the handsome and noble plant" and "certainly no other plant has

The Guiana Exhibition, is now open at 209, Regent Street

Containing among other Curiosities, a coloured Drawing, the Size of Nature.

THE VICTORIA REGIA,

The most beautiful specimen of the Botanical World hitherto discovered, painted from the Original Drawing by M. Bartholomew, Esq: Flower Painter in ordinary to HER MAJESTY.

Three Indians,

Who accompanied Mr. SCHOMBURGK, viz. a **Macusi, a Warrau, & a Paravilhana**, the first from the interior of Guiana who ever visited Europe, will be present in their Native Dress, and show the different customs of their tribe, and the use of their weapons.

A COLLECTION of Objects of Natural History, as **Animals, Birds, Fishes, Insects,** including a Specimen of the remarkable **Pirarucu,** (SUDIS GIGAS,) A Fresh Water Fish which occasionally attains the length of 12 Feet. In Geology, a Collection of specimens, showing the formation of that district of South America, from the Atlantic to the Equator. Warlike Implements, as Poisoned Arrows, Lances, Clubs, the Blowpipe, Wurali Poison, &c. Manufactures, as Hammocks, Baskets, Earthenware, articles of Dress and Ornaments. Drawings of Plants, Fishes, Landscapes, including among the latter Views of Pirara, on the Lake Parima; Ataraipu, on the River Essequibo; Esmeralda, on the River Orinoco, thus illustrating the Country, familiarly known as the

EL DORADO of Sir W. RALEIGH.

The whole forming a Collection made Mr. ROBERT H. SCHOMBURGK, in an Expedition in the Interior of Guiana, in the Years 1835-6-7-8 & 9.

Admission 1s.　　Catalogue 1s.　　Open from 10 'till Dusk.

E. & J. Thomas, Printers, 6, Exeter-street, Strand.

When Robert Schomburgk traveled to London in 1839, he brought with him three Indians, members of his boat crew, and a collection of various artifacts that were then shown as part of the Guiana Exhibition, "illustrating the country familiarly known as the El Dorado of Sir W. Raleigh." The greatest attraction, among many "curiosities," was "a coloured drawing, the size of nature" of *Victoria regia*.
THE LILY LIBRARY

Robert Schomburgk, letter to the secretary of the Royal Geographical Society, 1837:

The flower stalk is an inch [3 cm] thick near the calyx and studded with elastic prickles, about three quarters of an inch [2 cm] long. When expanded, the four-leaved calyx measures a foot [30 cm] in diameter, but is concealed by the expansion of the hundred-petaled corolla. This beautiful flower, when it first unfolds, is white with a pink centre; the colour spreads as the bloom increases in age; and, at a day old, the whole is rose-coloured. As if to add to the charm of this noble water-lily, it diffuses a sweet scent. As in the case of others in the same tribe, the petals and stamens pass gradually into each other, and many petaloid leaves may be observed bearing vestiges of an anther. The seeds are numerous and imbedded in a spongy substance. Ascending the river, we found this plant frequently, and the higher we advanced, the more gigantic did the specimens become; one leaf we measured was six feet five inches [2 m] in diameter, the rim five inches and a half [14 cm] high, and the flowers a foot and a quarter [38 cm] across.

Hooker 1847

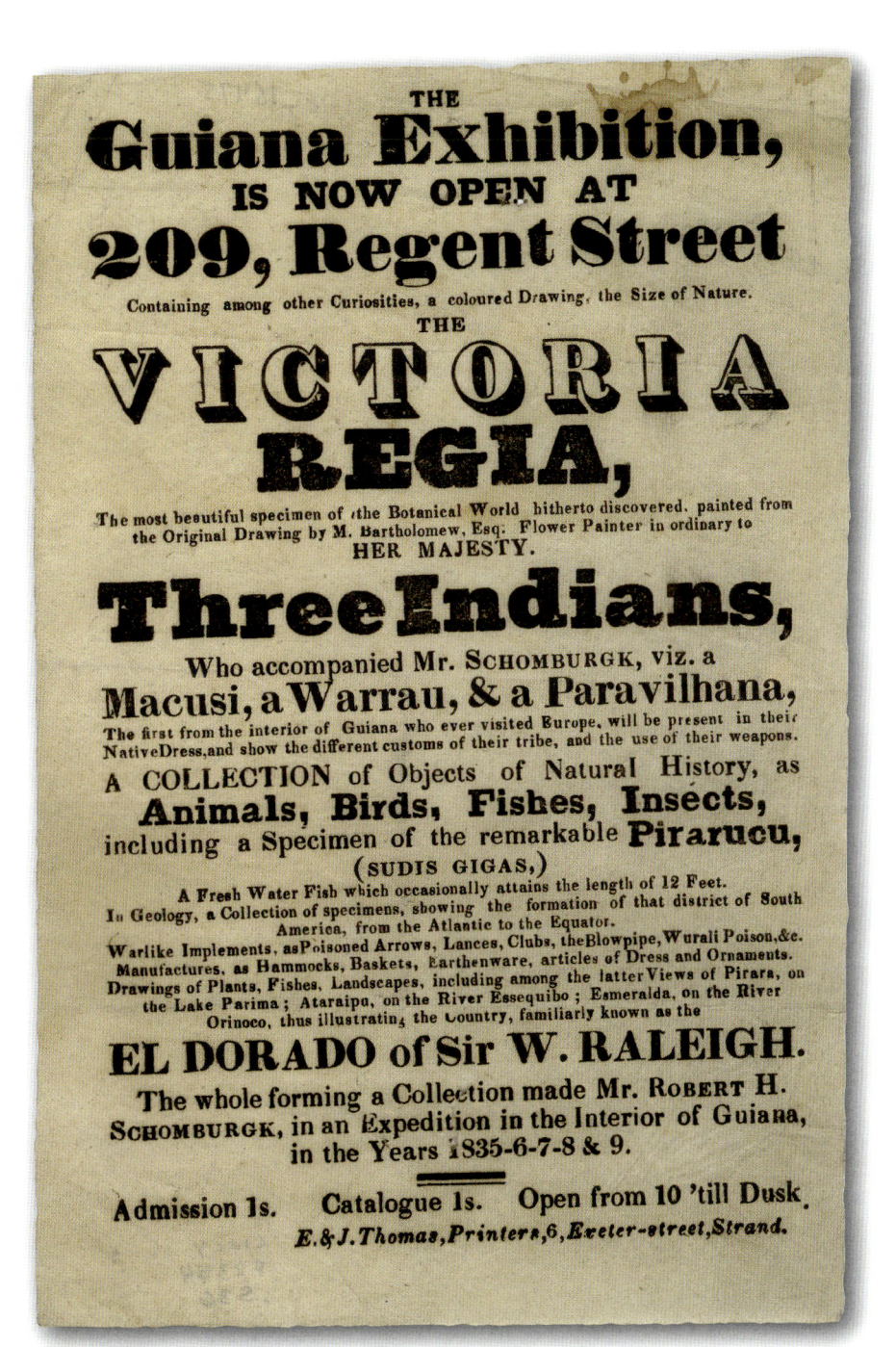

better claims to the royal name, for this is, without doubt, the Queen of Flowers" (Schomburgk 1873).

Instantly, the new lily, of which little was known other than what Schomburgk had described in his letters, became a compelling symbol of the new monarchy and the new South American colony. It was the talk of London and created a stir among England's horticultural elites. Her Majesty's royal botanists overlooked the fact that others had already collected the water lily several times in other parts of South America, discoveries that were understandably unknown to Schomburgk. Ignoring previous claims, they affixed the name to the flower and hailed Schomburgk as its discoverer. Even years later, despite evidence to the contrary, the British refused to give up their claim, attributing "the full and undivided honour of its discovery" to Schomburgk and declaring that accounts of other explorers "had remained so much involved in obscurity that even so learned a botanist as Sir R. Schomburgk does not appear to have been cognizant of its having been previously observed" (Anonymous 1857).

Needless to say, the members of the Geographical Society reconsidered their harsh criticism of Schomburgk's accomplishments, or rather his lack thereof. They directed him to continue his investigations of British Guiana.

FAME AND NEW EXPEDITIONS

In September 1837, Schomburgk began a new expedition that would take him on a circuitous route up the Essequibo, across Brazilian territory to Venezuela, then on to Esmeralda on the Orinoco. Since this was the easternmost point attained by Aimé Bonpland and Alexander von Humboldt in 1800, Schomburgk thus connected the two great geographical surveys. Returning via the Orinoco, Casiquiare Canal, Rio Negro, Rio Branco, and Tacutu River, Schomburgk closed a loop of nearly 5,000 km (3,100 miles). After a two-year absence, he returned to Georgetown with a wealth of data, observations, maps, and collections of natural history objects.

Any doubts about his aptitude as an explorer that may have still lingered in anyone's mind at that time were dispelled. In the summer of 1839, Schomburgk was invited to London, where he received the Patron's Medal from the Royal Geographical Society for his South American exploits. His fame as an explorer was assured.

Meanwhile, in 1841, a compilation of twelve color prints prepared from Schomburgk's drawings and sketches titled *Views in the Interior of Guiana* helped spread the *Victoria* craze. In an era when color images were still rare and expensive, this small set of highly embellished images portrayed a magical land filled with tropical riches and beauty. Schomburgk's water lily was emblazoned on the title page. In effect, the image became synonymous with Guiana and—since it bore the name of the young queen—of British rule over the South American domain. Once the Guiana plant was labeled with the regal name *Victoria regia*, she would remain, for 125 years, a visual icon of British dominance in that country.

Schomburgk returned to Guiana in 1841. This time, he traveled with his younger brother Richard on a joint Prussian-British commission to survey Guiana's eastern boundary with Venezuela and its western boundary with Dutch Surinam and to suggest a provisional southern border with Brazil. The task would take the brothers three long years to complete. It was during one of their forays in 1842 along the Rupununi River, a tributary of the Essequibo, that Robert and Richard found another population of the now famed water lily. Richard was no less astounded by *Victoria*—which he called a manifestation of "the productive powers of Nature"—than his brother had been

---

Anonymous correspondent to the *Gardener's Gazette*, 1840:

There is scarcely a Society in London but what has profited by Mr. Schomburgcks [sic] researches, and he has added much to our knowledge of this little explored, though highly rich and interesting country. He had been accompanied, on his return, by three of the Indians of the country, belonging to three different tribes, and who formed part of his boat's crew on his three expeditions. These three Indians are the first of their tribes who have ever visited Europe, and arrayed as nearly as possible in their native costume. Mr. Schomburgck's collection has just opened to the public at the Cosmorama-rooms in Regent-street and affords the best idea of the productive resources of this great, but unexplored country. There is a large drawing of that magnificent wonder of tropical vegetation, the Victoria regia, *discovered by this enterprising traveler, which has excited much notice amongst our botanists.*

Anonymous 1840

The title page of *Views in the Interior of Guiana* is dominated by a *Victoria* water lily depicted in a highly contrived setting, bearing little resemblance to the plains along the Berbice, where Schomburgk found her. While it might be lacking realism, this view projected a vision of a land of plenty, delight, and congeniality, inhabited by a wondrous lily and amiable natives.

RARE BOOKS AND MANUSCRIPTS COLLECTION, TEMPLE UNIVERSITY LIBRARIES

VIEWS
IN THE INTERIOR OF
GUIANA

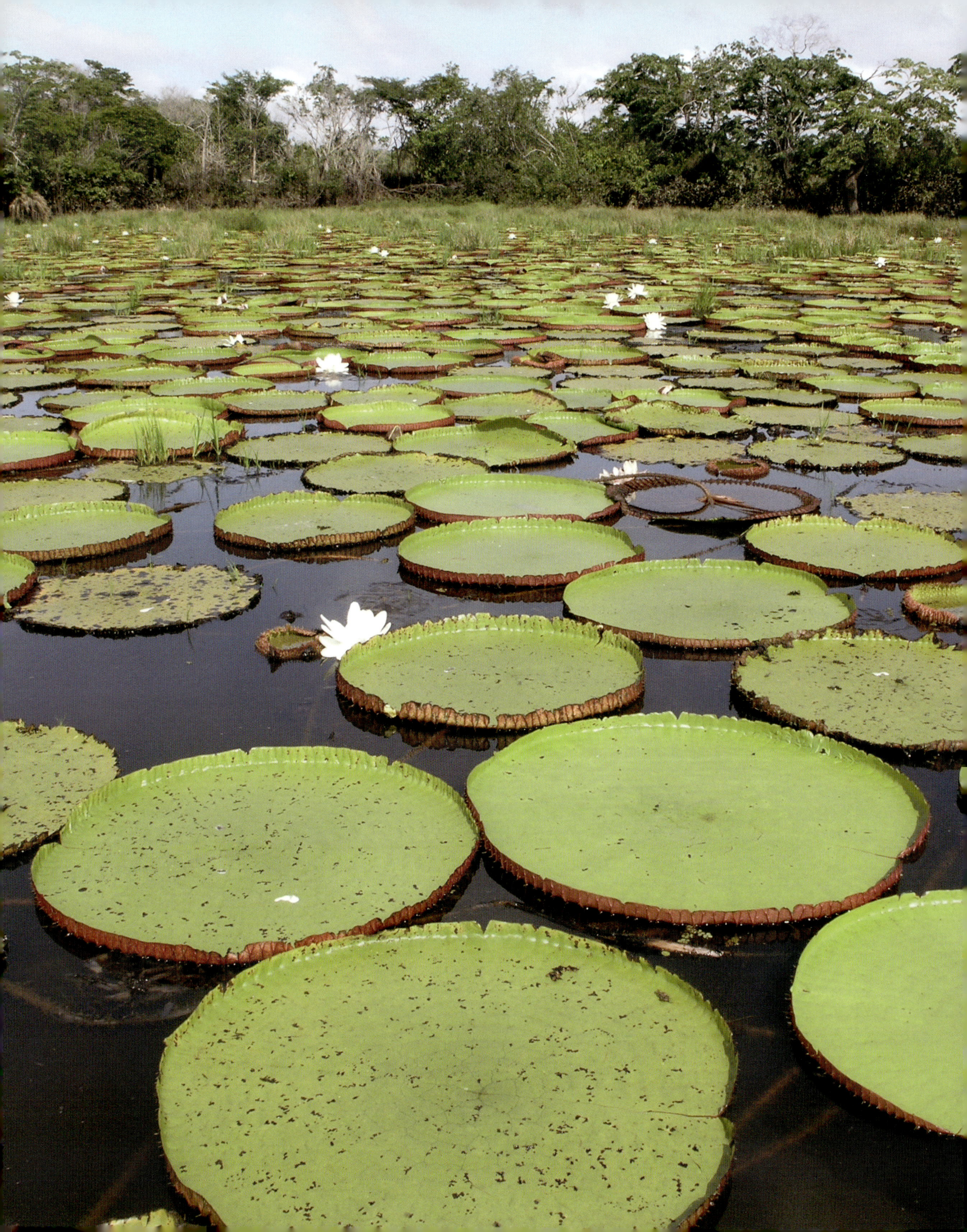

when he found it in the Berbice five years earlier. Richard proclaimed the grandeur of the Rupununi scenery "the most striking and the most sublime" he had ever seen (Schomburgk 1873).

A QUEEN'S KNIGHT

With the boundary survey completed, the Schomburgk brothers returned to England in 1844. Neither would ever return to Guiana or South America again. While in England, Robert was knighted by Queen Victoria. As Sir Robert Schomburgk, he entered the British diplomatic corps, trading, in effect, the dangers and uncertainty of an explorer's life for the comforts and security of a royal envoy.

His first assignment took him back to the Caribbean, on a diplomatic mission in Barbados in 1846. Two years later, he served as first consul to the Dominican Republic. He remained in the Antilles until 1857, when he was transferred across the world to Bangkok, capital of Siam (today's Thailand).

Bangkok's sweltering tropical climate strained Schomburgk's health and reignited illnesses he had contracted during his Guiana travels. By 1864, his condition had deteriorated to the point that he was forced to retire from diplomatic service. Schomburgk traveled to England in the summer of 1864, but a few months later, he returned to Germany, where he died in March 1865.

The Saxon explorer was laid to rest "to await his maker's call" in the Schöneberg district of Berlin, not far from the Royal Botanical Garden, where in a magnificent glass palace the giant water lily he discovered in Guiana more than a quarter century earlier was flourishing—living proof of the real treasures in the mythical El Dorado. "What could better give an idea of the luxuriance and richness of vegetation in Guiana," Schomburgk asked, "than the splendid *Victoria regia*, the most beautiful specimen of the flora of the western hemisphere?" (Schomburgk 1840).

Richard Schomburgk, 1873:

[T]he Rupununi, on its right bank, expanded into an extensive bay. It was an enchanting scene. So enchanting was the view which unfolded for our eyes that we were at a loss where to commence, in order not to overlook any object in this lovely picture, of which was the most prominent the Victoria regina, which I had longed so long to behold. The margin of this bay was bordered with this magnificent plant. The grandeur of tropical scenery was here the most striking and the most sublime I ever had as yet seen. . . . Long before we reached the bay the eastern breeze wafted the delightful odours towards us. The whole margin of this bay was bordered with the gigantic leaves of the Victoria, interspersed with the magnificent flowers, all shades from white to pink, scenting the air with their fragrance. On the leaves many aquatic birds were running to and fro, chasing the numerous insects which were humming around the brilliant flowers. May I observe that we stopped many hours to enjoy this sublime picture, and that our pencils were soon engaged in transferring to paper this striking feature of this remarkable spot. . . . I never was anywhere more forcibly impressed with the thought that the productive powers of Nature, on receding from the pole, had collected themselves in their greatest strength near the equator, and spreading their gifts with open hand and manifesting the abundant fertility of the soil.

Schomburgk 1873

One of the seasonally flooded ponds along the Rupununi River filled with *Victoria* lily pads.
TOMASZ ANIŚKO / LONGWOOD GARDENS

After Drawings by Mr. Schomburgk

chapter 6

PAPER WARRIOR

ALTOGETHER, IT TOOK THE VARIOUS EUROPEAN explorers thirty-seven years to make their discovery of the giant lily public. But it took even longer for European botanists to agree upon the appropriate name for the vegetable wonder.

The lily's earliest discoverers, Bohemian Thaddaeus Haenke and Frenchman Aimé Bonpland, who resided in the Spanish colonies, were unable to publish their findings and formally give the plant a scientific name. Their handwritten reports ended up in Madrid and Paris but never saw daylight. Understandably, both botanists immediately recognized the plant's similarity to the more common *Nymphaea* water lilies. But they left the task of accurately classifying and assigning the scientific name to their peers working in the herbaria of Spain and France, which was then, as today, standard protocol.

The issue of choosing a name for a newly discovered species had become a sensitive one by the time the Bohemian and French naturalists began cataloging the South American flora. In 1818, after his initial herborizing in and around Buenos Aires, Bonpland wrote to Dámaso Antonio Larrañaga, a Montevideo naturalist and author of hundreds of names for plants in that region. Bonpland wanted to be sure Larrañaga knew he would not take credit for Larrañaga's discoveries. "I have not yet sent them [the National Museum of Natural History in Paris] anything,"

Robert Schomburgk's giant water lily in John Lindley's 1837 pamphlet announcing the name of *Victoria regia*.
ROYAL HORTICULTURAL SOCIETY, LINDLEY LIBRARY

Aimé Bonpland, letter to Robert Gore, 1850:

Though I have assigned the mayz de l'eau *to the genus* Nymphaea, *I almost think it might constitute a new genus; and even if the description of the plant which I forwarded to France should have been lost or remain unpublished, I yet possess, among my manuscripts, a duplicate description; and as soon as I have been able to study in a fresh state several particulars of the* Nymphaea, *it will be easy for me to determine whether the* mayz de l'eau *belongs to the genus* Nymphaea, *or whether it may now form a new one.*

Hooker 1851

Bonpland explained, "and I won't send them anything until I see you and know for sure what your intentions are on this subject. I don't know how I can hope to publish on these works without your consent, because you have a thousand times more right to them and I consider them to be your property" (Larrañaga 1922–30, translated by Rose Torelli).

Nevertheless, people living in the Amazon and Paraná had known about the giant water lilies long before Haenke and Bonpland discovered them. Europeans had been in South America for three centuries before Haenke arrived with the Malaspina expedition. And by the time Bonpland arrived in Corrientes and learned about the colossal lily, she was already so familiar to the city's Spanish-speaking inhabitants that they'd called her *maíz de agua*, water maize, alluding to the similarities between the lily's seeds and Indian corn or maize.

Then there were the Indians who had lived in the Amazon and Paraguay-Paraná basins for millennia before the Spanish and Portuguese conquests. They had discovered the nutritional value of the water lily's seeds and had their own native names for the distinctive plant. A few of those names have been recorded, but with an estimated fifteen hundred languages existing in South America prior to the arrival of the Europeans, undoubtedly many more have been lost.

The Guarani Indians of the South America interior (today's Argentina, Bolivia,

People living along the Amazon gave the giant lily names such as *uaupé*, *turno*, and *forna*. These names reference the similarity of the lily pads to the huge pans used for roasting manioc, their staple food.
Tomasz Aniśko / Longwood Gardens

Brazil, and Paraguay) called the lily *abati-yú*, thorny maize. This was most likely due to the quality of the flour obtained from the seed as well as the challenge of gathering the spiny fruits. Another Guarani name, *irupé*, also written *yrupé*, remains in common use for the giant lilies in today's Paraguay-Paraná region, although translations vary. Alcide d'Orbigny (1840) translated *irupé* as water platter or lid, Domingo Parodi (1886) as shallow basket or sieve, and Julio S. Storni (1944) recorded *abatí irupé* in reference to the maize of warm waters. Other indigenous people spoke of the lily's awe-inspiring proportions. The Guaycuru Indians of Paraguay called her *gakauré-lodo*, the great water lily, while the Quechua speakers in the Ucayali River basin referred to her as simply *machu-sisac*, the big flower (Stransky 1951).

Along the Amazon and its tributaries, a number of other names have been recorded, although their meaning is not always fully understood: *dachocho*, *morinqua*, *mururú* or *mururá*, and *uaupé* or *uapé japona* (Pöppig 1832, Lawson 1851, Kidder and Fletcher 1857, Wallace 1889). The last name, translated as jacana's oven, refers to the jacana bird that often rests or builds its nest upon the giant lily's leaves, as well as the massive pans covering the ovens used for roasting manioc, a staple food in the Amazon. Likewise, the Portuguese names coined for the plant in Brazil, *furno* or *forno*, alluded to the similarity of the leaves to a pan covering a traditional manioc oven (Hooker 1851, Spruce 1908).

Following the example of Bonpland and d'Orbigny, the French were satisfied with translating the Spanish *maíz de agua* into *mayz de l'eau*. In contrast, the English, who came late to the naming game, accepted the scientific appellation assigned by their botanists and henceforth adopted that name for everyday use before even seeing the plant. In the United States, timid attempts at innovation produced names like Lincoln lily (Helper 1867), lily-boat (Pring 1952), or royal water-lily (Conard 1953), which were all eclipsed by the immense popularity and irresistible appeal of the lily's scientific designation *Victoria*.

Upon discovering the giant water lily in 1832, Eduard Pöppig recognized her close affinity to the Gorgon plant of Asia, *Euryale ferox*, and named his find *Euryale amazonica*. Leaves of the Gorgon plant, shown here, are nearly as large as those of the Amazonian nymph, but its flowers are diminutive by comparison.

TOMASZ ANIŚKO / LONGWOOD GARDENS

An 1838 portrait of young Queen Victoria assuming the throne of the United Kingdom by Thomas Sully.
THE METROPOLITAN MUSEUM OF ART, LENT BY MRS. ARTHUR A. HOUGHTON JR. L.1993.45

Robert Schomburgk, letter to John Fisk Allen, 1858:

I was animated by the desire to prove my gratitude for the fact, that I, a foreigner by birth, had met so much encouragement in my scientific travels from the British government, and from the Geographical Society of London; hence the thought struck me, that this plant, the most eminent of my botanical researches in Guiana, should bear the name of her, upon whom the nation rested their hopes, namely, that of Her Royal Highness Princess Victoria. I allude even in my description to the resemblance the water-lily bears to a gigantic rose, and the unison of the two colors of York and Lancaster in the Victoria regia.

Schomburgk 1865

FROM GORGON TO QUEEN

The earliest scientific name given to the giant lily, however, was not *Victoria* but *Euryale*, after one of the three Gorgon sisters of the Greek mythology—the other two being Medusa and Stheno. The Gorgons were terrifying creatures whose gaze turned anyone who dared behold them to stone. Many parts of the Old World, from India through China to Japan, are home to the Gorgon plant, *Euryale ferox*. This water lily has leaves nearly as large as those of her South American sister—whose vicious spines inspired British botanist

Richard A. Salisbury to christen her in 1805 after one of the Gorgons. If this was not horrifying enough, Salisbury also attached the specific epithet *ferox,* which means "fierce."

Eduard Pöppig, who carried his Amazonian discovery to Leipzig in 1832, recognized the features his nymph shared with the Gorgon plant of Salisbury. For this reason, he published the lily's first name as *Euryale amazonica*. Whether it was because of his reference to the gruesome Gorgon or an indirect allusion to the legendary Amazon women warriors, Pöppig's name did little to arouse European interest. There were few efforts to introduce the plant into cultivation. A strange silence followed his publication, which was surprising considering what was to come when the English announced their own name five years later.

In 1832, Robert Schomburgk, Pöppig's fellow Saxon, was busy mapping the British Virgin Islands and hoping to secure an assignment from the Royal Geographical Society in London to explore Guiana. Most likely Schomburgk was unaware of his countryman's historic botanical achievements in South America. When Schomburgk came upon the "vegetable wonder" in the Berbice five years later, he thought of her, like the other explorers before him, as a new species of *Nymphaea*. In a moment of diplomatic genius, however, Schomburgk decided to propose a specific epithet honoring the young Princess Victoria, who was soon to become queen.

Whether it was a brilliant political maneuver or shrewd opportunistic calculation, Schomburgk could not have chosen a name that would better advance his career or help the lily achieve worldwide fame. The stark contrast between his good fortune and the fate of the earlier discoverers must have left Schomburgk pondering if he indeed deserved the right to name the lily. Twenty years later, when the full story of her discovery came to light, the question was still on Schomburgk's mind. In 1858, writing to John Fisk Allen of Salem, Massachusetts, a pioneer in the Amazon lily's American cultivation, Schomburgk thought it necessary to defend himself. Schomburgk explained that when he found the great water lily in Berbice, his traveling library contained only the latest edition of Carl Linnaeus's *Systema Vegetabilium*, a hefty multivolume catalog of all known plants. He wrote, "The water-lily before me was certainly not described in that edition, or if so—in an erroneous manner. I considered myself authorized to use the privilege of a botanical discoverer, to give the name I liked to my new discovery" (Schomburgk 1865).

In 1837, a preserved specimen of Schomburgk's *Nymphaea victoria*, accompanied by a description and illustrations, arrived in London and soon sparked a rather bizarre turn of events. A "great paper-war," as Schomburgk called it, over the scientific name for the lily ensued. When it was all over, the name that warring factions agreed upon was attributed not to Schomburgk, but to a London-based botanist who had never set foot in South America. Of course, this must have rankled Schomburgk. "I claim the right to it," he wrote in his later years, "although, according to botanical precepts, my name does not stand as the author of it." Instead, he had to settle for "sufficient satisfaction" in "having brought the existence of this vegetable wonder to the knowledge of the civilized world," and giving "to thousands and thousands the pleasure of seeing it cultivated and in all its beauty" (Schomburgk 1865).

Robert Schomburgk, letter to John Fisk Allen, 1858:

There is no doubt that the plant had been seen by scientific travelers, previous to my discovering it in the river Berbice. They kept however their discovery a sealed book; and only after I had made known the existence of the Royal Water Lily to the civilized world, a number of claimants came forward! Had poor Thaddaeus Haenke returned to his native country, or had he sent his description of the vegetable kingdom under the tropics to any other part of Europe than to Spain, as then constituted, it would not have devolved upon me to give an account of the Victoria regia.

Schomburgk 1865

John Lindley, age thirty-three, professor at University College and one of the most influential botanists in mid-nineteenth-century London, played a pivotal role in designating the scientific name of the South American lilies.
ROYAL BRITISH COLUMBIA MUSEUM

THE GREAT PAPER-WAR

Ultimately, scientific appellation for *Victoria* belongs to John Lindley—a pivotal figure in the great paper-war. John Lindley was one of the most influential British botanists of that era. Although he lacked formal academic training or a college degree, Lindley became professor at University College and Chelsea Physic Garden in London; joined prestigious scientific societies in England, France, Germany, and the United States; and was awarded honorary doctorates from the universities in Basel and Munich.

Perhaps Lindley's greatest achievement, however, lay in saving the Royal Botanic Gardens, Kew. After the death of King George III and his botanical confidant, Joseph Banks, the gardens experienced many years of decline and were threatened with closure. Soon after Queen Victoria assumed the throne in 1837, Lindley led a committee charged with formulating recommendations for Kew's future. His report strongly defended the purpose of the botanical garden. A couple of years later, Kew became a public institution funded by the treasury and "Royal" in name only. This move not only assured the preservation of the gardens, but it also set them on the path to develop the world's finest collection of plants.

Through a multitude of public engagements, Lindley acquired the reputation of a formidable and quarrelsome opponent. "A warrior at heart," wrote William T. Stearn in the botanist's biography, "John Lindley waged battle after battle on such issues as the tax on glass, the mismanagement of royal forests and

VICTORIA: THE SEDUCTRESS

the artificial Linneaean 'sexual system' of plant classification; he was reputed to be even more forceful in speech than writing!" (Stearn 1999).

In his boyhood, Lindley had dreamed of becoming a plant collector, but his only travels outside England took him to Belgium, France, and Ireland—places then hardly suitable for discovering new plants. Instead, as the assistant secretary of the Horticultural Society of London (today's Royal Horticultural Society), Lindley was responsible for sending many explorers around the world on behalf of the Society and later naming and classifying their newly discovered plants.

When it came to naming plants, few botanists could compare with Lindley. With well over five thousand names to his credit, he was a prolific source of scientific designations for new plants coming to London, linguistically staking the British Empire's claim on the world's flora. Lindley never shied away from using plant names to immortalize those to whom he owed gratitude, a common practice then. Some of the names, such as *Cattleya*, *Cavendishia*, and *Loudonia*, recognize people who hired Lindley—William Cattley, a wealthy merchant; William Spencer Cavendish, president of the Horticultural Society; and John Claudius Loudon, a horticulturist and editor. Others, including *Drakaea*, *Paxtonia*, and *Miltonia*, honor Lindley's collaborators: Sarah Anne Drake, a botanical illustrator; Joseph Paxton, the co-founder, with Lindley and others, of *Gardeners' Chronicle*; and Charles Fitzwilliam, Viscount Milton and an orchid connoisseur. Explorers supplying Lindley with their discoveries were not forgotten either. He named the plants *Govenia*, *Hartwegia*, and *Schomburgkia* after plant collectors James Robert Gowen, Karl Theodore Hartweg, and Schomburgk himself, whose giant lily specimen, description, and drawing Lindley received in 1837.

These commemorative names show Lindley as a "warm-hearted and generous man on good terms with most of his botanical and horticultural contemporaries." But outside this circle of allies, he was known for "his notorious hot temper, his lack of tact in dealing with humble gardeners, his vigorously expressed opinions and resentment at opposition" (Stearn 1999). The intensity of this resentment can be inferred from his attitude toward the commemorative names assigned by non-British botanists. "It is full time, indeed, that some stop should be put to this torrent of savage sounds," Lindley stated in 1841, "when we find such words as . . . *Kraschenninikovia*, *Gravenhorstia*, *Andrzejofskya*, *Mielichoferia* . . . and hundreds of others like them, thrust into the records of botany without even an apology. If such intolerable words are to be used, they should surely be reserved for plants as repulsive as themselves, and instead of libeling races so fair as flowers, or noble as trees, they ought to be confined to slimes, mildews, blights, and toadstools" (Stearn 1999).

John Lindley, letter to Queen Victoria, 1837:

It has long been the practice between botanists to name the new plants that become known during their researches after individuals distinguished for their exalted station, and patronage of science; and where plants have been discovered of a sufficiently noble aspect to render them suitable for such a purpose, they have been dignified by the names of Royal Personages. It is therefore not less my duty than my inclination to concur with its zealous and enterprizing discoverer in distinguishing by your Majesty's illustrious name, by far the most majestic species in the family of the Nymphs—one of the most noble productions of the Vegetable Kingdom—first found in your Majesty's South American dominions by a gentleman traveling under the auspices of your Majesty's government and our knowledge of which dates from the period of your Majesty's happy accession to the throne of these realms. That the reign of Queen Victoria may be as much distinguished in the annals of history, as the majestic plant henceforward to bear the Royal name is preeminent in the flora of its native country, is the earnest prayer of Your Majesty's dutiful and loyal subject and servant.

Stransky 1951

When Schomburgk's *Nymphaea victoria* arrived in London on July 18, 1837, Lindley recognized that the South American lily differed from *Nymphaea* enough to warrant giving her her own separate genus. With a teenage Queen Victoria on the throne barely a month, he seized this opportunity

John Lindley, 1838:

Some drawings were sent home by Mr. Schomburgk in illustration of the previous account. He considered the plant a species of the genus Nymphaea, *and was desirous that it should be distinguished by the name of the Queen, a wish with which Her Majesty has been graciously pleased to comply. But it proves, upon an examination of the drawings and papers, which the Royal Geographical Society has placed in my hands for publication, that the plant is not a* Nymphaea, *as Mr. Schomburgk supposed, but a new and well marked genus; for this reason, it has appeared to me that the object of its discoverer will be best attained by suppressing the name of* Nymphaea victoria, *by which he had proposed to distinguish the plant, and by embodying Her Majesty's name in the usual way in that of the genus. I have therefore proposed to name it* Victoria regia.

Lindley 1838b

Jules Émile Planchon and Louis Van Houtte, 1850–51:

As a consequence of a habit too common among the English aristocracy, who are otherwise so generous and enlightened, [Lindley's] work was printed in only twenty-five copies (!) "for private distribution," that is to say, for a little circle of privileged and among friends: a thing most conceivable when it involves the literary intentions that spring up modestly in a family, or of which the effect is nicely calculated for the brief moment; a petty thing, despite its grand airs, when it is about science.

Planchon and Van Houtte 1850–51, translated by John Luttrell

to honor the young monarch in a way that no one else could: by naming the world's largest lily after her. To preclude others from formulating their own names, Lindley set out to publish *Victoria* before anyone else did. Unlike Schomburgk, Lindley was well acquainted with *Euryale*, so to justify creating a new genus, he also had to demonstrate how it differed from the Gorgon plant, *Euryale ferox*. He achieved both these goals in a highly unorthodox way: by issuing, "for private circulation," twenty-five copies of a pamphlet featuring Schomburgk's drawing and three pages of detailed description "with all the clearness which the specimens at his command could display," thus proving the distinction between *Victoria* and *Euryale* (Hooker 1851).

A BOTANICAL HEIST?

Although effective in the end, Lindley's machinations were met with great consternation in Europe. In their authoritative book *La Victoria Regia,* published in Belgium, Jules Émile Planchon and Louis Van Houtte called it a "petty thing, despite its grand airs" (Planchon and Van Houtte 1850–51, translated by John Luttrell). Lindley's pamphlet was then re-published for public distribution in the February 1838 issue of the *Miscellaneous Notices of the Botanical Register*. This delay of several months, however, later led Lindley's name for the lily to be vehemently contested.

Somehow, Baron Benjamin Delessert, wealthy banker, naturalist, and member of the French Academy of Sciences, was among the "little circle of privileged" included in the private circulation of Lindley's 1837 paper. Delessert took Lindley's paper containing Schomburgk's illustration of *Victoria regia* to a meeting of the Academy. At that meeting in Paris, Alcide d'Orbigny instantly recognized the drawing of the great water lily he had collected in South America some ten years prior. The French explorer had described his encounter with the giant lily in a book published two years earlier, but stopped short of assigning a name to his discovery at that time. If d'Orbigny had assumed that this public announcement would secure his moral right to the discovery and give his peers in Paris time to study the South American colossus before publishing the name, Lindley had proved him wrong.

Flower bud of *Victoria amazonica* reconstructed by Walter Fitch from specimens brought from Bolivia by Thomas Bridges. It was one of four plates that accompanied an article by William Hooker in the January 1847 issue of *Curtis's Botanical Magazine*.
LONGWOOD GARDENS LIBRARY AND ARCHIVES

4277

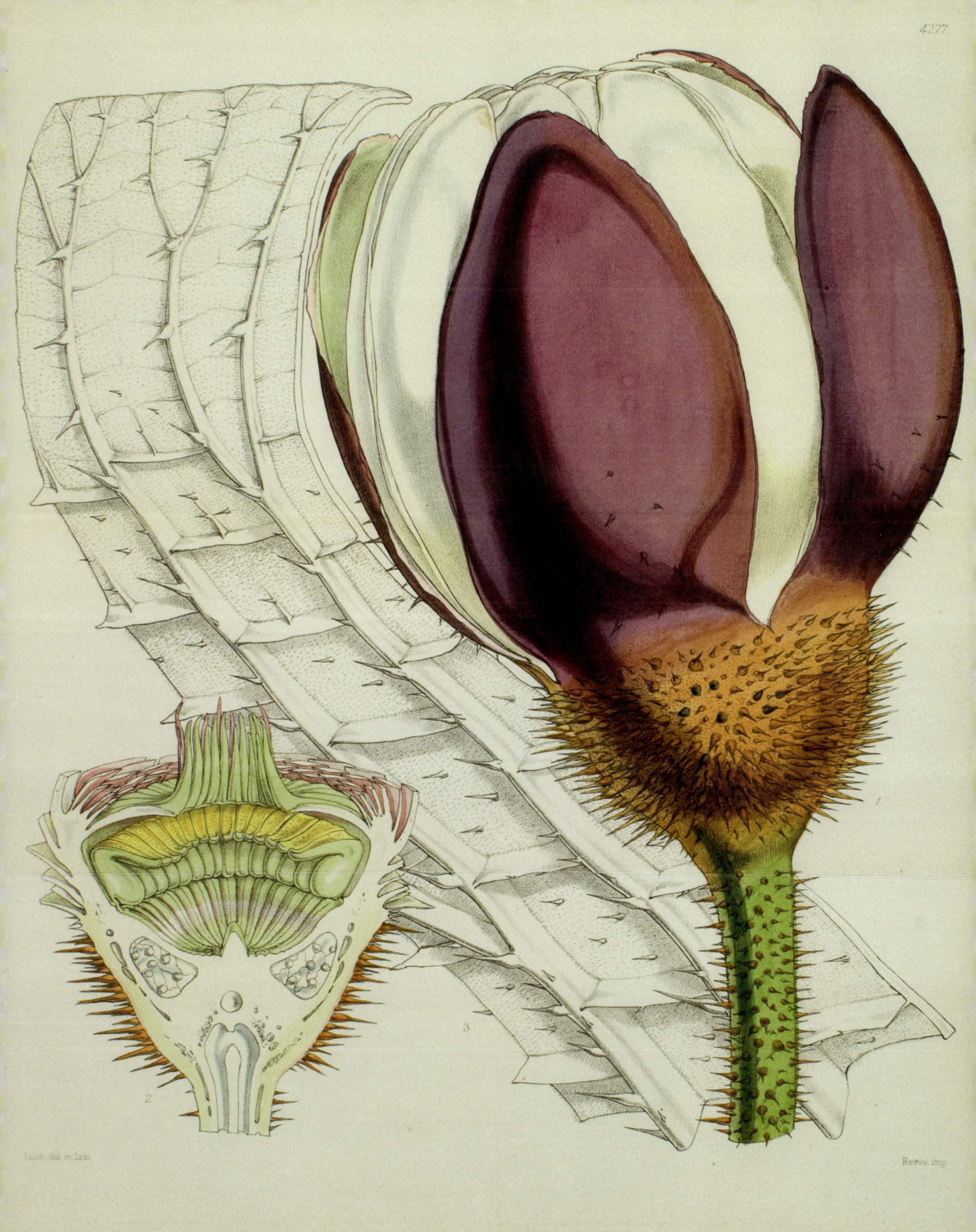

Jean Baptiste Antoine Guillemin of the National Museum of Natural History in Paris recounted that d'Orbigny's lily "had so many similarities to *Euryale* that botanists for the Paris garden did not hesitate to consider it congeneric." On top of that, the dried flowers and fruits d'Orbigny collected had vanished, leaving behind "a huge, somewhat deteriorated leaf that was bent in order to be put into the herbarium" (Guillemin 1840, translated by Rose Torelli). Clearly, in Paris, unlike in London, there was no sense of urgency about naming the lily.

Guillemin criticized Lindley for not clearly explaining the difference between *Euryale* and *Victoria* that would justify the establishment of a new genus. "The research that we have done has, in fact, shown the great affinity of these two genera," Guillemin stated. Ultimately, however, he agreed with Lindley's interpretation that the two lilies represented two distinct genera (Guillemin 1840, translated by Rose Torelli).

Lindley responded harshly to the criticism. Referring to papers published by Guillemin and d'Orbigny, Lindley alleged that "their object in putting them forth is evidently that of shewing that if I first published it I did not know how to describe it, and of claiming for the latter traveler the credit of having first discovered it" (Lindley 1840). He saw no fault of his own, and as a loyal subject of Queen Victoria, he had no intention of sharing the discovery with the French. "M. d'Orbigny's real object is to give an account of his own discoveries, and to complain of their having been anticipated by me in this country," Lindley wrote. "In what way however any blame attaches to me I am at a loss to understand," he declared. "The plant was discovered in an English Colony, by a distinguished naturalist in English pay, and by him it was communicated to me for publication" (Lindley 1840).

Pöppig remained, perhaps characteristically, silent on this issue of what some described as a "botanical heist of the first order" (Burnett 2000). Many other botanists did, too, avoiding being drawn into this great paper-war. Some, however, expressed understanding of d'Orbigny's disappointment that "someone else, because of happier circumstances, was able to name the plant first, not only robbing him of the triumph, but also giving it a name that offended French sensibilities and his own national pride" (Loescher 1852, translated by Kitty Byk). The great irony of the situation was that, in the words of French critic and novelist Alphonse Karr: "The war was on. Ink flowed freely. But the plant had still not arrived in Europe" (Karr 1853, translated by Rose Torelli).

Although there were only two people in all of Europe who had seen the *Victoria* lily—d'Orbigny and Pöppig—Lindley's name, "worthy of its dignity" (Planchon and Van Houtte 1850–51, translated by John Luttrell), caught the attention of the public. Even English botanists were interested, despite being accused by others, including Eduard Loescher of Hamburg (1852), of often ignoring the work of continental botanists and dismissing the value of plants discovered by them. Although the controversy surrounding Lindley's name was regrettable, it helped the plant gain greater recognition in botanical circles.

John Lindley, 1840:

I knew nothing of M. d'Orbigny, or of his discoveries, nor does he pretend that I did. But he says that he sent home specimens to Paris in 1828, only his friends at Paris did not make them known; that he talked about his "belles plantes" to M. Adolphe Brogniart, in 1834; that in 1835, at p. 289 of the "relation historique" of his travels, "il a indiqué sommairement sa découverte, sans lui imposer de nom botanique;" *and that he* "éprouvait une veritable peine" *when he found in 1837 that his plant was published by me with the* "nom pompeux" *of* Victoria regia. *In answer to all which I humbly submit to M. d'Orbigny that his specimens were not sent to me; that I am not M. Adolphe Brogniart; that I am very sorry for his distress of mind; and that* le nom pompeux de Victoria *is the name of the Queen of England.*

Lindley 1840

John Gray, president of the Botanical Society of London, authored in 1837 the earliest English publication describing the giant lilies under the name of *Victoria regina*.
HUNT INSTITUTE FOR BOTANICAL DOCUMENTATION

D'ORBIGNY STRIKES BACK

Defeated on the subject of the name of the genus, d'Orbigny wasted no time to ensure that credit for discovering the other *Victoria* was granted to France. In 1840, he published the name and description of *Victoria cruziana*, which he had found near Corrientes in 1828, emphasizing the characteristics distinguishing her from Schomburgk's *Victoria*.

Lindley and his camp were, however, determined not to let the French have this satisfaction. He immediately responded to d'Orbigny's claim on the pages of *Edwards's Botanical Register*, effectively ridiculing the French botanist's paper by calling it "so mean a result" (Lindley 1840). William Hooker of Kew added to the insult, alleging that d'Orbigny was "imagining that he had detected two species" (Hooker 1851). Hooker even derided d'Orbigny's fear that the English botanists "were anxious to steal a march upon him, in the publication of a second species of *Victoria*." Hooker said: "He is certainly under a great mistake; for we believe that no one but M. d'Orbigny ever imagined that there was a second species" (Hooker 1851). For many years, English botanists denied the existence of *Victoria cruziana* and reduced d'Orbigny's name to the status of a synonym of *Victoria regia*.

Anonymous, report of the proceedings of the Botanical Society, 1837:

At the meeting of the Society, held on Thursday, J. E. Gray, Esq., F. R. S. &c., President, in the chair, the Secretary read a communication from Mr. Robert H. Schomburgk, Corresponding Member of the Geographical Society, &c., dated New Amsterdam, Berbice, May 11th, 1837, on a new genus allied to the water-lily, named Victoria regina, *by permission of her Majesty. The communication was accompanied by magnificent drawings of the plant, one half the natural size, which may be seen at the rooms of the Society on any of the nights of meeting. . . . The thanks of the Society having been ordered to be returned to Mr. Schomburgk for his kind assistance, he was unanimously elected a Foreign Member.*

Anonymous 1837

PAPER WARRIOR

Meanwhile, Lindley had more problems than just the French botanists contesting *Victoria regia*. He also had to fight off attacks from within his own ranks. One prominent naturalist in London published his own name for the plant before Lindley's pamphlet was released publicly in February 1838. In the September 9, 1837, issue of the *Athenaeum*, John Edward Gray, president of the Botanical Society of London, published the name *Victoria regina*, designating it as "Queen Victoria" rather than the "Royal Victoria" of Lindley. The difference of a single letter may seem only a minor variation to some, but it is of paramount importance to botanists, especially those whose name, as the authority, follows the binomial. To further complicate things, an index to the *Athenaeum* listed Gray's article erroneously under *Victoria regia*. Gray's *Victoria regina* was then published in a number of other journals crediting Schomburgk as the author, while Lindley's *Victoria regia* still circulated privately and was known only to a small clique of insiders, starting with Queen Victoria herself, who received her copy (presumably the first one) in November 1837 (Hooker 1851).

Partial blame for the situation must be laid on Schomburgk himself, who sent two copies of the letter announcing his discovery to the Geographical Society. One of the two, accompanied by drawings and a pressed leaf, was forwarded to the Botanical Society of London, of which Schomburgk believed Queen Victoria to be the patron. The other went to Lindley, whom the Geographical Society commissioned to write up the description of the lily. John Gray, who received Schomburgk's material on behalf of the Botanical Society, observed that the new lily appeared to be intermediate between *Nymphaea* and *Euryale* and therefore altered the name proposed by Schomburgk to *Victoria regina*. He then presented it at the Society's meeting on September 7 and published it later in the *Athenaeum*. The Society members thought this occasion was so important, they elected Schomburgk as a Foreign Member and adopted *Victoria regina* as its emblem (Gray 1837).

REGIA, REGINA, OR AMAZONICA?

With two botanists competing for authorship of the queen lily's name, pens were drawn and ink was shed in the next battle of the great paper-war. Hooker at Kew found himself with the difficult task of refereeing arguments between the sparring opponents, both of whom were immensely respected in London's scientific community. There was little doubt that Gray's name, even though plagued by a misprint error, had priority over Lindley's. "Things being so," Hooker wrote, "I had little hesitation in stating my opinion . . . that the name *Victoria regina* should have preference" (Hooker 1851).

The dueling queen lily names ruled the pages of botanical and horticultural publications in England for some years. When the Amazonian nymph herself finally arrived to establish residence in the island kingdom, maneuvers to settle the question of the scientific name were renewed with even greater determination. In August 1850, Gray asserted that the "name of *Victoria regina*, which received the sanction

---

John Gray, 1850:

Shortly after the appearance of the description and figure in the Annals of Zoology and Botany, *and after Sir William Jardine had returned them, Captain Washington, R. N., then Secretary of the Geographical Society, borrowed from the Botanical Society the original description and drawing of the plant made by Mr. Schomburgk, with the intention of their appearing in the* Journal of the Geographical Society *with Mr. Schomburgk's journal of his travels. Instead of this being done, the papers found their way into the hands of Dr. Lindley, who printed, for private distribution, twenty-five copies of an essay on this plant, entirely derived from Mr. Schomburgk's paper, and illustrated with highly embellished copies of Schomburgk's drawing. In the essay he adopted the view which had been stated before the Botanical Society and British Association, that it formed a genus intermediate between* Euryale *and* Nymphaea, *but he called the plant* Victoria regia, *thus continuing the error of the printer of the* Athenaeum.

Gray 1850a

Frontispiece of a catalog for the 1862 exhibition of the Royal Horticultural Society featuring Queen Victoria's signature above the representation of the queen lily.
ROYAL HORTICULTURAL SOCIETY, LINDLEY LIBRARY

Victoria R
Patron

Paper Warrior 103

In 1850, James Sowerby, secretary to the Royal Botanical Society, reinstated Pöppig's epithet to give the giant lily the name Victoria amazonica, *still in use today.*
SMITHSONIAN INSTITUTION LIBRARIES, WASHINGTON, D.C.

John Lindley, an unrelenting paper warrior when it came to botanical matters, posed for this photograph shortly before his death in 1865.
ROYAL BRITISH COLUMBIA MUSEUM

of Her Majesty, was the one first used and published, and has the undoubted right of priority" (Gray 1850a). Lindley responded forcefully. He called Gray's statement a "tissue of mistakes" (Lindley and Paxton 1850–51). He then proceeded to invoke an "authority which we at least shall not presume to question" and, most convincing of all, stated: "Her Majesty's pleasure, that the name of *Victoria regia* should be affixed to the flower" (Lindley and Paxton 1850–51). In case this was not enough to subdue Gray, Lindley reminded him that Schomburgk was "entirely under the control and at the cost of the Geographical Society—a tolerably intelligible, although courteous hint, which most men would have known how to receive." His implication, of course, was that only that institution, and not the Botanical Society, had the right to name the lily (Lindley and Paxton 1850–51).

Once Lindley invoked the "authority" not to be questioned, Gray had no choice but to issue a declaration of surrender and a pledge of allegiance to *Victoria regia*. "I should be inclined," he wrote in December 1850, "to forgo the priority of publication and in future use the name of *Victoria regia* for the plant" (Gray 1850b). Hypocritically, Lindley had staked his claim by arguing that it was the right of the institution, in this case the Geographical Society, which had funded the presumed discovery, to designate the name for that discovery. It was a blatant disregard for the rule of priority governing publications of scientific names. Besides, the same reasoning could have been applied to the National Museum of Natural History in Paris, which had funded d'Orbigny's expedition.

Although he had averted mutiny within his own ranks for now, Lindley could not savor this victory for long: Another rebellion had already been brewing quietly in the halls of the Botanical Museum in Berlin. In April 1847, museum curator Johan Friedrich Klotzsch published a note in the *Botanische Zeitung* reminding readers that the unquestionable priority of Pöppig's name required the plant to retain the specific epithet of *amazonica*, whether the lily was classified as *Victoria* or *Euryale*. A printing error crept into Klotzsch's paper, however, and the name appeared as *Victoria amazonum* (Klotzsch 1847). Three years later, while the final sparring between Lindley and Gray was playing out on the pages of England's botanical journals, James De Carle Sowerby, secretary to the Royal Botanic Society, corrected Klotzsch's mistake, and the name *Victoria amazonica* appeared in print for the first time (Sowerby 1850).

"[Pöppig's] specific name *amazonica* ought to be retained," Sowerby argued, "or rather, it ought never to have been altered. As for the 'permission of Her Majesty,' our loyalty need not to be alarmed, for it appears most probable that the 'permission' only applied to the name *Victoria* along with the generic name *Nymphaea* in Sir R. Schomburgk's letter before it was revised, *regina* being an afterthought. Her Majesty will not be offended by that name being adopted which is most in accordance with accepted rules" (Sowerby 1850).

Lindley clearly underestimated the gravity of Sowerby's argument, decrying it as not worthy of "serious consideration" (Lindley and Paxton 1850–51). Hooker loyally backed Lindley and rejected Sowerby's proposal out of hand. "We put wholly aside *Euryale 'amazonica,'* Pöppig," he wrote, "well enough matched with one of the Furies, but

104   VICTORIA: THE SEDUCTRESS

totally unsuited to be in connection with the name of Her Most Gracious Majesty, whom it is intended to commemorate, and also as being inappropriate to a plant which is neither confined to the Amazon River nor was even originally detected there" (Hooker 1851).

Thus, the name *Victoria amazonica*, deemed "inappropriate" by the British botanical luminaries, was suppressed throughout Queen Victoria's vast empire until her death in 1901. The name that paired the beloved queen, projected as the ideal of femininity and domesticity, with the savage female warriors of the Amazon was just too much for British botanists and the public alike to stomach. However, contemporary author Adrienne Munich (*Queen Victoria's Secret* 1996) suggests "perhaps a sense that the label might be all too appropriate intensified the stakes in suppressing it." As a consequence, scientific integrity was subjugated to monarchic prerogatives, and the South American nymph remained, at least for the queen's lifetime, *Victoria regia*.

PEACE AT LAST

When the wheel of history turned again, and the empire built by Queen Victoria expired, so did Lindley's name. Unlike their predecessors, twentieth-century British botanists gave "serious consideration" to Klotzsch's and Sowerby's proposals and reinstated *Victoria amazonica* as an accepted name for the Amazon lily. Furthermore, they recognized the legitimacy of d'Orbigny's *Victoria cruziana*, which had been so blatantly denigrated by Lindley and Hooker.

A shadow of doubt was even cast on the originality of Lindley's *Victoria* after finding that the name had been previously used by Pierre-Joseph Buchoz, a French naturalist. In his 1783 *Herbier Colorie de l'Amerique*, Buchoz included an illustration of a plant he named *Victoria borbonica*, whose epithet alluded to Bourbon Island (today's Réunion) in the Indian Ocean. However, since the name lacked a formal description, it was not clear what plant it referenced. *Calophyllum inophyllum*, a tree native to that island, has been named as one possibility. Because of this ambiguity, Buchoz's *Victoria* was never validly established, but it did demonstrate how vulnerable Lindley's name was.

It is perhaps a great irony that although today's travelers to the Amazon may never hear the names *dachocho*, *morinqua*, or *mururú* spoken along the mighty river, sooner or later local inhabitants will tell them about *victória régia*. While this name has been relegated to the archives of botany everywhere else—including in Lindley's homeland—the settlers of mixed European, African, and American descent who supplanted the indigenous peoples of the Amazon throughout the nineteenth century adopted Lindley's name as the vernacular name for the giant lily and have effectively preserved it.

Ultimately, no single explorer or single nation could claim sole credit for discovering the South American nymph. Her out-of-this-world nature exceeded the ability of the nineteenth-century societies to fully tame such an awe-inspiring creature. Bohemia, Austria, and Spain can all point with pride to Haenke, *Victoria*'s first European discoverer. France, thanks to Bonpland and d'Orbigny, has the earliest dry specimens sent out of South America. Germany can claim Pöppig's publication as the first description of the vegetable colossus. England, although it did not triumph in the great paper-war, deserves recognition for giving the plant her lasting name of *Victoria*. In the end, it required a century of combined efforts of explorers and botanists from across Europe to bring this remarkable lily out of her wild primordial state and into the realm of Western civilization.

In 1783 Pierre-Joseph Buchoz, a French naturalist, assigned the name of *Victoria borbonica* to this plant from Bourbon Island. Its true identity being uncertain, it is thought to represent a plant known today as *Calophyllum inophyllum*.
UNITED STATES NATIONAL LIBRARY OF MEDICINE

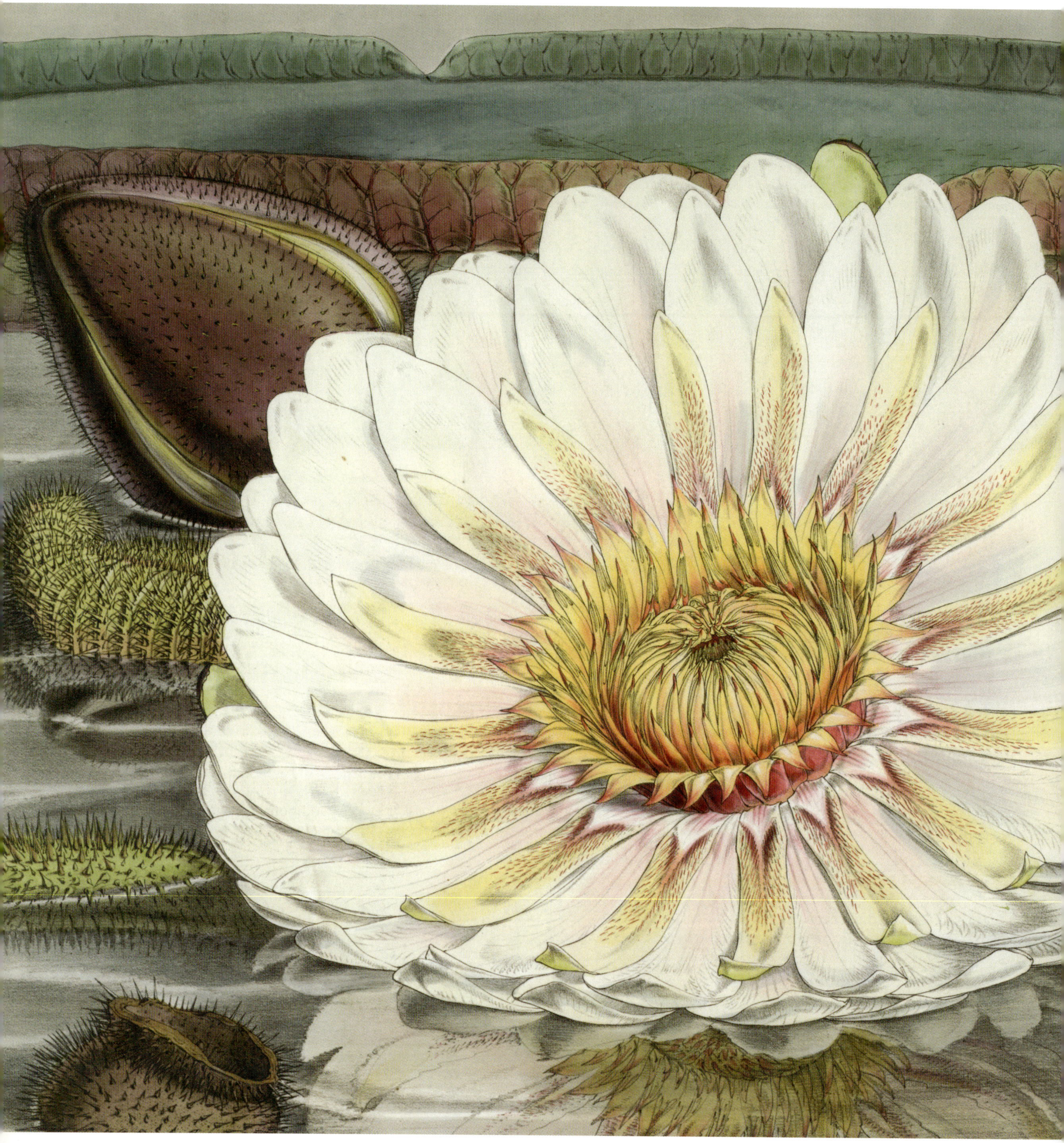

chapter 7

KNIGHTED GARDENER

ONCE THE NAMING OF THE COLOSSAL WATER LILY—inspired by recently enthroned Queen Victoria—became widely known, it was important to bring the South American wonder to England. William Hooker, director of the Royal Botanic Gardens, Kew, took the lead. Feeling pressure from the public's growing interest and desire to please his sovereign, Hooker made many attempts to procure either living plants or viable seeds. First, he asked Robert Schomburgk to "use his best exertions, and to employ those of his friends in British Guiana" to procure both seeds and the rhizomes of the marvelous lily. In 1840, Schomburgk obliged, and John Lindley expeditiously informed the public that "living plants of this vegetable prodigy have reached Demerara in safety, and that they may soon be expected in England" (Lindley 1840). Unfortunately, his announcement was premature. Schomburgk's collections arrived in "a state totally unfit for vegetation and germination" (Hooker 1851).

Despite Hooker's additional requests, it was not until August 1846—nine years after Lindley had named *Victoria* in absentia—that the lily's first living seeds arrived at Kew. They were purchased from Thomas Bridges, an explorer who had collected them in Bolivia a year earlier. Bridges had prepared the seeds for the long journey across the Atlantic by packing them in moist soil enclosed in a bottle. Unfortunately, only two

Victoria amazonica on the second night of flowering, a lithograph by Walter Fitch from William Hooker's 1851 book *Victoria Regia*.
THE MCLEAN LIBRARY, THE PENNSYLVANIA HORTICULTURAL SOCIETY

Joseph Paxton, painted by Thomas Ellerby, circa 1844.
DEVONSHIRE COLLECTION, CHATSWORTH, REPRODUCED BY PERMISSION OF CHATSWORTH SETTLEMENT TRUSTEES

William Hooker, 1846:

It is true that the Victoria has not yet produced its blossoms in England; but we have growing plants in the Royal Gardens of Kew, which germinated from seeds brought from Bolivia by Mr. Bridges. These have hitherto made satisfactory progress; although we have our fears that the plant being possibly annual and the season late (December), they may not survive the winter; or, at any rate, may not produce perfect flowers. Many are the disappointments and delays in Science! . . . We have, however, no reason to despair of being able to raise the Victoria regia and of seeing it bloom in this country. The time is not long since we first heard of this gorgeous water-lily; and the facilities of communicating with foreign countries are very different now from what they were in the days of Linnaeus and of the first importation of the tea-shrub!

Hooker 1847

seedlings grew out of this lot, and because the season was already so advanced, they perished when the "dark and cheerless" December days came without ever producing a flower (Hooker 1851).

Two years later, in 1848, another attempt was made by E. G. Boughton, Hooker's "liberal friend" from Leguan Island in the delta of the Essequibo River in British Guiana (Hooker 1851). Boughton thought that since the related water lilies of the *Nymphaea* tribe could be easily propagated by dividing their rhizomes, he would try to apply the same method to *Victoria*. Boughton hired several Indians to dig up the lily's rhizomes in the Upper Essequibo. Then he promptly dispatched them to England inside a Wardian case—a miniature greenhouse designed for carrying plants aboard ships. These were followed by a second shipment of seeds. Some were still enclosed within the fruit, and others were extracted from the fruit and immersed in muddy water, imitating their natural river conditions. All were pronounced dead upon their arrival at Kew in October.

Despite these setbacks, Hooker was not ready to give up, and with each attempt, he tried to modify the method used for shipping.

THE RACE IS ON

In February 1849, Hooker instructed two men living in Georgetown in British Guiana—Hugh Rodie, a former navy surgeon, and Mr. Lachie, of whom little is known—to procure some seeds and ship them this time in vials of pure water. To Hooker's delight, they arrived in excellent condition. In March, the seeds were planted at Kew in pots submerged in water and enclosed in a glass case. They germinated in large numbers. The plants grew well, thriving in the intense light of long summer days.

William Spencer Cavendish, sixth duke of Devonshire, portrait after Sir Francis Grant, circa 1850.
DEVONSHIRE COLLECTION, CHATSWORTH, REPRODUCED BY PERMISSION OF CHATSWORTH SETTLEMENT TRUSTEES

With more than fifty seedlings at hand, Hooker resolved to share them with "distinguished private cultivators" in various parts of the country (Lawson 1851). Only four ducal estates with gardeners known for their horticultural acumen, namely, Chatsworth of the duke of Devonshire, Syon House of the duke of Northumberland, Woburn of the duke of Bedford, and Dalkeith Palace of the duke of Buccleuch, were able to provide accommodations that might ensure the survival of the regal lily.

At Chatsworth, it was Joseph Paxton—superintendent of the renowned gardens of William Spencer Cavendish, sixth duke of Devonshire—who took up the challenge of competing with Kew and the other three ducal estates in raising the first English *Victoria*. At forty-six, Paxton was at the height of his career. He was widely credited with transforming Chatsworth into perhaps the finest plant collection in England, making the estate a veritable horticultural mecca for gardening aficionados. With a nation of gardeners watching and waiting, there was no more highly respected gardener than Paxton, and no establishment better equipped than Chatsworth to undertake the daunting task of tending to *Victoria*'s horticultural needs.

Paxton had come to Chatsworth from the Royal Horticultural Society's Chiswick Gardens more than twenty years earlier. He had impressed the duke of Devonshire, from whom the Society leased Chiswick. Eventually, the duke convinced Paxton to move to his private estate at Chatsworth. Nothing in Paxton's humble background or upbringing, however, foretold what would ensue after one fateful August day—which happened to be his birthday—when he traveled to London to receive from the staff at Kew the parcel containing the priceless water lily.

Thanks to the proximity of railroads to Chatsworth, Paxton was able to make the round-trip in a single day. After a 250-km (155-mile) train ride, he arrived at Chatsworth. He brought a small box, barely over 30 cm (12 inches) square but with ample accommodations for a young seedling. Paxton planted it immediately in a pot filled with water, which in turn he sunk in a bed heated to nearly 30°C (86°F). In the meantime, his staff hurried to prepare a larger tank for the proper reception of the regal lily. A week later, it was installed in a greenhouse, some 18 m (60 feet) long by 8 m (26 feet) wide, called Curvilinear House because its roof was a quarter circle. Planted into a hillock of soil that was mounded in the center

George Lawson, 1851:

It was not alone the difficulty of obtaining living plants or perfect seeds, and getting them safely transferred to English soil, that stood in the way of the lily's introduction to Britain. Its habits were new to our horticulturists, who were in a great measure ignorant of the natural conditions under which the plant was developed in the South American waters, and consequently were ill prepared to judge of the conditions requisite for its successful cultivation under artificial circumstances. Its gigantic size, and other peculiarities, rendered its treatment peculiarly difficult; no plant, requiring the same care, and attention, and favourable circumstances for its healthy development, had ever before come through the hands of the gardener.

Lawson 1851

On October 1, 1849, Joseph Paxton wrote in a letter to the duke of Devonshire: "We have been obliged to make the tank for the *Victoria* as large again as when your Grace saw it."
DEVONSHIRE COLLECTION, CHATSWORTH, REPRODUCED BY PERMISSION OF CHATSWORTH SETTLEMENT TRUSTEES

Joseph Paxton, letter to the duke of Devonshire, 1849:

My Lord Duke. Victoria *has shewn flower!! An enormous bud like a great poppy head made its appearance yesterday morning and by this evening it looks like a large peach placed in a cup, from what I can see it will be 8 or 10 days before it comes into flower and therefore I am in a great stew about going to Lismore at the time I appointed but I shall do whatever your Grace may wish. I have paid so much personal attention to it and it has been entirely under my own direction since I brought it from Kew that I should not like to be out of the way when it flowers. As this noble plant bears the Queen's name I think your Grace would like to send the first flower with a large leaf to Her Majesty. No account can give a fair idea of the grandeur of its appearance; I believe the plant will shew another bud in a few days, everybody here is mad about it even the labourers take great interest in it.*

Paxton 1849a

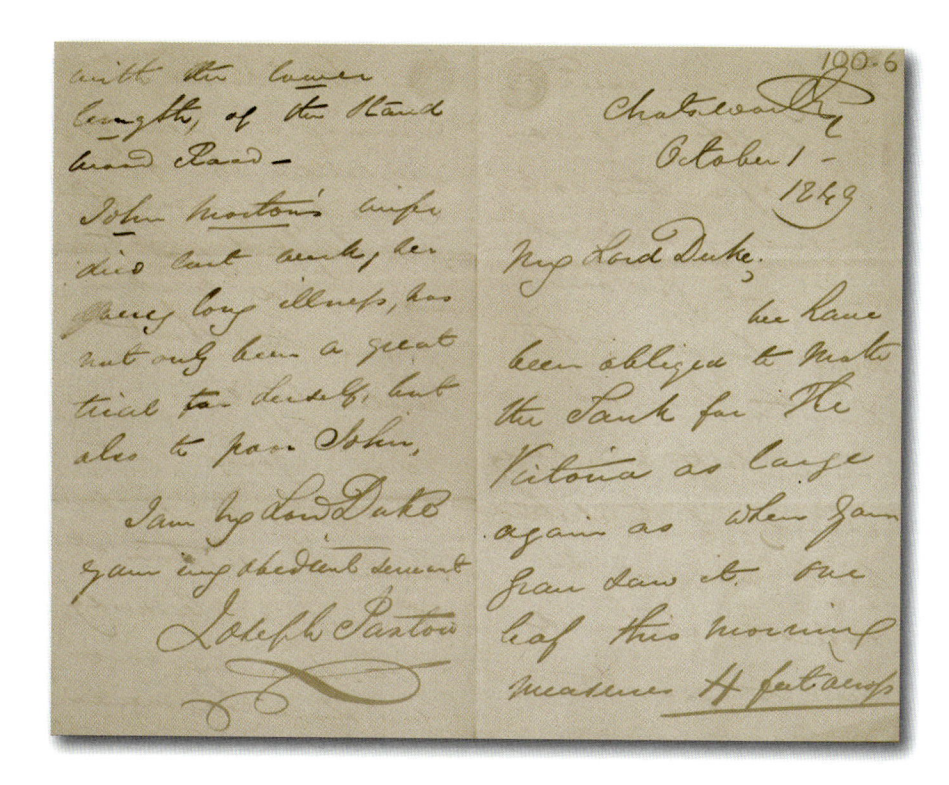

of the 3.7-m (12-foot) square tank, *Victoria* grew rapidly. Before the end of September, Paxton had to double the size of the tank. Astonishingly, in mid-October, the lily's immense leaf pads extended over an area 5.8 m (19 feet) across, which Paxton proclaimed "the most remarkable instance of the rapidity of vegetable development we have on record" (Hooker 1851). The nymph continued to thrive until early November, when her largest leaves, showing a dramatic dark purple upturned edge, reached an astonishing 1.5 m (5 feet) in diameter.

PAXTON'S TRIUMPH

Finally, on November 9, 1849, the much-anticipated flower opened in Chatsworth's greenhouse. It was the first to bloom outside *Victoria*'s native lands in South America. The duke was in Ireland at the time, but Paxton regularly sent him letters reporting *Victoria*'s progress. On November 11, he also dispatched a letter to William Hooker at Kew, informing him that the race for the first flower of *Victoria* was over. Chatsworth had crossed the finish line ahead of the other estates. "The sight of our plant is worth a journey of a thousand miles," he added to encourage Hooker to visit Chatsworth (Paxton 1849b).

Hooker came promptly to see Paxton's triumph. He also went to work right away on a book on *Victoria* that would be published in 1851. Kew gardeners hoped to come in second place, since their lily produced her first flower bud only two weeks later, on November 21. Unfortunately, it never fully opened. Kew's *Victoria* produced no new buds until the following year. Likewise, the other ducal estates had to wait until 1850 to see their first flowers.

With the duke's permission, Paxton soon arranged to deliver the subsequent flower to Queen Victoria herself. In the early hours of November 14, he set off for

Victoria blooming in the Curvilinear House at Chatsworth in November 1849. Annie, daughter of Joseph Paxton, is shown standing on one of the leaves.
LONGWOOD GARDENS LIBRARY AND ARCHIVES

Windsor accompanied by one of his gardeners. They carried a bloom plus a large leaf of *Victoria* to present to Her Majesty, who after twelve years of waiting could finally meet her floral namesake in person. When the duke of Devonshire returned from Ireland three days later, he described the South American lily in his diary with characteristic brevity: "It is stupendous" (Spencer, 1840–52).

As the fame of Chatsworth's lily spread, visitors clamored for a view of the vegetable wonder. Artists from the *Illustrated London News* came to create *Victoria*'s likeness, in which they included Paxton's daughter Annie gracefully posing on one of the floating leaves. Once printed, this image allowed Londoners to see for the first time what the mythical plant that carried the name of their beloved queen looked like. In truth, the presentation was somewhat distorted. The artists did not hesitate to exaggerate the flowers in both size and number. The rendering also began a fad of placing children on floating *Victoria* leaves, which in time reached every corner of the world where the lily was later introduced.

As November rolled into December and the days grew shorter and darker, Paxton's lily showed obvious signs of decline. The plant's succeeding leaves became progressively smaller. By Christmas, the

Joseph Paxton, letter to Sarah Paxton, 1849:

Here we are in as great a w[h]orl about Victoria *as ever. We expect Lord Carlisle tomorrow and then the curtain I beleive [sic] will drop. We have two artists Mr. Bartholemew & Mr. Holdin drawing away at it, Holdin sat up until half past two this morning. Sir William Hudson and Lady Newburgh have been also. Lady Newburgh who got upon the plank and examined the flower close to it.... Nothing I believe has caused so much stir in the fashionable world and also the world of gardening. You will have seen this* Gardeners' Chronicle *which I told you to get. There is a very good description of the plant there.... Anne is quite proud at being placed upon the leaf. She was put on for Lady Newburgh and the Duke.*

Paxton 1849c

The interior view of Chatsworth Lily House shows a 10-m-wide (33-foot) round central pool. The pool is surrounded by a walk covered by wooden planks, with smaller pools in each of the corners, and a flat ridge-and-furrow roof supported by slender, widely spaced columns. The end elevation and the perspective view of the exterior demonstrate the simple yet elegant concept of Chatsworth's greenhouse that Paxton would later replicate when designing the Crystal Palace.
LONGWOOD GARDENS LIBRARY AND ARCHIVES

new leaves were only 60 cm (27 inches) wide, a diminutive version of their former selves. Longer days in January, however, appeared to revive *Victoria*'s vigor, and new leaves began to increase in size. By spring, the plant was growing as luxuriantly as in the previous summer. She had, in Paxton's words, "fully realized our most sanguine expectations" (Allen 1854). Within a year since the first flower opened, Paxton's *Victoria* produced 125 additional flowers accompanied by 150 leaves, with up to 24 leaves present at any given time. Paxton found it remarkable that the giant water lily never ceased producing new flowers. It was "a property which we do not find any other cultivated plant to possess," he commented (Hooker 1851).

ARCHITECTURE INSPIRED BY A LILY PAD

Though the modifications to the Curvilinear House were adequate for the plant's first year, *Victoria*'s astonishing growth made it imperative to build a new home. Early in 1850, a larger house designed specifically for this aquatic giant was erected. Though similar in length to the Curvilinear House, it was increased in width to more than 14 m (45 feet) with a central circular heated tank over 10 m (33 feet) in diameter. This new Lily House had a flat roof that was designed using the ridge-and-furrow principle. Paxton decided to employ this design after observing the underside of the *Victoria* leaf, where a network of prominent veins imparted extraordinary strength to the leaf lamina it supported. Although Paxton had experimented with ridge-and-furrow design for many years, it was his first flat roof for such a large house.

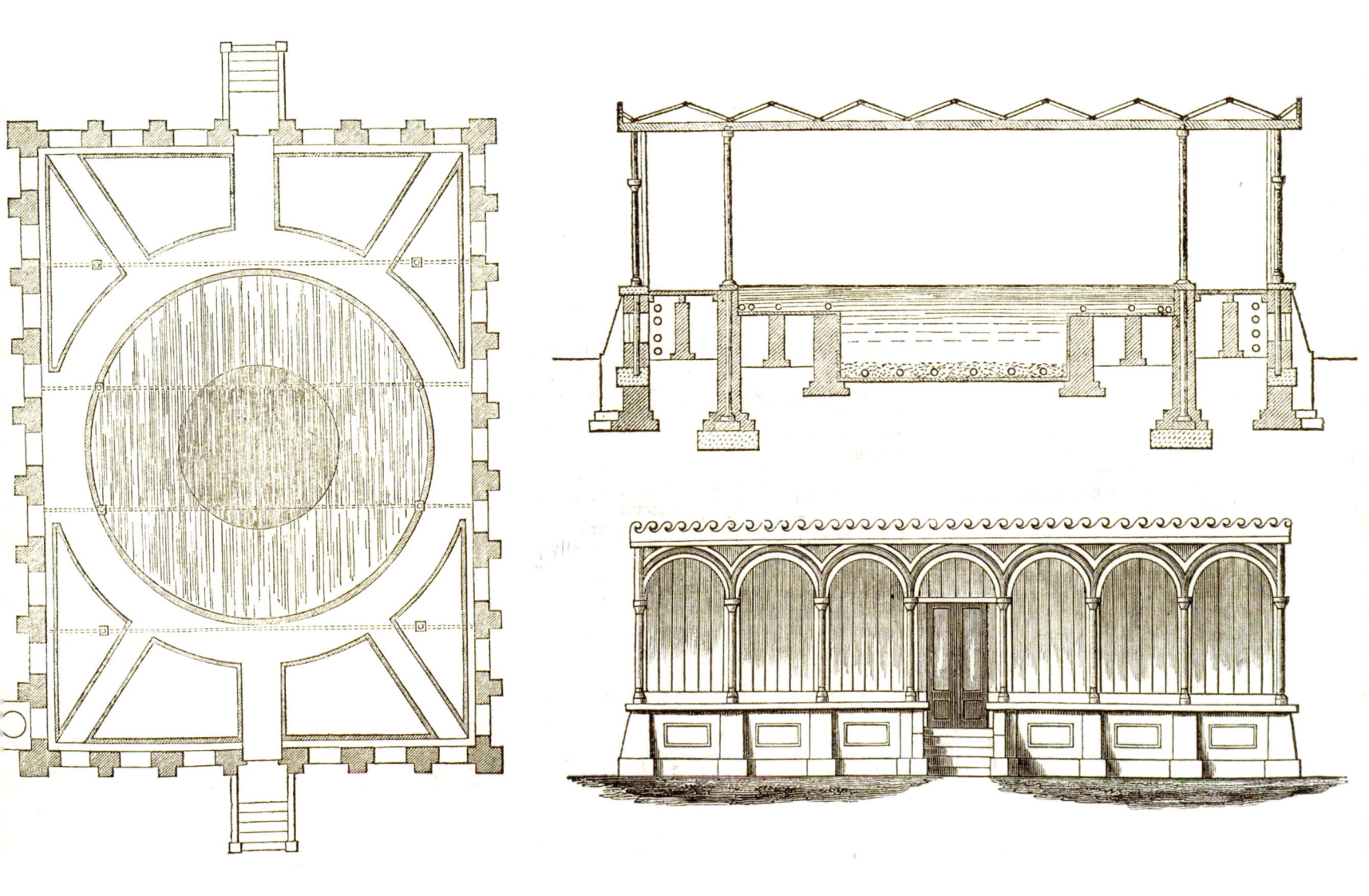

The speed with which the new Lily House was built is impressive even by today's standards. Paxton had at his disposal a large crew of workers; ready access to glass manufacturers, iron founders, and boiler suppliers; as well as a sash-bar machine of his own invention. Construction was essentially finished in April 1850. On June 26, the elegant glass pavilion received a young *Victoria* that had been raised from seeds saved from the previous year. She was gently planted into a spacious pool filled with balmy water. Chatsworth's extraordinary accommodations were designed to satisfy every need of the Amazonian beauty. Soon emulated by other gardens, the house and its occupant gave rise to the term "hothouse lily" as a metaphor for a "privileged Victorian woman, beautiful, delicate, protected, enclosed, and controlled through a special kind of nurture" (Darby 2002).

When designing the Lily House—which was to be the last of his buildings at Chatsworth—Paxton perfected elements he'd attempted or developed in many previous structures. His goal was to achieve simplicity, lightness, and efficient use of materials. For the first time, he combined the ridge-and-furrow

The ground floor and the transverse section of the Lily House at Chatsworth. The deeper central part of the pool contained soil for *Victoria*, while the more shallow outer ring of the pool was lined with large stone slabs.
LONGWOOD GARDENS LIBRARY AND ARCHIVES

KNIGHTED GARDENER 113

Chatsworth Lily House, sketch attributed to Sarah Paxton, wife of Joseph Paxton.
ROYAL BRITISH COLUMBIA MUSEUM, BRITISH COLUMBIA ARCHIVES

Joseph Paxton built the Lily House near Barbrook House, his home on the Chatsworth estate. The unmistakable façade of arched windows can be seen across from Paxton's house in this 1853 print.
DEVONSHIRE COLLECTION, CHATSWORTH, REPRODUCED BY PERMISSION OF CHATSWORTH SETTLEMENT TRUSTEES

principle (giving the flat roof the strength of a *Victoria* leaf) with rain gutters of his own patent and hollow cast-iron columns that both provided support for and carried water down from the roof. Once finished, Chatsworth's newest house proved the feasibility of Paxton's innovative design.

Shortly thereafter, Paxton was given the unprecedented opportunity to magnify this 18-m-long (60-foot) model more than thirty-fold into a vast glass palace for London's upcoming Great Exhibition of 1851. An immense building had to be erected in the middle of Hyde Park, but none of the 245 designs submitted by British architects fulfilled the requisite conditions. Out of desperation, members of the organizing committee came up with their own design for a brick-and-mortar building, which generated immediate objections over its high cost and undesirable lasting impact on Hyde Park.

These controversies were being hotly debated in the London press while Paxton was receiving accolades for his success with *Victoria* and the Lily House. "It was then that I turned my attention to the matter," he recalled, "when I was at once convinced that the least objectionable structure to occupy a public park would be an erection of cast-iron and glass, whilst at the same time a building of this description would be the very best adapted for the purpose of the Exhibition" (Paxton 1850–51). Even though the deadline for submitting a design had expired, the commissioners decided to consider Paxton's proposal.

What started as a quick sketch on a piece of blotting paper while Paxton sat, perhaps bored, in the board's meeting soon developed into a structural vision based on Chatsworth's latest greenhouse. The design not only satisfied all the organizers' initial

Residing in the Chatsworth Lily House, *Victoria* attracted numerous visitors eager to see the South American giant in person.
DEVONSHIRE COLLECTION, CHATSWORTH, REPRODUCED BY PERMISSION OF CHATSWORTH SETTLEMENT TRUSTEES

Chatsworth gardeners proudly posing in front of their famed Lily House, the groundbreaking design of which attracted so much attention.
DEVONSHIRE COLLECTION, CHATSWORTH, REPRODUCED BY PERMISSION OF CHATSWORTH SETTLEMENT TRUSTEES

The building of the Great Exhibition of 1851 in London's Hyde Park.
PRIVATE COLLECTION

requirements, but it also offered the possibility of extending the building in any direction and by any extent as dictated by the exhibition's evolving needs. In a mere ten days, Paxton prepared more detailed drawings, adapting the principle of the Lily House on a vast scale to design a massive structure 564 m (1,851 feet) long, 139 m (456 feet) wide, and covering 7.3 hectares (18 acres). He presented his plan on June 22. A month later, it was approved by the commissioners.

In November, Paxton presented a lecture to the Royal Society of Arts in London, one of the bodies organizing the Great Exhibition. He explained his concept for the building, illustrating his talk with numerous drawings, views, and diagrams as well as a machine he had invented that could speed up the production of 330 km (205 miles) of sash-bars. These were accompanied by a specimen of the *Victoria* leaf, which was 1.5 m (5 feet) in diameter. The underside of the leaf demonstrated a "beautiful example of natural engineering," in which the audience could see not only the veins but the "cantilevers" radiating from the center, with large bottom "flanges" and thin middle "ribs" joined by "cross girders" to prevent "buckling" (Paxton 1850–51). Paxton substituted the technical terminology of an engineer for the language a botanist might employ to describe the morphology and function of a leaf. The fabled water lily had crossed the divide separating the wilds of the Amazon from the cultured world of arts and technology.

John George Wood, a popular writer on natural history, proclaimed that Chatsworth's gardener "copied in iron the lines of the vegetable cellular structure which gave such a strength to the *Victoria regia* leaf." While in the *Victoria* leaf, "the capabilities of the Crystal Palace had lain latent for centuries," he continued, "the generalizing eye of genius was needed to detect it" (Wood 1877). In a few short months, the glasshouse of

Joseph Paxton, 1850:

It occurred to me that it only required a number of such structures as the Lily-house repeated in length, width, and height, to form, with some modifications, a suitable building for the exhibition of 1851. Hence arose the design for that structure, and the subsequent honour conferred on me by its unqualified adoption by Her Majesty's commissioners.

Paxton 1850

the Great Exhibition, "the most wonderful building in the world" as Wood called it, "sprang up like the creation of a fairy dream" on the green grounds of Hyde Park.

THE PALACE OF THE PEOPLE

The Great Exhibition opened on May 1, 1851. During the next five and a half months, it attracted a staggering six million visitors. After the exhibition closed that fall, Paxton's glasshouse was dismantled and moved to Sydenham Hill on the outskirts of London.

Joseph Paxton used Chatsworth's Lily House as the model on which he based the design for the building for the Great Exhibition of 1851.
DEVONSHIRE COLLECTION, CHATSWORTH, REPRODUCED BY PERMISSION OF CHATSWORTH SETTLEMENT TRUSTEES

KNIGHTED GARDENER 117

There, over the next two years, it was reassembled, enlarged, and eventually retitled the Crystal Palace, a name originally coined by a journalist at *Punch* magazine. Although the main nave was slightly shortened, the roof height was increased and two transepts were added, while two new wings extended the total length of the structure to 1,059 m (over half a mile). The whole structure was clad in about 15 hectares (37 acres) of glass, making it the largest conservatory ever built, a record that still stands. Around the vitreous palace, Paxton designed extravagant terraced gardens and an 80-hectare (198-acre) park outfitted with a dazzling plethora of fountains, statuary, and other attractions.

The public success of the Great Exhibition and Crystal Palace was phenomenal. Although many influential critics, such as William Morris and John Ruskin, objected on aesthetic grounds to the new mode of construction using prefabricated elements, Paxton's triumph was acknowledged by Her Majesty herself. In a striking example of upward mobility in Victorian society, Queen Victoria rewarded him with a knighthood. The serendipitous encounter with the giant American lily on his forty-sixth birthday had transformed Paxton's life from a caretaker of a country estate to that of an eminent architect and celebrity. In the words of Wood (1877), "an obscure gardener became Sir Joseph Paxton."

When reassembling the Crystal Palace at Sydenham Hill, Paxton added two large pools in the main nave, one at each of the transepts, answering the requests of the press for the queen lily to be included in the new scheme. Consequently, the pools were regularly stocked with *Victoria* lilies as their main feature, a tribute to the genius of Nature that provided the blueprint for the palace's construction.

The horticultural and engineering genius of Joseph Paxton earned him a knighthood from Queen Victoria, universal acclaim, and financial success.
DEVONSHIRE COLLECTION, CHATSWORTH, REPRODUCED BY PERMISSION OF CHATSWORTH SETTLEMENT TRUSTEES

An even more striking juxtaposition was created when another American colossus moved into the north transept next to *Victoria*. In 1854, a giant specimen of sequoia, *Sequoiadendron giganteum,* arrived in England. The mammoth tree had been recently discovered in California, though its existence was still doubted by the skeptics. Named Mother of the Forest, it was stripped of its bark, which was then shipped to New York, where it was reassembled and exhibited as a curiosity. Supported by internal scaffolding, the outer shell of the great tree rose to over 30 m (100 feet) high—perhaps the largest specimen of botanical "taxidermy" ever prepared. Crowds came to admire it, but others, among them American pioneer conservationist John Muir, deplored this act of skinning the Mother of the Forest, which sadly led to the death of the tree left standing in the Sierra Nevada a few years later. Soon, the hollow shell of the tree sailed from New York to London, beyond the reach of the outcry of the American public, where it joined the ranks of other wonders on view in the Crystal Palace. In a bout of patriotic fervor, the English decided to call the Californian giant *Wellingtonia*, another name, like that of *Victoria*, that John Lindley had hastily affixed—this time to recognize the duke of Wellington, a British war hero. Inside the Crystal Palace, the two vegetable giants—North America's Mother of the Forest and South America's Queen of the Amazon—kept each other company until 1866, when a fire broke out in the north transept and consumed the sequoia's outer shell.

Paxton was spared the view of the charred remains of his north transept, which would never be rebuilt. He had died a year earlier, as had Bridges, Hooker, Lindley, and Schomburgk, the entire quintet

The hollow shell of Mother of the Forest, a giant sequoia from California, towers over giant platters of *Victoria* in the north transept of the Crystal Palace in 1859.
ENGLISH HERITAGE, NATIONAL MONUMENTS RECORDS

J. Weeks and Co., letter to the *London Illustrated News*, 1851:

What an admirable place the Crystal Palace would be for the cultivation of this magnificent plant! It is hardly possible to conceive a more grand, novel, or interesting sight than the Victoria regia *would present, surrounded by all the species of Nymphaeaceae, in one noble central aquarium, where the public could view it without the danger of being stewed in a reeking atmosphere.... If the idea is carried out of converting the Crystal Palace into a winter garden (water being an essential feature in a garden), it would not be complete without it. I would in this case suggest that the aquarium be stocked with gold and silver fish, which would keep the water gently agitated, and would have a very lively appearance, and prove conducive to health. The whole might be enclosed by an ornamental iron railing to prevent accidents to the junior members of society.*

J. Weeks and Co. 1851

that had given the English their *Victoria* lily. The generation of explorers, botanists, and gardeners who together tamed the South American giant and delivered it to the glasshouses of Europe had disappeared.

Although missing its north transept, the Crystal Palace remained one of London's most popular destinations for eight decades, a place of artistic inspiration and entertainment for all, earning its nickname, the Palace of the People. However, despite attracting as many as two million visitors annually, more than any of London's other attractions at that time, it never met the profit expectations of the investors who financed its construction. In the early twentieth century, it was put up for sale and eventually became public property.

KNIGHTED GARDENER

A sphinx that guarded the queen lily and giant sequoia inside the Crystal Palace a century and half earlier, a nostalgic reminder of past splendors of Sydenham.

Tomasz Aniśko / Longwood Gardens

On the night of November 30, 1936, the Crystal Palace was destroyed in a horrific fire. In time, nearly all traces of its presence on Sydenham Hill have been erased. Today, those stepping off the train at the suburban Crystal Palace station enter a rather disappointing, nondescript, rundown park bearing little resemblance to the images gleaned from historic photographs. About all that remains of Paxton's creation are a few disintegrating terraces punctuated by headless statues, an assortment of grotesque concrete casts of prehistoric animals scattered around a pond, and several sphinxes from the lot that guarded the *Victoria* lily and giant sequoia in the north transept. The prevailing atmosphere is that of a past civilization, a fallen empire lying in rubble, the vestiges of which are already half-covered by spontaneous vegetation encroaching on the site.

Even then, Sydenham Hill's Crystal Palace outlasted its prototype, Chatsworth's Lily House, which was torn down after World War I. Like many Victorian-era conservatories, the Lily House fell victim to the financial hardships of postwar Britain. Half a century would pass before, in 1970, a new Display Greenhouse was built at Chatsworth. Designer George Pearce modeled the new greenhouse on his earlier construction at the Royal Botanical Gardens in Edinburgh. Both were built without interior support for the roof, a radical approach reflecting the spirit of Paxton's innovations. Chatsworth's new house also features a heated pool, which allowed *Victoria*

Joseph Paxton's death in 1865 marked the end of the generation of explorers, botanists, and gardeners who gave the *Victoria* lily to the English.
DEVONSHIRE COLLECTION, CHATSWORTH, REPRODUCED BY PERMISSION OF CHATSWORTH SETTLEMENT TRUSTEES

Paxton's Lily House served as the queen lily's residence for seventy years before it was demolished after World War I.
DEVONSHIRE COLLECTION, CHATSWORTH, REPRODUCED BY PERMISSION OF CHATSWORTH SETTLEMENT TRUSTEES

Edward Cavendish, tenth duke of Devonshire, visiting *Victoria* in the soon-to-be-demolished Lily House at Chatsworth.
DEVONSHIRE COLLECTION, CHATSWORTH, REPRODUCED BY PERMISSION OF CHATSWORTH SETTLEMENT TRUSTEES

to return to the location of her original residence in the British Isles. Below the entrance to the Display Greenhouse, a terrace was built with materials salvaged from the rubble of Paxton's Lily House. Large stone slabs that once lined the pool in the Lily House now make a ring surrounding a pebble snake, the Cavendish family emblem.

THE WORLD'S FIRST MODERN ARCHITECT

The influence of Paxton's innovative design of the Lily House reached beyond the Great Exhibition building, which some initially called the Victoria House. Editors of the popular *Gardeners' Chronicle* went so far as to predict the end of traditional greenhouses, whose costly high, wide, and heavy roofs required massive support walls and foundations. Instead, they envisioned how, thanks to Paxton's horizontal ridge-and-furrow structures, which were supported by light columns, "an acre or two of winter garden beneath a Victoria House, falls within the means of every wealthy person, and of every large city, in the United Kingdom." Such buildings would allow for the "enjoyment of flowers and green leaves all the winter long, in exchange for mud, snow, hail, frost, and floral desolation" (Anonymous 1851i). Prophetically, a century later, inexpensive prefabricated Dutch greenhouses replicated Chatsworth's model of a Victoria House, covering thousands of acres—first in Holland and then in other countries—on a scale unimaginable even to Paxton. The Dutch greenhouses enabled the widespread production of "hothouse" flowers and vegetables at an affordable price, putting them within reach of ordinary people.

The impact of the Crystal Palace was not lost on Victorian architects. Even though many of Paxton's contemporaries considered him a mere landscape designer, a number of Crystal Palaces emulating Paxton's design appeared in European and American cities following the Great Exhibition. None, however, surpassed his creation in size or extravagance.

Ruins of Chatsworth's Lily House as seen in the 1950s.
DEVONSHIRE COLLECTION, CHATSWORTH, REPRODUCED BY PERMISSION OF CHATSWORTH SETTLEMENT TRUSTEES

A more thorough understanding and appreciation of what Chatsworth's gardener contributed to architecture came later, when twentieth-century modernists recognized the Crystal Palace as the world's first modern building and praised its functionality, simplicity, and masterly utilization of new materials—glass and iron. Writing shortly after the disastrous fire at Sydenham, Le Corbusier, the Swiss icon of modern architecture, confessed: "When, two years ago, I saw the Crystal Palace for the last time, I could not tear my eyes from the spectacle of its triumphant harmony. The lesson was so tremendous that it made me feel how puny our own attempts still are" (Le Corbusier 1937). Le Corbusier described the structures envisioned by the knighted gardener as "the fruit of discovery, of the joy of creation, and of enthusiasm" and saw in them "the heralds of a new age."

Anonymous correspondent to the *Gardeners' Chronicle*, 1851:

When Mr. Paxton constructed at Chatsworth the Victoria House … he laid the foundation of a series of changes in the plans of conservatories, the end of which will doubtless be the gradual removal of all those lean-to, span-roofed, or upright fronted plant-houses with which gardens are now decorated. It will probably be found, too, that he will have introduced into very general use those winter gardens which so many have sought for and so few have found.

Anonymous 1851i

Stone slabs that once lined the pool in the Lily House were salvaged from the ruins and incorporated into the Snake Terrace—so called from the Cavendish family emblem in the center—below the entrance to Chatsworth's Display Greenhouse.
Tomasz Aniśko / Longwood Gardens

Chatsworth's Display Greenhouse, designed by George Pearce and opened in 1970, allowed *Victoria* to return to the site of her earliest residence in the British Isles.
Tomasz Aniśko / Longwood Gardens

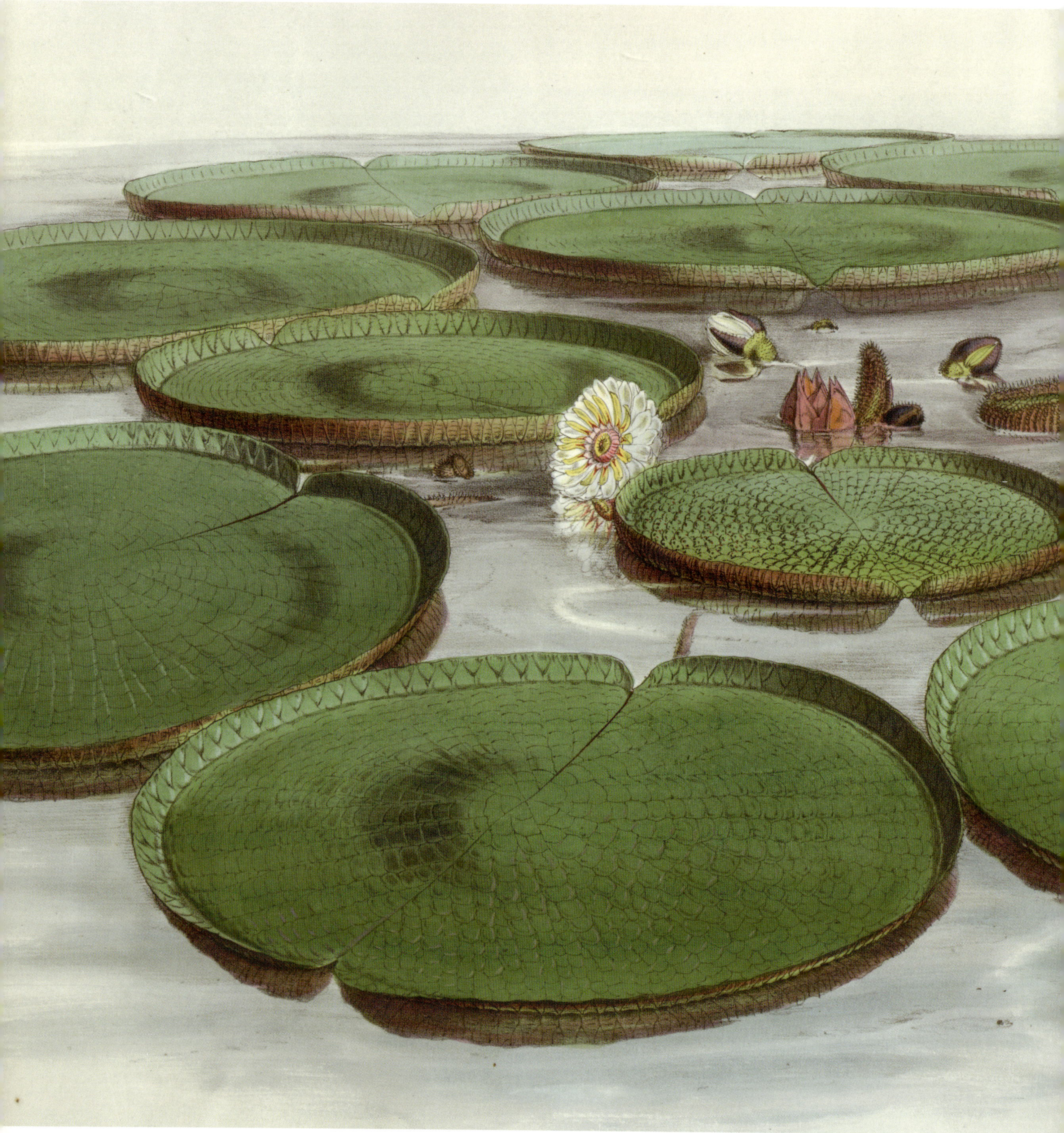

chapter 8

RULE, BRITANNIA!

Although Robert Schomburgk failed in his own attempts to introduce *Victoria* to cultivation in Great Britain, he nevertheless alerted many people to the plant's existence. The publication of Schomburgk's illustrations and descriptions sparked the desire to bring the now royal lily to her rightful place in Queen Victoria's dominion. This interest in *Victoria* intensified in 1840, when Schomburgk wrote a more extensive account of the new colony of British Guiana. This was followed a year later by his publication *Views in the Interior of Guiana,* which featured a highly embellished image of the giant water lily on the title page. Both publications furthered *Victoria*'s reputation as an iconic emblem—not only of Guiana but also of the riches of South America that were awaiting discovery by British explorers.

Accompanied by his younger brother Richard, Robert Schomburgk returned to Guiana and continued exploring the colony until 1844. While surveying Guiana's borders, the two explorers discovered additional populations of *Victoria* along the rivers demarcating the western frontier with Brazil. They showed the lilies with "gratification" to the officers of the West India Regiment who were proceeding to take a military border post in Pirara (Hooker 1847). Reverend Thomas Youde, a Protestant missionary who followed the officers to Pirara, tried

Victoria amazonica growing at the Syon House in London, an illustration by Walter Fitch from William Hooker's 1851 book *Victoria Regia*.
The McLean Library, The Pennsylvania Horticultural Society

Thomas Bridges was one of the first English explorers to search for *Victoria* in the Amazon basin.
Hunt Institute for Botanical Documentation

Thomas Bridges, 1847:

During my stay at the Indian town of Santa Anna, in the province of Moxos, Republic of Bolivia, during the months of June and July 1845, I made daily shooting excursions in the vicinity. In one of these I had the good fortune (whilst riding along the woody banks of the river Yacuma, one of the tributary rivers of the Mamoré) to come suddenly on a beautiful pond, or rather small lake, embosomed in the forest, where, to my delight and astonishment, I discovered, for the first time, "the Queen of Aquatics," the Victoria regia*! There were at least fifty flowers in view, and Belzoni could not have felt more rapture at his Egyptian discoveries than I did in beholding the beautiful and novel sight before me, such as it has fallen to the lot of few Englishmen to witness. Fain would I have plunged into the lake to procure specimens of the magnificent flowers and leaves; but knowing that these waters abounded in alligators, I was deterred from doing so by the advice of my guide, and my own experience of similar places.*

Hooker 1847

repeatedly to relocate the nymphs from the interior of the colony to the coast but was unsuccessful (Hooker 1847).

English colonists who had taken up residence on the coast were making their own efforts to uproot the lilies from their ancestral home and transport them to Britain. In 1848, one such expat, E. G. Boughton of Leguan Island in the delta of the Essequibo, a medical doctor and an acquaintance of William Hooker, director of the Royal Botanic Gardens, Kew, tried every possible method of shipping, including seeds kept in muddy water, entire fruits, and rhizomes carefully planted in a Wardian case. After a couple of weeks at sea, they arrived in London, but all were found to be "quite dead" (Lawson 1851).

One of the first English travelers to search for *Victoria* lilies beyond Schomburgk's hunting grounds in Guiana was Thomas Bridges. Bridges had collected plants in South America since 1828. His early activities had been centered in Chile, where he'd embarked on a journey over the Andes and across Argentina. Upon reaching the Atlantic, he sailed back to England in 1842.

With the *Victoria* craze rampant but no living plants in sight, Bridges undoubtedly realized how imperative it was to bring this plant into British cultivation. In 1844, he returned to South America and set up base again in Valparaíso, Chile. From there, he launched an expedition to Bolivia, arriving in December at Cochabamba, which had been Thaddaeus Haenke's home some thirty years earlier. Three months later, Bridges crossed the mountains northeast of Cochabamba and descended into the Amazon basin, following the Mamoré—the same river Haenke traveled in 1801—toward the Brazilian frontier. By July 1845, he reached the small town of Santa Ana on the Yacuma River, a tributary of the Mamoré.

It was during a hunting foray along the Yacuma River that Bridges finally came face-to-face with the mythical colossus he had heard so much about in England. Riding horseback along the banks of the river, Bridges arrived at a small oxbow lake that was covered by a large community of queen lilies. Bridges returned to Santa Ana to seek assistance from the local governor José María Zarate. The governor arranged for several Indians plus a yoke of oxen to draw a canoe overland from the river to the lake.

The canoe was only large enough for Bridges and two Indians, so collecting the immense leaves, spiny flowers, and fruits proved quite

In 1848 and 1949, three British naturalists, Alfred Wallace (left), Henry Bates (center), and Richard Spruce (right), undertook exploration of the Amazon, starting in Pará, Brazil. Along the way, each of them found the fabled lilies and would later publish vivid accounts of their encounters.
HUNT INSTITUTE FOR BOTANICAL DOCUMENTATION

a challenge. After several trips, however, Bridges had enough material to prepare pressed herbarium specimens of the leaves, preserve entire flowers in spirits, and extract an ample number of seeds, packed in wet clay, for his return to Europe.

When he returned to England in June 1846, Bridges promptly informed Hooker at Kew that he had seeds of *Victoria* available for a price of 2 shillings each and herbarium specimens at 30 shillings apiece. Hooker bought the seeds, two of which germinated. Unfortunately, with the approaching winter, the plants perished without producing a flower. At the same time, Bridges became very ill from a disease he believed he had contracted in Bolivia. Frail health forced him to return to Chile, where the warm and dry climate eased his condition, and he established a nursery in Valparaíso.

Although the plants grown from Bridges's seeds were the first ever outside South America, they did not bloom before expiring—thus missing the mark to be counted as a great horticultural achievement. Three years later, Bridges's feat was eclipsed by Joseph Paxton's success, and Bridges soon faded from memory. In time, he grew "very sore" upon the subject of *Victoria* because he "received no medal and scarcely mention honorable" for having introduced it in England (Johnston 1928). Despite his disappointment at

Thomas Bridges, 1847:

I returned in the afternoon, with several Indians to assist in carrying home the expected prize of leaves and flowers. The canoe being very small, only three persons could embark; myself in the middle, and an Indian in the bows and stern. In this tottering little bark we rowed amongst magnificent leaves and flowers, crushing unavoidably some, and selecting only such as pleased me. The leaves being so enormous I could find room in the canoe for but two, one before me and the other behind; owing to their being very fragile, even in the green state, care was necessary to transport them; and thus we had to make several trips in the canoe before I obtained the number required. Having loaded myself with the leaves, flowers, and ripe seed-vessels, I next mused how they were to be conveyed in safety; and determined at length upon suspending them on long poles with small cord, tied to the stalks of the leaves and flowers. Two Indians, each taking on his shoulder an end of the pole, carried them into the town; the poor creatures wondering all the while what could induce me to be at so much trouble to get at flowers, and for what purpose I destined them now they were in my possession.

Hooker 1847

Alfred Wallace, 1889:

I had heard of a plant growing in the pools in the marsh, which I was convinced must be the Victoria regia. *Senhor Nunez told me there were plenty near his house, and early next morning [near Monte Alegre, September 1848] he sent an Indian to try and get me one. After some search the man found one, with a half-opened flower, and brought it to me. The leaf was about four feet in diameter [1 m], and I was much pleased at length to see this celebrated plant. . . . It is found all over the Amazon district, but rarely or never in the river itself. It seems to delight in still waters, growing in inlets, lakes, or very quiet branches of the river, fully exposed to the sun. Here it grew in the pools left in the bog; but in June the water would be twenty or thirty feet [6 or 9 m] deeper, so its leaf and flower-stalks must increase in length rapidly while the water rises, as they did not seem to be very long now. I took the leaf home, in order to dry some portions of it. It is called by the Indians* uaupé japóna *(the jacana's oven), from the resemblance of the leaf, with its deep rim, to the clay ovens used for making* farinha.

Wallace 1889

Richard Spruce, 1849:

The crew of our vessel consisted almost entirely of Tapuya Indians, with whom I had frequent conversations respecting the plants of the environs of Santarém. Amongst others, they told me of a wonderful water-flower, called, in Lengua Geral, oape, *but in Portuguese,* furno, *from the similarity of its leaf in shape and size to the* mandiocca *furnaces of this country. They added that the leaf was purple underneath, and there furnished with numerous spines. To what could this description refer but the* Victoria? *My conclusion to this effect was strengthened when I arrived at Santarém. There everybody had seen the* furno, *and some wondered that I could ply them with eager inquiries respecting a plant which had been known by some of them for forty years, and had never been supposed scarce. Our countryman, Captain Hislop, one of the oldest settlers in Santarém, had, however, ascertained the plant to be the* Victoria, *from an account of Schomburgk's discovery of it in Guiana, which he had read in some periodical.*

Hooker 1851

not being inducted into Britain's horticultural pantheon, Bridges's zeal for plant collecting was undiminished. During the last ten years of his life, he traveled extensively, exploring the western coast of the Americas, finally settling down in San Francisco. In 1865, during a plant-collecting excursion to Nicaragua, Bridges was stricken with malaria. He subsequently died at sea on his return journey.

AN INTREPID TRIO

While Bridges followed some of the same trails blazed by Haenke earlier in the century, other British explorers traced parts of Eduard Pöppig's Amazonian route in reverse, starting at the mouth of the river rather than at its source. The first two, Alfred Russel Wallace and Henry Walter Bates, arrived in Pará (today's Belém) in the Amazon's estuary on May 28, 1848. The third, Richard Spruce, reached the shore of Brazil a year later. All three naturalists found the fabled water lilies along the broad stretch of the Amazon below Ega (today's Tefé), the small town where Pöppig had discovered the nymph seventeen years earlier.

Wallace, a master of drawing, mapmaking, and surveying at the Collegiate School in Leicester, had convinced his friend Bates, an apprentice to a hosiery manufacturer in the same city and a self-taught entomologist, to undertake an expedition to South America that would be financed by the sale of specimens collected along the Amazon. After they arrived in Pará, the twenty-something naturalists explored that region together for a year. Then they began their journey up the Amazon. Wallace left Pará in early August 1849; Bates followed a month later.

After a journey of twenty-eight days, Wallace reached Santarém at the confluence of the Amazon and Tapajós, his base for the next three months. From there, he launched collecting excursions nearby. One of the excursions took him some 150 km (93 miles) downstream from Santarém to the village of Monte Alegre.

While collecting along the Amazon, Henry Bates (left) often used native helpers to collect specimens such as caimans and turtles shown in this nineteenth-century hand-colored engraving.

IAM / AKG-IMAGES

A Frenchman named Nunez, who ran a small shop in Monte Alegre, provided Wallace with an empty house to stay in and a small canoe for day trips. Nunez told the young explorer there were giant lilies growing in the marshes around the village called *uaupé japóna*, or jacana's oven. He sent an Indian out to bring a specimen of a leaf and flower for Wallace, who instantly recognized the famed queen lily that was receiving so much attention in England. Wallace saved a portion of the leaf to take back with him to Santarém as proof of the fabled nymph's existence in the lower Amazon.

In the meantime, while Wallace was in Monte Alegre, Bates reached Santarém. He stayed there for a couple of days before continuing his journey west to Óbidos.

Shortly after Wallace returned to Santarém from Monte Alegre, Spruce arrived there from Pará. Spruce, who was previously a master of mathematics of the Collegiate School in York, had become a botanical explorer when the school closed in 1844. Early on, Spruce

Henry Bates, 1864:

Passing towards the farther end of the pool I saw, resting on the surface of the water, a number of large round leaves, turned up at their edges; they belonged to the Victoria *water lily. The leaves were just beginning to expand (December 3), some were still under water, and the largest of those which had reached the surface measured not quite three feet [1 m] in diameter. We found a* montaria *with a paddle in it, drawn up on the bank, which I took leave to borrow of the unknown owner, and Luco paddled me amongst the noble plants to search for flowers, meeting, however, with no success. I learnt afterwards that the plant is common in nearly all the lakes of this neighbourhood. The natives call it the* furno do piosoca, *or oven of the jacana, the shape of the leaves being like that of the ovens in which* mandioca *meal is roasted.*

Bates 1962

RULE, BRITANNIA! 129

Richard Spruce returned to England in 1864, after fifteen years of exploring South America.
LONGWOOD GARDENS LIBRARY AND ARCHIVES

Richard Spruce, 1849:

As soon as I conveniently could I planned an excursion to one of its habitats, a lake in the Ilha Grande de Santarém.... We started early, and took three hours, pulling with six oars, to reach the opposite shore. We disembarked at a sitio, *the nearest point to the lake, whither we were now to proceed overland; but we were told that the intervening campo had not yet been fixed (an usual process in the dry season), and that it was clad to the depth of six feet [2 m] with rank grass and rushes, so as to be quite impassable. We were advised to land at another* sitio *a little further down, where we should find a path leading through the woods to an* igaripé, *communicating with the lake. Following this course, we at length reached the* igaripé, *and were at once agreeably surprised by seeing the* Victoria *growing by the opposite shore of the* igaripé *itself.... We lost no time in crossing to the other side, where I sent a man to the outer ridge of the mass of plants, while Mr. King and I waded into the water to cut the leaves and flowers, which he towed round to the landing-place. We were now warned by the people not to venture among the plants, as their prickles are said to be venomous, but I got both my hands and feet considerably pricked without experiencing any ill effects.*

Hooker 1851

Richard Spruce, 1849:

The aspect presented by the Victoria *in its native waters is so novel and extraordinary that I am at a loss to what to liken it. The similitude is not a poetical one, but assuredly the impression the plant gave me, when viewed from the bank above, was that of a number of green tea-trays floating, with here and there a bouquet protruding between them; but when more closely surveyed, the leaves excited the utmost admiration, from their immensity and perfect symmetry. A leaf, turned up, suggests some strange fabric of cast-iron, just taken from the furnace, its ruddy colour, and the enormous ribs with which it is strengthened, increasing the similarity.*

Hooker 1851

had developed a keen interest in mosses, which had taken him to the Pyrenees and subsequently led him, in 1848, to a meeting with Hooker at Kew. It had been more than a decade since Hooker had showed Schomburgk's drawing to Queen Victoria, and still he was without an actual plant to prove the nymph's exceptional qualities worthy of the royal name. Thus, Hooker seized this opportunity to encourage Spruce to travel to the Amazon and search for the great lily there.

A few months later, Spruce departed for Pará, where he embarked on a brig owned by Captain Hislop, an old Scottish settler. The brig brought him to Santarém by the end of October 1849. When Wallace and Spruce met, they had much to share regarding their experiences on the Amazon. Wallace verified his encounter with *Victoria* in Monte Alegre with a preserved leaf fragment, convincing evidence that reports of the colossal water lilies were true.

Soon, Spruce was told of giant water lilies growing in a lake on Ilha Grande, an island situated at the confluence of the Amazon with Tapajós, and decided to find them himself. The island was covered with an impassable growth of grasses and rushes. Fortunately, there was also a small channel, or *igaripé,* called Tapiruari connecting the river with the inland lake. After a several-mile hike to reach the channel, Spruce spotted the much-sought nymph floating along the opposite bank of the *igaripé*.

Her leaves were much smaller than those described by Schomburgk and others, although Spruce had been told they would grow larger later in the season. Back in Santarém, Spruce prepared specimens of the flowers and leaves of the queen lily. He dispatched them to England in a "barrel of spirits" on November 15, 1849, unaware that a week earlier the first *Victoria* had flowered in England (Hooker 1851).

While Wallace and Spruce were sharing stories of finding the colossal water lilies, Bates was preparing to depart from Óbidos, about a three-day journey upriver from Santarém. He was bound for Barra (today's Manaus), located at the confluence of the Amazon and Rio Negro. Along the way, in early December, he stopped at the straggly village of Villa Nova (today's Parintins) on the border separating the Brazilian provinces of Pará and Amazonas. As soon as the boat anchored near the village, Bates set off to explore the surrounding area, accompanied by his servant Luco. Upon entering the forest, they discovered a "broad placid pool whose banks, clothed with grass of the softest green hue, sloped gently from the water's edge to the compact wall of forest which encompassed the whole" (Bates 1962). On the far end of the lake, Bates spotted large platter-like leaves, which he recognized as belonging to *Victoria*. Since it was December, only the start of the lily's growing season there, his search for the flowers was in vain. Four months later, Bates had another memorable encounter with the elusive nymph. While traveling along one of numerous *igaripés* strung along the Amazon between Barra and Ega, he "rowed for half a mile through a magnificent bed of *Victoria* water lilies." By then, they were showing countless flower buds that were just beginning to expand (Bates 1962).

Wallace spent the next two years collecting along Rio Negro before heading back to England in 1852. Bates continued his travels up and down the Amazon for another nine years. The last of the three explorers to leave South America was Spruce, who stayed until 1864. Although they were the first British explorers to observe, collect, and report on the queen lily in the Amazon, by the time they returned to England, *Victoria* was hardly a novelty there. Nevertheless, their vivid accounts of the splendors and horrors associated with the reclusive and mysterious tropics of the Americas—of which the giant lily was becoming an icon—perfectly answered British Victorian society's growing obsession with the New World's wonders.

By late 1849, when the three naturalists saw their first wild lilies in the lower Amazon, England was already abuzz over the triumphant flowering of the queen lily at the duke of Devonshire's Chatsworth estate. And several more plants were thriving in other parts of England, albeit in their vegetable phase.

VICTORIA IN BLOOM

Although the Royal Botanic Gardens, Kew, had successfully germinated the seeds sent from British Guiana earlier that year and generously shared the young seedlings with four estates, Kew did not come in first or even second in the race for a *Victoria* flower. This was "due to the want of a suitable tank for its accommodations" (Bean 1908).

William Hooker, 1851:

If the Victoria *at Kew was tardy in producing its flowers, this circumstance arose from no want of skill and care on the part of the able Curator. It is mainly, if not entirely, owing to the fact of our having then no sufficient command of soft water. The case is altered now, thanks to the liberality of the Commissioners of Woods and Forests, and thanks to an enlightened public, who, while deriving pleasure and instruction from the treasures contained in these gardens, are not backward in expressing the desire they feel for their prosperity.*

Hooker 1851

Anonymous correspondent to the *Cottage Gardener and Country Gentleman*, 1857:

The Royal Gardens at Kew, from which the plant originated, have yet to learn, it appears, how to erect a building at all suitable for its growth. The "new house" there at present, erected, we believe, at a cost of £2,000 or £3,000, according to the general opinion entertained of it, is anything but creditable to the conductors of so public an establishment, and our own private opinion respecting this matter, we should observe, is precisely parallel to that of the public. The exterior, in our opinion, has nothing to recommend it, and the tank in the interior assuredly has that about it which strongly reminds us of one of those green and slimy, undisturbed pools occasionally to be stumbled upon by the excursionist in some of the shady nooks and corners of old England.

Anonymous 1857

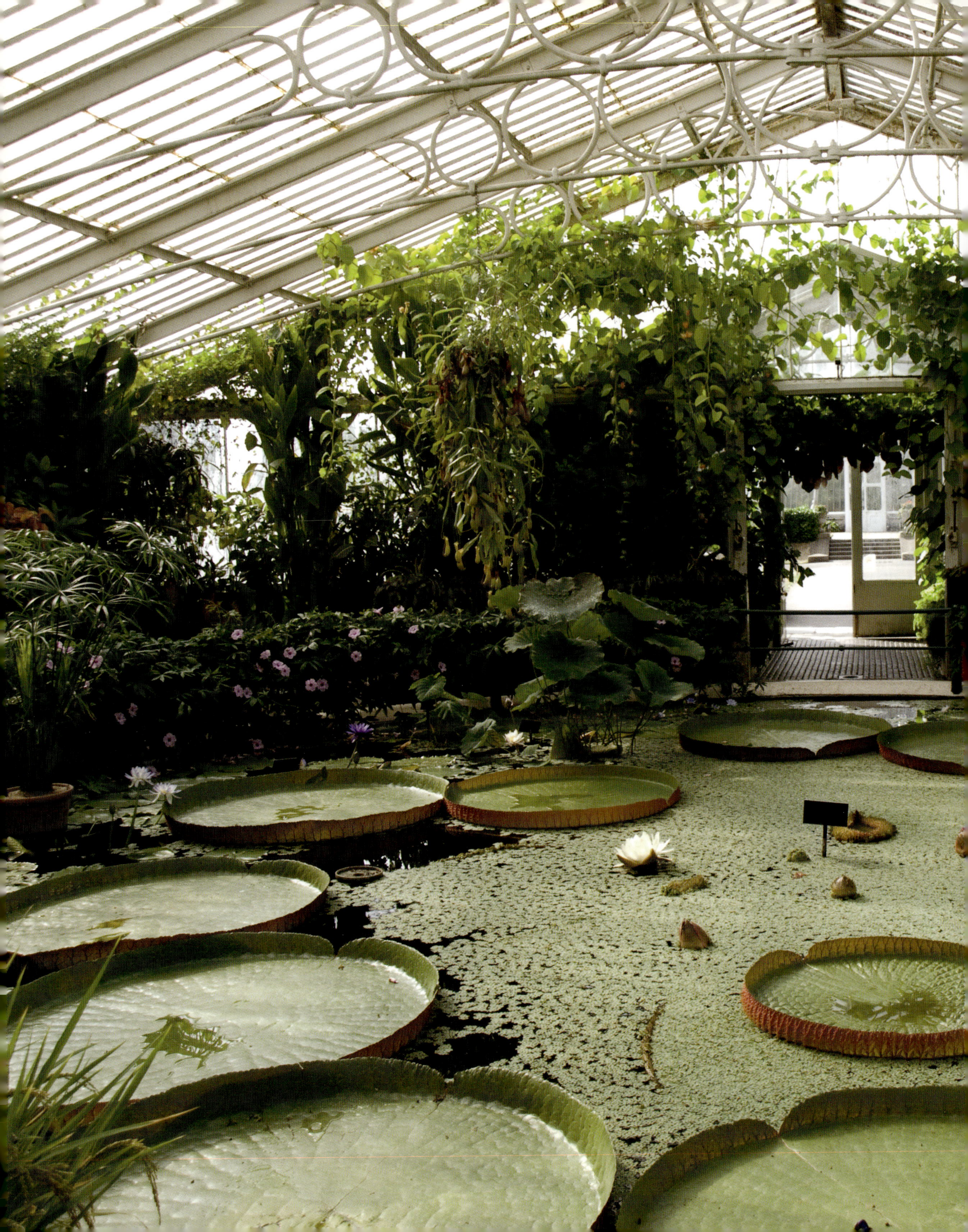

Kew's less-than-perfect tank was in an old propagation house. However, when the lily was planted again in the same tank in April 1850, diligent care compensated for any shortcomings, and the first bloom opened on July 20. Kew's plant continued to flower prodigiously until winter.

To provide the nymph with accommodations worthy of her regal status, Hooker proposed building a special greenhouse over 30 m (nearly 100 feet) long. This ambitious proposal was vetoed, but Hooker succeeded in securing funding for a smaller structure about half that size. The new greenhouse opened in 1852 and became known as the Victoria House. It won approval from crowds of visitors as well as praise from a correspondent who wrote in the *Cottage Gardener* that it was "worth going the length of the Kingdom to see" (Desmond 2007).

A few years later, opinions changed on whether the Victoria House was suitable for growing the Amazonian wonder. After William Hooker died in 1865, his son Joseph Dalton took over the directorship of Kew. He moved *Victoria* to a new glasshouse called the T-Range, named for the T-shape of its floor plan. Joseph installed a large tank at the intersection of the three arms to house the queen lily. Meanwhile, the 1852 Victoria House was converted into an Economic Plant House for growing medicinal and culinary herbs, but following the extensive damage it suffered during World War II and a series of renovations afterward, it was returned to its original function as the Water Lily House.

Like Paxton, who had taken one of the first flowers from his plant to Windsor Castle to present to Her Majesty in 1849, Hooker made a similar pilgrimage from Kew to the Isle of Wight a year later. He carried the precious bloom in a circular tin box for the queen and her family, who were staying at Osborne House. Upon his arrival, the bloom was taken to the queen, who later at dinner expressed her delight that the flower was "in the most beautiful state possible" (Allan 1967).

Despite all the attention focused on the progress of Kew's Amazonian lily, one other ducal estate achieved bloom status before the Royal Botanic Gardens. Opposite Kew, on the left bank of the Thames, was the duke of Northumberland's Syon House. After a small seedling arrived from Kew in early September 1849, it thrived under the diligent care of the head gardener, Iveson. On April 10, 1850, the Syon House lily opened her first bloom—three months ahead of Kew.

Thanks to extensive renovation, the venerable 1852 Victoria House at the Royal Botanic Gardens, Kew, again serves as home for the giant lilies.
Tomasz Aniśko / Longwood Gardens

Iveson, letter to William Hooker, 1850:

Our Victoria House, originally a lean-to, was converted into a span roofed one as soon as the plant filled the original space devoted to it, and the tank was enlarged to nearly twenty-two feet [7 m] square, but I have found during the summer that it would have covered a space double the size of the tank in which it is now growing; indeed, two or three healthy leaves were obliged to be removed every week, in order to allow the young ones to expand. The largest leaf was six feet [2 m] in diameter, with a footstalk eighteen feet long [6 m]! ... Up to the present time (11th November, 1850) there have been eighty flowers; the largest measured was fourteen inches [36 cm] in diameter, and since the heat of the sun has declined, the white part of the petals has a much more clear and fresh appearance on the second day of the flower which adds very much to its beauty.

Hooker 1851

Today, the conservatory of Syon House features an aquatic tank, which, although a more recent addition, provides a symbolic link to the momentous occasion on April 10, 1850, when the ducal estate became only the second garden in Britain to flower *Victoria*.

TOMASZ ANIŚKO / LONGWOOD GARDENS

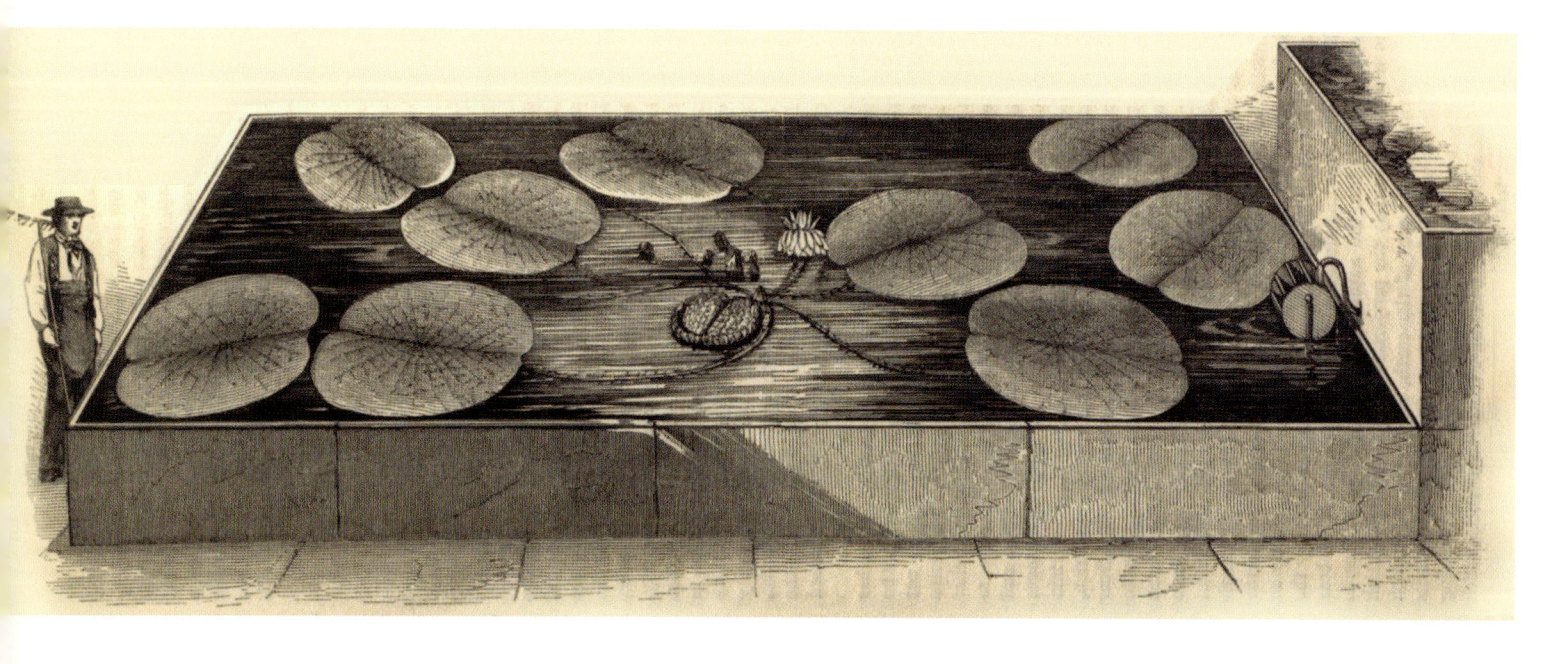

The Amazonian nymph flowered at Syon House, only the second such place in England, after Chatsworth.

THE LUESTHER T. MERTZ LIBRARY OF THE NEW YORK BOTANICAL GARDEN

134 VICTORIA: THE SEDUCTRESS

During the summer months of 1850, Iveson exhibited the mammoth leaves and treasured flowers at horticultural shows in the Chiswick Gardens. One anonymous correspondent to the *Florist and Garden Miscellany* described Syon's lily blossom as "opening beautifully" and "throwing off volumes of fragrance every time the large bell glass with which it was covered was removed" (Anonymous 1851b).

In 1851, the duke of Northumberland opened Syon House to visitors, many of whom were in London for the Great Exhibition. When they entered the mansion, they were greeted by the queen lily, her leaves and flowers reclining on a table beneath an impressive glass case. After touring the estate's extensive art collections, one guest proclaimed that they paled by comparison with those of the conservatories, which were "richly luxuriant, and must have been costly in the extreme" (Anonymous 1851a). Of these, the most impressive was "a special conservatory, containing a large tank of tepid water" which housed the "singular aquatic plant the *Victoria regia*."

The royal Kew and the ducal Chatsworth and Syon were soon joined on the growing list of successful flowerings by Woburn, seat of the duke of Bedford, some 80 km (50 miles) northwest of London; and Dalkeith, seat of the duke of Buccleuch outside Edinburgh in Scotland. At Dalkeith Castle, the first Scottish garden to accommodate *Victoria*, the nymph resided in an elegant 1832 dodecagonal conservatory featuring massive Doric columns that carried the weight of the elaborate cast-iron girders of the roof. The conservatory, although now in ruin, can still be visited in Dalkeith Park.

Soon, England's lesser nobility and gentry succumbed to the giant lily obsession. Baronet George Thomas Staunton of Leigh, near Havant

At the time of the Great Exhibition in London in 1851, the elegant conservatories of Syon House displayed "richly luxuriant" collections of plants, the latest addition being the *Victoria regia*.
Tomasz Aniśko / Longwood Gardens

In 1884, the Tropical House, 19 m (62 feet) long and 9 m (30 feet) wide, at Abraham Dixon's Cherkley Court was home to the latest arrival from the Amazon, *Victoria amazonica* var. *randii*.
LONGWOOD GARDENS LIBRARY AND ARCHIVES

in Hampshire, exemplified this aspiration. In 1852, he built an octagonal Victoria House with a circular tank, 9 m (30 feet) in diameter, on his estate. The first plants, procured from Kew, flowered there the following year (Gladwyn 1992). Today, the Victoria House at Leigh—now municipally owned and renamed Staunton Country Park—has been restored and continues to showcase the Amazonian nymph.

Some thirty years later, it was the merchant and industrialist Abraham Dixon of Cherkley Court, near Leatherhead, who was perhaps the first in England to grow the new variety of the Amazonian lily called *randii*, after Edward S. Rand, who had collected it in Brazil. In 1885, a correspondent to the *Gardeners' Chronicle* reported that "one of the wonders of the Vegetable Kingdom" had attained "unusual perfection" in Dixon's conservatory and asserted it was "one of the finest in foliage and flower that has ever been produced in this country" (Anonymous 1885b).

ICON OF THE EMPIRE

These early pioneers were carefully watched by Britain's gardening public. Their success was noted, inducing many—as a writer to the *Gardeners' Chronicle* put it—"to become cultivators of so truly curious and magnificent a water plant, who have hitherto considered it beyond their reach" (Anonymous 1850b). Within only a year of her introduction, *Victoria* was declared "established, as a stove-plant, in the gardens of Great Britain; that is, among those horticulturists who will incur the expense of a tank large enough for its cultivation" (Anonymous 1850a).

The Amazonian lily arrived in Britain at a time when preoccupation with horticultural novelties had reached levels not previously seen. The influx of exotic plants from all corners of the world stirred people's imaginations. *Victoria* rose to the top with amazing speed, outshining all other botanical

Victoria grown in Dixon's Cherkley Court.
LONGWOOD GARDENS LIBRARY AND ARCHIVES

curiosities of that era. Her ability to attain colossal proportions within a span of only a few months defied the public's traditional experience with plants, whether they were grown in hothouses or out of doors.

Instantly embraced and universally admired, *Victoria* assumed the throne of the Vegetable Kingdom and became a symbol of Britain's imperial splendor and colonial might. "To England, and to English enterprise alone," one patriotic correspondent wrote in the *Cottage Gardener and Country Gentleman*, "are both eastern and western hemispheres indebted, in the first instance, for the possession, in its present cultivated state, of one of the most beautiful of natural productions" (Anonymous 1857). Horticultural publications exalted the virtues and ingenuity of "the successful cultivator" who was able to grow the wondrous lily and had "a right to almost equal honour with the enterprising and adventurous discoverer" (Anonymous 1857).

Starting in 1851, a number of commercial nurserymen contested for the honor of being *Victoria*'s "successful cultivators." The prestige associated with the queen lily, however, was not the sole motivation behind these enterprises. It was apparent that the *Victoria* craze was stimulating unprecedented interest in growing a variety of aquatic plants.

The epicenter of these efforts by commoners to domesticate the royal lily was ironically King's Road in Chelsea, a borough of London, along which several prominent nurseries were strung. Knight and Perry's nursery, for instance, installed in one of its greenhouses a slate tank 9 m (30 feet) long and 7 m (23 feet) wide, partly to accommodate *Victoria*, and partly to demonstrate how the increasingly popular tribe of aquatic plants could be managed. The results exceeded expectations. "There is scarcely

The front store of Knight and Perry's nursery on King's Road in Chelsea around 1850.
GETTY IMAGES

a private garden at present," wrote one commentator, "in which a house so complete and a collection so comprehensive exists" (Weale 1854).

Nearby, Veitch's nursery erected many "aquariums under glass," among them a "noble one" for *Victoria*, which in a few years was proclaimed a sight that "must be seen to be appreciated" (Abercrombie 1857). Purportedly the first nursery to flower the queen lily on March 15, 1851, Veitch's tank was only about 4.5 m (15 feet) long and 3.7 m (12 feet) wide, which nevertheless afforded enough room to grow leaves in excess of 1.2 m (4 feet) wide (Anonymous 1851c).

Weeks's nursery, another Chelsea establishment, took a different approach. Instead of installing an indoor tank, it routed hot water pipes into an outdoor pond 6.4 m (21 feet) in diameter for its *Victoria* (Anonymous 1851k). To protect the plant from the cold, a temporary covering was placed over the pond at night or during stormy weather. The lily performed surprisingly well under these conditions. Visitors noted that Weeks's plant developed a prominently raised leaf margin, "a natural desideratum of much interest," and that it had overall a "more noble appearance in the open air, than when growing in the hot-house aquarium" (Anonymous 1851k).

George Lawson, 1851:

Aquatic plants generally are beginning to receive more attention than they ever before received from cultivators; and our opinion is not the result of an over-sanguine enthusiasm, but of a considerate observation of the present tendency of horticultural taste, when we say that ere long the exotic aquarium and the open-air pond, for the culture of aquatics, will be considered indispensable adjuncts to every garden of any extent.

Lawson 1851

138   VICTORIA: THE SEDUCTRESS

The kingdom's botanical gardens were not far behind the ducal estates and the enterprising nurserymen in inviting *Victoria* into their collections. Professor Charles Giles Bridle Daubeny, keeper of England's oldest garden, the Oxford Botanic Garden, was so inspired by the sight of an Amazonian nymph flowering at Chatsworth in 1849 that he decided to build a Victoria House. When it opened in 1851, Daubeny instituted an admission fee of a shilling to recoup the construction cost (Heine and Mabberley 1986). His initiative backfired, however, when angry Oxford residents stayed away and instead sent aggrieved letters objecting to being charged to visit the queen lily. By 1859, facing the rising expenses of caring for *Victoria*, Daubeny discontinued growing the lily. A century and a half would pass before the South American nymph returned to Oxford.

To the west, across the Irish Sea, Glasnevin Botanic Gardens in Dublin built a Victoria House in 1854. The garden's first attempt to grow the queen lily was not successful. It took another year and another batch of seeds donated by the Oxford garden before Dubliners could enjoy their own homegrown *Victoria*.

To the north in Scotland, the Royal Botanic Garden, Glasgow, erected its Victoria House in 1855 equipped with a tank 6.7 m (22 feet) long and 6 m (20 feet) wide. The lily took up residence there on May 12 and showed her first flower to some two thousand spectators on the last evening of August (Clarke 1855).

In London, following the example of Kew, the Royal Botanical Society Garden introduced the queen lily into its greenhouses in Regent's Park. During the 1850s, "very excellent plants" were grown there annually (Anonymous 1857). Queen Victoria herself showed the Regent's Park's display of the Amazonian lily to the French president (later emperor) Napoleon III when he arrived in London to visit the Great Exhibition of 1851 (Conard and Hus 1907).

The pinnacle of public fascination with the colossal lily was perhaps achieved with the opening of the Crystal Palace in 1854, in London's suburb of Sydenham. This largest glasshouse ever built featured two large pools allotted to *Victoria*. The ingenious design of the building's immense ridge-and-furrow roof, devised by Chatsworth's gardener, Joseph Paxton, was widely attributed to the structure of the queen lily leaf.

By the time *Victoria* took up residence in the Crystal Palace, she had already extended her reign beyond the shores of the British Isles: The rest of Europe had been claimed by her in one country after another. Still, the gardeners ruled by Queen Victoria boasted of the superiority of lilies grown in her kingdom. "We are not aware of any establishment on the Continent," one of them wrote, "however favoured, in which it has been grown to greater perfection than in this country" (Anonymous 1857).

END OF AN EPOCH

The 1850s saw an astonishing explosion of popularity of the Amazonian lily among Victorian society, but by the end of the decade, the public had grown used to her widespread presence. The novelty was slowly wearing off. In addition, the year 1865 saw the departure of five men who contributed greatly to the introduction of *Victoria* to

Anonymous correspondent to the *Cottage Gardener and Country Gentleman*, 1857:

[A]rt and science in this country owe a deep and lasting debt to the introduction of the Victoria regia. *Reposing on the still and placid waters of the bays of the most powerful rivers of the New World, it had for ages flowered and floated in all its beauty, until it met the gaze of the ardent and delighted botanist, who little thought that in giving the world this magnificent aquatic he gave it as well the germ of that Palace which now crowns the hill of Sydenham. . . . But, with all that we have said and attributed to this plant, let it be particularly remembered that the leaf of the* Victoria *does not present on its under surface any palpable plan of a palace, or of anything, to an ordinary eye, at all resembling it; or let the observer even discern, if he can, the analogy existing between it and the house erected for its growth at Chatsworth; yet, nevertheless, from it originally was drawn the first crude and unexpanded idea that eventually gave the world the existing Palace, and to the author of that happy and auspicious idea a name and fame "which history hereafter will be glad to chronicle."*

Anonymous 1857

The South American lily occupies a pool in the 1970 Display Greenhouse at Chatsworth, providing a telling reference to the first flowering of *Victoria* in Britain.
TOMASZ ANIŚKO / LONGWOOD GARDENS

cultivation. Robert Schomburgk, Thomas Bridges, William Hooker, John Lindley, and Joseph Paxton all died within months of each other. With their passing, an epoch in the history of *Victoria* ended.

During the three decades since her discovery, the Amazonian nymph was taken from her wild state, where she lived in almost complete obscurity, to a position of prominence and privilege in England's best gardens. When this queen of flowers was given the name of the queen whose empire circled the globe, Britons, oblivious to the nymph's existence in 1837, were enamored with her a dozen years later. The lily became a metaphor of the colonial bounty of Guiana, of the tropical riches of South America, and of Her Majesty Queen Victoria herself.

In present-day Britain, the meaning of this metaphor has for the most part eroded. Nevertheless, the tamed and domesticated *Victoria* resides on this island quite comfortably: Her position as a cultural icon is secure. Although the number of gardens where she is cultivated today has declined sharply since the heyday of the Victorian era—mirroring perhaps the fate of Britannic rule as a whole—the queen lily remains a permanent, popular resident in major botanical gardens, such as those at Kew and Edinburgh, and some historical estates, including Chatsworth and Staunton.

And it is not only the colonial heritage of these venerable institutions that justifies continued expenditures to grow the South American lilies. The youngest of botanical gardens, the Eden Project in Cornwall—which opened in 2002 to project global concerns of biodiversity conservation—would not be complete without the wonder nymph. The queen lily's monarchic lineage is less relevant to today's British society. Instead, *Victoria* embodies all of the life forms that are dependent on the great rivers of South America.

Thus, the story, which began with a handful of explorers from Britain who barely made it out alive from Amazonia with little more than scruffy-looking dry specimens, a handful of seeds, or literary attempts to describe the aquatic creature, has come full circle. In a century and half, the giant water lily has become a champion of saving vanishing flora, and her presence in British gardens affords a path to understanding the natural world of South America, which today is in peril.

The Princess of Wales Conservatory at Kew, opened in 1987, features *Victoria* as part of its tropical display.
TOMASZ ANIŚKO / LONGWOOD GARDENS

VICTORIA: THE SEDUCTRESS

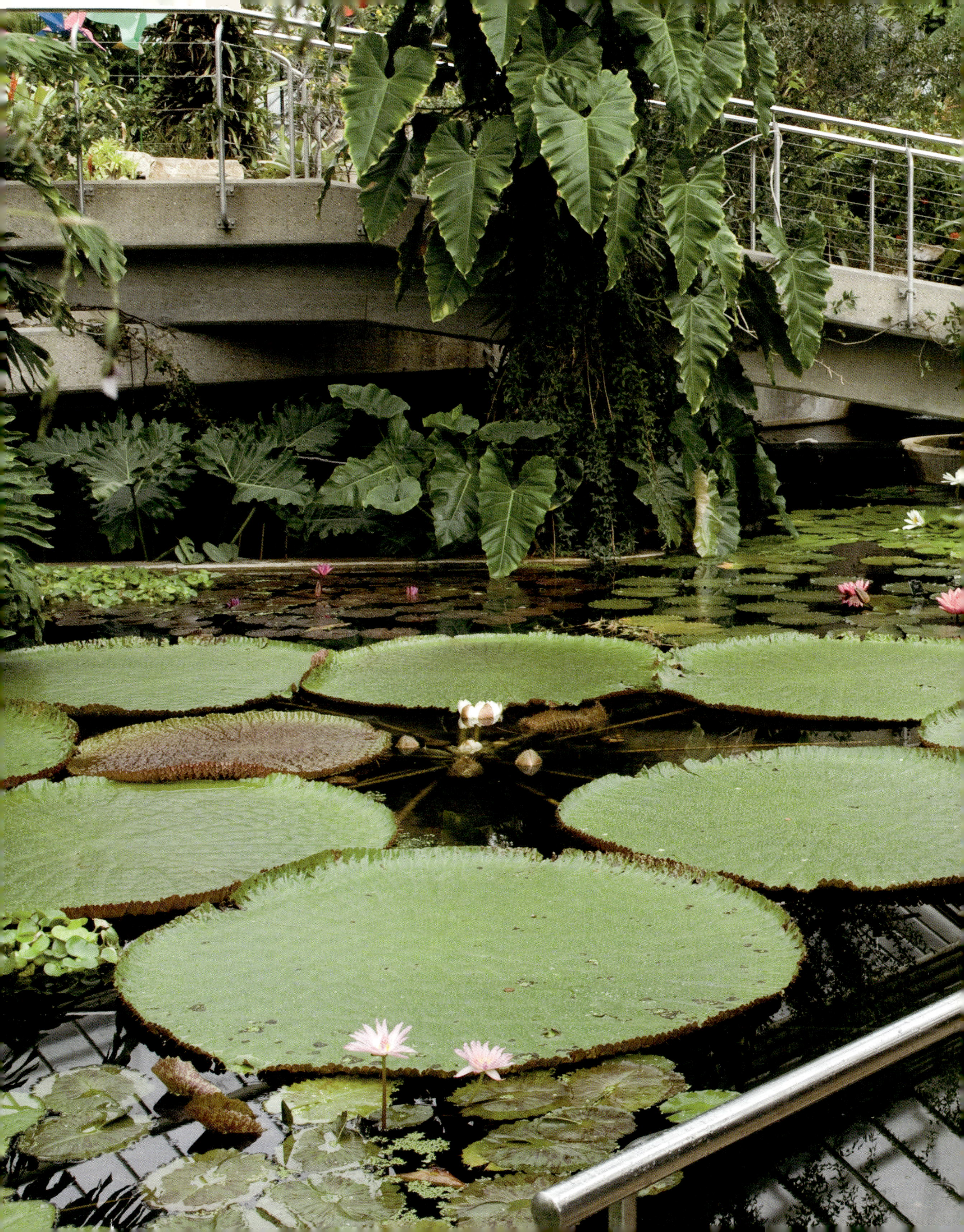

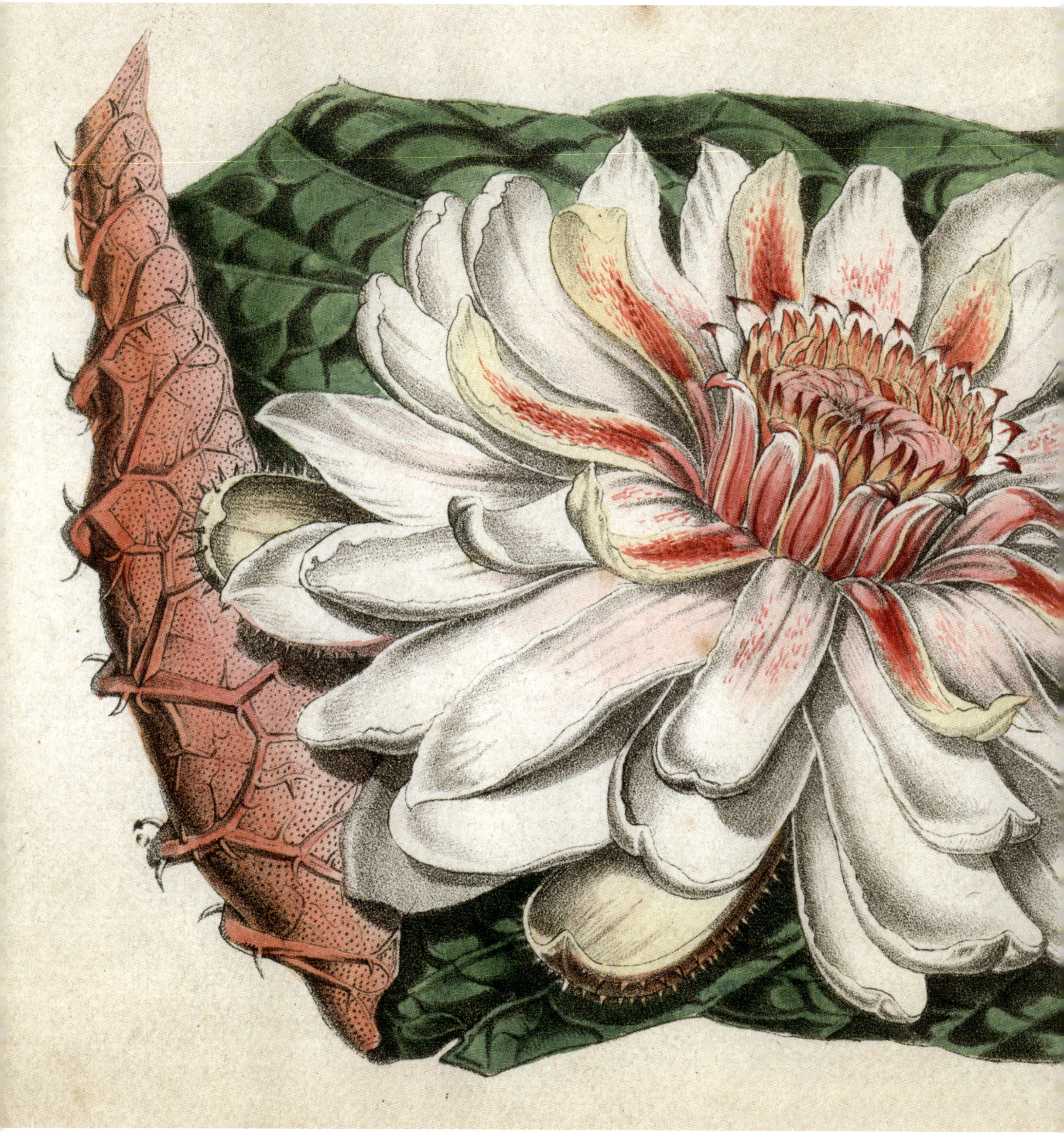

chapter 9

WORLD CONQUEST

As Victoria fever swept the British Isles, the unprecedented attention and publicity attached to the tropical nymph reverberated across Europe. Once a few plants had successfully grown and were flowering in England, the seed that had taken three decades to cross the ocean from South America suddenly became easily obtainable for horticultural connoisseurs with adequate facilities to nurture the queen lily.

The first to welcome *Victoria* on the continent was Louis Van Houtte in Ghent, Belgium. In February 1850, when Joseph Paxton germinated the seeds collected from the plant growing at Chatsworth, he had spared one seedling and sent it to Van Houtte, one of Europe's foremost horticulturists. A tiny plant with only four leaves, none larger than 15 cm (6 inches) in diameter, reached Van Houtte's nursery in Gentbrugge outside Ghent on May 26, 1850.

To ensure *Victoria*'s successful acclimation to her new residence, Van Houtte offered to employ Eduard Ortgies, a young German gardener who, under Paxton's direction, had been tending the royal lily at Chatsworth since her arrival a year earlier. Even though Paxton had only four seeds germinating at that time and was inundated with requests, he obliged Van Houtte's plea, parted with one of his precious seedlings, and sent Ortgies off to Belgium to care for it. Arriving on site at

A second-night flower and a section of a leaf of *Victoria amazonica* from Eduard Loescher's 1852 book *Die königliche Wasserlilie Victoria Regia*.
Library of the Gray Herbarium, Harvard University

Van Houtte's nursery on April 1, 1850, Ortgies was immediately charged with building a new greenhouse to receive *Victoria* later that year. The move occurred in early August, and one month later on September 5, the lily's long-awaited flower opened, satisfying Van Houtte's desire to be the first in continental Europe to achieve *Victoria*'s success.

A month later, Van Houtte's lily stopped flowering for a few weeks as the plant matured her first fruits. She then resumed blooming in mid-November. Under the watchful eye of Ortgies, the South American nymph flourished despite the typically gloomy Flanders sky. Soon, Van Houtte was showing off the wondrous plant at horticultural exhibitions in Brussels. Ortgies continued to look after the royal resident for another five years until he moved to Switzerland as head gardener at the Zurich Botanical Garden.

Citizens of Brussels were so enchanted by Van Houtte's *Victoria* that within a couple of years, the Royal Society of Zoology and Horticulture resolved to add an elegant greenhouse, regally decorated with an elaborate ironwork crown on top, to its zoological garden. Confined to its own ornate iron-and-glass cage, the Amazonian nymph joined the ranks of more animate exotic creatures that the Brussels zoo had collected from all over the world. *Victoria* was perhaps the only plant in history that transcended its vegetable form and competed for visitors' attention with the wild animals that surrounded her. Amusing the Belgian crowds at the height of the country's colonial expansion, *Victoria* enjoyed the noisy company of zoo animals for twenty-five years before resettling in a place more customary for a water lily, the National Botanic Garden. If this was the first instance of the queen lily taking residence among the beasts of the wild, it was not to be the last.

CROSSING THE RHINE TO GERMANY

While Van Houtte was enjoying the first Belgian *Victoria*, German horticulturalists were not far behind. Only a year after she flowered in Gentbrugge, several gardens east of the Rhine took up the challenge of raising the fabled South American wonder.

George Lawson, 1851:

Scientific foreigners visiting England have shown an eager desire to behold the royal water-lily, and have evinced a deep interest in its history; the result will no doubt be the extensive cultivation of this plant in other lands. But the lily will likewise be reared by English hands in many parts of the world. The banner of England encircles the entire globe, and in every region where that banner is seen to float on the tropical breeze, there, in the silvery lake beneath it, will be also seen the royal Victoria *water-lily, the namesake of our illustrious British Queen—the attendant satellite of her sovereign's power.*

Lawson 1851

Louis Van Houtte's nursery in Belgium was the site in 1850 of the first flowering of *Victoria* on the European continent.
LONGWOOD GARDENS LIBRARY AND ARCHIVES

Brussels's Victoria House, opened in 1854, stood in the city's zoological garden for a quarter of a century, before relocating to the National Botanic Garden of Belgium.
Paul Borremans / Collection of the National Botanic Garden of Belgium

Fully aware that two German explorers, Eduard Pöppig and Robert Schomburgk, had discovered her, a number of renowned gardeners were eager to bring her to flowering triumph in Germany in 1851. Two succeeded: Heinrich Ludolph Wendland, superintendent at the royal Herrenhausen Garden near Hanover, and Eduard Loescher of the Hamburg Botanical Garden.

Of the two, Wendland earned the winner's laurels. His *Victoria* opened her first flower on June 29, 1851. A year prior, Wendland had procured the seeds from England—obtaining them from both the Royal Botanic Gardens, Kew, and Syon House, two gardens that faced each other on opposite banks of the Thames. To give his plants an early start, Wendland germinated the seeds in late November and early December. By March, he was able to select the two strongest seedlings to transplant into a waiting tank, some 9 m (30 feet) long and 6 m (20 feet) wide. The queen lily repaid his attention and care by producing more than fifty flowers over the course of that summer and fall.

Loescher in Hamburg received a young *Victoria* from Wendland in late May 1851. He had at his disposal a greenhouse, 10 m (33 feet)

Louis Van Houtte, 1850–51:

Started from seed at Chatsworth itself, in February 1850, our plant, upon its arrival at Ghent, the 26th of May in the same year, had only four leaves, of which the largest (nevertheless mature) measured only 0.15 m [6 inches] in diameter. From the 26th of May until 6th of August, confined provisionally to a glazed basin comparatively too narrow for it, it produced successively ten larger and larger leaves, the last measuring 0.75 m [30 inches] in diameter. Finally, on the 6th August, it was possible to give it more space, air, and light. It profited quickly; because a month later (the 5th of September) its first flower opened, and already its vast leaves extended over an area more than 25 m [82 feet] in circumference. Since then, during the uninterrupted production of its first ten flowers, leaves and flowers showed themselves larger and larger, the maximum of the first being 1.62 m [5 feet] (the 20th of October); the maximum of the second being 0.30 m [1 foot].

Planchon and Van Houtte 1850-51, translated by John Luttrell

WORLD CONQUEST

> **Eduard Loescher, 1852:**
>
> *The result [of previous incomplete reports on Victoria] was that some people expected a veritable monster of a plant and many did not even realize that it was a water plant. A tremendous step forward occurred when through the magic of science small shelters were created under the harsh northern skies to house this queen of the tropical rivers of South America and to force her to display her charms to the civilized world. If we wish to dispel some of the more fantastic stories circulating, it is the duty of the gardener who has the privilege of watching the plant from germination to full growth, to fully inform the news-thirsty public.*
>
> Loescher 1852, translated by Kitty Byk

> **Wilhelm Hochstetter, 1852:**
>
> *Everything I read and heard about the majestic water lily* Victoria regia *and about the successful attempts to grow it in England, Belgium and northern Germany fed my desire to grow the plant in the local Botanical Garden. I was determined to be able to see, with my own eyes, this wonder of the plant world germinate, grow and prosper, and to overcome any difficulties by careful nurture. At last I finally was given control of the garden this year and was able to carry out my plan. With the agreement of my superior, Professor Hugo von Mohl, I ordered seed from my friend Wendland in Herrenhausen and on March 18, 1852 I received a vial of* Victoria *seeds in the mail.*
>
> Hochstetter 1852, translated by Kitty Byk

square that was specially designed for *Victoria* and came equipped with a heated tank, but Loescher contended with many technical problems. Since his tank lacked a water circulation system, each day thirty buckets of water had to be removed as an equivalent amount of fresh water was added. Heating the tank proved challenging, and the water temperature often dropped to 15°C (59°F). Despite these problems, Loescher succeeded in bringing the South American lily to bloom on August 28 (Otto 1851a).

The event excited immense public interest. Thousands showed up at the Hamburg garden. No other plant had attracted as many visitors (Otto 1851a). The September 12 issue of *Botanische Zeitung* reported that, in order to prevent too great a crowd from storming the greenhouse, admission tickets were issued at four schillings each. And since only a limited number could be admitted at once, hundreds were disappointed by a long wait or were turned away (Anonymous 1851h).

While Loescher came in second in the race to flower *Victoria*, he succeeded in publishing the first German book dedicated to the royal lily. His *Die königliche Wasserlilie Victoria Regia: Ihre Geschichte, ihr Wesen und ihre Kultur* appeared in Hamburg in March 1852, only six months after the historic flowering—an enviable achievement even by today's standards.

The date of Loescher's publication unexpectedly acquired particular significance when in August of that year, Wilhelm Hochstetter, superintendent of the Botanic Garden of the University of Tübingen in Württemberg, published his own book, *Die Victoria Regia: Ihre Geschichte, Natur, Benennung und Cultur* (Stransky 1951). In 1852, Hochstetter received *Victoria* seeds from Wendland at Herrenhausen and successfully brought his lily to bloom the same year, making the Tübingen garden the first in southern Germany to accomplish this. The seed arrived in March, germinated by late April, and in early June, the burgeoning lily was ready for her permanent home. Hochstetter lacked the facilities available at Herrenhausen and Hamburg, so he improvised by having a large tank built of oak staves. The wooden tank was brought to the garden on a wagon and carried into the greenhouse by thirty men.

Hochstetter's day of triumph came on the afternoon of August 7, when the greenhouse was filled with delightful fragrance, foretelling the opening of the flower a couple of hours later. In the evening, the illuminated house was overflowing with crowds eager to see the famed nymph's flower in "all its virginal beauty" (Hochstetter 1852, translated by Kitty Byk). Within days of this event, the Tübingen gardener finished his monograph of *Victoria* and sent it off to the printer.

When Hochstetter's book was published, however, Loescher accused him of plagiarism. Hochstetter claimed that he had not seen Loescher's book, or *Werkchen* (little work), as he referred to it (Stransky 1951), before completing his own—a claim that many found hard to believe since numerous passages in the two books were strikingly similar. Loescher was not willing to give up his literary priority, so a stormy exchange between him and Hochstetter ensued on the pages of German horticultural and botanical journals that lasted a couple of years before subsiding.

By 1852, gardeners in many cities across Germany—from Hamburg in the north, and Berlin in the east, to Stuttgart in the south, and Bonn in the west—prepared to

In 1878, *Victoria* took up residence in Bonn in a specially designed circular house on the grounds of the Royal Botanic Gardens. Its low dome is visible next to the conservatory on the left and the Poppelsdorfer Palace in the center.

BOTANISCHE GÄRTEN DER UNIVERSITÄT BONN

introduce the queen lily to their citizens. Hochstetter shared his surplus seedlings with several gardens in Württemberg, including Wilhelma, the royal gardens in Cannstadt outside Stuttgart.

Because *Victoria* is no longer present in Herrenhausen and the Hamburg and Tübingen gardens have since relocated, Wilhelma is probably the sole garden in Germany that pioneered cultivation of the South American lily and continues to exhibit her today. In Wilhelma's early days, *Victoria* was grown indoors. But beginning in 1956, she was given a home outside in a vast circular heated pool, some 30 m (99 feet) in diameter, in the center of a spectacular Moorish-style garden (Herkert 2004). In the 1950s, Wilhelma also began incorporating animal exhibits into the historic estate, so, as earlier in Brussels, the queen lily once again found herself in the company of flesh-and-blood creatures that typically inhabit zoological gardens.

VICTORIA IN BERLIN

One major city that almost missed the mark in 1851 was Berlin. The first attempts there were made in the gardens of the Schönhausen royal

Wilhelm Hochstetter, 1852:

In the evening of 12 June the new 15' [5 m] long and 12' [4 m] wide water tank, made from oak, was brought by wagon to the greenhouse and carried by 30 men to its final location, while a large crowd watched the proceedings.... The area where the Victoria *would be located was separated from the rest of the greenhouse by a simple wooden divider and the glass roof was only 2' to 5' [60 to 165 cm] above the water level of the* Victoria *basin. This was all the financial resources of the botanical garden allowed, which was in laughably poor contrast to the splendid glass palaces in England.*

Hochstetter 1852, translated by Kitty Byk

Eduard Loescher, 1854:

My article opposing Mr. Hochstetter in the Hamburger Gartenzeitung *1853, page 523, contains indisputable facts and proof on which my assertion of literary theft of my material is based, no need to repeat them here. Hochstetter's words of finding "some value" do not suffice considering the extensive use of my material (not just the ten parts mentioned), particularly since he insists that he saw my book only after finishing his own manuscript. If what I wrote is of value I cannot be blamed for resenting if it is published by another firm. After all it is not likely that readers would go to the trouble of comparing the relevant passages in both books to determine my input. If I wish to protect my work it is up to me to point out which of my material was used, and since I know my book intimately I certainly am qualified. While I reserve for myself the right to defend myself it does not mean that I appoint myself as judge and certainly I do not consider legal action necessary.*

Stransky 1951, translated by Kitty Byk

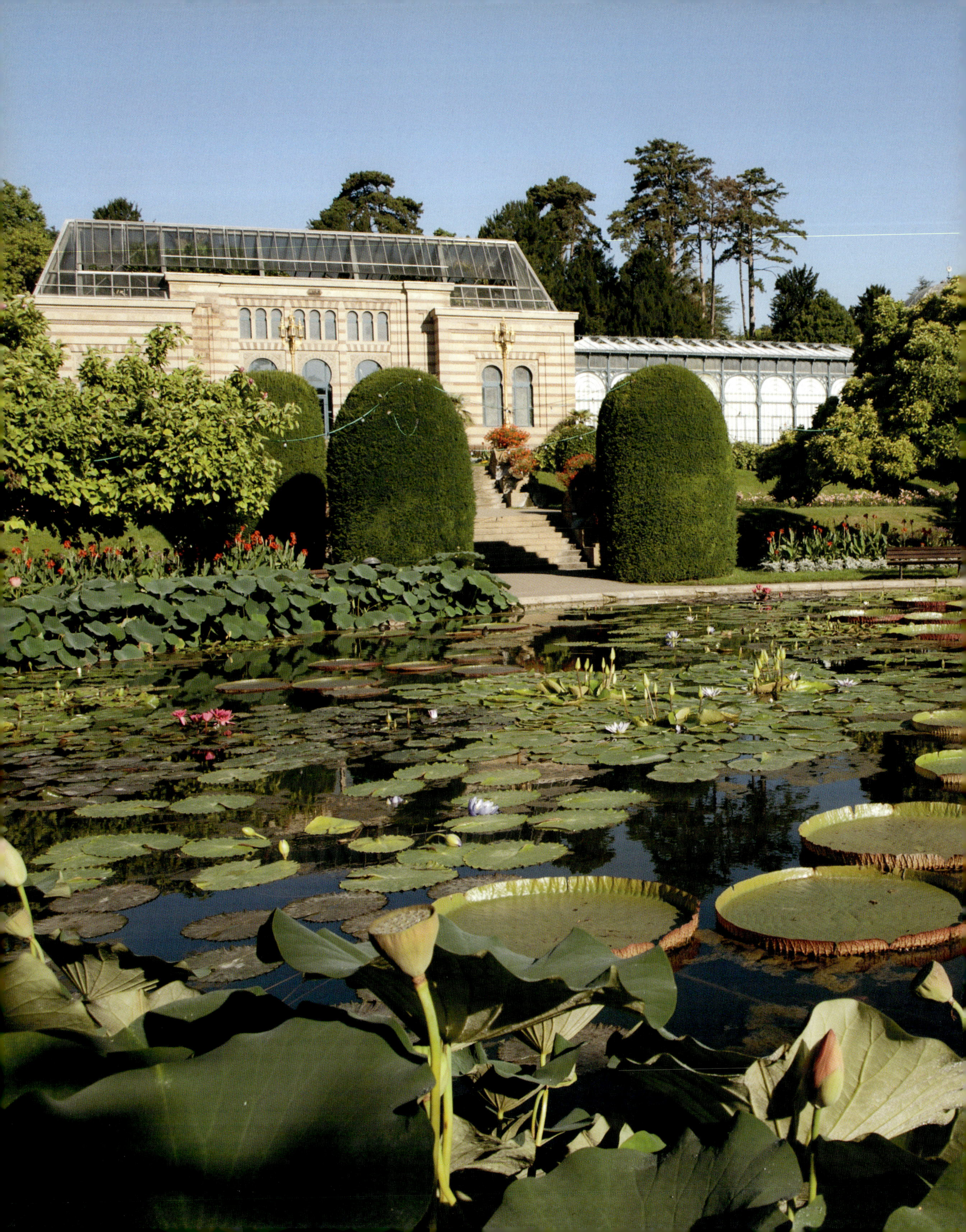

palace outside Berlin and in the greenhouses of August Borsig, a locomotive magnate, in Berlin's Moabit district (Otto 1851a). Working in a small greenhouse, Schönhausen's head gardener, Theodor Eduard Nietner, placed *Victoria* in a tank not much bigger than 1 m (3 feet) wide and 1.5 m (5 feet) long. The giant lily progressed as far as setting flower buds, but due to the cramped space or the lateness of the season, they refused to open (Stransky 1951).

Borsig, on the other hand, took advantage of the locomotive factory adjoining the grounds of his estate and had a special circular Victoria House built, heated with warm runoff water redirected from the factory. Even with these technological advantages, however, Borsig had to wait until July 19 the following year to see the flower. Although it was a private estate, Borsig's garden was open to the visiting public on regular occasions. The flowering of Borsig's *Victoria*—Berlin's first—stirred as much excitement among Berliners as those a year earlier in Hamburg and Tübingen. Unfortunately, nothing remains of Borsig's garden today. The Victoria House and other conservatories, the villa, and the ironworks were swept away by the winds of history in the twentieth century. Now a busy street traverses the former estate, while the remaining fragment of the garden is known as Essener Park.

Another little green oasis in today's Berlin, Heinrich von Kleist Park in the Tempelhof-Schöneberg district of the city was also the site of an 1852 cultivation triumph. Through most of the nineteenth century, the Royal Botanic Gardens Schöneberg occupied this area. In 1851, it received *Victoria* seeds, most likely from Loescher in Hamburg. Following Borsig's example, garden director Alexander Braun built a special greenhouse to accommodate the royal lily. In May 1852, Schöneberg's first Victoria House, designed

In Stuttgart's Wilhelma the Amazon lily moved to the heated outdoor pool in 1956.
Tomasz Aniśko / Longwood Gardens

WORLD CONQUEST 149

The South American lilies have been living in the Victoria House of the Botanical Garden in Berlin-Dahlem for more than a century.
AUTHOR'S COLLECTION

by garden superintendent Carl David Bouché, received the lily, which had been grown from seeds allegedly carried from Hamburg by Bouché himself. In Berlin, Schöneberg's *Victoria* flowering came in a close second to Borsig's, a mere three days later than her sister at Moabit (Lack 2004).

As in other gardens where *Victoria* made her appearance, the popularity of the South American lily forced Schöneberg's administration to extend opening hours and restrict the number of visitors each day (Potonié 1882). Under the watchful eye of Schöneberg's gardeners, visitors were required to leave bags and coats at the door before entering *Victoria*'s domain. Eventually, the extended hours became permanent at Schöneberg, and the South American lily was credited with making the botanical garden more accessible to Berliners (Lack 2004). Thirty years later, *Victoria* moved out of Bouché's original house and into more spacious and elegant quarters designed by city architect Friedrich Schulze.

Then, at the turn of the century, the Amazon lily and the entire botanical garden relocated from Schöneberg to the Dahlem district of Berlin. A new Victoria House opened in Dahlem in 1909. Integrated into the largest conservatory complex in Germany, the South American giant was given a private chamber on a sunny terrace backed by an immense tropical greenhouse and overlooking a spectacular Italian garden below. In the language of architecture, *Victoria*'s supreme position was forcefully established. As the capital of imperial Germany, Berlin could not have created an edifice better suited for the queen of the Vegetable Kingdom. Conservatory architect Alfred Koerner received the Order of the Red Eagle, Prussia's second highest medal, for his design.

The Amazon lily continued to rule over the floral riches of Dahlem's botanical collection through the turbulent years of World War I, the depression of the 1920s, and—despite coal shortages and widespread rationing—through the early years of World War II. In 1943, however, the bombs of the Allies' air raid left the Victoria House and the rest of the conservatory in ruins. When reconstruction began after the war, the Victoria House was the first building to reopen. It opened in 1950, well ahead of the additional eighteen years it took to rebuild the entire conservatory complex. Thus, except for a seven-year absence, the queen lily has occupied the preeminent place among one of the world's largest plant collections for over a century.

From the places of the initial introduction in Hanover, Hamburg, Tübingen, and Berlin, *Victoria* spread to nearly all corners of Germany, never failing to attract large crowds of spectators. She reached Dresden by 1866, Bonn by 1878, Cologne in 1881, Strassburg (today's Strasbourg) in 1884, Breslau (today's Wrocław) in 1885, and Karlsruhe by 1891. In a country richly endowed with botanical gardens, the ability to grow and exhibit *Victoria* became a matter of prestige and rank. Smaller gardens strived to replicate the success of leading institutions. By the turn of the century, any German garden able to afford facilities to accommodate the queen lily was probably doing so. In areas where *Victoria* could not be grown year-round, the gardeners emptied her basin during the winter months, lowered the temperature to reduce heating costs, and stocked the house with various winter plants. Few of the Victoria Houses built during that era survive today; most have been rebuilt or replaced by newer structures, often more than once.

ESTABLISHING ROOTS

The same year *Victoria* took up residence in Berlin, she crossed Germany's southern border into Austria. The earliest record of the Amazon lily in that country comes from Tetschen (today's Děčín) Castle, a few kilometers inside Bohemia, then part of the Austrian Empire. Once home of Bohemian kings, Tetschen was in the hands of the Thun-Hohensteins, a dynasty of prominent Austrian statesmen. When the queen lily's seeds arrived in early 1852, they were put in the care of Franz Josst, the castle's head gardener. When the *Bohemia* newspaper reported the opening of the first "magically beautiful blossom" of *Victoria*, it noted that the historic event took place precisely at 4:30 in the afternoon of July 11 (Gicklhorn

The 1870 view of the greenhouses of Tetschen (today's Děčín) Castle, where *Victoria* flowered in 1852.
STATE REGIONAL ARCHIVES LITOMĚŘICE, BRANCH DĚČÍN

A circular basin that once held *Victoria* on terraces below Tetschen (today's Děčín) Castle.
TOMASZ ANISKO / LONGWOOD GARDENS

Beginning in 2001, a century and half after her introduction in Vienna, *Victoria* has taken residence in the magnificent Great Palmhouse of Schönbrunn.
TOMASZ ANIŚKO / LONGWOOD GARDENS

1961). Although Tetschen's greenhouses once occupied several south-facing terraces below the castle, today nothing is left of them except a modest circular stone basin—most likely the South American nymph's first home in the Austrian Empire.

In 1852, shortly after Tetschen, *Victoria* also made an appearance outside Vienna at Schönbrunn, the summer palace of Emperor Franz Joseph. One of Austria's leading botanists and explorers of that era who oversaw the cultivation of the South American lily in the imperial gardens, Heinrich Wilhelm Schott obtained the seeds from Loescher in Hamburg. In the early years, she was grown on and off, but starting in 1890, *Victoria* was regularly featured in her own greenhouse, which opened to the public on August 18, Franz Joseph's birthday (Stransky 1951).

The death of the emperor in 1916 and the hardships and coal shortages in the aftermath of World War I interrupted *Victoria*'s presence at Schönbrunn. She came back to the palace in 1926, but World War II forced her out in 1941. *Victoria* returned briefly to Schönbrunn in the early 1950s, when she was given a room in a small greenhouse. Since 2001, however, the queen lily has maintained residency in Schönbrunn's most impressive greenhouse, the Great Palmhouse. This 1882 conservatory is 25 m (eight stories) tall and a quarter of a hectare (over half an acre) in size. After a turbulent century and a half, Vienna has provided *Victoria* with accommodations reflecting Her Aquatic Majesty's noble status. Moreover, today's visitors do not have to wait for the emperor's birthday to call.

Austria, and later Austria-Hungary, embraced *Victoria* as ardently as Germany. The nymph was prized not only in the conservatories of the nobility, but also in university botanical

WORLD CONQUEST 153

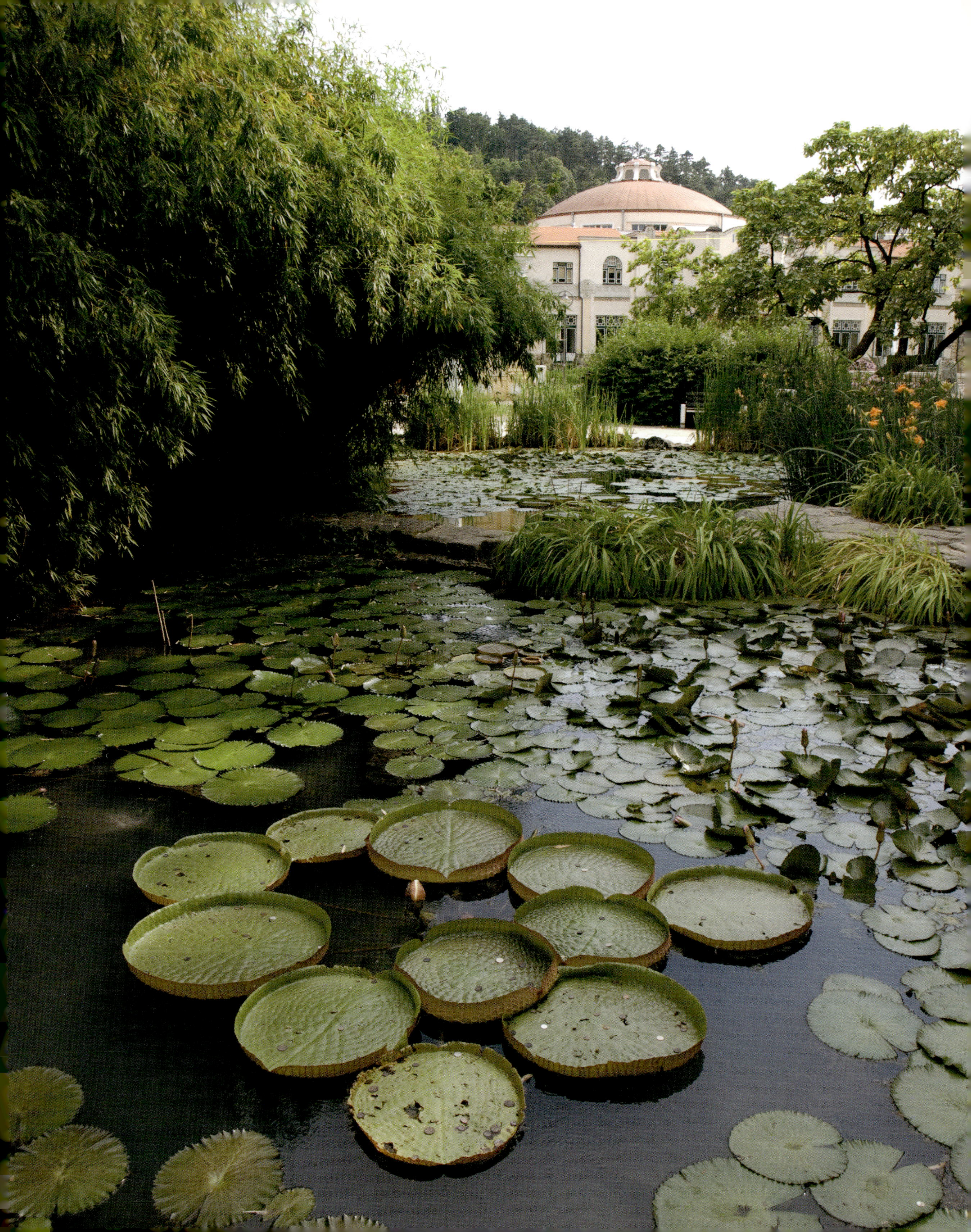

gardens, such as those in Graz, Budapest, and Vienna. After World War I and the breakup of the Habsburg Empire, *Victoria* migrated further east. By 1930, she reached the great arc of the Carpathians, settling in Cluj-Napoca in Romania and in Piešťany in today's Slovakia.

Piešťany must be counted among the most extraordinary places the Amazon lily has been introduced. Known since the Middle Ages for its thermal springs, the Piešťany spa attracted generations of visitors seeking to cure their illnesses through drinking and bathing in warm mineral waters. Among the spa's devotees was Ferdinand I, the former tsar of Bulgaria living in exile in Slovakia. Whether it was due to his blood relation to Queen Victoria—Ferdinand's father was Victoria's cousin—or his keen interest in botany and gardening, Ferdinand suggested during one of his walks in the park in Piešťany that the spa should build outdoor pools fed by thermal springs to house the South American lily.

His novel idea finally came to fruition when the pools were inaugurated in 1930. In time, the presence of this vegetable wonder—with such a strikingly exotic appearance considering the lily's outdoor environs—became a hallmark of Piešťany. What could be better proof of a thermal spring's curative and life-sustaining properties than the image of a tender tropical nymph thriving outdoors in the spa's balmy pools? Predictably, several nearby hotels adopted the name *Victoria regia*, as did an annual festival that included a flower parade, a flower-arranging competition, and a local liquor based on the water from the thermal springs. To ensure that guests did not miss the spectacle, the pools were illuminated at night, and the opening of each *Victoria* flower was announced by Piešťany's radio station.

NORTH INTO RUSSIA

The northward migration of *Victoria* out of Belgium, remarkably, did not lag behind its southern expansion. As early as 1853, the Amazon lily was growing in Stockholm in her own greenhouse at Rosendal, the residence of King Oscar II of Sweden. Shortly after that, the royal lily migrated to Riga, Latvia, then part of the Russian Empire, where she was cultivated in the greenhouses of Wagner's nurseries, a leading horticultural establishment at the time. Wagner supplied young *Victoria* to the Imperial Botanical Garden in St. Petersburg, where the queen lily flowered for the first time in 1854 (Regel 1871).

In Piešťany, Slovakia, *Victoria* has been residing in outdoor pools fed by thermal springs since 1930.
TOMASZ ANIŚKO / LONGWOOD GARDENS

Sweden's first Amazon lily was grown in 1853 in a specially built Victoria House on the grounds of Rosendal, a royal residence in Stockholm.
KUNGLIGA BIBLIOTEKET, NATIONAL LIBRARY OF SWEDEN

WORLD CONQUEST 155

Georgy Trespe (in the white jacket and hat) supervises the planting of *Victoria* at the Botanical Garden of Moscow State University in 1925.
BOTANICAL GARDEN OF MOSCOW STATE UNIVERSITY

Eduard Regel, 1885:

Every year I had the opportunity to present the flower of Victoria *to the Highnesses. This year, we were able to show two flowers at the same time, one on day one, white, the other one on day two, red. In order for the flowers to keep, they were put into a glass container filled with water which was put on a display table, surrounded by a bouquet of other flowers, such as orchids and other aristocratic flowers, protecting their queen. But, behold!, whereas the flower, when it is attached to the plant, closes after the first night, and opens up again on the second evening and withers afterwards, these two flowers remained open for three days, and in full bloom, and the white flower remained white, and the red flower did not change its color either.*

Regel 1885, translated by Daniela Freitag

Unfortunately, subsequent attempts to bring seedlings to St. Petersburg often failed. Out of thirty plants purchased for the garden over the course of fifteen years, only one arrived in St. Petersburg alive, hand-carried on a train. To improve their odds, imperial gardeners tried to produce seeds in St. Petersburg, but a number of challenges yielded mixed results (Regel 1871). Without supplemental lighting, at that latitude the Amazon lily flowered briefly between mid-July and early August, when the sun rose high enough to approximate tropical conditions. Each year that *Victoria* flowered in St. Petersburg, her bloom was presented to Their Imperial Highnesses. In 1885, two plants successfully bloomed in the Imperial Garden—one on the first night, the other on the second night—creating a spectacle at the palace of Tsar Aleksandr III.

Aleksandr Tsinger, a physicist and writer, reported an earlier attempt to introduce *Victoria* to Russia in his 1927 bestselling book *Zanimatelnaya Botanika* (Entertaining Botany). Allegedly, the owner of an estate in Tula province, some 200 km (125 miles) south of Moscow, imported *Victoria* seeds directly from Germany before they reached St. Petersburg in 1854. An estate gardener and his son were tasked with caring for the royal lily and told that if they brought the plant to flower, they would be freed from serfdom. They cared for the lily in a large heated basin. She grew huge leaves, but after a year and a half, there still were no flowers. Faced with the rising cost of upkeep and repairs, the owner ordered the basin drained and the plant discarded. As the lily lay on the bottom of the empty basin, helpless "as fish on sand," the gardener's son found emerging flower buds among the leaves. He and his father rushed to refill the basin and revive the queen lily, but it was to no avail. The owner was so saddened by the whole affair that he ordered both the basin and the greenhouse destroyed and forbade anyone to mention *Victoria* in his presence. The gardener and his son were not rewarded for their diligent care of the water lily, although in 1861 serfdom was abolished in all of Russia (Tsinger 1951).

Muscovites would have to wait until the early 1900s to see *Victoria* flower in their city. In 1887, Christian Gabekost, a nursery owner in Moscow, attempted to grow the

VICTORIA: THE SEDUCTRESS

South American lily in one of his greenhouses, but the plant never flowered. He built a small tank heated from the sides and below by fermenting horse manure that had to be replaced several times during the summer. In the end, swapping the manure proved to be too much trouble, and Gabekost gave up.

In 1908, however, the Botanical Garden of Moscow State University built a more appropriate basin. It was there that *Victoria* was presented to the citizens of Moscow in her full glory (Trespe 1925). The lily produced fifteen flowers that summer and attracted fifty thousand visitors, many of whom had to stand in lines for hours to see her. In 1911, in response to the public's unprecedented interest, Moscow's Zoological Gardens commissioned architect Karl Gippius to design and build a special tank-equipped greenhouse for *Victoria*'s care and exhibition. Again, Muscovites came in huge numbers. Never before had the zoo experienced such large crowds.

World War I brought shortages of coal in Russia, as in most of Europe, forcing Moscow State University to stop caring for the queen lily in 1915. When she returned in 1924, long lines formed again. More than thirty thousand Muscovites passed through the garden gates to witness one of the seventeen flowers that opened that summer. After the intense upheaval brought on by the war and the Russian Revolution, *Victoria*'s triumphant return was also a matter of local prestige. "Regardless how complete or

The South American lily in the greenhouse of the Botanical Garden of Moscow State University in the 1930s.
BOTANICAL GARDEN OF MOSCOW STATE UNIVERSITY

The South American lily has been growing in its northermost in Helsinki since 1892.
AUTHOR'S COLLECTION

Alphonse Karr, 1853:

Unfortunately, there are only a few people who could see one of the most magnificent plants that exists bloom in their home because building such a greenhouse and the heating equipment is expensive. However, the city of Paris owes itself this luxury. It is more interesting and pleasurable than a bear. And it would cost less than the upkeep of the eight or ten hyenas which comprise the collection of the menagerie of the Jardin des Plantes. I truly hope that the museum will entrust the director of greenhouses, Mr. Neumann, with a young Victoria regia. *All of Paris will quickly come to admire this magnificent Nymphaeaceae thanks to its rapid growth, a growth that is as extraordinary as its splendor and size. It would be shameful to hesitate. Even for a private gardener, it would be quite miserable to have a warm greenhouse without preparing a sanctuary for* Victoria regia.

Karr 1853, translated by Rose Torelli

interesting a botanical garden or some other collection might be," wrote Georgy Trespe, the director of the garden, "without *Victoria* it, however, is not full and complete" (Trespe 1925).

SPREADING THROUGH EUROPE

The Amazonian lily reached her northernmost habitat, above 60° latitude, in 1892, when she was raised in the botanical garden of Helsinki, Finland, then part of the Russian Empire. An aboveground tank was fitted beneath a low roof in one of the garden's smaller greenhouses. Despite the somewhat cramped conditions, *Victoria* thrived under the Finnish sky, producing scores of flowers and leaves 2 m (7 feet) in diameter.

Fifty years later, when the world was engulfed by World War II, the Amazon lily became, for the Finns, a symbol of survival and rebirth. In February 1944, Helsinki found itself the target of a fierce air raid, and some of the bombs landed in the botanical garden with devastating results. Shattered glass exposed the delicate conservatory plants to frigid temperatures, killing nearly all of them. The basin used for growing *Victoria* froze solid. The following spring, however, gardeners were astonished to discover in the sediment in the bottom of the tank a few sprouting seeds of the royal lily. It was a hopeful sign of life returning to the war-ravaged city.

While *Victoria* was making spectacular advances in central and eastern Europe, her westerly progression sorely lagged. Despite the fact that French naturalist Aimé Bonpland had sent seeds to Paris as early as 1835, it would take more than two decades for the South American lily to find a home in the Jardin des Plantes of the National Museum of Natural History, after she had already found homes in many European cities (Barral 1859). Why was there such a delay on the part of the French? Was it residual resentment toward a plant carrying the name of a monarch? Or was it wounded national pride over the insult of English botanists naming the South American lily ahead of her

In the Netherlands, *Victoria* first flowered at the Amsterdam Botanical Garden in 1859.
University of Amsterdam Library Special Collections

French discoverer? Regardless of the cause, influential writer and critic Alphonse Karr lamented the delay and the fact that Parisians were deprived of "one of the most magnificent plants." Karr insisted, "The city of Paris owes itself this luxury" (Karr 1853, translated by Rose Torelli).

Thirty years later, the perception of *Victoria* in France had changed so much that the municipal council of Lyon felt embarrassed that their city did not have a proper house for the Amazonian lily. The council promptly funded both its design and construction in the Tête d'Or Park. That summer, the first *Victoria* flower finally opened in Lyon, delighting the citizens and, it was hoped, allaying council members' concerns over the city's reputation.

The Netherlands welcomed *Victoria* first in Amsterdam in 1859, then Leiden in 1872, and Rotterdam in 1887. While the first two cities accommodated the queen lily on the grounds of the venerable botanical gardens, Rotterdam chose to build a special Victoria House in the city's zoological garden, following the peculiar example of Brussels (Wilke 1891).

In her southerly expansion, *Victoria* arrived first in Sicily in 1855, planted in an outdoor pool at the Royal Botanical Gardens in Palermo (Console 1857). By the time the nymph developed flower buds, however, the cooler October weather arrested their development, and the plant died a few months later. Another attempt also failed the following year. Finally, in 1857, the first flower opened on October 1. It was an event of such importance that *Victoria*'s flowering was promptly touted on the pages of *Revue Horticole* by the gardens director (Console 1857).

WORLD CONQUEST

Beginning in 1851, the queen lily was introduced into many public gardens in India, such as the Victoria Gardens in Bombay (today's Mumbai), shown here.
AUTHOR'S COLLECTION

Ironically, although the countries in southern Europe were blessed with a climate that was most congenial to *Victoria*, they showed the least interest in cultivating her. Beyond Sicily, it was well into the twentieth century before the Amazon lily appeared in public and private Italian gardens—Padua Botanic Garden in the 1930s followed, after World War II, by Villa Taranto, Villa Bricherasio, and La Mortella.

Likewise, Spain, the country that had ruled the native lands of *Victoria* for three centuries prior to her discovery, showed little interest in the lily's cultivation. History records only one Spanish appearance—in the gardens of the Vistillas Palace in Madrid sometime before 1882 (Díaz-Pérez 1976). Palace owner Mariano Téllez-Girón y Beaufort-Spontin, twelfth duke of Osuna, was known for his extravagant expenditures, and the queen lily display could probably be counted among those.

BEYOND EUROPE

Initially, *Victoria*'s expansion outside Europe followed the trade routes of the British Empire. Soon after her successful flowering in England, the South American lily was sent east to India and Ceylon (today's Sri Lanka) and west to the Caribbean islands. In 1850, William Hooker of Kew dispatched seeds to Hugh Falconer, superintendent of the Royal Botanic Gardens, Calcutta. When celebrated Scottish explorer Robert Fortune visited the garden a year later, he saw *Victoria* growing luxuriantly on one of the ponds. He predicted, with unabashed patriotic flair: "It will soon reign as the queen of flowers in every land, and, like our beloved sovereign whose name it bears, the sun will never set on its dominions" (Fortune 1852).

Edward Chitty, 1852:

It is indeed gratifying to Dr. Gilbert McNab and myself, that we have at length succeeded in growing to maturity that justly-termed "gorgeous," "extraordinary," "most magnificent," water lily—that "vegetable wonder"—that "Queen of Aquatics," the Victoria regia, *for the first time in Jamaica. It is gratifying, not simply to feelings of vanity, but because our labours and constant attention, and watchings, are crowned by success; and our friends and selves have seen this wonder; and because the plant is, as we feel confidently assured, now safely established in this most beautiful island of Jamaica, where, because it is so beautiful, every thing else that is beautiful ought to be congregated.*

Chitty 1852

Victoria amazonica in a pool at the Castleton Gardens in Jamaica in the early 1900s.
LONGWOOD GARDENS LIBRARY AND ARCHIVES

In the fall of 1851, James McNab, curator of the Royal Botanic Garden, Edinburgh, sent four seeds of *Victoria*, presumably procured from Kew, to his brother Gilbert, a medical doctor in Jamaica. The seedlings were planted on June 18, 1852, to commemorate the anniversary of the victory of Waterloo. The plant flowered for the first time on September 8 (Chitty 1852). The lily was employed so frequently to inspire patriotic jubilation among the English queen's subjects, it is no wonder that the plant fell out of favor with the French.

From Jamaica, the Amazon lily spread to Trinidad. By 1852, she was adorning the ponds of the British governor's house there (Chitty 1852). Next, *Victoria* landed on the west side of the Andes and found a home in Río Magdalena, the principal river of Colombia. She flourished so well that within a few years the lily was pronounced "a troublesome weed" (Bollaert 1861).

Paradoxically, the queen lily was cultivated relatively late in her native South America. In Argentina, where the nymph can be found growing wild along Paraná, barely 250 km (155 miles) northwest of Buenos Aires, the earliest records of the lily's cultivation date back to 1901. By that time, *Victoria* had already traveled around the world (Valla 1976). Even today, she is rarely seen in Argentine gardens and is virtually unknown to the Argentinean public. It is much easier to see *Victoria* in Europe than in South America.

In British Guiana (today's Guyana), where the giant water lily had been previously confined to the country's interior, the plant was subsequently introduced to the coastal settlements, where it invaded the network of canals built for the sugarcane plantations. Late nineteenth-century travelers visiting Georgetown, the colony's capital, were awestruck by the proliferation of the "magnificent *Victoria regia*" in the city's canals (Crookall 1898). Leo Edward Miller of the American Museum of Natural History in New York was less

One of the many canals of Georgetown, British Guiana, filled with *Victoria amazonica* around the turn of the twentieth century.
PHOTOGRAPHS AND PRINTS DIVISION, SCHOMBURG CENTER FOR RESEARCH IN BLACK CULTURE, THE NEW YORK PUBLIC LIBRARY, ASTOR, LENOX AND TILDEN FOUNDATIONS

poetic in his description of Georgetown's water lilies. He likened them to "huge pies" and warned "an overenthusiastic admirer" that "the plant is lovely from a distance only" because her sharp spines "effectively prevent any intimate advances" (Miller 1918).

AN ASIAN INFUSION

After her early introduction to India and Ceylon, *Victoria*'s next stop in world conquest was Singapore, a nineteenth-century British possession tied to other colonies through trade routes and diplomatic channels. Apparently, the first person to grow the South American colossus in Singapore was Hoo Ah Kay, or Whampoa, a ship chandler and "the happy possessor of many, many dollars as the result of his labors" (Hornaday 1885). His fabled Whampoa Gardens were filled with various attractions, both botanical and zoological, which, in the early 1870s, included the queen lily. Although these gardens have long since disappeared, Whampoa shared *Victoria* with the Singapore Botanic Gardens he helped establish. The lilies can still be admired there today.

Outside these and other European outposts, the Amazon lily's inroads into the rest of Asia were delayed well into the second

Victoria amazonica in Whampoa Gardens in Singapore around 1877.
SINGAPORE BOTANIC GARDENS

half of the twentieth century. The hermetic nature of the cultures of China, Japan, and Korea, their apprehension about Western influences, and their adherence to traditional horticultural principles all proved to be formidable obstacles preventing *Victoria* from being included in East Asian gardens. After two world wars, however, many aspects of these ancient cultures gave way to a barrage of Western ideas and rapid modernization. As part of their historic transformation, China, Japan, and Korea came to embrace the South American lily with the same force as others had before them. Today, Asia hosts some of the most daring presentations of *Victoria* anywhere. Strikingly nontraditional, immense conservatories showcase the giant lilies as the manifestation of their people's growing

The queen lily growing in one of the ponds of the Singapore Botanic Gardens in the late nineteenth century.
MÉDIATHÈQUE DE L'AGGLOMÉRATION TROYENNE

WORLD CONQUEST 163

Sakuya Konohana Kan in Osaka, the largest of *Victoria*'s palaces in Japan, opened in 1990.
YOKO ARAKAWA / LONGWOOD GARDENS

aspirations, economic might, and rising prosperity.

In modern Japan—where at least twenty public gardens cultivate *Victoria*—the most radical departure from revered horticultural traditions appears in the Sakuya Konohana Kan, or Great Conservatory. It celebrates the exuberant Amazonian colossus in a huge interior space. Its design was modeled on the lily's flower, a nod perhaps to London's Great Exhibition of 1851, which reflected the lily's leaf. The conservatory opened in 1990 on the grounds of the World Expo in Osaka. The South American vegetable marvel complemented the latest technological achievements on display there. Rising to 30 m (98 feet) and encompassing nearly 0.7 hectare (2 acres), Sakuya Konohana Kan is among the world's largest conservatories.

Another impressive exhibit of Amazon lilies was created in the grand conservatories of the Kyoto Botanical Garden in 1992. But perhaps the most spectacular indoor display of South American lilies is in the 2003 conservatories of

A stunning display of colorful birds enlivens the scene inside the conservatory of Kachoen in Kakegawa City, where *Victoria* shares a vast pool, 37 m (120 feet) long and 16 m (51 feet) wide, with smaller members of the water lily tribe.
KAKEGAWA KACHOEN

VICTORIA: THE SEDUCTRESS

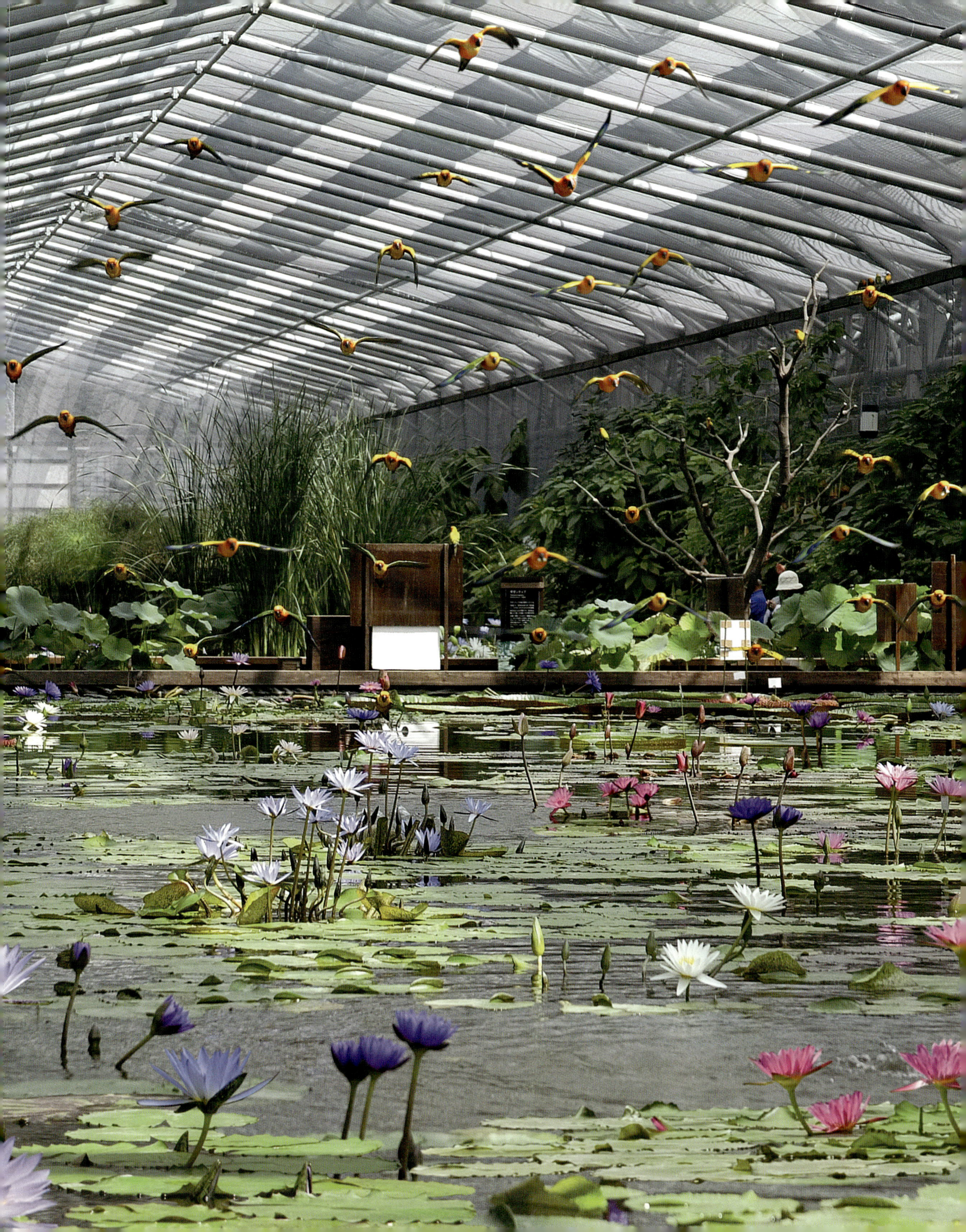

The South American lily growing inside the Victoria House at the Adelaide Botanic Garden in 1877.
NATIONAL LIBRARY OF AUSTRALIA

Kachoen, a flower and bird garden in Kakegawa City. The garden includes a dazzling combination of flocks of exotic birds darting freely over a vast pool filled with *Victoria* and accompanied by a rainbow of *Nymphaea* lily flowers—a sight to behold.

ON TOP OF DOWN UNDER

For a long time, the southern- and easternmost location reached by the queen lily was Adelaide, Australia. In 1849, Richard Schomburgk, who had assisted his famous brother Robert in mapping Guiana's borders, emigrated from Germany to Australia. There, he became the second director of the Adelaide Botanic Garden. In 1868, he had a Victoria House built for the regal lily. Schomburgk later confessed, however, that since he had left Europe before *Victoria* was cultivated there and before any Victoria Houses were built—hence lacking practical expertise in their construction—he was "rather timid and doubtful regarding the success" of the Adelaide structure (Schomburgk 1873).

The seeds arrived from Germany, sealed hermetically in a vial of pure water. They germinated in time to have two plants ready for planting in July, the middle of Australia's winter. Two months later, on September 28, 1868, Australia's first flower "expanded in its beauty" (Schomburgk 1873). Schomburgk faithfully reported the whole event, without omitting any details, to the members of Adelaide's Philosophical Society the following day.

The development of *Victoria* 'Longwood Hybrid' in 1961 marked the beginning of a new chapter in the global expansion of the queen lily. Hailed as more adaptable and hardy than either parent species, the hybrid enticed many who had previously failed to raise the queen lily.

One continent curiously devoid of *Victoria* was Africa. Despite Aimé Bonpland's early attempts to introduce it to the French colonies in northern Africa, followed by the Breslau Botanic Garden's efforts to send seeds to the Congo in the 1880s (Bornemann 1886), the queen lily found it difficult to settle on that continent. In the early 1960s, Longwood Gardens began sending seeds to African countries, including Egypt, Kenya, Nigeria, South Africa, and Zambia. This was met with limited success.

Yet one tiny island off the coast of Africa, Mauritius, proved to be amiable to *Victoria* cultivation. The lily was brought to Mauritius from Brazil before 1904 and planted in the Jardin de Mon Plaisir near Port-Louis, known today as Sir Seewoosagur Ramgoolam Botanical Garden. In time, it grew to be arguably the most stunning outdoor display of royal lilies anywhere (Puchooa and Khoyratty 2004).

New Zealand was another place where the 'Longwood Hybrid' helped bring the exhilaration of seeing the vegetable colossus to the public. In a tropical conservatory of the Auckland Domain, the city's oldest park, the vigorous hybrid "literally became a celebrity overnight" when she produced her first flower, reported the *New Zealand Herald* in 1984. In 1989, *Victoria* migrated even further south, below the 41° parallel, to the botanical garden in Wellington, where a special indoor pool was built for her. Consequently, New Zealand surpassed Australia as the world's most southern and western location inhabited by the South American lily. There, more than 140 years after her first leap across the Atlantic, *Victoria*'s journey reached the metaphoric end of the earth.

In the 1980s, *Victoria* arrived at the site of its southernmost residence, the Lily Pond inside the Begonia House of the Wellington Botanic Garden in New Zealand. WELLINGTON CITY COUNCIL, NEW ZEALAND

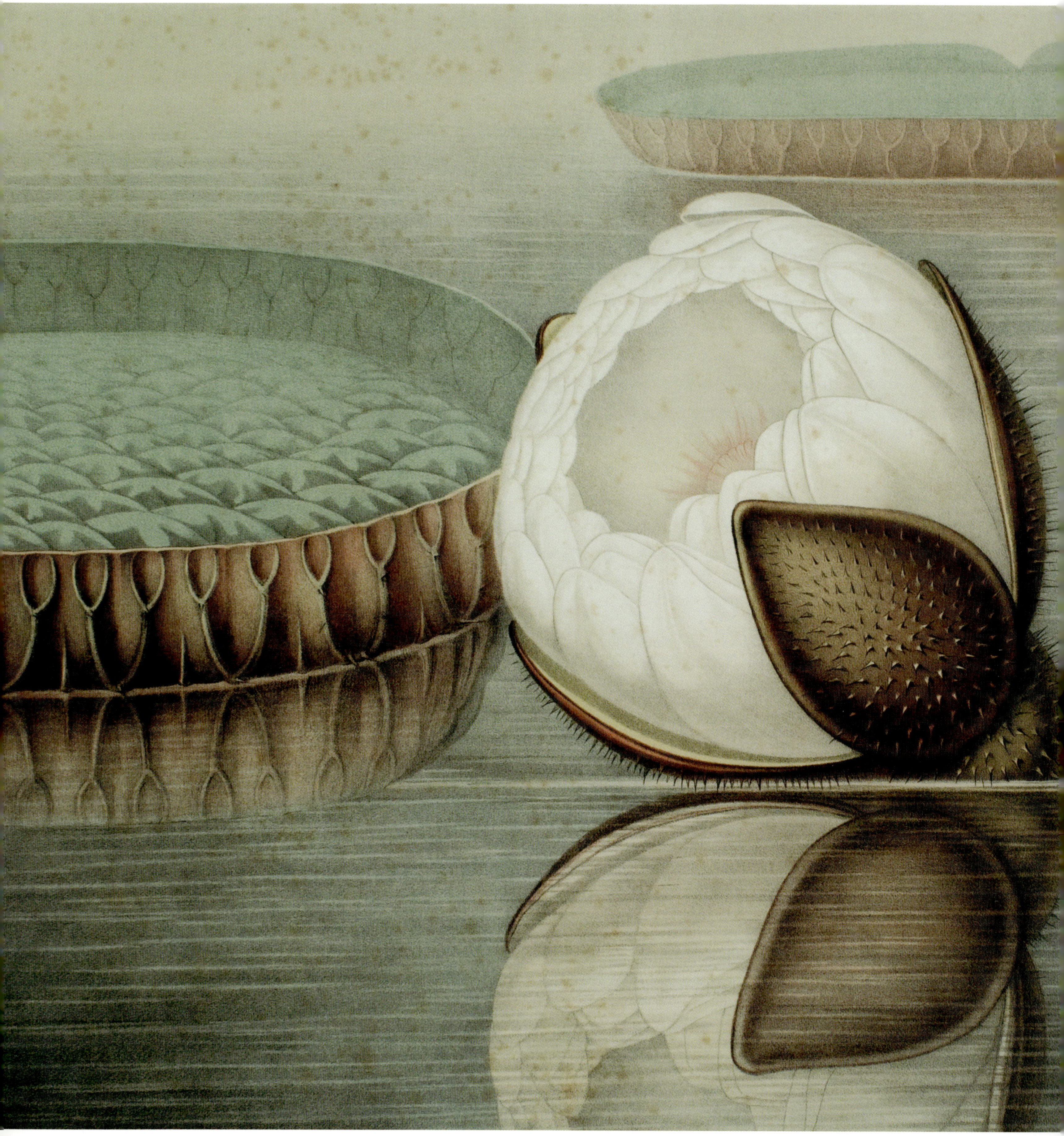

chapter 10

TRUE AMERICAN

THE NEWS IN NOVEMBER 1849 THAT *VICTORIA* had flowered at Chatsworth was heralded in England and beyond. Visitors began to flock to see this vegetable wonder and Paxton's crowning achievement. Among the many horticultural cognoscenti who came to view the following year's flowering was Andrew Jackson Downing, a celebrated American architect, landscape designer, and writer who championed the Gothic Revival style. As a book author and an editor of the *Horticulturist* magazine, he had lasting influence on United States horticulture. Downing was so impressed by the sight of the giant water lily at Chatsworth that, upon his return home, he used the *Horticulturist* to publicly challenge America's "liberal amateurs" to flower the first *Victoria* in the United States.

One of the two "amateurs" Downing called by name was Caleb Cope of Philadelphia; the other was Noel J. Becar of Brooklyn (Downing 1850). Of the two, Cope answered Downing's challenge.

Caleb Cope was born to a distinguished Quaker family in Greensburg, Pennsylvania, in 1797. His great-great-grandfather, Oliver, purchased land from William Penn in 1681, and his grandfather, also named Caleb, was known during the Revolutionary War as "a Quaker gentleman of Loyal proclivities." Caleb's father, William, died when Caleb was still an

Opening flower bud of *Victoria amazonica*, color lithograph by William Sharp, 1854.
LONGWOOD GARDENS LIBRARY AND ARCHIVES

Caleb Cope portrait painted by Thomas Sully, 1852.
THE MCLEAN LIBRARY, PENNSYLVANIA HORTICULTURAL SOCIETY

> **John Ellis, letter to Andrew Downing, 1851:**
>
> *It would be doing injustice to Mr. Downing, did I fail to mention that the first living plants of the* Victoria *which have grown in this country, were produced from seed furnished by him to the proprietor of these gardens, out of a supply presented to him last autumn, at Chatsworth. These were lost by the gardener then in charge of the place, as I understand by an accidental over-heating of the tank, consequent upon a sudden change of the weather during the night.*
>
> Cope 1851a

infant. At age eighteen, he was invited to Philadelphia to work in his uncles' counting-house, which was engaged in shipping and general merchandise. "From a fatherless boy in my uncles' establishment in 1815," Cope once said, "I rose to be the senior partner in one of the largest mercantile houses, if not the very largest, in the United States" (Morton 1897).

In 1838, Cope married his cousin Abbey Ann, and the couple moved into a home on the corner of Quince and Walnut Streets in Philadelphia. Cope's financial prosperity and interest in public affairs led to his involvement in numerous Philadelphia institutions, such as the Academy of Natural Sciences, the Academy of Fine Arts, and the Magdalen Society. In 1842, Cope also became president of the Pennsylvania Horticultural Society, a post he held for the next ten years.

After his wife's death, Cope purchased a country estate outside Philadelphia near Holmesburg in 1845. Named for the crystal spring that traversed the grounds, Springbrook was a 43-hectare (107-acre) property located on the Bristol Pike stage route between Holmesburg and Frankford. The property featured spacious lawns studded with a variety of noble trees that surrounded an elegant three-story mansion. Built by wealthy merchant Josiah W. Gibbs, who had lost his fortune in risky cotton speculation, the estate was situated on rising ground. It commanded impressive views of the surrounding countryside, including the Delaware River and New Jersey riverfront to the east. From the observatory atop the mansion, one could even see the panorama of Philadelphia some 10 km (6 miles) south.

Springbrook provided Cope with a long-awaited opportunity to pursue his horticultural passions. His thriving shipping partnership made it easier for him to acquire exotic plants, and his new country estate provided ample space to grow and display his favorite botanical treasures. About a third of the land was taken up by the mansion, lawns, a lake, gardens, and other pleasure grounds. On the south side of the house there were fourteen conservatories and graperies, with a combined area of over 1,000 m², eleven of them heated.

INHABITING SPRINGBROOK

The greenhouse Cope assigned to *Victoria*, which became known as the Lily House, was about 9 m (30 feet) long by 10 m (33 feet) wide. In its center, Cope installed an octagon-shaped tank 7.3 m (24 feet) in diameter. It was heated by a lead pipe that circled the inside of the tank twice. Following Paxton's design at Chatsworth, Springbrook's Lily House was supplied with tempered water, dropping on a small tin wheel to agitate the water in the tank and dissipate the slimy mucus that might otherwise build up on a placid surface.

When Downing had publicly challenged Cope to grow and flower America's first *Victoria*, he had also supplied Cope's gardener, John Ellis, with seeds he had obtained at Chatsworth earlier that year. The seeds germinated, but the young seedlings were lost when the tank accidentally overheated due to a sudden overnight change in weather (Boyd 1929).

The three-story mansion surmounted by an observatory was built at Springbrook by Josiah Gibbs, who in 1845 sold it to Caleb Cope.
CLARION UNIVERSITY OF PENNSYLVANIA

The mansion and greenhouses at Springbrook around 1880.
THE ATHENAEUM OF PHILADELPHIA

True American

Caleb Cope, notes, 1851: *Victoria Regia*. A letter containing 12 seeds of the plant was recd. by me from Sir Wm. J. Hooker per Steamer *Asia* on the 20th March 1851. 21st March placed four seed[s] in a small tank of water in the forcing House, each seed being planted separately in a small seed pan in sand and loam.

THE MCLEAN LIBRARY, PENNSYLVANIA HORTICULTURAL SOCIETY

Caleb Cope, letter to William Hooker, 1851:

I have in my kitchen-garden a small basin for catching the rainwater and overflow from the aquarium and other houses. It is about 8 or 10 feet [2 to 3 m] in diameter. Into this basin I planted one of the Victorias, *on the 25th of June last. The plant has grown remarkably well, the largest leaves attaining a diameter of more than 4 feet [1 m]. It has not yet, however, bloomed, and may not, as cold weather is near at hand. Sash, blocked by whiting, has remained over the basin during the whole time.*

Cope 1851b

Undeterred by this failure, Cope requested additional seeds for Springbrook the following year from William Hooker, director of the Royal Botanic Gardens, Kew, who had supplied the first *Victoria* to Chatsworth. On March 20, 1851, a package from Hooker containing twelve seeds arrived in Philadelphia via the steamer *Asia*. The next day, four seeds were planted in small pans and placed in a tank in the forcing greenhouse. The fate of the remaining eight seeds was not recorded. Most likely they either rotted upon arrival or were saved for replanting in case the first four failed.

The first seed germinated on April 10. Two more followed on April 14 and May 22, but the fourth seed failed to germinate and eventually rotted. The first seedling was transferred to the Lily House on May 24. It thrived and quickly increased in size. With summer approaching, Ellis was able to discontinue heating the tank on June 21.

Cope also wanted to test *Victoria*'s performance outdoors, so on June 25, the

One of the greenhouses at Springbrook around 1862.
THE LIBRARY COMPANY OF PHILADELPHIA

second seedling was placed in a cement basin about 3 m (10 feet) in diameter in the kitchen garden. Although it was outdoors, this basin was fed warm water that flowed out of the tank in the Lily House. The outdoor plant grew much more slowly than her companion, but nevertheless her leaves eventually reached more than 1.2 m (4 feet) in diameter. Records do not show the fate of the third and the last seedling.

On August 13, Cope discovered with "great delight" the first flower bud rising in the Lily House tank (Cope 1851c). Six days later, still without a flower, Cope took one of the *Victoria* leaves, which was 193 cm (6 feet) in diameter, to the Pennsylvania Horticultural Society's show in the Chinese Saloon, as the lower story of the immense Philadelphia Museum Building was called at that time. A correspondent of Downing's *Horticulturist* reported that this "object of the greatest attraction ... assuredly merited all the admiration bestowed upon it" (James 1851a). In the absence of the real bloom of *Victoria*, however, a wax flower brought from Europe was exhibited alongside the leaf.

Caleb Cope, letter to Andrew Downing, 1851:

I am sorry that you were not here to witness the excitement which prevailed on the 21st ult. [ultimo mense, or last month], when the Victoria *bloomed for the first time in this country, and when my grounds seemed to be in complete possession of the public. Since that event we have had a weekly contribution of a flower, the fourth one maturing last evening.... The interest felt by the public appears not only unabated, but on the increase, so that every show day we have crowds of visitors from all parts of the country.... The committee on plants and flowers of the Horticultural Society were present on the second flower blooming. They measured the petals, which they found seven inches [18 cm] in length, and the crown or disk of the flower three inches [7 cm], thus making the diameter of the whole seventeen inches [43 cm]. This is three inches larger than any flower produced in England. The leaves are also six inches [15 cm] larger than any grown there. The natural conditions of the plant in our country are, undoubtedly, more favorable than they can possibly be in England. There the water is 85° [29°C] generally, and the atmosphere at 75° [24°C]; here it is just the reverse, which is undoubtedly more like its native country.... Although all this has been accomplished at a great expense of money and personal exertion, I do not regret what I have done. I think I never have been so richly repaid in a similar effort.*

Cope 1851a

A walled garden at Springbrook around 1862.
THE LIBRARY COMPANY OF PHILADELPHIA

Pennsylvania Horticultural Society's Gold Medal awarded to Caleb Cope in 1851.
THE MCLEAN LIBRARY, PENNSYLVANIA HORTICULTURAL SOCIETY

Pennsylvania Horticultural Society's Committee on Plants and Flowers, 1851:

Without entering into an elaborate description, your committee beg leave to say that they found the plant growing in a circular tank some twenty-four feet [7.3 m] in diameter in a beautiful and costly house constructed expressly for its growth and display.... Your Committee are proud that the first flowering of this Queen of Aquatics in the United States was produced by the liberality and munificence of a member of the Pennsylvania Horticultural Society. Aside from which the influence to be expected from so munificent an expenditure, in the field of Horticulture, will give a new impulse to persons of wealth; the example set will create a desire to do likewise.

Boyd 1929

Caleb Cope, notes, 1851:

SpringBrook [sic] was quite a scene of excitement this afternoon and evening. Hundreds of persons were in attendance to witness the final development of the flower which commenced opening yesterday. The committee on plants and flowers of the Penna. Hor. So. were present, and measured the flower, which they pronounced to be 17 inches [43 cm] in diameter.

Cope 1851c

A HORTICULTURAL TRIUMPH

All Cope's troubles were rewarded a week later, on August 21, 1851, when the flower opened at Springbrook between 5:00 and 6:00 P.M.—the first *Victoria* to bloom in the United States. To ensure that onlookers would be able to view the floral spectacle into the late evening, Cope had a large lamp placed on one of the *Victoria* leaves. "This floating light house answered an admirable purpose," he noted (Cope 1851c).

When a second flower opened six days later, a large number of guests were there to see it. The following evening, an even larger crowd showed up to view the flower's transformation from the chaste white female phase to the blushed purple male phase. Among the visitors were members of the Pennsylvania Horticultural Society's Committee on Plants and Flowers, who faithfully recorded the exact measurements of the flower and its leaves. After their visit, the committee recommended that the Pennsylvania Horticultural Society award Cope its Gold Medal "for his liberality and energy in bringing into successful and mature growth that truly wonderful water lily" (James 1851b). The committee also recommended awarding twenty-five dollars to Cope's gardener John Ellis.

News that the famed giant water lily had flowered at Springbrook traveled fast. After the third flower opened on September 1, crowds of spectators "thronged the grounds the whole day" (Cope 1851c). They included several students from Philadelphia's School of Design for Women, the first visual arts college for women in the nation (today's Moore College of Art and Design), who came to try their drawing skills on *Victoria*.

Thomas Meehan portrait painted by James Longacre Wood, 1901.
THE ACADEMY OF NATURAL SCIENCES, EWELL SALE STEWART LIBRARY AND THE ALBERT M. GREENFIELD DIGITAL IMAGING CENTER FOR COLLECTIONS

Caleb Cope, letter to William Hooker, 1851:

The excitement produced by the successful cultivation of the Victoria *in this side of the Atlantic has been very great, and I am happy to say that no one has affirmed that the glowing accounts of the plant were at all exaggerated. Indeed the universal sentiment is that no tongue or pen can exaggerate it. Our worthy friend and accomplished botanist, Dr. Darlington, who spent a night with me recently, has enjoyed the sight as much as anybody.*

Cope 1851b

To give even more people an opportunity to marvel at the *Victoria* bloom, Cope agreed to take the sixth flower to Philadelphia for a special showing at the Pennsylvania Horticultural Society, which was planned for September 17. However, a heat wave accelerated the development of the flower bud, and it opened on September 15, one day earlier than anticipated. The next morning, Cope rushed to the city to inform the organizing committee that the bloom had opened the evening before. The decision was made to commence the exhibit that very same day. Before seven o'clock that night, Cope had the flower and four leaves of *Victoria*—the largest nearly 2 m (7 feet) in diameter—delivered to Philadelphia.

Fueled by newspaper reports, public curiosity about *Victoria* grew. Cope continued exhibiting new flowers: On September 19, he delivered the seventh flower for another viewing at the Pennsylvania Horticultural Society. Five days later, he brought the next bloom, accompanied by two leaves, to the Delaware Horticultural Society show in Wilmington, where they were enthusiastically pronounced as a "horticultural triumph" (Emerson 1851).

Robert Buist's greenhouses at Twelfth Street in Philadelphia, where he grew *Victoria* distributed by Caleb Cope.
LIBRARY COMPANY OF PHILADELPHIA

Gouverneur Emerson, address before the Delaware Horticultural Society, 1851:

The horticultural triumph... as it has been recently achieved in Europe, with the aid of science, skill, and wealth there so abundant, has been promptly repeated on this side of the Atlantic by Mr. Caleb Cope, President of the Philadelphia Horticultural Society, with whose company we are favored on the present occasion. When it is considered that in Europe, the aid of princely munificence has been called into requisition in obtaining the first successful development of the Victoria regia *at Chatsworth, Kew, and Zion [Syon] House, the horticultural feat accomplished by our tasteful and spirited fellow-citizen, must be the more highly appreciated. The éclat of Mr. Cope's achievement is only equalled by the kindness he has displayed, not only towards his personal friends, but the public at large, to all of whom his superb conservatory had been freely opened. More than this, many horticultural exhibitions have like the present, been supplied by him during the blooming period, with flowers and leaves of the* Victoria regia, *which has greatly extended the gratification furnished by a sight so perfectly unique.*

Emerson 1851

SPRINGBROOK IN BLOOM

While the first American *Victoria* was receiving accolades in Philadelphia, Cope sent letters to Downing and Hooker reporting his success. He described the size and vigor of Springbrook's *Victoria*, which exceeded the results obtained in any of the ducal estates in England. Cope attributed this to the more favorable climate in Philadelphia than in England. He suggested it was more natural for the plant to have the air temperature warmer than the water temperature, a condition that was reversed in England.

While the *Victoria* residing in the Lily House enjoyed diligent care and the aura of celebrity, her sister plant in the kitchen garden's basin was struggling. Cope explained that the other plant's poor growth was due to the shortage of fresh water in the basin as well as the fact that the water temperatures were too low for the nymph. The outdoor plant never attained the size of her sheltered kin, even in the heat of the summer. To make things worse, cooler weather in October arrested the outdoor plant's growth. By early November, she was rapidly declining. Cope's gardeners made a desperate attempt to move the lily from the kitchen garden to the Lily House, but to no avail—her remains quickly decayed. Ironically, this episode of two siblings separated at birth—one flourishing and basking in her queenly glory, surrounded by crowds of admirers, the other succumbing to unjust and harsh conditions—echoed the nature-versus-nurture literary tales of the Victorian era made popular by Hans Christian Andersen, Charles Dickens, the Grimm brothers, and their contemporaries.

The *Victoria* in the Lily House continued blooming through the winter months, producing flowers with surprising regularity. After opening her forty-fourth flower on February 12, 1852, however, she halted for a short while. That month, Thomas Meehan, a Kew-trained English émigré, joined Springbrook's gardening staff. Meehan had come to Philadelphia four years prior to work at the famed nursery of Robert Buist and had quickly become an influential figure in American horticultural circles. By spring 1852, *Victoria* had, under Meehan's care, ripened perfect seeds from which the first generation of offspring germinated without difficulty. Cope instructed Meehan to announce in the pages of the *Horticulturist* that April that he would "be happy to supply any one forming a tank for the *Victoria* with a plant for it," while Meehan himself "should be pleased to give any desired information to those desiring it" (Meehan 1852). As it often happens with plants, prolific fecundity can quickly lead from scarcity to abundance or overabundance. Among the first to take Cope up on his offer was Meehan's former employer, nurseryman Robert Buist.

Meehan remained with Cope and Springbrook's *Victoria* until 1853. In August of that year, he exhibited the 128th American flower at the Pennsylvania Horticultural Society's show. Was anyone getting tired of seeing *Victoria* flowers? Not according to Meehan (1852): "It would not be extravagant to call the beauties of the plant unsurpassable. . . . Nor is this ever-blooming principle one long routine of wearisome monotony, for no two flowers can be said to be exactly alike. At the appearance of every bud there is something to anticipate—some new beauty, as yet unknown, to excite our curiosity, and raise up expectation."

In the summer of 1854, America's first *Victoria* was still alive after having produced two hundred flowers. The number of seeds and seedlings reared from these flowers is not known, but it has been acknowledged that Springbrook's *Victoria* provided the main source of seeds in the United States during that time.

Under Cope's care, Springbrook became the most attractive country seat around Philadelphia. Although its extensive plant collections were highly esteemed as some of the best in the country, it was *Victoria* that brought a continuous stream of visitors eager to view the "Queen of Flowers" and turned this quaint garden on the banks of the Delaware River into a national horticultural treasure.

Gouverneur Emerson, address before the Delaware Horticultural Society, 1851:

In his conservatory floats the Queen of Flowers in all her beauty, attended by her natural but strange-looking subjects, the orchids, suspended around in groups and mingling their fragrance with her own. In fact, the whole scene presented in the lily-house is unique and highly impressive, well calculated to awaken poetical conceptions, among which it is easy to imagine a shrine consecrated to an oriental goddess, or grotto dedicated to water-nymphs, and presided over by Aegle, the fairest of Naiades.

Emerson 1851

Pennsylvania Horticultural Society's Committee on Nominations, 1851:

Its orchidean collection and its varieties of the cactus tribe may be pronounced without rival in this country, either in extent or beauty of arrangement. The crowning glory of his Victoria regia *has already received its special and appropriate mention from the Society: but we have not yet seen on record all that might be said of the princely surroundings in which its cultivation has been perfected and its beauty exhibited; and we cannot speak too often of the liberal hospitality with which facilities have been furnished to citizens and strangers to see this queen of water flowers, nor of the more than hospitality with which specimens of its magnificent flower and leaf have been furnished to more than one horticultural exhibition in more than one State.*

Boyd 1929

SPRINGBROOK CHANGES HANDS

Unfortunately, things took a dramatic turn for the worse in 1857 when the country's financial panic and economic crisis led to the United States's first depression, which caused Cope's mercantile and shipping business to collapse. At the same time, Cope's dishonest business partners defrauded him out of cash reserves nearing two hundred thousand dollars. Cope's suddenly desperate financial situation forced him to sell Springbrook to George H. Stuart, another merchant prince of Philadelphia, for just over seventy thousand dollars.

A week later, Springbrook's plant collections—3,200 plants, including *Victoria*—were sold off as well. The sale began on May 20 and continued until the whole collection was gone (M. Thomas and Sons 1857). Within a few years, Cope managed to pay off his creditors; afterward, he decided to retire from commercial life. When he died in 1888, Cope was duly remembered for his financial successes and charity work. But it was his horticultural achievements, crowned by raising the first *Victoria* in America, which secured his place in history.

Cope's Springbrook successor, George Stuart, was well aware of Cope's legacy and mindful of the public's great affection for the estate. Stuart made every effort to preserve Springbrook's former glory. He also continued growing *Victoria*, which one correspondent to the *Horticulturist* who visited the estate in 1862 found to be "very flourishing" (Anonymous 1862). After nine years, however, Stuart put Springbrook on the market, attributing the sale to the high cost of upkeep plus the rapidly declining air quality, due to the construction of new factories nearby. Stuart suffered from asthma and was frequently forced to drive to Philadelphia late at night to escape the polluted atmosphere of Holmesburg.

Springbrook's next and final owner was Edwin Forrest. As the first American-born tragedian to achieve stardom performing in the great Shakespearean plays, Forrest was the highest paid actor of that era. He never used Springbrook as his primary residence. After his death, the estate was converted into a home for retired actors. The Edwin Forrest Home, as it became known, operated at Springbrook until the 1920s, when the estate was sold again and then demolished to make way for a working-class neighborhood. Today, all evidence of Caleb Cope and America's earliest and most daring horticultural endeavor here has vanished.

M. Thomas and Sons, auction catalog, 1857:

Shade, afforded by majestic and rare specimens of forest trees, is abundant wherever desired. The wood and water of the place are, indeed, so bountiful as to invest the grounds with a charm which is seldom found to exist so near a great City. . . . The collection of plants is known to be one of the finest in this country. No expense has been spared to add to it everything beautiful or interesting that could be obtained from any part of the world; many things exist in it which, from the difficulty of importing them alive, are never seen in this country; and others, from the rare opportunities they afford for propagation, are seldom seen in even the princely establishments of Europe. The Victoria lily is still blooming here in perfection, and the numerous varieties of air plants or orchideae, now at an age for blooming profusely, afford almost daily an opportunity of enjoying the richest treasures of the floral world. The subscribers are persuaded that the proprietor of these described grounds has extended a wide gratification to visitors from all parts of the world, in allowing them to share with himself in enjoying his plants; and that all may now have a chance to possess them, he has decided to offer them at public sale only, and separately.

M. Thomas and Sons 1857

M. Thomas and Sons, auction catalog, 1857:

The main plant of the Victoria occupies the centre of the tank. Around it are a number of small ones in boxes, intended by the proprietor for gratuitous distribution amongst those disposed to try the cultivation of the plant in other parts of the country. The writer feels a certain degree of sadness in learning that the old plant of the Victoria, which had contributed to the enjoyment of thousands, as well as received, in by-gone times, so large a share of his own attention and care, has been discarded for one of its own offspring—a "true American."

M. Thomas and Sons 1857

Today a neighborhood of row houses occupies the former Springbrook estate in the Holmesburg section of Philadelphia.
Tomasz Aniśko / Longwood Gardens

Anonymous correspondent to the *Horticulturist*, 1862:

We have just returned from our second visit, and rejoice to say that the mansion, the beautiful lawns and trees, not only, but all the green and hot-houses, so far from retrograding, are all in a decidedly improved condition. Even the Victoria regia house, and the fern and orchid houses, appeared in the best possible order. The Victoria regia is very flourishing; the whole tank is bordered with fine plants, and the walls are festooned with most beautiful ferns and other rare plants. Luxuriance, abundance, and health seemed to predominate, and I know it will gratify the readers of the Horticulturist *to know that Mr. Stuart has more than sustained its former glory.... It is indeed a rare thing to find such a place as Springbrook change owners without suffering in character. We are glad to learn that Mr. Stuart has not allowed its glory to be marred.*

Anonymous 1862

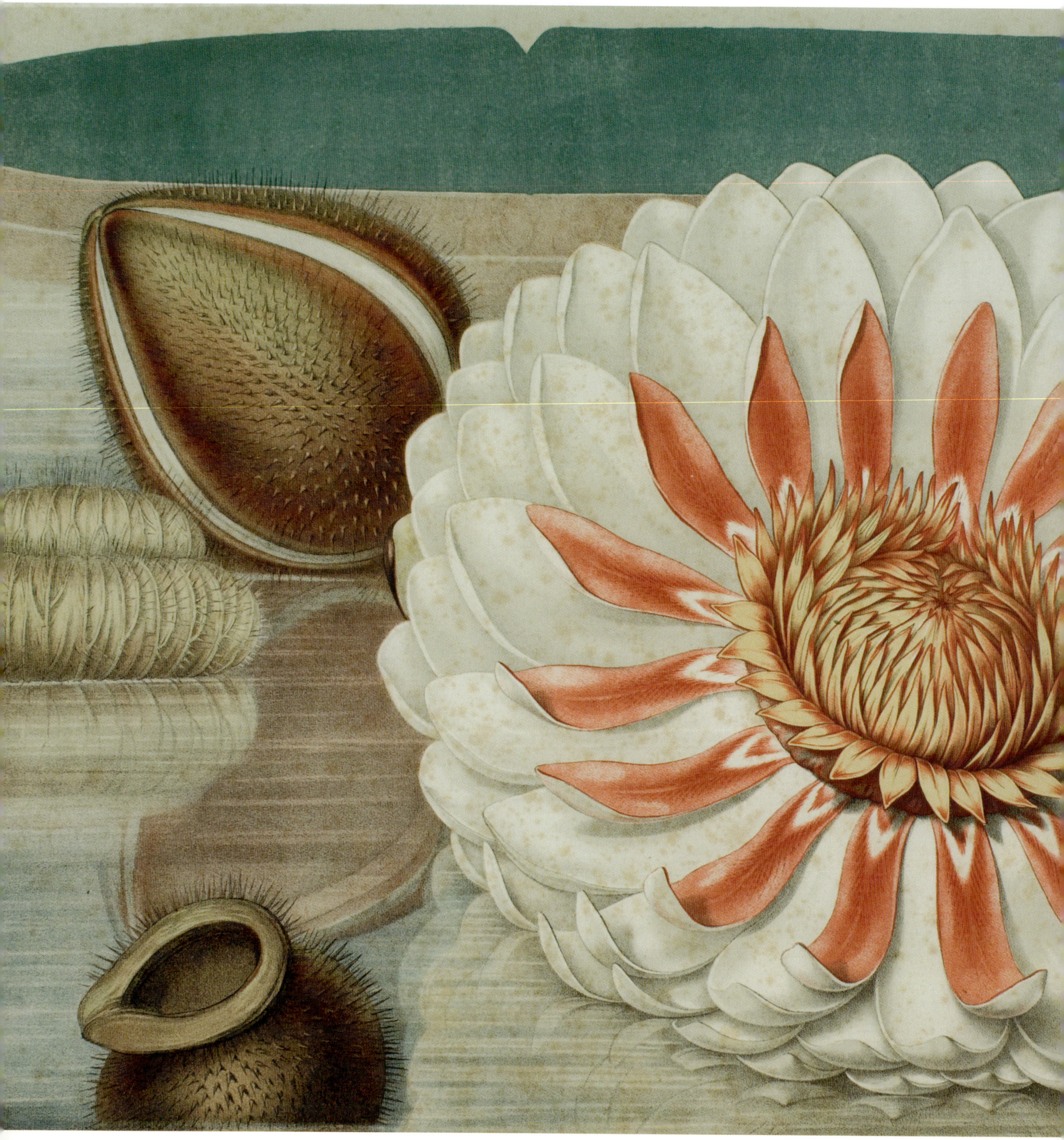

chapter 11

TRANSCONTINENTAL

NEWS OF ROBERT SCHOMBURGK'S 1837 DISCOVERY of a giant South American water lily traveled quickly through the horticultural cognoscenti of the United States. "We noticed the discovery of this splendid flower," wrote editor Charles Mason Hovey in the 1838 issue of the *Magazine of Horticulture, Botany, and All Useful Discoveries and Improvements in Rural Affairs* (Hovey 1838).

Despite taking notice, American gardeners initially left the task of removing this "splendid flower" from her wild state and cultivating her to their British counterparts. Once Joseph Paxton achieved *Victoria*'s successful flowering at Chatsworth in 1849, and Caleb Cope of Philadelphia triumphed with America's first *Victoria* a mere two years later, the garden gates of the entire North American continent were open wide to the queen lily.

Like so many vegetable immigrants before her, the seeds of the Amazonian giant fell on very fertile American soil. Although America's gardeners lacked the sophistication and affluence of European horticulture at the time, they took up the cultivation of *Victoria* with as much enthusiasm as their counterparts in England or Germany. In a few short years, William Hooker of the Royal Botanic Gardens, Kew, noted that *Victoria* had been dispatched around the world and flourished in many places. "Nowhere, however," he wrote, "has this

Second-night flower of *Victoria amazonica*, a lithograph by William Sharp from John Fisk Allen's 1854 book *Victoria Regia or the Great Water Lily of America*.
LONGWOOD GARDENS LIBRARY AND ARCHIVES

The Yellow Mansion of James Dundas on the corner of Broad and Walnut Streets in Philadelphia. The far end of the garden featured a domed Victoria House occupied by the South American lily.
FRANK H. TAYLOR, LIBRARY COMPANY OF PHILADELPHIA

John Scharf and Thompson Westcott, 1884:

His [James Dundas's] taste for horticultural pursuits was strongly marked, and his liberality rendered his gardens and conservatories quite celebrated. In beauty and rarity they were not surpassed by any in Philadelphia. His gardener had become quite a well-known personage, and generally took a number of prizes at the exhibitions of the Horticultural Society. Few conservatories in the country can show so good a collection of air-plants as the one he had in charge, and the great tank containing the Victoria regia *was an unfailing resort for the curious.*

Scharf and Westcott 1884

splendid aquatic succeeded so well (under glass be it observed) as in the United States, and nowhere has its introduction been so highly prized" (Anonymous 1857).

ROOTED IN PHILADELPHIA AND NEW YORK

Thanks to Cope, Philadelphians were ahead of the rest of the country. "The success which has crowned the efforts of Mr. Cope, and the abundant reward which the plant and its flowers afford its beholders, are inducing others to attempt its cultivation," Thomas Meehan, Cope's gardener, reported in 1852 (Allen 1854). Cope distributed seeds to prominent Philadelphians, including Robert Buist, a nurseryman and Meehan's former employer; and James Dundas, a banker and vice president of the Pennsylvania Horticultural Society. Whereas Cope and Dundas had expensive greenhouses built for *Victoria*, Buist erected a small tank in one of his nursery's existing growing houses (Allen 1853). Dundas's gardener, John Pollock, not only succeeded in growing the giant lily in an elegant and spacious Victoria House, but he was also able to grow *Victoria* in an open-air pool (Seaman 1892). In 1860, at the Pennsylvania Horticultural Society's August meeting, Pollock was praised for presenting "a very beautiful and perfect" flower of the Amazon nymph (Anonymous 1860c).

In the early 1870s, planning began for Philadelphia's 1876 Centennial Exhibition on the grounds of Fairmount Park. Many local horticultural enthusiasts expressed the desire to include a special display house built for *Victoria*. Some even "made liberal offers of money to aid in the construction and support of such a house" (Barry et al. 1874). These plans never materialized, but some years after the Centennial, the queen lily took residence in the outdoor pools near the Moorish-style Horticultural Hall, one

VICTORIA: THE SEDUCTRESS

The giant leaf pads of *Victoria* featured prominently among elaborate flower beds laid out in front of Horticultural Hall in Fairmount Park in Philadelphia.
AUTHOR'S COLLECTION

Henry Olcott, 1861:

The tank in the center of this hall [of the American Institute's horticultural show in New York's Palace Garden] is intended for two extraordinary specimens of the Victoria regia *or gigantic American lily, of which the leaves are twenty-one feet [6 m] in circumference and the flower a foot [30 cm] in diameter. One of these is the original plant imported by Mr. Caleb Cope a dozen of years ago, and is exhibited by Mr. Stuart, of Philadelphia. The other, shown by Mr. James Dundas, another gentleman from Philadelphia, and from this lily is expected a mammoth flower, which will burst and exhibit its glories on the 29th inst. [instante mense, or this month].... The flower is not yet fully opened, but will probably be so Friday afternoon or evening, and one must watch it for a whole day to see the beautiful changes which its tints undergo. The opportunity of seeing so rare and wonderful a plant as this, will probably not occur in a generation again, and none should neglect to take advantage of it when thus fortunately presented.*

Olcott 1861

TRANSCONTINENTAL 183

Victoria amazonica in a heated outdoor pool, called Tropical Pond, in Prospect Park, Brooklyn, in the early twentieth century.
Brooklyn Public Library, Brooklyn Collection

of the Exhibition's few permanent remaining structures. There, she instantly became a popular attraction during the summer.

From Philadelphia, *Victoria* was quickly taken to other cities up and down the East Coast. Leaves and flowers of Cope's plant were shown to New Yorkers at their Horticultural Exhibition for the first time in 1852 (Anonymous 1852). For several years, *Victoria*'s flowers traveled by express train from Philadelphia to New York, where she was presented at various horticultural galas. When Cope sold his estate at Springbrook to George Stuart, the new owner continued this tradition. Soon he was joined by Dundas, and in 1861, both Philadelphians exhibited their plants side by side in the same tank at the horticultural show of the American Institute in New York (Olcott 1861).

In later years, New Yorkers took to the cultivation of *Victoria* with the great energy characteristic of that bustling metropolis. Over the next century and a half, the regal lily could be found at a number of prominent addresses, from the New York Botanical Garden and Wave Hill in the Bronx, to the Brooklyn Botanical Garden and Prospect Park in Brooklyn. She even briefly checked into the cozy conservatory of a posh Manhattan residence on the corner of Eighth Avenue in 1864, where she looked out onto the new Central Park.

If it were not for lack of funding, Central Park itself would have had a proper edifice for the South American giant. Original 1857 plans included a conservatory that would enclose a little lake on the east side between Seventy-third and Seventy-fourth streets for the cultivation of *Victoria* and other aquatics (Hoffmann 1889). Unfortunately, no building came of these ambitious plans, and eventually the proposed lake was turned into the formal pond known today as the Conservatory Water.

A NEW FLOWER FOR NEW ENGLAND

Even before *Victoria* was established in New York, she had made a longer leap from Philadelphia to Massachusetts. The first to cultivate Cope's seeds there was John Fisk

---

Anonymous correspondent to the *New York Times*, 1864:

*It seems to me that every man, woman and child should make it a point to see it [*Victoria *in the conservatory on the corner of Eighth Avenue]. It is said that no complete specimen, if any, of this magnificent production of the Amazon region has ever before been seen among us. The cultivator has spared no pains and expense in bringing it to perfection. Indeed, we may rank him almost as an artist, not only in the loving devotion he has shown in producing so rare a specimen of floral beauty, but in the highly tasteful setting he has given to this brilliant Koh-inoor of flowers. . . . The public must go and judge for themselves, for nothing like it has ever been seen in our cold North. You are transported into fairy-land and giant-land.*

Anonymous 1864

John Fisk Allen, a miniature portrait by an unknown artist.
PEABODY ESSEX MUSEUM

Allen of Salem. A successful sea merchant and avid horticulturist, Allen was best known for his work with grapes and credited with introducing the 'Zinfandel' variety to the United States. Allen obtained the seeds of the Amazon lily in late 1852. By mid-January the following year, he had sprouted *Victoria* in one of his grapehouses. Six months later, on July 21, 1853, New England's first flower opened (Allen 1853).

Predictably, this event stirred up as much interest among the citizens of Salem as it had earlier in Philadelphia and New York. The Reverend John L. Russell, vice president of the Essex Institute in Salem, saw in "the crowds of wondering admirers" who came to see Allen's magnificent lily a sign of "a public taste of a superior order springing up" (Russell 1856).

By late summer, Allen knew he needed a larger greenhouse to accommodate a tank of "more ample dimensions" for the expanding royal resident (Allen 1853). Since relocating *Victoria* was impossible, Allen had his old greenhouse dismantled and a larger structure built over the queen lily pool. Before construction was complete, however, the colder September weather settled in, and the tropical nymph began to visibly suffer. Despite this setback, *Victoria* vegetated throughout the fall and early winter months, budding continuously. But in January 1854, excessive snow and ice accumulated on the roof of the greenhouse, reducing the amount of heat and light reaching the lily, and

Charles Hovey, 1853:

Mr. Allen has fitted up a suitable place for his plant in one of his grapehouses; and besides the cost of doing this, the constant exhalation of moisture from the tank has done much injury to the crop of fruit, and lessened the product one half. We presume, however, that he feels amply repaid for this in the success which has attended his efforts, in flowering such a magnificent plant, and in being enabled to show to his friends and the public such a splendid specimen of the floral treasure of the tropics.

Allen 1853

John Russell, address before the members of the Essex Institute in Salem, 1854:

Its artificially produced blossoming, under remarkable conditions of vigor and luxuriance, displays what patience can do, and what degree of success shall follow. The creation, so to speak, of a new feature of attraction in our city, elevates our standard of horticulture which is already high. The crowds of wondering admirers, who have been attracted by its novelty, give assurance that there is a public taste of a superior order springing up; a taste which can appreciate a work so actively undertaken and laudably accomplished.... There were many eager eyes beside mine own watching its developing loveliness, and I believe that its rare beauty, thus gradually disclosed, touched many a heart. We stood as worshippers at its shrine; indeed! who could but feel that the August Presence was there in one of the many forms of mysterious wonder of this fair world.

Russell 1856

The Amazon lily growing in an outdoor pool at Sandyside, the garden of John Simpkins in Yarmouth, Massachusetts, in 1888.
LONGWOOD GARDENS LIBRARY AND ARCHIVES

> **John Fisk Allen, 1854:**
>
> *Had it not been for the unusual cloudy weather, I have good reasons for supposing that the plant would have survived [the winter of 1853–54]. After October, when continuous cloudy and stormy weather prevailed, it would suffer severely; reviving and giving hopes of its recovery on the re-appearance of sunshine. An excessive fall of snow, attended with great cold and high wind, on the last days of December, and repeated early in January, so covered up the house with ice and snow as effectually to shut out the light and warmth of the sun for a week or more. Continued cloudy weather during January completed its destruction, having survived rather over one year, and continuing to send up flower buds to the last.*
>
> Allen 1854

the one-year-old plant died. Undeterred, Allen obtained fresh seeds from both Cope in Philadelphia and Hooker at Kew and continued to cultivate the lily for some years.

Inspired by Allen's example, other Massachusetts gardeners took on the challenging South American giant. In Worcester, D. Waldo Lincoln, the city's mayor and an eminent patron of horticulture, grew the lily in an open-air pool (Seaman 1892). Congressman John Simpkins also raised *Victoria* outdoors, in Yarmouth, where she flourished "with greater luxuriance and success than in any private garden in the United States" (Anonymous 1888). For his efforts, Simpkins earned a silver medal at the annual exhibition of the Massachusetts Horticultural Society in Boston in 1887 (Anonymous 1887). Meanwhile, in Northampton, William W. Lee, owner of a cutlery manufactory, built a heated pond some 13 m (42 feet) in diameter on the grounds surrounding his factory in 1891. Crowds poured in to witness the spectacle of the Amazon nymph. "During the season the ponds are visited by thousands of people," Lee observed, "and on Sundays, and in the evenings when illuminated, the enjoyment of the public is most gratifying to me and worth many times the expense of maintenance" (Anonymous 1892).

AQUATIC NURSERIES

As *Victoria* expanded north from Philadelphia, she established two important outposts in New Jersey: Bordentown on the bank of the Delaware River and Clifton in Passaic County.

Bordentown was the birthplace of the first aquatic nursery in the United States. One year after its opening in 1876, owner Edmund D. Sturtevant had *Victoria* thriving in an outdoor pool (Sturtevant 1879). In 1886, Sturtevant received seeds of *Victoria amazonica*, collected by Edward Rand near Pará (today's Belém), Brazil. The plants grown from these seeds developed leaves with taller, distinctly wavy margins. Widely distributed by Sturtevant, they soon became known in cultivation as variety

In 1894, William Tricker introduced *Victoria cruziana*, initially thought to be a variety of *Victoria amazonica*. It was distributed under the name *trickerii*. Here it is growing in a heated pond in the garden of Scotto Nash in Clifton, New Jersey.
LONGWOOD GARDENS LIBRARY AND ARCHIVES

randii (Conard 1953). This new variety received a silver medal from the Massachusetts Horticultural Society when it was exhibited in September 1886 (Anonymous 1886).

Sturtevant's outdoor pool, which measured about 6 m (20 feet) wide and 9 m (30 feet) long, was situated close to a greenhouse. Heating pipes that extended from the greenhouse warmed the pool, except on the hottest summer days (Sturtevant 1883). Sturtevant saw his success as proof that the thrill of the queen lily did not need to be restricted to men of considerable wealth who could afford to build an aquatic house. "I am confident," he wrote, "that if it were more generally known with what little trouble and at what comparatively small expense it can be grown in perfection in the open air, its culture would become more common" (Sturtevant 1883). Over the next decade, Sturtevant became a leading promoter of the outdoor culture of aquatic plants, supplying seeds, plants, instruction, and encouragement. He contributed immensely to the popularization of the Amazonian wonder in the United States.

In Clifton, New Jersey, William M. Tricker opened another influential aquatic nursery in the early 1890s. His catalogs offered both the typical form of *Victoria amazonica* and the variety *randii* (Anonymous 1895d). In 1894, Tricker received from Europe what he believed to be yet another variety of the Amazonian species. Subsequently distributed under the name *trickerii*, it turned out to be *Victoria cruziana*, originally brought to Europe from Corrientes in Argentina and possibly the earliest case of the Santa Cruz lily's introduction into the United States (Conard 1953).

William Tricker, 1897:

From the first these seedlings exhibited a feature which marked them as entirely distinct from the original form, the leaves being light green and mottled with reddish brown on the face, purplish below. The rapid growth and the early cupping of the leaf were also very noticeable. In its permanent quarters the growth of the plant was still more remarked, and it was soon evident it would outrun the older plants of the other variety, which in fact it did, at a very early date. The first flower was produced about July 15, and during August the same plant produced twelve magnificent flowers; these on first opening were pure white, and the second day a lively rose color. At one time as many as nine flowers and buds were visible in different stages of development, while var. randii *produced but half that number, and seldom had more than five presentable leaves at one time.*

Tricker 1897

"It made such a record and proved to be so entirely distinct from anything before seen in the United States," noted Tricker in 1897. This new Argentinean *Victoria* outperformed the older form when grown outdoors and in time helped spread the popularity of *Victoria* around the country.

HEADING SOUTH

Victoria's southerly migration out of Philadelphia took her first to Baltimore, where members of the Maryland Horticultural Society had admired homegrown Amazonian lilies as early as 1853 during the autumnal exhibition (Saunders 1853). From Baltimore, she headed straight to the nation's capital in Washington, D.C. There, the queen lily lived in the White House greenhouses built in the early 1850s (which were later demolished to make room for the construction of the West Wing in 1902). Surprisingly, one guest visiting these greenhouses in 1860 left a less-than-flattering account of the decrepit conditions the South American nymph had to endure there. "Dirt and disorder, decayed leaves, under potted half starved plants, met your view at every turn," he wrote, condemning the condition of the house as a disgrace to either the gardener in charge, or to the nation, in not providing sufficient help to properly care for the plants. To complete this scene of despair, "the aquarium was filled with dirty, green, stagnant water, in the midst of which floated two leaves of an unhappy aquatic, which you would have to be informed was the peerless *Victoria*" (Anonymous 1860b).

Ironically, while *Victoria*'s early home near the executive branch of the government was not favorable, thirty years later, she found great success at the other end of Washington's Pennsylvania Avenue. It became the site of a record-breaking triumph for growing *Victoria*.

At the foot of Capitol Hill, on the grounds of the United States Botanic Garden, stood the Bartholdi Fountain, created by Frédéric Auguste Bartholdi, a French sculptor best known for his iconic Statue of Liberty. Originally designed for the Centennial Exhibition in Philadelphia, the fountain was later purchased by the federal government and reassembled in Washington. In 1891, William R. Smith, superintendent of the United States Botanic Garden, obtained seeds of *Victoria* from Sturtevant in New Jersey. After Smith started the young plants, he placed one in the basin, about 12 m (40 feet) across, surrounding the fountain. Although the water was unheated, the lily flourished. Soon, her leaves reached a whopping 2.24 m (7 feet) in diameter, then the largest on record (Seaman 1892). An estimated forty thousand people came to see the flowers. "From our experience here," wrote one of them, "there does not seem any reason why these extraordinary plants cannot be grown anywhere in the Southern States wherever there is a small pond and any one who will take the pains of starting them" (Seaman 1892).

Since that time, the Bartholdi Fountain has been relocated to a nearby park and sadly deprived of the company of its queen lily. But *Victoria* has appeared at other locations in Washington: The United States

A water lily pond in Riverton, New Jersey, at a nursery owned by Henry Dreer, to whom William Tricker sold his business in 1897. The pond featured two forms of Victoria *commonly cultivated in the United States at the turn of the twentieth century—*randii *of* Victoria amazonica *(in the front) and* trickerii *of* Victoria cruziana *(in the back).*
AUTHOR'S COLLECTION

National Arboretum has shown the South American nymph on and off in its Aquatic Garden since the 1970s. Similarly, the National Zoo hosted *Victoria* on a number of occasions in one of its ponds.

While the southern United States offered the most congenial climate for cultivating the Amazonian colossus, the American Civil War and its economic aftermath halted most nonessential horticultural pursuits. Nevertheless, by the 1880s, the queen lily was reported to be thriving in a "carp pond" in Georgia (Seaman 1892). And in the 1950s, the central Georgia town of Thomaston, outside Atlanta, boasted a remarkable display of *Victoria*. Albert Matthews, a successful inventor and industrialist, built a pool over 70 m (231 feet) long in his Thomaston garden called Crystal Hill (Hudson 1956). The South American wonder basked in the southern sun with an array of lesser tropical water lilies. More recently, starting in 1993, *Victoria* also made an appearance in Georgia's capital city when William H. Anderson of Conyers, Georgia, nurtured one plant for the Atlanta Botanical Garden (Anderson 1993).

Further south, Florida was naturally predisposed to embrace the giant lily without reservation. Although Florida was blessed with a climate better attuned to the Amazonian wonder than any other state in the Union and had an unmatched public passion for all things tropical, the Sunshine State had to wait for its first view. Perhaps the earliest to feature *Victoria* in a major way was the McKee Jungle Gardens in Vero Beach, on Florida's Atlantic Coast. The gardens, which opened in 1932, were renowned for their aquatic displays, including a major presentation of *Victoria*. Unfortunately, the gardens closed in the mid-1970s, but when they reopened a quarter century later, the South American giant once again dazzled visiting crowds.

Today, Florida boasts more gardens with giant lilies than any other region of the country. In northern Florida, the Kanapaha Botanical Gardens in Gainesville displays queen lilies in ponds

A record-breaking *Victoria* thrived in the basin of the Bartholdi Fountain on the grounds of the United States Botanic Garden in Washington, D.C., in 1891.
MARIETTA COLLEGE LIBRARY

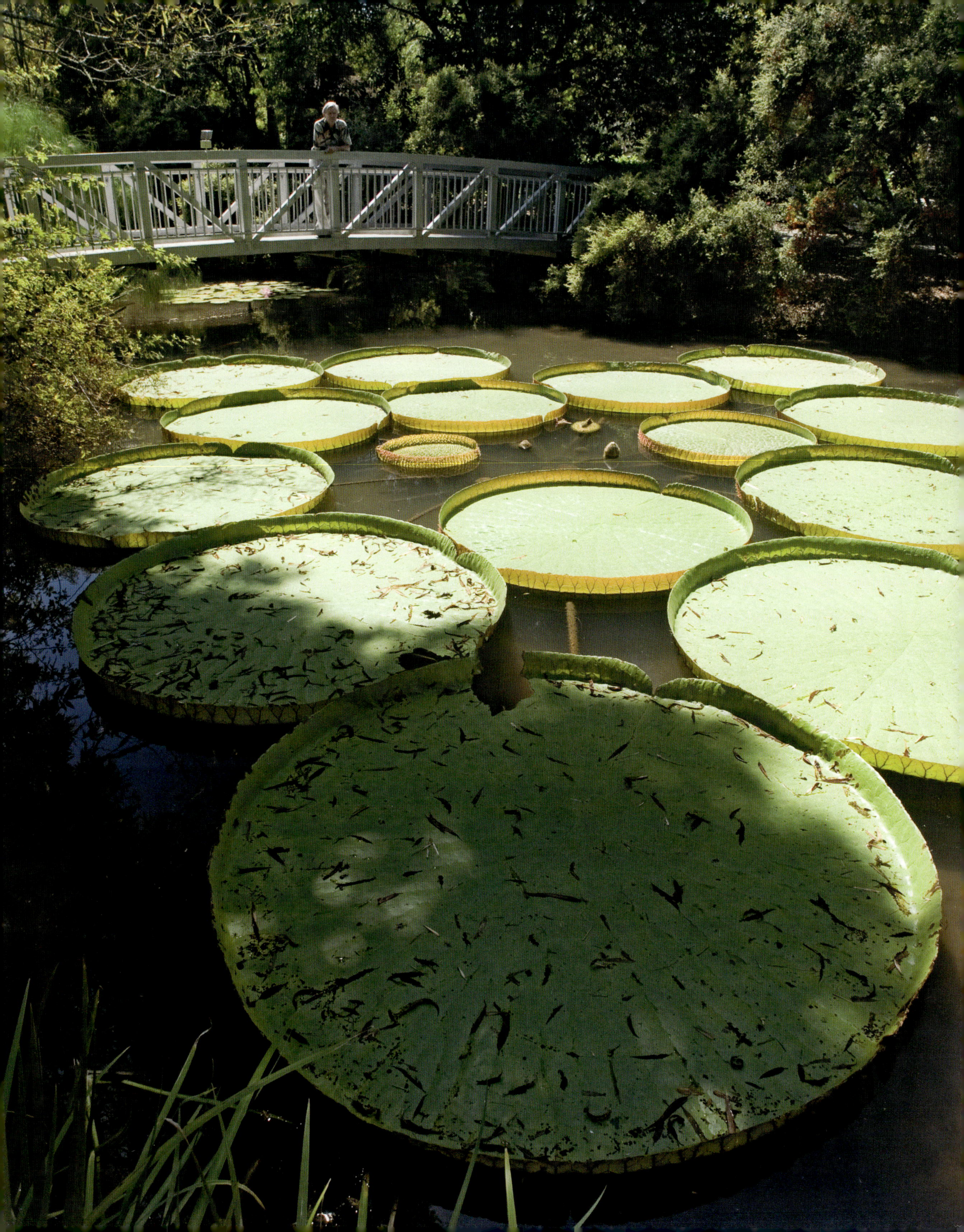

frequented by alligators. In Cocoa Beach, Kit and Ben Knotts have earned worldwide acclaim for their breeding work with *Victoria,* which is on display in their beautiful oceanfront garden. Near the southern tip of the peninsula, Fairchild Tropical Botanical Garden in Coral Gables has incorporated a Victoria Pool into its luscious plantings. But perhaps *Victoria*'s latest and most dramatic Florida residence is on the state's west coast—in the Naples Botanical Garden, where the South American nymph inhabits Brazil-themed pools joined by exuberant water cascades.

The southernmost state in the Union, Florida offers *Victoria* a congenial climate and the attention of dedicated gardeners. The results of the genuine fascination with and affection for the South American nymph can be observed today in many parts of the state. At far left, opposite page, is Kanapaha Botanical Gardens in Gainesville. Left to right, above, are Naples Botanical Garden, Knotts' Garden in Cocoa Beach, and McKee Jungle Gardens in Vero Beach.
TOMASZ ANIŚKO / LONGWOOD GARDENS

WESTWARD HO!

At the same time that *Victoria* was holding court in private and public gardens along the eastern United States, she also began her westward migration. After crossing the Appalachians, the nymph established residence in every state strung along the 40th parallel from Pennsylvania to Colorado, where she leaped over the Rockies to reach California.

In Pittsburgh, near Pennsylvania's western edge, the queen lily was given her own elegant Victoria House at the renowned Phipps Conservatory when it opened in 1893 (Guttenberg 1894). Just across the border from Pennsylvania, Ohio led the pack of the Midwestern states, successfully cultivating *Victoria* as early as 1855 (Murray 1856). Nicholas Longworth of Cincinnati, a "pioneer of horticulture in the expanding West" and the "father of American grape-culture" (Bailey 1953), is credited with the lily's introduction there. Initially, Longworth nurtured his *Victoria* in a greenhouse. Three years later, however, he shared a surplus seedling with a neighbor, Charles Anderson, who

Grassyfork Fisheries in Martinsville, Indiana, the world's largest goldfish hatchery in the mid-twentieth century, exhibited *Victoria* lilies in their demonstration pools.
AUTHOR'S COLLECTION

attempted to grow the queen lily in a small open-ground pond. Although the first year was not successful, by 1859, the outdoor lily grew so vigorously that she even surpassed the specimen in Longworth's greenhouse.

In 1860, the news reached Ohio that *Victoria* had flowered outdoors in Dundas's garden in Philadelphia—initially thought to be the first outdoor flowering in the country. Swiftly, a proud, albeit anonymous, Cincinnatian countered in a letter to the Philadelphia-based *Gardener's Monthly and Horticultural Advertiser,* claiming the priority for Charles Anderson.

West of Cincinnati, *Victoria* landed in a most unlikely place: the small town of Martinsville, Indiana, then home to Grassyfork Fisheries. Grassyfork was hailed by its owners as the world's largest goldfish hatchery. There, among six hundred fishponds spread over as many hectares, the giant water lily delighted customers who visited the hatchery in the early decades of the twentieth century.

THRIVING ON THE GREAT PLAINS

Further west, the queen lily's next stop would eventually be recognized as the finest showcase of water lilies anywhere in the world. In St. Louis, Missouri, America's Gateway to the West, Henry Shaw captivated the city with his remarkable undertaking.

Shaw—an English immigrant who had made a fortune selling hardware supplies to pioneers heading West—developed what became the Missouri Botanical Garden and Tower Grove Park. His inspiration for the garden was Chatsworth, the estate of the duke of Devonshire, located near Sheffield, Shaw's birthplace.

Anonymous correspondent to the *Gardener's Monthly and Horticultural Advertiser*, 1860:

In your paper for October it is claimed that the Victoria regia *was this summer grown for the first time in the open air in this country. We did suppose that our hog-killing city (Porkopolis) in these western wilds was behind you in all things but hog-killing; but I now discover my error. In the summer of 1858, Charles Anderson, whose residence adjoins Mr. Longworth's, obtained from him a root of the* Victoria, *and planted it in his small pond. It did not grow well that year. The supposed cause was, that there was not enough earth in the pond. In 1859 ground was put in the pond, and a new root planted. It grew more vigorously than in Mr. Longworth's greenhouse, which is within one hundred yards of Mr. Anderson's pond.*

Anonymous 1860d

James Gurney standing on a leaf of the giant South American lily, which he introduced to St. Louis in 1894.
TOWER GROVE PARK

Anonymous, tribute to James Gurney in the *St. Louis Star*, 1910:

With infinite patience and care and skill the gardener while in the service of Her Majesty, Queen Victoria, produced the wonderful royal lily, Victoria regia, *for the first time beyond its native home in the waters of the Amazon. With the contemplation of this triumph of his skill there is associated the... recollection of the humble gardener's exultation when the first lily was inspected by Her Majesty, Queen Victoria, who came to the artificial lily pond on the arm of Napoleon III. Prince Albert, consort of the Queen, was a member of the group of admirers of the beautiful flower and he led by the hand a little boy, his son, the late King Edward.... Mr. Gurney remembers the intense interest taken by his royal visitors in the beautiful floral specimen. Especially was this true in regard to the Queen, who asked many questions concerning the propagation and development of the wonderful lily of the Amazon, which had been the marvel of the aborigines and the admiration of discoverers, and which now as an exotic blooming in her own dominions bore her name.*

Anonymous 1910

Shaw had traveled to England in 1851 to attend London's Great Exhibition. By then a man of considerable wealth, he had stopped first at the acclaimed ducal estate in Devonshire. He saw Chatsworth at the height of its development, complete with Paxton's latest achievement—the Victoria House and its queenly resident—and believed it was something to aspire to (Grove 2005).

Back in America, Shaw decided that his adopted home of St. Louis deserved a public botanical garden of comparable stature. To accomplish this Herculean task, he recruited the services of another Englishman, James Gurney. Trained at several highly regarded horticultural establishments, including London's Regent's Park and Woburn, the estate of the duke of Bedford, Gurney brought to St. Louis a wealth of plant knowledge then unattainable in the western frontier lands.

During his tenure at Regent's Park, Gurney had been in charge of growing one of England's first *Victoria* lilies. When it flowered, the young gardener was given the honor of showing it to his monarch, Queen Victoria, who was visiting Regent's Park with both the

George Pring (right) photographed with fellow gardener George E. McClure shortly after joining the staff of the Missouri Botanical Garden in 1906.
MISSOURI BOTANICAL GARDEN

Prince Consort and Louis Napoleon, then president of France and soon to become Emperor Napoleon III (Conard and Hus 1907). This encounter left a lasting impression on Gurney and likely helped to solidify his lifelong dedication to *Victoria*, which he carried with him to St. Louis.

In St. Louis, Gurney created probably the finest displays of aquatic flora that America had seen. By 1894, this included the queen lily (Grove 2005). *Victoria* captured people's imaginations. Newspapers were abuzz about the aquatic colossus, and a special evening reception for dignitaries was organized (Anderson 1965). In 1895, crowds coming to see the Amazonian wonder lilies swelled the number of visitors in the garden and park by a third, reaching a record thirty thousand on one September Sunday (Trelease 1896).

By the turn of the twentieth century, the Amazonian nymph was a mainstay at both Tower Grove Park and the Missouri Botanical Garden, an unmistakable hallmark of St. Louis and of Gurney's English traditions. Gurney remained at the Missouri Botanical Garden after Shaw's death in 1889. Then in 1903, he became superintendent of the neighboring Tower Grove Park.

Responsibility for the South American lilies and the rest of the aquatic collection in the Botanical Garden passed to another young English immigrant trained at Kew, George H. Pring. Pring started in 1906 and moved up the ranks to become superintendent of the garden in 1928, a post he held until his retirement in 1963. Building on Gurney's success with *Victoria* and other water lilies, Pring expanded the aquatic displays at the Missouri Botanical Garden and elevated them to a class unmatched anywhere. To Gurney's *Victoria amazonica*, he added the second species, *Victoria cruziana* (Anderson 1965).

At the neighboring Tower Grove Park, *Victoria* has been featured in meandering earthen ponds fancifully woven among exuberant seasonal arrangements of tropical plants. The presentation evokes the backwaters of the Amazon, or at least the way the public imagines them. In contrast, the Missouri Botanical Garden has framed the South American lilies in formal pools. In both locations, *Victoria* has enjoyed a dazzling complement of *Nymphaea* water lilies and other aquatic subjects.

The Missouri Botanical Garden's first *Victoria* pool was built on the south side of a small conservatory called the Linnaean House, which conveniently piped hot water into the pool. In 1913, a larger water garden was built in front of the newly erected Palm House. Four years later, pools in that garden were given concrete walls and redesigned to their present-day form.

When the futuristic Climatron replaced the old Palm House in 1960, a new, more contemporary pool was added for *Victoria*, with a plexiglas tunnel permitting views of the lilies from below. Although immensely popular, the new pool presented a range of challenges for the staff, from wearing a scuba outfit to clean the "Aquatunnel" to maintaining the required water temperature. With time, shade from nearby vegetation had a detrimental effect on *Victoria*. When the Climatron was renovated in 1988, the pool was eliminated.

Even though Pring grew both *Victoria* species in St. Louis as far back as 1915, he never attempted to cross them—surprising, perhaps, considering his prodigious hybridization of *Nymphaea* water lilies

Since 1894 *Victoria* has been enchanting visitors coming to the Missouri Botanical Garden. A formal pool, shown here, was heated with water redirected from the nearby Linnaean House.
MISSOURI BOTANICAL GARDEN

(Anonymous 1915). But in the late 1950s, when Pring was helping Russell Seibert, director of Longwood Gardens and his son-in-law, create a new world-class aquatic display, he suggested making such a cross. Eventually, Pring's and Seibert's combined efforts gave birth to a new lily that reflected the best traits of both parents and was christened 'Longwood Hybrid'. When this hybrid was grown for the first time in St. Louis in 1963, she became an instant hit with both the public and the staff at the Missouri Botanical Garden. The new hybrid's most important advantage was her ability to flourish outdoors in unheated water and to develop leaves of "spectacular size and elegant proportions" (Anderson 1965). As Pring reported to Seibert in July of that year, 'Longwood Hybrid' was "really going to town here" (Pring 1963).

FROM THE HEARTLAND TO THE COAST

Once Gurney and Pring, the two Englishmen in St. Louis, proved that *Victoria* could thrive on North America's Great Plains, others followed their example. In fact, Missouri's western neighbor, Kansas, provided a spectacular illustration of what horticultural ingenuity can accomplish in the most unlikely places. If little Dorothy from *The Wonderful Wizard of Oz*—the classic 1900 children's book by Frank Baum, which portrayed Kansas as a harsh and desolate place—had returned to Topeka in the mid-twentieth century, she might not have recognized her home state. There, in the city's Gage Park, she would find a fanciful scene not unlike the one from Oz in the 1939 film: a vast pool, surrounded by thousands of rosebushes, featuring giant South American lilies along with countless *Nymphaea*.

From Topeka, following Interstate 70 to the Continental Divide, is *Victoria*'s next dramatic outpost: the Denver Botanic Garden, where the queen lily has made a home since the 1980s. What would seem to be the most improbable of juxtapositions—the fragile Amazonian nymph amid craggy snow-capped mountains—was made possible by the pioneering efforts of garden director Merle M. Moore and gardener Joseph V. Tomocik. In 1984, the two introduced the first *Victoria cruziana,* brought from Longwood Gardens in Pennsylvania. Six years later, in 1990, Robert H. Meade, a geologist and hydrologist with the United States Geological Survey and an authority on Amazon hydrology, presented the garden with its first *Victoria amazonica* seeds. And beginning in 1999, Nancy Styler, a founder of the Victoria Conservancy—a group promoting cultivation of the South American giants and sharing their seeds—provided young seedlings of both species.

Doran Lily Pool was named for the Topeka attorney who spearheaded fundraising for its 1930s construction. There, despite all the odds and the challenges of the Kansas climate, *Victoria* was luxuriously accommodated among an assortment of other aquatic subjects.
AUTHOR'S COLLECTION

West of Denver stretches a territory that has never been conquered by *Victoria*'s charms. In fact, one has to travel 2,000 km (about 1,200 miles) through the mountains and deserts before seeing another Amazonian lily. She can be found in San Francisco, on the western edge of the continent.

When it came to horticultural endeavors, California was not far behind the East Coast. As early as 1878, the public there was "commencing to show a lively taste for ponds and aquariums" and hoped to see the South American lilies "in a short time" (Anonymous 1878). The first attempt to cultivate *Victoria* in San Francisco failed, because the seeds grown by one floral firm were pronounced "defective" (Anonymous 1878). On the second try, however, at least two locations in the city boasted success with the famed Amazonian wonder. The first was planted in a tank in one of the conservatories at the "costly and grand" Nob Hill mansion of Mark Hopkins, one of the founders of the Central Pacific Railroad (Anonymous 1878). It was followed a year later by a specimen "in magnificent health," displayed in the newly opened conservatory in Golden Gate Park, known today as the Conservatory of the Flowers (Anonymous 1879).

In 1894, Edmund D. Sturtevant, the enterprising aquatic nurseryman from New Jersey, relocated his operation to Hollywood, California, where he opened it under the name Cahuenga Water Gardens. For years, Sturtevant supplied the sprawling estates in Hollywood and around Los Angeles with a range of aquatic and exotic plants.

Victoria lilies in an aquatic house of the conservatories at Lyndhurst Castle in Tarrytown, New York, at the end of the nineteenth century.
LONGWOOD GARDENS LIBRARY AND ARCHIVES

During the World's Columbian Exposition in Chicago in 1893, Victoria was displayed in that city in a number of outdoor ponds heated seasonally with water diverted from the nearby conservatories, including this one in Lincoln Park.
AUTHOR'S COLLECTION

Of course, the fabled Amazon nymphs were among them. *Victoria* performed well outdoors there, even without supplemental heating, although cool California nights were blamed for her having leaves with less than record-smashing dimensions (Sturtevant 1895).

FILLING IN THE GAPS

The queen lily's territorial claims along the 40th parallel—the circle of latitude stretching west from Philadelphia to the Pacific—were supplemented by rapid expansion to the north and south. In the north, after winning over New York City, *Victoria* befriended many of the era's *nouveau riche* industrialists in that state. In Tarrytown, the lily embellished the conservatories of railroad magnate Jay Gould at Lyndhurst Castle. In Rochester, she graced a 20-m (66-foot) long tank in the greenhouses of Kimball Castle, belonging to tobacco tycoon William S. Kimball (Beard 1886).

Despite Sturtevant's and Tricker's efforts in the late nineteenth century to popularize *Victoria* among wider masses, "indulgence in the new cult involved considerable labor and expense, and only the few could enjoy such a floral luxury" (Tricker 1897). A turning point perhaps was the 1893 World's Columbian Exposition. Millions of spectators converged in Chicago, where the Amazonian colossus put on a mind-boggling display in water basins gracing the entrance to the Horticultural Building (White and Igleheart 1893). *Victoria*'s popularity likely sparked interest among the many visiting public officials to feature the vegetable wonder in their own city, a trend that soon spread from Chicago's Lincoln Park to St. Paul's Como Park in Minnesota.

South of the 40th parallel, Tennessee introduced the queen lily to places far different from the usual botanical gardens or wealthy estates. In fact, before 1859, a special circular Victoria House, 10 m (33 feet) in diameter, was built on the grounds of the Hospital for the Insane in Nashville (Anonymous 1859). The institution was known for its extensive ornamental gardens, of which the Amazon nymph became a part. These gardens were cared for by hospital patients—a nineteenth-century prototype of today's horticultural therapy.

While the hospital no longer exists, a traveler to Nashville today may nevertheless be surprised to find *Victoria* has made a home in, of all places, the Opryland Hotel. One of Nashville's prime attractions, the hotel's spacious indoor atrium gardens encompass over 3.5 hectares (9 acres) featuring exuberant fountains, waterfalls, and even a small lake with an island in the middle. The Amazon lily, however, is stationed in the outdoor pools in front of the hotel's lobbies, where it prefers Nashville's summer heat and open skies to the relative comfort of the air-conditioned atrium.

In 1860, Nicholas Longworth, the Cincinnati pioneer of *Victoria* culture, sent the lily down the Ohio and Mississippi rivers to New Orleans, convinced that she could be grown effortlessly there. "It will be their own fault," he believed, "if all their low, shallow streams of water are not covered with the plant, and abound in flowers nearly all the season" (Anonymous 1860c). Although Longworth's vision of Amazon lilies taking over the Mississippi delta never materialized, by the 1880s, the lilies were well established in a number of New Orleans gardens. An anonymous witness described the opening of a *Victoria* flower in one of these gardens, judging that from "appearances and expressions of pleasure, between two and three hundred people were very much delighted thereby" (Anonymous 1885a). Today, *Victoria* can be seen in multiple Louisiana public gardens, including the New Orleans Botanical Gardens, the Audubon Zoo, and the Louisiana Purchase Gardens and Zoo.

If a traveler wandering along the Gulf Coast from New Orleans to Texas in the 1960s happened upon Galveston on the barrier island by the same name, he or she might have discovered *Victoria* thriving in the garden of Hans Guldmann. Thanks to his acquaintance with Pring in St. Louis, Guldmann was among the first to obtain seeds and introduce the queen lily to the Lone Star State (Pring 1961).

Twenty-five years later and some 600 km (373 miles) northwest of Galveston, the city of San Angelo welcomed the South American nymph when aquatic gardener Ken Landon was put in charge of a neglected early-1930s swimming pool in Civic League Park. Challenging himself to create the world's most comprehensive collection of *Nymphaea* water lilies, Landon spent some fifteen years turning his aquatic dream into reality. By the late 1980s, *Victoria* joined San Angelo's stunning array of water lilies and grew to huge proportions, clearly benefiting from Landon's expert care and the blazing Texan sun. With some two hundred varieties of *Nymphaea* in his collection, Landon surrounded the queen lily with the largest aquatic royal court ever assembled.

Of course, accounting for all places in the United States where *Victoria* has found a home would be impossible. Considering the plant's ephemeral nature, it is clear that American gardeners succeeded in cultivating the giant lily in all corners of the continent—barring the highest mountains, driest deserts, and most frigid northern extremities. Whether motivated by curiosity, genuine fascination, commercial interests, or the prospect of prestige and recognition, the queen lily's American enthusiasts found ways to overcome many obstacles. They allowed one of Nature's most inspiring creations to flourish and garner public acclaim in America's big cities, great plains, prairies, mountain foothills, the shores of two oceans, plus the Gulf of Mexico—places that could not be farther removed from the lily's native home in the backwaters of South America's great rivers.

In Europe, *Victoria* culture was primarily pioneered by the members of the aristocracy. In the United States, however, it was the emerging class of entrepreneurs who led the way, followed closely by anyone able to dig a pond, fill it with water, and, in the northern tier of the country, find a way to keep it warm. By the late nineteenth century, inexpensive seeds were easily available from a variety of aquatic nurseries. For those unwilling or unable to cultivate the giant lily from a seed, young plants were available for a few dollars more and shipped to any place reachable within three days (Conard and Hus 1907). Thus, *Victoria* entered the realm of American commerce and popular culture. A century and a half since her introduction into cultivation, the Amazonian lily has, in many ways, become the American lily.

Crowds gather to admire the South American lilies in a tropical lily pond of Como Park in St. Paul, Minnesota.
AUTHOR'S COLLECTION

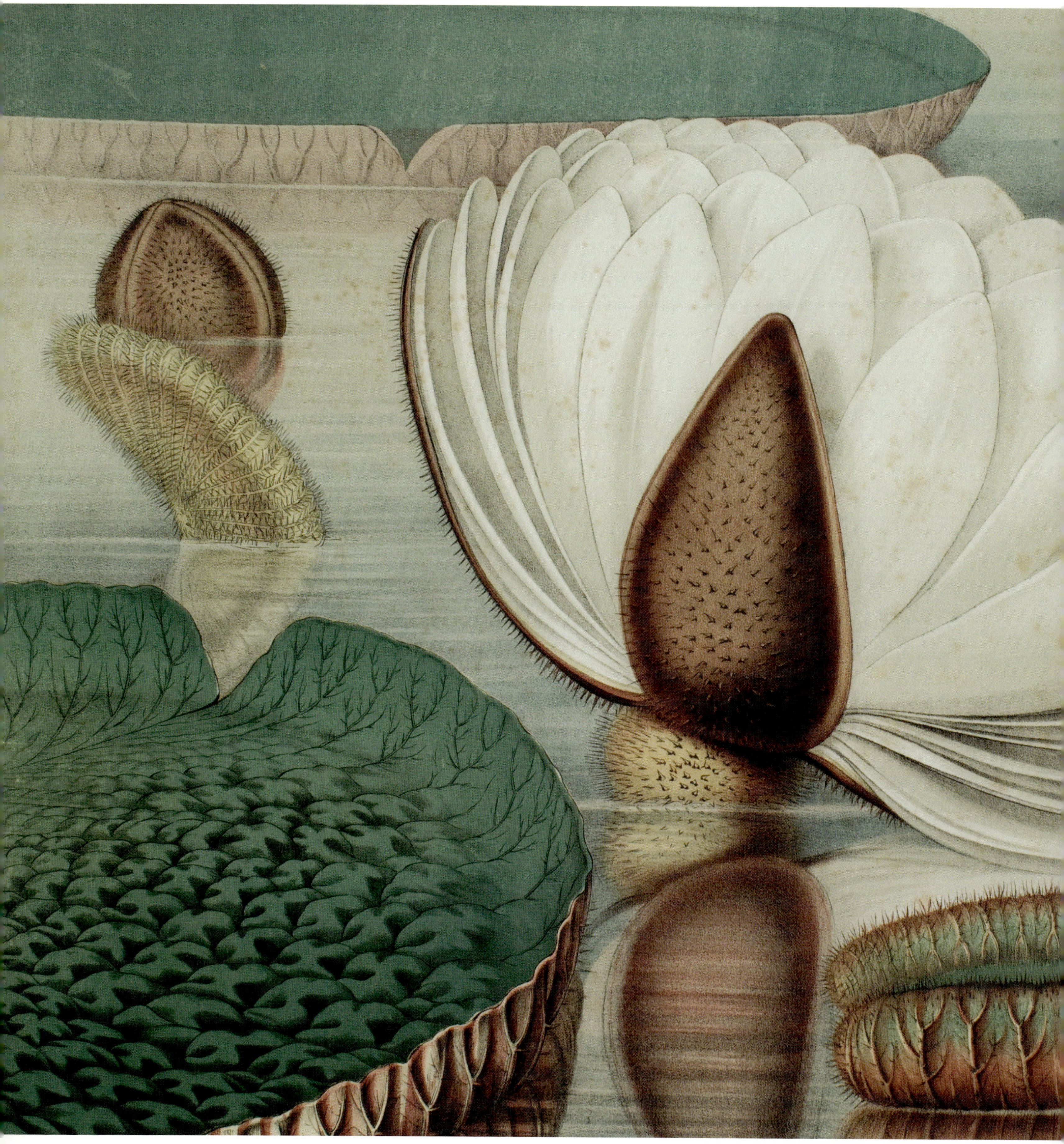

chapter 12

THE BIRTH OF THE HYBRID

IN 1955, LONGWOOD GARDENS—THE FORMER ESTATE of Pierre S. du Pont, near Kennett Square, Pennsylvania— became a public garden. Russell J. Seibert, then director of the Los Angeles State and County Arboretum, was asked to be Longwood's first director. Among many novel ideas Seibert brought to Longwood was his appreciation for water lilies, especially *Victoria*. At that time, Longwood had no aquatic plants in its collections, "except for periodic algae invasions of the fountain systems," as Seibert noted. He was determined to change this.

Seibert's earliest encounters with *Victoria* can probably be traced back to the 1930s, during his teaching years at the Missouri Botanical Garden, then home to undoubtedly the finest display of water lilies in the United States. As a graduate assistant at St. Louis's Washington University, Seibert instructed botany classes at the Botanical Garden. He came to know garden superintendent George Pring, from whom he regularly obtained plants for his classes. During those days, Seibert must have walked by the famed outdoor pools countless times. These featured *Victoria* flowers, which had been skillfully raised each year under the watchful eye of Pring. A few years later, when Seibert married Pring's daughter Isabelle, his connection to *Victoria* became familial.

First-night flower of *Victoria amazonica*, a lithograph by William Sharp for John Fisk Allen's 1854 book *Victoria Regia or the Great Water Lily of America*.
LONGWOOD GARDENS LIBRARY AND ARCHIVES

A DRAMATIC NEW ADDITION

Within his first three months at Longwood, Seibert proposed building heated outdoor pools for tropical water lilies. The area he recommended was a grassy courtyard enclosed between the conservatory's Exhibition Hall and a smaller greenhouse used for potted azaleas. In the spring of 1956, Seibert wrote to Henry B. du Pont, president of the board, to request earmark funding for the water lily pools. He reasoned that the pools would provide "floral displays during the hot summer periods when the conservatory floral displays are at a low ebb" and added that the tropical plants would introduce "a group of plants not yet featured at Longwood Gardens but in which there exists an increasing public interest" (Seibert 1956b).

In March 1956, the first plans were drafted. They included one central pool, over 15.25 m (50 feet) in diameter, flanked by a series of three varying sized pools in each of the four quadrants. They were to be built of concrete with a pale sky-blue-tinted finish and filled with water heated to a minimum of 21°C (70°F) and filtered every sixteen hours. In addition, floodlighting was to be installed for evening displays of night-blooming lilies. The plans also called for equipping the potted azalea house with five indoor tanks and converting it into a support facility necessary for raising young water lily plants. The total cost of the construction was projected at $68,500.

In the fall of that year, the contract for construction of the pools was finalized, and by the following spring, the work was well advanced. Preparations were under way for planting in the pools by the end of May.

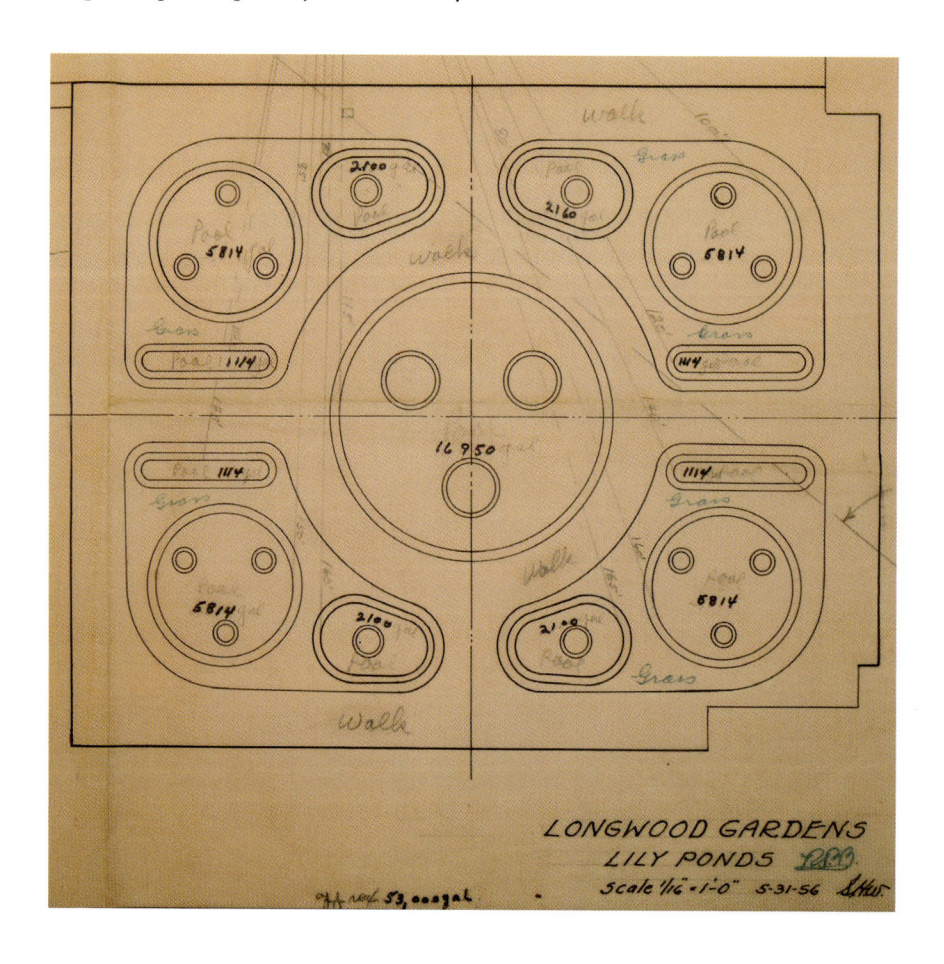

Russell Seibert, report to Longwood Gardens Board of Trustees, 1955:

Serious consideration and preliminary sketches for proposed tropical water lily pools will be started after the first of the year. These pools should logically be placed in the grass court adjoining the rear of the conservatory. The tropical water lily pools would make a very attractive display supplementing our water gardens and fountains. The addition of this spectacular summer flowering color would greatly augment our display for the enjoyment and benefit of the public.

Seibert 1955

The design of Longwood's outdoor pools was drafted in the spring of 1956.
LONGWOOD GARDENS LIBRARY AND ARCHIVES

Construction of Longwood's lily pools in the spring of 1957.
Gottlieb A. Hampfler / Longwood Gardens

Russell Seibert, letter to George Pring, 1957:

The pools are coming along very nicely in spite of a great deal of rainy weather. Additional concrete pouring is required on three of the remaining pools. I would think that by next week all of the concrete work should be completed. Most of the piping is in. Our valve house is just about installed. Most of the filtering, heating equipment is in. So that by the end of April, we should be starting to test the pools and the equipment. There is certainly no question but what by the end of May everything will be set—barring of course, an over-abundance of miserable weather.

Seibert 1957a

While the pools and support facilities for the water lilies were being built, it became clear to Seibert that the success of this new display hinged on finding the right person to provide meticulous care for the plants. No gardener at Longwood had experience growing water lilies. However, with Pring as his father-in-law, Seibert had an obvious advantage. Tapping Pring's considerable expertise, Seibert requested his consulting services for designing the pools, training the new gardener, obtaining plants and seeds from the collections of the Missouri Botanical Garden, and, ultimately, overseeing the first planting at Longwood. As early as September 1956, Seibert asked Edgar S. Anderson, director of the Missouri Botanical Garden, to give Pring leaves of absence in order to consult for Longwood: "I trust that publicity regarding these pools can be (and I know that

The Birth of the Hybrid

George Pring (left) and Patrick Nutt inspecting water lilies and *Victoria cruziana* seedlings growing in the tanks installed in a greenhouse previously used for potted azaleas.
Gottlieb A. Hampfler / Longwood Gardens

Russell Seibert, memorandum to Henry du Pont, 1956:

This over-all program would necessitate the employment and training of one young man interested in the growing, care and breeding of tropical water lilies. It is proposed that G. H. Pring of the Missouri Botanical Garden, the outstanding breeder of tropical water lilies in the world, be retained on a consulting basis to train a new man into the field of growing and particularly the specialty of breeding tropical water lilies at Longwood. By doing so, this important field of work can be carried on without interruption of experienced knowledge known to the present time. This program, if carried on without break in continuity, can lead to quick results and the introduction of new and improved series of Longwood varieties of tropical water lilies.

Seibert 1956c

Mr. Pring will insist that it will be), so released as to give the Missouri Botanical Garden full credit for being the outstanding contributor to the knowledge and development of tropical water lilies in the world" (Seibert 1956a).

It was probably not entirely a coincidence that the man Seibert selected for the job of caring for Longwood's water lilies was, like Pring himself, a "Kewite"—a graduate of the highly esteemed training program at the Royal Botanic Gardens, Kew. Following in the footsteps of Thomas Meehan, James Gurney, and Pring, Patrick A. Nutt had emigrated to the United States a few years earlier. He did not realize that his destiny was to carry on a century-long legacy of English gardeners tending to the needs of the queen lily in America.

Born in 1930, Nutt grew up in Hendon, now part of greater London, not far from the famed Perry's Aquatic Nursery. Visits to Perry's intrigued the young boy and sparked what would become a lifelong interest in water lilies. When World War II broke out, nine-year-old Patrick did not give up his dreams of growing water lilies. In fact, after a bombing raid in his neighborhood, he built his first lily pool from a rubble-salvaged sink.

After the war ended, Nutt completed training as a gardener, first at the Royal Horticultural Society's Garden, Wisley, and later at Kew. This was followed by a botany degree from the University of London Night School. Equipped with such a solid education, he was recruited in 1953 to take charge of the gardens at Malabar Farm in Lucas,

George Pring (left) and Russell Seibert instruct Patrick Nutt in planting Longwood's first water lilies in May 1957.
GOTTLIEB A. HAMPFLER / LONGWOOD GARDENS

Ohio, the estate of Louis Bromfield, noted author and conservationist. After Bromfield's death in 1956, Nutt began looking for another position. Thanks to an incidental visit by a friend of Walter H. Hodge, Longwood's head of education and research, Nutt learned about the opening at Longwood.

In February 1957, Nutt moved to Longwood to raise the first *Victoria* plants, a ritual he would repeat for the next thirty-eight years. Perhaps the culminating moment in his career came in 1988, when Nutt was inducted into the Water Lily Hall of Fame by the International Water Lily Society. At the ceremony held in Ripley Castle in England, Nutt stood beside the duke of Devonshire, who was receiving the same honor on behalf of Joseph Paxton.

CULTIVATING A QUEEN

In June 1957, as workers were finishing putting flagstone walks between the pools, Longwood's first three *Victoria cruziana* were planted in the large central pool. Earlier that year, Pring had sent seeds of *Victoria* from St. Louis. Only two seedlings grew successfully from that batch, so a third plant had been sent via airmail from the Missouri Botanical Garden to complete the set. Although *Victoria*'s initial growth in the outdoor pool was slow, the plants took off once summer's hot weather arrived in July. Soon the first spectacular flowers were produced. That fall, Nutt was able to save several fruits produced by flowers that had self-pollinated. The seeds recovered from these fruits were used to grow the next generation the following year. This routine continued until Nutt switched to cross-pollinating the flowers by hand in 1960.

Patrick Nutt, 2006:

I was first introduced to Victoria regia, *as it was named at that time, in 1951. This was my first year as a student at the Royal Botanic Gardens, Kew. This was also the very same year George Pring was serving as the president of the Kew Guild, possibly the first American, a well-deserved honor. He gave a lecture at that time to the staff and students, the topic being tropical water lilies. Little did I realize that six years later I would be fortunate enough to study and work under George at Longwood.*

Nutt 2006

Patrick Nutt, 2005:

As children, we would often salvage materials that were left over from bombing raids in the area. One day I found an abandoned porcelain sink from the site of a demolished house. I loaded it into a barrow made from other discarded items (bicycle parts) and brought it home. I put the sink in our garden, and it became my first water garden.

DiMartino 2005

Patrick Nutt with *Victoria cruziana* in 1959.
Patrick A. Nutt / Longwood Gardens

Patrick Nutt, 1996:

Longwood's original seed source of Victoria cruziana *was the Missouri Botanical Garden in St. Louis. George Pring, my mentor at the time, had been growing very fine* Victoria *there since before World War II. His source of seed was probably William Tricker of Saddle River, New Jersey, who was responsible for the 1894 introduction of a* Victoria *"more amenable to outdoor culture" than the more famous at that time* Victoria regia, *to quote Henry Conard.*

Nutt 1996

Russell Seibert, letter to George Pring, 1957:

The lilies are now beginning to look as though they belong in the new pools and have expanded quite well and rapidly—flowering is quite good. I have a feeling however, that the Victorias *are growing abnormally slow. Perhaps it is due to their set back and then too, it may be due to unduly high pH of the water 9.5 to 10.4. Nevertheless, they are not standing still but slowly increasing in size. The flagstone walks are well on their way and about two more weeks should finish them up, then we can start being "in business" as far as display is concerned.*

Seibert 1957b

The response to Longwood's newest addition was instantly encouraging. *Victoria* and other water lilies were the highlight of the summer season and "a prime attraction for camera enthusiasts" (Seibert 1959). From the day of her premiere, *Victoria* captured the public's attention and soon acquired the status of the most iconic plant in Longwood's collections. The reign of *Victoria* at Longwood had begun.

Although Pring recommended *Victoria cruziana* for Longwood's outdoor pools, he also urged Seibert to try to grow the more difficult *Victoria amazonica*. Pring reasoned that the water heating and circulatory system of the Longwood pools might enable this more tender species to flourish successfully outdoors. Nutt remembers, "Besides growing *Victoria amazonica* for comparison with the type already grown, Pring was particularly interested in the possibility of cross-pollinating the two species. He had had a goal of a *Victoria* hybrid for many years but he had not had the facilities to grow both species in the same pool or nearby at the Missouri Botanical Garden. As far as he knew, this had not been previously accomplished" (Nutt n.d.).

The following year, in April 1959, Seibert brought back seeds of *Victoria amazonica* from the Royal Botanic Gardens, Kew. George E. Wolstenholme, curator of the Botanic Gardens in Georgetown, British Guiana (today's Guyana), had sent seeds a month earlier. The seeds were immediately planted in water lily house tanks. The Georgetown seeds, which arrived green and appeared immature, all failed to germinate. One of the Kew seeds did manage to germinate, but not until June, too late for planting in the outdoor pools. The small plant was kept indoors through the remainder of the growing season, but eventually died when winter's short and dark days arrived.

Undeterred, Longwood's staff pursued other possible sources to obtain the *Victoria amazonica* seed. In October 1959, while on a plant collecting expedition in Indonesia, Walter Hodge arranged for seeds to be sent from Kebun Raya, also known as Bogor Botanic Gardens. There, *Victoria amazonica* had been cultivated successfully in several ponds. That same fall, Thomas J. Walsh, director of the National Botanic Gardens Glasnevin in Dublin, Ireland, visited Longwood. After hearing Seibert describe their difficulties with *Victoria amazonica,* Walsh offered to share seeds from plants growing in the Glasnevin conservatories. The seeds arrived from Ireland in December 1959, and the following February, they were planted alongside those from Indonesia. Only one of the Bogor seeds germinated, but nearly all of Glasnevin's

Longwood's first *Victoria* display in the summer of 1957 was enthusiastically received by visitors.
GOTTLIEB A. HAMPFLER / LONGWOOD GARDENS

Three *Victoria cruziana* plants fill the large central pool in July 1958.
GOTTLIEB A. HAMPFLER / LONGWOOD GARDENS

Patrick Nutt, letter to George Pring, 1960:

I attempted cross pollination with cruziana, *making reciprocal pollinations and did obtain a few seeds, but due to the difficulty I had in removing the thick leathery anthers and their position, I cannot be sure the flowers were perfectly emasculated. Anyway, I will find out if the seeds germinated. I checked the chromosome count of the two* Victorias. *Both are diploids,* cruziana *has 12 pairs,* amazonica *having 10 pairs. Our geneticist, Dr. Lighty, did not think that this would have any effect on the F1 generation. I made these pollinations between 9:30 and 11 P.M. and was afforded the best opportunity to view the flowers at their best as they were quite turgid as compared with their rather limp appearance in daylight.*

Nutt 1960

seeds sprouted successfully. Nutt noted that this Irish *Victoria* had leaves of a deeper crimson color and more prominent upturned margins, which differed somewhat from those he remembered from his days at Kew. Nevertheless, since the Glasnevin form appeared to possess superior vitality, it was selected over the Bogor form for outdoor planting. Thus, in June 1960, *Victoria cruziana* and *Victoria amazonica* met for the first time in Longwood's pools.

Only one *Victoria amazonica* was planted in the pools. She grew vigorously, considering the cooler weather that summer. Her largest leaves measured 1.6 m (5 feet), considerably larger than *Victoria cruziana* under the same conditions. Yet she produced only half as many flowers. Also, although the Glasnevin plant bloomed for the first time at the end of July, her flowers were not large enough to attempt the crossing with *Victoria cruziana* until September.

Victoria amazonica (front) grew side by side with *Victoria cruziana* in Longwood's pools for the first time in 1960.
GOTTLIEB A. HAMPFLER / LONGWOOD GARDENS

During the months leading up to the first cross, Nutt searched far and wide for any information that might shed some light on how to approach the process. In the end, it was *La Victoria Regia*, the 1851 work by Jules Emile Planchon and Louis Van Houtte, that provided a meticulous account of hand-pollination. Nutt followed the instructions with one small modification. Rather than use a cork float to keep the flower up out of the water, Nutt tried styrofoam. He made four cross-pollinations. On September 10, 13, and 15, *Victoria amazonica* was used as the pistillate, or female, parent. On September 17, a reciprocal cross was made with *Victoria cruziana* as the pistillate parent. Since *Victoria* flowers are protogynous (born female and then turn male, shedding pollen on the second night of flowering), Nutt used flowers that had opened the previous evening as the male parents.

Within two weeks, the ovaries of all four flowers had commenced to swell and the peduncle had curved characteristically, denoting at least partial fertilization. All four pods were separated from the peduncles on October 25, the peduncles having almost decayed by that time. The pods were then placed in plastic pans, filled with water and kept under the bench in a greenhouse. Two weeks later, all four pods burst, the seeds floating to the water surface.

Patrick Nutt:

Both Victoria cruziana *and* Victoria amazonica *are protogynous, that is to say a flower whose stigmatic surface is receptive to pollen before the pollen is shed by the same flower.* Victoria *flowers appear to have a built-in survival mechanism that allows them to pollinate themselves, but I would consider the resulting seed inferior to cross-pollinated seed. In order to increase chances of cross-fertilization between* Victoria amazonica *and* Victoria cruziana, *it was decided to use pollen from another flower that had opened the previous evening, using a first-night flower from the seed parent. This gave the pollen tubes the maximum length of time to reach the ovules, for the flower soon begins to sink beneath the water on the morning after the second night of flowering.*

Nutt n.d.

Comparison of the leaves of *Victoria cruziana* (top left), *Victoria amazonica* (top right), and their hybrid (bottom).
GOTTLIEB A. HAMPFLER / LONGWOOD GARDENS

Pods collected from *Victoria amazonica* that were pollinated with *Victoria cruziana* pollen had thirty to sixty seeds per pod. The one pod produced by *Victoria cruziana* as the female parent had almost three hundred seeds. The seeds were then placed in moist sand and subjected to five weeks of after-ripening. Those harvested from *Victoria cruziana* were kept at 16°C (61°F), and those harvested from *Victoria amazonica* at 21°C (70°F), after which they were all transferred to cool storage at 7°C (45°F).

The hybrid seeds were sown on February 20, 1961. Eighty-five percent of the seeds produced by *Victoria cruziana* germinated at 29°C (84°F), but all failed to germinate at 24°C (75°F). Paradoxically, those produced by *Victoria amazonica* failed to germinate at either 29° or 24°C. It appeared that in order to germinate, the hybrid seed required warmer temperatures typically associated with *Victoria amazonica*, the more tender parent species. Puzzled that the hybrid seed produced from a cross with *Victoria amazonica* as the female parent had failed to germinate, Nutt asked Richard W. Lighty, Longwood's geneticist, to examine the seeds. After dissecting the seeds under his microscope, Lighty found no abnormalities that could explain failed germination.

AN AMERICAN HEIR

On March 30, the five most vigorous hybrid seedlings were potted up and repotted again on April 21. Nutt noted, "Even at this early stage, hybrid vigor was noticeable, the hybrid seedlings being larger and more vigorous than those of the two parent species growing in the same tank" (Nutt n.d.). In early June, when water in the pools had reached a temperature of 25°C (77°F), a single hybrid *Victoria* was planted in the central pool alongside *Victoria amazonica* and *Victoria cruziana*. By the end of

Hybrid *Victoria* flowered for the first time on July 18, 1961.
GOTTLIEB A. HAMPFLER / LONGWOOD GARDENS

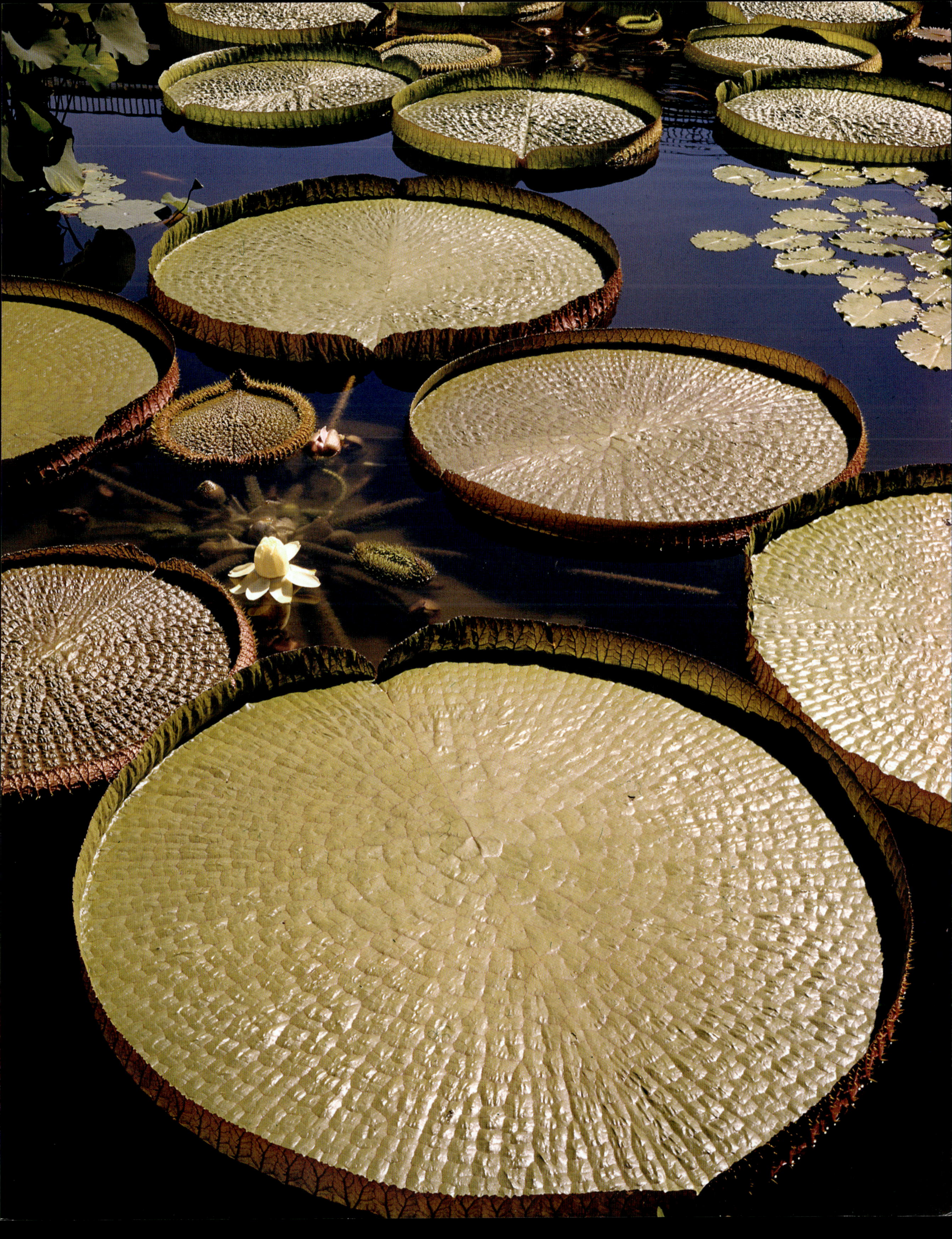

Longwood lily pools in 1963. The central pool features one of each, *Victoria amazonica*, *Victoria cruziana*, and 'Longwood Hybrid'.

Gottlieb A. Hampfler / Longwood Gardens

Patrick Nutt, letter to George Pring, 1961:

The plant produced in all, 46 fully opened flowers, more than either parent type this year. It is apparently fertile, for I selfed it twice with resulting fertilization and seed. It proved as hardy as V. cruziana, *for on October 18th when* V. amazonica *was just about finished, the hybrid possessed seven good leaves and was flowering. The water temperature had dropped to 70 degrees F [21°C].*

Nutt 1961

Victoria: The Seductress

July, the hybrid plant was growing at a prodigious rate, her leaves reaching 2 m (7 feet) in diameter, far surpassing both parent species.

Her first flower opened on July 18, before either one of the parents. As time passed, the hybrid outperformed both of the species in many ways. She exhibited greater vigor and strength; she developed more and larger leaves, which were able to better handle adverse weather, such as periods of high wind; she produced more and larger flowers, which opened earlier in the evening; and finally, she tolerated cooler water and air temperatures, which meant the plant maintained a presentable appearance later into the season.

By the end of the first growing season, it was evident that hybrid *Victoria* possessed many highly desirable traits and should be widely introduced into cultivation. Donald G. Huttleston, Longwood's taxonomist, announced the results of the first *Victoria* hybridization in the United States in the pages of the *American Horticultural Magazine* in 1961, indicating that the plant's name was expected to be 'Longwood' (Huttleston 1961). A year later, in the same magazine, Nutt published the formal description of the new variety of *Victoria* and gave her the name 'Longwood Hybrid' (Nutt 1962).

Later that summer of 1961, Nutt performed several pollinations involving the hybrid plant. While the hybrid produced fertile seeds of the second, or F_2, generation, when self-pollinated, her backcross with *Victoria cruziana* as a pollen parent was unsuccessful. Nutt continued making various backcrosses between F_1 and F_2 hybrids and their parent species until the late 1960s, but eventually came to the conclusion that none of them was superior to or possessed the vigor of 'Longwood Hybrid'. To those urging naming additional cultivars of hybrid *Victoria*, Nutt answered: "With all due respect to the various hybridizers, I feel that some of them could follow the example of the late Lionel de Rothschild when he was hybridizing his famous Exbury rhododendrons and azaleas. His very good judgment and ruthless selection resulted in the destruction of all inferior hybrids by consigning them to the bonfire" (Nash 1997).

UPDATING THE ROYAL GROUNDS

It is not exactly clear who deserves credit for the original design and layout of the thirteen lily pools at Longwood, as both Pring and Seibert were intimately involved. For the most part, the pools stood the test of time, although the twelve smaller pools (three in each corner) turned out to be too small for the growing collection of water lilies. Also,

Donald Huttleston, 1961:

It is clearly intermediate, but also displays a remarkable degree of hybrid vigor which promises to make it far superior to the parents for display purposes. The leaves grow much more rapidly and reach a larger size. Even by August 1st, leaves had attained the diameter of 6 feet 5 inches [2 m], whereas the greatest leaf diameter previously obtained here by V. amazonica, *the larger of the parents, was 5 feet 3 inches [2 m] in September of 1960. The flower also is larger and opens earlier in the evening. Longwood Gardens expects to give this hybrid a cultivar name, 'Longwood'. This will be done after the current growing season when all the records are in.*

Huttleston 1961

Edgar Anderson, 1965:

The development of a new hybrid between plants which are well known to you is a fascinating thing to watch.... Hybridization produces not the new but the unexpected.... Victoria amazonica has much larger leaves than V. cruziana *but the stiff upright rims which give* Victorias *their distinctive charm are proportionally lower and do not develop as early in the life of the plant as they do in* V. cruziana. *These characters worked out about as had been expected.... The rims were intermediate in proportion but they were of course on much larger leaves than those of* cruziana *and rose dramatically above the surface of the water, making the plants conspicuous from a distance. The big surprise was the color on the exposed outer side of the rim. This is dark pink in* amazonica, *and greenish in* cruziana *with the red pigment restricted to the very edge. The hybrids were brighter than either parent, a strong coppery red, one of those shades which delight photographers because it always comes out so well on color film.*

Anderson 1965

Peter Shepheard's rendering of his 1987 design for Longwood's lily pools.
LONGWOOD GARDENS LIBRARY AND ARCHIVES

Construction of Longwood's new lily pools designed by Peter Shepheard.
LARRY ALBEE / LONGWOOD GARDENS

the grass strips separating the pools from the paved walks were difficult to maintain and subject to heavy wear. By the mid-1980s, after thirty years of continuous use, the pools required extensive renovations. It was also decided that their 1950s modernist style had lost some of its appeal.

Sir Peter Shepheard was a renowned English landscape architect and University of Pennsylvania professor who had served as Longwood's garden and landscape adviser since 1977. When asked to review the plans for renovation, Shepheard proposed redoing the whole courtyard. "I had to be very rude about it to get them to realize how horrible it was," he remembered (Downs 2004). The large central pool was retained, but Shepheard redesigned the twelve smaller pools into four large straight-edged pools, which increased their display areas by 50 percent. All the grass strips were removed, and the entire surface between the pools was paved with Pennsylvania bluestone. The new design called for replacing all the white-painted pool edging, which Shepheard abhorred, with brick that was slightly sloped and darker in color than bluestone paving. As a result, instead of being punctured by thirteen pools, the courtyard acquired broad paved walks that appeared to float on the surface of the water.

When the 1988 *Victoria* growing season ended that fall, the demolition of the 1957 pools began. After a $1.2 million remodel, *Victoria* moved into her spacious new home in June 1989. The area now consisted of five large pools occupying over 1,022 m² (11,000 square feet) and holding more than 600 m³ (21,000 cubic feet) of water. Shepheard's design gave *Victoria* and the accompanying water lilies upscale accommodations with a more contemporary feel. A quarter of a century later, the design has not lost its luster or functionality, and the architect's genius is still present in that space—but one has to ponder what the future versions of Longwood's *Victoria* court may look like.

GENETIC PROBLEMS, WILD SOLUTIONS

From her first appearance in 1957, *Victoria* enjoyed the expert care of Nutt and his assistants, who without fail facilitated a spectacular display year after year. The first indication of any troubles threatening the cultivated *Victoria* reached Longwood in the mid-1980s, when R. Maxwell of the Glencairn Park in Belfast, Northern Ireland, sent Nutt a worrisome letter: "This last two years we have been growing *Victoria amazonica* in the gardens, but were unable to set viable seed. We had obtained our seed from the Dublin Botanic Gardens, but unfortunately they have this last year been without viable seed. It seems that *Victoria amazonica* in cultivation has a degenerative streak" (Maxwell 1985).

Longwood's line of this *Victoria* also came from Dublin; by the early 1990s, Longwood found itself unable to produce seeds of *Victoria amazonica*. Similar signals came from other gardens. When Nutt wrote to Sir Ghillean T. Prance, director of the Royal Botanic Gardens, Kew, requesting seeds of *Victoria amazonica*, Prance responded that the situation with *Victoria* seeds at Kew was "not very helpful" (Prance 1991). It appeared that the *Victoria* cultivated in Europe and the United

Peter Shepheard at Longwood in 1989.
LARRY ALBEE / LONGWOOD GARDENS

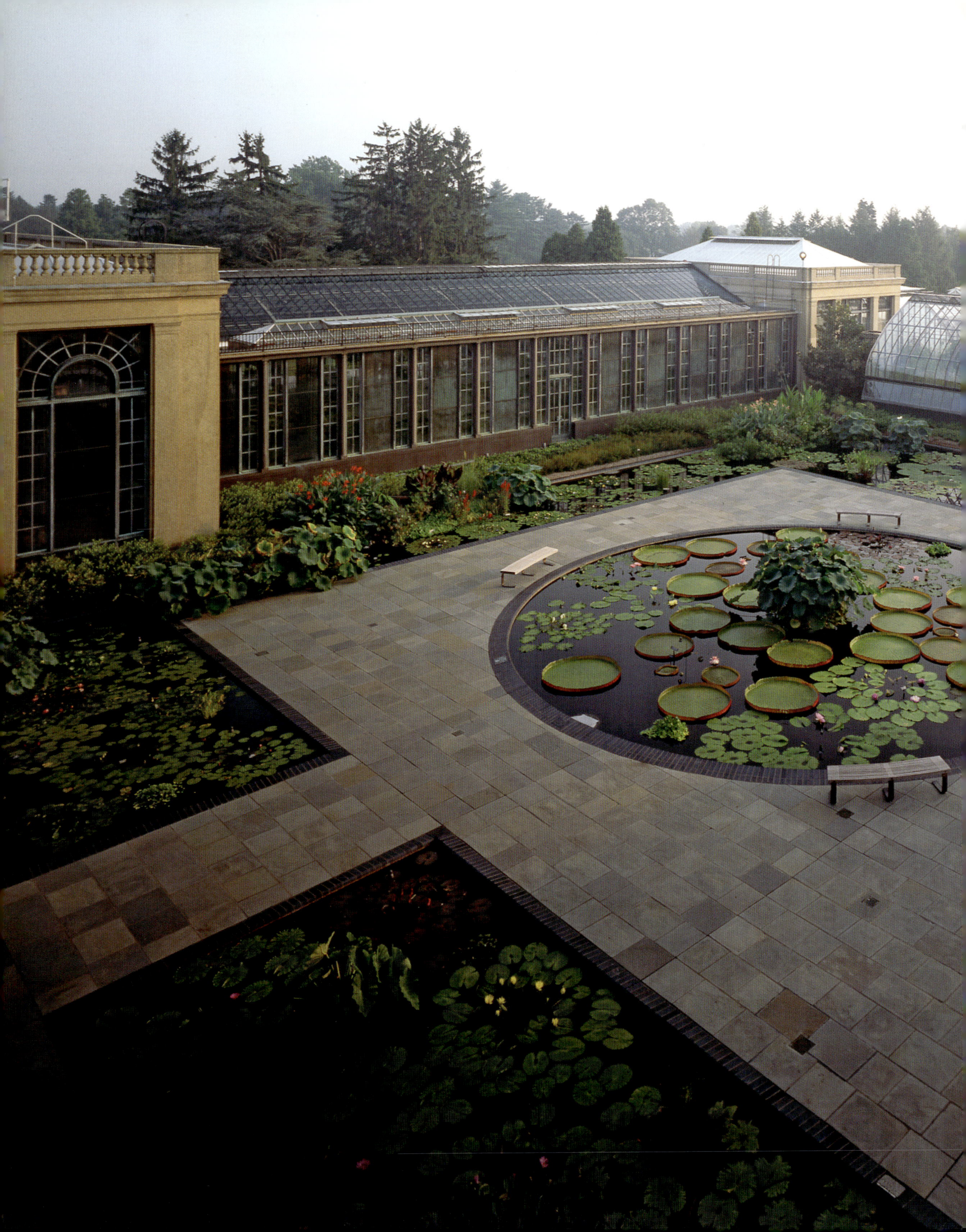

States were succumbing to a genetic degeneration—the unfortunate result of inbreeding caused by years of repeated self-pollination. Was the reign of *Victoria* coming to an end after nearly 150 years?

To avert this gloomy prospect, *Victoria* followers in the United States mobilized their resources. In November 1991, two Floridians, aquatic plant growers Donald W. Bryne and Peter D. Slocum, led an expedition to Manaus, Brazil, to collect seeds from wild populations of *Victoria*. Their hope was that the wild provenance seeds could restore the vitality to *Victoria* in cultivation. When the expedition returned, the seeds were shared widely—including with Longwood. They germinated, and the ensuing plants were anxiously watched throughout the 1992 season. The results were exhilarating: The Manaus seed produced superior plants exhibiting vigor not seen in cultivated plants. Nutt and his peers across the United States sighed in relief.

But the troubles with *Victoria* were not over yet. A year later, *Victoria cruziana* at Longwood became afflicted with sterility, so neither this species nor hybrid seeds were produced. Fortunately, there were still some seeds left from the 1992 season, and these were sown successfully in 1994. Nevertheless, Nutt was alarmed by the prospect that the 'Longwood Hybrid' might disappear unless the genetic vitality of *Victoria cruziana* could be restored. The likely cause of the sterility, he thought, was "cross-pollinating from a limited gene pool" (Nutt 1994).

Nutt wrote many of his correspondents around the world, asking for assistance in obtaining new or wild seeds of *Victoria cruziana*. Help came from the Kanapaha Botanical Garden in Gainesville, Florida. Director Don Goodman rushed Nutt approximately twenty seeds.

Peter Shepheard's design of the lily pools increased their display areas by half compared to their 1957 layout.
LARRY ALBEE / LONGWOOD GARDENS

THE BIRTH OF THE HYBRID

Patrick Nutt demonstrating *Victoria* pollination technique to his successor, Timothy Jennings.
Larry Albee / Longwood Gardens

Patrick Nutt, letter to Ghillean Prance, 1994:

The very same situation has cropped up with Victoria cruziana *as happened with* Victoria amazonica *several years ago. I fear we have been working with parent plants that are closely related. Even if we have obtained seedlings from other botanical or display gardens, one discovers that the parents of these plants probably originated at Missouri Botanical Garden. Last year our large plant, which should have served as the female parent for the hybrid, was totally sterile. To continue to produce a hybrid, I am in need of genetical diversity. I would very much like to obtain seed from plants growing in the wild. . . . Any assistance you could supply as regards location, a possible contact or any information would be greatly appreciated. Fortunately, we have viable two-year old hybrid seed that has produced fine seedlings for this year.*

Nutt 1994

"We have profited over the years from the receipt of Longwood *Victoria* seed and I am happy to return the favor," he wrote (Goodman 1994). The Kanapaha seeds germinated successfully in early 1995, plants grew vigorously, and flowers proved perfectly fertile. Once again, Nutt was able to repeat the cross between *Victoria cruziana* and *Victoria amazonica*. When he retired later that year, Nutt left Longwood with a parting gift—a few jars filled with the seeds of *Victoria* 'Longwood Hybrid'.

Victoria 'Longwood Hybrid' growing in outdoor pools at Longwood Gardens in 2009.
Larry Albee / Longwood Gardens

Victoria: The Seductress

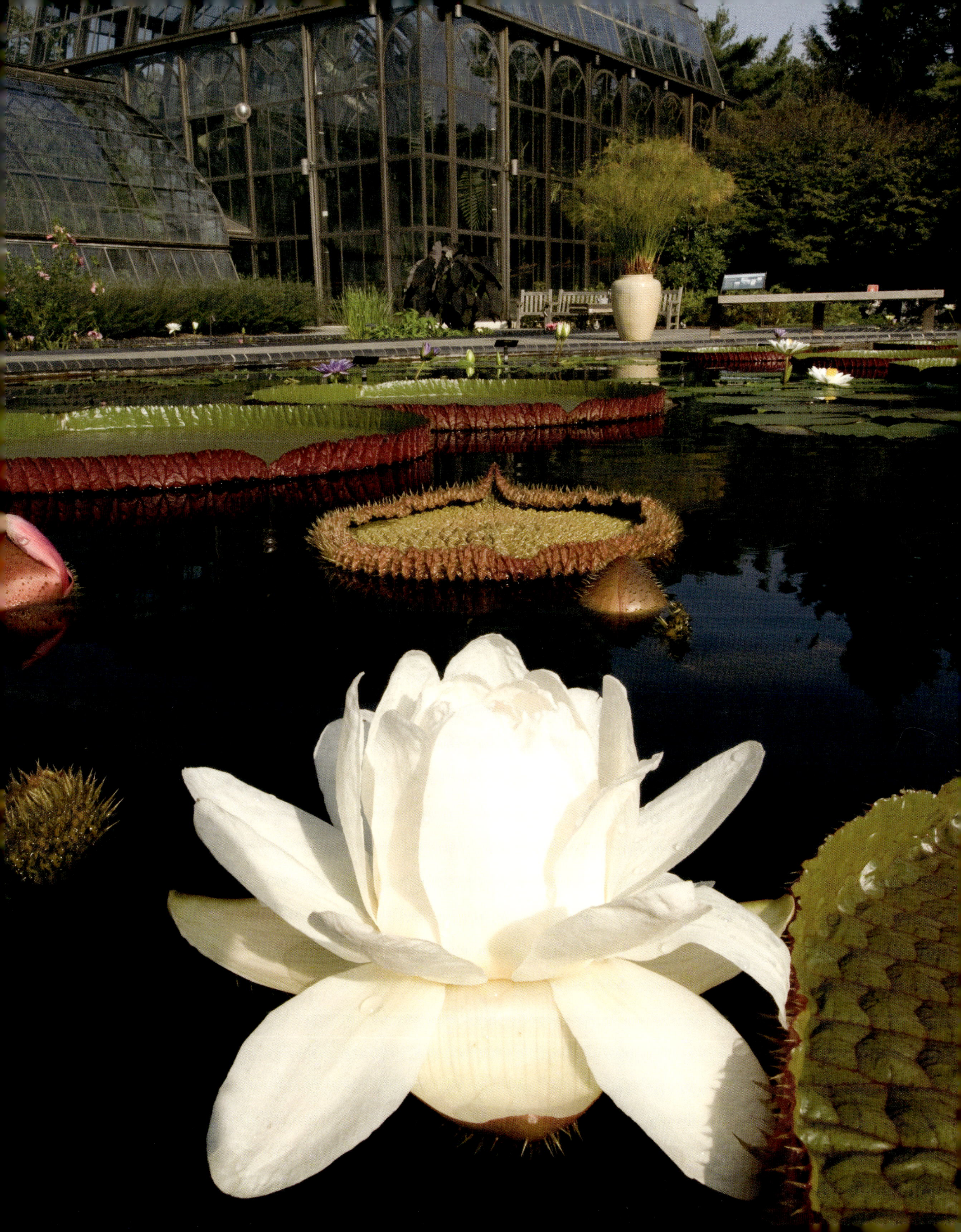

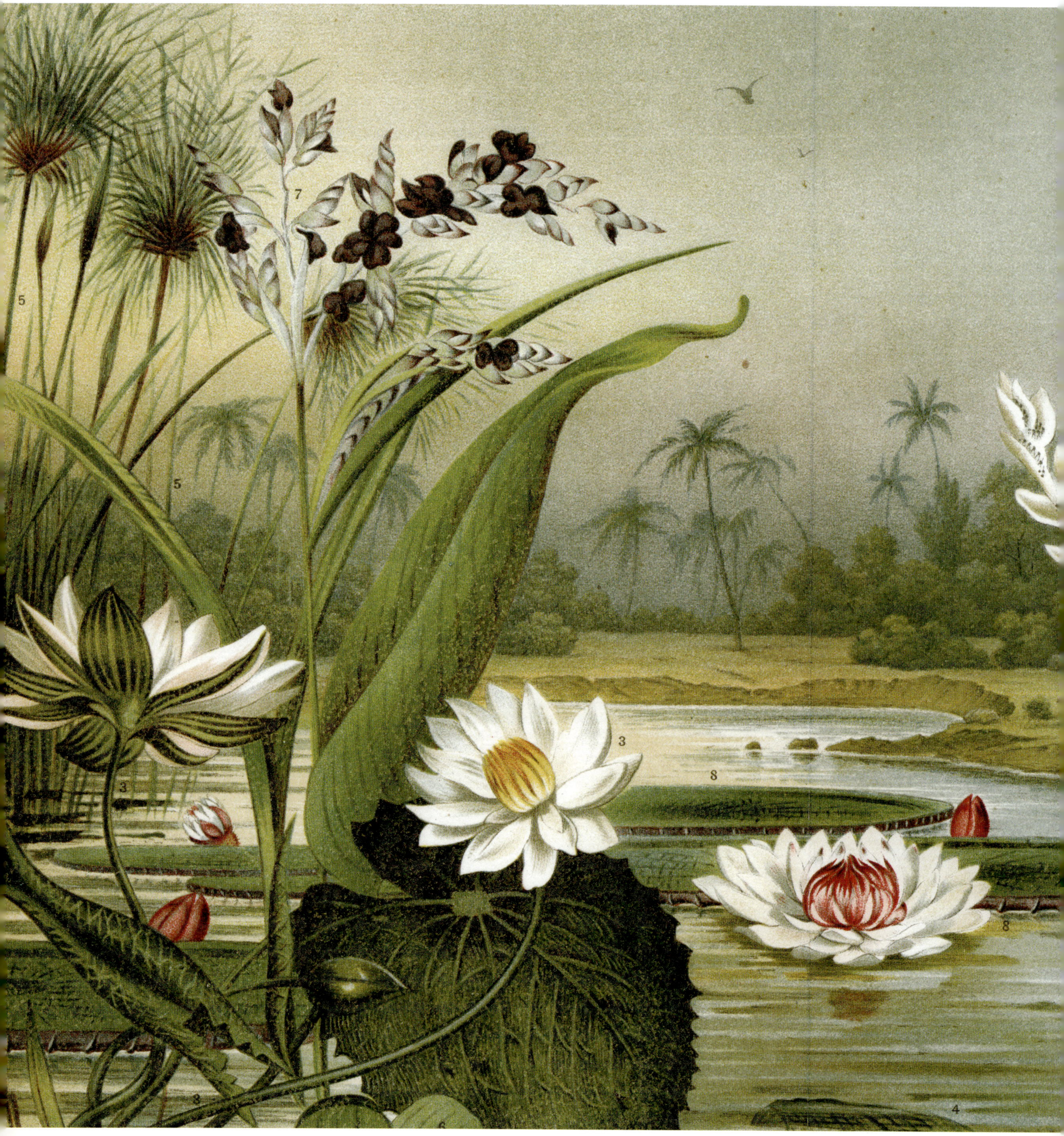
7
5
5
3
3
8
8
3
4

chapter 13

LIFE IN CAPTIVITY

THE RAPID EXPANSION OF *VICTORIA*'S DOMAIN around the world would never have happened if scores of gardeners had not found various ways to approximate her native environment under highly contrived conditions. Satisfying the queen lily's needs—which were often only vaguely understood—and allowing her to flourish in places far from South America was often viewed as a gardener's ultimate challenge.

These early triumphs in raising the giant lily inspired many gardeners to attempt cultivation further north, while others were encouraged to test her tolerance of outdoor conditions in temperate climates. Successful results were eagerly announced, but when occasional failures happened, many skeptics voiced doubts over *Victoria*'s long-term prospects for survival in cultivation.

One report described the Amazonian nymph living happily in the open air in England at Messrs. Weeks's establishment in Chelsea. In response, a correspondent to the *Cottage Gardener and Country Gentleman* pointed out that this open-air tank was nevertheless protected by an awning and that water in the tank was heated to 29°C (84°F). "Although great credit is due to the enterprising spirit of the Messrs. Weeks in carrying out this experiment so successfully," he wrote, "still we are far from being

While the queen lily's true domain was in South America, in cultivation she was usually surrounded by plants from several other continents, shown in this illustration from a late nineteenth-century German encyclopedia.
AUTHOR'S COLLECTION

In 1895, Scotto Nash of Clifton, New Jersey, planted *Victoria amazonica* in a heated pond.
ARCHIVES OF THE GRAY HERBARIUM, HARVARD UNIVERSITY

> **Anonymous correspondent to the *American Gardening*, 1895:**
>
> *Our mind has recently awakened to this true love by a ramble through the wild garden, that has been tamed by the loving care and skillful hand of Mr. S. C. Nash, at Clifton, N. J. Here the beautiful in Nature has been fully appreciated; here the* Victoria regia *of the Amazon and the sacred lotus of the Orient, are happily blended with their humble cousins, the nymphaeas of our native ponds. How beautiful to see so many forms and nationalities in such close proximity, growing together in perfect harmony, without contentions, jealousies or strifes, each performing its own functions in its own way, teaching man a lesson of faithfulness in the discharge of duties! What a lesson there is in this garden for the student of rural architecture and landscape gardening. Here nature has not been robbed of her rights, she has been left entirely alone, only kindly assisted in her efforts to please, by the introduction of a goodly number of distant relatives.*
>
> Anonymous 1895a

convinced that the plant is capable of being grown in the 'open air' in England; and the complete failure, too, this year of the plants in the marble basins of the greenhouse division of the Crystal Palace tends even more strongly to confirm us in our opinion of the utter impossibility of attempting to acclimatize a tropical plant of this description, even within a greenhouse, in Great Britain or any other country above the latitude of 45° or 50° north" (Anonymous 1857).

THE OUTDOOR CHALLENGE

Although Messrs. Weeks's example did not inspire many British followers to redirect the hot water pipes from their greenhouse to outdoor pools, there were numerous imitators in late nineteenth-century America. This new gardening fad began in the 1870s, when Eduard Sturtevant in Bordentown, New Jersey, successfully grew *Victoria amazonica* in an open-air tank with water that was kept warm by heating pipes (Sturtevant 1879, Lockwood 1885). Nearby, in Clifton, New Jersey, Scotto C. Nash eschewed building a tank and instead connected hot water pipes from a greenhouse boiler to a pond he had excavated from a roadside swamp (Anonymous 1895c, 1895e). According to Nash, what was once an "erstwhile dreary swamp" became a "garden fair" thanks to the Amazonian nymph, who was accompanied by the usual assortment of other aquatic plants.

One important advantage of growing the queen lily outdoors (besides the obvious cost savings of not erecting a greenhouse) was her greater accessibility to the public. In 1891, William Lee, owner of a cutlery manufactory in Northampton, Massachusetts, built a pond nearly 13 m (43 feet) wide for *Victoria* on the factory's grounds. The following year, the queen lily flourished, and when Lee opened the garden to the public, she attracted thousands of visitors (Anonymous 1892). A few years later, in Brooklyn, New York, Prospect Park had three outdoor pools built for aquatic plants. One of them had a heating system installed to accommodate *Victoria*, which was, as one observer noted, "of absorbing interest to the multitudes who visit the park" (Tricker 1897).

Experience had taught *Victoria* enthusiasts that young lilies could be planted around and north of Philadelphia in the open air in early May so long as provisions were made to maintain the water temperature at about 27° to 29°C (80° to 84°F) until summer weather arrived. William Tricker of Clifton, New Jersey, commented, "As a general rule, the season is too short, as it is not safe to plant without artificial heat until the end of June" (Tricker 1897). Heating the water in an outdoor pool or pond was equally beneficial in late summer when the giant lilies were reaching their prime, but when cooler air temperatures could prematurely put an end to their growth. Tricker noted, however, that in rare instances, in "exceptional localities," plants were growing and flowering surprisingly well, even without supplemental heat.

At Longwood Gardens outside Philadelphia, giant water lilies are planted in the outdoor heated pools in late May.
TOMASZ ANIŚKO / LONGWOOD GARDENS

Since 2002, an outdoor heated pool at the Botanical Garden in Amsterdam has been a summer home for the *Victoria* lily.
TOMASZ ANIŚKO / LONGWOOD GARDENS

In continental Europe, the Weeks's experiment gave others the courage to try growing *Victoria* in the open. August Borsig, a German pioneer in lily cultivation, not only had the first Victoria House in Germany, but he also successfully raised the giant lily in an outdoor pool in Berlin in 1852. The feat was achieved in part by using a pool that was heated with excess water from Borsig's nearby locomotive factory. According to one observer, Berlin's unusually hot summer weather that year contributed to the success as well (Anonymous 1853).

Elsewhere in Germany, Borsig's example was emulated a number of times. At Rosenhöhe outside Darmstadt, a garden of the duke of Hessen had an outdoor pool fitted with heating pipes dedicated to growing the giant lilies. For his trouble, the duke was rewarded with a *Victoria* flower that opened in his garden on July 24, 1905 (Henkel et al. 1907). Half a century later near Stuttgart, Wilhelma—a former estate of the king of Württemberg—welcomed the queen lily into perhaps the finest lily pool yet constructed.

Since 1956, at the former estate of the king of Württemberg near Stuttgart, *Victoria* has resided in an enormous heated pool each year between May and October.
TOMASZ ANIŚKO / LONGWOOD GARDENS

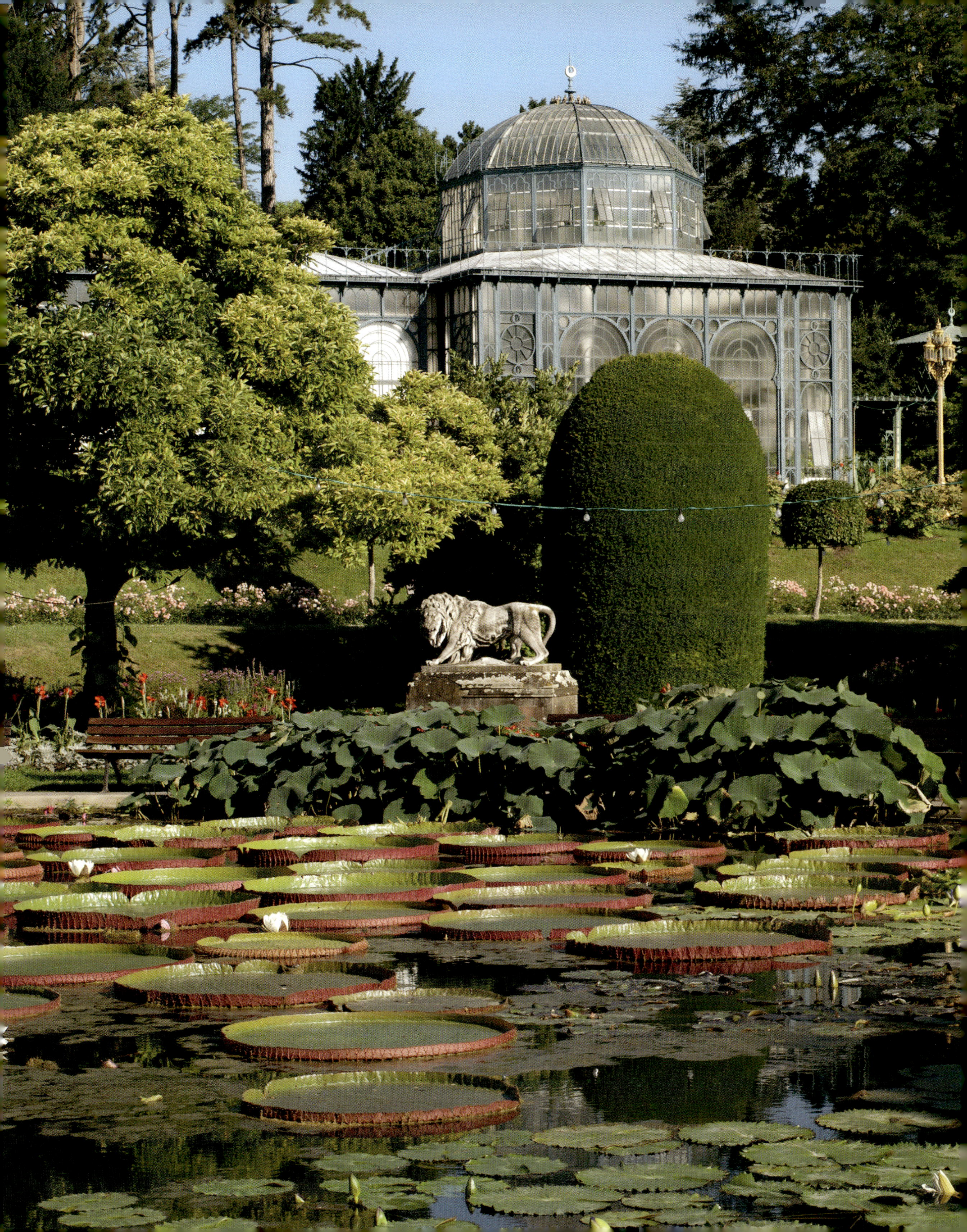

At 30 m (98 feet) across, it is likely the largest heated *Victoria* pool anywhere. In order to keep the water temperature at about 28° to 30°C (82° to 86°F), the pool's supplemental heat is kept on from May to October, except on the hottest summer days (Herkert 2004).

The most daring attempt to defy the northern European climate, though, took place in Moscow, 55° north latitude. In 1907, architect Karl Gippius had heating pipes installed in an outdoor pond in his garden on Zubovsky Boulevard. To everybody's amazement, *Victoria* thrived under these conditions, despite a cool and rainy summer. By early August, the lily had eight large leaves. Regrettably, however, she failed to produce flowers before the close of the growing season (Trespe 1925).

Many who attempted growing the giant lilies outdoors in temperate climates took a cue from the Weeks, who used a temporary covering placed over *Victoria*'s basin at night and during stormy and windy weather (Anonymous 1851d, 1851k). At the Botanical Garden of the University of Tübingen in Germany, it was impossible to redirect heating pipes to an outdoor tank, so Wilhelm Hochstetter tried to raise the lilies in a large tub placed in a sunny spot outside. Initially, to lessen the effect of moving *Victoria* to a colder environment, he periodically added warm water and covered the tub with a window frame to minimize heat loss and maintain higher temperatures. In time, Hochstetter lifted the window and discontinued adding water, hoping the lily would acclimate to lower temperatures. The plant made little progress, however, forming new leaves reluctantly, while the older ones developed spots and holes and eventually deteriorated (Hochstetter 1852).

More encouraging results were achieved in the Botanical Garden of the University of Basel in Switzerland. There, in the foothills of the snowcapped Alps, a small pond, about 7.5 m (25 feet) long and 2.5 m (8 feet) wide, was prepared in the gardens and covered with windows in April 1863. Adding hot water to the pond elevated and then maintained its temperature at about 25°C (77°F). In May, the sun warmed the glass-covered pond enough to end the tedious task of repeatedly pouring in hot water. Keeping the glass windows in place throughout the summer often raised the temperature inside above 43°C (109°F) without any apparent detriment to the plant. Then, on August 22, the first flower opened, demonstrating that even in the cool Swiss climate, it was possible to cultivate the Amazonian lily in the open (Krieger 1867).

In the United States, Caleb Cope was the first to test the lily's tolerance of a temperate climate in Philadelphia in 1851. Cope had one plant already thriving in a pool inside a Lily House and

---

Caleb Cope, letter to Andrew Downing, editor of the *Horticulturist*, 1851:

Mr. Longworth, who regards so much of what is new in his favorite path, as humbug, says, in a letter which I received from him to day, that "there is but one plant in the world—the Victoria." He adds, however, that he will present me with a fresh-milk cow, if he fails to grow the lily without heat. By this he means that he can grow it in his pond.... The plant in our kitchen garden, which has had fire heat at no time, is very beautiful, and would bloom, I think, if it had been planted a month earlier. As it is I am not without hope that it will yet give us a flower.

Cope 1851a

Lafayette Goodell, 1893:

[Victoria] can be grown and flowered without artificial heat with good success even in cold New England, with little expense. I have flowered it in this way for three years. The most important point to ensure success is, to get a strong growth early in the season. To accomplish this, I set out a good plant about the first of June, and then made a frame around it of planks ten or twelve feet [3 or 4 m] square and wide enough to come five or six inches [12 or 15 cm] above the surface of the water and covered it with hot-bed sash; this gave nearly all the advantages of artificial heat: the temperature of the water and soil often rose to one hundred degrees [38°C], which caused very rapid growth, soon filling the frame with the leaves. Both sash and frame were then removed to give the plant more room. My plants made leaves five feet [2 m] across and were in flower for a month.

Goodell 1893

Unheated lily pools, under construction at the Missouri Botanical Garden in 1917, would soon welcome *Victoria* as part of the garden's summer display.
MISSOURI BOTANICAL GARDEN

another one growing in his kitchen garden. Although the outdoor basin was unheated, warm water flowed into it from the indoor pool. Over this basin, Cope placed a sash window for the entire season (Cope 1851b). The lily in the kitchen garden made relatively slow progress compared to her "more favored companion in the aquarium," but she nevertheless produced leaves nearly 1.2 m (4 feet) wide.

Others who, like Cope in Philadelphia, were blessed with long, hot summers in the eastern United States went a step further and did not heat

William Tricker, 1897:

*Last season one plant of this variety [*Victoria cruziana*] produced some pods of seed, one of which bursted earlier than was expected, and not having been bagged the seed was scattered. So far as was possible the seeds were picked up, but a number escaped notice and sank. Early in July, 1897, a number of seedling* Victoria *plants made their appearance on the surface of the water (which is about two feet [61 cm] deep). During the winter but little water remained in the pond, and at one time what was there must have been frozen nearly solid; in spring the water was drawn off, the bottom, consisting of pure stiff clay, was pounded firm, and a layer of sand put upon it; the young plants referred to above are firmly rooted in the clay bottom and have every appearance of being strong and vigorous. The partiality for a comparatively low temperature is a remarkable feature of this variety.*

Tricker 1897

LIFE IN CAPTIVITY

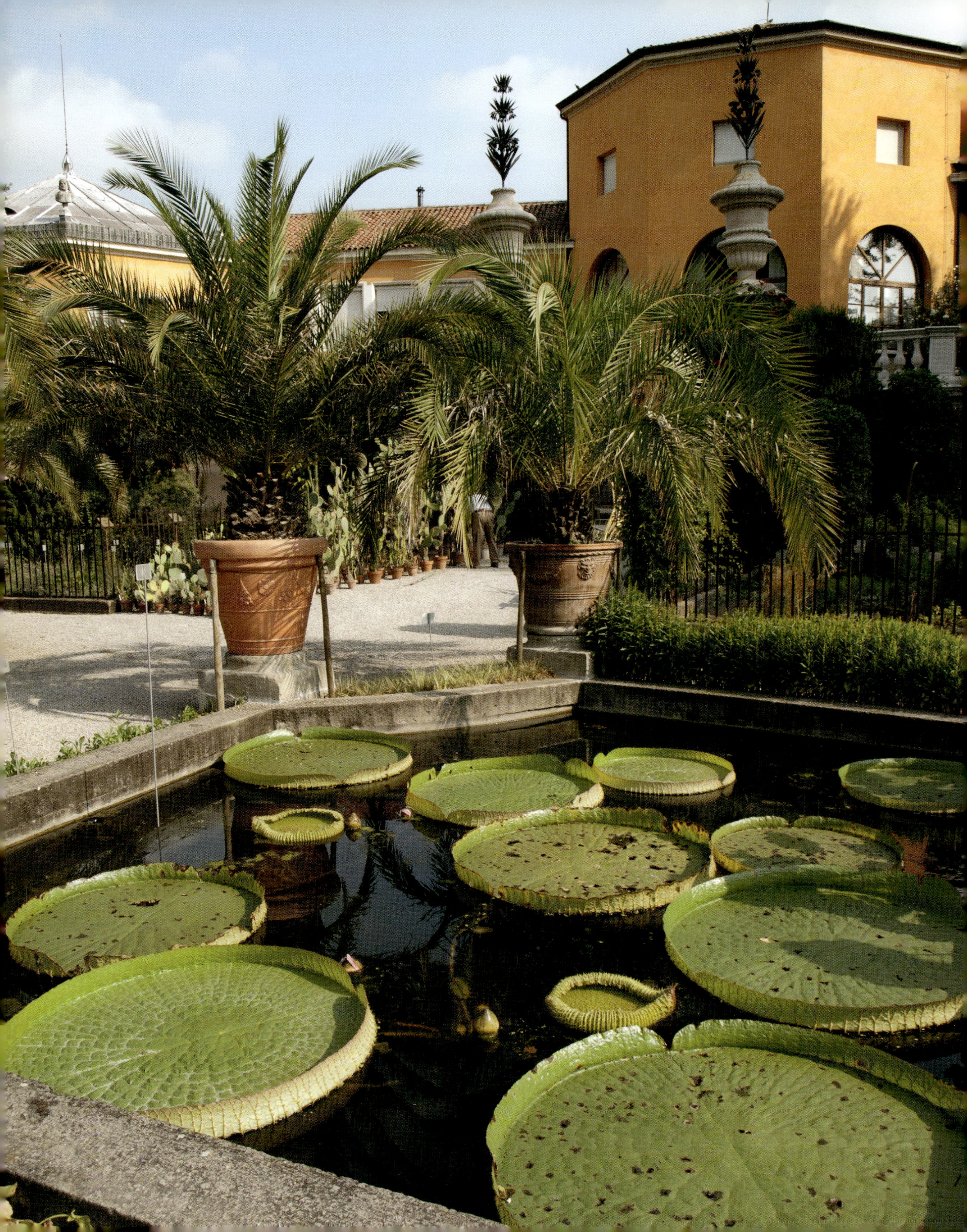

or add hot water to their outdoor ponds or pools. Placing windows over the lily early in the season seemed to give young *Victoria* enough of a head start to make her thrive when hotter weather arrived. In some cases, it even allowed for removal of the windows at the height of the season.

Taking this approach, in 1893 Lafayette W. Goodell, founder of the Pansy Park seed and plant catalog from Dwight, Massachusetts, reported that *Victoria* "can be grown and flowered without artificial heat with good success even in cold New England, with little expense" (Goodell 1893). Apparently, he had done this for three years. By simply placing a hotbed sash window over the surface of the water, he was able to raise its temperature enough for the lily to thrive. Once the entire space under the window frame was filled with bulging lily pads, he removed the frame, allowing the plant to expand unobstructed.

In 1888, Congressman John Simpkins tried yet another variation on enhancing *Victoria*'s living quarters. Following Sturtevant's example in New Jersey, Simpkins heated a 9-m (30-foot) wide outdoor pool for the queen lily at his Sundyside garden in Yarmouth, Massachusetts. In addition, on cooler or windy days, the pool was covered with a cotton canopy that was stretched over a frame and placed a couple of feet above the water, while the sides of this light structure were closed with tight-fitting shutters (Anonymous 1888). Given such plush accommodations, the Sundyside *Victoria* produced luxuriant growth and flowered reliably through the middle of September.

As Cope's experiment with his kitchen garden had proven, Philadelphia's climate was not quite amiable to *Victoria amazonica*. However, this situation changed when her southern kin, *Victoria cruziana*, was introduced into cultivation in the late nineteenth century. Coming from cooler regions of South America, this species proved perfectly adapted to outdoor summer conditions in and around Philadelphia, provided the lily was planted in June in shallow, quickly warming pools that received plenty of sun (Conard and Hus 1907). Not far north from Philadelphia, in Riverton, New Jersey, *Victoria cruziana* was even reported to sprout from self-sown seeds that overwintered at the bottom of the pond (Tricker 1897, Conard and Hus 1907).

HER MAJESTY'S SOUTHERN PREFERENCES

Those living south of Philadelphia had far less trouble helping either species of *Victoria* flourish in the open air. In the Washington, D.C., area, only 200 km (124 miles) from Cope's city, both the Amazonian and the Paraná nymphs performed splendidly without artificial heat or cover, although in some years they might not have flowered in time to ripen seeds (Bisset 1929). Likewise, in St. Louis both the Missouri Botanical Garden and Tower Grove Park were universally praised for their outstanding summer displays of giant lilies growing in unheated pools.

Giant lilies have been grown in the open air at the Botanical Garden of Padua, Italy, since the 1930s.
TOMASZ ANIŚKO / LONGWOOD GARDENS

Victoria has thrived in an unheated pool at Les Cèdres on France's Côte d'Azur since the 1950s.
TOMASZ ANIŚKO / LONGWOOD GARDENS

In southern Europe, which is about the same latitude as Washington, D.C., the queen lily found agreeable accommodations in an unheated outdoor pool at the Royal Botanical Garden in Palermo, Sicily. After two failed attempts, a *Victoria amazonica* planted there opened her first flower on October 1, 1857 (Console 1857). One hundred years later, the tropical nymph thrived in a vast unheated pool in Les Cèdres, the garden of Julien Marnier-Lapostolle, maker of Grand Marnier liqueur, which was located on France's Côte d'Azur (Marnier-Lapostolle 1958).

In Italy, *Victoria* has resided in the outdoor pools of the Padua Botanical Garden since the 1930s. To the east, on the coast of the Black Sea, the Sukhumi Botanical Garden in the Abkhazia region of the Russian Empire welcomed *Victoria* into one of its outdoor basins in 1910, where she basked in the summer sun for a couple of years without supplemental heat (Trespe 1925).

In the Southern Hemisphere—but a few degrees closer to the equator than Washington, D.C., or Palermo—gardeners at the Botanic Gardens of Adelaide, Australia, tried unsuccessfully for many years to grow *Victoria amazonica* in an outdoor lake. Finally, in the exceptionally hot summer of 1959–60, when the water temperature in the lake reached nearly 28°C (84°F), the lily flourished. Her first flower buds appeared in February, and from that point on, she bloomed weekly until the close of the growing season in April. This event received much attention since it was the first time the giant lily was successfully cultivated in the open anywhere in Australia (Lothian 1960).

Many brave cultivators sought to reach the limits of *Victoria*'s endurance—and were undoubtedly repaid with repeated disappointments. Although they tried to grow the giant lily under less-than-ideal circumstances, thanks to them, the nymph was liberated from the confines of the aristocratic Victoria Houses and taken outdoors, where she could then mingle with ordinary folks under the open sky. At the same time that the South American lily's exact environmental requirements were being defined, more affordable outdoor facilities were being designed, tested, and widely popularized.

As expected of a tropical creature, high temperature proved to be a critical factor in *Victoria*'s successful development. Whether heated artificially or warmed by the rays of the summer sun, water has to reach a temperature of 27 to 29°C (80 to 84°F) to sustain the vigorous growth of *Victoria amazonica*, or about 3°C (5.4°F) less for *Victoria cruziana* (Tricker 1897, Nutt 1962). The Amazonian lily's growth may be checked if the water is allowed to cool below 24°C (75°F) during the day or 19°C (66°F) at night (Clifford 2005). Temperature increasing a few degrees above 30°C (86°F) has no ill effect, but in the days when heat supply to the pool was controlled manually, it was common to severely overheat the water, which often led to the lily's sudden demise (Wilke 1891).

Victoria grown out-of-doors in the Sukhumi Botanical Garden in Abkhazia, Russian Empire, in 1912. SERGEI MIKHAILOVICH PROKUDIN-GORSKII / LIBRARY OF CONGRESS

THE BEST CONDITIONS

While the queen lily appears to be very particular when it comes to water temperature, she is much more flexible with regard to other environmental factors. The volume of soil provided, for example, can vary widely. *Victoria*'s peculiar roots do not extend very far from the crown of the plant, a quality that makes the giant lily quite adaptable to growing in containers of various sizes. Although larger containers help to raise larger lilies, while extremely small pots can arrest or retard their growth, *Victoria* has been grown splendidly in planters that were either 90, 120, or 180 cm (35, 48, or 70 inches) in diameter (Herkert 2004, Clifford 2005, Jennings 2011).

Even more remarkable is *Victoria*'s adaptability to waters of strikingly different depths. Whereas in the wild she sometimes inhabits bodies of water 7 m (23 feet) deep, in cultivation, one-tenth of this is more than adequate. Because of the considerable cost of building and then heating a pool or an aboveground tank, the fact that *Victoria* seems perfectly satisfied with shallow water is a great advantage. At a minimum, the depth of the water should allow the growing tip of the lily's underwater rhizome to be submerged at all times, given the height of the container in which she is planted and the fact that the rhizomes can grow about 30 cm (12 inches) out of the soil in a single season.

LIFE IN CAPTIVITY   231

Victoria being transplanted from a small pot to her permanent location in a greenhouse of the Botanical Garden of Moscow State University around 1930.
BOTANICAL GARDEN OF MOSCOW STATE UNIVERSITY

Draining water from a pool in which *Victoria* was grown at the Botanical Garden of Moscow State University around 1930 shows that the water was only about knee-deep. Note the mound of soil in the center of the pool.
BOTANICAL GARDEN OF MOSCOW STATE UNIVERSITY

The question of *Victoria*'s requirements for water quality and purity was on the minds of gardeners from the earliest attempts to cultivate her. John Smith, the gardener and later curator of the Royal Botanic Gardens, Kew, declared that the "hard pump water from the gravel" used in the gardens "will not answer" (Hooker 1851). Instead, he recommended using rainwater, "doubtless the best, and the freest from anything injurious."

Like most plants, *Victoria* despises excessive salinity in her water and soil. Initially, in coastal areas, gardeners feared even the indirect effects of seawater carried by sea breezes. Soon, however, reports of giant lilies growing successfully in proximity to the sea showed that these fears had been overstated. In 1852, Edward

Chitty of Kingston, Jamaica, announced that the lilies dwelling in his garden, situated 800 m (one-half mile) from the coast, were thriving despite the influence of the sea breeze, which blew "with considerable violence at most times" (Chitty 1852). In recent years, Kit and Ben Knotts of Cocoa Beach, Florida, have proven that the giant lilies can flourish in their beachfront garden, surrounded by sand dunes.

Before water-filtering equipment became widely available, gardeners caring for aquatic plants worried a great deal over the buildup of algae and other harmful impurities, especially in indoor pools. Joseph Paxton at Chatsworth was convinced that it was important to keep the surface of the water in the basin in which *Victoria* grew in a constant state of agitation. He achieved this by installing a small overshot waterwheel. Many followed Paxton's example, but others objected, believing that such movement was nonexistent in *Victoria*'s native waters. "This we consider quite unnecessary," stated Smith of Kew, "having evidence before us of a plant producing above sixty flowers in the course of five months without any artificial motion being given to the water" (Hooker 1851). Instead, Smith recommended simply adding a small amount of water each day "to increase the freshness and wholesomeness of the entire body."

In cultivation, it is one thing to try to approximate the depth and temperature of the lily's native Amazonian waters, but it is quite another to imitate the fertility of the sediments carried by the river. Countless fertilizers have been tried and tested over the past century and a half. Their composition—containing both mineral and organic ingredients—also varies greatly. They all, however, seem to follow the same approach: to provide easily absorbable nutrients in small,

In the garden of Kit and Ben Knotts in Cocoa Beach, Florida, the giant lilies thrive despite proximity to the Atlantic.
TOMASZ ANIŚKO / LONGWOOD GARDENS

LIFE IN CAPTIVITY 233

Three versions of the apparatus designed to keep the water in the lily pool in a state of gentle agitation, used at Chatsworth, top, Syon House, middle, and Cherkley Court, bottom.
LONGWOOD GARDENS / THE LUESTHER T. MERTZ LIBRARY OF
THE NEW YORK BOTANICAL GARDEN

frequent doses. This essentially mirrors what a continuous deposition of alluvium does in the Amazon or Paraguay-Paraná river systems. This principle also applies to the occasional cohabitation of *Victoria* with koi fish in the same pond, as at La Rinconada in Santa Cruz, Bolivia, or the Wilhelma in Stuttgart, Germany. Not only do the fish cause no harm to the spiny plant, but their defecations provide a steady supply of daily fertilizer to the lilies.

While *Victoria*'s immense pads are a sight to behold and their rapid expansion inspires awe, compared to most plants, their life span is short. In Nature, older leaves have to make room for the constant production of younger ones. Even lilies in good health allow their oldest pads to gradually decay when they are only about a month old. The process usually begins with deterioration of the raised lip, which gives the outermost senescing leaves the appearance of being completely flat. Eventually, once the entire older leaf deteriorates, its place on the surface of water is taken by a younger one. In cultivation, the aging, unsightly leaves are regularly removed, giving a somewhat false impression that *Victoria* is an impeccable icon of vitality and obscuring the fact that her leaves are subject to natural succession and death.

DISSECTING THE QUEEN'S POLLINATION

One aspect of the lily's fascinating life in the wild that has not yet been replicated in cultivation—a situation unlikely to change—is her intimate relationship with scarab beetles. Among these nocturnal pollinators, the most common are three species of the genus *Cyclocephala* (Prance and Prance 1976). While their close relatives are also found in North America, they have not shown any interest in *Victoria* flowers.

Robert Schomburgk's initial report from Guiana mentioned the presence of twenty to thirty beetles inside *Victoria* flowers. He accused the insects, however, of infesting the blossoms, "to their great injury, often completely destroying the inner part of the disc" (Hooker 1851). Following Schomburgk, many other travelers to South America made similar observations, but they recognized the scarab beetles as critically important pollinating agents (Valla and Cirino 1972). Their accounts, however, did not convince everybody that the beetles helped pollinate the flower. As one skeptic surmised twenty-five years after Schomburgk's report: "The question why the *Victoria* flower can produce fruits and seeds in its native environment without human intervention is as far as we know not yet solved sufficiently" (Oudemans 1862, translated by Ger Meeuwissen).

With or without "human intervention," the cultivated *Victoria* has produced seeds ever since she was brought out of her native South America and left her entourage of scarab beetles behind. This fact intrigued some of the greatest minds of the nineteenth century. In 1865, German botanist Robert Caspary, who was working in Königsberg (today's Kaliningrad), concluded that because *Victoria* opened only one flower at a time and usually just one plant was cultivated, the seeds that had been

The removal of the oldest pads offers a rare opportunity to admire the fascinating structure of the underside of the *Victoria* leaf.
TOMASZ ANIŚKO / LONGWOOD GARDENS

LIFE IN CAPTIVITY 235

produced in Europe (by that time for sixteen generations) had resulted from self-pollination (Caspary 1865). This, Caspary pointed out, was in clear opposition to Charles Darwin's doctrine of the necessity or advantage of cross-pollination.

Darwin consulted with Smith at Kew on this matter and responded with a counter-argument. At Kew, Darwin explained, flowers left to themselves, and "probably not visited by insects," produced only eight to fifteen seeds in each fruit; those hand-pollinated with pollen from the same plant had fifteen to thirty seeds; and those pollinated with pollen brought from another plant growing at Chatsworth contained sixty to seventy-five seeds. He argued that this convincingly demonstrated the benefits of cross-pollination (Darwin 1876).

The low seed count in flowers left to themselves compared to those helped by "human intervention" stems from the fact that a tight ring of paracarpels, or inner staminodia, separates the fertile stamens above from the stigmatic cup below. In the wild, this defensive ring is penetrated by the beetles carrying pollen on their bodies, an adaptation favoring cross-pollination of the flowers. In cultivation, hand-pollination, even within the same flower, helps to overcome this partiality toward foreign pollen and improves the results of self-pollination by delivering the domestic pollen, usually carried on a brush, straight to the stigmatic cup.

Experiments carried out at the Amsterdam Botanical Garden in 1861 showed how effective paracarpels may be in preventing a flower's own pollen from falling into the stigmatic cup. Of seven flowers tested, two were left undisturbed, while the remaining five had paracarpels removed and pollen brushed inside the stigmatic cup. The two untouched flowers decomposed shortly, while the hand-pollinated ones produced ripe fruits, each containing a considerable number of seeds, provoking a conclusion that *Victoria* cannot possibly reproduce herself unassisted (Oudemans 1862).

Victoria's flowers can self-pollinate because their stigmas remain receptive on the second night of the flowering when stamens shed their pollen (Arcangeli 1908, Prance 2002). In the wild, this pollen lands on the back of the beetles scrambling out of the flower to be delivered to the stigmatic cup of the next flower they choose to visit. In captivity, the pollen may also land, especially if helped by a gardener, in the stigmatic cup below. In the wild, too, if cross-pollination fails for some reason, self-pollination may take place, although the result is fewer viable seeds (Leppard 1978).

SELF- VERSUS CROSS-POLLINATION

In cultivation, a large quantity of seeds was rarely desirable. If a pool or basin was large enough for only one plant to be grown each year, a handful of viable seeds were all that was needed. Even with a reduced seed set, self-pollination answered such low

---

Louis Van Houtte, 1850:

In its flowering it demands a most assiduous attention: first of all, if one is to properly manage the freshness and purity of its petals, the flowers must be somewhat supported above the water-level, which is achieved by means of a disc fashioned of cork or of light wood, notched in the side, and hollowed out in the center in order to hug the base of the calyx. Then, if we intend on harvesting the fertile seeds, on the second evening, when the flower is fully bloomed, we must cut in the middle of the internal ring of its sterile stamens with a penknife, taking care to shake the pollen off the stamens on the concave base of the flower (stigmatic cup): for this we employ a small colorist brush. Without this precaution, the fertilization of the plant in our enclosures would be achieved only under strongly restrained limits. The day after the fertilization, we cut the petals which are already fully stained, remove the peduncle from the float, leaving the fertilized ovary to submerge underwater.

Planchon and Van Houtte 1850–51, translated by Adam Koppeser

Inbreeding, resulting from flowers self-pollinating repeatedly over many generations, can manifest itself in a plant's retarded growth and failure to flower, even under favorable conditions. Diminutive *Victoria* pads can barely be recognized in the center of this pool at the Botanical Garden in Dresden, Germany. In 2010, several gardens in Europe reported such problems.
TOMASZ ANIŚKO / LONGWOOD GARDENS

demand adequately. Besides, it was the only available option when there were no other flowering lilies nearby.

Repeated over many generations, however, self-pollination brought about unintended consequences. Perhaps the first to notice this was Johann F. Wilke, superintendent of the plants department at the Rotterdam Zoological Garden. In 1891, he reported that some *Victoria* plants may be weakened as a result of inbreeding brought about by repeated self-pollination (Wilke 1891).

Once in a while, this problem recurs in cultivation—even as recently as 1996 in the United States and 2010 in many European gardens—but since it is easily correctable through the acquisition of new seeds, ideally from wild populations, it is usually just as easily forgotten. The signs of inbreeding to watch out for include reduced vigor of the plant growing in an otherwise favorable environment, a failure to flower or develop fertile seeds, or various abnormalities in the development of floral parts.

The number of self-pollinated generations that can pass before inbreeding takes a toll on giant lilies is not known, but the benefits of cross-pollination are widely recognized today. Thus, there is no longer any need to take chances growing seeds obtained through selfing.

Among the benefits of cross-pollination one can also count the possibility of raising hybrids of *Victoria amazonica* and *Victoria cruziana*. In the days when the only species known in cultivation was the Amazonian one, an anonymous correspondent to the

Emasculated first-night flower prepared to receive pollen from a second-night flower.
Larry Albee / Longwood Gardens

Hans Guldmann, letter to Patrick Nutt, 1961:

I do not find pollinating the Victoria *essential. Left to itself it forms a fair number of seeds, but this can be greatly improved by pollination immediately after opening on the first night with pollen from a flower that is blooming for the second night. . . . Some time ago when I needed about ten thousand seeds for some tests, I grew two plants and used this method to advantage. One may also save pollen from a previous second night bloom, but fresh pollen seems more viable. Too, with less success, one may find a few dehiscent anthers the morning after the first night and use this pollen on the same plant's stigma. Incidentally, I believe this is the period that the plant apparently pollinates itself. I use a quarter-inch round camel hair watercolor brush for this purpose. Just sweep across the pollen laden anthers of the second night flower then insert it into the opening formed by the stamens of the first night flower and give the brush a few sharp taps—the pollen will fall onto the stigma. After applying, gently brush the pollen onto all parts of the stigma for better distribution.*

Guldmann 1961

Gardener's Chronicle wrote: "It is much regretted that this fine water lily is tender... and if it were possible to render its constitution hardier by crossing it with some less tender kind, the subject is one worth the attention of the hybridizer" (Anonymous 1850b).

This wish became a reality when, only a few decades later, the hardier *Victoria cruziana* was introduced into cultivation; soon, a hybrid between the two species followed. The hybrid not only surpassed both parents in vigor and appearance, but it also exhibited tolerance that was characteristic of the hardier species. The relative ease with which the two nymphs pollinated each other ultimately led to the development of second-generation hybrids through backcrossing the primary hybrid with either of the species. As a result, however, the authenticity of many cultivated *Victoria* today is questioned, and the uncontrolled intercrossing and selfing of hybrids of unknown pedigree is often suspected.

Whether cross-pollinating or selfing, in the absence of scarab beetles, a gardener's helping hand greatly improves the seed set (Nutt 1962). The particulars of each gardener's technique in delivering the pollen to the stigmatic cup vary somewhat—such as whether to do it with a brush or a finger—but the critical decision is the timing of this operation. Those who want to ensure cross-pollination perform it on the first night of bloom, starting with the removal of the still-closed stamens along with staminodia for easier access to the stigmatic cup. This way, they avoid accidental self-pollination. On the second night of bloom, when stamens begin shedding pollen, self-pollination can be easily accomplished. At the royal garden Herrenhausen near Hanover, Heinrich Wendland even delayed this "human intervention" into *Victoria*'s private life until the morning following the second night of bloom. Apparently, he was always able to gather copious amounts of seeds (Regel 1871).

Once the pollination is completed and ovules are successfully fertilized, the ovary begins to swell rapidly. Its further development, ripening, and eventually dehiscence take place under water. To prevent the seeds from falling to the bottom of a pool or pond, Louis Van Houtte, a Belgian pioneer of *Victoria* cultivation in Europe, devised a method still widely in use today. An ovary showing signs of swelling was wrapped in

After washing off the gelatinous arils, *Victoria* seeds are usually stored in distilled water, which from time to time is changed to keep it fresh.
Tomasz Aniśko / Longwood Gardens

muslin—now usually replaced by cheesecloth—fastened around the peduncle with a thread or wire, and allowed to submerge (Planchon and Van Houtte, 1850–51).

When *Victoria* is grown in the open air, the ripening fruits should be removed from the pool or pond at the end of growing season, placed in a container filled with water, and brought indoors (Nutt 1962). The number of seeds that develop inside each fruit can vary greatly, from only a few, as observed by Smith at Kew, to as many as five hundred (Clifford 2005).

In nature, the gelatinous arils that surround the seeds freed from the decomposing fruit help them to first rise to and then float on the surface of the water, facilitating their dispersal. In cultivation, seeds are usually separated from these arils and washed several times. The water is then changed frequently to keep it fresh (Nutt 1962).

After harvesting the seeds, a ripening period is required to improve their germination. Patrick Nutt of Longwood Gardens recommended storing the seeds of *Victoria cruziana* for eight weeks at about 15°C (59°F), and those of *Victoria amazonica* at 21°C (70°F) (Nutt 1962). Once the seeds attained a brownish-black color associated with full ripeness, they were washed again, placed in distilled water, and kept at about 7°C (45°F) until sowing (Nutt 1962). Others found that storing seeds at temperatures as high as

14°C (57°F) gave comparable results (Clifford 2005). While it is generally accepted that seeds need to be kept moist—either submerged in water or mixed with wet sand—Eduard August von Regel, director of the Botanical Garden in St. Petersburg, reported that storing seeds dry and wrapped in cotton improved their germination (Regel 1871).

Although properly stored seeds of *Victoria* may remain viable for up to five years, their germination rate diminishes rapidly as the seeds age (Trespe 1925, Clifford 2005). To the frustration of many gardeners, the giant lily's germination is not well synchronized. A small number of seeds may germinate the same year they were harvested, and not all of the seeds will germinate the following spring. Instead, small batches may continue to sprout randomly for the next three or four years (Valla 1976).

In the wild, this randomness is a useful adaptation that helps *Victoria* cope with the unpredictable nature of flooding rivers and improves the chances that at least some seeds will germinate in response to a lasting deluge. Under cultivated conditions, however, this can give the impression of low viability, disappointing gardeners who would like to see all seeds germinate when they choose to sow them. After Edward Chitty in Jamaica waited eleven months to see some of the *Victoria* seeds come up after sowing, he concluded: "This shows the patience and watchfulness required to raise some things from seed, and the folly of ever despairing or throwing up the ground, etc., as hopeless, because the seed has long lain dormant" (Chitty 1852).

Anyone who can successfully grow *Victoria* is soon blessed with more seeds than he or she can possibly use. The practice of freely sharing the surplus seeds started with

Mature *Victoria* seeds, the black "pearls" of the floral kingdom.
TOMASZ ANIŚKO / LONGWOOD GARDENS

Joseph Paxton at Chatsworth and William Hooker at Kew. Thanks to their generosity, and soon that of others, *Victoria* was able to travel the world and win the hearts of gardeners everywhere only a few years after her introduction into cultivation. This tradition has continued admirably till this day, although the acquisition of wild seeds from South America has become more complicated since the Convention on Biological Diversity in Rio de Janeiro was adopted in 1992.

The giant lily's prolific seed production allowed the Knottses in Florida, gardening on a small parcel in Cocoa Beach, to save enough seeds each year to share them with anyone who asked. One year, after they grew eighteen plants, they were able to harvest more than twenty-eight thousand seeds (Knotts 2004). As their reputation grew, so did the number of requests. In a few years, the Knottses became the world's main supplier of *Victoria*, sending out nearly ten thousand seeds to some one hundred sixty gardens around the globe each year.

Considering the plethora of organizations and societies dedicated to specific plants, it may come as a surprise that there is no group solely dedicated to *Victoria*. One such initiative was founded in the United States in 1996 and named Victoria Conservancy, but it was short-lived. Today, enthusiasts interested in growing the queen lily can link up with each other through a number of aquatic gardening societies, such as the International Waterlily and Water Gardening Society, and Water Gardeners International, which share not only seeds but also advice and encouragement.

Organized or not, faithful and enthusiastic followers of *Victoria* can be found around the world. As long they are willing to perform daily chores, diligently looking after the phenomenal lily, and bear the not-so-trivial expense of maintaining appropriate facilities to imitate the annual floods of the Amazon and Paraná, *Victoria*'s life in captivity will continue into the foreseeable future.

Patrick Nutt of Longwood Gardens holds a handful of *Victoria amazonica* seeds. Thanks to prolific seed production, the queen lily has been freely shared among gardeners ever since she was introduced into cultivation in 1849.
TOMASZ ANIŚKO / LONGWOOD GARDENS

LIFE IN CAPTIVITY 241

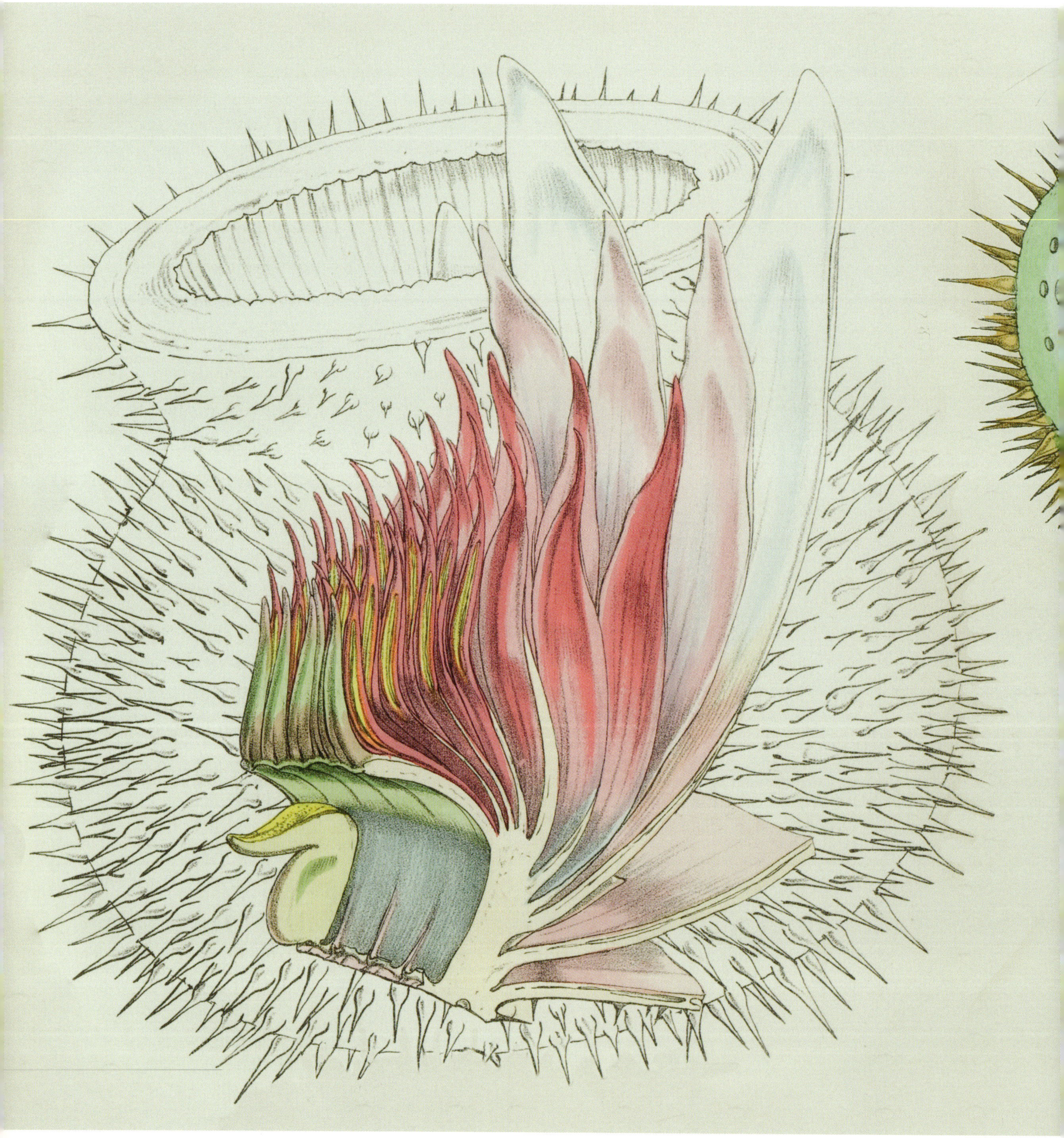

chapter 14

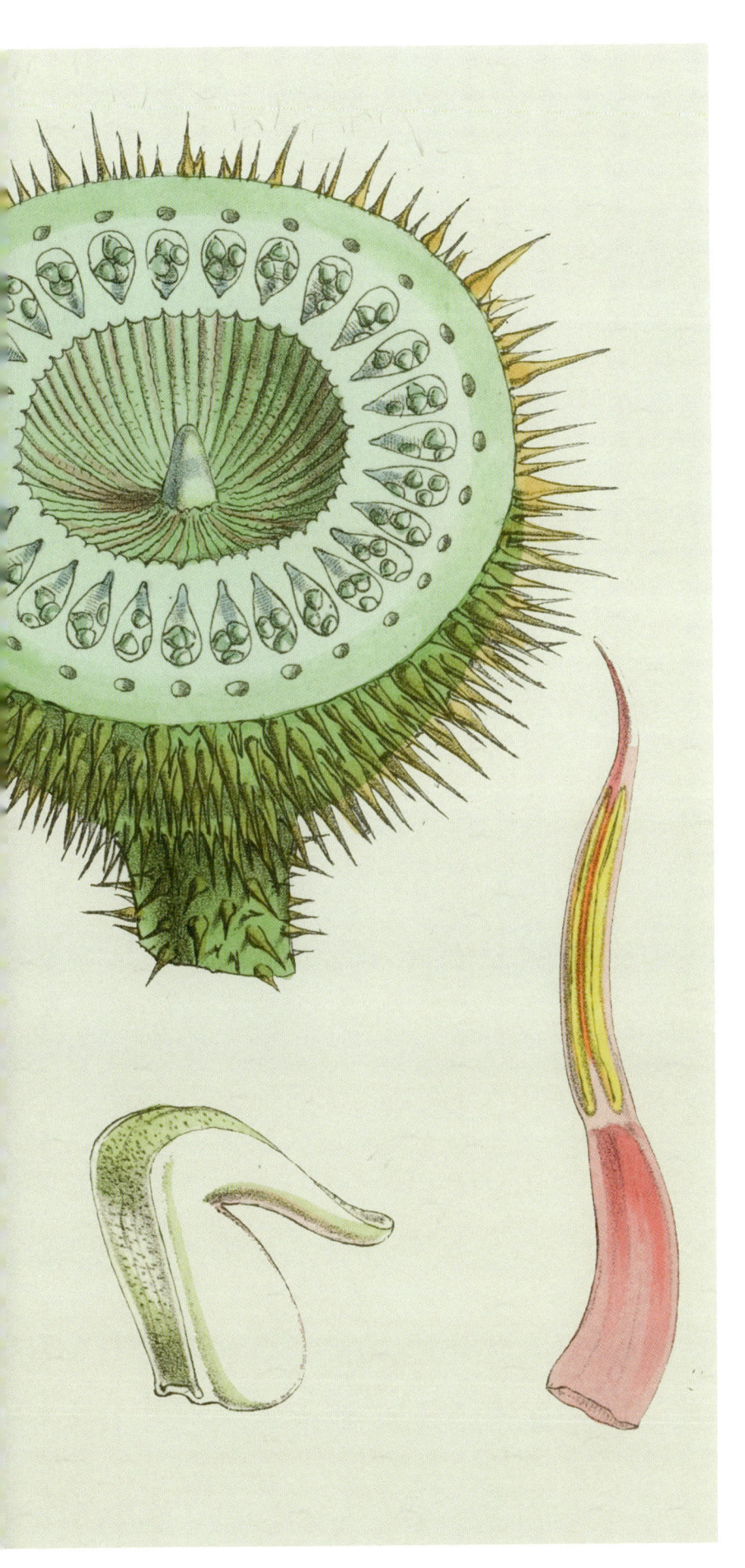

THE ORIGIN

THE ORIGIN OF *VICTORIA*, THE QUEEN OF FLOWERS, may be inextricably linked to the origin of all flowering plants. In 1920, Paraguayan writer and intellectual Viriato Díaz-Pérez contemplated *Victoria,* wondering whether he was standing "before [a] contemporary or before some miraculous survivor of a giant primitive flower" (Vidal y Careta 1920, translated by Emily Vera). To him, the lily's flowers and leaves evoked the "vegetation of the immense slimy swamps where prehistoric monsters lived."

This metaphor of the giant lily as a relic from the age of "monsters" may not be as far-fetched as it appears. Spanish paleontologist Francisco Vidal y Careta thought that *Victoria*'s "miraculous" survival from the prehistoric past was possible because the immense expanse and stability of Amazonia afforded a refuge where the giant lily outlasted her contemporaries of the Tertiary geologic period, 65 to 2.6 million years ago. "The day that *Victoria regia* is found … in fossil state," he predicted, "we will have no hesitation or doubt to affirm its preexistence in other geological periods" (Vidal y Careta 1920, translated by Emily Vera).

Vidal y Careta's prophecy came close to being fulfilled when a team of researchers from Cornell University excavated Upper Cretaceous deposits in the Old Crossman Clay Pit near Sayreville, New Jersey (Gandolfo et al. 2004). When these

A cross-section of the flower and fruit of *Victoria amazonica* from the January 1847 edition of *Curtis's Botanical Magazine*, one of four plates prepared by Walter Fitch based on preserved specimens brought from Bolivia by Thomas Bridges.
LONGWOOD GARDENS LIBRARY AND ARCHIVES

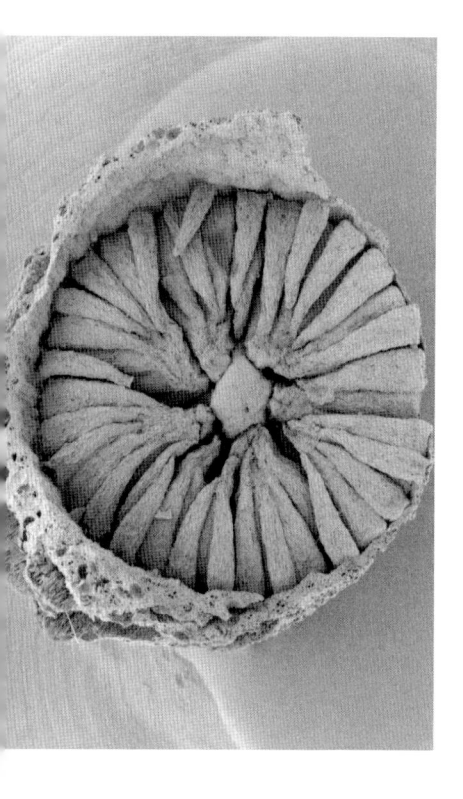

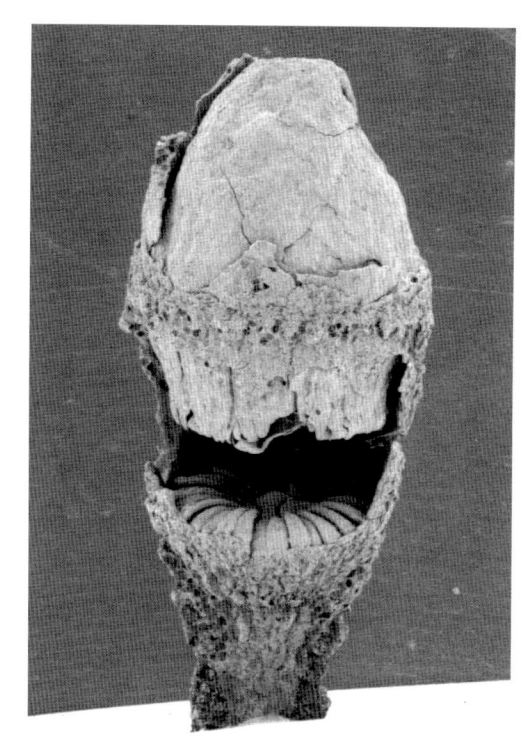

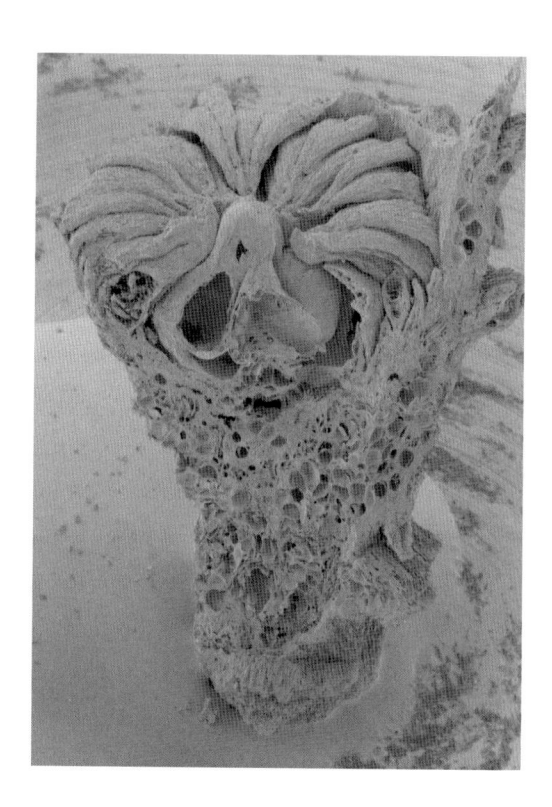

Scanning electron micrographs of the *Microvictoria svitkoana* flower bud reveal a striking resemblance to the modern *Victoria* flower.
MARIA A. GANDOLFO / CORNELL UNIVERSITY / NATIONAL ACADEMY OF SCIENCES

deposits accumulated some ninety million years ago, dinosaurs still roamed Earth, large parts of North America were covered by shallow seas, and the future New Jersey enjoyed a warm subtropical or tropical climate.

The area around Sayreville was a vast swamp, teeming with life and subject to floods that delivered fluvial deposits that eroded from the Appalachians to the west. Fragments of plants that fell into the swamp were often covered by these sediments. During the dry season, wildfires frequently broke out and swept through the area. Subjected to high temperatures in the absence of oxygen, buried plant pieces were fossilized through a process of charcoalification by which the volatile elements of organic material were driven off, leaving behind carbon residue that preserved the original structure in astonishing detail.

Among the fossils that the Cornell team found were exquisitely preserved flower buds that had many features of the modern-day *Victoria*, including a stigmatic cup surrounding a central apical residuum and topped by a ring of paracarpels. These similarities led Cornell's scientists to name this extinct lily *Microvictoria svitkoana*. The generic appellation *Microvictoria* alludes to the fact that the flowers were a miniature version of today's queen lily. The fossilized buds were only about 3 mm (one-tenth of an inch) long. Even taking into account considerable shrinkage resulting from charcoalification, this did not suggest flowers of impressive size. Nevertheless, their striking resemblance convinced Cornell scientists that *Microvictoria* was a sister genus to *Victoria*. Their discovery thus dated the giant lily's closest relative on Earth to the age of the dinosaurs.

The remarkable morphological similarity between *Microvictoria* and *Victoria* implies that the intimate relationship between the queen lily and the pollinating beetles, reflected in the unique architecture of her flower, is indeed an ancient one. Most likely, however, the beetles entrapped in *Microvictoria* were proportionally much smaller than the scarab beetles visiting the giant lily today (Gandolfo et al. 2004). To address Díaz-Pérez's question about *Victoria*, the New Jersey fossils suggest that today's *Victoria* is a "survivor"—yet not of a "giant primitive flower," but a rather diminutive one.

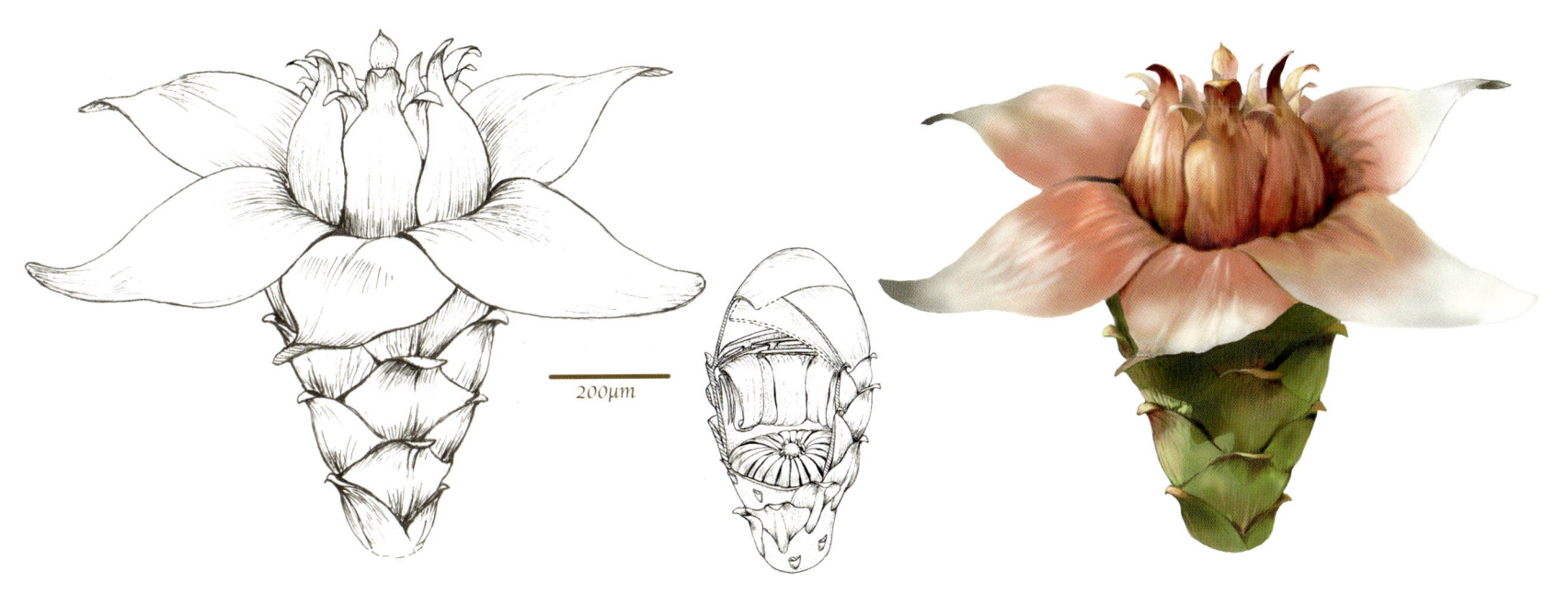

A reconstruction of the flower of *Microvictoria svitkoana* based on the ninety-million-year-old fossil excavated by the Cornell University team in Old Crossman Clay Pit in New Jersey.
MICHAEL ROTHMAN

Fossilized flowers of such great antiquity are rare. Yet fossil records of leaves, pollen, and seeds that link water lilies to flowering plants during the Early Cretaceous, about 130 million years ago, have long been known (Ervik and Knudsen 2003, Thien et al. 2009, Ronse De Craene 2010). It appears that aquatic habitats and their floodplains have long played a critical role in the evolution of the earliest flowering plants, even though the high number of their impressions from the Early Cretaceous may be due in part to the aquatic environment being more favorable for fossilization than the terrestrial one (Endress and Doyle 2009).

This paleontological evidence has been corroborated by conducting morphological studies of living plants and by breaking down their genetic codes. Together, these methods allow scientists to reconstruct evolutionary lineages and trace relationships between modern species with a high degree of confidence. In light of these findings, various water lilies of the family Nymphaeaceae and the closely related aquatic family of Cabombaceae—which together form a taxonomical order of Nymphaeales—belong to the oldest lineages of flowering plants (Borsch et al. 2008, Löhne et al. 2008).

THE FLOWERING FAMILY TREE

Mapping the genealogy of flowering plants results in so-called phylogenetic trees, where individual branches represent various lineages. Using this metaphor of a tree, water lilies form one of the lowest—earliest—branches that sprouted at the very base of the tree. Plants that ascended from these most basal branches share many features of their flowers, most notably the spiral or whorled arrangements of their floral parts, an indefinite number of floral organs, and the central apical residuum, which is clearly visible in the *Microvictoria* fossils and in living *Victoria* flowers (Ronse De Craene 2010).

These primitive flowers are often protogynous, meaning that their pistils are receptive before stamens shed the pollen. They also exhibit a gradual transition between various floral parts, such as sepals and petals, or have infertile staminodes

THE ORIGIN   245

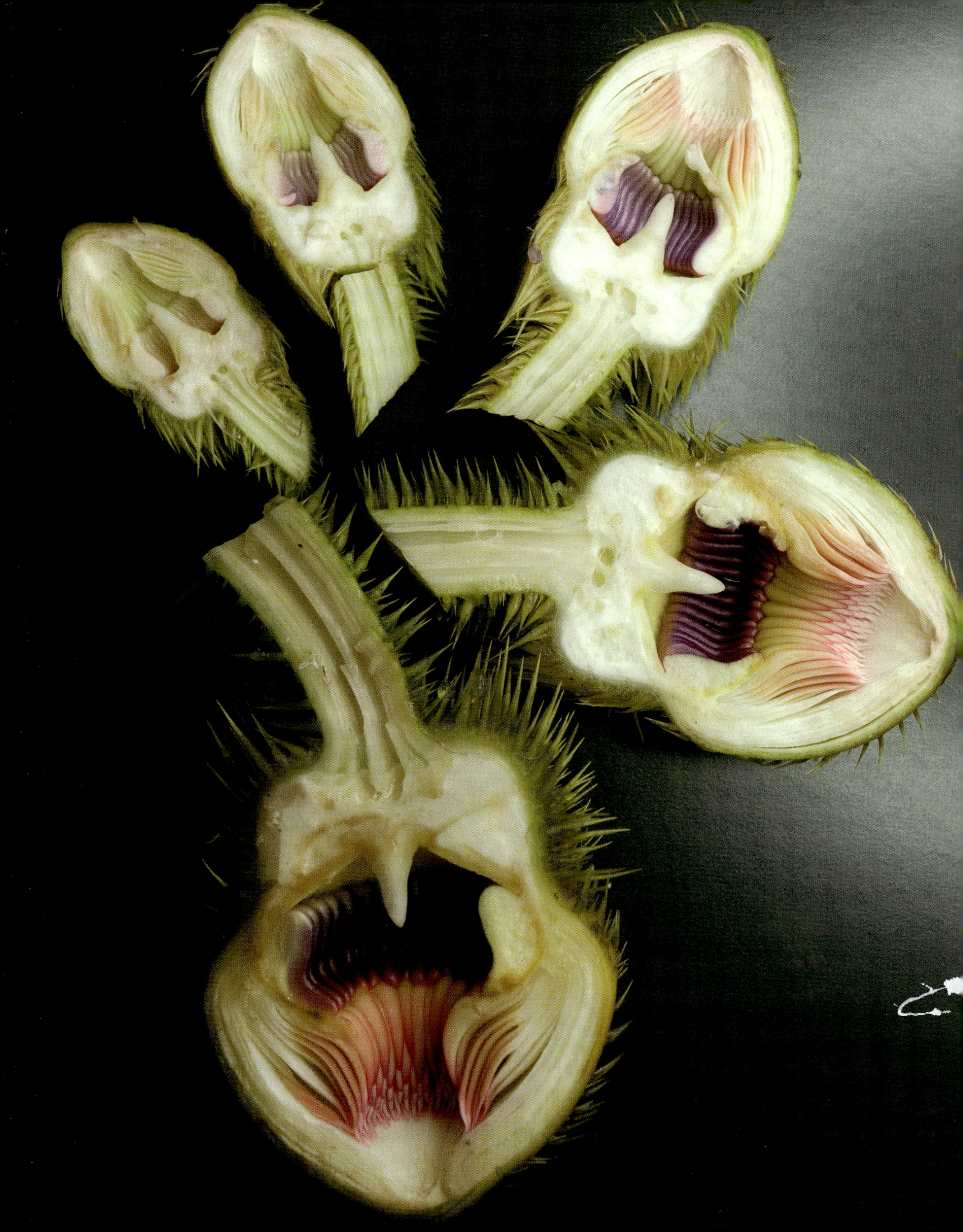

separating fertile stamens from petals or carpels. Although infertile themselves, the staminodes take on special roles in pollination, either by preventing self-pollination or by providing allure and rewards such as food, scents, or visual attractants to visiting insects (Ronse De Craene 2010).

After Nymphaeales emerged, it branched out into two families, Nymphaeaceae and Cabombaceae. This is estimated to have taken place between seventy-three and forty-six million years ago (Löhne et al. 2008, Borsch et al. 2011). The success of water lilies as a new branch was conditioned on several evolutionary innovations, including transitioning from the spiral to whorled arrangement of floral parts and increasing their numbers; differentiating sepals and petals; and developing a hypanthium, a cup-shaped extension of the floral axis (Ronse De Craene 2010).

As soon as the earliest flowers appeared in the swamps of the Cretaceous, insects found them irresistible. Beetles were probably the first to discover many benefits of foraging inside the flowers in exchange for carrying a load of pollen from one plant to the next. Beetles were followed by butterflies, and bees were last (Baker and Hurd 1968). Many of the primitive flowers' features, such as the hypanthium enclosing the ovary, point to the necessity of protecting precious ovules from the reckless behavior of voracious insects (Baker and Hurd 1968).

Although infertile, outer staminodes of the *Victoria* flower, which separate stamens from petals, play an important role in pollination by controlling beetles' access to the stigmatic cup below.
Tomasz Aniśko / Longwood Gardens

A sequential arrangement of *Victoria* flower buds at various stages of development. Their internal structure reveals many features indicating the ancient origin of giant water lilies.
Tomasz Aniśko / Longwood Gardens

THE ORIGIN   247

Victoria flower features a large hypanthium. This cup-shaped extension of the floral axis protects ovules from beetles foraging inside the stigmatic cup.
TOMASZ ANIŚKO / LONGWOOD GARDENS

In the case of *Victoria*, her long affair with beetles may also explain the enormous size of her flowers. Over the course of millions of years, flowers that could entrap a greater number of beetles crowding inside the floral chamber were more successful in pollinating their ovules and producing more seeds, which preferentially selected for increased flower size (Thien et al. 2009).

Richard Salisbury recognized Nymphaeaceae as a family in 1805. Nymphaeaceae includes several genera of water lilies: *Nymphaea*, which lent its name to the whole family; *Barcleya*; *Nuphar*; the two sister genera, *Victoria* and *Euryale*; and the most recent addition, *Ondinea* (Schneider et al. 2003, Borsch et al. 2011). *Nuphar* is thought to have split first from the family during the Paleocene. Then, between the Late Oligocene and Middle Miocene, the remaining genera developed their own branches (Borsch et al. 2011). The most recent common ancestors of modern *Euryale* and *Victoria* emerged nearly thirty-eight million years ago. Some twenty million years later, the giant lilies of what later became the Old World and the New World took separate paths (Borsch et al. 2011).

FAMILY MATTERS

Despite its ancient roots, the family of water lilies has changed a great deal since its inception. Many of its characteristics are considered to be derived, meaning they were not present in their ancestral forms but evolved more recently as adaptations to either the aquatic life or the mode of pollination (Les et al. 1997). Water lilies underwent a secondary loss of cambium, or lateral meristem-producing vascular tissues, which they did not need in an aqueous environment (Borsch et al. 2008). Their stamens became flat and laminar, and they also increased in number—a means of attracting and feeding pollinating insects. Broadening of the hypanthium containing the floral chamber allowed for a greater number of stamens as well as petals surrounding it (Schneider et al. 2003).

Among water lilies, *Victoria* and her sister *Euryale* are viewed as the most evolved. In the past, they were sometimes separated into their own family, Euryalaceae (Kite et al. 1991, Les et al. 1997). They differ from other water lilies in their annual rather than perennial growth habit. Their flowers also have an inferior ovary that is positioned below the point of attachment of the remaining floral parts. In contrast, the ovary is superior in *Nuphar* and intermediate in *Nymphaea*, *Barclaya*, and *Ondinea* (Borsch et al. 2008).

Since their separation in the Early Miocene about twenty-three to eleven million years ago, *Victoria* and *Euryale* have drifted apart. Today, the sister genera are easily distinguished by a number of characteristics (Löhne et al. 2008, Borsch et al. 2011). While *Victoria* continued the affair with the pollinating beetles that had been established by her ancestors, *Euryale* freed herself from this relationship and found a way to reproduce through self-pollination. For this reason, *Victoria*'s flower has retained a prominent ring of carpellary appendages on which pollinating beetles feed, whereas such structures are absent in *Euryale* (Borsch et al. 2008).

In the warm Early Miocene climate, water lilies were widespread throughout the northern latitudes. Thanks to that period's land bridges, their migration across what is now the North Atlantic and the Bering Strait was unhampered (Löhne et al. 2008). Fossils of plants resembling *Victoria* and *Euryale* have been found in the

When *Euryale* became independent of the pollinating beetles, her flower lost the ring of carpellary appendages inside the stigmatic cup that is so prominent in *Victoria* flowers.
LARRY ALBEE / LONGWOOD GARDENS

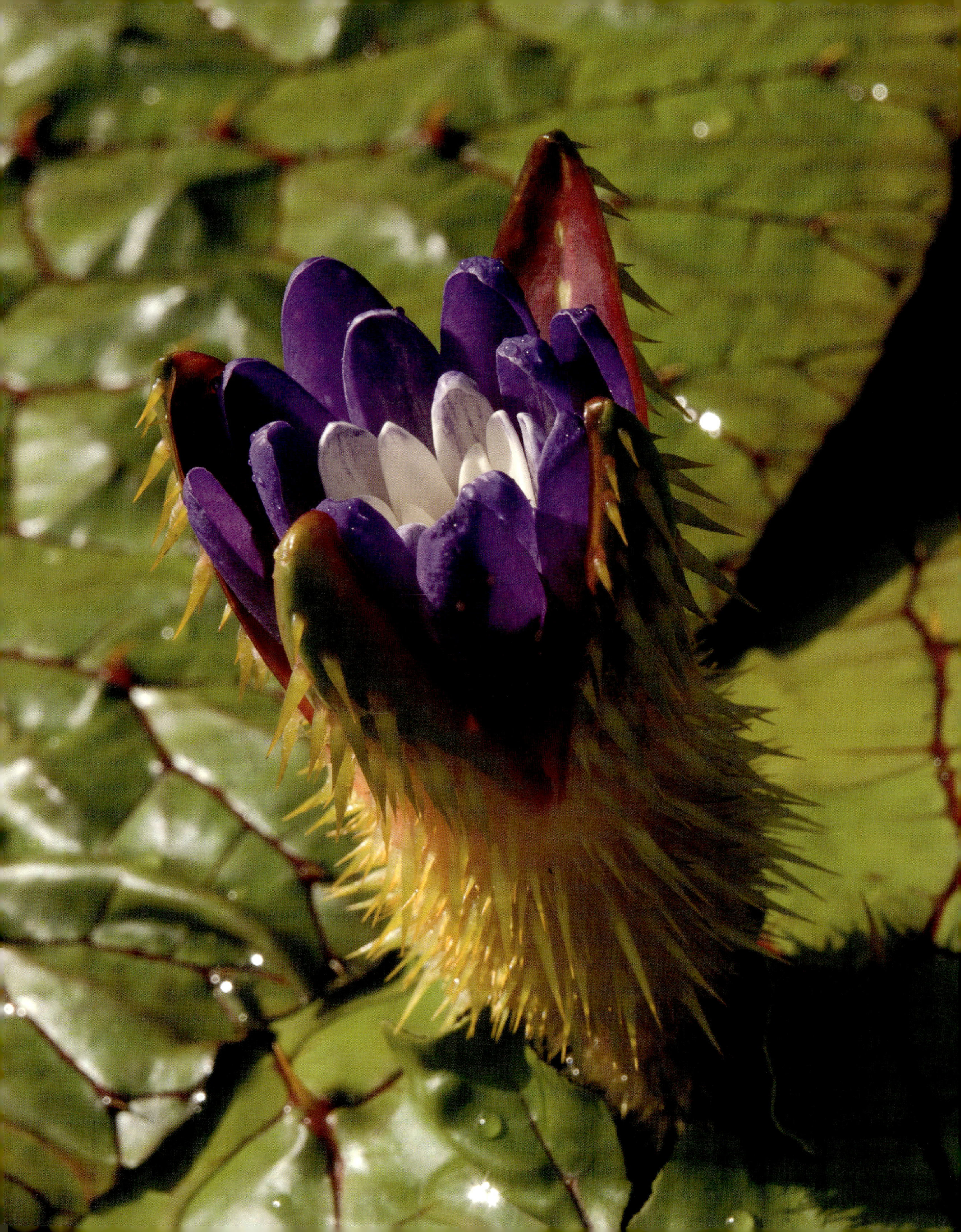

Netherlands, Germany, Russia, and Japan, while today's northernmost populations of *Euryale* in Chinese and Russian Manchuria are considered relics from the time when this region enjoyed a milder climate (Skvortzow 1925, Löhne et al. 2008).

The cooling Late Miocene climate led to mass extinctions in the Northern Hemisphere. *Euryale* and *Victoria* made a southward migration to the warmer regions of Asia and the Americas, respectively (Löhne et al. 2008). This dislocation, followed by the re-establishment of the Antarctic ice sheet, effectively separated the two lineages, which continued to evolve in isolation from each other. Coincidentally, during the Miocene, North America and South America became reconnected, offering *Victoria* a warm passage to the tropics (Löhne et al. 2008). On the other hand, *Euryale* migrated south to China, Japan, and India and somehow managed to survive in the chilling climate along the Manchurian floodplains (Skvortzow 1925).

Like *Victoria*, *Euryale* inhabits shallow bodies of waters left behind by meandering sediment-rich rivers. She has adapted to harsher climates by shortening her lifecycle to as little as four and half months, reducing her flower and leaf size, and becoming independent of pollinating beetles. *Euryale* flowers self-pollinate, usually without even opening, and often under water. This self-pollination led in turn to a secondary reduction in the number of floral parts. While both *Victoria* and *Euryale* have four sepals, the latter has about half as many petals, stamens, and carpels as her sister *Victoria* (Les et al. 1997).

Despite millions of years of separation, *Victoria* and *Euryale* retained enough common features to make their close relationship clearly evident. Both have very large platter-like floating leaves with

Flowers of *Euryale*, like those of *Victoria*, have four sepals but only about half as many petals, stamens, and carpels, a secondary reduction due to *Euryale*'s switch to self-pollination.
Tomasz Aniśko / Longwood Gardens

Instead of being positioned in the middle of the leaf axils, *Victoria* flowers are shifted slightly up the spiral toward the growing tip. This displacement affords both the leaf and flower bud enough space for development.
Tomasz Aniśko / Longwood Gardens

A cross-section of the three sister water lilies—*Nymphaea* (left), *Victoria* (center), and *Euryale* (right)—which, though separated millions of years ago, are often grown today in the same aquatic gardens. They may one day be reunited under the name of *Nymphaea*, oldest of the three.
LARRY ALBEE / LONGWOOD GARDENS

John Lindley, 1838:

Although Victoria *is possibly the same as the* Euryale amazonica *of Pöppig, yet it is, in my opinion, quite distinct from the latter genus. I am not aware that any one in this country, of any botanical reputation, has called this opinion in question. . . .* Victoria *has the inner petals rigid, and curved inwards over the stamina, into which they gradually pass: in* Euryale *there is no transition of this kind. In* Victoria *is a double row of hornlike sterile stamens, curving over the stigmas, and adhering firmly to their back;* Euryale *has no such structure. In* Victoria *there are thirty-six large, reniform, compressed, fleshy stigmas; in lieu of this very singular character,* Euryale *has only the margin of a cup, with six, seven, or eight crenatures.* Victoria *has twenty-six cells to the ovary;* Euryale *only from six to eight. And, finally, to say nothing of minor distinctions, the ripe fruit of* Victoria *lies at the bottom of a regularly truncated cup, which stands high above the water; while the flower of* Euryale *sinks into the water after flowering, and the fruit, when ripe, is invested with the decayed remains of the calyx and corolla.*

Lindley 1838a

---

petioles attached near the center of the leaf, while their juvenile leaves are submersed. Both also exhibit a rather curious arrangement of flowers and leaves. These arise in what appear to be separate spirals: Rather than having each flower bud positioned in the middle of the leaf axil, it is shifted slightly up the spiral toward the growing tip. This displacement is easily explained. With the enormous size of both leaves and flowers, there would be no adequate space for bud development if the flower buds were positioned exactly above the leaf (Endress and Doyle 2009).

Botanists have struggled with sorting out the differences and similarities between *Victoria*, *Euryale*, and *Nymphaea*. Both Aimé Bonpland and Robert Schomburgk initially thought of *Victoria* as a type of *Nymphaea*. Eduard Pöppig recognized it as *Euryale*. John Lindley, who designated *Victoria* as a distinct new genus in its own right, acknowledged, "Notwithstanding a *prima facie* resemblance to *Euryale*, *Victoria* is in fact more nearly allied to *Nymphaea*" (Lindley 1838b). Adolphe Brongniart, in turn, thought the distinctions between *Euryale* and *Victoria* pointed out by John Lindley related only to minor characteristics (Lindley 1838b).

Today, phylogenetic studies are shedding new light on the origin of and relationships among water lilies. These studies may put into question the long-established definitions of *Victoria*, *Euryale*, and *Nymphaea*. The old argument about whether *Victoria* is distinct enough from her sister *Euryale* to deserve her own genus may be laid to rest in the future by molecular evidence showing that both sisters nest within *Nymphaea* (Endress and Doyle 2009). It would be a great irony indeed if, by applying the most sophisticated modern methods, botanists concluded that *Victoria* and *Euryale* should be reclassified as *Nymphaea*. This would validate the intuition of early explorers who assigned their discoveries of the giant South American lilies to that long-known genus.

DEVELOPMENT OF A QUEEN

In examining *Victoria*'s remarkable features, one can appreciate how she evolved within and was shaped by her environment. Her immense, solitary, terminally born flowers reflect an adaptation for pollination by beetles. Likewise, the high number of floral parts (50 to 70 petals, 150 to 300 stamens, and 25 to 40 carpels) is thought to be a response to the voracious feeding by these insects (Les et al. 1999). The beetles must also be given credit for the fact that *Victoria*'s flowers raise their temperature on the first night of flowering and release a delightful fruity scent. The large size of the flower, the sheltered floral chamber lined inside with starchy carpellary appendages, and the movements of petals and staminodes are also intended for the beetles' comfort and safety (Borsch et al. 2008).

The fruits, which develop under water, are well protected from birds flying overhead, and needle-sharp spines repel any swimming herbivores. Once mature, the fruits rupture, assisted by the inflating seed arils. These balloon-like arils bring the seeds to the surface and allow them to float as the water disperses them (Borsch et al. 2008). The mammoth, rapidly expanding leaves provide a clear advantage in the struggle to conquer as much of the water surface as possible before it is taken over by other aquatic subjects. The spiny armory on the underside of the leaves, petioles, and peduncles discourages any herbivores in the water from taking a liking to the soft and succulent tissues.

The notion that *Victoria* existed as two species—which met with so much resistance in Victorian England—was still not entirely settled in the 1960s. At that time, Edgar Anderson of the Missouri Botanical Gardens wrote: "Exactly how they ought to be classified is still a matter for scientific dispute to which a study of the hybrids and

The *Victoria* seeds are superbly equipped for water dispersal thanks to inflated balloon-like arils. This means of conveyance carried the giant lilies into the remote parts of the Amazon and Paraná-Paraguay river basins throughout much of South America.
Tomasz Aniśko / Longwood Gardens

William Tricker, 1897:

Later it became a difficult matter to obtain seed of the true Victoria regia, *and being desirous of securing it I determined to try a new field for supply, and during the winter, 1893–94, received from a European house some seed purporting to be of the true* Victoria regia. . . . *From the first these seedlings exhibited a feature which marked them as entirely distinct from the original form, the leaves being light green and mottled with reddish brown on the face, purplish below. The rapid growth and the early cupping of the leaf were also very noticeable. In its permanent quarters the growth of the plant was still more remarked, and it was soon evident it would outrun the older plants of the other variety, which in fact it did, at a very early date. . . . At one time as many as nine flowers and buds were visible in different stages of development, while var.* randii *produced but half that number, and seldom had more than five presentable leaves at one time.*

Tricker 1897

Flowers of *Victoria amazonica* discovered near the confluence of the Rio Branco and Rio Negro (right) are smaller than the form growing along the main stem of the Amazon near Manaus (left). Flowers pictured here were collected on the morning following their first-night opening and came from plants growing in the same pool.

TOMASZ ANIŚKO / LONGWOOD GARDENS

These Brazilian introductions showed that the South American nymph exhibited considerable morphological variability throughout her range. In 1894, another American nurseryman, William Tricker of Clifton, New Jersey, planted seeds of *Victoria amazonica* ordered from Europe. When they produced very distinct-looking lilies, he concluded that he had on hand yet another variety. She differed from the other type in cultivation in the United States because she produced leaves that were light green on top with a very high raised edge. In addition, the whole plant demonstrated a preference for cooler temperatures, a highly desirable trait for plants grown in the open. Like the variety *randii* earlier, this form was widely distributed across the United States as variety *trickerii* of *Victoria amazonica*. But soon her true identity was revealed. Upon more careful examination, Tricker's form turned out to be nothing more than *Victoria cruziana* masquerading in European gardens under the name of her Amazonian kin (Malme 1907).

Yet another variant of the giant lily was found in 1995 on an expedition led by Scott A. Mori of the New York Botanical Garden. Researchers located the lily downstream from the confluence of the Rio Branco and Rio Negro in Brazil, along the northern fringes of *Victoria*'s range (Mori 1995). When Donald Bryne, an aquatic plant nurseryman from Lake City, Florida, learned about this report, he decided to investigate it (Bryne 2008). A veteran of many expeditions to Brazil, Bryne knew it was highly unusual for the lily to thrive so far from the Amazon, beyond the reach of its white waters. In 2007, he led a team that traveled from Manaus up the Rio Negro to the point where it joins the Rio Branco. The plants they found there were noticeably smaller in all aspects than those around Manaus. In addition, the leaves did not have even a hint of a raised edge, and the flowers lacked the strong purple tinge on the second night of flowering (Bryne 2008). University of

Florida researchers conducted a molecular study of the Rio Branco lilies, but the taxonomic status and name of this variant have not yet been resolved (Anonymous 2007, Bryne 2008).

A SPONTANEOUS HYBRID?

By the turn of the century, botanists and gardeners alike were finally becoming acquainted with two species of *Victoria*—one being assigned to the Amazon and its tributaries, the other to the Paraguay and Paraná river system. In 1894, Swedish explorer Gustav O. Malme traveled through the region of Mato Grosso (also written as Matto Grosso). He arrived in the Brazilian town of Corumbá on the border with Bolivia. Corumbá lies near the western edge of the Pantanal, an immense swamp from which the river Paraguay gains its strength. The area is also home to the northernmost reaches of the Paraguay-Paraná watershed, where it connects to the watershed of the Amazon.

When Malme arrived in Corumbá in July 1894, he found *Victoria* in a lagoon by the river Paraguay. He diligently prepared specimens and later deposited them in the Regnellian Herbarium of the Swedish Museum of Natural History in Stockholm. "I did not think," Malme wrote later, "it was worth bringing home live seeds to Europe, especially since there was no possibility to grow the plant in Sweden at the time and furthermore I thought it was *Victoria regia* that I was dealing with" (Malme 1907, translated by Inger Wallin). Before reaching Stockholm, however, Malme stopped in Rotterdam, where he saw *Victoria regia* cultivated. To his surprise,

Giant lilies of Santa Ana in Bolivia were thought to represent *Victoria amazonica* when they were collected by Thomas Bridges in 1845, but Gustav Malme later recognized them as *Victoria cruziana* f. *mattogrossensis*, the same plant he had discovered in Corumbá. Santa Ana lilies have moderately high upturned leaf margins, either green or purple-red, and spineless sepals.
TOMASZ ANIŚKO / LONGWOOD GARDENS

THE ORIGIN

The Haage und Schmidt facility in Erfurt, Germany, where *Victoria amazonica* and *Victoria cruziana* were crossed before 1923.
THE BAILEY HORTORIUM, CORNELL UNIVERSITY

this plant differed significantly from the one he collected in Corumbá. After studying other herbarium specimens in Stockholm, he concluded that the Mato Grosso lily was more closely related to *Victoria cruziana* from Argentina and Paraguay than to the Brazilian species.

When Malme returned to Corumbá eight years later, he was determined to collect live seeds and have them grown in the recently opened Victoria House of Stockholm's Bergius Botanical Garden. He arrived in December 1902 during a dry season and found the old lagoon all but dried up. By the following July, however, the lilies were back in large numbers, and Malme was able to retrieve a couple of plump ripe fruits.

Back in Stockholm, the Corumbá lilies germinated successfully in early 1904 and were soon growing side by side with *Victoria regia* in the same basin, allowing for detailed comparison. Malme noted that while the leaves of *Victoria amazonica* had an upturned margin that was slanted outward, those of the Corumbá lilies had a margin that in its lower part was slanted inward; it was only slanted outward at the very top, as if it were "squeezed in the middle" (Malme 1907, translated by Inger Wallin).

Malme also pointed out that the plants from Mato Grosso differed from *Victoria cruziana* in a number of ways and therefore designated them as a new form, *mattogrossensis*. Their upturned leaf margin was only about half as tall as in *Victoria cruziana*. Malme also described the underside of the leaf as bluish-violet as opposed to green with only a bluish-violet cast. Where flowers of *Victoria cruziana* had smooth sepals or only a few weak prickles at the base, form *mattogrossensis* had variably spiny sepals reminiscent of those of *Victoria amazonica*, except the spines were shorter and pointing down rather than straight outward (Malme 1907). All these defining features could be described as intermediate between what had been known as true *Victoria amazonica* and *Victoria cruziana*. This later led to speculations on the hybrid origin of the Pantanal lilies. To add to the mystery, Malme also concluded that the *Victoria* plant collected more than half a century earlier in Bolivia by Thomas Bridges should be classified with Corumbá lilies as the form *mattogrossensis*.

Later writers purported that in Mato Grosso, where the tributaries of the Paraná and the Amazon interlace, both species of *Victoria* coexist and grade into one another (Conard 1953, Pott and Pott 2000). In addition, lilies of the Moxos plain in Bolivia, previously assumed to represent the typical *Victoria amazonica*, extend this transition zone further north, well into the watershed of the Amazon. Despite all this, we are still awaiting proof that spontaneous *Victoria* hybrids exist in either Panatanal or Moxos.

GERMAN AND SWEDISH HYBRIDS

Once both *Victoria amazonica* and *Victoria cruziana* were introduced into cultivation in the late nineteenth century, it was inevitable that sooner or later they would intercross and produce a hybrid, unless genetic barriers that could not be overcome existed. The earliest report of *Victoria amazonica* and *Victoria cruziana* successfully crossing with each other came from Haage und Schmidt, a seed company from Erfurt, Germany. In 1911, Haage und Schmidt built a greenhouse for aquatic plants with a tank large enough to grow three *Victoria* plants (Trespe 1925). Details of what happened inside this aquatic house are not known, but the company's catalog of 1923 offered for the first time *Victoria hybrida imperialis* alongside *Victoria cruziana* and *Victoria regia* (Haage und Schmidt 1923).

The hybrid was described as having leaves with a higher edge than *Victoria amazonica* and growing better at lower temperatures. Her seeds were also the most expensive of the three lilies. They were priced at two hundred million marks for a single seed, while the Amazonian nymph sold for only thirty million. These astronomical figures reflected Germany's hyperinflation, which peaked in 1923. The hybrid was also listed in

The 1923 catalog of Haage und Schmidt seed company, in which *Victoria hybrida imperialis* was offered for the first time.
THE BAILEY HORTORIUM, CORNELL UNIVERSITY

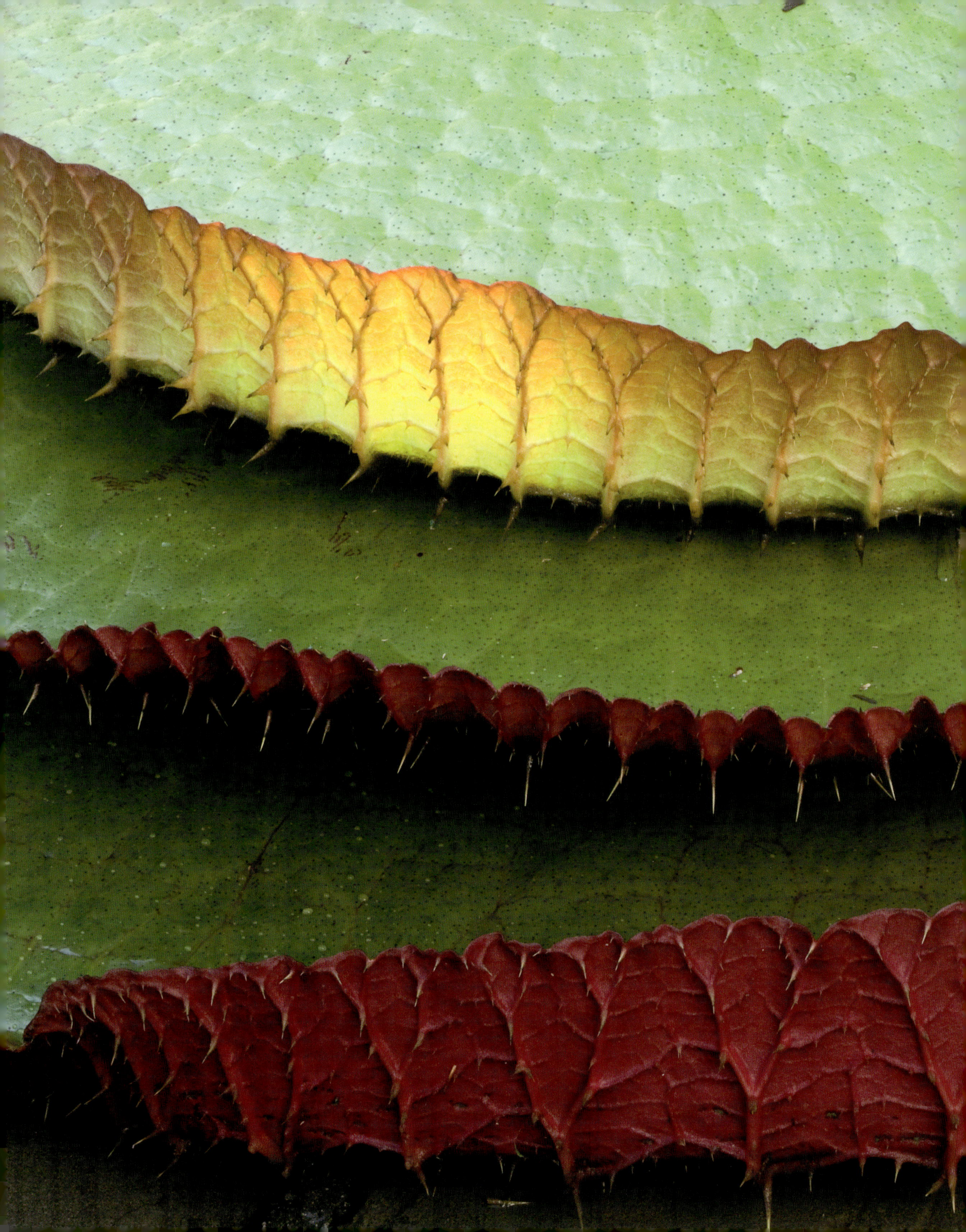

the English language edition of the Haage und Schmidt catalog for the 1922–23 season, describing it as a "very vigorous grower and very hardy" (Haage und Schmidt 1922–23).

The hybrid from Erfurt was soon growing in a number of Victoria Houses in Europe, including the Botanical Garden of the University of Basel, the Botanical Garden in Berlin-Dahlem, and the Bergius Botanical Garden in Stockholm (Trespe 1925, Langlet and Söderberg 1927, Lack 2004). She was praised for her ability to thrive in northern latitudes without supplemental heat during the summer. Researchers in Stockholm were able to confirm the hybrid nature of the Erfurt lily when they found that she had twenty-two chromosomes, a number expected from a cross between *Victoria amazonica,* with twenty chromosomes, and *Victoria cruziana,* with twenty-four chromosomes (Langlet and Söderberg 1927). They were surprised, however, that when *Victoria hybrida imperialis* was crossed in Stockholm with *Victoria cruziana,* it produced an offspring with twenty-three chromosomes. This was named *Victoria pseudocruziana* (Langlet and Söderberg 1927). With so much interbreeding taking place in two small European greenhouses over the span of a few years, it is not difficult to imagine what must have been happening among the millions of lilies sprouting each flood season between Moxos and Pantanal.

When World War II swept through Europe, the Erfurt and Stockholm hybrids probably vanished. Yet plants of uncertain identity producing leaves with red-violet undersides, characteristic of *Victoria amazonica*, and very high rims, typical of *Victoria cruziana*, did appear in the botanical gardens in Munich and Berlin in the 1960s (Eckardt 1969, Seibert 1969).

Interest in giant lily hybrids was revived when Longwood Gardens released its own cross under the fitting name of 'Longwood Hybrid' in 1961. This hybrid has since been distributed and grown around the world. Backcrosses to either of the parent species were attempted, too, but since their offspring were inferior to the first generation hybrid, they were discontinued. While 'Longwood Hybrid' had *Victoria cruziana* as a seed parent, a reverse cross named 'Adventure' was jointly introduced in 1999 by the Missouri Botanical Garden in St. Louis and two private gardens in Colorado and Florida. Shortly thereafter, four backcrosses of 'Longwood Hybrid' and 'Adventure' were developed by Kit Knotts of Cocoa Beach, Florida, and named 'Atlantis', 'Challenger', 'Columbia', and 'Discovery'. These names honored the NASA space shuttles whose launches at Cape Canaveral Knotts watched from her garden (Knotts 2004).

ONE, TWO, OR MORE SPECIES?

While the diversity of *Victoria* in the wild is still poorly understood today, the results of numerous cross-pollinations that took place in such gardens as Erfurt, Stockholm, Longwood, St. Louis, and Cocoa Beach may shed some light on whether there are one, two, or more species of the South American nymph. Crossing species with an unequal number of chromosomes (twenty-four from *Victoria cruziana* and twenty from *Victoria amazonica*) should generally lead to sterile offspring due to unpaired chromosomes (Johnson 2005). But *Victoria* first generation hybrids are fully fertile when self-pollinated or backcrossed to one of the parents. Furthermore, all of their offspring are fertile, too—clearly indicating that there are no limits to hybridization among *Victoria*, a highly unusual condition for presumably an interspecific cross.

Upturned leaf margins of *Victoria cruziana* (top), *Victoria amazonica* (middle), and *Victoria* 'Longwood Hybrid' (bottom).
LARRY ALBEE / LONGWOOD GARDENS

Cross-sections of flowers of, left to right, *Victoria cruziana* from Paraguay, *Victoria* 'Longwood Hybrid', *Victoria amazonica* from the Amazon near Manaus, and *Victoria amazonica* from the Rio Branco. Flowers were collected in the morning following their first-night opening.
LEZHONG WANG / LONGWOOD GARDENS

To explain this paradoxical situation, Matthew Johnson (2005) proposed that the difference in the chromosome counts of *Victoria amazonica* and *Victoria cruziana* is the result of chromosome fusion or splitting, where two shorter chromosomes fuse to form one longer or vice versa. In either case, their pairing would not be hampered in the hybrid, because two of the ten chromosomes from the *Victoria amazonica* set could each pair with two chromosomes from the *Victoria cruziana* set of twelve, allowing for proper recombination.

This difficulty with categorizing *Victoria* into clearly defined species is not unlike the challenges facing her sister *Nymphaea*. Studies of white water lilies of Europe and Asia found high levels of polymorphism, which led botanists who were trying to untangle this puzzling array of variants to arrange them into between one and ten species (Volkova et al. 2010). A prevailing opinion recognizes three species: *Nymphaea alba*, *Nymphaea candida*, and *Nymphaea tetragona*. But of these three, *Nymphaea candida* is thought to be a hybrid that originated in the area where the ranges of the other two species overlap (Volkova et al. 2010). Today, *Nymphaea candida* occupies an area between *Nymphaea alba* and *Nymphaea tetragona*, exhibits intermediate features, and is highly variable morphologically, a scenario reminiscent of that describing *Victoria* in South America.

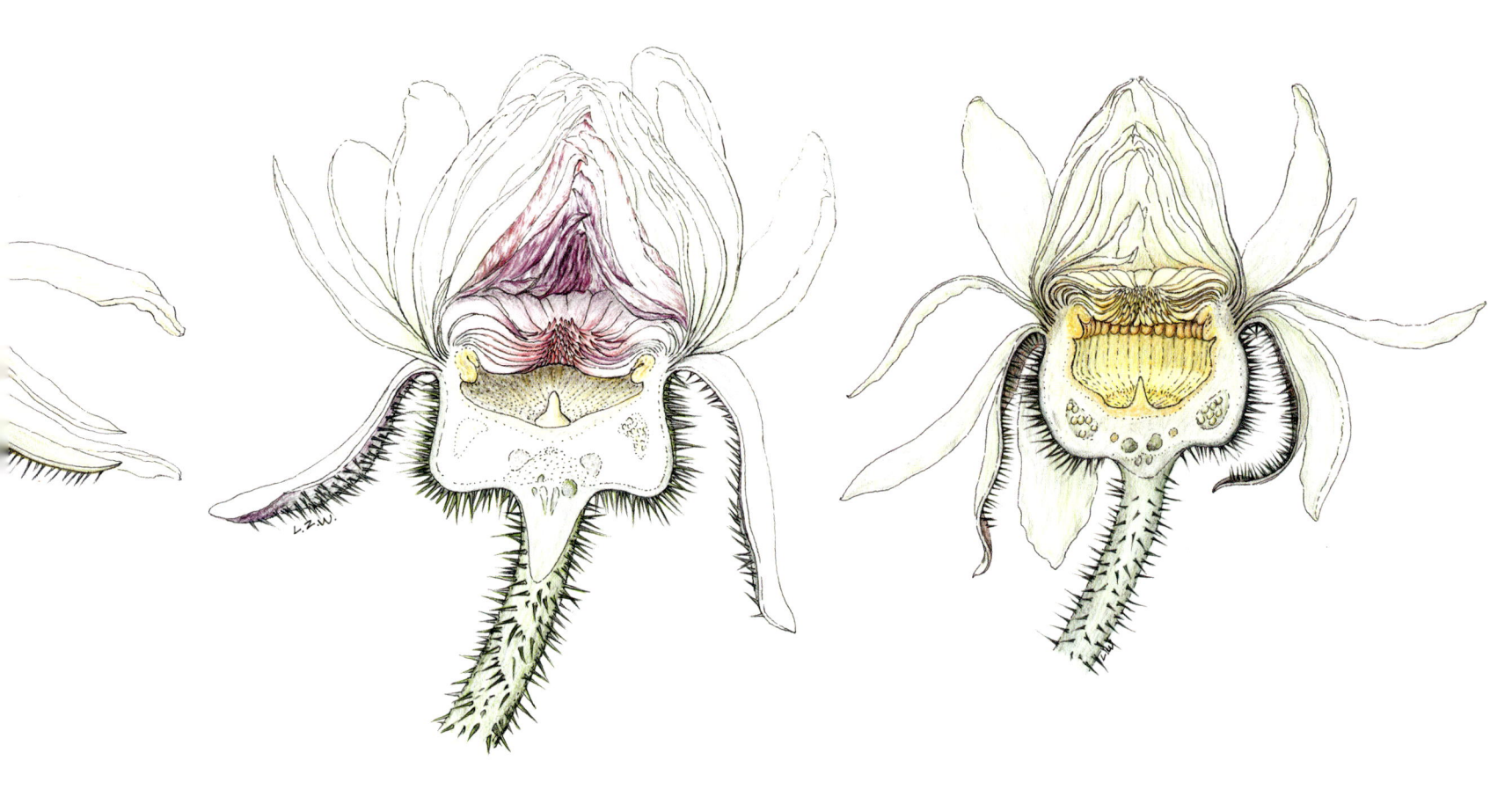

The distinction between *Victoria amazonica* and *Victoria cruziana* is obvious when comparing plants from Guyana and Argentina. Coincidentally, these two, which were used to establish the original definitions of each of the species, also represent *Victoria*'s most northern and southern populations. When plants in the center of the continent are considered, however, the situation becomes far less clear. It seems likely that on the vast plains of Moxos and Pantanal, intercrossing among many forms of giant lilies is widespread and has been so for a very long time. However, the question remains whether this spontanous hybridization began after the two species evolved independently in the Amazon and Paraná river systems and then came into contact where the two watersheds meet, or if this perplexing medley of hybrids in the center of South America represents a primal state of *Victoria* from which both species evolved, literally downstream.

Anderson hoped in 1965 that the study of hybrids in cultivation would provide "decisive evidence" to show how *Victoria* should be classified. However, it now appears that only extensive field investigations throughout the entire distribution range, backed by rigorous molecular analysis, can provide new insight into the complex nature of the giant lilies of South America.

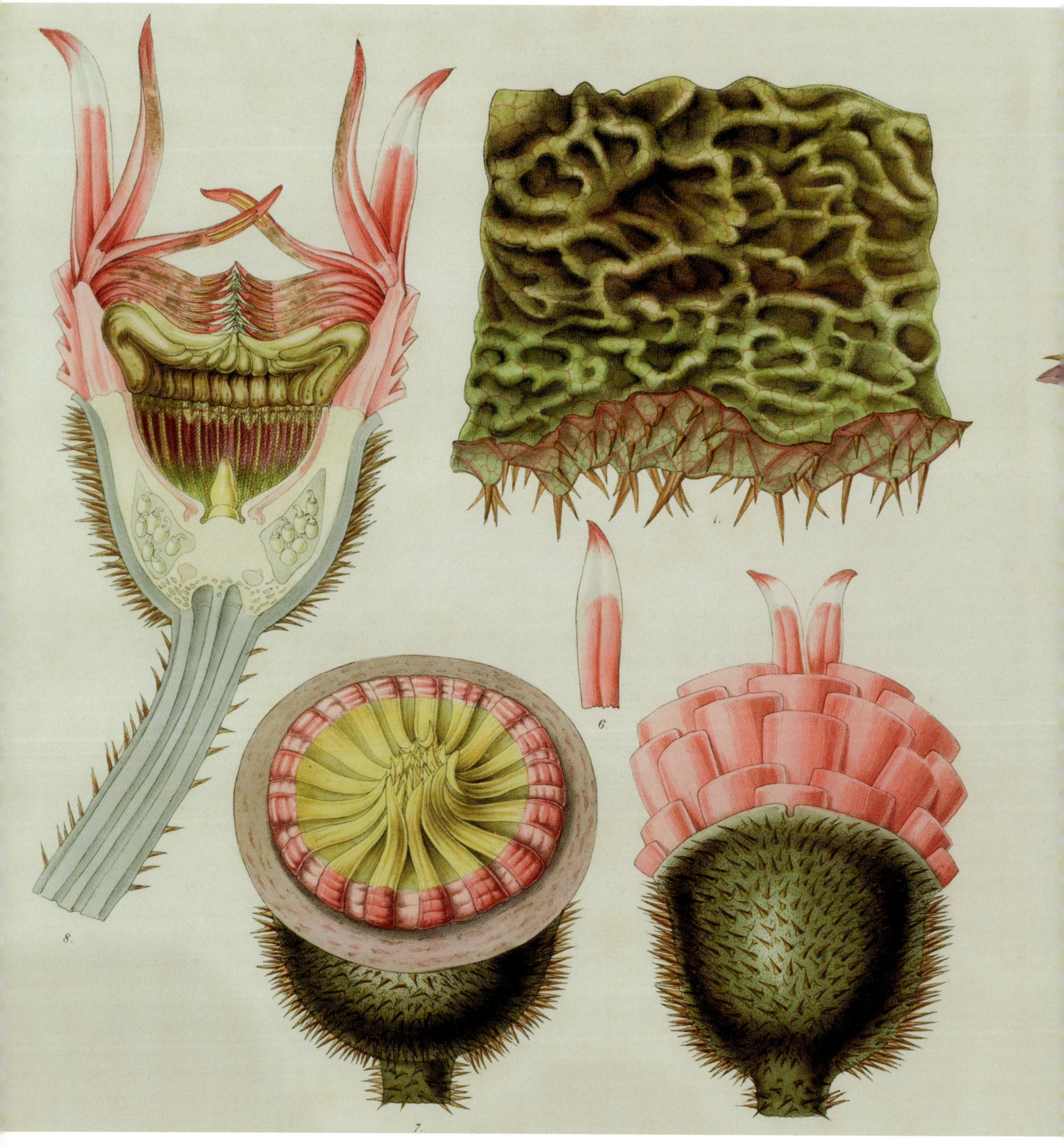

6.
8.
7.

chapter 15

A CREATURE OF CONTRADICTIONS

Giant lilies have perplexing diversity, eluding our attempts to define and classify them. Yet this is only one manifestation of *Victoria*'s complex personality. Full of contradictions and never bending to our expectations, the nymph has evaded those who have tried to describe and understand her ever since she was discovered. After two centuries of exchanging arguments and counterarguments, there is still no consensus on what should otherwise be a simple matter to settle: whether *Victoria* is annual or perennial.

The earliest cultivators of the queen lily in both Europe and America were often disappointed when their precious plant was gone after only one season of growth. This led many to conclude that she was an annual. "It suffers in cloudy weather from the want of its native tropical sun," lamented John Fisk Allen (1854) of Salem, Massachusetts, after his *Victoria* ceased to produce flower buds or new leaves.

When Allen was certain that the nymph was dead, he had her uncovered to examine the condition of her roots. What he found was "a tuber or a rhizoma of a beet red color, partially decomposed; with countless number of rootlets, some yet alive, others dead, and a mass of decomposed matter below all." This was not an encouraging sight in the least. Allen's comment also

Details of flower and leaf structure of queen lily from *La Victoria Regia* (1850–51) by Jules Planchon and Louis Van Houtte.
Longwood Gardens Library and Archives

In temperate climates, the arrival of colder weather in the fall defines the end of life for *Victoria* cultivated outdoors. Plants are started from seed each year and discarded at the conclusion of the growing season.

TOMASZ ANIŚKO / LONGWOOD GARDENS

> **Anonymous correspondent to the *Gardener's Magazine of Botany, Horticulture, Floriculture, and Natural Science*, 1850:**
>
> *The old plant [at Chatsworth], in the meantime, though resting in winter, continued in perfect health, and progressing rapidly in growth, with the advancing spring, thus apparently setting at rest the question which had been raised, as to whether the species was annual or perennial. The rapidity with which its growth had been matured, and its seeds perfected, gave rise to the opinion that it was but of annual duration, which notion obtained apparent confirmation in the fact of the decay of almost all the other unbloomed plants that had been raised, on the approach of winter. On the other hand, an account of its being successfully transplanted at Georgetown, in Demerara, and the description given of the rootstock, or trunk, by collectors, led to the hope of its being perennial; whilst Mr. Bridges, who sent the earliest seeds which reached England, spoke of it as decidedly perennial. The continued growth of the Chatsworth plant, after flowering and seeding, may be taken as nearly conclusive evidence of the latter.*
>
> Anonymous 1850c

demonstrated the widespread confusion over how to characterize the underwater parts of the plant and whether they fit the definition of "a tuber or a rhizoma."

Yet others, looking at the same stem of the plant, saw it differently. "The thick brown rhizome, buried in the mud, preserves vitality for a long period," wrote George Lawson of Edinburgh in 1851. He further noted "the process of decay going slowly on at its base, while its upper and younger part continues development, and year after year produces an abundant supply of fresh foliage and flowers—a constant growth of adventitious roots going on the same time to supply the place of the old ones lost from time to time by the gradual decay of the tuber." He surmised that this proved "satisfactorily" that *Victoria* was of "a perennial character" (Lawson 1851).

Accounts provided by explorers encountering the nymph in her native state were only partially able to settle this argument. On the one hand, *Victoria*'s close affinity to the unquestionably annual *Euryale* suggested that she might be annual, too. On the other hand, Robert Schomburgk, whose discovery in Guiana put the giant lily on the world's stage, believed the South American lily was perennial (Allen 1854).

Richard Spruce, an explorer traveling in South America in the 1850s, "wished to obtain proof as to whether its duration was annual or perennial, but was unable to decide, although the evidence seemed in favour of the latter" (Spruce 1908). Rather than referring to the submerged body of *Victoria* as a tuber or rhizome, Spruce recognized it as a thick central root "penetrating so deep that we could not dig to the bottom of it with our *terçados* [machetes]" and thought that it "might be annual." Yet he could not reconcile this with the fact that the giant lily "was never wanting all the year round" (Spruce 1908), as the locals assured him. More recent reports from Amazonia, however, describe the lily as an annual living for only several months each year (Anderson 1965, Cowgill and Prance 1989).

The confusion over *Victoria*'s status as an annual or perennial even appeared on the pages of the classic American *Standard Cyclopedia of Horticulture* (Bailey 1953). After describing the giant lilies in the wild as perennials, the publication stated that in cultivation, "whether grown indoors or out, plants are only annuals, and seedlings are of necessity raised every spring." The reason given was their failure to form tubers or rootstock as the more common *Nymphaea* lilies did.

While in cultivation *Victoria* is often grown as an annual—with the seeds being planted in late winter and the lily dying in late fall—experience has shown, starting with Joseph Paxton at Chatsworth, that under favorable conditions, plants can overwinter and live for several years. Allen was able to keep one nymph alive for four

A four-year-old *Victoria* growing indoors at the Botanical Garden of Adam Mickiewicz University in Poznań, Poland.
TOMASZ ANIŚKO / LONGWOOD GARDENS

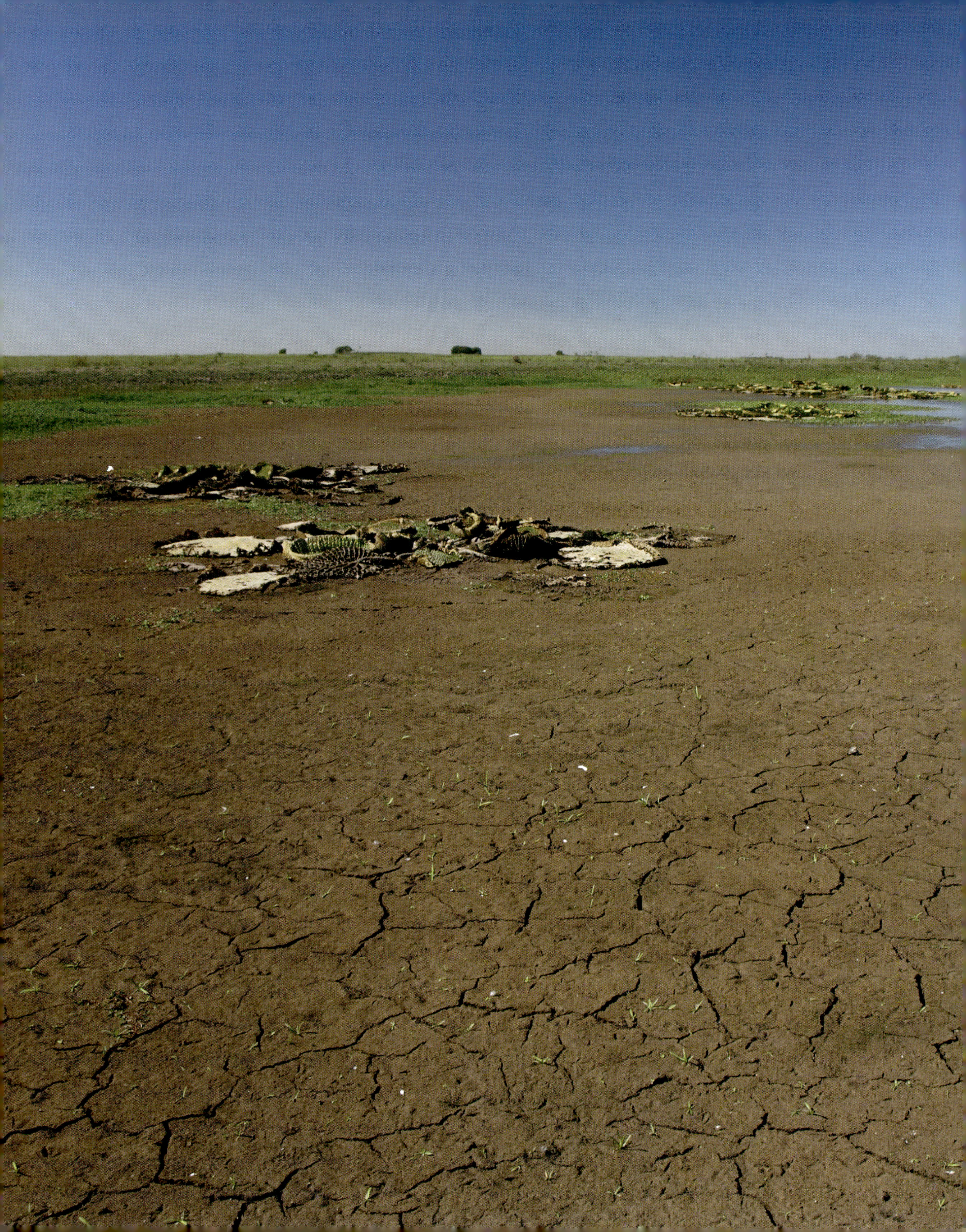

years, during the course of which she produced over two hundred flowers (Conard 1953). Comparable results are often reported for plants grown indoors in northern climates, even though the winter months are clearly a challenge for the queen lily, leading to declining leaf size and the suspension of flowering (Fabian and Micle 1962, Gawlak 2009). An even longer lifespan can be achieved when *Victoria* is cultivated outdoors in the tropics. One seven-year-old plant was reported growing in a pond of the Museu Goeldi in Belém, Brazil (Prance and Arias 1975, Leppard 1978).

WHEN FLOODWATERS RISE

One fundamental difference between highly contrived cultivated settings and those in the wild is the stability of the water levels. The lily has evolved in an environment that cycles annually through a flood stage followed by a dry season. Her life begins with the arrival of the floodwaters and ends when they recede. Her seeds, scattered and buried in mud, await the next inundation.

Hailing from equatorial areas where the temperature and day length hardly fluctuate throughout the year, *Victoria* has learned to grow, flower, and fruit for as long as there is water to float her colossal leaves. While garden ponds and pools can imitate the flooded plains of South America, here, the flood pulse never ends, enabling the nymph to live for several years. Whether this qualifies the queen lily as a perennial or not is a matter of semantics rather than biology.

Martin Leppard, who studied *Victoria amazonica* near Manaus in the 1970s, concluded that she is "a perennial that tends to grow as an annual in the natural habitat, coerced to do so by unfavourable water levels arising during the course of a year" (Leppard 1978). However, this argument could easily be turned around to present the Amazonian nymph as an annual that tends to grow as a perennial in cultivation, "coerced" by favorable water levels.

In parts of South America that retain water between annual floods, individual *Victoria* plants were observed to last for several years (Prance and Arias 1975). However, the apparent year-round presence of the giant lilies, which suggests a perennial habit, is more likely a result of various areas remaining submerged at different depths below the river's flood level (Prance and Arias 1975). When floodwaters rise, one area may become too deep for *Victoria*, leading to her demise, while

Giant water lilies on their last breath in a drying pond along the Paraná, near the town of Victoria in Argentina. The receding floodwaters mark the end of life for these lilies, but their seeds buried in the mud will await the next inundation.
TOMASZ ANIŚKO / LONGWOOD GARDENS

Locations that retain some water between the annual floods allow *Victoria* to extend her lifespan to several years.
TOMASZ ANIŚKO / LONGWOOD GARDENS

shallower areas may enable the lily to thrive. The reverse happens when the floodwaters recede. While the nymph is not present throughout the year in any of these locations, she can be found in one of them at any time.

In addition, repeated attempts to locate the giant lilies sprouting from rhizomes that have survived the dry season have yielded no results, although statements about the rhizomes surviving "in moist sediments" have been made (Junk and Piedade 1997, Meade and Pierce 2000).

It's important to note that *Victoria*'s stem does not branch, produces no vegetative propagules or axillary buds, and cannot be divided or propagated through vegetative means. All observed regeneration, both in nature and in cultivation, is in the form of young seedlings (Meade and Pierce 2000).

All this confusion should not be blamed on *Victoria*, though. Rather, it stems from forcing our inadequate concepts of annual and perennial plants upon her. These definitions were based on our experience with the flora of temperate regions, where winters end the growing season each year. There, annual plants perish after dispersing their seed, while perennial ones lie dormant until the return of spring, when they renew themselves vegetatively. In contrast, although *Victoria* sometimes grows for several years, she is incapable of becoming dormant to wait out an unfavorable dry season. She can live through only a single flood event, although that event may be prolonged for several years.

A CLASS UNTO HERSELF

Victoria's peculiar stem also posed problems for plant anatomists and systematists. Detailed studies of this curious structure began as soon as the first generation of lilies that arrived in Europe in 1849 started to expire. "The specimen of *Victoria* which flowered in the Gardens of the Royal Botanic Society, was found floating, dead, upon the surface of the water a few weeks ago," wrote Arthur Henfrey, professor of botany at King's College in London, "and by the kindness of the Society's Curator, Mr. Marnock, I obtained one of the pieces, when it was sliced down through the middle to ascertain the cause of death" (Henfrey 1852).

Although Henfrey's autopsy of the nymph did not yield the cause of death, it did reveal intriguing features of the giant lily's anatomy. For instance, it stated that while the stem's outer layer was made of spongy tissue, underneath was a denser cortical layer, and at the center, a mass of interlacing fibers. Vascular bundles were isolated, scattered, and "exceedingly simple." Henfrey also noted that roots occurred only at the bases of the petioles. *Victoria*'s roots were made of fleshy, spongy tissue, varied in color from white to brown, and were bundled in clusters of twenty to forty. As new leaves were produced in the center of the plant, a succession of root clusters formed. Meanwhile, the oldest roots on the other end of the rhizome disintegrated.

Victoria's stem is often called a rhizome, even though it is neither horizontal nor entirely underground. This fact alone demonstrates how helpless the language of science has been when confronted with the South American colossus. The rhizome presents a stark contrast to the long, slender, and constantly swaying petioles and peduncles. It is motionless, short, and stalky at 30 cm (12 inches) in diameter and barely 60 cm (24 inches) in length. This prompted Thomas Bridges to call it "the trunk," while Henry Conard referred to it as "the tuber" (Hooker 1847, Conard 1953). As its bulging growing tip keeps throwing out new leaves and flowers, it slowly creeps out of the sediments—which are being deposited by the floodwaters—and is propped up by stilt-like adventitious roots. Meanwhile, the opposite end buried in the soft mud slowly decomposes, leaving behind a hollow cavity. The continuous rejuvenation is thus inseparable from the plant's inevitable decay.

In the olden days of plant classification, before the phylogenetic approach was widely adopted, all flowering plants were either divided into so-called monocots, which develop a single cotyledon, or embryonic leaf, or dicots with two cotyledons. A number of anatomical and morphological characteristics differentiated the two groups.

The queen lily, however, did not fit within these well-established patterns, leading scientists to group her with either the monocots or dicots, depending on which characteristics were given higher priority. While *Victoria*'s germination sequence was thought to approximate that of the monocots (Henfrey 1859), her stem's anatomical organization showed parallels with both the monocots and dicots (Henfrey 1852, Weidlich 1980). This uncomfortable situation might never have been resolved if it were not for advances in phylogenetic research. The phylogenetic system deprived the monocot-dicot schism of its taxonomical supremacy, took *Victoria* and other water lilies out of that conundrum, and gave them, along with a number of primitive flowering plants, a class to themselves: the basal angiosperm.

OF LAND AND WATER

Victoria lives in both the terrestrial world—providing nutrients and anchorage for her roots and rhizomes—and the aqueous environment, supporting her floating leaves and suppressing competing vegetation that might otherwise quickly colonize exposed land.

A cross-section of *Victoria* roots shows they are made of fleshy, sponge-like tissue.
TOMASZ ANIŚKO / LONGWOOD GARDENS

New roots form at the bases of the youngest petioles, while the oldest roots, on the other end of the rhizome, continuously disintegrate.
TOMASZ ANIŚKO / LONGWOOD GARDENS

Victoria's stem, referred to as a rhizome, trunk, or tuber, consists of an epidermis, cortex, stem vascular bundles, and pith. The middle region of the cortex contains aerenchyma with large air spaces and occasional small vascular bundles. The middle portion of the cortex is bounded internally and externally by more densely arranged parenchyma. The pith contains vascular bundles embedded in parenchyma.
TOMASZ ANIŚKO / LONGWOOD GARDENS

Faithful to her amphibious lifestyle, the nymph spends her embryonic youth as a resting seed buried on land. She sprouts into adolescence in the shallow waters of the early phases of the annual inundation, and she reaches her prime at the height of the flood season. Her juvenile leaves, developing under water, resemble the leaves of many submerged aquatic plants. They are narrow, grass-like, and later arrow-shaped with narrow, pointed lobes. Her leaves are also pliable, offering minimal resistance to flowing water. But with a rising flood, these completely unremarkable leaves undergo a sudden metamorphosis and reach out to light and air.

These two essential ingredients—the sun's energy and the atmosphere's carbon dioxide—condition the nymph's phenomenal growth. Spreading on the surface of the water, the now-familiar enormous lily pads occupy a very restrictive and defined habitat, spliced between the aqueous and the aerial environments. The upper leaf side floats open to the air and bright sky, while the underside is immersed in dark, murky waters. Stomata, or vents through which carbon dioxide can enter the leaf, are usually found on the underside, but there would be little use for them in *Victoria*'s floating pads, so instead, they have relocated to the upper side.

The two sides of the *Victoria* leaf are strikingly different. The upper side (top) is spineless, smooth, and covered by a water-repellent waxy layer. The underside is exceedingly spiny, reinforced with the scaffolding of protruding veins, and variously infused with purple or violet.
LARRY ALBEE / LONGWOOD GARDENS

The two sides of the leaves could not look more different. One side is inviting—smooth, glistening with a silky sheen, and unwettable thanks to a waxy layer. The other deters, displaying a horrifying armory of spines from its maze of enlarged veins. The round shape of the platter-like leaf, delineated by an entire undivided margin and combined with a long, flexible petiole connected in the middle rather than at the leaf base, as commonly seen in other plants, is superbly designed to assure the greatest possible stability and resistance to the force of wind and waves (Sculthorpe 1967). But even when built to perfection, these giant lily pads cannot withstand the destructive power of fast currents, hence the nymph's fondness for quiet, slow-moving waters.

The connection between the floating leaves and flowers basking in the intense light and the submerged roots and stems anchoring the lily to the nutrient-rich sediments is maintained by snake-like petioles and peduncles. The air needs to be delivered from the leaves to the lily's crown, which is confined to the gloomy underwater world. It travels through the petioles in two spacious canals surrounded by a number of smaller ones. Unlike typical petioles, those of the giant lily have no predetermined length and must continuously stretch. This occurs both to keep up with the rising floodwaters and to permit

Entangled peduncles and petioles, superficially very similar in appearance, form an impenetrable defense of the stem's growing tip.
TOMASZ ANIŚKO / LONGWOOD GARDENS

Flower buds of *Victoria* appear on the anodic side of the associated leaves.
TOMASZ ANIŚKO / LONGWOOD GARDENS

maturing leaves to take a position farther from the plant's center, where new leaves expand (Anderson 1965, Sculthorpe 1967).

The maximum length that petioles attain in Nature can only be speculated to exceed 7 m (23 feet) (Meade 2001). This estimate is based on the depth of the water in which *Victoria* has been found. In cultivation, petioles more commonly measure 4.5 to 5.5 m (15 to 18 feet) (Hooker 1851, Allen 1854). Such a phenomenal lengthening of the petioles is only possible thanks to a zone of meristematic cells situated at each petiole's base. This meristem permits the petioles to grow by adding new cells, most likely in response to the tension caused by rising water that pulls the floating leaf upward (Schneider 1976). The petioles (connected to the leaves) and the peduncles (connected to the flowers) are entangled under water like snakes on Medusa's head and can be difficult to tell apart. Externally, peduncles differ from petioles because they lack adventitious roots at their bases; internally, they exhibit four main air canals accompanied by eight smaller ones.

Spinning around the central axis of the rhizome is one flower bud closely associated with each new leaf and ensheathed by the fused stipules of that leaf. Instead of being positioned in the axils of a new leaf, *Victoria*'s flower buds appear on the anodic side of their associated leaves—the side that is in the upward direction of the spiral along which the leaves and flowers are arranged circling the stem (Schneider et al. 2003). As a result, flowers and leaves make up two sets of intertwined, upwardly spiraling, lateral appendages of the stem. The phyllotactic formula describes how many turns of this spiral and how many leaves or flowers separate those that are perfectly aligned above each other. Thus, a formula of 3/8

Cross-sections of peduncles, above, and petioles, below, show wide air canals, facilitating the distribution of oxygen into the underwater parts of the plant.
TOMASZ ANIŚKO / LONGWOOD GARDENS

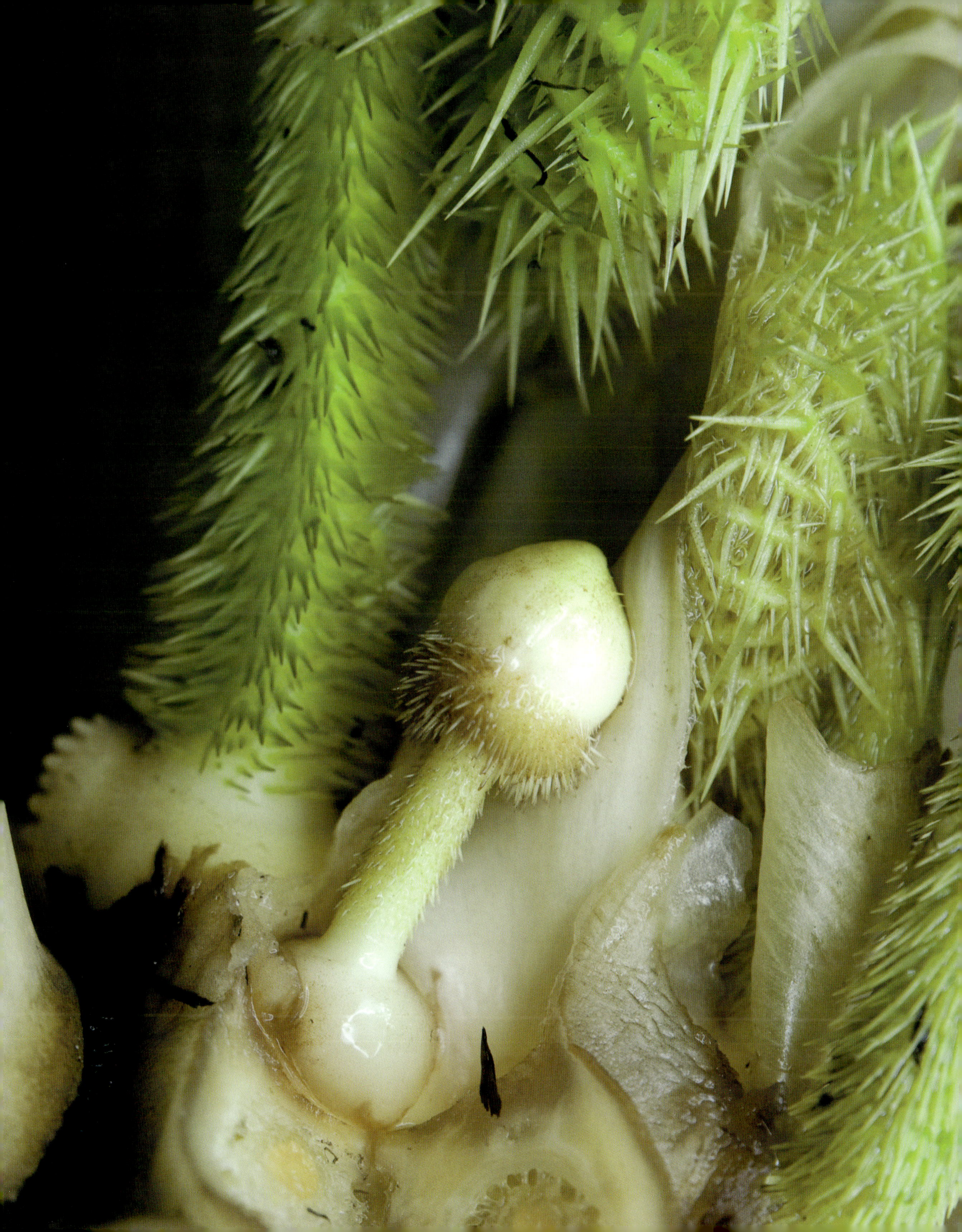

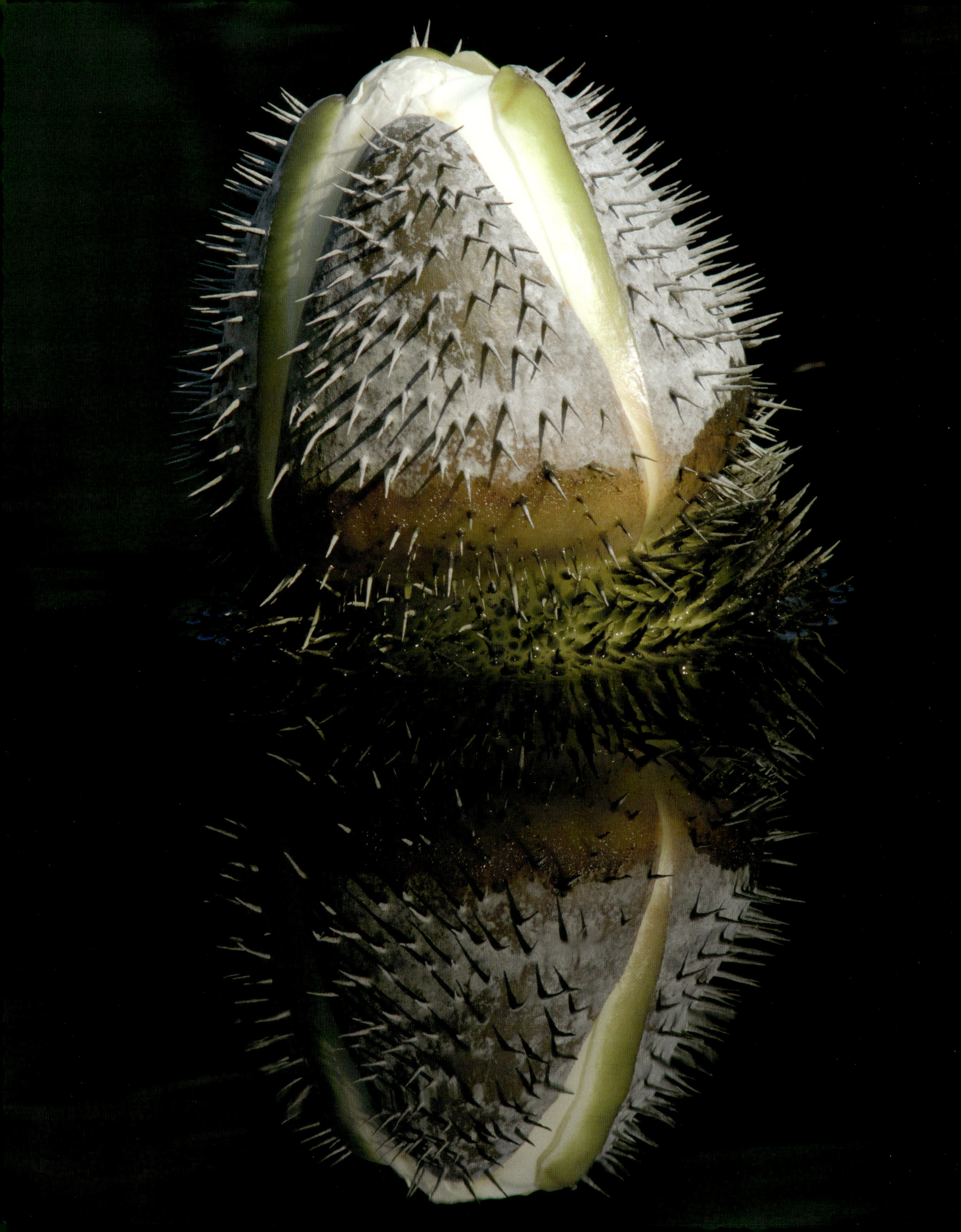

given for *Victoria* by Wayne H. Weidlich (1980) implies that the spiral has to circle the stem three times, and eight leaves have to develop before the ninth leaf will be positioned directly above the first one. Others calculated this formula to be 7/18, 9/23, or even 55/144, but they all lead to approximately the same spacing of about 140 degrees between two subsequent leaves or flowers (Oudemans 1862, Seidel 1869, Conard 1953).

As a rule, one flower develops for each unfolded leaf. Occasionally, a flower will appear to be missing when a bud aborts early in its development, usually the result of unfavorable growing conditions. Such events cause no disturbance in the organization of the spiral or the spacing between the consecutive leaves (Sculthorpe 1967).

In 1903, Frederick W. Moore of the Royal Botanic Gardens, Glasnevin, Ireland, reported an exceedingly rare event: Two flowers had opened simultaneously on the same plant while only one leaf had developed with these buds. "This is a unique experience in my cultivation of this glorious aquatic, extending now over many years," Moore wrote. "These twin flowers developed together, appeared together, opened together, and withered together" (Moore 1903).

AN EXQUISITE FLOWERING

The flower reaches the surface of the water and opens about two days after its corresponding leaf has unfolded (Weidlich 1980). Its regal presence, fleeting nature, nocturnal lifestyle, female-to-male transformation, violent affair with the six-legged pollinators, choreographed movements of floral parts, incomparable fragrance, passionate hot flushes, and, ultimately, rapid descent to a misery of decay and stench all epitomize *Victoria*'s gregarious, seductive, and scandalous personality.

Four sturdy sepals of *Victoria*'s bud hide inside a dazzling attire of numerous floral parts of several categories.
LARRY ALBEE / LONGWOOD GARDENS

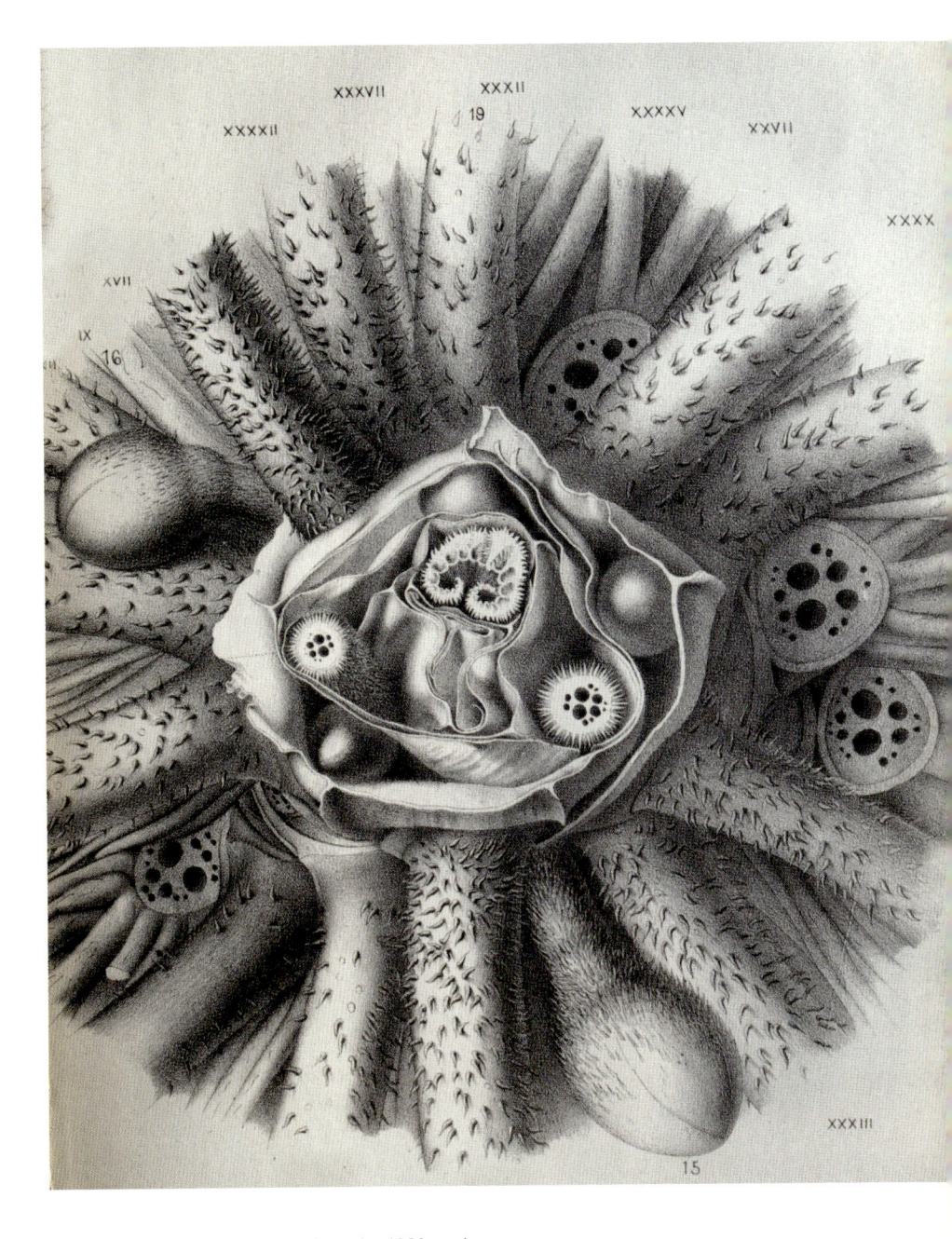

The top view of *Victoria*'s stem from the 1869 work of C. F. Seidel, *Zur Entwickelungsgeschichte der Victoria Regia Lindl.*, published in Dresden. It shows the leaves and flowers being spirally arranged.
MISSOURI BOTANICAL GARDEN LIBRARY

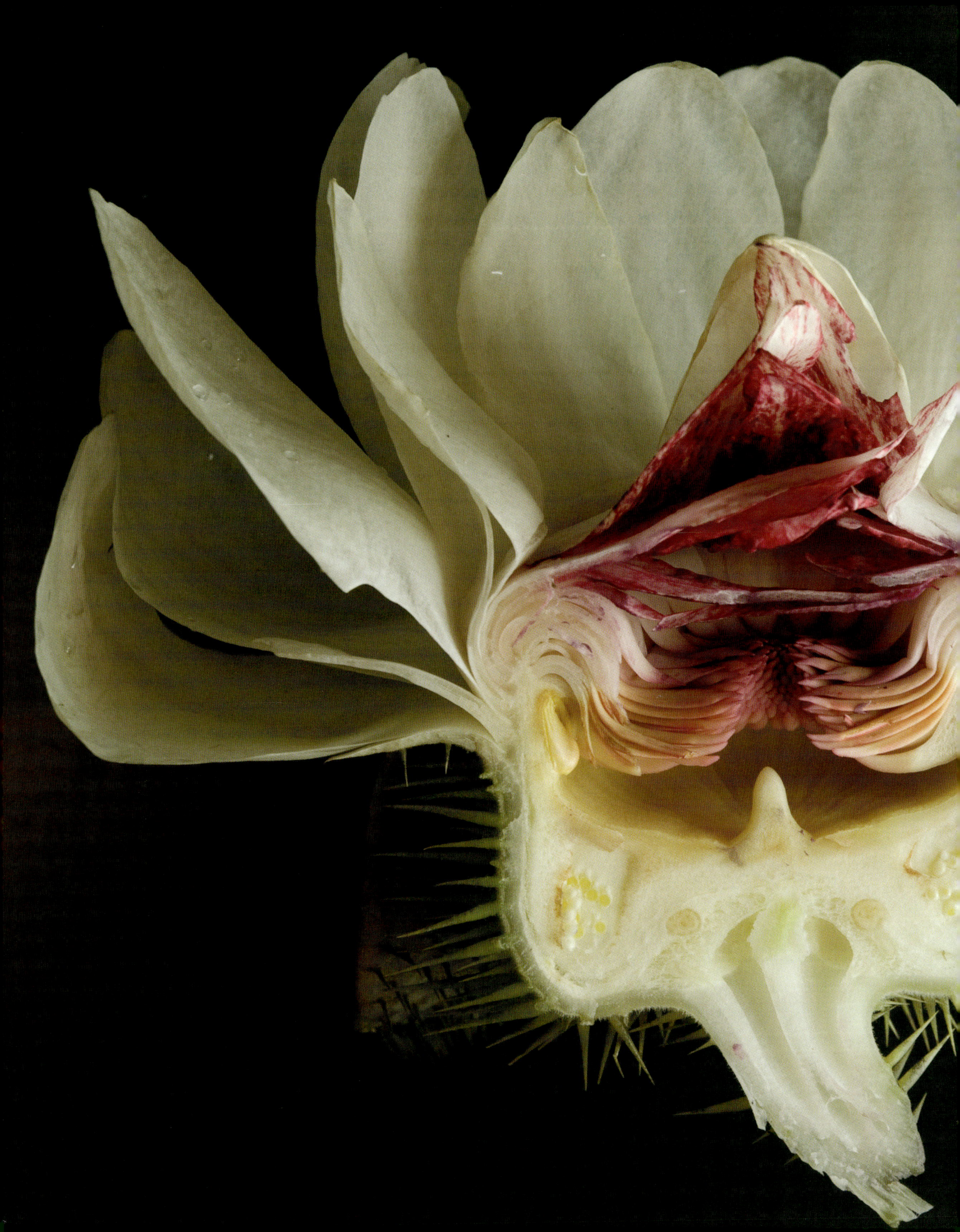

The nymph's flowers, magnificent in their sheer size and proud posture and splendidly reflected on the water's surface, captivate with their intriguing architecture. Showing four straightforward green sepals on the outside—spiny in *Victoria amazonica*, and smooth or with only a few spines in *Victoria cruziana*—the flower bud hides inside a dizzying array of floral parts, many unparalleled in the plant world. Their arrangements and purpose mystified botanists for a long time.

Behind the thick sepals are fifty to seventy thin and delicate petals. Further in are about fifteen to thirty-five outer staminodia, or modified sterile stamens, enclosing 150 to 300 tightly packed fertile stamens. These are thick and flattened, and instead of being differentiated into the usual anther and filament, they have a pair of elongated pollen sacks on their inner face. Below the stamens are twenty-five to forty inner staminodia, also called paracarpels, guard cones, or pistillodes (Knoch 1897, Prance and Prance 1976, Schneider 1976).

Immediately underneath is a ring of curious structures referred to as carpellary appendages, stylar processes, or food bodies. They surround the floral chamber, also known as a stigmatic cup, forming the gynoecium, which is made of twenty-five to forty fused carpels. These carpels in turn radiate around a mysterious raised conical projection called the floral apex, apical residuum, or receptacular residue (Schneider 1976, Borsch et al. 2008, Ronse De Craene 2010). Although these various classes of floral parts give the impression of being grouped in separate whorls, they are in fact carefully aligned along a greatly compressed spiral

A cross-section of *Victoria*'s flower reveals a puzzling arrangement of various floral parts spiraling around the central axis, starting on the outside with sepals, followed by petals, then outer staminodes, which transition into fertile stamens. These in turn give way to inner staminodes, below which are carpellary appendages surrounding the floral chamber and ending with the protruding apical residuum in the middle.

Tomasz Aniśko / Longwood Gardens

Aside from the gigantic size, the immaculate beauty of the *Victoria* flower was not lost on early cultivators of the Amazonian nymph. John Fisk Allen of Salem, Massachusetts, wrote of her petals as a "most delicate tissue of lace."

LARRY ALBEE / LONGWOOD GARDENS

Eduard Loescher, 1852:

With quiet tension the few privileged to witness the feast stood watching the object of their anticipation, only a few low remarks broke the silence.... Every eye was focused on the center of the water, where the flower, with the reticence of a bride, still hid among the great reddish brown sepals. They as well as the thorny cover formed an honor guard, keeping any assault from outside at bay. But soon these grim guardians had to yield. The flower, feeling free at last, unfolded its petals, one after another, surrounding itself with a sumptuous white gown until she stood forth in all her glory.... There seems to be movement in her interior, restless stirrings to right and left and her warm breath fills the area with a magical scent. But see—there is a pause and the inner petals remain chastely closed hiding her innermost secrets throughout the night! Towards morning even the petals close and seek shelter under the sepals—all is quiet until sunlight wakes the maiden, no longer a cool white bride, but ready to surrender with a blush of shame. Then the corolla opens to rest on the water, the color deepens and the inner petals unfold, forming a flaming crown; all in the space of two hours. After this the outer petals rest quietly while the filaments, squirming restlessly, spread their pollen. About midnight the flower begins to close and at dawn it sinks below the water surface hiding the fruit of its mysterious love.

Loescher 1852, translated by Kitty Byk

(Schneider 1976). If following this spiral from the outermost sepals to the receptacular residue in the middle does not induce dizziness, trying to grasp the confusing terminology applied to these floral elements certainly will.

Allen (1854) could not contain his admiration when describing the lily's petals: "Imagine a most delicate tissue of lace, with the interstices filled with some semi-transparent white substance, yet so soft and tender as to bruise under a slight pressure." Upon revealing itself, the flower—the embodiment of purity and virginity—gives in under cover of darkness to its innate, all-consuming fever of desire, perfuming the air with a delightful aroma and signaling its receptivity to flying suitors. Then begins the metamorphosis that captivates observers to this day. On the following evening, the previously white petals appear, in Allen's words, "as if the crimson had been accidentally rained in many different-sized drops upon them, with here and there a petal upon which the shower descended with such a force as to color the whole."

Caleb Cope of Philadelphia compared the metamorphosed second-night flower of *Victoria* to "a crown of some of the ancient kings of England."
Tomasz Aniśko / Longwood Gardens

Caleb Cope, 1851:

So novel is the appearance of the transformed flower, that were we not conversant with its nature to metamorphose, we could not believe it possible to be produced from the same plant. The petals become reflexed, lie prostrate on the water, and expose to view a disc so beautiful in color and form that I am sorry I cannot find language to describe it adequately. In its form it resembles a crown of some of the ancient kings of England, especially so when the flower has reached its climax. The disc, which first appears quite smooth and flat, becomes, in a very short time, perpendicular petalous-looking anthers, surrounded by others of crimson, embosomed in pure white. Thus it floats in its glory through the night, declines as the rays of light approach, the succeeding morn, and ultimately sinks into the element from whence it arose so noble and grand.

Allen 1854

Although eluding description, the unique scent of *Victoria* is irresistible.
TOMASZ ANIŚKO / LONGWOOD GARDENS

Thomas Meehan, 1854:

When they expand in the evening, they may be of any shade, varying from the purest white to the richest cream, till they close in the morning, as if to exhibit the change in their calyx from a greenish to a crimson hue. Soon after, the flower expands a second time, and exhibits the same flower quite metamorphosed—sometimes of the deepest pink—sometimes rich with crimson—and sometimes feathered with crimson and white, as if in playful mimicry of the delicate markings of a prize tulip.

Allen 1854

Of course, *Victoria* is not the only flower that changes color. This phenomenon is quite widespread and occurs among one in every five families of flowering plants (Weiss 1995). Color change can alert pollinators to the current phase of the flower's development. The color associated with the early phase can indicate that a flower provides a nectar reward, offers pollen, or has receptive stigmas. Following the color change, the flower is generally unrewarding and sexually unviable (Weiss 1995). Such advertising is of great benefit to pollinators as it saves them time and energy while foraging. Although floral color change is common in more advanced plant families, it is rare among those that evolved early, such as water lilies, suggesting that early pollinators, such as beetles, were relatively unspecialized and not particularly visually oriented when compared to more advanced butterflies or bees. Flowers like those of *Victoria*, which are pollinated at night, are generally very light in color in their receptive phase to provide contrast with the surroundings. After that phase ends, their color darkens, blending with the background (Weiss 1995).

This elegant form of signaling between flower and pollinating insect, however, cannot fully explain *Victoria*'s color change, because the nocturnal beetles visiting her are lured by the scent and the warmth of the flower, not by the color. In this case, the appearance of a purple pigment—identified as pelargonine, one of the anthocyanins—in the petals is merely thought to be a by-product of the intense physiological processes of generating heat in the flower and releasing scent associated with the thermogenic flare (Micle et al. 1969, Weiss 1995).

Astonishingly, the same scent that *Victoria*'s flower releases to lure in the scarab beetles hovering over the waters of Amazonia attracts humans just as effectively. *Victoria*'s highly unusual scent has been compared to many things. John Ellis, a gardener to Caleb Cope in Philadelphia, thought it strongly resembled "highly cultivated pineapples" (Cope 1851a). Near Philadelphia, in Wilmington, Delaware, Gouverneur Emerson compared it to "the mingled odors of the pineapple and melon" (Emerson 1851). But in Kingston, Jamaica, Edward Chitty concluded, "To describe the fragrance is utterly impossible, except by saying that it is the perfume of the *Victoria regia*." Visitors to Chitty's garden who came to witness an opening of the giant lily flower "severally likened it to a pine, a melon, a quince, a ripe papaw, an over-ripe jackfruit, a rich apple; and yet all agreed it was not either of these, but that of the *Victoria regia* only" (Chitty 1852).

Modern analysis has revealed the secret ingredients that make *Victoria*'s scent so unique are indeed a rare combination. Roman Kaiser, a noted Swiss scent hunter, identified the key ingredients in the queen lily's fragrance as 2-methylbutanoate, methyl tiglate, and methyl caproate, with a sprinkle of minor components (Kaiser 2006). When it comes to fragrance, these molecules are fairly simple and widespread in nature, but their combination is uniquely specific to *Victoria* and not found in any other flower. Researchers from the Royal Botanic Gardens, Kew, described a slightly different concoction of five major compounds and many minor ingredients, but they still summarized it as having a "strongly fruity odor" (Kite et al. 1991).

A TORRID AFFAIR

The flower releases its sweet, fruity scent starting around mid-afternoon. The fragrance reaches its highest intensity shortly after the flower opens at sunset, and then it begins to diminish around 10:00 P.M. (Prance and Prance 1976). Under the cover of night, scarab beetles, intoxicated by *Victoria*'s scent, descend clumsily onto the soft padding of the white flowers and make their way into the cozy warmth of her floral chamber. The walls of the chamber are lined with starch-rich carpellary appendages on which beetles feast all night, taking breaks only for their mating rituals. Once the appendages are consumed, which happens sooner if more beetles end up inside the same flower, the rambunctious guests proceed to gnaw on anything they can get their mandibles on, including the walls and the floor of the floral chamber. Since the exit doors, the staminodes, are closed, the frenzy continues until the following evening, when the beetles are released. Each is packed with a load of pollen, leaving behind a scene that appears to be complete devastation—the floral chamber looted, its walls vandalized, its floor soiled with beetle excrement.

Interestingly, no real harm is done to the ovary amid all the rioting. During this seemingly chaotic and destructive night, pollen grains brought by the beetles from other flowers drop onto the floor of the chamber. Within hours, they germinate and eventually fertilize the ovules lying within the ovary. Then, *Victoria*'s mating ritual is complete.

All the frolicking between the bloom and beetles is conditioned on the flower's ability to raise its temperature to keep insects active all night long. This flare-up requires a sudden burst of energy that only happens if an adequate amount of oxygen is provided

---

Henrick Witte, 1872:

A soft indescribable sweet scent [of Victoria*] fills the greenhouse in a few moments in such a way that it even penetrates through the cracks in the doors. It is as if incense smoke, although much more pleasant than that, turns the greenhouse into a temple which can evoke a mood of reverent tribute in a person, who is not insensitive to the beauty of Nature and thereby letting his imagination wander freely.*

Witte 1872, translated by Ger Meeuwissen

Anonymous correspondent to the *Gardeners' Chronicle*, 1851:

Could not the essential oil containing the delicious odour which is so powerful in the flower of this plant as to remain in the air for some hours, be fixed and retained, so as to become an essence, and made use of as a scent for the toilet? It might become a fashionable article of commerce under the name "Balm of Victoria," as I am very certain it would be in great request.

Anonymous 1851e

Following flowering, the spiny ovary sinks under water and develops there into a large berry-like fruit.
TOMASZ ANIŚKO / LONGWOOD GARDENS

to the flower—hence the purpose of the wide air canals running through the peduncles and petioles. Except for a couple of nights spent above the surface of the water, the bulk of floral development, from bud to fruit, takes place under water, where oxygen is absent or in extremely low concentration (Gessner 1960).

The oversized air ducts and spongy aerenchyma, which comprise most of the nymph's body, greatly facilitate the diffusion of gasses, but they alone would not allow the underwater parts of the lily to breathe in enough air. To adapt to such extreme conditions, *Victoria* performs what is known as pressurized ventilation, or thermo-osmotic gas transport (Grosse et al. 1991, Junk and Piedade 1997). This ventilation is driven by the pressurization of gas contained in the aerenchyma of the leaves.

The phenomenon of gas flowing through aquatic plants as a result of differences in pressure was first observed by Wilhelm Pfeffer of the University of Tübingen in the late nineteenth century (Grosse et al. 1991). Air pressure buildup inside the leaf occurs due to the temperature gradient between the leaf aerenchyma and the leaf surface, the latter being cooler. Intense light, which warms up the interior of the leaf, and transpiration, which cools the leaf's upper surface, create a steep temperature gradient, resulting in higher air pressure in the aerenchyma. In *Victoria,* this increased pressure can generate a flow of

5 liters (1 gallon) per hour through a single petiole, greatly improving oxygen supply to the underwater portions of the plant (Grosse et al. 1991).

After its short, passionate affair with the beetles, the exhausted flower presents a sad picture. Its glorious crown of petals, staminodes, and stamens has collapsed into a mass of discolored, tattered tissues—a striking visual reversal of a rags-to-riches tale. As if embarrassed by its dramatic fall from grace, the flower soon sinks under water. There, out of sight, the remaining floral parts decay, leaving behind the spiny ovary, which develops into a large berry-like fruit over the next several weeks. Once mature, the fruit literally falls apart as its walls rupture, pushed from inside by the swelling of the arils surrounding hundreds of seeds (Sculthorpe 1967, Schneider 1976). Out of this mucilaginous pulp, seeds rise to the surface, lifted by their arils—by then fully expanded and inflated by entrapped gases like miniature balloons—to be carried away from their mother plant by floodwaters.

These tiny vessels of life sail off in search of their new homes, but the majority of them are destined to fail. Some will be caught by fish, others by birds. Many will lodge at the wrong harbor, one that is too deep, too shallow, or too crowded. Still more will end up in places that may remain dry through the next flood season. Finally, most of those that reach the promised lake or river channel will succumb to fierce competition from their own kin. These staggering losses are mitigated, however, by *Victoria*'s amazing reproductive potential: Each plant produces thousands of seeds in a single year. Even if only one seed grows to maturity in the next flood season, the nymph's survival is assured, as it has been over millions of years.

This dynamic pairing of vulnerability with vitality, so characteristic of the perplexing nature of *Victoria*, riddled with contradictions and paradoxes, reveals her to be a true child of the ever-changing landscape shaped by the meandering rivers of South America, a landscape that belongs to neither land nor water.

At the end of the growing season clumps of seeds can be seen floating among *Victoria* leaves along the Paraná near Santa Lucia, Argentina.
Tomasz Aniśko / Longwood Gardens

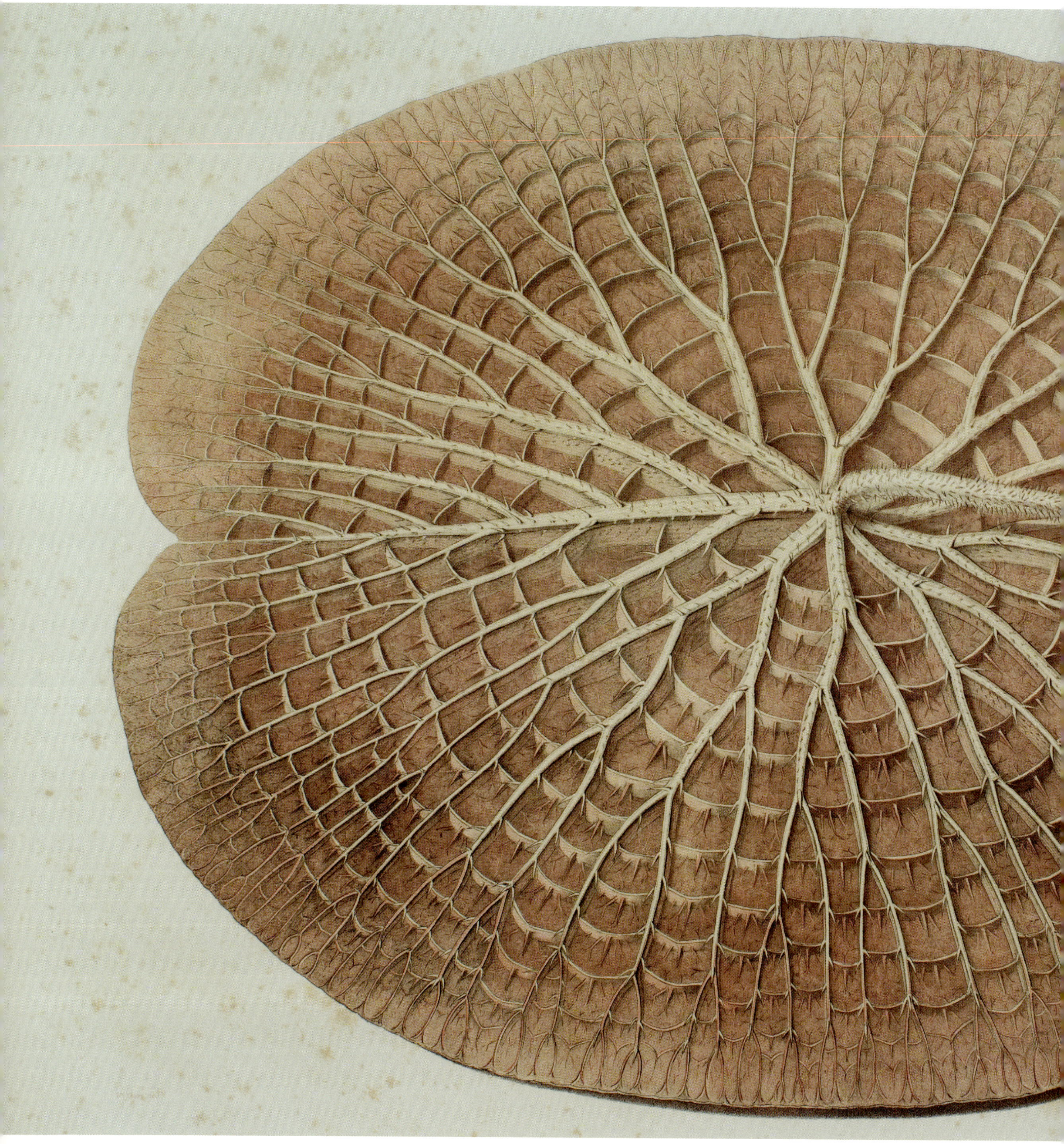

chapter 16

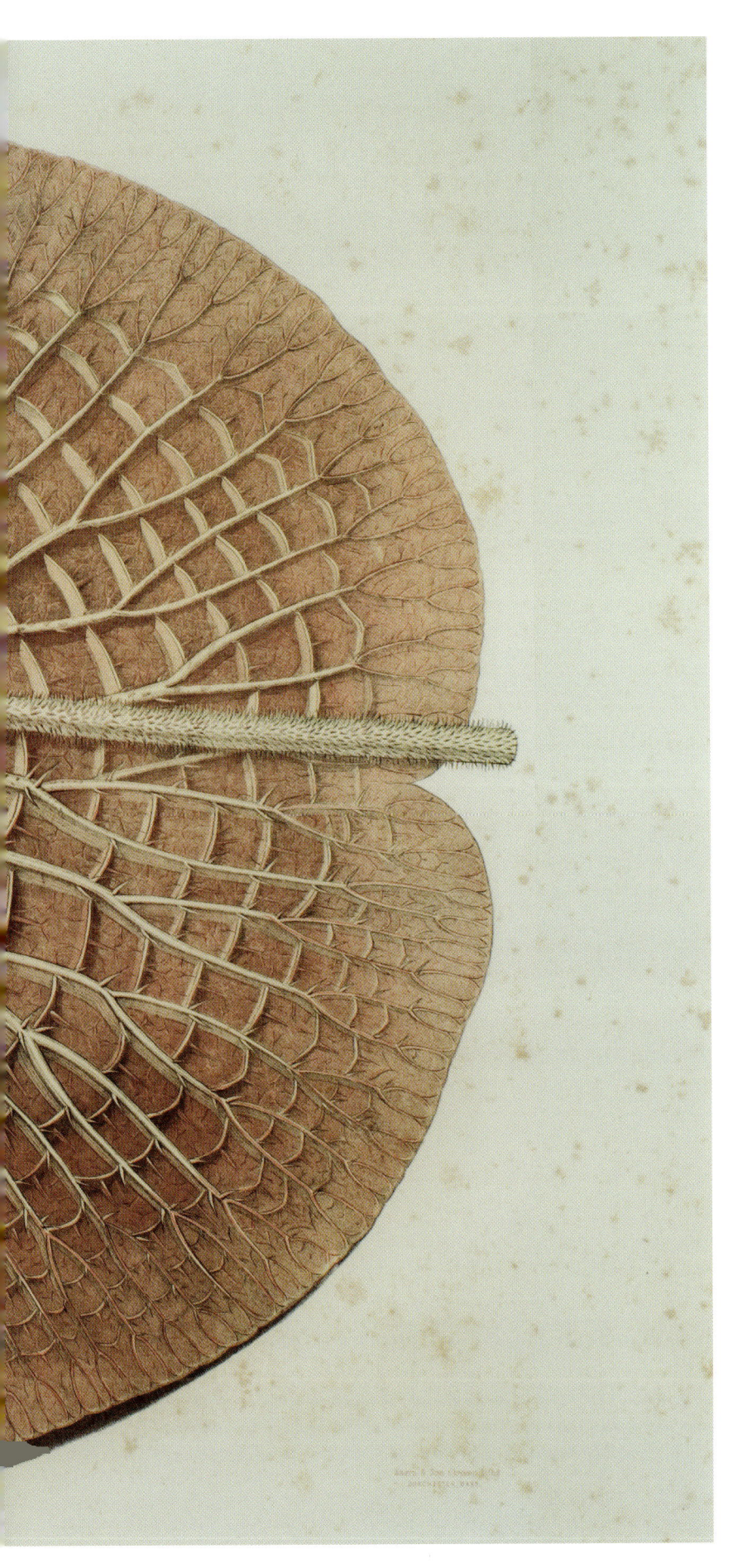

SIZE MATTERS

When it comes to the world's largest water lily, size matters. Undoubtedly, *Victoria* would never have received such admiration and attention if it were not for her larger-than-life presence. Our cultural obsession with all things colossal, things beyond the constraints of everyday experience, has made the South American nymph a perfect object of adoration. Ironically, despite her scale—which is unmatched by any other plant—some of *Victoria*'s admirers felt compelled to grossly exaggerate the size of her leaves and flowers, much like the sailors of past centuries did when inventing tales of sea monsters.

"In front of me, as far as the eye can see, the surface of the lake is covered with colossal leaves of a beautiful satiny green, above which emerge splendid flowers as large as barrels." So began French writer Louis Henri Boussenard's hair-raising description of an encounter with *Victoria* on the pages of the Parisian *Journal des Voyages* (Boussenard 1901, translated by John Luttrell). These barrel-size flowers of Boussenard's imagination were accompanied by leaves 9 m (30 feet) in diameter, 60 cm (24 inches) thick in the center, and held by ribs "as thick as a leg," which were capable of supporting a man walking on them. According to Boussenard, *Victoria* was like "a raft made of cross-ties and planks." The brave explorer resolved to subdue the vegetable monster and "to dry it and roll it up for

Underside view of *Victoria amazonica* leaf, a lithograph by William Sharp from John Fisk Allen's 1854 book *Victoria Regia or the Great Water Lily of America*.
Longwood Gardens Library and Archives

Louis Boussenard, 1901:

At first glance the largest among these almost round leaves seem to me to measure from eight to nine meters [26 to 30 feet] in diameter! It is the smallest of these of which the edges raise themselves gracefully; and some others still that, before they open themselves, appear in the form of great balls prickling with spines, like fabulous chestnuts covered with their spiny husk. I recognized the wonder of the equinoctial lakes, the incomparable Victoria regia. *. . . I would like to be able to preserve it and, to accomplish that, to dry it and roll it up for the purpose of bringing it back to France. The attempt is folly. Nevertheless, we try. The Indian . . . slices the petiole and embeds one of the grappling hooks under the median stem. We secure the cable on land and, once disembarked, we pull with all our might. Despite its extreme weight, we slowly haul the leaf up to the bank. We raise even a part of it. . . . There is nothing to be done! It weighs more than five hundred kilograms [1,100 pounds], and I must resign myself to abandon it.*

Boussenard 1901, translated by John Luttrell

The cover of the September 1901 issue of the *Journal des Voyages* depicting an encounter described by Louis Boussenard, an early French master of science fiction, with a colossal *Victoria* whose barrel-size flowers were home to a poisonous snake.

AUTHOR'S COLLECTION

the purpose of bringing it back to France." Assisted by his Indian guide, the nymph-hunter pulled his trophy to the edge of the lake and attempted to haul the giant leaf up the bank, only to discover that the Leviathan of the Amazon weighed more than half a ton, far beyond anything that could be lifted with bare hands. Instead, he plunged his knife into the lily's corpse, "soft, spongy, filled with liquid," to excise a small piece for inspection. Instantly, he saw the nymph's "skin of a beautiful violet color" with "veins as large as cord" seeming to "writhe like snakes." Since *Victoria*'s body "decomposes very quickly, fades, withers," the nymph-hunting hero allowed the "mutilated wonder to fall again into the lake."

Boussenard attempted to haul the flower, larger than the "canoe itself," onto the bank. Unfortunately, it was full of insects, making the Frenchman disgusted and fearful. His Indian companion reached inside the flower, "up to his arm," to clean it up, but he "swiftly" pulled his hand from the floral cavity. A venomous coral snake was wrapped around his wrist and biting "furiously." A painful death seemed imminent, but thanks to the curative properties of rum applied internally in liberal quantity, all ended well. The next day, the Indian awoke "fresh as a daisy, without the shadow of an ill effect" (Boussenard 1901, translated by John Luttrell).

Boussenard's climax paints a picture of a snake-infested beastly nymph, which was no doubt borrowed from the mythological Medusa, whose head was covered with serpents. Boussenard was one of many writers who followed Jules Verne's blend of natural history and fantasy to create the new genre of science fiction. To entertain his thrill-seeking audience, the Frenchman transformed *Victoria* into a monstrous man-killing creature and grotesquely magnified the size of the nymph's leaves and flowers. This deception was not entirely unbelievable for readers who had seen lilies with leaves over 2 m (7 feet) wide featured in European gardens for nearly a half century prior to the story's publication. If *Victoria* could reach such extraordinary proportions while cramped in small tanks of Victoria Houses in London, Brussels, or Berlin, could she not achieve gargantuan dimensions when living free and unconstrained in her native waters?

Such caricatures were not limited to Parisian magazines of questionable credibility. When Richard Spruce, a British explorer, arrived in Santarém on the Amazon, he met one Captain Hislop, who claimed to have seen *Victoria* with leaves nearly 3.7 m (12 feet) in diameter. Spruce himself never found leaves larger than 1.2 m (4 feet) wide, but he did not dare "doubt of the fact, having the testimony of many component observers" (Hooker 1851). So he searched along the Amazon for the enormous lilies from Captain Hislop's tales—much like others had searched for the mythical El Dorado or the tribe of female warriors from whom the Amazon river got its name. Spruce concluded that "measuring-tape was needed to correct the illusions caused by the exaggerated statements of others, or even by the apparent evidence of my own senses" (Spruce 1908).

OF MYTHICAL PROPORTIONS

While Boussenard's account of 9-m (30-foot) wide leaves must be dismissed as a figment of his imagination, the question remains: Under ideal circumstances, how big can *Victoria*'s leaves really be?

Understandably, nearly everyone who has ever met *Victoria,* either in the wild or in cultivation, ponders the same question that preoccupied Spruce. As a result, there are endless accounts of the width of

---

Louis Boussenard, 1901:

Unhappily, the base of the corolla is full of insects, contact with whom disgusts me and whose stings I fear.... Very calmly the Indian, who doesn't partake of my aversion, ... plunges his arm slowly, up to his shoulder, into the preserved corolla. And almost as swiftly he retracts it, with a quickness that astonishes me in view of his customary apathy. A cry of terror escapes me, and I feel myself tremble to the marrow of my bones. Around his wrist and forming a moving bracelet, a small snake twists and unrolls itself with rage.... [V]ivid red with black bands, it bites furiously the thumb of the Indian. Its fangs are deeply implanted in the flesh, and its ferocious little eyes sparkle like diamonds. I recognize the terrible élaps, *or coral snake, whose bite kills the most vigorous of men in less than an hour.... My pallor, my agitation, my offers of help make the Indian shrug his shoulders. With his admirable calm, he seizes with his left hand, between the thumb and index finger, the snake by the base of its head, with a strong grip, he makes it release its bite, smashes it against the wood of the* pirogue, *and says in his raspy voice, "Give me some rum."*

Boussenard 1901, translated by John Luttrell

her leaves, the height of her upturned leaf edges, the length of her petioles, and the diameter of her flowers. Nymphs kept in captivity often had each of their leaves and flowers counted and measured throughout the entire growing season. It was perhaps the only time in botanical history that leaves and flowers and other parts of a plant were diligently measured from the first day they were encountered.

In the world of exploration, the pursuit of the largest lily pad on the planet can be compared to similar obsessions with finding the world's tallest tree or climbing the highest mountain. Naturalists who find record-breaking *Victoria* plants experience the same rush of excitement as hunters bragging about their trophies and fisherman gesturing about the size of their catch. Cultivators of the South American lily give in to the same competitive impulse that keeps pumpkin-weighing contests alive.

Yet today, more than two centuries since *Victoria* was discovered, we still do not know how large her leaves can become in her natural environment. In 1842, when Robert Schomburgk and his brother Richard traveled the Rupununi River in Guiana, they measured a *Victoria amazonica* leaf 2.29 m (8 feet) across (Schomburgk 1873). A century and a half later, this record has still not been surpassed for plants in the wild. The largest *Victoria cruziana* on record in the wild was reported in 1999, when two Americans, Walter Pagels and Lindsay Weaver, measured a leaf with a diameter of 2.13 m (7 feet) near the town of Victoria in Argentina, in the Paraná delta (Pagels and Weaver 1999). The lily's ephemeral nature and the relative inaccessibility of her native habitat make it difficult, if not impossible, to attempt a systematic study that would establish her maximum dimensions in the wild. There is little doubt, however, that one day leaves that are even larger will be found somewhere in South America.

In contrast, botanists cultivating *Victoria* in Europe and then in the United States have had ample opportunities to conduct detailed studies of the giant lily, including rigorous leaf measurements. The first plants introduced from Guiana and grown in the greenhouses of Europe produced leaves that reached a maximum diameter of between 1.57 and 1.70 m (5 and 6 feet), far less than Schomburgk reported (Allen 1854, Hochstetter 1852, Planchon and Van Houtte 1850–51). In the 1850s, the earliest American cultivators, Caleb Cope in Philadelphia and John Fisk Allen in Salem, beamed with pride when their nymphs outperformed those in Europe, achieving 1.98 and 1.83 m (7 and 6 feet) across, respectively (Cope 1851a, Allen 1854). Europeans came close to these results in 1866, when a leaf 1.93 m (6 feet) wide was measured in the Dresden Botanic Garden (Seidel 1869).

The introduction of *Victoria amazonica* seeds from Brazil later in the nineteenth century took the rivalry for the largest leaf to a new level. Starting in 1884, cultivators in Cherkley Court in Leatherhead, England, announced they had raised lily pads up to 2.13 m (7 feet) across. Then, over the next ten years, others recorded leaves exceeding 2 m (7 feet) in diameter in several gardens on the continent. The Rotterdam Zoo led the pack with its 2.20 m (7 feet) record (Anonymous 1885b, Graebener 1891, Wilke 1891, Beissner 1893). Rotterdam's record remained unchallenged for a century, until a leaf 2.49 m (8 feet) wide was reported from Wyld Court (today's The Living Rainforest), near Hampstead Norris in Berkshire, England, in 1996 (Findon 1996).

For the most part, plants of *Victoria amazonica* grown outdoors trailed a few centimeters behind their counterparts, who enjoyed the comfort and protection of heated indoor pools. One exception was an early success in Washington, D.C., where awe-inspiring pads 2.24 m (7 feet) wide—then the outdoor world

---

Richard Spruce, 1849:

We were fortunate in finding the plant in good flower, but all the people at Santarém who had seen the plant asserted that the foliage is much larger in winter. Captain Hislop assures me he had seen many leaves twelve feet [4 m] across, whereas the largest we saw measured little more than four feet [1 m], and they were packed as close as they could lie. But I can easily conceive how, in the wet season, their size must be considerably increased, for whereas the plant is now growing in less than two feet [60 cm] of water, the igaripé *will be filled in winter to the topmost banks, or at least fifteen feet [5 m] deeper than present, while its breadth will also be greatly augmented, so that the petioles of the Victoria, lengthening, doubtless, with the rise of the waters, will bring the foliage to a much greater surface, whereon they will have room to dilate to above double the size they now exhibit. I cannot doubt of the fact, having the testimony of many component observers; but I hope to confirm it one day by personal examination.*

Hooker 1851

The enormous leaves of *Victoria* have been measured since the day this giant nymph was first discovered.
TOMASZ ANIŚKO / LONGWOOD GARDENS

record—were raised in the basin of the Bartholdi Fountain at the foot of Capitol Hill in 1891 (Seaman 1892). Later, some expressed doubts about the credibility of this astonishing result. "It must have been measured with a rubber tape," wrote George Pring of the Missouri Botanical Garden (Pring 1960). Whether real or fictitious, this record was unsurpassed by an outdoor-grown *Victoria amazonica* until 2006, when plants with leaves up to 2.35 m (8 feet) across were reported from Kebun Raya in Bogor, Indonesia (Kunii et al. 2006).

The largest leaves of *Victoria cruziana* in the wild, reported by Pagels and Weaver, were only 13 cm (5 inches) smaller than the record-holding *Victoria amazonica* the Schomburgks found along the Rupununi. A much greater size difference persists among cultivated plants, though. The records for the indoor-grown plant of *Victoria cruziana*, 1.96 m (6 feet), and an outdoor one, 1.88 m (6 feet), are about 0.5 m (20 inches) smaller than those achieved by the Amazonian species (Guldmann 1961, Henderson 1973). This discrepancy suggests that either much still remains to be learned about the proper culture of *Victoria cruziana* or that plants in cultivation do not represent the full genetic potential of that species.

Although these records are remarkable in their own right, they have all been surpassed by the 'Longwood Hybrid' introduced in 1961. From the start, she showed the vigor expected of a hybrid and produced leaves larger than either of her parent plants. In her first season in Longwood Gardens' outdoor pools, the hybrid reached 2.01 m (7 feet) in diameter. Eighteen years later, she attained 2.24 m (7 feet), tying Washington's 1891 record. Thus far, the largest leaf of an outdoor-grown 'Longwood Hybrid' was reported by Kanapaha Botanic Garden in Gainesville, Florida. In 2007, garden director Don Goodman measured one leaf at a whopping 2.36 m (8 feet) across (Goodman 2008).

Still, 'Longwood Hybrid' achieved even more impressive results indoors. In 1972, the Royal Botanic Garden, Edinburgh, set a new world record with a leaf 2.54 m (8 feet) wide (Henderson 1973). In 1995, the Royal Botanic Gardens, Kew, took the lead with a leaf 2.59 m (9 feet) in diameter (Anonymous 1995). Several years later, both royal gardens were overtaken by Wyld Court, already the world record holder for *Victoria amazonica*. In 2002, it raised a 'Longwood Hybrid' with leaves 2.65 m (9 feet) across (Anonymous 2011).

A NEW WORLD RECORD

While these record-setting results are astonishing, they also showed that *Victoria* gained just 11 cm (4 inches) in leaf diameter over thirty years of perfecting her growing methods. Many felt that perhaps this indicated the giant lily's outer limits. But then enormous lily pads up to 2.60 m (9 feet) across were observed in the wild in Bolivia, sending shockwaves around the botanical world (Ribero 2006a).

When grown at Longwood Gardens in 1979, leaves of *Victoria* 'Longwood Hybrid' reached a maximum diameter of 2.24 m (7 feet).
RICHARD F. KEEN / LONGWOOD GARDENS

Tonchi Ribero, a plantsman, artist, and restaurateur from Santa Cruz, Bolivia, saw these record-shattering nymphs near the town of Trinidad in Beni province, along the Tijamuchi, a tributary of the Mamoré. In 2000, he had some of these young plants collected and brought back to Santa Cruz for planting in a large koi pond in La Rinconada, his garden outside the city. Only one of them survived transplanting, but when she died in 2002, she was replaced by seedlings that sprouted spontaneously from seeds produced by the lone nymph.

The same year, another batch of young plants was fetched from Trinidad and planted at La Rinconada, but again only one survived (Ribero 2006b). Still, Ribero now had a self-reproducing population of giant lilies sharing the pond with more than a thousand koi fish. Ribero noted that the leaves of his *Victoria* were becoming larger each year. In fact, in 2005, they set a new world record of 2.78 m (9 feet). This reported gain of 13 cm (5 inches) over the previous record of 2.65 m (9 feet) was received with as much disbelief and euphoria among *Victoria* enthusiasts as was Bob Beamon's historic long jump at the 1968 Olympics among sports fans.

In 2007, 'Longwood Hybrid' grown outdoors at the Kanapaha Botanic Garden in Gainesville, Florida, produced leaves with a diameter of 2.36 m (8 feet).
TOMASZ ANIŚKO / LONGWOOD GARDENS

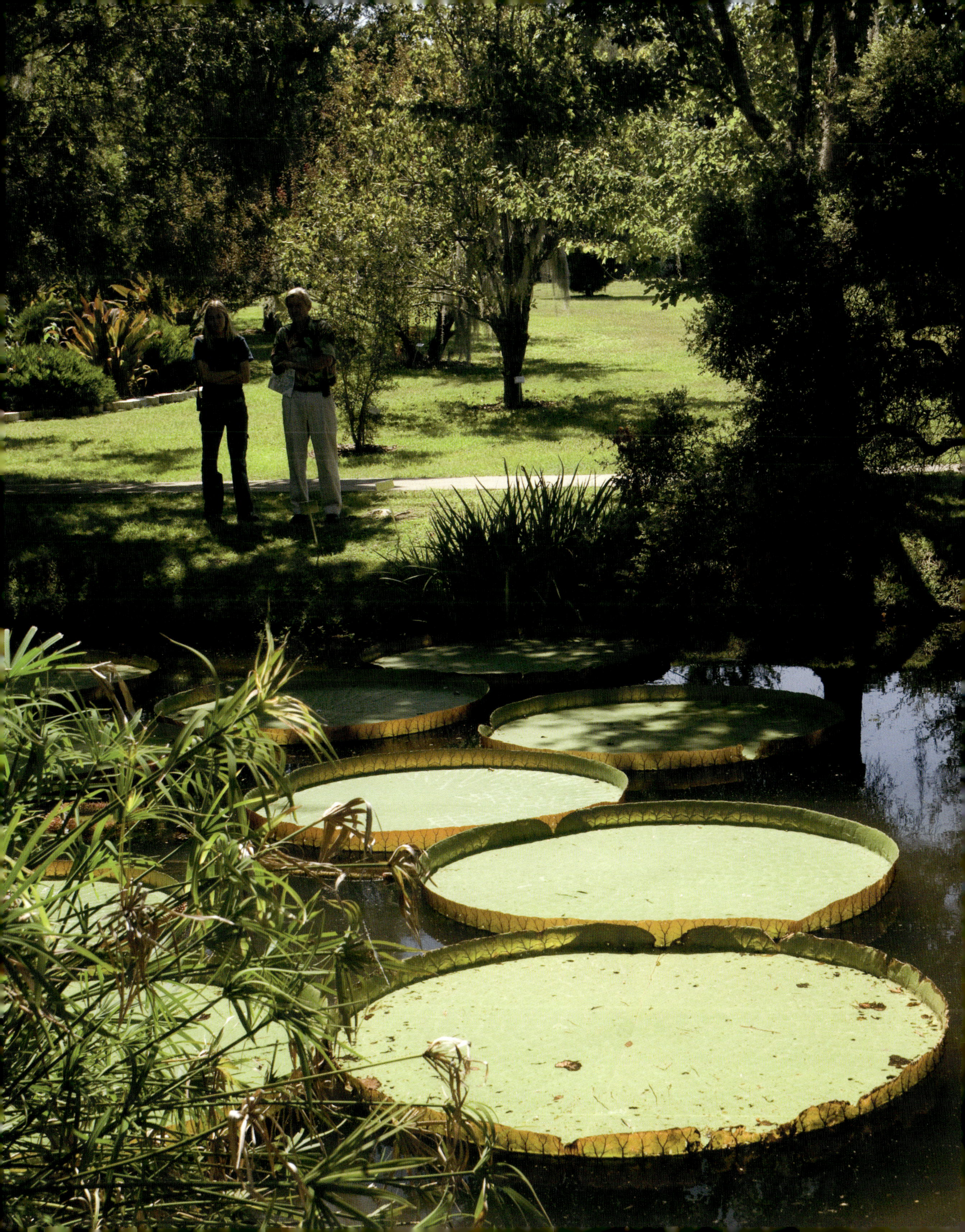

294 VICTORIA: THE SEDUCTRESS

Amazingly, Ribero's lilies kept getting bigger with each passing season until in 2010, the largest leaf at La Rinconada measured an astounding 2.93 m (10 feet) across (Ribero 2011). A year later, however, Ribero's *Victoria* population became a shadow of its former splendor as it finally exhausted its vitality. Seed germination was poor and plant growth weak. Whether Ribero or anyone else will be able to surpass the 2.93-m (10-foot) world record and cross the 3-m barrier remains to be seen.

In contrast to this relentless pursuit of larger and larger lily pads, it should be noted that *Victoria* shows a remarkable plasticity. Under certain conditions, she can be made into a miniature version of herself—not unlike trees that are artfully transformed into Japanese bonsai or Chinese penjing. "Cultivation," wrote one correspondent to the *Cottage Gardener and Country Gentleman* in 1857, "sometimes contracts, as well as expands, the subject; and this reminds us of a gentleman with whom we are acquainted, who has flowered the *Victoria* in a box a foot and a half [46 cm] square!" (Anonymous 1857).

Tonchi Ribero of La Rinconada, Bolivia, with the 2005 record lily pad measuring 2.78 m (9 feet) across.
ROBERTO VASQUEZ

La Rinconada garden outside Santa Cruz, Bolivia, where the world's largest *Victoria* lilies, originally procured from Beni province, have been growing since 2000.
ROBERTO VASQUEZ

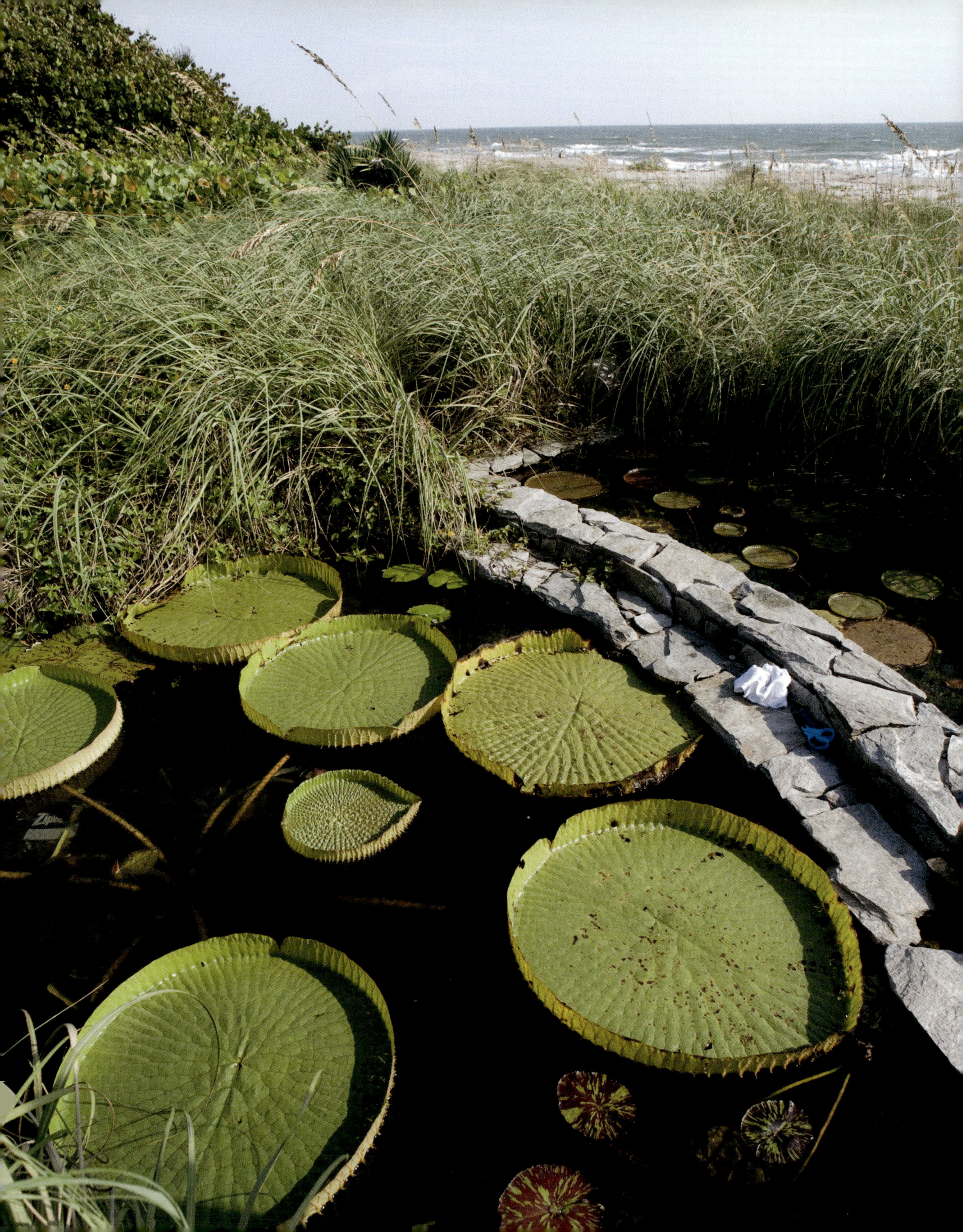

Manuel Belgrano of the Darwinion Institute of Botany in Buenos Aires inspects dwarfed *Victoria cruziana* growing in the shallow waters along the Riachuelo near Corrientes.
Tomasz Aniśko / Longwood Gardens

One sure way to have a miniature lily is to grow her in a small container. As Pring observed from growing many generations of *Victoria* at the Missouri Botanical Garden, "The size of the plant may be governed by the amount of soil given the roots, and a small specimen may be grown in an ordinary half barrel" (Pring 1949). Flowering specimens can be raised in pots with a diameter as small as 20 cm (8 inches) (Tricker 1897). In such cases, their leaves may not exceed 30 cm (12 inches) across. It is less clear, however, how to explain miniature plants occasionally found in the wild. Low fertility of the soil or low water level during the peak flood season may play a role.

FIRST LEAVES FIRST

The first three leaves that a juvenile *Victoria* develops bear no resemblance to the floating pads the queen lily is famed for. This initial trio remains completely submerged and well hidden from view. The first leaf is slender and linear; the second is hastate, meaning that it is shaped like an arrowhead with the

In the garden of Kit and Ben Knotts in Cocoa Beach, Florida, a fully grown *Victoria* occupies the center pool, while dwarfed lilies of equal age are grown in small pots in an adjoining canal above.
Tomasz Aniśko / Longwood Gardens

SIZE MATTERS

Victoria's first three leaves, developed under water, bear little resemblance to the floating pads that the nymph produces later.
Tomasz Aniśko / Longwood Gardens

basal lobes turned outward; and the third is sagittate, which differs from the hastate in that the basal lobes are directed downward. None of these leaves has defensive spines, which suggests they evolved to sprout in waters too shallow for large aquatic herbivores to enter. The fourth leaf is spiny and breaks the surface of the water, but it may not be easily recognized as a future giant lily pad. Another three floating leaves must develop before they acquire *Victoria*'s unmistakable appearance, and a few more before the upturned leaf margin develops.

The frequency with which new leaves appear can vary significantly, depending upon light and temperature conditions as well as plant vigor. In a greenhouse of the Dresden Botanical Garden in Germany, new leaves emerged on average at four-day intervals, although the actual frequency varied between three and seven days (Seidel 1869). By comparison, plants grown outdoors in Kebun Raya, Indonesia, produced new leaves every two to three days (Kunii et al. 2006), but in Buenos Aires, Argentina, leaves appeared every six to ten days (Valla and Martin 1976).

While the rate of leaf production also varies with the season, *Victoria* sends new pads to the surface continuously throughout her lifetime. To make room for new leaves, the oldest ones must senesce and disintegrate—a process that may accelerate if older leaves are overlapped by younger pads. This continual succession sets a limit on the lifespan of an individual leaf. In wild populations that occur at the confluence of the Paraguay and Paraná, leaves lasted between eighteen and twenty days (Valla and Martin 1976). Under cultivated conditions, their lifetime can be extended somewhat. In an outdoor pool in Buenos Aires, leaves lasted twenty-five to thirty days before deteriorating, while they survived for thirty to forty days in Kebun Raya. A still greater lifespan, up to fifty-six days, was reported for plants grown indoors in Amsterdam (Oudemans 1862).

The longevity of the leaves combined with the rate at which new ones are produced determines the number of healthy leaves a plant has at any given time. These can range from as few as five (Allen 1854) to as many as nine (Pagels and Weaver 1999), or even fifteen (Kunii et al. 2006).

A plant with only five leaves gives the impression that the leaves follow a five-ranked arrangement. In reality, their spatial distribution around the axis of the plant is much more complicated. Leaves are placed in a spiral in such a way that they are sequentially separated by a turn of 137 degrees and 30 seconds (Oudemans 1862). Theoretically, 144 leaves would have to develop before a new leaf could emerge exactly above the first one, while the spiral along which the leaves aligned would have to circle the stem 55 times. This arrangement, or phylotaxy, is therefore described by a 55/144 formula. Others calculated *Victoria*'s formula to be 3/8, 7/18, or 9/23, all giving a turn of about 140 degrees between two sequential leaves (Seidel 1869, Weidlich 1980).

The expansion of a giant lily leaf as it emerges curled up to spread its spiny body on the water's surface may be one of Nature's most captivating phenomena. Early observers often found themselves at a loss to describe this curious spectacle. The rolled-up leaf bristling with sharp spines has been likened to a hedgehog, a prickly shell, and even a sea urchin (Cope 1851a, Emerson 1851, Anonymous 1857). The young leaf that rises above the water as "a mere clenched mass of yellow prickles" is transformed the next day into "a crimson salver, gorgeously tinted on its upturned rim" (Higginson 1863).

Unlike the first three leaves, the fourth leaf, seen here on top, reaches the surface of the water and develops protective spines.
TOMASZ ANIŚKO / LONGWOOD GARDENS

To avoid overcrowding, sequential leaves of *Victoria* are spaced at about 137 to 140 degrees. Older leaves are distributed around the periphery of the plant and are gradually replaced by younger ones developing in the center. In cultivation, the oldest deteriorating leaves are regularly removed to improve the appearance of the plant.
LARRY ALBEE / LONGWOOD GARDENS

The speed with which *Victoria*'s leaves expand is truly astonishing. A patient observer can almost see it happening. The unfolding phase may take three days, after which the leaf lies flat on the surface of the water with its wrinkles smoothed out and enters into an accelerated expansion stage. The reported rates of expansion can vary from 20 to more than 60 cm (8 to 24 inches) in a twenty-four-hour period (Anonymous 1856, Anonymous 1857, Higginson 1863, Seidel 1869, Valla and Martin 1976).

Robert Caspary, who studied *Victoria* at the Royal Botanical Gardens Schöneberg in Berlin, noticed that the expansion rate changed during each day and night cycle. It reached one maximum around noon and another around midnight, as if the leaf took a deep breath at twelve-hour intervals (Anonymous 1856). Usually, this stretching exercise slows down three days later. Then, within seven to ten days from its start, it comes to a halt, regardless of the final size of the leaf (Valla and Martin 1976, Lamprecht et al. 2002c, Kunii et al. 2006). In rare instances, it may take up to nineteen days for the leaf to fully expand (Seidel 1869).

John Ellis, letter to Andrew Downing, 1851:

When we contrast the seed in its first state of germination, and by an acute observation perceive its feeble cotyledon, like a thread, endeavoring to reach the water's surface, but unable—with its colossal leaves between six and seven feet [2 m] in diameter, well may we call it a Vegetable Wonder, and the Queen of Aquatics. We hail with delight the promised leaf, and watch its daily unfoldings with increasing interest. When we view its shell-like appearance when first above the water's surface, quilled together into ridge and furrow of transparent golden hues, with its dark crimson veins flowing through its much admired tissue, its superb salver edge, and its huge rope-like stems, covered with elastic spines of surprising strength, as though destined to protect its noble structure from all invasion. When we look at the short period it has taken to germinate a seed no larger than a pea, and to bring to maturity a plant that fills a tank twenty-four feet [7 m] in diameter . . . well may we affirm that it deserves the attention and culture of every true lover of nature who can afford the expense.

Cope 1851a

Edmund Sturtevant, 1895:

The flowers are lovely beyond description; but the monster leaves of the plant are its glory. It is most fascinating to watch the expansion and growth of these leaves on a plant of normal size. Out of the heart of the plant rises to the surface of the water an oblong ball or wrinkled mass of vegetable tissue about ten inches [25 cm] across and covered thickly with long sharp thorns. The next day it is expanded into a lovely bronze-colored salver some eighteen inches [46 cm] in diameter and having an upturned rim tinted crimson. From this time on, its growth is about eight inches [20 cm] a day until it attains full size.

Sturtevant 1895

The emerging rolled-up leaf of *Victoria* has been compared to a hedgehog, a prickly shell, and a sea urchin.
Tomasz Aniśko / Longwood Gardens

THE SOMBRERO'S BRIM

The upturned rim on *Victoria*'s leaves draws almost as much attention as their diameter. The rim is universally recognized as a feature that greatly adds to the beauty of the queen lily. Spruce compared it to "the brim of a Spanish sombrero" (Hooker 1851). Both its color and height have been meticulously recorded since the day Joseph Paxton grew the first plant at Chatsworth in 1849. There, the edge rose 8 cm (3 inches) and was "of the most beautiful dark purple color" (Allen 1854).

This came short of the 14-cm (6-inch) high rim measured by Schomburgk in the wilds of British Guiana in 1837 (Hooker 1851), but by the late nineteenth century, leaves with quite respectable rims measuring 13 to 15 cm (5 to 6 inches) were showing up in European gardens (Anonymous 1885b, Graebener 1891). Later, although the leaves of *Victoria cruziana* measured slightly smaller in diameter than those of their northern cousin, the plant had rim heights that easily surpassed earlier results. For that reason alone, the leaves of *Victoria cruziana* are often preferred in cultivation. In the wild in Argentina, these plants are commonly observed with rims up to 18 cm (7 inches) high (Pagels and Weaver 1999).

Because higher rims are desired in cultivated *Victoria*, considerable attention has been paid to their purpose and the conditions favoring their development. One can usually expect to see higher rims at the peak of the summer season. They are also more prominent in vigorous, healthy plants growing in full sun. Most likely the raised edge gives the leaf a greater rigidity, providing improved stability against strong winds that might otherwise lift the leaf off the surface of the water, fold it, and, in effect, destroy it (Lamprecht et al. 2002c). High rims also prevent leaves from overlapping each other. For this reason, they are often higher in populations where lilies are crowded. In extreme cases, entire leaves assume a cup-like form (Valla and Martin 1976). Leaves armed with high rims are also able to smother and push aside other aquatic plants, an immensely beneficial trait in this fiercely competitive environment (Pagels and Weaver 1999).

Typically, the expansion of the lily pad is completed within seven to ten days after rising to the surface of the water.
LARRY ALBEE / LONGWOOD GARDENS

The striking upturned rims of the *Victoria cruziana* leaf are widely admired. Therefore, this lily is often chosen in cultivation over *Victoria amazonica*, which develops larger pads but with lower rims.
TOMASZ ANIŚKO / LONGWOOD GARDENS

VICTORIA: THE SEDUCTRESS

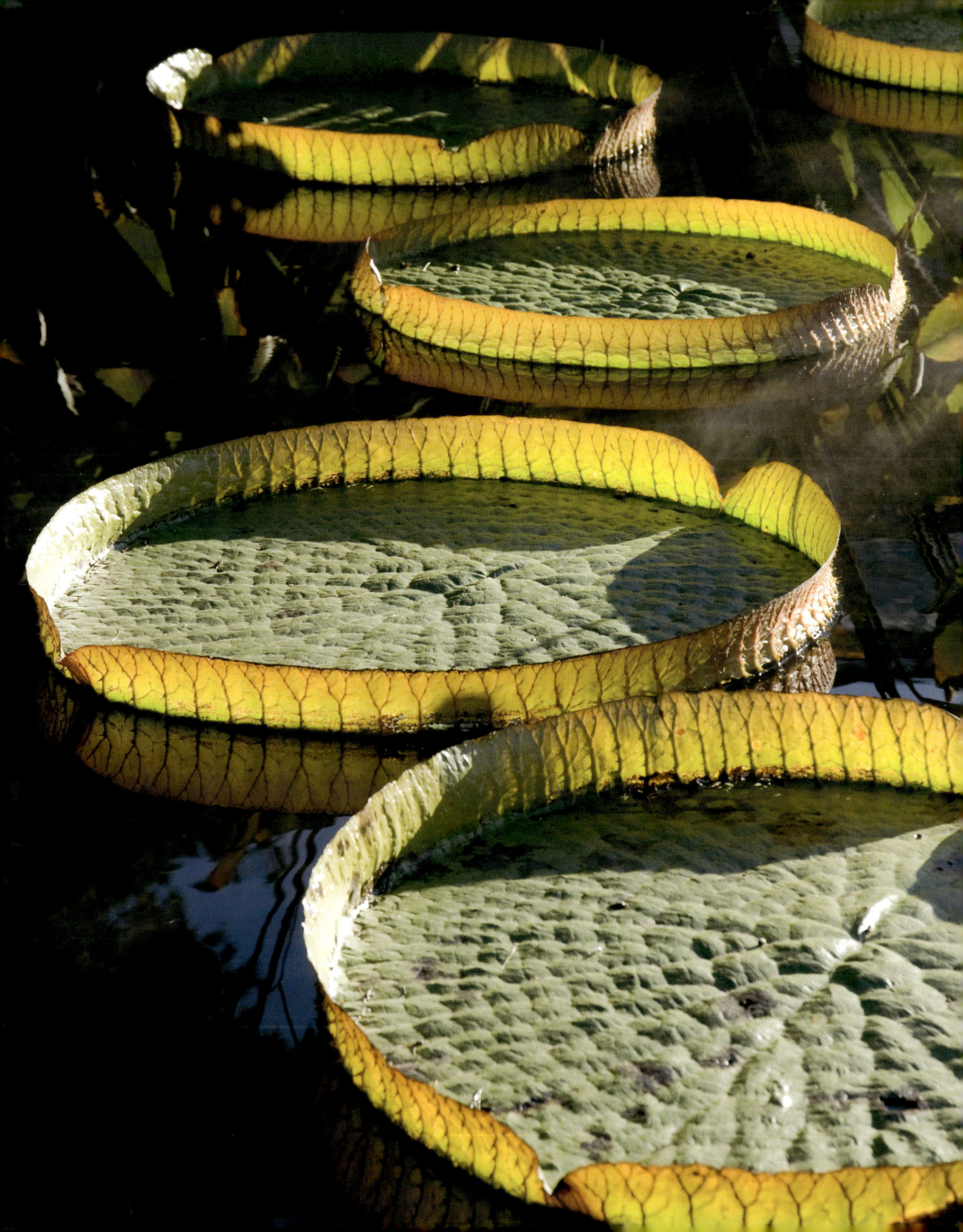

Strong wind can pick up *Victoria* leaves and fold them. Since they are incapable of straightening on their own, this inevitably leads to their demise.
TOMASZ ANIŚKO / LONGWOOD GARDENS

In her relentless struggle to make territorial claims against other aquatic invaders, *Victoria* employs countless needle-sharp spines that project outward from the surface of her upturned leaf margins. These push against competing vegetation and mercilessly shred it to pieces (Guldmann 1965). Yet the fact that all her underwater parts are thickly studded with spines while the upper leaf surface lacks them suggests that their primary purpose is to defend against large aquatic herbivores. Since *Victoria* is not known to fall victim to fish predation (Cowgill and Prance 1989), there is only one possible candidate: the manatee. In the Amazon basin, the giant lily and the manatee have shared the same rivers for millions of years, while the likely ancestors to the modern Amazonian manatees also lived in the

Upturned leaf margins prevent *Victoria* leaves from overlapping, which is especially critical in crowded populations like this one near Corrientes, Argentina.
EDWIN E. HARVEY

304 VICTORIA: THE SEDUCTRESS

SIZE MATTERS 305

Rainwater does not accumulate on the leaves of *Victoria*, despite their upturned margins.
Tomasz Aniśko / Longwood Gardens

John Fisk Allen, 1854:

When in the young stage of growth, and when unfolding, the leaf is exquisitely beautiful, equaling, in the estimation of many, the flowers themselves. When fully grown and mature, the texture of the leaf is thin and very tender; its color is of a pale green on the face or disk, but highly colored, and of a purplish crimson tint beneath. The edge or margin is turned up, to the width of from two to four inches [5 to 10 cm], and when the sun shines upon this raised edge in the young leaves, a most beautiful varying crimson color is present to the eye.

Allen 1854

Paraná river system (Domning 1982). There is little doubt that during their long course of coexistence, *Victoria*'s spines provided an effective deterrent against these soft-lipped creatures (Clute 1921).

While they clearly provide many benefits, *Victoria*'s upturned leaf margins also create a significant challenge. In areas with heavy rainfall, the lily can easily receive upward of 20 liters (5 gallons) of water on each pad a day. The rim, which only has two notches around its perimeter, interferes with water draining off the surface of the leaf. If rainwater were allowed to collect on the leaf's upper side, it would effectively choke the stomata located there, stop the diffusion of gases in and out of the leaf, and ultimately suffocate the nymph. To facilitate drainage, the lily has countless minute holes, 0.2 to 0.3 mm in diameter, that perforate the whole leaf except those areas occupied by the ribs.

Jules Planchon, a French botanist who studied the first lilies grown by Louis Van Houtte in Ghent in 1850, coined the term "stomatodes" to describe these peculiar perforations (Planchon and Van Houtte 1850–51). Planchon believed they permitted the escape of harmful gases rising from the bottom of a pond—gases that might otherwise be trapped between the ribs under the leaf. A few years later, however, Peter Clarke, curator of the Royal Botanic Garden in Glasgow, noted that the stomatodes had an equally important role in draining excess water from the upper surface of the leaf (Clarke 1855).

It is easy to observe how water mysteriously vanishes from the surface of a *Victoria* leaf, even after a torrential rainfall. However, Juan Jose Valla and Maria Elena Martin, Argentinean botanists working at the University of Buenos Aires, had to resort to a little trickery to prove that gases indeed pass through these same perforations. First, they poured soapy water on a section of the leaf. Next, they blew air underneath the leaf, raising that section slightly off the water. Shortly thereafter, soap bubbles appeared above the stomatodes, indicating that the air underneath was escaping, which soon returned the leaf to its normal flat position (Valla and Martin 1976).

AMAZING UNDERSIDE

Whether it is likened to a giant tea tray or a Spanish sombrero, the sight of a floating lily pad is captivating. The underside of the leaf, however, can be even more so. There, one finds a striking network

Jules Planchon, 1850–51:

A single viewing distinguishes without difficulty, on the surface of the foliar disc, small blemishes or reddish punctuations, the structure of which merits an attentive examination. Studied under the microscope on a still young leaf, these points appear as many small indents hollowed onto the surface of the leaf, restricted by a circle of rosy cells, and whose translucent center owes its transparence to the absence of chlorophyll in the parenchyma portion that separates the two epidermises at this point. As the leaf develops proportionately, the indents, whose number remains the same, spread out more and more; at the same time, their bottom foundation tears; the cells beneath are destroyed, as well as the corresponding portion of the inferior epidermis; quite simply, in the original indents, single superficial depressions are replaced by genuine perforations, riddling the thin parenchyma of the leaf, from section to section, like a plethora of pinholes. . . . these are sui generis *organs, developed normally and regularly on the leaves of the* Victoria, *and whose existence is probably as rare as the need to which they seem to respond. Would these not be, indeed, a means of extrication for gases, which, rising via bubbles of a muddy or silty bottom foundation, would otherwise remain imprisoned under the leaf's inferior relief compartments, if Nature did not manage this problem? . . . [T]he name stomatode proposed for these openings will have the advantage of fixing on them the attention of observers, and perhaps to permit them to be found again in other plants.*

Planchon and Van Houtte 1850–51, translated by Adam Koppeser

Minute perforations called stomatodes effectively drain water from the *Victoria* leaf. They are seen as darker dots on the upper surface of the leaf or as luminescent spots when viewed against light.
LARRY ALBEE / LONGWOOD GARDENS

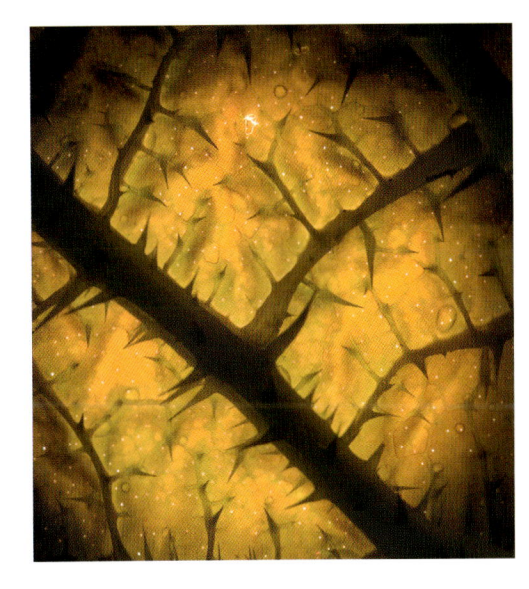

The underside of the *Victoria* leaf presents an awesome sight, combining structural ingenuity, captivating beauty, and a horrifying armory of spines.
Tomasz Aniśko / Longwood Gardens

of unusual veins, very thin but projecting down several centimeters from the lower leaf surface and gradually tapering toward the edge. This framework of narrow ribs spans the entire underside and is joined by a network of web-like cross-veins. It was recognized early on as a means to "afford the requisite firmness and support" (Allen 1854).

This ingenious design provides the delicate leaf surface with a surprising rigidity and has fascinated structural engineers ever since Paxton was inspired to apply the same principle to the construction of glass roofs. As one engineering expert admitted after carefully studying the underside of *Victoria*'s leaf, he "could not suggest an improvement in any important detail," explaining that "wherever an engineer is confronted with a problem of stiffening a circular flat plate, supported near the center, his design will look very much like the one developed by the water lily of the Amazon" (Anonymous 1927).

While supporting ribs, which are much taller than they are wide, lend a greater stiffness to the lily pad, their internal design exemplifies the principle of economy. Mostly hollow and made of spongy tissue, the ribs are much stronger than they would be if they were solid and used the same amount of building material.

Over time, many people have been tempted to check the limits of the lily pad's strength. They quickly learned, however, that "notwithstanding its gigantic size and elaborate structure, the texture of the leaf is so very delicate that should a straw fall perpendicularly from the height of five feet [1.5 m], so as to strike between the ribs, it would penetrate its substance" (Allen 1854). With leaf density calculated at about 0.34 g/cm^2, or 0.14 g/cm^2 if ribs are excluded, a mature leaf weighs only a few kilograms (Lamprecht et al. 2002b, 2002c). Of that, 94 percent is water, leaving very little solid material from which the leaf is built, between 7 and 12 mg/cm^2 (Trespe 1925, Kunii et al. 2006).

Sometimes in the wild, long-toed birds, most often jacanas or lily-trotters, can be spotted walking on or even building their nests upon *Victoria* leaves (Lovejoy 1978), but one would look in vain for a cayman or any other creature of substantial weight scrambling onto a lily pad. Cultivators must be careful to avoid breaking the exceedingly fragile surface of the leaf when testing its buoyancy. This is usually done by using thin wooden planks or plywood to evenly distribute the weight of the load without puncturing the leaf. Such precautions have shown that a single leaf can successfully sustain weights ranging from 40 to 90 kg (88 to 198 pounds), depending on its size (Loescher 1852, Witte 1872, Beissner 1893, Conard 1953).

Another test showed that the leaf could sustain an even heavier load in the form of sand that was spread evenly on its surface. In this case, the lily pad collapsed when the sand's weight exceeded 136 kg (300 pounds) (Anonymous 1927). An even more impressive test performed in the greenhouses of Regent's Park in London in 1870 purportedly showed that a leaf 1.67 m (6 feet) in diameter supported 193 kg (426 pounds) of gravel "when an unlucky throw tilted it to one side and it sank" (Seaman 1892). The most outrageous claim, however, was made in 1885 by Samuel Lockwood, who alleged that in Ghent, a *Victoria* leaf bore a load of bricks totaling 345 kg (760 pounds), a number that was "nearly equal to five men of average weight" (Lockwood 1885).

Edgar Anderson, 1963:

Some years ago I became intrigued with the design [of the Victoria *leaf] and carried photographs and samples to Dr. Alexander F. Langsdorf of the Engineering School at Washington University. He had great respect for the design. It was "an almost perfect solution for the problem of stiffening a circular flat plate supported near the middle." The veins, he said, were more efficient if flat, since the end-to-end stiffness of a supporting vein would be proportional to the cube of the vein's height but only directly proportional to its width. . . . Dr. Langsdorf then proceeded to illustrate these and other principles of the design from illustrations of various kinds of machinery; I remember in particular a series of boilers with circular plates at their ends. Between one machine and another he could show mechanical parallels of most of the water lily design. . . . Immediately however he had a question for me: "Why should water lily leaves be stiff?"*

Anderson 1963

SIZE MATTERS 309

Despite its amazing buoyancy, the *Victoria* leaf is very light and fragile. When it is lifted out of the water, it wilts and deflates within minutes.
TOMASZ ANIŚKO / LONGWOOD GARDENS

Samuel Lockwood, 1885:

I have some notes which I think were made some thirty years ago, from which we will extract, though the figures seem incredible. It was stated in Science pour Tous, *that in the aquarium of the Botanical Garden at Ghent, the head gardener, M. Van Houtte [sic, Van Hulle], was interested to learn the force required to immerse one of the floating leaves in the water. One leaf supported a child; another was not submerged by the weight of one of the gardeners. He was led to experiment as to the limit of this resistance—loading the surface of the largest leaves with bricks. It was found to bear a weight of 760 pounds [345 kg] avoirdupois—that is to say, nearly equal to five men of average weight.*

Lockwood 1885

William Hooker of the Royal Botanic Gardens, Kew, was probably the first to suggest that the astonishing buoyancy of *Victoria*'s pads was due to air spaces contained in their bulky ribs as well as air trapped in deep compartments that were formed by branching and anastomosing ribs underneath (Hooker 1851). A decade later, Corneille Oudemans of the Botanical Garden in Amsterdam demonstrated the presence of air trapped underneath the leaf by placing an inverted glass filled with water on the upper leaf surface and puncturing several holes in the leaf from below (Oudemans 1862). From each of these holes, Oudemans noticed large bubbles escaping into the glass. He speculated that gases trapped underneath the leaf originated from the sludge accumulated at the bottom of the pond where the plant was growing.

Of course, this contradicts Planchon's theory about the purpose of the stomatodes (to ventilate the underside of the leaf and prevent the gases from being trapped there). Nonetheless, Hooker's explanation for the lily pad's buoyancy was widely accepted and recently supported by theoretical calculations showing that a leaf 1.5 m (5 feet) wide can trap 50 to 55 liters (2 cubic feet) of air, which perfectly matches its corresponding load-carrying capacity (Lamprecht et al. 2002c, Lack 2004). How scientists can reconcile this elegant, indeed Archimedean, argument with the presence of the gas-leaking stomatodes remains to be seen.

Large *Victoria* pads can support 40 to 90 kg (88 to 198 pounds), provided the weight is evenly distributed and the surface is protected from being punctured. At Tower Grove Park in St. Louis, Missouri, quilted pads were used under the frame of thin wooden slats on which these police officers were able to stand and pose for a picture.
TOWER GROVE PARK

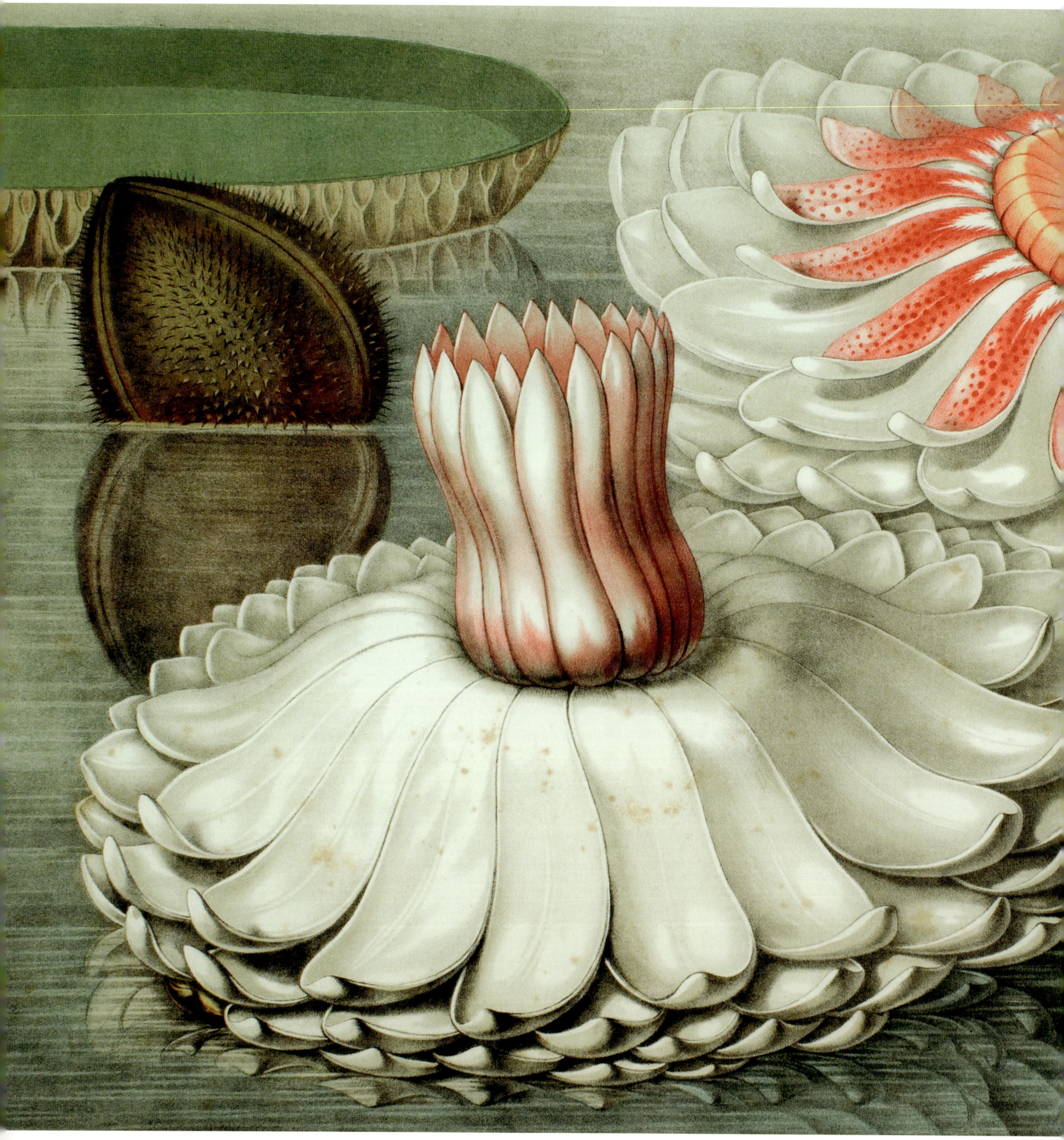

chapter 17

NIGHTFALL FEVER

IN 1850, IN GHENT, BELGIUM, LOUIS VAN HOUTTE grew the first *Victoria* on the European continent. He and French botanist Jules Planchon were also the first to note that the giant lily produced "heat of very remarkable intensity," raising the temperature inside the flower 6°C (11°F) above the outside air temperature (Planchon and Van Houtte 1850–51).

The phenomenon of flowers generating heat, today called thermogenesis, had been known since the late eighteenth century. In 1778, French naturalist and early evolutionist Jean-Baptiste Lamarck—also remembered for his theory of inheritance of acquired characteristics known as Lamarckism—had reported that the common woodland lily, *Arum maculatum* or *pied-de-veau* (calf's foot), had inflorescences that were warmer than the rest of the plant. To Lamarck, they appeared to be "burning."

In 1789, Lamarck's casual observation prompted Jean Senebier, a Swiss pastor and naturalist, to measure the temperature of the *Arum maculatum* inflorescence. Senebier reported that the lily's temperature rose to more than 27°C (81°F), or nearly 9°C (16°F) above the air. More studies followed, and by the time Van Houtte and Planchon made their announcement in 1850, heat-producing flowers had been discovered in about a dozen various species (Caspary 1855).

Intermediate stages of the opening of *Victoria amazonica* flower on the second day of blooming, a lithograph prepared by William Sharp based on plants grown by John Fisk Allen in Salem, Massachusetts, and published in Allen's 1854 book *Victoria Regia or the Great Water Lily of America*.
LONGWOOD GARDENS LIBRARY AND ARCHIVES

Intrigued by the report coming from Ghent, Johann Georg Christian Lehmann—a German botanist and founder of the Hamburg Botanical Garden—asked Eduard Otto, the garden's inspector, to study *Victoria* when it flowered for the first time there in 1851 and to verify the Belgian findings. Lehmann had observed a similar increase in temperature in *Nymphaea alba*, a European cousin of the South American water lily. On the evenings of September 24 and October 17, Otto measured the inside temperature, each time taking a single reading at the moment of the flower's opening (Otto 1851c, 1852b). He and Lehmann were gratified to see that the flowers in Hamburg produced the same burst of heat as those in Ghent. Further, Otto noticed that temperature readings decreased as he inserted the thermometer deeper into the floral chamber, below the ring of stamens. He repeated these measurements the following year, on August 8, recording the temperature every 10 minutes between 6:50 and 7:20 P.M. while the flower was opening (Otto 1852a). The same year in Berlin, where the first *Victoria* bloomed at the Royal Botanical Garden Schöneberg, garden curator Johann Klotzsch reported similar warming of a flower that was cut off from the plant (Klotzsch 1852).

GATHERING HEAT

Although this phenomenon had already been positively confirmed by several botanists, its cause or purpose still eluded them. In 1852, Eduard Loescher of Hamburg, author of the first German monograph on *Victoria*, acknowledged that on the evening of its opening, the flower's temperature rose several degrees above the air. However, he admitted that he did not know the cause and considered this phenomenon to be of "little importance."

Otto established that the flowers are indeed warmer than the air and that the heat most likely emanates from the anthers. However, it was another German botanist, Robert Caspary, who investigated the relationship between periodic changes of flower temperature, daily fluctuations of air temperature, and changing light conditions. In August 1854, Caspary recorded the temperature of *Victoria* flowers at the Schöneberg garden in Berlin. That October, he repeated his measurements on a plant blooming in the famed gardens of locomotive magnate August Borsig in Berlin-Moabit. Using five thermometers over the course of three days and two nights, Caspary measured the temperature of the flower, water, and air. He took readings hourly or more, an exhausting exercise that kept him awake for forty to forty-five hours. To the three flowers he measured in 1854, Caspary added another four in 1855. That year, he published the first comprehensive reports describing heat generation by *Victoria* flowers.

Forty years later, *Victoria* had become a familiar sight in European conservatories. At that time, Eduard Knoch was preparing his doctoral dissertation at the University of Marburg, Germany, which studied the physiology of the giant lily's flowers. For the first time, he associated the diffusion of scent from the opening flower with its increased

---

Jean-Baptiste Lamarck, 1778:

When the blossom has grown to a certain state of perfection or development, it is warm to the extent that it seems burning, and is not at all at the temperature of the other bodies; this state only continues for a few hours; I observed this phenomenon in one variety of this plant, that M. de Tournefort named arum venis albis, italicum, maximum.

Lamarck 1778, translated by John Luttrell

Eduard Otto, 1851:

At the request of Professor Lehmann, who thought he had formerly noticed an increase of temperature in the flowers of Nymphaea alba *at the moment of opening, as compared with that of the surrounding atmosphere, we made experiments in this garden (the Hamburg Botanic Garden) with the* Victoria regia *on 24th of September last (1851), which produced the following striking results. The temperature in the hothouse being 17 ¼° Réaum. [22°C], and that of the tank being 16 ½° Réaum. [21°C], the thermometer on being plunged into the flower at the moment of expanding its anthers, at 7 h. 11 min. P. M., rose to 21 ½° Réaum. [27°C] . . . the bulb being placed among the anthers. On being sunk into the blossom below the anthers, a decrease of temperature took place gradually. In thus preliminarily noticing the above fact, we deem it proper to say, that owing to the number of visitors who crowded to see the plant in flower, it was impracticable to pursue the experiment any further.*

Otto 1852b

Infrared imaging shows the temperature of the staminodes surrounding the opening leading to the floral chamber at 30 to 32°C (86 to 90°F).
LARRY ALBEE / LONGWOOD GARDENS

NIGHTFALL FEVER 315

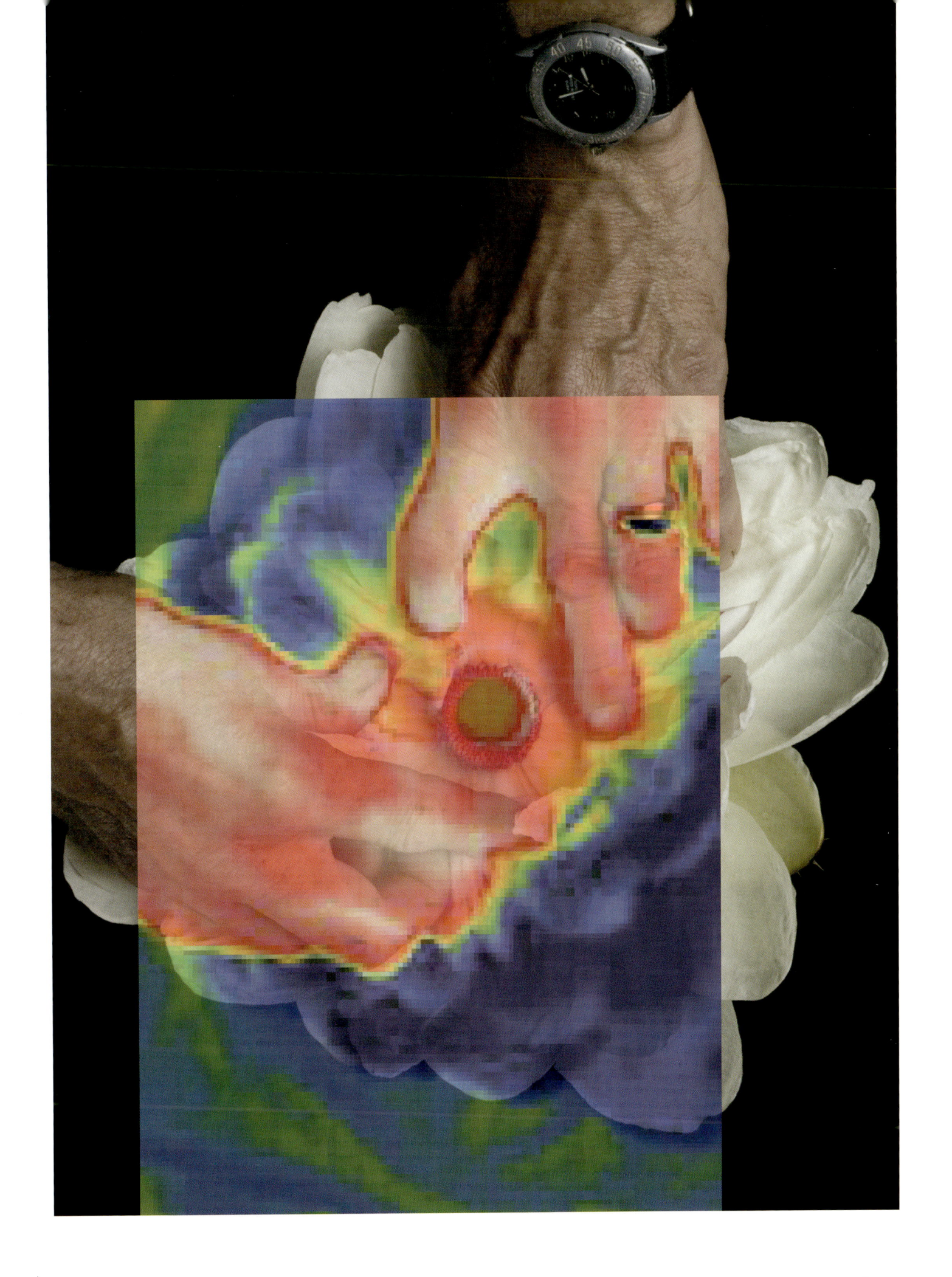

Robert Caspary conducted the first systematic study of temperature of *Victoria* flowers in 1854 and 1855.
Hunt Institute for Botanical Documentation

temperature (Knoch 1897). Knoch proposed that this system was designed to attract pollinating insects. His claim, however, was based on temperature measurements made solely on plants growing in various European greenhouses, where there were no insects pollinating *Victoria*.

Since the time of Schomburgk's 1837 discovery, South American travelers had observed that *Victoria* flowers release a delightful aroma and that scarab beetles flock to the blooms. Yet it was not until 1936 that the rise in flower temperature was documented in wild plants growing in the Amazon. This helped validate Knoch's hypothesis (Valla and Cirino 1972).

After Van Houtte and Planchon first recorded a 6°C (11°F) temperature difference between the *Victoria amazonica* flower and the surrounding air, subsequent studies that produced comparable results took place. In Hamburg, Otto recorded the temperature of the opening flower that varied between about 27 and 31°C (81 and 88°F), which was 3 to 8°C (5 to 14°F) above the ambient temperature. In Berlin, Klotzsch measured only about 24°C (75°F) inside the flower, but this was more than 11°C (20°F) higher than the air temperature.

Caspary's measurements showed that the opening flowers were 10 to 11°C (19 to 20°F) warmer than the air, reaching a maximum temperature of 34°C (93°F). He also observed that the temperature of the flower, although higher than the ambient temperature, was affected by it. As the air warmed up, so did the flower. In contrast, Caspary noted that the temperature difference between the flower and the air tended to be greater in a cooler atmosphere. *Victoria* flowers do not maintain a stable temperature the way warm-blooded creatures do, but Caspary's observations suggested the flower had a limited ability to compensate for changes in air temperature.

More than a century after Caspary, Juan Jose Valla and Donato Ricardo Cirino of the University of Buenos Aires studied *Victoria cruziana* in her native habitat near Esquina, Argentina. They noted that the largest temperature difference between the flower and the air, more than 9°C (16°F), was recorded on a cool evening when the air temperature was barely above 23°C (73°F) (Valla and Cirino 1972). Similarly, when Ghillean Prance of the New York Botanical Garden studied *Victoria amazonica* in the wild in Brazil, he observed that when the evening air temperature was between 21 and 22°C (70 to 72°F), flowers were about 9°C (16°F) warmer (Leppard 1978). Later, a team from the University of Adelaide, Roger Seymour and Philip Matthews, working in Guyana, recorded that the maximum temperature difference was a little above 9°C (16°F) when the ambient temperature was about 25°C (77°F) (Seymour and Matthews 2006).

Rather astonishingly, the same approximate 9°C (16°F) maximum temperature difference was measured in *Victoria cruziana* flowers growing in places as diverse as the outdoor ponds of an aquatic plant nursery in Brookshire, Texas (Schneider et al. 1990), and a conservatory of the Botanical Garden in Berlin-Dahlem (Lamprecht

Robert Caspary's measurements (left) in Berlin in 1854 and 1855, collected hourly from seven flowers of *Victoria amazonica* on the first (red squares) and second (yellow squares) night of flowering show dependence of the flower temperature on the air temperature. A similar relationship was observed at Longwood in 2008 and 2009 (right) when temperature was recorded in ten flowers of *Victoria* 'Longwood Hybrid' every minute. In Berlin, flowers were on average about 8°C (14°F) warmer than the air during the first night (6:00 P.M. to 6:00 A.M.) and 4°C (7°F) on the second night. At Longwood, flowers averaged more than 5°C (9°F) warmer than the air on the first night and nearly 2°C (4°F) on the second.

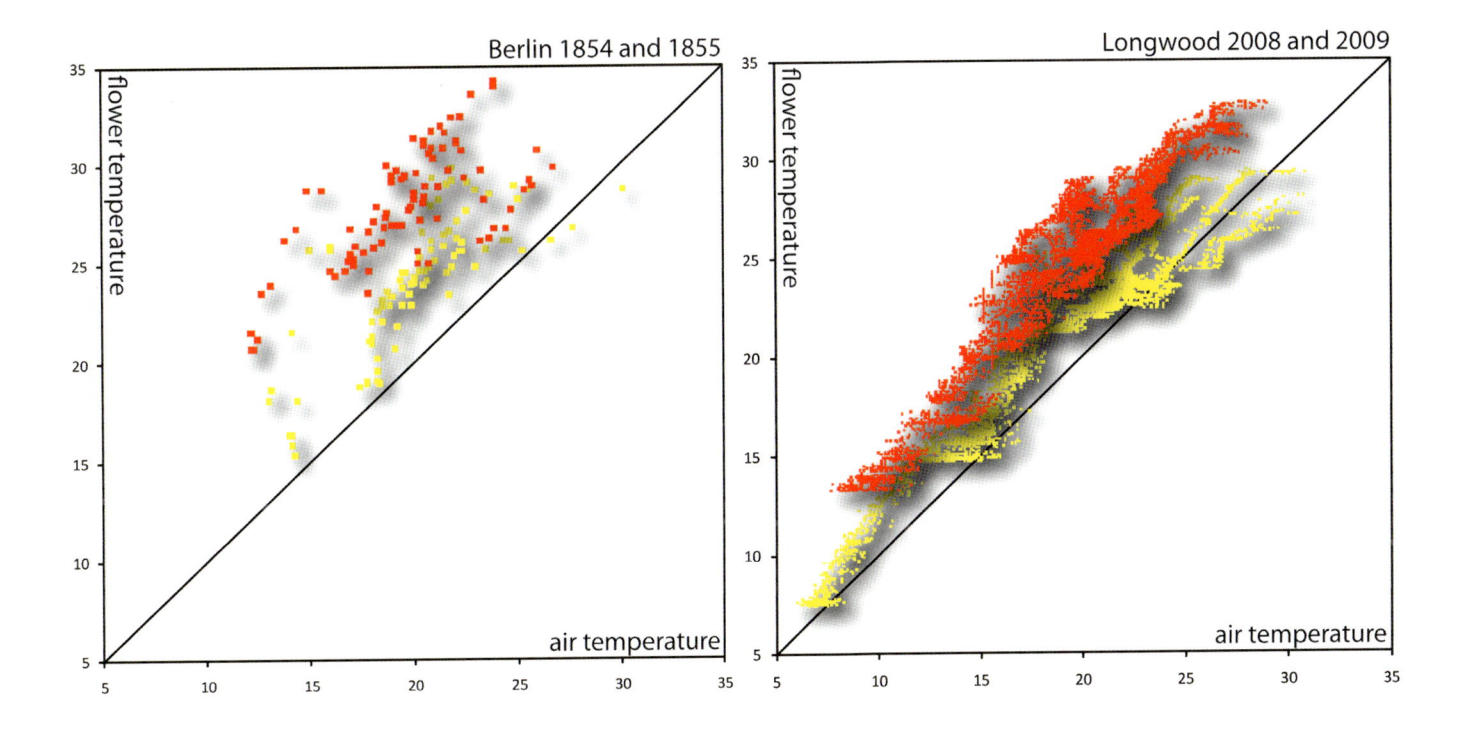

6:53 P.M.

7:00 P.M.

7:10 P.M.

7:18 P.M.

7:23 P.M.

et al. 2002a). Likewise, recorded temperature inside the flowers of *Victoria* 'Longwood Hybrid' grown outdoors at Longwood Gardens in 2008 and 2009 showed the flowers warming to a maximum of about 9°C (16°F) above the ambient temperature.

However remarkable these results are, in comparison to some other thermogenic plants, *Victoria*'s heat burst of 9 to 11°C (16 to 20°F) may appear only lukewarm. *Nelumbo nucifera*, the sacred lotus often cultivated side by side with the South American lily, can heat up to more than 20°C (36°F) above the ambient temperature, while *Symplocarpus foetidus*, skunk cabbage, a distant North American relative of Lamarck's *pied-de-veau*, can be as much as 35°C (63°F) warmer than the surrounding air.

OPENING CEREMONIES

The thermogenic process in *Victoria* flowers begins sometime before sepals separate and flowers open, but the exact timing depends on growing conditions. When Caspary made his measurements in the fall of 1855, he noticed that the flowers of *Victoria amazonica* were warmer than the air at 3:00 P.M., which was the earliest hour he took temperature readings. Almost a century and a half later, Ingolf Lamprecht and his team (2002a) studied *Victoria cruziana* in Berlin-Dahlem using instruments far superior to Caspary's. They noted a slight temperature increase in the morning preceding a flower's opening.

On September 3, 2009, at Longwood Gardens, a flower of *Victoria* 'Longwood Hybrid' began opening soon after sunset at 6:31 P.M. and was fully open by about 7:20 P.M. Infrared imaging showed that the temperature inside the flower was about 22 to 25°C (72 to 77°F) (red and yellow areas), while the temperature of the petals and the ambient air was 18 to 20°C (64 to 68°F) (blue areas). The fully open flower exposed the entrance to the tunnel leading to the floral chamber, surrounded by stamens and staminodia, the temperature of which was elevated to 28 to 29°C (82 to 84°F) (white areas).
LARRY ALBEE / LONGWOOD GARDENS

The opening of the flowers of *Victoria amazonica* inhabiting the waters of the Rupununi River in Guyana, about 5° north latitude, is timed with the sunset. Shown here is a flower six minutes after sunset.
TOMASZ ANIŚKO / LONGWOOD GARDENS

At Longwood Gardens between July 24 and October 17, the time when the temperature of the first-night flower peaked shifted from 4:40 to 8:40 P.M. (red squares). During the same period, sunset advanced from 7:23 to 5:18 P.M. and sunrise retreated from 4:51 to 6:13 A.M.

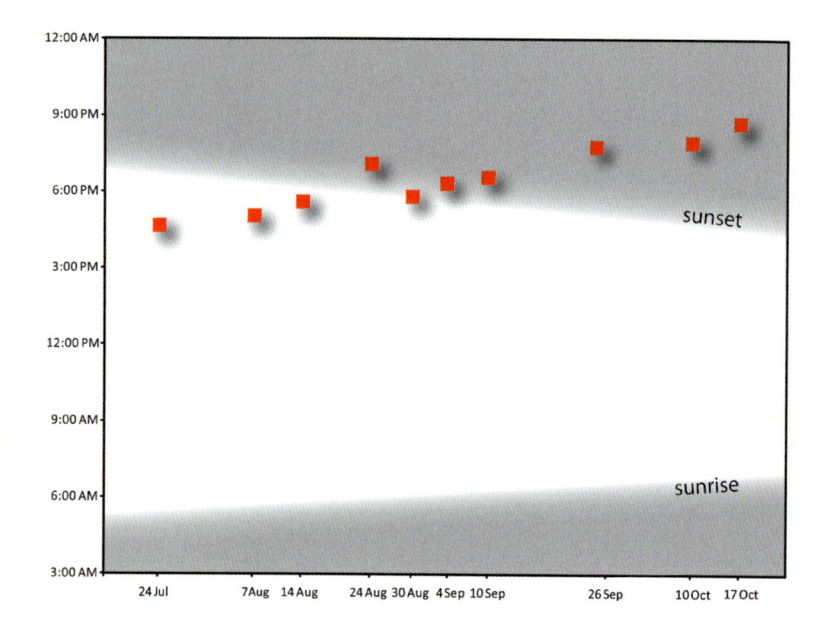

In her native habitat, *Victoria* opens her flowers just after sunset. Near the equator, this occurs around 6:00 P.M. In higher latitudes, the time of opening changes with the season. In Europe, flowers open in the summer between 4:00 and 5:00 P.M.; in autumn, it happens later in the afternoon or evening (Lamprecht et al. 2002b).

Like the timing of the *Victoria* flower opening, the timing of the heat burst inside the flower also changes between summer and fall. On July 24, 2009, at Longwood Gardens, it was recorded around 4:40 P.M. By October 17, however, it had shifted to 8:40 P.M. Curiously, this shift to a later time occurred when the sunset advanced in the opposite direction, from 7:23 to 5:18 P.M.

In the tropics, the flower opens at or near sunset. It might appear that the sunset triggers the heat burst, but results from the northern climes suggest a different explanation—one that shifts the attention from sunset to sunrise.

A comparison between the time of sunrise and the time of the heat burst in *Victoria* grown at Longwood shows an approximate twelve-hour delay at the height of summer. In equatorial regions, where all days are about twelve hours long, a sunrise trigger would mean that the flowers' heat burst would occur in apparent synchrony with the sunset. North or south of the equator, however, sunset synchrony prevails only during the time shortly before and immediately following the autumnal equinox.

At Longwood between July 24 and August 14, as the sunrise advanced from 4:51 to 5:23 A.M., the floral flare-up shifted from 4:40 to 5:35 P.M.—roughly twelve hours later, although between two-and-a-half hours and one hour before sunset. In October, however, floral temperature peaked between 8:00 and 8:40 P.M., or two-and-a-half to three-and-a-half hours after sunset. Toward autumn, as the sun's position shifted closer to the horizon and the amount of daylight declined, the time response of *Victoria* flowers at Longwood also extended from twelve hours to more than fourteen hours by mid-October. Likewise, Caspary's detailed records in Berlin showed that the flower reached its peak temperature on August 18 about an hour before sunset, while his October measurements showed that the flower's temperature reached its maximum between 8:00 and 9:00 P.M., or three to four hours after sunset.

The internal alarm clock of *Victoria* appears to be reset with each sunrise, but on overcast days, this resetting may not be so punctual. One August morning, a heavy cloud cover and 40 mm (1.6 inches) of rain at Longwood postponed the expected heat burst in *Victoria* flowers that evening by about an hour and a half. Similarly, Valla and Cirino, studying *Victoria cruziana* near Esquina, found that cloudy skies during the day delayed the opening of the flowers.

Infrared imaging shows that paracarpels and carpellary appendages are the warmest part of a *Victoria* flower. On the first night (left), their temperature reached 32°C (90°F) (white areas), but on the second night (right), their temperature was only about 24°C (75°F) (green areas).

LARRY ALBEE / LONGWOOD GARDENS

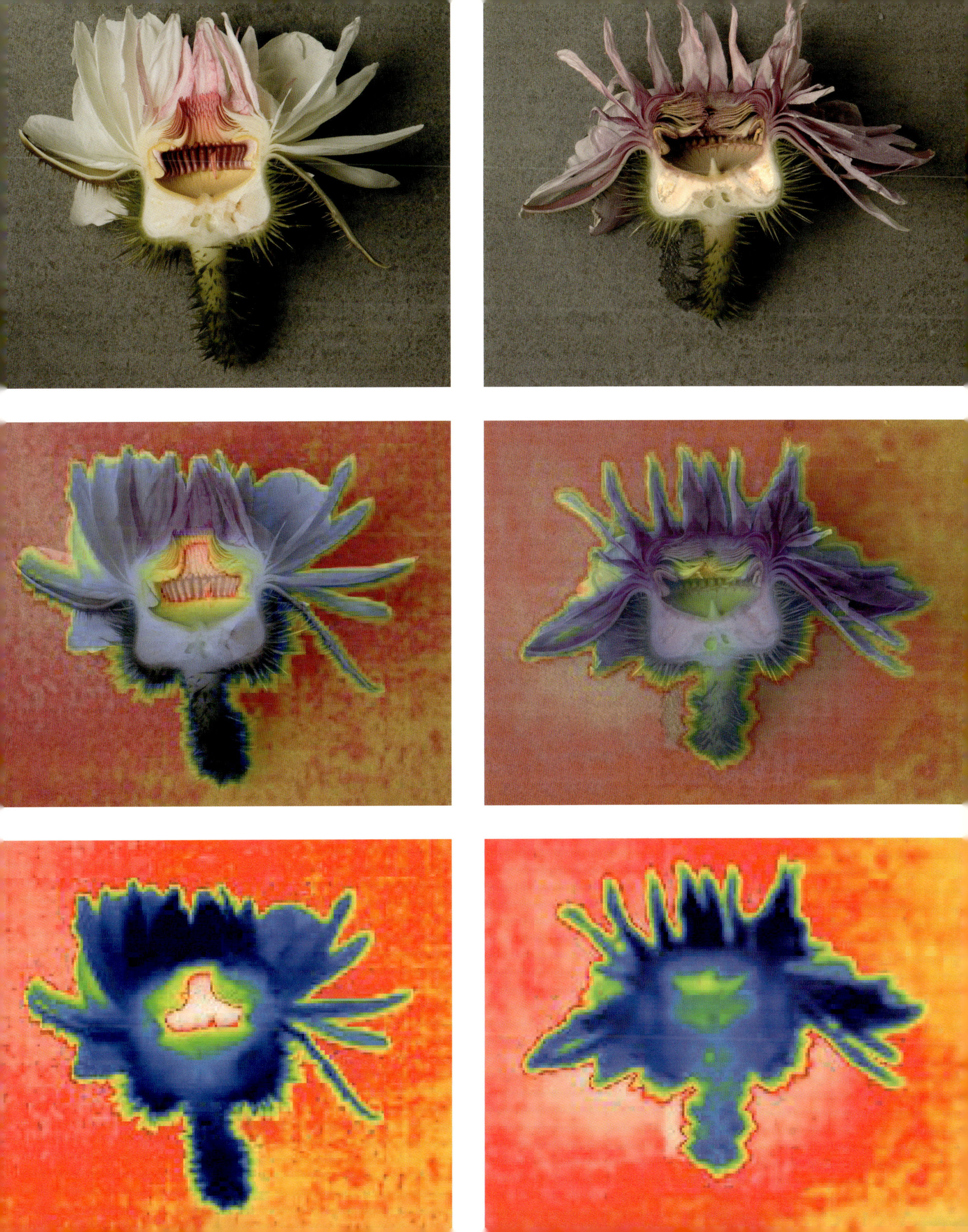

Staminodia, stamens, and paracarpels close the tunnel leading to the floral chamber, trapping pollinating beetles inside during the day. The beetles are then released on the second night of flowering.
TOMASZ ANIŚKO / LONGWOOD GARDENS

The reported timing of the floral flare-up in relation to the opening of the flower varies to such a degree that scientists remain mystified as to what mechanism regulates these two processes. In the wild, *Victoria cruziana* flowers growing near Esquina, Argentina, showed an increase in temperature starting at 6:30 P.M., coinciding with flower opening (Valla and Cirino 1972). In contrast, the temperature of *Victoria amazonica* in the Rupununi River in Guyana peaked about one-and-a-half hours after the flowers opened (Seymour and Matthews 2006). An even greater delay was observed on the Amazon near Manaus, Brazil, where *Victoria amazonica* flowers reached maximum temperature four to five hours after the flowers opened (Leppard 1978).

INTO THE FURNACE

Flowers of thermogenic plants do not warm up uniformly but have specialized organs that carry out the task of heat production. In the 1850s, Otto and Caspary noted that stamens were the warmest part of a *Victoria* flower and suggested they were also the source of heat.

One hundred and fifty years later, Lamprecht and Schmolz (2004) used modern infrared imaging to show that the innermost sterile stamens or staminodia (also called paracarpels) were the warmest. These paracarpels form a ring surrounding the narrow opening leading to *Victoria*'s floral chamber. Valla and Cirino established that the paracarpels were not only the warmest part of the flower but also the main source of scent.

Contrary to these findings, Knoch proposed that the primary source of heat and scent were the starch-filled carpellary appendages positioned just below the paracarpels and, to a lesser extent, the paracarpels themselves. The carpellary appendages not only have an ample supply of fuel (starch) to generate heat, but they also have a sponge-like internal structure connected to the system of large air canals, linking the entire plant. This structure facilitates rapid delivery of oxygen and removal of carbon dioxide, both essential functions for maintaining high rates of respiration. On the first night of flowering, the carpellary appendages appear plump, hard, and shiny. Within twenty-four hours, however, they become shriveled and their color darkens. Edward Schneider and his collaborators from Southwest Texas State University showed that it was the rapid consumption and depletion of starch in the carpellary appendages that led to their withering by the second night of flowering (Schneider et al. 1990).

Seymour and Matthews agreed that the carpellary appendages were the main source of heat on the first night, but they observed that as beetles consume the appendages, the task of warming the flower gradually shifts to the paracarpels. The beetles' ferocious first night of foraging on carpellary appendages reduces the flower's capacity to generate heat, and its temperature gradually drops over the course of the night. At the same time, the carpellary appendages reduce their contribution to the overall heat output—from nearly 70 percent on the first night to about 15 percent on the second night. Meanwhile, the paracarpels take the lead in warming the flower. Thus, seemingly contradictory arguments for paracarpels or for carpellary appendages being the flower's furnace may in the end refer only to different stages of one process (Seymour and Matthews, 2006).

Scarab beetles feasting inside a *Victoria amazonica* flower not only devour the starchy carpellary appendages but also burrow into the ovary, with no apparent detrimental effect to the subsequent fruit set and seed production.
Tomasz Aniśko / Longwood Gardens

The rapid heat generation by *Victoria* flowers can raise their internal temperature more than 4°C (7°F) per hour. Some label it a metabolic explosion (Lamprecht et al. 2002a). On a per-weight basis, feverish *Victoria* flowers have metabolic rates that are ten times higher than a resting man (Lamprecht et al. 2002c). Such an extraordinary burst of heat is made possible by the plant switching its usual respiratory pathway to an alternative one, which captures only a third of the energy but releases the rest as heat. This process is accompanied by a remarkable reorganization of mitochondria, the cellular organelles responsible for energy metabolism. At the end of the thermogenic flare-up, the worn-out mitochondria present the rather sad picture of an internal structure that is damaged or entirely broken up (Skubatz et al. 1990).

A SYMBIOTIC RELATIONSHIP

Knoch's thesis, which associates the heat burst of *Victoria* flowers with their scent and the pollinating insects, inspired follow-up research. This research has added immensely to our understanding of how this symbiotic relationship works.

One would expect that the heat burst facilitates both the volatilization and the rapid diffusion of aromatic scent molecules, in turn attracting pollinating insects to

A scarab beetle emerging from a flower on the second night has to find its way out of the floral chamber through a maze of fertile stamens, whose anthers are now shedding pollen. The beetle will carry the pollen to another flower, which will open for the first time that evening.
TOMASZ ANIŚKO / LONGWOOD GARDENS

Victoria flowers. Although this understandably has a positive effect on pollination, some argue that the flowers' rise in temperature—which ranges from 9 to 11°C (16 to 20°F)—has only a minor effect on the diffusion of the scent molecules. Volatility is increased, but only by about 50 to 70 percent, perhaps not the kind of return worth the effort and expenditure *Victoria* puts into heating her flowers (Lack 2004). Nevertheless, the scent might do more than just signal to the beetles the presence of *Victoria* flowers. Some suggest it also plays a role in stimulating the beetles' mating behavior (Lamprecht et al. 2002a).

Since the improved diffusion of scent alone may not justify the immense energy expended by *Victoria* flowers—after all, most fragrant flowers do not generate heat—scientists turned their attention to the other actor in this pollination drama: *Victoria* flowers are pollinated by several species of scarab beetles of the genus *Cyclocephala*. When the flowers open on the first night, beetles enter the floral chamber through the narrow opening lined by the paracarpels. Lured by the warmth and abundance of food provided by the starch-filled carpellary appendages, the beetles remain in the floral chamber until the second night, when they depart in search of another first-night flower. *Victoria*'s internal floral temperatures of around 32 to 34°C (90 to 93°F) approximate the optimal temperature for sustaining agility in the pollinating beetles, thus providing the insects with an energy reward. Researchers estimate that inside the balmy floral chamber, beetles can reduce their metabolic rates to about a fifth of what they require outside the flower (Seymour and Matthews 2006, Seymour 2007).

By elevating the temperature inside the floral chamber, *Victoria* promotes the beetles' feeding, digesting, and mating. She also ensures that their body temperature is adequate for flying to the next flower on the second night. Most flowers visited by pollinating insects provide them a reward in the form of food, such as nectar or pollen. *Victoria* and other thermogenic flowers go one step further, adding a direct metabolic incentive. This explains why the temperature of the flower—which peaks at or shortly after opening, as if intended to lure and guide beetles to the flower—remains above the ambient temperature throughout the period that the insects

A thermographic camera shows a *Victoria* flower against the background of the water (top); the entrance to the tunnel leading to the floral chamber (middle); and warm paracarpels and carpellary appendages lining the tunnel (bottom). The temperature in the tunnel (shown in white and red) is about 30 to 32°C (86 to 90°F), while the air temperature and that of the petals (shown in blue) is about 22 to 24°C (72 to 75°F).

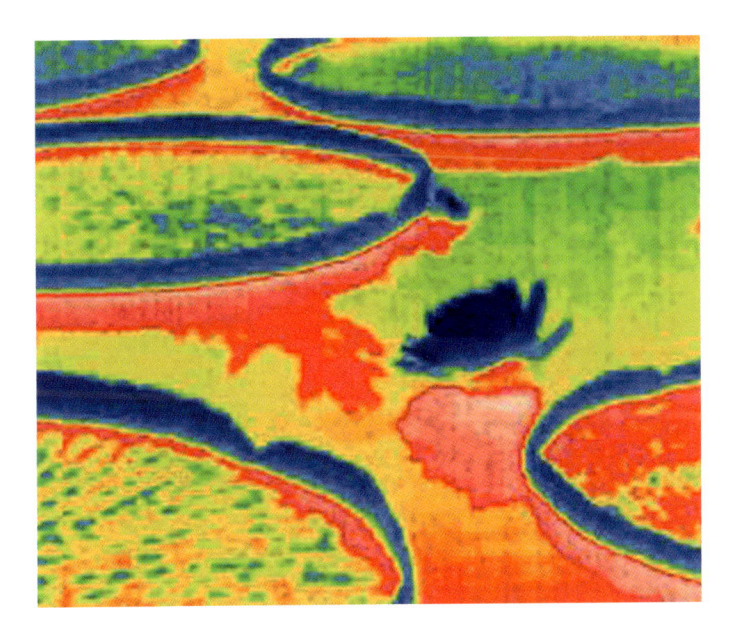

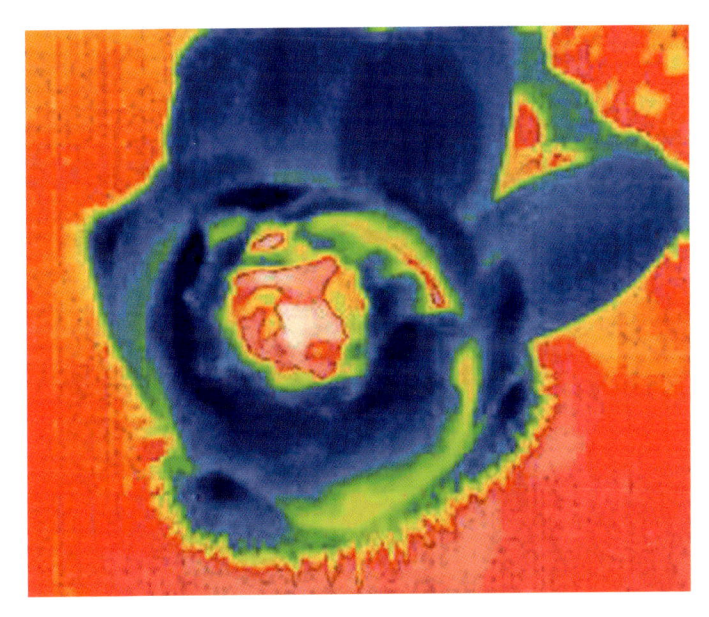

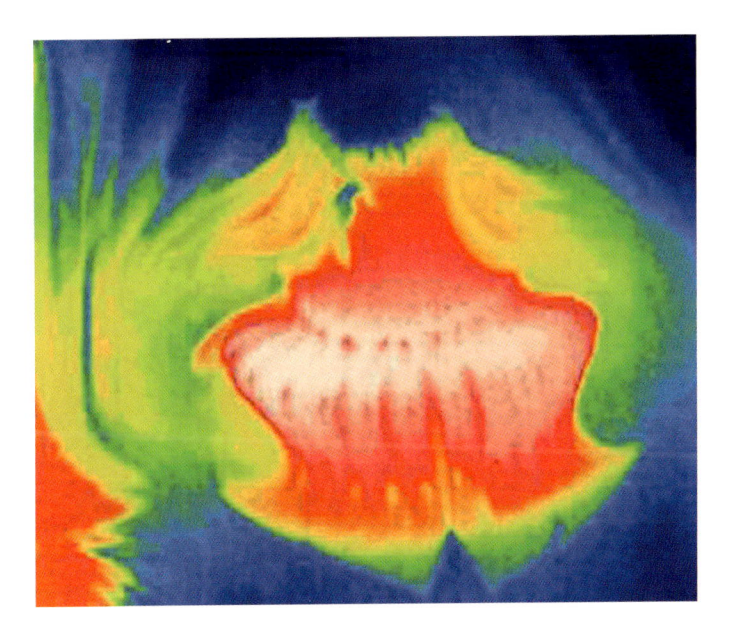

TOMASZ ANIŚKO / LONGWOOD GARDENS

On the morning following the first-night opening, the *Victoria* flower closes, trapping in its floral chamber any beetles that might have been lured into it and sheltering them from birds, lizards, and other predators.

Tomasz Aniśko / Longwood Gardens

occupy the floral chamber, until the second night. Aside from the energy benefits of food and warmth, *Victoria* flowers offer beetles an attractive mating place, fully protected from predators such as birds or lizards.

Since *Victoria* flowers open and attract the beetles at night when visual cues are reduced or absent, the question arises as to how these insects find the flowers in the first place. In addition, how do they locate the narrow opening leading to the floral chamber? Although *Victoria*'s fruity scent can bring the pollinators into the flower's general vicinity, it may not be as effective in guiding them into a tunnel the size of a wedding ring set in the middle of a lake.

Humans have devised technological solutions to overcome our lack of night vision. Thermographic cameras create images that allow us to "see" an object in complete darkness as long as the temperature of this object differs from that of its surroundings. Thermal images of *Victoria* flowers clearly show the flowers on the surface of the water and illuminate the entrance to the floral chamber. One is tempted to think that this is also how nocturnal insects "see" at night, but to do this, they would need to be able to sense infrared radiation. No such sensors have been identified in the scarab beetles pollinating *Victoria* yet, but they have been found in other night-foraging insects, which use them to locate food (Takács et al. 2009).

Curiously, after Robert Schomburgk's 1837 account of the beetles inside the flowers of *Victoria amazonica*, all subsequent reports referred to *Victoria amazonica*. None mentioned *Victoria cruziana*. Working near Esquina along the Paraná, Valla and Cirino captured a few types of small beetles marauding at night in the vicinity of *Victoria cruziana* flowers. The following morning, however, when none were found inside the flowers, the researchers deduced that these beetles were not

326 Victoria: The Seductress

involved in pollination. They explained this apparent lack of pollinators by the proximity of the Esquina site, about 30 degrees south latitude, to the southern limit of *Victoria* distribution. Flowers in the Esquina population produced an adequate amount of seeds through self-pollination. This modification of her reproductive system apparently enabled *Victoria cruziana* to flourish in areas where pollinators were absent.

THE THERMOGENIC FAMILY TREE

Even though production of heat is uncommon among plants, *Victoria* is not alone in her affair with scarab beetles. Thermogenic plants are found among several families, including Annonaceae, Araceae, Arecaceae, Aristolochiaceae, Cycadaceae, Cyclanthaceae, Magnoliaceae, Nelumbonaceae, and Nymphaeaceae. Researchers estimate that in the New World tropics, some nine hundred species of thermogenic plants are pollinated by scarab beetles of the genus *Cyclocephala* alone (Seymour and Matthews 2006).

The fact that thermogenic plants appear only among the most archaic groups of seed plants, which diversified during the Jurassic and Cretaceous—the same time beetles underwent an explosive diversification—indicates that their intimate relationship and mutual dependence may indeed be an ancient one dating back a hundred or more million years to the very dawn of flowering plants (Seymour and Schultze-Motel 1997). The widespread occurrence of scented flowers among these archaic families also suggests that scent preceded color as a primary pollinator attractant—drawing insects not only to the source of food but, in the case of thermogenic flowers, to mating sites (Pellmyr and Thien 1986).

Many of *Victoria*'s features are also found in other thermogenic flowers. Typically, they are protogynous (their female phase of development precedes the male phase), and they attract pollinators during the female phase. Some of the stamens in such flowers may be modified into staminodia, which produce scent and provide food as a reward for the insects. Many trap the pollinators inside the flower during the female phase and free them when flowers enter the male phase, a process that promotes pollen distribution via the departing insects.

Often, thermogenic flowers are pollinated by beetles, have an internal chamber where insects can aggregate, and offer food in the form of flower parts or a prodigious amount of pollen. Characteristically, beetle-pollinated flowers are relatively large and bulky, providing an easy landing platform for these clumsy flyers. In addition, they release a scent ranging from sweet and fruity to nauseating in order to attract a specific kind of beetle (Seymour and Schultze-Motel 1997). Fortunately, *Cyclocephala* beetles prefer *Victoria*'s fruity scent. Indeed, humankind's affair with the regal *Victoria* would be very different if these beetles had favored a foul odor.

Humans and scarab beetles share the same fondness for the *Victoria* flower's fruity scent.
TOMASZ ANIŚKO / LONGWOOD GARDENS

Fitch, del et lith.

chapter 18

QUEEN'S DOMINION

AFTER ROBERT SCHOMBURGK'S DISCOVERY of the colossal lily in British Guiana was announced in 1837, it soon became apparent that the plant was not restricted to this small sliver of the South American continent. Once Eduard Pöppig's earlier paper finally received its well-deserved attention and recognition, *Victoria*'s existence in Ega (today's Tefé) along the Amazon became widely known. Subsequent expeditions by British explorers Alfred Wallace, Henry Bates, and Richard Spruce in 1849 extended the nymph's range from Pöppig's Ega downriver to Monte Alegre, some 1,200 km (745 miles) to the east. In 1840, Alcide d'Orbigny brought to light Thaddaeus Haenke's 1801 and Aimé Bonpland's 1821 discoveries. This widened *Victoria*'s range into Bolivia and Argentina, the latter more than 3,500 km (2,175 miles) south from Schomburgk's Guiana site.

By 1850, it was clear that the queen lily ruled over a vast territory in South America. Yet one could crisscross the entire continent on land or water without ever seeing *Victoria*. Since the arrival of the Europeans three centuries earlier, travelers and explorers had plied the waters of the Amazon, Paraná, Paraguay, and other great South American rivers, completely oblivious to the existence of this wondrous water nymph. Even today, despite the fact that we have every reason to believe that

Victoria amazonica in Guiana as it was imagined by Walter Fitch, an illustration for William Hooker's 1847 article in *Curtis's Botanical Magazine*, "chiefly done" from scenes in Robert Schomburgk's book *Views in the Interior of Guiana*.
LONGWOOD GARDENS LIBRARY AND ARCHIVES

William Hooker,
***Curtis's Botanical Magazine,* 1847:**

Seeing, indeed, that V. regia *has been detected in Bolivia (Río Mamoré), in the Amazons; in Berbice and in Corrientes (Paraná) rivers . . . we must conclude that this magnificent water lily is, like the generality of aquatics, a plant of wide distribution, and probably a not uncommon inhabitant of the still waters of all those great rivers which intersect the immense plains eastward of the Andes. . . . It does not appear that the* Victoria regia *has been found in any water flowing into the Pacific; probably because of the rapid movement of those streams.*

Hooker 1847

Thomas Bridges, 1847:

This splendid plant has, undoubtedly, a very extensive geographical range; the town of Santa Anna is situated between the 13th and 14th parallels of south latitude, which I consider about its most southern limit, because I sought in vain for it farther south, in the department of Santa Cruz de la Sierra. May we not justly suppose that it is also found as far north of the Equator? Thus occupying about 28° of northern and southern latitude. Dr. Weddel[l], the botanist of the French expedition across the American Continent, informed me that he had found it about the same latitude in Brazil. It occupies, without doubt, many of those immense lakes lying between the rivers Mamoré, Beni and the Amazons; that central part of the Continent, yet but little known.

Hooker 1847

Victoria is widespread throughout the immense watersheds of the Amazon and Paraná, it is not easy to find her there.

Most reported sightings or collections of herbarium specimens and seeds tend to cluster around major settlements, such as Manaus in Brazil, Asunción in Paraguay, or Corrientes in Argentina. Coincidentally, these were important stopovers for early naturalists exploring the interior of the continent. Other sightings align with frequently traveled rivers: the Mamoré, Paraguay, Paraná, and South America's main artery, the Amazon. But beyond the areas that are accessible from these main throughways lie secluded backwaters sustained by the annual pulsing of the great rivers. These areas comprise *Victoria*'s true home.

MIGHTY RIVERS

South America's largest rivers, the Amazon and Paraná, both receive much of the rainwater running off the eastern slopes of the Andes, the world's longest mountain range. It is their unique hydrology that shaped the environment in which the world's largest lily was conceived by the forces of evolution.

The Amazon, mightier of the two, vies with the Nile for the title of world's longest river. (And with the length of both being constantly revised as improved measuring techniques become available, this contest may continue into the foreseeable future.) No river, however, comes close to rivaling the Amazon as the largest on the planet—whether this attribution is based on the volume of water it discharges into the ocean or the area of its drainage basin. Here, the Amazon's dominance is truly staggering. Its average discharge is greater than the next seven largest rivers combined and accounts for about one-sixth of all river flow on Earth. The Amazon's vast drainage basin covers some 40 percent of the South American continent and exceeds 7,000,000 km^2 (2,700,000 square miles), more than double the size of the Nile's basin. The Paraná, the Amazon's smaller kin, drains an area of more than 2,500,000 km^2 (965,000 square miles), making the combined area of both river basins larger than that of Australia or continental Europe. And though the Paraná is some 2,000 km (1,243 miles) shorter than the Amazon, it still scores as the world's ninth longest river.

The overwhelming scale of the Amazon escapes human comprehension, which may be the reason for the disagreements about the names assigned to its various sections. The main stem flowing out of the Andes is called the Ucayali until it joins the Marañón in the lowlands of Peru. According to Peruvian and Colombian convention, it is first called the Amazon at this confluence. In Brazil, however, this section is called the Solimões, and it is not until it is joined downstream by the Rio Negro near Manaus that it becomes the Amazon of the Brazilians.

Combined watersheds of the Amazon and Paraná cover an area larger than continental Europe. Hypothesized distribution ranges according to Walter Lack (2004), red for *Victoria amazonica* and blue for *Victoria cruziana*, are defined by each of the two watersheds. Yellow circles represent *Victoria* populations described in the text.
Tomasz Aniśko / Longwood Gardens

QUEEN'S DOMINION 331

The Amazon carries an unimaginable quantity of sediments that have eroded off the slopes of the Andes—estimated at well above a billion tons per year. This is of great consequence to the history of life in the Amazon basin (Meade 2007). These sediments are a vital source of mineral nutrients, supporting both lush tropical vegetation and the greatest concentration of biodiversity on the planet. This life-giving alluvium is replenished annually when the Amazon and its tributaries overflow and flood a vast swath of land.

The Amazon's water level fluctuates on average 10 m (33 feet) in a typical year, whereas flood waves can swell the discharge of its tributaries by tenfold. The volume of water ultimately discharged to the ocean, however, varies seasonally by only a factor of two or three (Meade et al. 1991). This apparent paradox is explained by the seasonal shift of discharges between the Amazon's far-flung northern and southern tributaries. Frequent storms in the tropics are spawned within the intertropical convergence zone. Because the zone drifts cyclically, first to the south then to the north of the equator, peak precipitation in the basin's southern extremities falls six months earlier than in its northernmost parts. This seasonal shift of maximum rainfall from south to north, combined with the storage capacity of the vast floodplains, effectively diminishes the fluctuation of discharge in the river's main stem.

The Amazon basin encompasses a huge area, elevated up to approximately 200 m (650 feet) above sea level. One can travel 1,500 km (930 miles) from the Atlantic coast to Manaus and gain only about 20 m (66 feet) in elevation. The river at Iquitos, another 2,000 km (1,240 miles) upstream from Manaus, is still only about 110 m (360 feet) above sea level.

WATER COLORS

The broad Amazon basin is bound to the north and south by Precambrian and Paleozoic rocks of the Guianan and Brazilian shields. Having weathered more than six hundred million years, these rocks release very few nutrients into the runoff. The Amazon's tributaries draining these areas, such as the Tapajós or Xingu, are known as clear water rivers, although their color is often blue or green due to the reflection of the sky. The clear water rivers carry little sediment and are very low in mineral nutrients.

The Amazon basin itself is thinly covered with layers of sediments of meager fertility. These layers were left by a vast inland sea formed by the rise of the Andes some twenty-five million years ago. When the Andes blocked the ancestral Amazon's westward flow to the Pacific, it forced the river to reverse course and find a new outlet into the Atlantic (Meade 2007). Although clear and low in nutrients, the rivers that have their source in these sediments, such as the Rio Negro, are blackened by the tannic and humic substances released by decomposing forest litter. These organic compounds also make the black water rivers distinctly acidic.

Of paramount importance to life in the Amazon basin are the so-called white water rivers, such as the Madeira or Marañón, which drain the rapidly eroding slopes of the Andes. The heavy load of sediments carried by these rivers makes the water turbid

White waters inundating the várzea in the Amazon floodplains carry a heavy load of sediments, which give them a turbid, milky appearance.
TOMASZ ANIŚKO / LONGWOOD GARDENS

and gives it the color of *café au lait*. High in dissolved mineral compounds, white water rivers create the most fertile soils in the basin. In the low water season, many channels and branches of the Amazon become cut off from the main stem and the agitation of the white waters by the river currents ceases. The sediments then gradually settle to the bottom. As a result, their color becomes similar to that of the black water rivers, though their chemical properties remain very different. In addition, lakes filled with white water during the flood season may collect black water flowing in from the surrounding upland areas during the dry season.

Due to the continual buildup of sediments deposited by these white water rivers and the ongoing erosion of their river banks, the Amazon and its tributaries meander through the valleys. As these meanders grow larger, they form longer necks that are eventually cut off when the river finds a shorter channel, leaving behind countless oxbow lakes.

The Amazon's annual inundation affects about 3,000,000 km^2 (1,158,000 square miles) of floodplains (Myster 2009). Different plant communities form throughout the floodplains, depending on the duration, depth, and regularity of the flooding and whether the floodwaters that inundate them are white, black, or clear. Areas flooded by white waters are known as the *várzea* and make up the largest portion of the Amazon floodplains. Those flooded by black waters are called the *igapó*. Almost without exception, *Victoria* inhabits the fertile *várzea* and avoids the nutrient-poor *igapó*.

The fertile shallow lakes and channels of the *várzea* provide an ideal habitat for *Victoria* along the Amazon.
TOMASZ ANIŚKO / LONGWOOD GARDENS

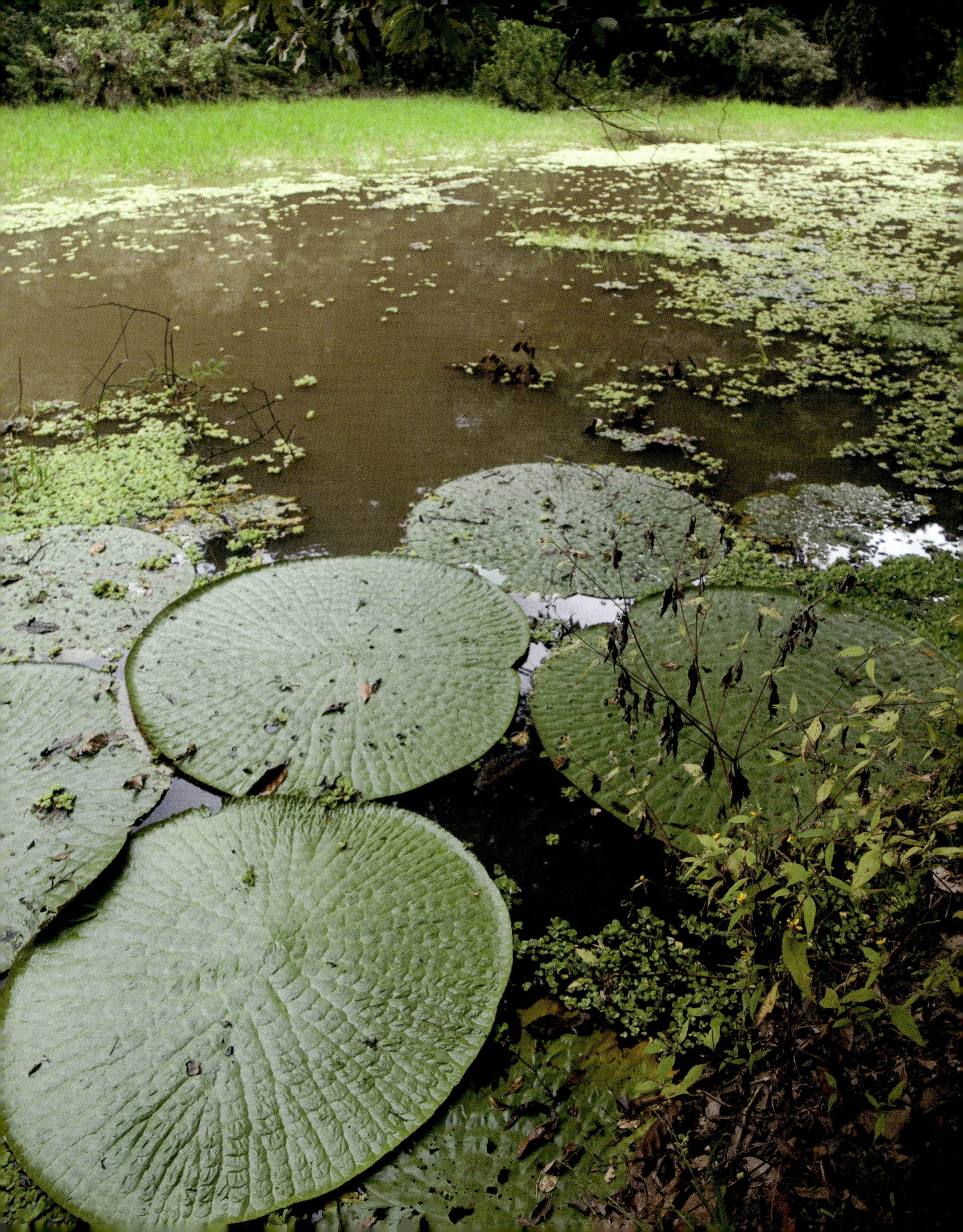

Enriched with Andean-derived sediments, the *várzea* also supports the region's rainforests and riparian savannas, which in turn sustain an unmatched wealth of fish, bird, and animal life. The most significant force shaping the *várzea* is the Amazon's flood pulse. The pulse takes about six months to traverse the entire Amazon basin, beginning in the Andean foreland basin in the west and diminishing in size as it spreads eastward (Bannerman 2008). As the white waters cross the *várzea*, they erode riverbanks in some places while depositing sediments and building new banks in others. The landforms of the floodplain are ever changing, and the course of the rivers is constantly shifting. After the flood pulse passes, it leaves behind countless lakes and narrow channels filled with water and rich sediments. Once they are cut off from the main stem of the river, these lakes and channels are destined to be completely filled with sediments carried by annual floods, creating a pattern of striking scars on the surface of the earth.

Sediment deposits slowly change the elevation of a given site, which in turn alters the depth to which the site is flooded and the length of time it is under water. Most of the *várzea* contain several ecological zones. The lowest lying is the *chavascal*, submerged for six to eight months. The *restinga baixa* is higher, under water up to 5 m (16 feet) for four to six months. The *restinga alta* is even higher, flooded to about 1 m (3 feet) for two to four months (Bannerman 2008).

Plants living in these habitats have developed unique adaptations to the *várzea*'s alternating aquatic and terrestrial phases. For instance, fruiting season coincides with flooding season so that floating seeds will be dispersed by water. Morphological innovations, such as adventitious and stilt roots, provide stable anchorage in the soil, which is subject to continuous sedimentation and erosion. And internal anatomical organizations facilitate gas exchange between the plants' submerged roots and the leaves that remain above the water. Because light cannot penetrate the depth of the murky white waters, there are few submerged plants in the *várzea*. There are, however, many floating plants. These often coalesce into floating meadows (Sternberg 1975).

MOST FAVORED HABITATS

Victoria is superbly adapted to the rhythm of the flood pulse and the cyclic transformation of the land, from the emergent to the submerged phase. Her floating seeds are carried by the floodwaters for a while and then sink and are buried in the sediment. They spend the dry season awaiting the next inundation. Once the lily is submerged, sprouted, and growing again, she continuously produces adventitious roots that spread to form a firm stilt-like anchorage in loose sediments. Her entire body is full of open airspaces and wide conduits that channel oxygen from the floating leaves to the roots under water.

The shallow waters preferred by *Victoria*, such as these in Mamirauá Reserve near Tefé, represent a transitional stage of the infilling of a formerly open lake or channel that is being transformed into a dry floodplain.
TOMASZ ANIŚKO / LONGWOOD GARDENS

With each flood, the Amazon deposits new sandbanks, like this one near Tefé, while at the same time undercutting and eroding riverbanks elsewhere, gradually changing the course of its many channels.
TOMASZ ANIŚKO / LONGWOOD GARDENS

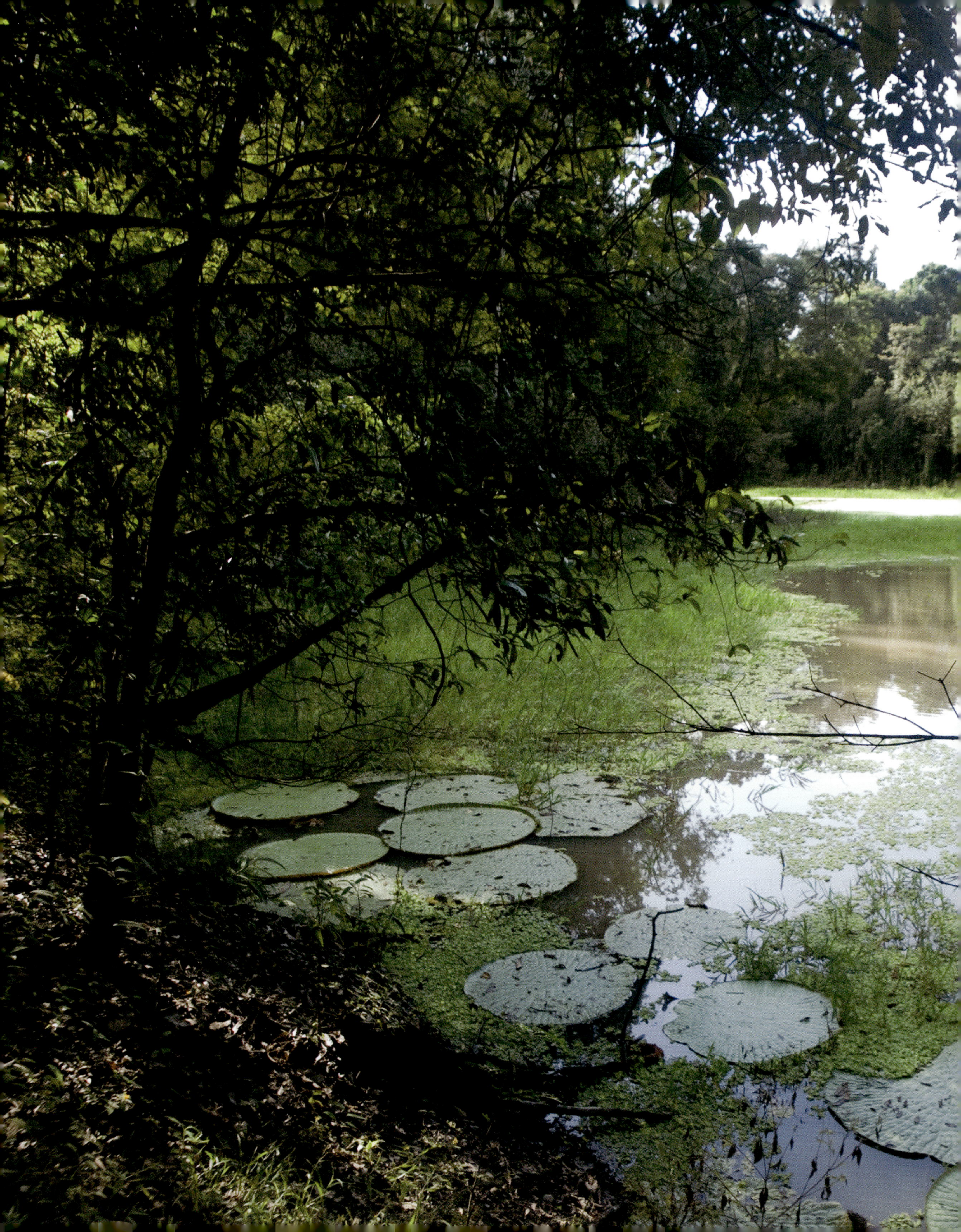

The queen lily's most favored habitats seem to be the shallow lakes and channels in the transitional stage between open water and dry infilled floodplain (Meade 2009a). She avoids deep waters, especially when subject to fast currents, preferring shallower depths between 0.5 to 1.5 m (2 to 5 feet) (Leppard 1978). Opinions vary as to the maximum inundation the lily can withstand, but there are reports of *Victoria* in water as deep as 7 m (23 feet) (Meade 2001).

The more critical factor seems to be the depth to which the water level drops during the dry season. *Victoria* seeds can survive buried in wet depressions even if the lake above dries out completely between floods. But the lily cannot establish herself in areas where water remains too deep for her seedlings' first floating leaves to reach the surface. Typically, seeds germinate in water that is less than 0.5 m (2 feet) deep (Meade 2001), but seedlings growing in water about 1 m (3 feet) deep have been observed under cultivation. Once a sprouting seedling successfully spreads its floating leaves, it can keep pace with floodwaters, which rise at an average rate of 5 cm (2 inches) per day and up to 10 to 15 cm (4 to 6 inches) per day for several weeks in high water years (Junk and Piedade 1997).

When the *várzea* is inundated, the water surface is initially free of vegetation. Soon, however, plants begin their frantic race to colonize it with astonishing speed. *Victoria* competes in this race for space and light, too. In the backwaters of the Amazon near Manaus, more than two dozen species of aquatic plants have reportedly engaged in this mortal combat with the queen lily (Leppard 1978). Thanks to her prodigious growth rate, the sheer immensity of her leaves, and their raised spine-armored rims, she can generally keep all other plants at bay.

Like other aquatic plants of the Amazon floodplain, the giant lily has a relatively short life cycle, a phenomenal ability to colonize the water surface, and high reproduction rates. Two key elements facilitate

The concentration of *Victoria* along the banks suggests that the middle of the lake is still too deep for germinating seedlings to reach the surface with their first floating leaves.
TOMASZ ANIŚKO / LONGWOOD GARDENS

QUEEN'S DOMINION

her rapid development: an abundant supply of mineral nutrients from sediments carried by white waters and intense sunlight unimpeded by the canopy of terrestrial plants. In addition, *Victoria*'s prolific seed production is an adaptation to the nearly complete loss of living plants caused by her habitat's cyclic desiccation (Junk and Piedade 1997).

Today, we know that *Victoria* occurs in the backwaters along the main stem of the Amazon at least as far west as Iquitos in Peru (Anderson 1965). However, because she favors secluded lakes and channels some distance from navigable streams, even as keen a plant collector as Pöppig—who descended the entire length of the Amazon in 1832, traversing a huge swath of *Victoria* territory—did not see his first lily until reaching Ega, about 1,000 km (620 miles) downstream from Iquitos. Even in Ega, Pöppig's encounter with the nymph might never have happened if he hadn't accidentally lost his boat during an unplanned excursion into the *várzea* and been forced off his intended course.

Most modern reported sightings of *Victoria* in the Amazon basin come from the river's main stopping points, which are easily accessible by plane. Starting with Iquitos in the west, there are border towns downstream where the Amazon crosses into Brazil, leaving Peru on its right bank and Colombia on its left. They include Tabatinga, where Pöppig stayed in August 1831; Leticia; and Benjamin Constant, where British traveler Roger Perry found the lily near the mouth of the Itaqui River, in "a stretch of sheltered water, still, black and discoloured by rotting vegetation" (Perry 1963).

Continuing downriver, many travelers call on the port of Ega (today's Tefé) as Pöppig did in 1832. Here, two rivers, the Japurá flowing from the north and the Tefé flowing from the south, join the Amazon. Farther east is Amazonia's largest city, Manaus, the meeting place of the Amazon and the Rio Negro, where tourists come from around the world to experience the Amazon and its amazing plant and animal life. Among its most coveted sights are the charismatic pink dolphin and, of course, the queen of all lilies.

Near Manaus, tour boats bring travelers face-to-face with *Victoria* in her own native surroundings. Thanks to an international airport and the presence of the National Institute of Amazonian Research, better known as INPA, Manaus has also become a hub from which many scientists studying *Victoria* launch their expeditions (Leppard 1978, Prance 1991).

Some 250 km (155 miles) downstream from Manaus is Itacoatiara, another port at the confluence of the Madeira, a major tributary. Itacoatiara offers ample opportunities to seek out *Victoria*. Robert Meade, a United States Geological Survey potamologist, chose Silves, located some 40 km (25 miles) from Itacoatiara, as the launch point for eight expeditions between 1999 and 2004—part of a systematic study of the giant lily's floodplain habitat and its changes in various seasons (Meade 2009b).

Thomas Bridges, 1847:

The Victoria *grows in 4–6 feet [1 to 2 m] of water, producing leaves and flowers, which rapidly decay and give place to others. From each plant there are seldom more than four to five leaves on the surface, but even these in parts of the lake where the plants were numerous, almost covered the surface of the water, one leaf touching the other. . . . From what I observed of the nature and habits of this most interesting plant, I conclude that it cannot and does not exist in any of the rivers, where the immense rise and fall, of twenty feet [6 m], would leave it dry, during many months of the year, especially in the season when there is no rain.*

The lagoons, being subject to little variation in the height of their waters, are the places where it grows in all its beauty and grandeur. The Victoria *appears to delight in parts of the lake fully exposed to the sun, and I observed that it did not exist where the trees overshaded the margins.*

Hooker 1847

Below Itacoatiara is Santarém, where the Amazon meets the Tapajós. Richard Spruce had a fruitful stay here in 1849, collecting specimens of *Victoria* on Ihla Grande, which were sent to London in a "barrel of spirits" (Hooker 1851). While in Santarém, Spruce also received flowers of the lily gathered in the Rio Arapiuns. This river runs into the Tapajós before its confluence with the Amazon and unites the two great rivers in the wet season. Reports of *Victoria* at many other locations in the vicinity convinced Spruce that the plant was "plentifully distributed through the whole of this region" (Hooker 1851).

Sometimes *Victoria* is reported in lakes and channels that are filled with what appears to be black water. This can occur when rich sediments carried by the floodwaters settle on the bottom in low water season, or when local black water rivers and streams fill in these depressions, displacing white waters. In either case, it is the annual inundation by the Amazon's white waters that delivers a fresh load of sediments and maintains the soil's fertility.

Somewhat different from this typical scenario are recent sightings of *Victoria* at the confluence of the Rio Branco with the Rio Negro, about 300 km (186 miles) north of the Amazon's main stem and well beyond the reach of its white waters (Bryne 2008).

Victoria's enthusiasts regularly visit the queen lily's habitats in many parts of South America.
TOMASZ ANIŚKO / LONGWOOD GARDENS

The fertile waters of the Rio Branco support populations of *Victoria* and other white water specialist species of flora and fauna, despite being surrounded by black water rivers and separated from the Amazon by some 300 km (186 miles).
Tomasz Aniśko / Longwood Gardens

Richard Spruce, 1849:

The igaripé, where we gathered the Victoria, *is called Tapiruari. Two flowers were brought to me a few days afterwards, from the adjacent lake, which seems to have no name but that of the* sitios *on its banks. Mr. Jeffreys also sent me flowers from the Rio Arrapixuna [today's Arapiuns], which runs into the Tapajoz [today's Tapajós], above Santarém, and the wet season unites the Tapajoz and the Amazon. I have information likewise of its inhabiting abundantly a lake beyond the Rio Mayaca, which flows into the Amazon some miles below Santarém. Mr. Wallace, who recently visited Monte Alègre, had a leaf and flower brought to him there. I have seen a portion of the leaf, which he dried. Lastly, I have distinct intelligence of its occurring in the Rio Trombétes [today's Trombetas], near Obidos, and in the lakes betwixt the rivers Tapajoz and Madeira; thus proving that it is plentifully distributed through the whole of this region, both north and south of the Amazon.*

Hooker 1851

While the Rio Negro is the largest black water river, the Rio Branco, its largest tributary, is unique in Amazonia. Though surrounded by black water rivers, it carries a significant load of soil-enriching sediments. The Rio Branco is not as turbid as the Amazon, Madeira, or Mamoré, but its waters are nevertheless rich in nutrients and support the *várzea* along its course (Naka et al. 2007). This vital supply of nutrients permits *Victoria* and a host of other white water specialist species to thrive far from the Amazon's main stem. The Rio Branco also nurtures a composition of fish and bird communities that are more similar to those of the Amazon than those of the Rio Negro (Naka et al. 2007). It also suggests that finding the giant lily farther upstream along the Rio Branco might be possible.

TRAILING HISTORY AND THE QUEEN

Following the Rio Branco north, one enters the Tacutu, a tributary that defines the border between Brazil and Guyana. There, only a narrow stretch of savanna separates the watersheds of the Amazon and the Rupununi, a tributary of the Essequibo and the location of the Schomburgk brothers' 1842 encounter with *Victoria*, as well as the Berbice, where Robert Schomburgk memorably discovered his first queen lily in 1837. The proximity of the watersheds, combined with the periodic flooding of the Rupununi savannas, provides an exchange of waters. It also allows for an exchange of *Victoria* seeds between the Amazon and the rivers of Guyana, which flow north and drain directly into the Atlantic.

Further testifying to *Victoria*'s reclusive character is the fact that she was first discovered in Bolivia, near the southern fringes of her native

The Rupununi savannas stretching between the watersheds of the Amazon and Essequibo abound in lakes and channels that are inhabited by thriving populations of *Victoria*. The Schomburgk brothers discovered the lily here in 1842.
Tomasz Aniśko / Longwood Gardens

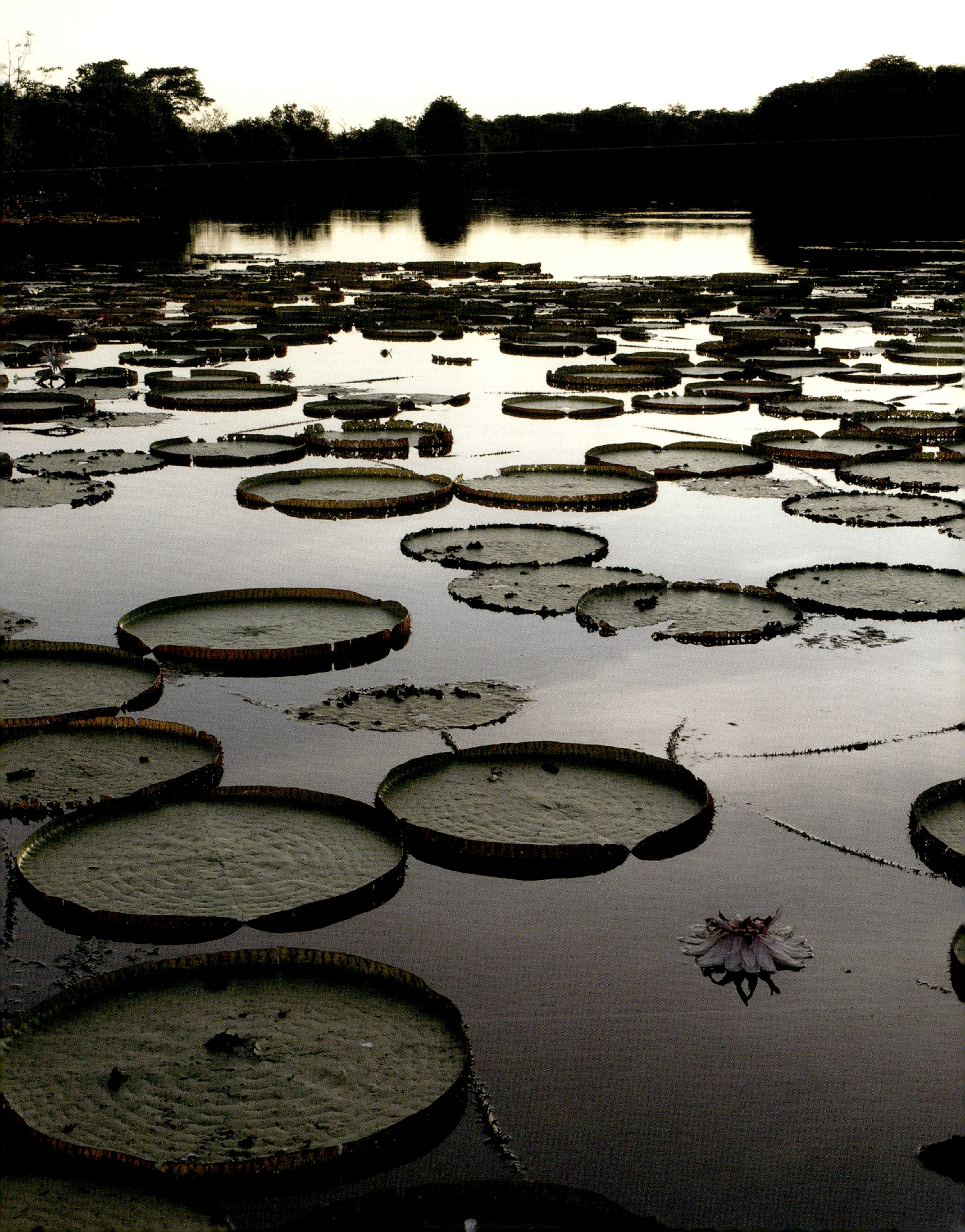

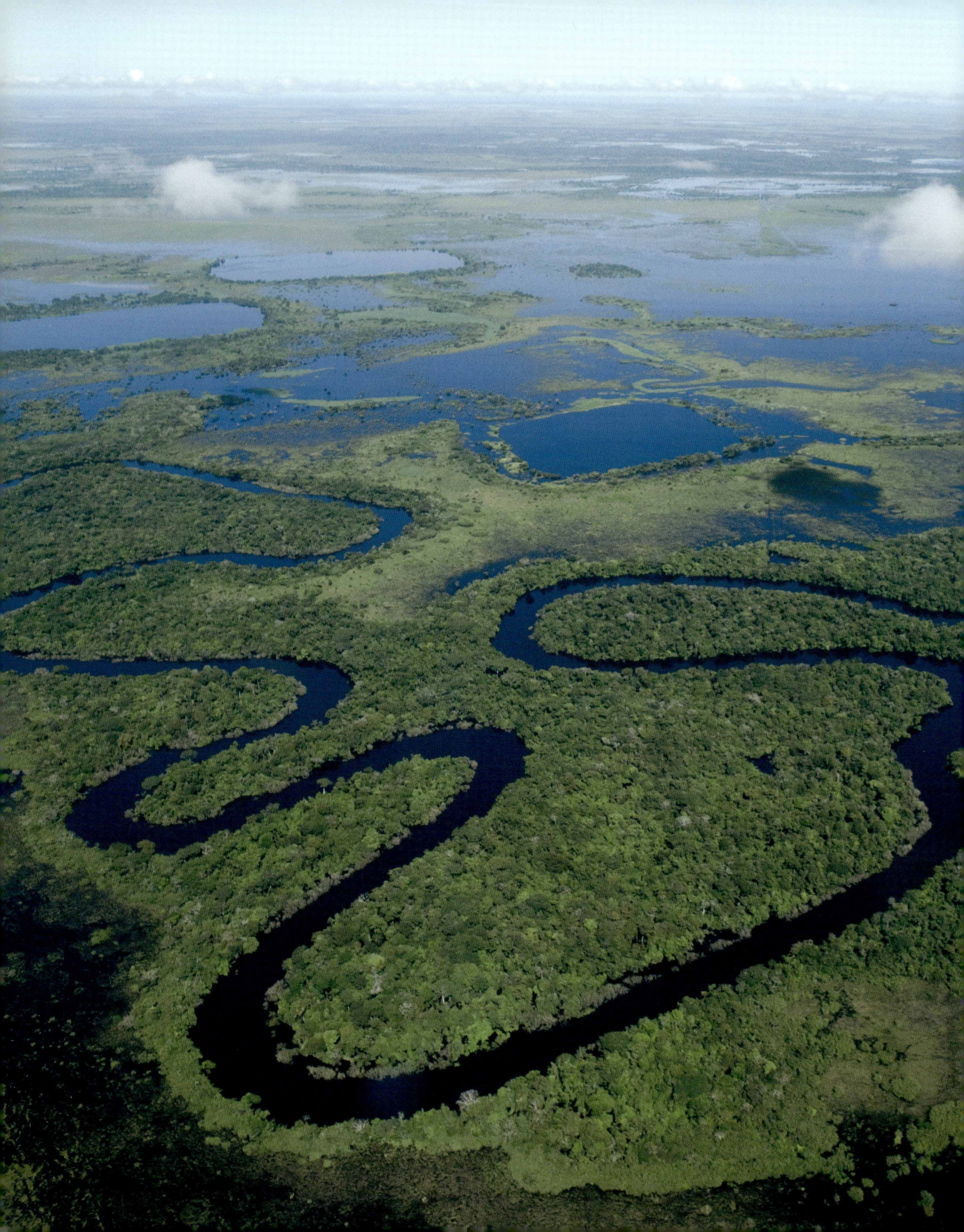

range, long before she was found in the Amazon's main stem. Many rivers cross the savannas of the Moxos plain in Bolivia, and they flood with the same regularity and force as the Amazon. The Mamoré, which collects most of these waters, is rich in Andean sediments and is a prime habitat for the giant water lilies. After it is reinforced by the waters of the Madre de Dios, which drain the slopes of the Andes in southern Peru, the Mamoré transforms into the Madeira, the Amazon's largest tributary.

For four to ten months, the Mamoré and its tributaries, the Yacuma, Apere, and Tijamuchi, inundate the seasonal savannas between the Bolivian towns of Trinidad and Santa Ana. It was here that the earliest discoveries of the queen lily took place. Haenke found *Victoria* on these savannas in 1801, d'Orbigny in 1832, and Thomas Bridges in 1845. As in the *várzea* along the Amazon, the duration of the aquatic phase varies with slight changes in elevation, but here it is the lowest-lying *bajíos* that are inundated for up to ten months, while the *semialturas* stay under water for up to four months, and the *alturas* are flooded only briefly or not at all.

The savannas of the Moxos plain in Bolivia are under water for four to ten months. The Tijamuchi River meanders across the plain shortly before it joins the Mamoré. Thaddaeus Haenke, Alcide d'Orbigny, and Thomas Bridges each made their discoveries in these floodplains.
TOMASZ ANIŚKO / LONGWOOD GARDENS

W. H. Campbell, letter to John Balfour, 1850:

I enclose in this a dozen seeds of Victoria regia, *brought from the Essequibo . . . by an itinerant collector, who seems to know their value, as he charges a dollar (4s. 2d.) a dozen for them. . . . I visited the locality of the plant in the Essequibo, above a hundred miles [160 km] from the sea, in 1846, and it appeared to me a small lagoon, rather than a lake, over which the river flows in the rainy season. It is surrounded on all sides with a dense "bush" (natural forest), through which we had great difficulty in dragging a small corial (wood-skin boat), in which we embarked on the lagoon . . . a most gloomy spot, the favourite resort of caymans, where the sun can scarcely penetrate even at noon, and with an atmosphere oppressively damp and hot. So far as I could judge by sounding and examining the stems of the plant, it appears to grow at a depth of twelve or fourteen feet [4 m], in an oozy, slimy, muddy sort of compound, with which, I presume, sand must be mixed, for higher up the river are immense tracts of loose sand . . . which must be swept along with the torrent every rainy season.*

Lawson 1851

In 1845, Bridges stayed in Santa Ana on the Yacuma River and announced that he "felt more rapture" at finding the queen lily than Giovanni Belzoni had when making his "Egyptian discoveries" (Hooker 1847). In the rainy season, Santa Ana is spared inundation thanks to levees surrounding the town. For those wet months, it becomes a veritable island in a sea of floodwaters, cut off from the rest of the world and reachable only by small boat or single-engine plane. Today, visitors arriving in Santa Ana during the flood can experience Bridges's euphoria by seeing scores of giant lilies along the levees. But travelers will be bitterly disappointed during the dry season when the waters recede, leaving *Victoria*'s seeds buried in the plain beneath grazing cattle.

East of Santa Ana, the Moxos plain is bound by the Guaporé River, where French explorer Hugh Algernon Weddell found the aquatic nymph in 1845. Upstream on the border between Brazil and Bolivia, the watersheds of the Amazon and Paraná are separated by a narrow, low divide. On the other side of this invisible line, running between the towns of Santa Bárbara in Brazil to San Rafael in Bolivia, is the Pantanal. Here, the Río Paraguay collects waters from the world's largest wetland and delivers them farther south to the Paraná.

A BOLIVIAN HYBRID?

The earliest reports of *Victoria* in the Pantanal came from Gustaf Malme, a Swedish botanist traveling through Brazil and Paraguay. In 1894, he discovered the giant lily near the town of Corumbá, on the border with Bolivia.

After carefully examining his collections, Malme was mystified by the Pantanal lilies' true identity. Even though he had expected to find *Victoria amazonica*, the plants he saw appeared much more like *Victoria cruziana*, which had been reportedly farther south along the same river, near Asuncíon in Paraguay. On his second expedition to Brazil in 1903, Malme successfully collected seeds of the Pantanal lily, brought them to Stockholm, and grew them at the Bergius Botanical Garden. Four years later, when Malme published his studies, he announced that *Victoria* near Corumbá differed from *Victoria cruziana* in several characteristics. For instance, the raised lip of the leaf was only half as high, and the underside of the leaf was a more intense violet. This led him to segregate the Pantanal lily as the variety *mattogrossensis* of *Victoria cruziana* (Malme 1907). Malme also concluded that the plants Bridges saw and collected near Santa Ana in Bolivia should be classified as this variety.

Gustaf Malme, 1907:

In July 1894 I found Victoria *at Corumbá in Matto Grosso, in a lagoon by the river Paraguay just below the town of Ladario. . . . On my way home I passed through Rotterdam . . . to look at* Victoria regia *that was grown there. I was surprised to see that the direction of the leaf edge (and color) was different in this plant from the plant I had seen in Matto Grosso. After arriving in Stockholm, I found also that my collections from Corumbá should be classified as* Victoria cruziana, *even though they did not quite agree with Caspary's description. . . . Around Christmas time 1902, I was again in Corumbá and I was then eager to acquire seeds from the before mentioned* Victoria *species for the Bergius Garden in Stockholm. But the . . . lagoon was at that time almost totally dried up and there was no trace of any* Victoria. *I found out from the inhabitants of the city, however, that it also existed on the other side of the city in a bay around Bahia Blanca. A mild case of fever caused me to avoid any excursions along the swampy sides of the river especially since no flowers or ripe fruits would be available at that time. . . . I revisited the site in Corumbá on 22 July 1903. The plants existed in abundance and I fished out a couple of ripe fruits.*

Malme 1907, translated by Inger Wallin

In the wet season, *Victoria* springs up in the floodwaters that turn the Bolivian town of Santa Ana into a veritable island.
TOMASZ ANIŚKO / LONGWOOD GARDENS

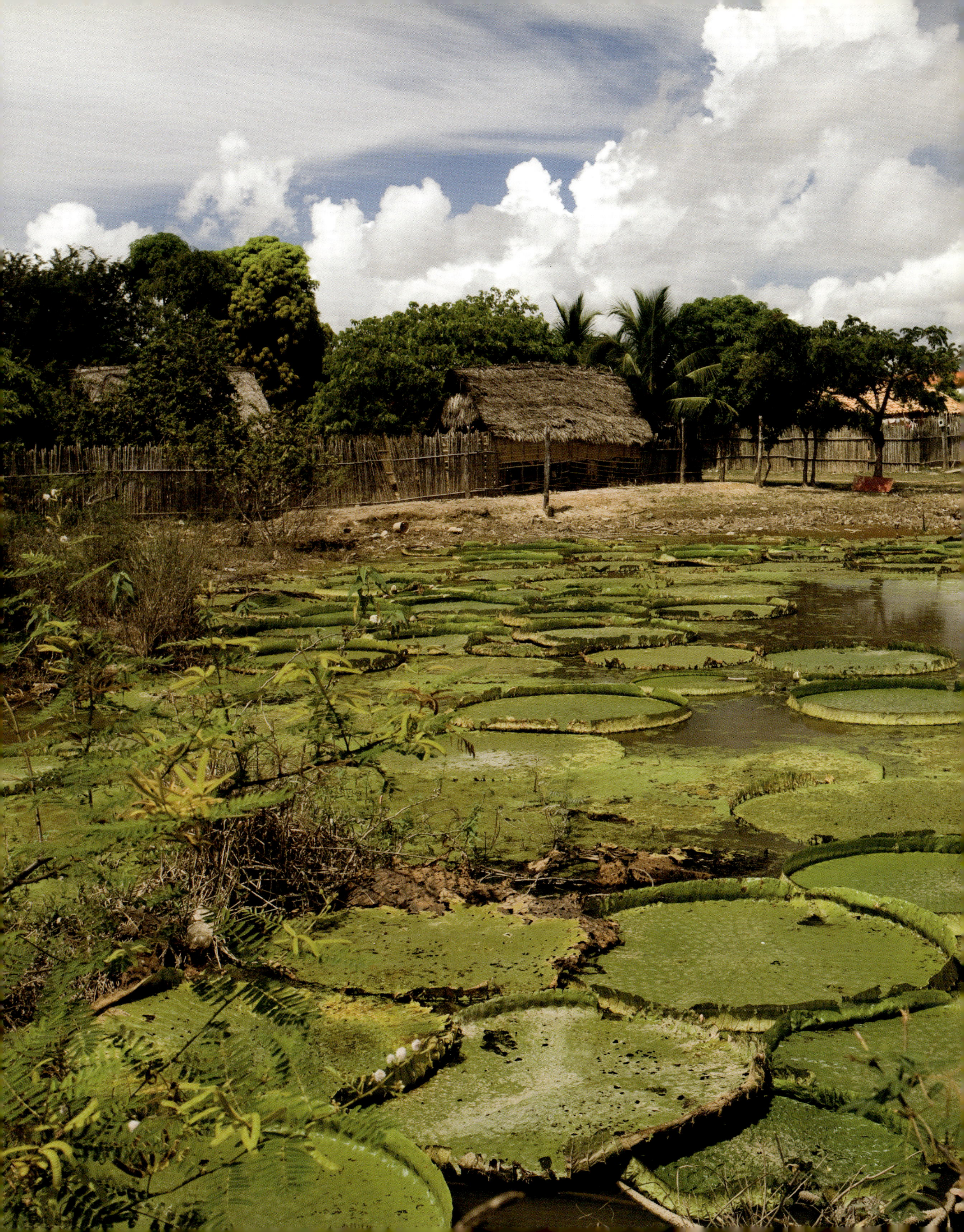

Giant lilies of the Pantanal were classified by Swedish botanist Gustaf Malme as *Victoria cruziana* var. *mattogrossensis*. Here, the Pantanal lilies are being enveloped by smoke rising from countless bushfires breaking out at the onset of the dry season.
CHRISTOPHE COURTEAU / MINDEN PICTURES

A century later, the question remains unanswered: What is the true nature of the giant lilies inhabiting the southernmost fringes of the Amazon watershed and the northernmost extremes of the Paraná watershed, from Santa Ana in Bolivia to Corumbá in Brazil? Could this region—where the two great river systems interlace, come close, and almost touch each other over a low divide—have provided an opportunity for two *Victoria* species to mingle and spawn a hybrid offspring?

By the time the Paraguay crosses from Brazil into its namesake country and reaches the capital city of Asuncíon, there is no doubt that this is *Victoria cruziana* territory. Beginning with Bonpland's discovery in 1857, this species has been repeatedly collected in the vicinity of Asuncíon, as well as along the stretch of river downstream that defines the boundary between Paraguay and Argentina until its confluence with the Paraná.

The city of Corrientes has welcomed many explorers who found and collected *Victoria* where the sediment-rich Paraguay meets the sediment-poor Paraná. The earliest were two Frenchmen, Bonpland in 1821 and d'Orbigny in 1827. Thomas Page, a United States Navy officer, later followed, exploring the rivers of Argentina and Paraguay in 1854. Upon his arrival in Corrientes, Page resolved to see the famed "queen of the floral tribes" (Page 1859). He succeeded, taking a boat up the Riachuelo, the same Paraná tributary that had rewarded Bonpland with his discovery more than thirty years earlier.

Once the Paraná, devoid of the lilies above Corrientes, receives the rich alluvium of Paraguay, it transforms itself into a life-sustaining force, spilling fertile turbid waters onto broad floodplains. While the Paraguay increases the flow of the Paraná by only one quarter, its load of sediments grows by 70 percent (Neiff 1990). As she does along the Amazon, here, too, *Victoria* dwells in shallow lakes that are revived each time the Paraná floods and delivers a new layer of alluvium.

The productive floodplains along the Paraná support a greater number of settlements than those along the Amazon. The settlements are also more accessible thanks to a network of roads and several bridges that span the riverbanks. For this reason, most *Victoria* sightings in this region—from Corrientes in the north to Diamante in the south—align with a highway that trails close to the east side of the Paraná and crosses over many of its left-bank tributaries, such as the Riachuelo, Santa Lucia, or Guaiquiraró. Below Diamante, the Paraná splits into several arms to form a delta, a confusing maze of ever-shifting channels.

Victoria settles in shallow lakes and channels that are refilled annually by sediment-rich floodwaters along the Paraná and its many tributaries, including the Santa Lucia, shown here.
TOMASZ ANIŚKO / LONGWOOD GARDENS

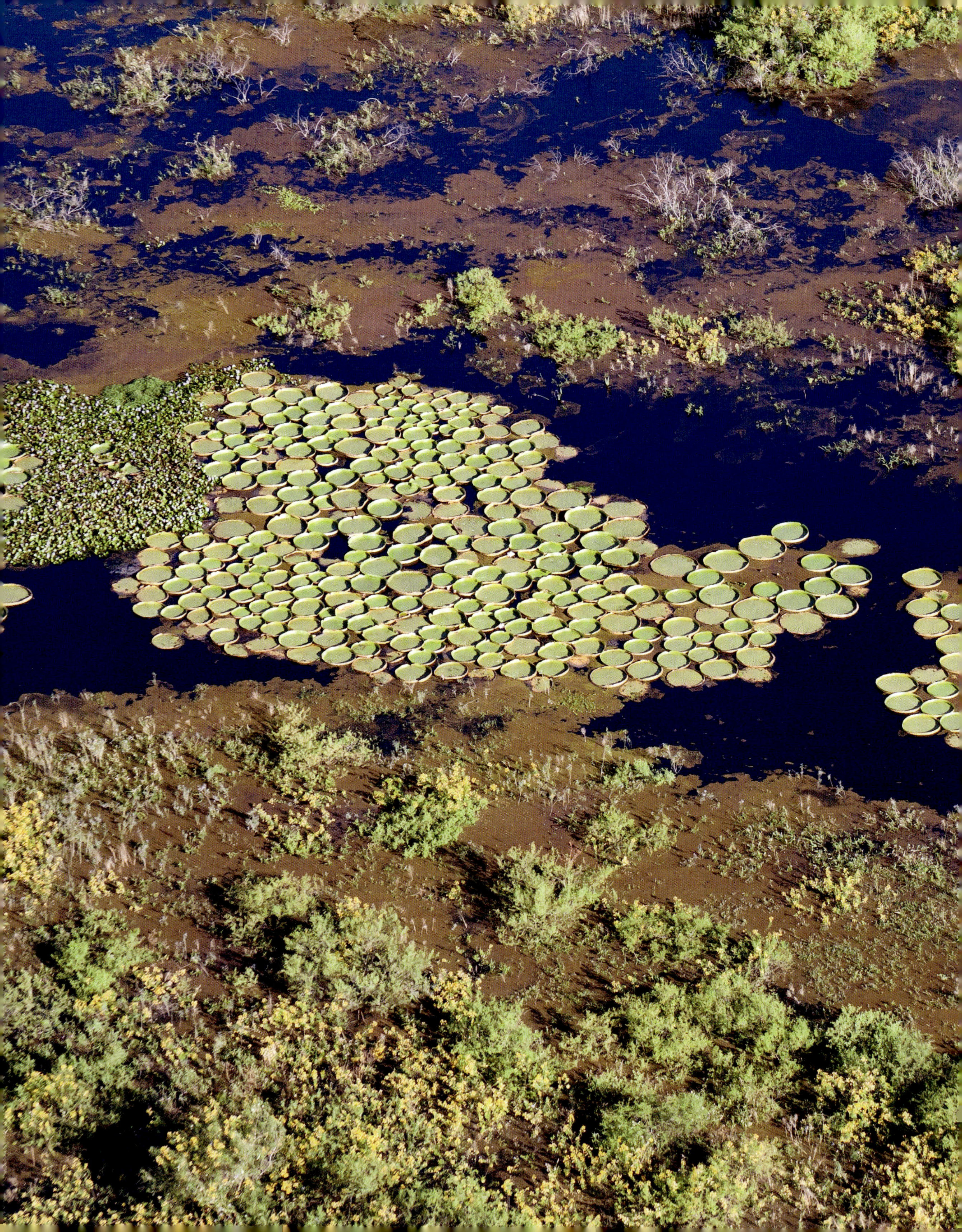

Today, travelers can find thriving *Victoria* lilies near the confluence of the Riachuelo and Paraná, a short distance south of Corrientes, just as Thomas Page, a United States Navy officer, did in 1854, and before him, Aimé Bonpland, a French explorer, in 1821.
EDWIN E. HARVEY

Thomas Page, 1854:

Wishing to see the country adjacent to the river during the rainy season, and with the hope of adding something new to our collections, I determined to make a little boat-cruise up the Riachuelo, a small stream that rises in the interior and empties into the Paraná nine miles [14 km] below Corrientes. I was fortunate in obtaining some rare birds, and in seeing—what alone would have repaid for a longer journey—the "Queen of the Nymphaeaceae" upon its native waters. Extensive shallow lagoons, pure and limpid, were gemmed with islands of the Victoria regia, *or* mais del agua *(corn of water), as it is called in the country; for it is not only the queen of the floral tribes, but ministers to the necessities of man.... What infinite study is found in its leaves—those great pages of Nature's book! I never wearied in examining their mechanism. Here, spreading over the lagoons, they looked as if they would bear the weight of men, and were covered at all times after dawn with myriads of water-fowl, gleaning the "corn," unless anticipated by the natives.*

Page 1859

QUEEN'S DOMINION

By now, *Victoria* has long abandoned the comforts of the tropics and ventured into the upper reaches of the subtropics in latitudes above 30 degrees, equivalent to that of Charleston, South Carolina, in the Northern Hemisphere. That far south, low winter temperatures set the limit of the queen lily's domain, and they achieve this around the small town called, coincidentally, Victoria, only 250 km (115 miles) from Buenos Aires (Burkart 1957, Pagels and Weaver 1999). Since the conditions throughout the Paraná delta are fairly consistent, it is possible that one day the giant lilies may be found even farther south.

Victoria's presence in the Paraná below Corrientes is fairly common knowledge. But reports of her occurrence along the river Uruguay are rare. The Uruguay joins the Paraná shortly before they empty their waters into the Río de la Plata, an estuary opening to the Atlantic. In 1850, Bonpland received fruits that were collected near Restauración (today's Paso de Los Libres) on the Argentinean side of the Uruguay, described as "taken from the waters of the Mirime" (most likely today's Miriñai) (Hamy 1906, translated by John Luttrell). A century and half later, in 2006, José Francisco Pensiero of the National University of Littoral at Santa Fe confirmed *Victoria*'s presence in the backwaters of the Miriñai, not far from Paso de los Libres (Monteverde 2009). In 2003, Cláudio Vinícius de Senna Gastal discovered another population further south on the Brazilian side of the river Uruguay in Laguna Saladeiro, near the small town of Barra do Quarai (Monteverde 2009).

Downstream from there, the Uruguay bids farewell to Brazil and becomes the border separating Argentina on the west bank and the country of Uruguay on the east. In 1968, Arturo

This *Victoria* community thrives in shallow waters in Diamante National Park, on the left bank of the Paraná, shortly before the river splits into a many-channeled delta.
TOMASZ ANIŚKO / LONGWOOD GARDENS

Many sightings of *Victoria* along the Paraná come from areas that are traversed by numerous highways. This one was spotted along the Guaiquiraró, south of the town of Esquina.
TOMASZ ANIŚKO / LONGWOOD GARDENS

This colony of *Victoria* flourishes in one of the Paraná channels crossed by a road and bridge connecting the cities of Santa Fé and Paraná, situated on the opposite banks of the river.
TOMASZ ANIŚKO / LONGWOOD GARDENS

Thus far, the southernmost populations of *Victoria* have been discovered around the town of Victoria in the Paraná delta.
TOMASZ ANIŚKO / LONGWOOD GARDENS

Burkart, a Buenos Aires botanist traveling this stretch of river on the Argentinean side, found the giant lily in the backwaters of the Perucho-Verne, a Uruguay River tributary near Villa San José, located nearly as far south as the sites around the town of Victoria along the Paraná.

ANCESTRAL SEPARATION AND MIGRATION

While low temperatures likely define the southern limit of *Victoria*'s distribution today, many believe it was the cooling of the earth's climate during the Miocene that separated her from her closest relative, *Euryale*, in Asia and brought her to South America (Löhne et al. 2008). Until the beginning of the Miocene about 23 million years ago, even the northern fringes of Asia, Europe, and North America enjoyed a warm climate. The ancestral lineages to modern *Victoria* and *Euryale* were distributed widely across these continents. In 1879, Constantin Ettingshausen, a professor at the University of Graz in Austria, examined various plant fossils uncovered on the Isle of Sheppey off the coast of England, dating back to the Eocene, fifty-five to thirty million years ago. He recognized two water lily species, which he believed were related to the modern *Victoria*. He named them *Victoria sheppyensis* and *Victoria najadum* (Ettingshausen 1879).

The global cooling that followed in the Late Miocene led to mass plant and animal extinction in the Northern Hemisphere and the dislocation of warm climate plants to the tropical regions of South America, Africa, and Asia. As this happened, the lineage that ended up in South America was estranged from its sister lineage, which migrated to southern Asia. This separation between *Victoria* and *Euryale* is estimated to have happened between twenty-three and eleven million years ago (Löhne et al. 2008).

The ancestral *Victoria* arrived in South America at the time of that continent's dramatic transformation, coinciding with the rise of the Andes and the formation of the Amazon and Paraná river systems. Both of these processes influenced the aquatic nymph's evolution and shaped her into the great natural marvel she is today. The record of the giant lily's intricate dependency on the rivers' unique water flow and resulting landforms can be found and read from her present distribution.

The 2006 discovery of *Victoria* in the backwaters of the Miriñai, a tributary of the Uruguay, added to the growing body of evidence that these grassy plains were once home to the giant lilies.
CLÁUDIO VINÍCIUS DE SENNA GASTAL

The Perucho-Verne is a tributary of the Uruguay near Villa San José in Argentina. Arturo Burkart found *Victoria* there in 1968, marking the first documented record of the nymph's existence along that river.
TOMASZ ANIŚKO / LONGWOOD GARDENS

QUEEN'S DOMINION 353

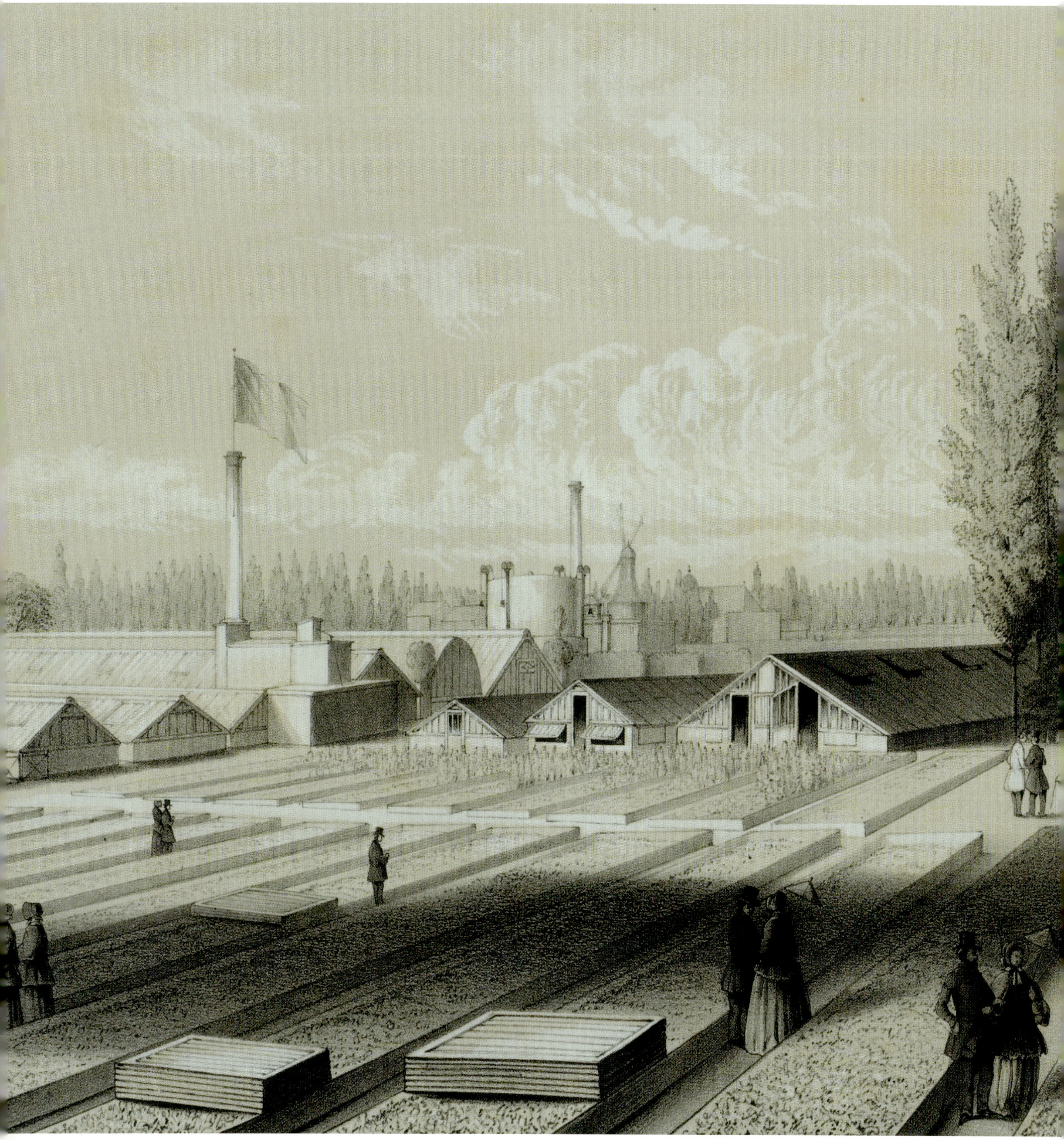

chapter 19

PALACES AND POOLS

When the Royal Botanic Gardens, Kew, distributed young *Victoria* seedlings to various horticultural establishments in Great Britain in early August 1849, not one had adequate facilities to match the immensity of the South American giant. Existing greenhouses were hastily equipped with improvised tanks and refurbished with makeshift implements to serve the royal lily's needs. Within a few weeks, however, the enlarged tanks proved to be too small to accommodate the aquatic wonder, which was expanding at an astonishing rate.

Before the end of September, Joseph Paxton at Chatsworth had to double the size of his first 3.7-m-square (12-foot-square) tank, which he had planted in early August. At Syon House in London, head gardener Iveson placed *Victoria* in a tub, the top of which was enlarged to 1.8 m (6 feet) square with the help of sheet lead. As the lily rapidly overtook this little body of water, Iveson had a slate tank, 6.7 m (22 feet) long and 3.7 m (12 feet) wide, built just in time to receive the plant shortly after Christmas 1849. But soon, even this tank was not large enough to contain the bulging colossus. Iveson altered the greenhouse itself so a larger tank, 6.7 m (22 feet) square, could be installed. At last, the queen lily was given ample space to grow. *Victoria* repaid these favors by throwing impressive 1.5-m (5-foot) wide leaves and showing her first flower in April 1850 (Anonymous 1850b).

In 1850, Louis Van Houtte built a circular Victoria House, 11 m (36 feet) wide, on the grounds of his nursery in Gentbrugge in Belgium.
Longwood Gardens Library and Archives

Anonymous correspondent to the *Gardeners' Chronicle*, 1850:

[Victoria at Syon House] was then a very small affair, the largest leaf not being more than four inches [10 cm] in diameter. No convenient receptacle having been previously provided for it, three Nelumbium tubs . . . were procured; one of these was filled with water, and in this . . . our aquatic was plunged. The other two tubs were placed one above and the other below this one, for the purpose of circulating and changing the water . . . which was led by means of a siphon out of the higher tub into the one in which the plant was, from thence into the lower tub, and out of that it was again pumped into the higher one. . . . It was shifted first into a pot, and then into a basket, while it remained in the Nelumbium tub . . . which was at last enlarged to six feet [2 m] square at the top by means of sheet lead, and even under these circumstances it made very satisfactory progress. A slate tank, twenty-two feet [7 m] long, twelve feet [4 m] wide, and two feet six inches [76 cm] deep, becoming shallower as its sides were approached, was about this time constructed for its reception. . . . Since the house has been altered the tank has been enlarged to twenty-two [7 m] feet square, each corner containing Nymphaeas of different colors, and there are also two Nelumbiums near the centre, whose foliage, rising, as it does, above the surface of the water, gives to the whole an artistic appearance which it would not otherwise possess.

Anonymous 1850b

ENTHRONING A SOVEREIGN

Like Paxton at Chatsworth, others soon realized that a special kind of greenhouse had to be constructed to afford the adequate space *Victoria* required to show her glory. As a consequence, in 1850 a new model of greenhouse was designed specifically to suit the needs of the Amazon lily. At Chatsworth, Paxton refined his earlier ideas and created the groundbreaking Lily House with its flat ridge-and-furrow roof. In Belgium, Louis Van Houtte, one of Europe's leading horticulturists, revived a concept proposed some three decades prior by John Loudon, an influential Scottish botanist and horticulturist.

In 1822, Loudon had published *An Encyclopaedia of Gardening*, in which he proposed a design that he considered ideal for aquatic plants. It had a circular form and contained two cisterns: a central one for plants naturally growing in rivers and another one around the periphery of the house for plants inhabiting ponds and lakes. The dome-like roof was low over the outer tank for the shorter plants and high in the middle for

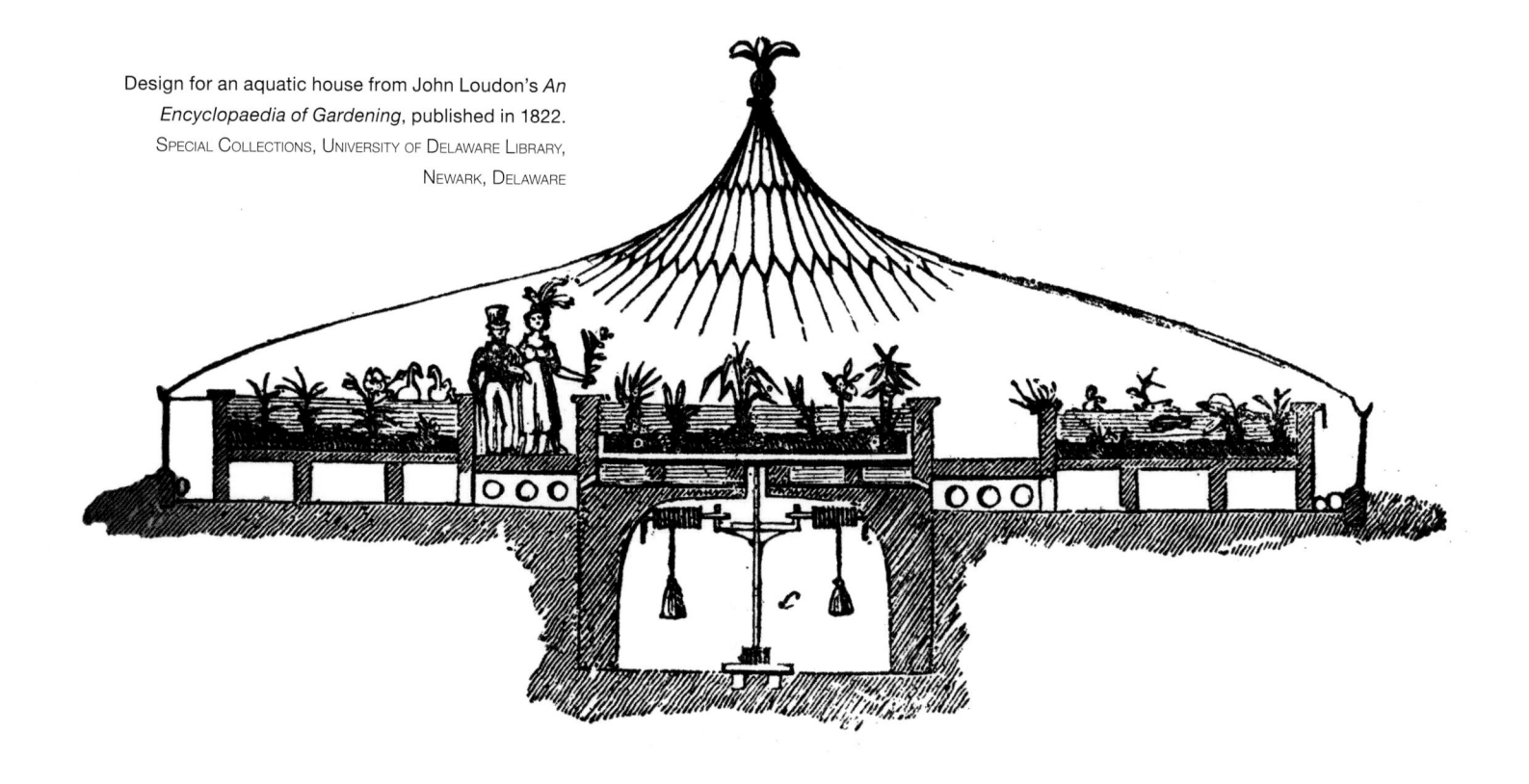

Design for an aquatic house from John Loudon's *An Encyclopaedia of Gardening*, published in 1822.
SPECIAL COLLECTIONS, UNIVERSITY OF DELAWARE LIBRARY, NEWARK, DELAWARE

taller plants. To emulate the movement of water in the central tank, Loudon designed a clever wind-up mechanism of descending weights. This powered the turntable upon which submerged plants were placed.

When Van Houtte built the Victoria House on the grounds of his nursery in Gentbrugge in 1850, he eliminated the turntable and the outer cistern in Loudon's design. Its central tank, 8.2 m (27 feet) in diameter, occupied most of the interior, but the low domed roof closely resembled the Scotsman's design. It employed small pieces of glass that overlapped like fish scales and fitted into a filigree of thin iron sash bars. Van Houtte's 11-m (36-foot) wide "elegant and spacious glass rotunda" sheltered *Victoria*, "well enthroned as sovereign," while *Nymphaea* water lilies floated around her, "less her sisters than her humble vassals" (Planchon and Van Houtte 1850–51, translated by Adam Koppeser). Aside from *Nymphaea*, Van Houtte refrained from planting tall plants, which would obstruct the view of *Victoria*. A narrow walk around the raised pool enabled visitors to admire the Amazon lily from all sides, while the delicate lace-like structure of the roof, fitted with countless small panes of glass, resembled an elegant filigree parasol sheltering the rare creature inside.

Although they took different approaches to solving the same engineering problem, both Paxton's and Van Houtte's houses proved successful in their own ways. Both featured a central aboveground round pool, although the one at Chatsworth was almost 2 m (7 feet) wider than the one in Gentbrugge. This core element remained essentially unchanged as Victoria Houses modeled on Paxton's and Van Houtte's designs began sprouting across Europe. Both also provided an expanse of placid water free of columns supporting the roof, arguably the best backdrop to showcase the Amazon lily's beauty.

The interior of Van Houtte's Victoria House in Gentbrugge was taken up by a round pool, 8.2 m (27 feet) wide, and protected by a dome of thin iron sash bars fitted with small pieces of glass.
LONGWOOD GARDENS LIBRARY AND ARCHIVES

Designed in 1852 by Richard Turner, the Lily House at the
Royal Botanic Gardens, Kew, is the oldest still-standing Victoria House.
Tomasz Aniśko / Longwood Gardens

But there the similarities ended. The house at Chatsworth was more than twice as large as the one at Gentbrugge. It required about five times the amount of glass used by Van Houtte and utilized the latest technological advances, such as prefabricated cast-iron elements and large glass panes. Architectural details—combined with a flat ridge-and-furrow roof disguised behind an ornate cornice and a façade of arched windows—gave Paxton's house the aura of a stylish garden pavilion, a sharp contrast to Van Houtte's modest house. The round pool, fitted into a rectangular structure at Chatsworth, left the corners available for smaller pools where the lesser members of the aquatic tribe, *Victoria*'s "humble vassals," could be grown, something Van Houtte was not concerned about.

Paxton's design climaxed in London's Crystal Palace and its later permutations in Europe and in America. Despite its astonishing success, however, this model did not inspire many other similar Victoria Houses. A year after Chatsworth, a smaller and simpler version of the Lily House was built in the Oxford Botanic Garden. It lacked many of the decorative features of Paxton's structure, and instead of a round pool, it had a rectangular one occupying most of the interior. A slightly larger variant of the Oxford house was erected in the Glasgow Botanic Garden in 1855. Its pool was shorter and closer to a square.

THE ROYAL ROOFLINE

When Richard Turner, the acclaimed builder of Kew's grand Palm House, was tasked with designing an aquatic house for *Victoria* in 1852, he took some cues from Paxton's

The rectangular Lily House built in 1851 at the Oxford Botanic Garden featured
a flat ridge-and-furrow roof modeled on Joseph Paxton's Lily House at Chatsworth.
Longwood Gardens Library and Archives

358 Victoria: The Seductress

PALACES AND POOLS 359

The Victoria House designed in 1852 by Johan Åbom for King Oscar II of Sweden stood in Rosendal in Stockholm until 1877.
ROYAL LIBRARY, NATIONAL LIBRARY OF SWEDEN

Lily House. Turner made the pool the same diameter as Paxton's and enclosed it in a house about as wide: 15 m (49 feet) square. He also added a vestibule over the entrance, which extended the length of the whole structure to 18.7 m (61 feet), nearly identical to Chatsworth's Lily House. One might have wondered if a new architectural canon for an aquatic edifice was being formed. However, where Turner departed from Paxton's design was in the roof. Rather than repeating the ridge-and-furrow design, he used a more traditional single-span roof. Whatever his motivation, over time Turner's model had greater longevity. Chatsworth's Lily House fell into disrepair and was dismantled in the early twentieth century, but Turner's structure, with a few renovations, has continued to accommodate the queen lily to this day, making it the oldest still-standing Victoria House in the world.

Turner was not alone in his preference for a single-span roof over the ridge-and-furrow style. In 1852, Johan Fredrik Åbom, a leading Swedish architect, built a rectangular house at Rosendal, the summer residence of Swedish King Oscar II. It was fitted with a round pool and covered with a single-span roof. The Rosendal house, however, did not fare as well as Kew's. It was demolished in 1877 to make room for a new Winter Garden.

In Germany, a year before Turner's house was constructed at Kew, a 10-m (33-foot) square house was built for *Victoria* at the Hamburg Botanical Garden. It had a single-span roof sloping east, west, and south. Inside, there was a round basin nearly 8 m (26 feet) in diameter in the center, with tables in each corner displaying potted plants (Otto 1851a).

Likewise, the first Victoria House at the Royal Botanical Gardens Schöneberg in Berlin, built in 1852, was a simple, unassuming square structure with a single-span roof. Designed by Carl Bouché, inspector of the Schöneberg garden, it had a central sixteen-sided basin close to 8 m (26 feet) in diameter that accommodated one or two *Victoria* plants, along with an assortment of *Nymphaea* water lilies and sacred lotus along the edge (Caspary 1855). In smaller tanks fitted along the walls there grew aquatic *Alisma* and *Aponogeton*, while tubs with other tropical plants occupied the remaining space. This Victoria House became so popular with Berliners that garden administrators were forced to impose restrictions on access and visitation time (Potonié 1882).

Although they never became the dominant style of this architectural genre, rectangular Victoria Houses were constructed throughout the nineteenth century. In 1868, the Adelaide Botanic Gardens in Australia opened such a house. It was covered with a single-span roof, but inside it featured an unorthodox oval-shaped pool, 11 m (36 feet) long and 8 m (26 feet) wide. "I am proud to say, [it] exceeds in its dimensions the

Rectangular Victoria Houses built in England between 1849 and 1852. The Kew structure is extant.
ANNA ANIŚKO

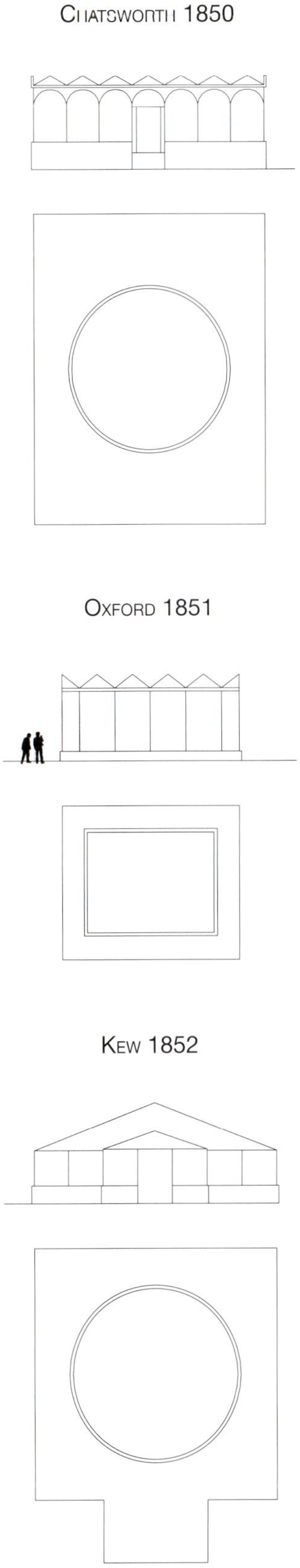

CHATSWORTH 1850

OXFORD 1851

KEW 1852

The 1868 Victoria House in the Adelaide Botanic Gardens, the first such structure in Australia, featured an indoor oval pool, 11 m (36 feet) long and 8 m (26 feet) wide.
NATIONAL LIBRARY OF AUSTRALIA

PALACES AND POOLS 361

The circular Victoria House designed in 1878 by Julius Bouché for the Royal Botanic Gardens in Bonn-Poppelsdorfer.
BOTANISCHE GÄRTEN DER UNIVERSITÄT BONN

The first Victoria House in the Netherlands was built in 1872 in the Leiden Botanical Garden. The impressive structure, 15 m (49 feet) wide, had its low dome surmounted by an ornate cast-iron crown.
HORTUS BOTANICUS LEIDEN

tanks intended for like purpose not alone in the Colonies, but in England itself," proclaimed Richard Schomburgk, the garden's director and brother of Robert Schomburgk, who had discovered *Victoria* in Guiana (Schomburgk 1873). Adelaide's record was broken in 1887, when an even larger oval-shaped pool, 15 m (49 feet) long and 10 m (33 feet) wide, was constructed inside a rectangular Victoria House at the Rotterdam Zoological Garden in the Netherlands (Wilke 1891).

ROUND TRUMPS RECTANGULAR

Although the fame and reputation of both Chatsworth and Kew inspired rectangular Victoria Houses across Europe and beyond, another style would soon prevail. The circular form, devised first by Van Houtte in Gentbrugge in 1850, was emulated one year later in Berlin by August Borsig, Germany's locomotive magnate. Next to his factory on the bank of the river Spree in the Moabit district of the city, Borsig created much-admired gardens, situating a grandiose Italianate mansion and conservatories among them. The conservatories were built with cast-iron elements produced in Borsig's foundry and heated by excess steam harnessed from the factory (Gaerdt 1894). The practically unlimited supply of steam and ready access to construction elements explains how Borsig managed to build the first Victoria House in Berlin so early—even before the Royal Gardens in Schöneberg. When Borsig opened his gardens and conservatories to the public, they quickly became one of Berlin's favorite attractions. Even the German Empress Victoria, daughter of Queen Victoria, often came with her family to stroll the gardens and visit her mother's namesake.

The European nobility's eagerness to tame and possess *Victoria* as a mark of horticultural acumen, as well as to share and publicly display the nymph, was soon adopted by the rising class of newly wealthy industrialists, who were often from very humble backgrounds. This practice reveals much about the way the privileged of that era viewed their place in society. Botanical collections of exotic rarities were a means to project and cultivate an image of "a guardian and lord of Nature simultaneously" (Neumeyer in Kohlmaier and von Sartory 1986). The "guardian" protected and took care of Nature's treasures within the confines of his domain, while the "lord" was able to exercise his power over Nature to hunt, trap, and tame any living creature.

Some were quick to criticize the round Victoria Houses as impractical because they were exposed to the elements on all sides, and therefore costly to heat (Loescher 1852), but Van Houtte's and Borsig's early success encouraged others to follow. These rotunda-like structures varied greatly in style to reflect the taste and financial status of their owners. In 1866, the Botanic Garden in Dresden erected a modest circular house 7.6 m (25 feet) in diameter with a 6-m (20-foot) wide pool inside (Seidel 1869). Instead of a cupola on top of the roof, which provided ventilation in Van Houtte's house, Dresden's angled roof had large sections that opened as windows to the outside, an early precursor of today's open-roof greenhouses.

A larger 10-m (33-foot) wide circular Victoria House was built in 1878 in the Royal Botanic Gardens in Bonn-Poppelsdorfer. Designed by Julius Bouché, son of Carl David of the Schöneberg garden, it had a low domed roof created from thin arched iron girders, which gave the impression of a finely spun net and covering for the lily's heated tank (Stoverock 2001).

While Victoria Houses enjoyed unprecedented popularity in Great Britain, Belgium, and especially Germany in the 1850s and 1860s, the Netherlands—the horticultural hotbed of Europe—was curiously lagging behind. Only the Amsterdam Botanical Garden widened one of its greenhouses for *Victoria* by adding a half dome to both of its sidewalls. While this oddly shaped structure was adequately suited to accommodate a large tank, even with further improvements, it never became what the Dutch really wanted: "a temple devoted to the queen of water plants" (Witte 1872, translated by Ger Meeuwissen).

This somewhat embarrassing situation finally ended in Leiden in 1871, when the government and Leiden University combined resources to build an impressive circular Victoria House. Its delicate, beautifully proportioned roof was surmounted by a cast-iron crown rather than a cupola. A walkway surrounded the 10-m (33-foot) wide central tank, and there was a 1-m (3-foot) wide tank along the building's perimeter. To maintain symmetry, the furnace room was situated opposite the entrance. At 15 m (49 feet) in diameter, the Leiden house surpassed earlier designs. When its first *Victoria* flowered a year later, the house was proclaimed "not only worthy of this beautiful plant but also worthy of the Leiden University" (Witte 1872, translated by Ger Meeuwissen).

AN OCTAGONAL INNOVATION

Early in its evolution, the circular Victoria House sprouted a minor mutation that in time would replace it completely. In 1851, when Caleb Cope of Springbrook was preparing a rectangular house to raise America's first *Victoria*, he chose an octagonal

Circular Victoria Houses built in Belgium, the Netherlands, and France between 1850 and 1888. None are extant today.
ANNA ANIŚKO

GENTBRUGGE 1850

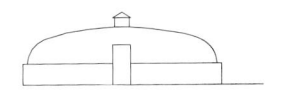

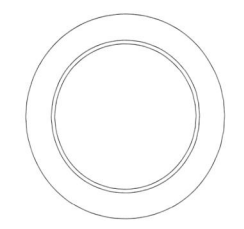

LEIDEN 1871

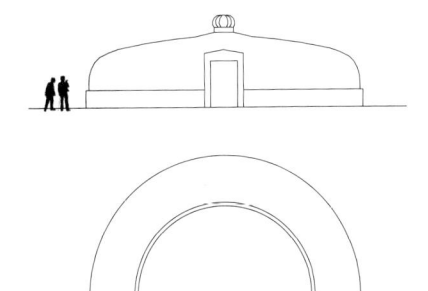

LYON 1888

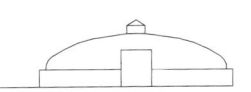

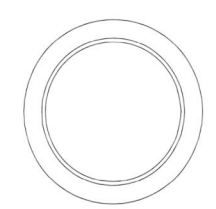

The 1854 Victoria House designed by Alphonse Balat was moved in 1879 to the National Botanic Garden of Belgium in Brussels.
COLLECTION OF THE NATIONAL BOTANIC GARDEN OF BELGIUM

rather than a circular footprint for the tank inside (M. Thomas and Sons 1857). Cope's tank, 7.3 m (24 feet) in diameter, was modest in comparison to later structures but revolutionary for its time.

The octagonal design took on new prominence with the opening of the Victoria House in Brussels in 1854. Designed by Alphonse Balat, principal architect to the Belgian royal family, it is arguably the most refined standalone Victoria House. Reaching 4 m (13 feet) high and 14 m (46 feet) wide, Balat's house featured a dome supported by graceful trusses rising from the eight corners of the octagonal foundation. At the top, a large, elaborate ironwork crown rose over a low lantern. The interior of the dome was extended with vertically terminating recesses on all eight sides of the house. Instead of hiding the braced girders and wrought-iron ribs under the glass surface of the dome, Balat transformed them into decorative elements that were visible on the outside.

Balat's house premiered in the Brussels Zoological Garden but was relocated to the National Botanic Garden twenty-five years later. When this garden was moved outside the city to Meise in 1941, the Victoria House traveled again (Diagre-Vanderpelen 2008). It can be seen there today, although it is no longer used as an aquatic house.

Two decades after designing the Victoria House, Balat created another glass dome, this time for the king himself. When King Leopold II assumed the throne of Belgium in 1865, he asked Balat to design a complex of immense greenhouses for the Royal Castle at Laeken. When it was finished thirty years later in 1895, the complex

Alphonse Balat's Victoria House in its third and present location in the National Botanic Garden of Belgium in Meise.
PAUL BORREMANS / COLLECTION OF THE NATIONAL BOTANIC GARDEN OF BELGIUM

366 VICTORIA: THE SEDUCTRESS

covered 2.5 hectares (more than 6 acres). The largest house in this complex, the Winter Garden (opened in 1874), was a colossal rotunda, 60 m (197 feet) wide and 30 m (99 feet) high. It was not intended for displaying *Victoria*, but its dome nevertheless bore more than a passing resemblance to Balat's earlier design for her. Like its predecessor, the Winter Garden was surmounted with an ironwork crown.

Twenty years after the rectangular Victoria House at Rosendal was torn down, the nearby Bergius Botanical Garden in Stockholm, Sweden, began constructing a dazzling new octagonal Victoria House. Designed in 1899 by head gardener Ivar Anders Örtendahl, it featured a 10-m (33-foot) wide pool inside a double-glazed, high-pitched dome, 18.5 m (61 feet) in diameter. Following a series of renovations in the late twentieth century, its original iron frame was replaced with aluminum elements (with the exception of the eight main load-bearing trusses).

The ironwork ornaments of the cupola and the entrance—which had been lost during the 1940s—were diligently reproduced in 2001, returning this Swedish *Victoria*'s palace to its former glory. Standing on the shore of Brunnsviken bay, a former lake now connected to the Baltic Sea, the Örtendahl structure was one of the largest of its kind in the nineteenth century. Today, it is an unforgettable sight. Surrounded by frigid waters and tormented by icy winds, this minuscule tropical sanctuary stands defiant and shelters its precious inhabitant despite all odds, only seven degrees south of the Arctic Circle.

While the Swedes were building their Victoria House in Stockholm, an equally impressive structure was being inaugurated across the Baltic Sea on the eastern shore of the Bay of Finland in St. Petersburg. Designed for the

An octagonal Victoria House designed by Ivar Örtendahl for the Bergius Botanical Garden in Stockholm in 1899.

Tomasz Aniśko / Longwood Gardens

Octagonal Victoria Houses built in Belgium, Sweden, and Romania between 1854 and 1960. All are extant.
ANNA ANIŚKO

BRUSSELS 1854

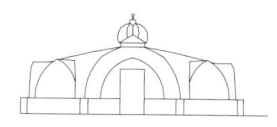

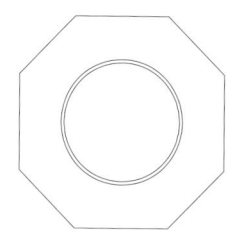

STOCKHOLM 1900

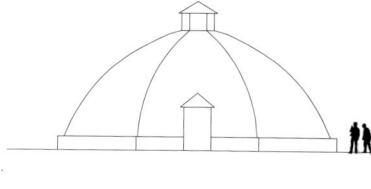

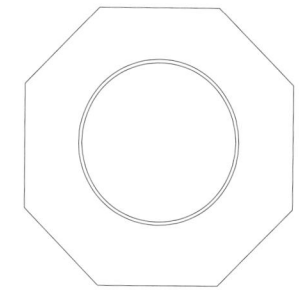

CLUJ-NAPOCA 1960

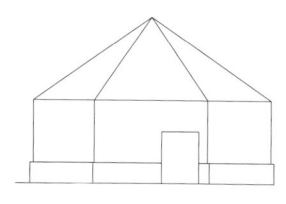

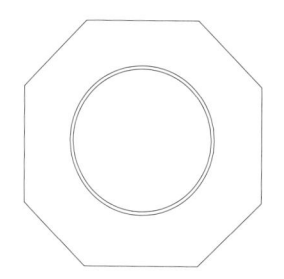

An octagonal Victoria House at the Imperial Botanical Garden in St. Petersburg featured an impressive circular tank 13 m (43 feet) in diameter.
BOTANICAL GARDEN OF KOMAROV INSTITUTE, ST. PETERSBURG

Imperial Botanical Garden (today's Botanical Garden of Komarov Institute), St. Petersburg's Victoria House was scenically situated on Aptekarsky Island in the mouth of the Neva River. It boasted an octagonal structure with a straight sloping roof and a huge round tank 13 m (43 feet) in diameter—likely the largest ever in a Victoria House. The house and garden were severely damaged during the siege of Leningrad in World War II, but following a thorough restoration, it continues to accommodate South American water lilies to this day.

Architectural creativity and angular variations of the Victoria House canon did not end with the octagonal design. After Germany's unification in 1871 and Berlin's designation as the imperial capital of the Second Reich, a new Victoria House was conceived for the Royal Botanic Garden Schöneberg. (Bouché's early rectangular structure had gradually fallen into decay.) In 1882, Friedrich Schulze, an architect in Berlin's building administration, designed a more imposing edifice for the Amazonian lily: a decagonal (ten-sided) structure some 15 m (49 feet) in diameter, with a central pool about 10 m (33 feet) across, surrounded by a walkway 1.5 m (5 feet) wide and a ring-shaped tank of the same width along the wall

(Ring 1883). It was covered by a bell-shaped dome more than 5 m (17 feet) high and culminated in a small ventilating cupola, giving it an overall profile that was higher than that of earlier houses with circular or octagonal bases. To improve the structure's appearance and prominence, it was built on a site that was raised a meter and half (5 feet) above the surrounding area (Potonié 1882). Schulze's house stood in Schöneberg for twenty-five years until 1907, when the garden relocated to a new site in the Dahlem district of Berlin.

In 1897, the Swiss used Schöneberg's decagonal Victoria House as a model for their structure at the University of Basel's new botanical garden. With a diameter of 13 m (43 feet) and a basin 8 m (26 feet) wide, it was slightly smaller than the Berlin prototype, but it nevertheless had a similar ten-sided base, arched trusses, and elevated ventilating cupola on top of the roof. The Basel design also featured several technological innovations, including a system of anchors and ropes that could pull a shade cloth on the roof's exterior up or down.

The spacious interior of the 1882 Victoria House in the Royal Botanic Garden Schöneberg in Berlin featured a circular pool, 10 m (33 feet) wide, under an decagonal glass dome.
GENERAL RESEARCH DIVISION, THE NEW YORK PUBLIC LIBRARY, ASTOR, LENOX AND TILDEN FOUNDATIONS

The design for the 1897 Victoria House in the Botanical Garden of the University of Basel was inspired by the structure built fifteen years earlier in Berlin-Schöneberg.
BOTANISCHER GARTEN DER UNIVERSITÄT BASEL

The 1897 Victoria House in the Botanical Garden of the University of Basel was meticulously reconstructed before it turned one hundred.
HEINZ SCHNEIDER / BOTANISCHER GARTEN DER UNIVERSITÄT BASEL

PALACES AND POOLS   371

Decagonal Victoria Houses built in Germany and Switzerland between 1882 and 1902. The Basel and Halle structures are extant.
ANNA ANIŚKO

BERLIN-SCHÖNEBERG 1882

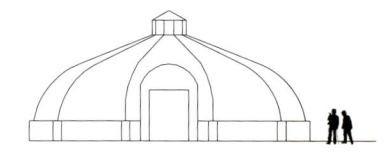

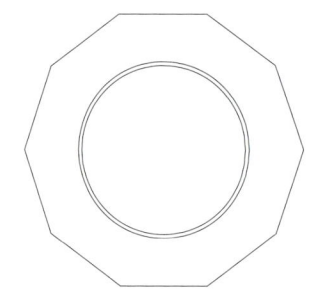

BASEL 1897

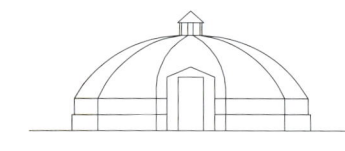

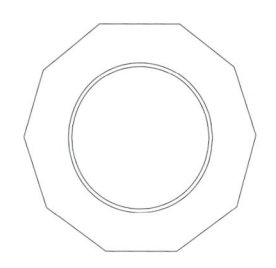

HALLE 1902

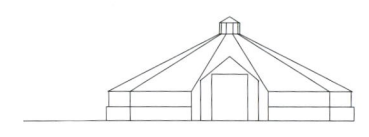

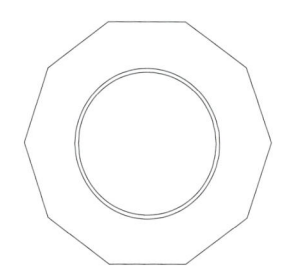

In the twentieth century, the ravages of two world wars took a heavy toll on Europe's Victoria Houses. Although the Basel house survived both wars, by the 1960s, it was showing alarming signs of aging and deterioration. Miraculously, the house was saved when surrounding greenhouses were demolished to make room for expansion of the university's library. Little was done at that time to reverse the progression of inevitable structural decay, but in 1996, a faithful and meticulous reconstruction was carried out using authentic building techniques. Today, the Basel house showcases *Victoria* with as much splendor as it did more than a century ago (Schmid 1997).

THE POLYGONAL CANON

As Van Houtte's circular house morphed over time into an eight-sided and then ten-sided structure, it was inevitable that someone would eventually build a Victoria House based on a twelve-sided plan. In 1884, a dodecagonal house, 12.5 m (41 feet) in diameter and 4.5 m (15 feet) high, was erected in the botanical garden of the local university in Strassburg, Germany (today's Strasbourg, France). Designed by Georg Peter Hermann Eggert, it enclosed a round pool 7 m (23 feet) wide that was surrounded by a walkway and a ring-shaped basin along the perimeter (Jost 1911). When the city came under French control in the aftermath of World War I, the Victoria House became the sole example of a polygonal aquatic house in France. Until recently, visitors to Strasbourg were able to admire *Victoria* in this historic house, but due to structural deterioration, it has been closed to await proper restoration.

Strasbourg's Victoria House complemented a structure in Lyon, 500 km (310 miles) to the south. This circular house was built in 1888 in Tête d'or Park, the largest

A 1924 view of the Victoria House in the Botanical Garden of the University of Strasbourg.
JARDIN BOTANIQUE DE L'UNIVERSITÉ DE STRASBOURG

urban park in France. Designed by Oddos, it originally featured a then-classic central pool, about 8 m (26 feet) in diameter, that was surrounded by a walkway 1 m (3 feet) wide and covered by a low curved glass dome. In 1929, the house was widened to permit the addition of a ring-shaped basin along the outer perimeter for growing *Nymphaea* water lilies. Half a century later, the dome-like roof of small glass panes—meticulously arranged on a gently curved frame—was replaced with a straight sloping one that had large, more energy-efficient sheets of glass. The historical character and the beauty of the structure unfortunately fell victim to more practical considerations.

In the second half of the nineteenth century, numerous standalone Victoria Houses were built in Europe, but only a handful of them survive today. In addition to those mentioned in Basel, Meise, Strasbourg, Stockholm, and St. Petersburg, extant examples can be found in Halle, Leipzig, and Budapest. The octagonal Victoria House in the Leipzig Botanical Garden stands unheated, stripped of glass, and longing for its former inhabitant. Its shell is dwarfed by a 1998 rectangular structure that replaced it as a home for the grand lily of the Amazon. The Leipzig house is a pointed reminder of the fragility of these iron and glass houses.

The decagonal house in Halle, built in 1902 on the grounds of the Botanical Gardens of Martin Luther University, still accommodates *Victoria* lilies, but a series of intrusive renovations have taken a toll on its historical authenticity. Similarly, in Budapest, the 1893 octagonal Victoria House at Füvészkert—the botanical garden of Eötvös Loránd University—underwent a complete renovation in 2009. Unique for its octagonal tank inside, the building had large sheets of glass applied to it during renovation. Regrettably, this obscured its historic character, which may not be apparent to those visiting today.

The polygonal canon of the Victoria House has shown remarkable resilience since its inception in the 1850s. Even a century later, it was still used as the model for

The extant dodecagonal Victoria House built in Strasbourg in 1884.
ANNA ANIŚKO

STRASBOURG 1884

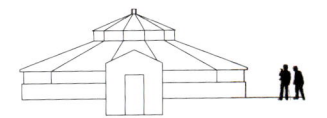

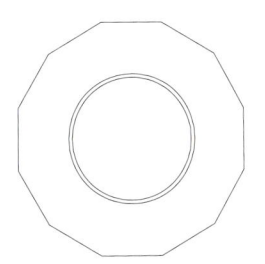

The interior of the 1888 Victoria House in Tête d'or Park in Lyon.
JARDIN BOTANIQUE DE L'UNIVERSITÉ DE STRASBOURG

A disused octagonal Victoria House in the Leipzig Botanic Garden stands in front of a 1998 rectangular structure where the South American lilies are grown today.
TOMASZ ANIŚKO / LONGWOOD GARDENS

new structures to house the South American lily. In Finland in 1953, the Botanical Garden of Helsinki University erected its Victoria House based on a dodecagonal footprint, evoking the classic form and proportions of the freestanding aquatic houses of yesteryear. Similarly, in Romania, the 1960 octagonal Victoria House built in the botanical garden in Cluj-Napoca was fitted with a 9-m (30-foot) wide pool. Although at 10 m (33 feet) high it was much taller than its predecessors, the structure followed the long-established tradition in principle.

Aesthetic considerations aside, the advantages of polygonal houses over the circular ones hailed by their nineteenth-century proponents proved to be significant for longevity. The polygonal footprint permitted straight, sloping roofs that, unlike their curved predecessors, could be built using larger panes of glass, making them cheaper to construct, easier to maintain, and more energy efficient. While the round structures are no more—with the exception of the Lyon house, which has been transformed beyond recognition—several polygonal houses with either curved or straight roofs managed to defy the destructive forces of corrosion, wartime chaos and depravation, and rising fuel costs and shortages. Today, they provide a glimpse into an era when Europeans fell under the spell of the South American wonder lily and created a unique architectural form: the Victoria House.

The 1893 octagonal Victoria House at Füvészkert, the botanical garden of Eötvös Loránd University in Budapest, after renovation in 2009.
Tomasz Aniśko / Longwood Gardens

The 1960 octagonal Victoria House in Cluj-Napoca features a roof 10 m (33 feet) high, considerably higher than those found in similar structures.
Tomasz Aniśko / Longwood Gardens

The Victoria House built in 1953 in the Botanical Garden of the University of Helsinki reflected the nineteenth-century style of a polygonal aquatic house.
Tomasz Aniśko / Longwood Gardens

CONTEMPORARY TRANSFORMATIONS

Yet the triumphant domination of polygonal structures was short-lived: The evolution of Victoria Houses was about to make the next radical turn. The same concerns about the expense of heating round houses, which rendered them obsolete, prompted architects to look for more and better ways to incorporate Victoria Houses into larger conservatories made up of a series of greenhouses that were designed specifically for different groups of plants.

An early example of this trend, dating from 1899, can be seen in the Münster Botanical Garden in the Westphalia region of Germany. There, a decagonal house, 10 m (33 feet) wide, was placed contiguous with another warm house—a simple low structure with a single span roof that in turn was attached to a similar cool house. The entrance to the Victoria House led through a small vestibule connecting it to the warm house.

When in 1897 the Royal Botanical Garden in Berlin began relocating from Schöneberg to the Dahlem district, a new conservatory complex covering 0.8 hectares (2 acres) was designed by royal architect Alfred Koerner. Koerner positioned his Victoria House, 17 m (56 feet) long and 15 m (49 feet) wide, on the axis with the iconic Great Tropical House and connected both structures with a passageway. The distal end of the Victoria House took on a form of half of what otherwise would be a fourteen-sided rotunda, while a rectangular frame with a single span roof made up the other half.

Inside was a pool for *Victoria*, 10 m (33 feet) long by 8 m (26 feet) wide, rectangular at one end and rounded off at the other to fit under the half-dome roof. This large pool was complemented by smaller tanks for other aquatic plants along the

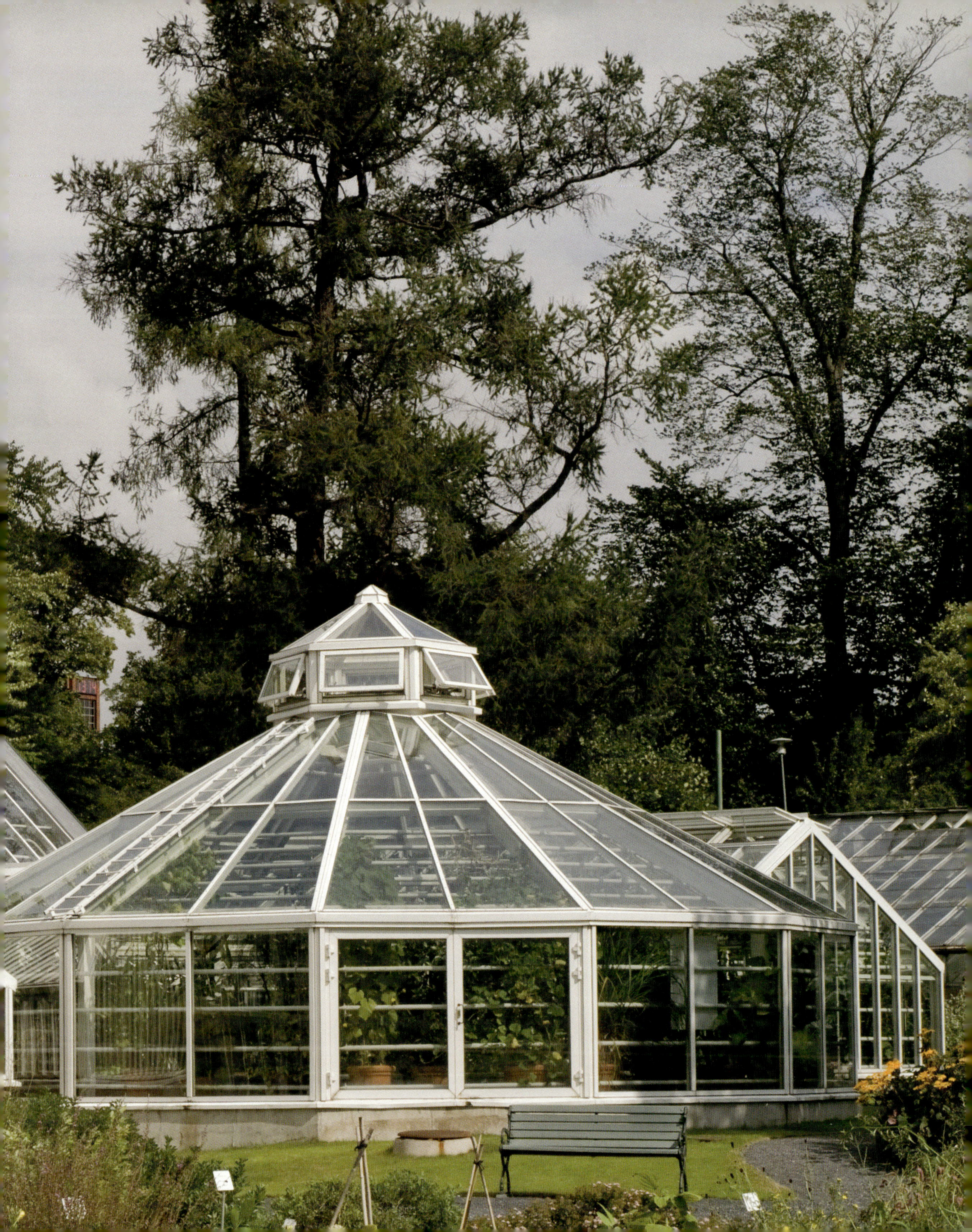

Zum
Konzert

house perimeter. In this form, the Victoria House complemented the Great Tropical House, 60 m (197 feet) wide and 23 m (75 feet) high, which towered over it from almost every vantage point. Dahlem's house was also unusual in that it had a lower story below the tank where submerged plants could be viewed. It also served as an entrance to the whole conservatory complex. Although the Victoria House was finished in 1909, it was not opened to the eager public until the entire garden's official inauguration in 1910. Like the rest of the conservatory complex, it was destroyed in an air raid during World War II; it was later rebuilt and reopened in 1950.

Koerner's Dahlem conservatory design received high praise. He himself was recognized with the Order of the Red Eagle, one of Prussia's highest medals (Lack 2004). His innovative integration of the Victoria House into the conservatory complex was also well received, as it permitted visitors to tour all of the greenhouses without stepping outside—a welcome feature in colder climates. Koerner's layout established a new model that was emulated in botanical gardens across Europe and beyond.

In 1923, the University of Bonn began replacing old greenhouses, including the round 1878 Victoria House in the Poppelsdorf Botanical Garden. Its new Victoria House was connected to the dominant Palm House, analogous to the Dahlem layout. Bonn's house, which was much simpler in design, had its distal end shaped as a half dome of an octagonal rotunda.

In Munich, too, new conservatories erected in the Nymphenburg Botanical Garden had a Victoria House attached directly to the Palm House, the largest in the whole complex. Similarly, in the National Botanical Garden of Belgium in Meise, the Plant Palace, which opened in 1960 and was made up of thirteen interconnecting greenhouses, had its axis defined by the Palm House on the north end and the Victoria House on the south end. All the other houses were subordinate and laid out east and west. The 27-m (89-foot) long by 22-m (72-foot) wide Victoria House had its free end in an octagonal half rotunda, while the opposite rectangular end was inserted into the conservatory complex. Inside, it featured a pool, 17.5 m (57 feet) long by 15 m (49 feet) wide, much larger than its predecessor in Dahlem.

Parallel to these models—which effectively crossbred the freestanding Victoria Houses with large conservatory complexes—

The 1909 Victoria House in the Berlin-Dahlem Botanical Garden is attached to the Great Tropical House, which towers over it. The lower level allows for viewing submerged plants.
TOMASZ ANIŚKO / LONGWOOD GARDENS

Palaces and Pools

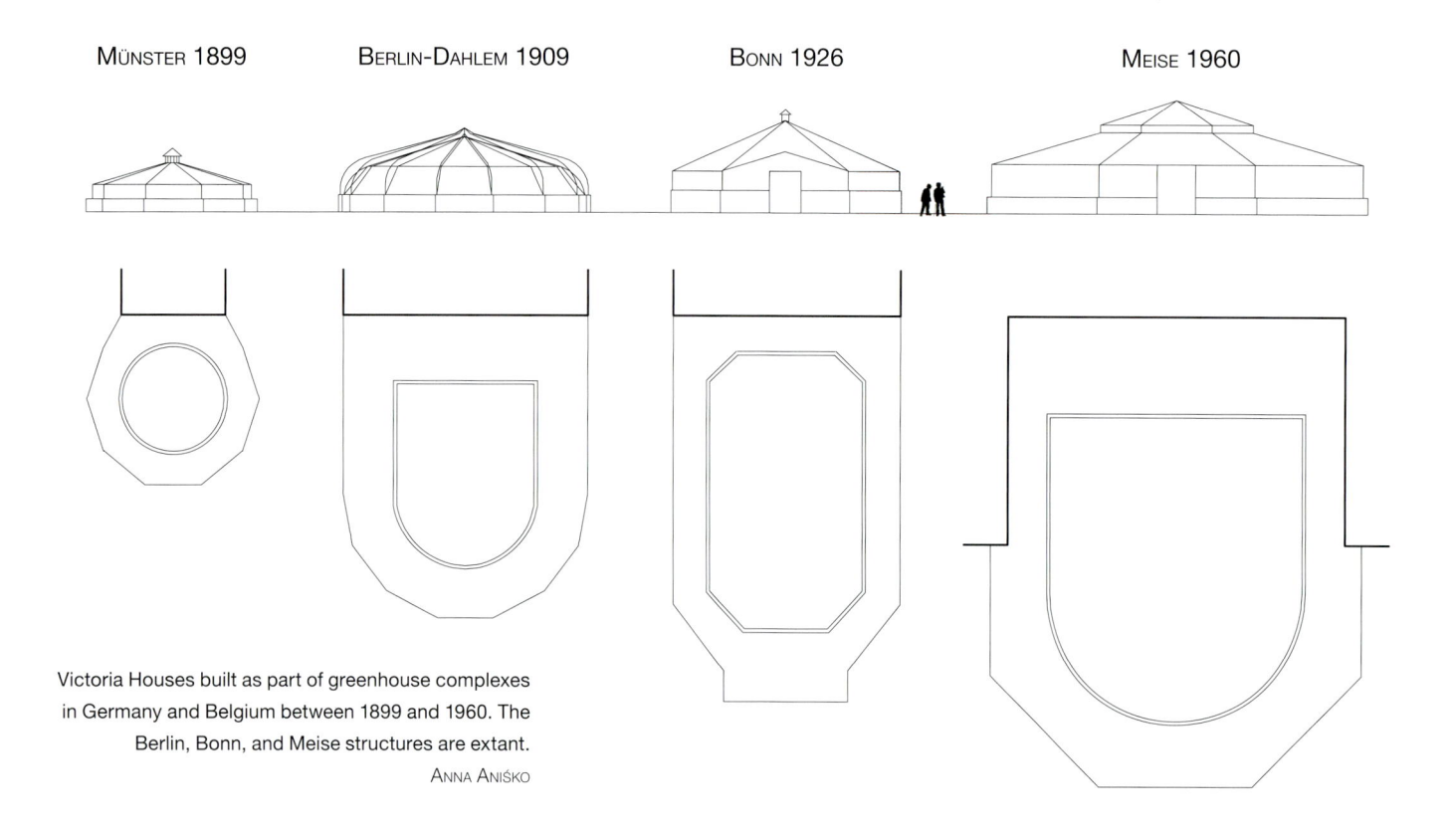

MÜNSTER 1899   BERLIN-DAHLEM 1909   BONN 1926   MEISE 1960

Victoria Houses built as part of greenhouse complexes in Germany and Belgium between 1899 and 1960. The Berlin, Bonn, and Meise structures are extant.
ANNA ANIŚKO

In Meise outside Brussels, the 1960 Plant Palace in the National Botanical Garden of Belgium includes a Victoria House that is 27 m (89 feet) long by 22 m (72 feet) wide.
TOMASZ ANIŚKO / LONGWOOD GARDENS

there were more radical changes taking place in how *Victoria* structures were designed. In the late nineteenth century, New York firm Lord & Burnham began the trend of completely integrating Victoria Houses into the overall layout of the conservatory, as seen in their structures in Golden Gate Park in San Francisco in 1878 and Schenley Park in Pittsburgh in 1893. Connected on both ends to other houses of the complex, they gradually lost their distinctive architecture and evolved to function as aquatic rooms in much larger plant palaces. The Allegheny Conservatory in Schenley Park, known today as the Phipps Conservatory, featured an elegant octagonal Victoria Room with a curved, two-tiered dome roof that was connected on three sides to lower rectangular houses. It no longer defined the main axis of the conservatory but instead terminated one of its two main wings. A matching Fern Room terminated the other.

Over the course of the twentieth century, integrating the queen lily room into a maze of smaller greenhouses forming a conservatory complex became the dominant style. Initially, these rooms retained some degree of prominence among the other houses in the complex. This can be seen in the Botanical Garden in Leiden, Netherlands. Here, while the 1938 square Victoria House (which replaced an 1872 circular house) was designed at the intersection of three attached rectangular houses, it was elevated on top of a masonry head house. In later variants of this model, however, *Victoria* rooms became externally indistinguishable from other houses. The 1970 Display House at Chatsworth, the 1983 Glasshouses of the Botanical Gardens in Jena, Germany, and the 2000 Pavilions of the Liberec Botanic Garden in the Czech Republic illustrate this development.

In the latter half of the twentieth century, the complexes of small interlinking greenhouses gave way to spacious conservatories with large-scale exhibits of world flora. Rooms devoted solely to *Victoria*—the last vestiges of her former prestige—disappeared. In their place, pools featuring an assortment of

The 1893 Victoria Room of the Phipps Conservatory was given an octagonal two-tiered dome and was attached on three sides to other houses of the complex.
TOMASZ ANIŚKO / LONGWOOD GARDENS

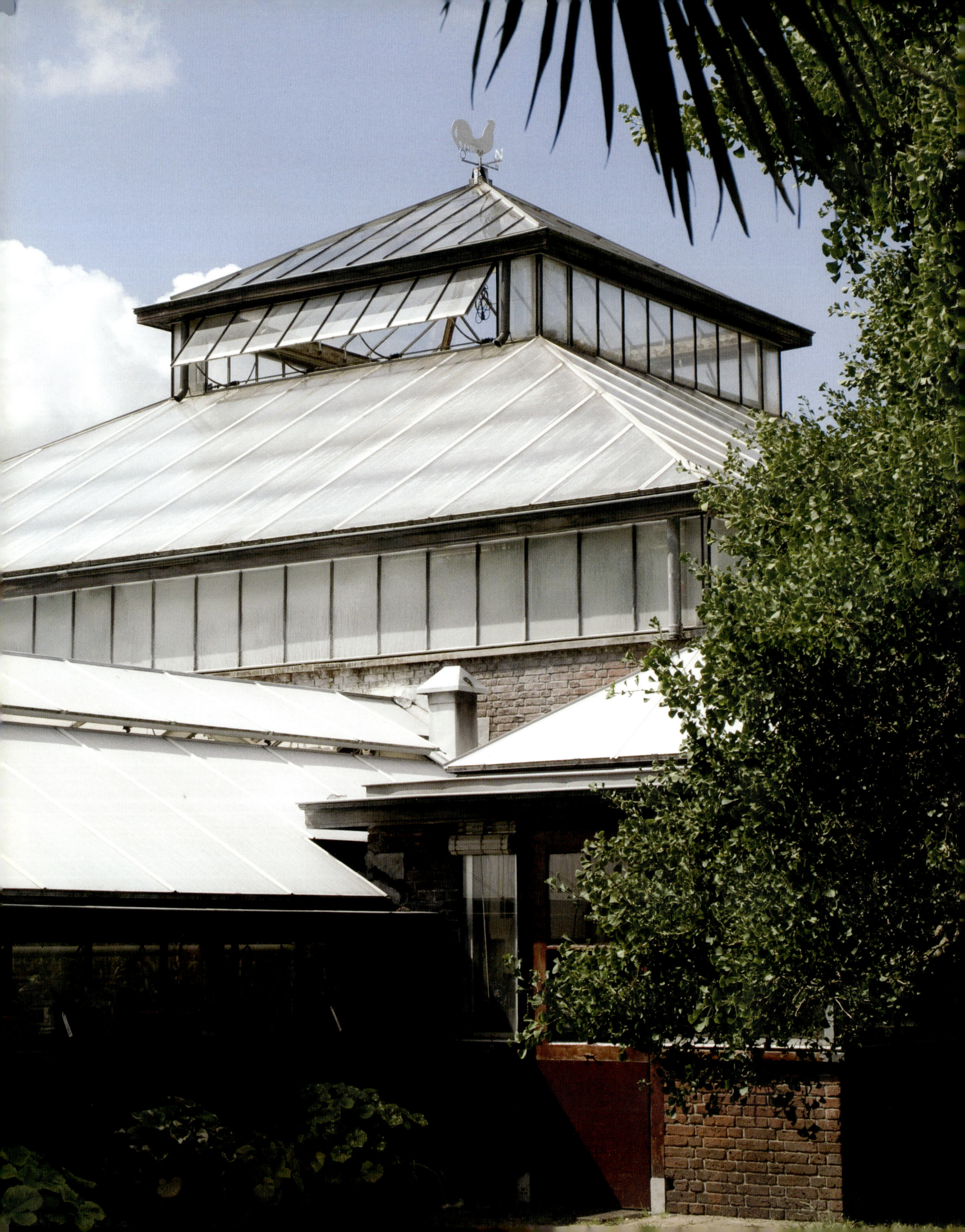

aquatic plant life, including the giant lilies of South America, were incorporated into larger displays of tropical vegetation.

Some of these broke sharply with traditional greenhouse design. For example, extravagantly modern structures like the 1960 Climatron at the Missouri Botanical Garden in St. Louis, the 1987 Tropicarium in Frankfurt's Palmengarten, the 1995 Tropenhaus at the Graz Botanical Garden in Austria, and the 2000 Tropical Conservatory of the Beijing Botanical Garden all assimilated *Victoria* into displays of reconstructed mangroves or rain forests.

For the evolution of the Victoria House, this could mean only one thing: the gradual demise of the building's distinctive architectural form, which would eventually lead to its extinction. Deprived of her privileged position, the queen of the Vegetable Kingdom was dethroned. Instead, she was amalgamated into shared exhibits with her

The conservatory complex that opened in the Liberec Botanic Garden in 2000 accommodated *Victoria* inside its Neotropis Pavilion, which was externally indistinguishable from the other pavilions.
TOMASZ ANIŚKO / LONGWOOD GARDENS

In 1938, an unconventional second-story Victoria House was built in the Botanical Garden in Leiden to replace the 1872 standalone house. It is connected on three sides to other sections of the greenhouse complex.
TOMASZ ANIŚKO / LONGWOOD GARDENS

PALACES AND POOLS 383

The 1960 Climatron at the Missouri Botanical Garden in St. Louis included *Victoria* lilies in its rain forest exhibit.
TOMASZ ANIŚKO / LONGWOOD GARDENS

Opened in 1987, the Tropicarium of the Palmengarten in Frankfurt features giant water lilies, both indoors and outdoors, as part of the exhibit in the Mangrove House.
TOMASZ ANIŚKO / LONGWOOD GARDENS

384 VICTORIA: THE SEDUCTRESS

former "humble vassals," and gradually even her regal name lost its former luster and was dropped from the appellations applied to the new structures she inhabited. Today, one often finds *Victoria* not in a "temple" devoted solely to her as the nineteenth-century Dutch desired, but in various Aquarium, Mangrove, Rain Forest, and Neotropical Houses.

But the evolution of the Victoria House did not come to an end at the turn of the twenty-first century. On the contrary, in 1982 Romanian architects had already created a striking geodesic version of the classic Victoria House, along with a matching Palm House for the Botanical Garden in Jibou. A bold and courageous aesthetic statement, the Jibou Victoria House appears as a futuristic capsule containing strange life forms transported from a world away, which landed among the pristine bucolic scenery of the Carpathian Mountains.

The 1999 Victoria House designed by architect John O'Connell and sculptor Simon Verity for La Mortella on the Italian island of Ischia broke from the traditional interior arrangement and decorum. Although it features a simple single-span-roofed structure on the outside, inside it has a pool nested below a curved wall studded with craggy rocks. An enormous boulder is sculpted into a mask—a stone reproduction of an earlier motif that was designed for the front curtain of *Façade*, a 1922 musical. William Walton, proprietor of La Mortella, wrote the composition for *Façade*. This symbolic stone mask doubles as a fountain that is constantly renewing water in the pool below. Is it a theatrical stage, a mysterious grotto, or a temple of meditation? The interpretation of this intimate, surreal space inhabited by giant lilies is left to the visitor's imagination.

The 1982 geodesic Victoria House in the Jibou Botanical Garden (foreground) is complemented by a larger Palm House of similar construction standing nearby.
TOMASZ ANIŚKO / LONGWOOD GARDENS

The 1995 Tropenhaus in the Botanical Garden of Graz shelters *Victoria* under its striking slanted roof.
TOMASZ ANIŚKO / LONGWOOD GARDENS

PALACES AND POOLS   385

The 1999 Victoria House at La Mortella has simple lines and classical proportions, but it encloses an exuberant and imaginative interior.
Tomasz Aniśko / Longwood Gardens

Yet another radical transformation of the Victoria House took place in 2007 in Australia, at the Amazon Waterlily Pavilion designed by Steve Duddy for the Adelaide Botanic Gardens. This third-generation edifice replaced the 1957 structure, which in turn supplanted the original 1868 house. While the original pool inside was retained, the outer shell of the new pavilion embraces the contemporary architectural vocabulary and the latest technological advances. Its roof, like the one at the first Lily House at Chatsworth a century and half earlier, was also inspired by the structure of the *Victoria* leaf. Transparent and airy, the Adelaide pavilion is built almost entirely of glass—six and a half tons of it. The design gives new meaning to the concept of a queen's house and sets its evolution on a new course for the twenty-first century.

The Amazon Waterlily Pavilion at the Adelaide Botanic Gardens presents a remarkable twenty-first-century interpretation of the venerable Victoria House ideal.
Adelaide Botanic Gardens

Palaces and Pools 387

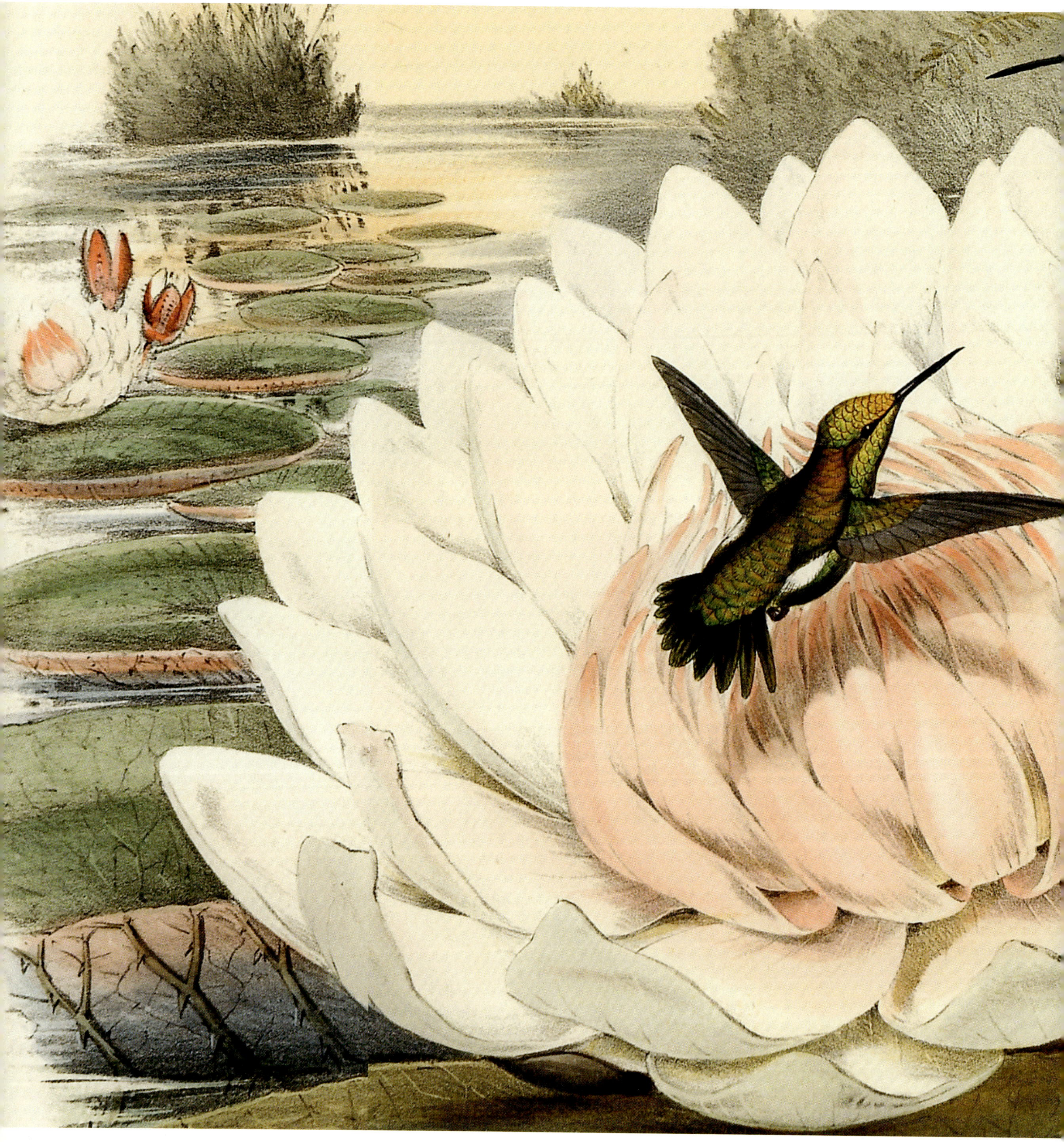

chapter 20

INSPIRED ARTS

SINCE THE DAWN OF CIVILIZATION, PLANTS HAVE BEEN an inexhaustible source of inspiration for all forms of art. Representations and interpretations of flowers, fruits, leaves, vines, and trees of countless specimens have filled canvases, verses, musical scores, carpets, fabrics, and façades created by many cultures. Plants have been transformed into every artistic medium known to humankind and endowed with symbolic meaning. They have nurtured and sustained our language, imagination, and aesthetic canons. As a result, many plant species have become cultural icons and have spurred social phenomena.

The giant water lily is included among these. "That *Victoria regia* has inspired beautiful verses, melodious songs, sublime landscapes . . . who would doubt it!" wrote Francisco Vidal y Careta in 1920 (translated by Emily Vera). Unlike plants of the Old World like the Egyptian papyrus, Greek acanthus, or Chinese bamboo, which had millennia to define their place in our collective consciousness, the Amazonian nymph has done so in a mere century and a half. Indeed, despite our short engagement with the South American giant, the extent to which she has impacted the world of art—which was already saturated with floral references and imagery—is surprising.

A highly improbable juxtaposition of Poortman's emerald hummingbird and *Victoria amazonica*, deliberately chosen for the lily's fame rather than appropriateness, created by John Gould for his work *A Monograph of the Trochilidae* (1861–1887).
SPECIAL COLLECTIONS, LINDERMAN LIBRARY, LEHIGH UNIVERSITY

Inspired by the leaves of the South American lilies, floating cities called *Lilypads* are designed to house the climatic refugees of the future.
VINCENT CALLEBAUT ARCHITECTURES

borrows from the ribbed model of the lily leaf. "This resembles nothing so much as the underside of a *Victoria regia* water lily in concrete," wrote Smith, exalting the superlative qualities of Nervi's building, which in his view had "few equals in our time."

The *Victoria* leaf's paradoxical strength is irresistibly alluring to architects, who are often challenged to design vast self-supporting structures with minimal building material. Even more directly than in the works of Paxton, Wright, or Nervi, the *Victoria* leaf can be seen in the 2008 design of a floating city—not yet built—developed by Belgian architect Vincent Callebaut. His prototype of a self-contained and self-sufficient amphibious city called the *Lilypad* is modeled on a giant lily leaf magnified 250 times. Callebaut envisioned the *Lilypad* to house the "climate refugees" of the future who will be driven from coastal areas flooded by rising seas in response to global warming. Even if the *Lilypad* turns out to be just another utopian ideal, it has provoked much conversation among architects on how to address the challenges brought about by climate change.

Before Callebaut, another architect dreamed of houses and cities that would combine the ingenuity of humans with the vitality of Nature to mitigate the effects of industrialization. Bruno Taut, an influential German architect and urban planner, also found inspiration in the leaves of *Victoria*. In 1920, Taut wrote a script for the movie *Die Galoschen des Glück* (The Lucky Shoes). In the story, a desolate youth escapes a blighted city and is magically transported into a beautiful fairy-tale city built on floating lily pads and made of opalescent domes reflected in the water.

Taut never realized this vision, either as a movie or as a city. But David Nielsen (2010) argues that Taut's most iconic building, the 1914 *Glashaus* designed for the Werkbund Exhibition in Cologne, expressed the same concept of architecture bringing Nature back into cities. Referencing the Victoria Houses found in many European gardens in those days, Taut's structure had a central pool spilling into a water cascade that was covered by a striking prismatic glass dome. The reinforced-concrete structure of the dome was reminiscent of the network of veins on the underside of a *Victoria* leaf. Although the building was dismantled shortly after the exhibition closed, the *Glashaus* had a profound influence on early modernist architecture.

A PERMANENT IMPRESSION

As long as the *Victoria* leaf floats in water, its weight-carrying capacity appears to contradict the laws of physics. Removed from its aquatic milieu, however, it deflates within minutes and desiccates, revealing its true fragile character. The leaf's ephemeral nature may explain why a number of sculptors chose to create realistic representations of *Victoria* that were close to Nature's original design yet were created in a long-lasting if not permanent medium.

Such life-size casts of the queen lily leaf were created for the Botanical Garden in Amsterdam and the Conservatory of Flowers in Golden Gate Park in San Francisco. Amsterdam's bronze impression of the *Victoria* leaf, created by Hein Kramer, stands at the entrance to the Drie Klimatenkas, or the House of Three Climates, the garden's largest conservatory. The lily pad is pitched vertically to show off the intricate venations of its underside. It is also large enough to double as a screen and hide unsightly trash containers. The work by Stephen Hirt in San Francisco is even more realistic. Made of bronze, steel, and glass, Hirt's *Victoria* features several lifelike leaves and flowers in their natural horizontal orientation yet suspended on fantastically contorted petioles above a pool where a living lily floats.

While the Amsterdam and San Francisco pieces are unique and irreproducible, Arizona artist John Wayne Jackson has devised a more affordable option. Jackson specializes in making limited-edition casts of large leaves using a concrete formula of his own invention. He has created permanent, lifelike *Victoria* leaves that can be hung as wall decorations. Jackson first added the *Victoria* leaf to his portfolio in 2008, working from a living model that was flown to his Scottsdale studio from Longwood Gardens.

Bruno Taut's most iconic building, the *Glashaus*, was shown at the 1914 Werkbund Exhibition in Cologne, Germany.
Foto Marburg / Art Resource, New York

In the San Francisco Conservatory of Flowers, Steven Hirt's *Victoria* of bronze, steel, and glass hovers in the air, suspended above a pool occupied by living lilies.
DAVID WAKELY

Aspiring to "bring permanence to that which would otherwise wither and die," Jackson created what could be considered a faithful reproduction of the *Victoria* leaf if not for the dyes and stains that are liberally applied to the stone's surface.

FURNITURE AND FINE ART

Jackson's work follows a well-established tradition of representing *Victoria* in a variety of decorative pieces. This tradition began soon after the nymph appeared in England for the first time in 1849. Designers of that era quickly exploited the lily's popularity by incorporating her motif in mantelpieces, chandeliers, gas brackets, carpets, fabrics, wallpapers, vases, pitchers, cups, saucers, and cigar boxes, among others. Some historians suggest that pieces created during this outburst of the *Victoria* craze heralded the birth of the Art Nouveau style later in the nineteenth century (Elliott 1996).

One would be mistaken to assume, however, that *Victoria*'s charm works only on artists creating decorative pieces for popular consumption that may not necessarily win approval from curators of fine art museums. In 1998, Chicago-born Keith Edmier—whose work is displayed in some of the world's most prestigious art galleries, including the Tate Modern in London and the Museum of Modern Art in New York—created *Victoria Regia (First Night Bloom)* and *Victoria Regia (Second Night Bloom)*. These two works were rendered in a concoction of nontraditional materials, including polyester resin, silicone rubber, dental acrylic, acrylic paint, polyurethane, and steel. Rising 3 m (10 feet) high and painstakingly detailed, Edmier's

A life-size bronze cast of Hein Kramer's *Victoria* leaf stands at the entrance to Drie Klimatenkas in the Amsterdam Botanical Garden.
TOMASZ ANIŚKO / LONGWOOD GARDENS

Two life-size works by Keith Edmier, *Victoria Regia (First Night Bloom)* from the Collection Akzo Nobel Art Foundation, Arnhem, and *Victoria Regia (Second Night Bloom)* from the Collection Angelika Taschen, Berlin, shown here in 2007 in the Hessel Museum of Bard College.
KEITH EDMIER

Steve Messam's installation of *Lily* for the 2010 Tatton Park Biennial, a contemporary art exhibit in Cheshire, England.
STEVE MESSAM

representations of *Victoria* may be seen as botanical equivalents of Madame Tussaud's wax figures, but they are much more than just hyperrealistic models. Holland Cotter (2008), an art critic for the *New York Times*, writes that while Edmier's "exacting craftsmanship" has "the chill of the mortician's art," eroticism pervades his work. "It is most overt in botanical imagery," Cotter states, pointing to two *Victoria* pieces, "the repeated sculptures of various monstrous flowering plants, which in nature are both male and female or conspicuously one or the other." With his art, Edmier has lifted the lily out of her tranquil, secluded aqueous habitat and put her on display for everyone to examine—and be startled by—the nymph's perceived nudity and sexuality, monstrous or not.

Moving past the symbolic and contemplative realism of Edmier's work are humorous and engaging sculptural pieces that double as furniture, created by Fernando and Humberto Campana, Brazilian artists based in São Paulo. In 2007, the Campanas exhibited a new outdoor edition of *Vitória Régia* seats at the Victoria and Albert Museum

VICTORIA: THE SEDUCTRESS

in London to mark the museum's 150th anniversary. True to the Campana brothers' signature use of commonplace, often recycled materials and bright colors, *Vitória Régia* was crafted from rolled fabrics, carpets, rubber mats, and nets. This innovative use of everyday materials, combined with one of the Amazon's most iconic metaphors, captures the vibrancy and energy so characteristic of the Campanas's designs. In addition, the works have the form and functionality of a stool, speaking to the instinctive urge most people get to sit upon the lily's floating leaves.

While *Victoria* leaves have been transformed into art pieces that stand stiffly upright, or are suspended in the air, or take the form of a four-legged stool, they have not often performed the function that Nature intended—that is, to float. In 2010, however, Steve Messam, an environmental artist from northern England, created a site-specific installation titled *Lily* for the Tatton Park Biennial, a contemporary art exhibition in Cheshire, England. Messam's works often create visual elements in wider landscapes to encourage viewers to perceive familiar environments or objects in completely new ways. His installation at Tatton consisted of scores of lily pads up to 5 m (16 feet) in diameter, made of foam and fabric, painted fiery red, and floating in the park's lake. He envisioned *Lily* as an homage to the history of Tatton. The linear arrangement of lily pads stretching for 1.5 km (nearly a mile) suggests the original course of the river Lily, which was dammed in the twelfth century to create the lake now known as Tatton Mere. Messam's choice of *Victoria* referenced Joseph Paxton, who designed Tatton's fernery and Italian garden, while the red color recalled Humphry Repton, the great eighteenth-century landscape designer who worked on enhancements to Tatton's estate. Repton's designs were customarily first presented as a collection of before-and-after views known as *Red Books* (for their binding). Messam intended this river of red *Victoria* leaves to be viewed not only by park visitors walking around the lake or taking boat rides, but also by passengers of planes flying in and out of the nearby Manchester airport. Ironically, the excessive buoyancy and unruly drifting of the lily pads in windy weather forced Messam to remove his installation after the first month. *Victoria* as art clearly did not measure up to the real thing.

As Messam's experience shows, making *Victoria* into an art piece that can float comes with its own set of challenges, but placing other artwork in the water among live giant lilies has been tried and tested many times. In St. Louis, the Missouri Botanical Garden's outdoor water lily pool, *Victoria*'s summer home, has become a favorite spot for displaying sculptural works of some of the best-known twentieth-century artists.

In 1972, Alexander Calder's *Five Rudders* was exhibited together with *Victoria* in the water lily pools at the Missouri Botanical Garden. Today, Calder's work can be viewed at the Milfred Lane Kemper Art Museum in St. Louis.
MISSOURI BOTANICAL GARDEN

It is a veritable aqueous gallery. In 1972, the lily pool hosted *Five Rudders*, a 1964 piece by Alexander Calder, an acclaimed master of stabiles and mobiles, abstract sculptural forms that are stationary or moving. In *Five Rudders,* Calder combined both of these forms to create a bright red stabile base and five mobile biomorphic elements that were painted contrasting black above. In the garden's pool, Calder's kinetic creation performed together with *Victoria*. As the rudders responded to the wind by gently rotating around the base, so did the plant's leaves on the water's surface, anchored by long petioles to their submerged rhizome. Through these seemingly choreographed, almost hypnotic movements, the nymph engaged in a dialogue with the sculpture and became an art object herself.

Calder's artwork established a precedent that led to the water lily pool being invaded by Swedish sculptor Carl Milles's three *Angel Musicians* fifteen years later. Renowned for his fountains and monumental works, which appear in many major cities across Europe and America, Milles's *Angels* were inspired by a dream in which winged creatures with pipes, horns, and flutes enveloped him in music. The 1950 statues—now permanently exhibited in the lily pool and elevated on granitic shafts—hover high above the water surface, each dancing and playing a wind instrument. Emanating the

The water lily pool at the Missouri Botanical Garden in St. Louis is transformed into an outdoor gallery where the South American nymphs create an otherworldly ambience for Carl Milles's *Angel Musicians* and Dale Chihuly's *Walla Wallas*.
TOMASZ ANIŚKO / LONGWOOD GARDENS

VICTORIA: THE SEDUCTRESS

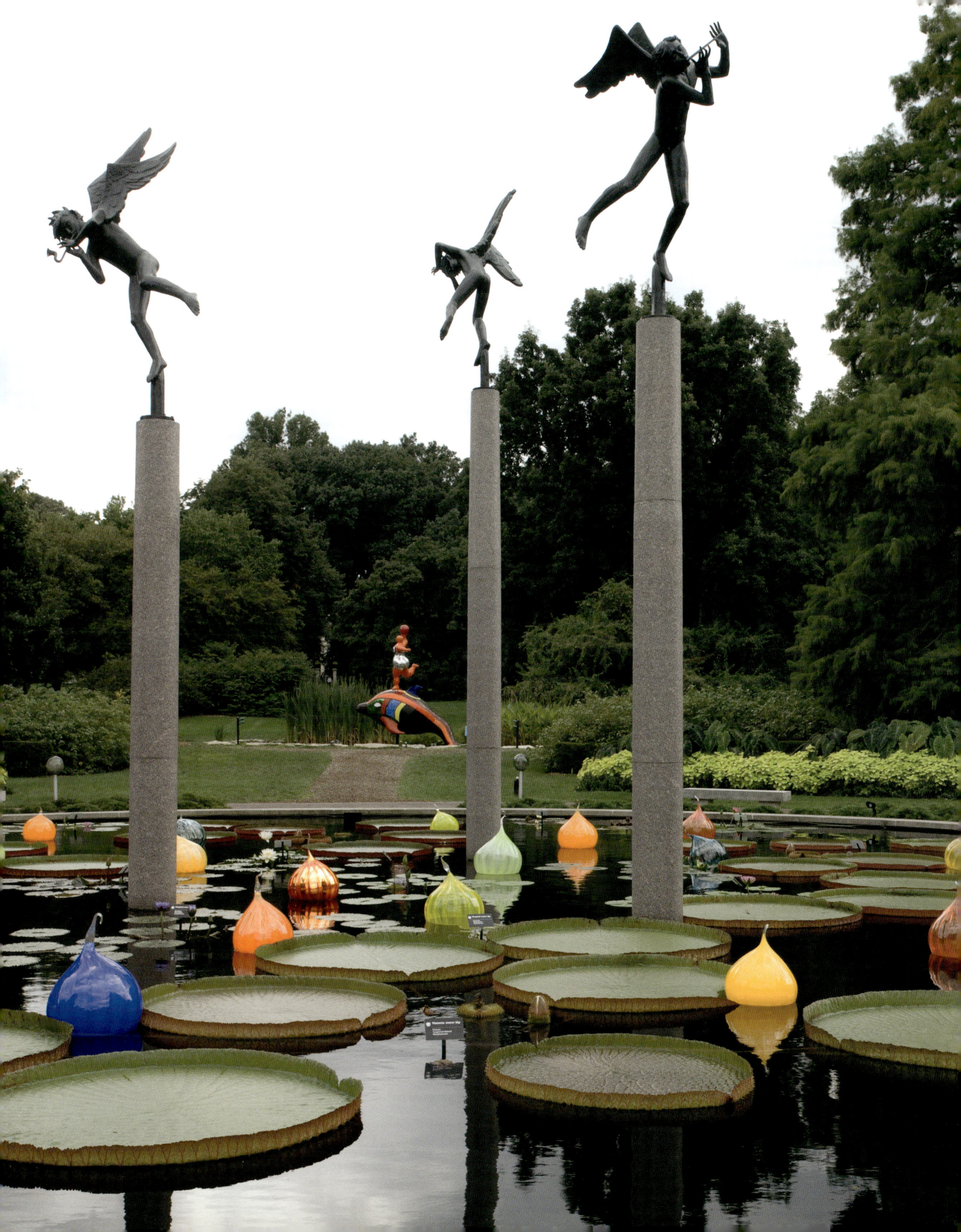

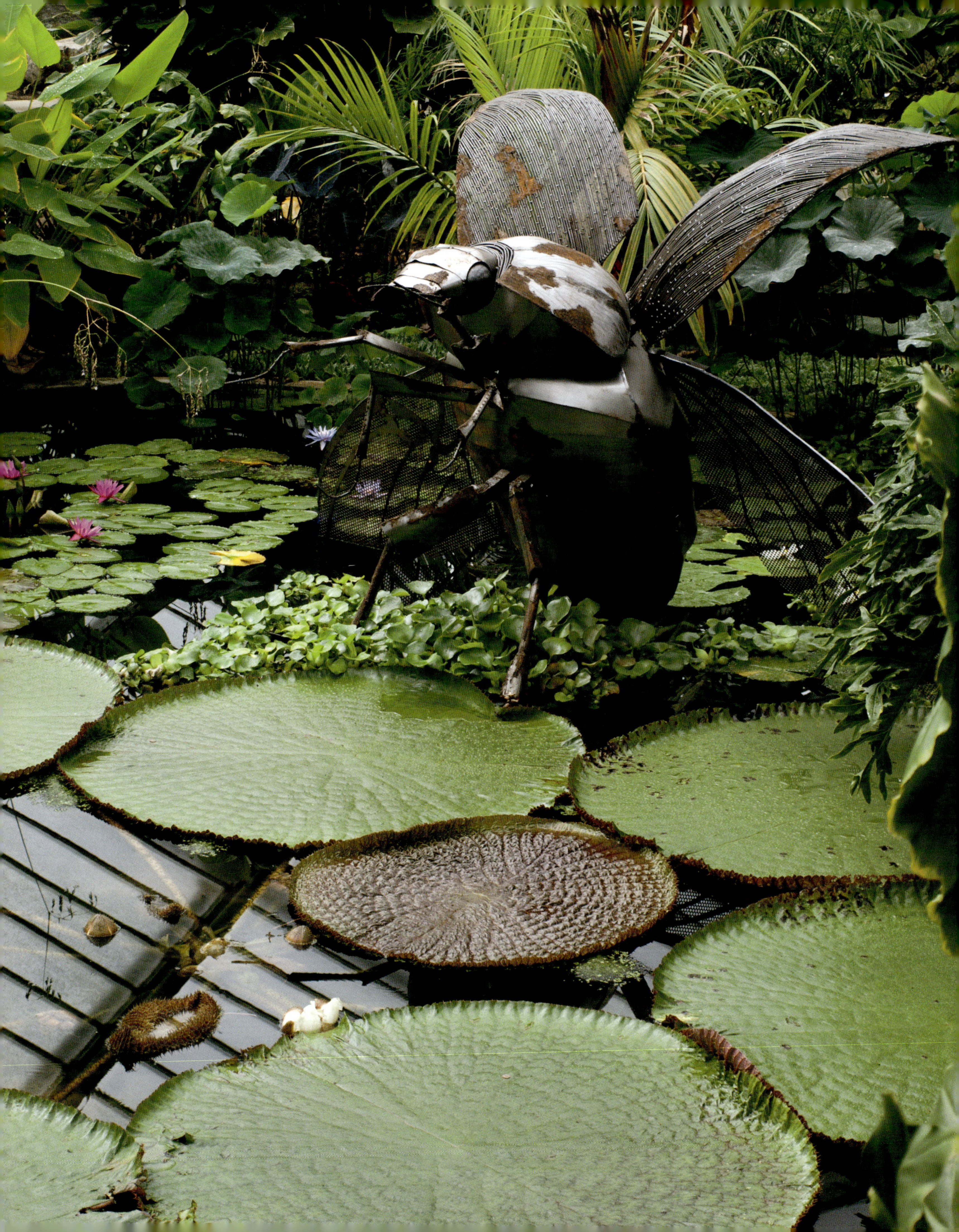

innocence and playfulness of childhood, Milles's *Angels* appear perfectly at home in the fairy-tale-like atmosphere created by the out-of-this-world colossal lilies.

Below the *Angels* and among the lilies float the latest additions to this aquatic gallery. In 2006, cheerfully colored, bulbous blown-glass pieces created by Dale Chihuly, a celebrated American glass sculptor, were added to the pool. Chihuly's pieces are known as *Walla Wallas* after the sweet onions grown near Walla Walla in Washington. They may also be likened to Hershey's Kisses, a popular type of American chocolates—an association that is far more appealing than onions and more fitting for a wonderland inhabited by aquatic nymphs and musical angels.

FROM FAIRY TALES TO FAÇADES

Other artists bringing their pieces to gardens have also sensed the giant lily's surreal qualities. In the Fairchild Tropical Botanic Garden in Coral Gables, Florida, French sculptor Claude Lalanne of the husband-and-wife duo Les Lalanne chose the *Victoria* pool to display her *Dimetrodon II*. This 1998 topiary sculpture featured a fictitious dinosaur made of stainless steel, copper, and living plants. It is difficult to image a more fitting scene for such a fantastic creature. Les Lalanne's work relies on the natural forms of animals and plants, embodying the pair's credo that "the supreme art is the art of living." In this context, the tropical nymph epitomizes this idea as much as the artwork itself.

In contrast, Ross White's 2010 installation in the lily pool at the Royal Botanic Gardens, Kew, alluded to a creature that actually existed. White's gigantic steel *Beetle* emanated industrial strength as it hovered precariously over *Victoria* flowers in the Princess of Wales Conservatory as part of an educational exhibit on pollinators in 2010. White, a British theater designer, captured the steel-bodied insect as it approached the flower. He also added patches of rust to its metallic armor to emulate the pollen carried by the scarab beetles in the Amazon. Despite this attempt at realism and ecological pedagogy, White's installation retained fairy tale ambience. Readers of Hans Christian Andersen's stories may recognize this arrangement as the scene from *Thumbelina* when a mischievous cockchafer picks up the little maiden off her lily pad. One only had to imagine Thumbelina on the *Victoria* leaf for the whole act to come alive.

Victoria water lilies surround Claude Lalanne's *Dimetrodon II*, a unique copper, steel, and stainless steel topiary that was part of the 2010 Les Lalanne exhibit at the Fairchild Tropical Botanic Garden in Coral Gables, Florida.
TOMASZ ANIŚKO / LONGWOOD GARDENS

Ross White's 2010 installation, *Beetle*, in the Princess of Wales Conservatory at the Royal Botanic Gardens, Kew.
TOMASZ ANIŚKO / LONGWOOD GARDENS

INSPIRED ARTS 401

This innocent expression of theatrical whimsy at Kew may have not been entirely intentional. Yet there is no doubt that the installation in the Victoria House at La Mortella—the garden of British composer William Walton and his wife, Susana, on the Italian island of Ischia—is a superbly choreographed spectacle. One of Walton's best-known musical compositions was *Façade— An Entertainment*, written in 1922 to the poems of Edith Sitwell. The poems were recited from behind a curtain so as to hide the performers' visual personalities. The curtain, designed by English painter and printmaker John Piper, featured a large mask in its center. Performers spoke through a megaphone held behind this mask. *Façade* was as controversial as it was successful, launching Walton's career as one of twentieth-century Britain's greatest composers.

When Susana Walton decided to build a Victoria House at La Mortella in 1999, she commissioned Irish architect John O'Connell and Simon Verity, a British stone sculptor. Their assignment was to create not only a place to grow *Victoria,* but also a stage to represent the many years her husband spent in the garden composing his music. This was accomplished by creating a stone version of *Bocca,* Piper's mask from *Façade.* Verity sculpted the mask out of an enormous boulder, which took up the center of a massive wall. This provided a backdrop for a pool—or a stage on which *Victoria* performed—at its base. In Verity's version, water flows continuously out of *Bocca*'s gaping mouth while a Muse in the form of a bird whispers in his ear. The eyes of the mask were sculpted differently: One appears to be looking inward, while the other is seeing the outer world.

Susana Walton completed this stunning scene by applying her extraordinary skill in making

A grotto-like interior of the Victoria House at La Mortella features *Bocca* by Simon Verity, which recalls a mask designed by John Piper for the performance of *Façade—An Entertainment,* the 1922 composition written by William Walton.

DMITRY TERESHCHENKO / GIARDINI LA MORTELLA

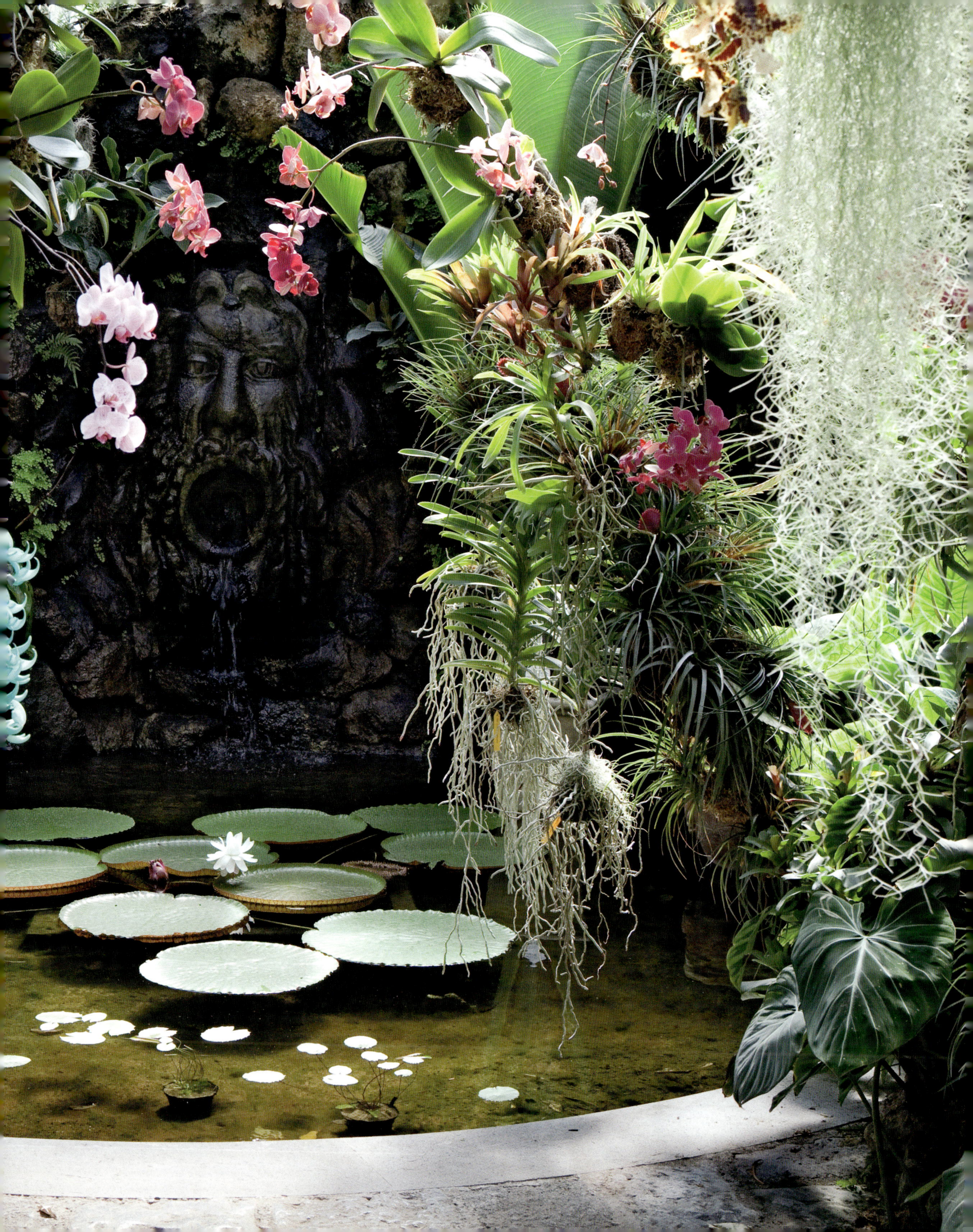

plant compositions. Here, the tropical nymph is given center stage to perform the mysterious act of raising her flower out of the water, opening it at sunset, transforming herself from female to male, and finally disappearing into the depths of the pool. The result was so spectacular that one year later, after the opening of the Victoria House at La Mortella, the scene was re-created at the Chelsea Flower Show in London. A crowd favorite, it attracted a lot of attention, including—in the tradition of royal patronage—a visit by the Prince of Wales to view the lilies named after his great-great-great-grandmother (Walton 2002).

In La Mortella's Victoria House, one can almost hear *Bocca* spewing his verses of poetry, the Muse whispering into his grotesque ear, and perhaps even Walton's musical accompaniment. But it was the giant water lily's ever-changing nature that inspired American composer Lei Liang to write his *Harp Concerto* during a stay at La Mortella in 2008.

Much like the transformation of the giant lily flower, Liang's concerto for harp and chamber orchestra explored the idea of musical transformation. "I remember," he wrote, "the early mornings before dawn when I visited Victoria House with a torch light, hoping to catch a glimpse of this secret beauty! And the day before I left, I finally was able to witness the complete process. *Victoria* was truly magical" (Liang 2009). Although Liang's *Harp Concerto* is not descriptive of the water lily, its length, pace, and acoustic and emotional subtleties allow the listener to visualize the nymph's flower spreading its blushing petals, fluffing them like a bird-of-paradise, and performing the mysterious transformation.

Lei Liang wrote *Harp Concerto*, inspired by the flowering of the South American lily, during his stay at La Mortella. Here, he is accompanied by Susana Walton (sitting) and garden director Alessandra Vinciguerra.
LEI LIANG

If Liang's contemporary concerto represents one end of the musical landscape, *Victoria*-inspired tangos, boleros, and waltzes of the late nineteenth and early twentieth century perhaps define the other. The amorous, seductive, and choreographed movements of her flowers appealed to composers writing dance music of that era. In Germany, Wilhelm Popp composed a waltz for flute and orchestra titled *Victoria Regia*, while Eduard Künneke wrote a tango-bolero with the same title. In 1927, Argentinean Constantino Gaito composed the ballet *La Flor del Irupé*—a nod to the great lily that inhabited the Paraná and Paraguay rivers of his native country. His compatriot Francisco Garcia wrote the fiery *Irupé, Tango Brilliante*.

THE QUEEN ON FILM

The association of *Victoria* with dance even found its way to the silver screen. In *The Imaginarium of Doctor Parnassus*, a 2009 fantasy film by Terry Gilliam, Maggie Steed portrays an aging woman lured through a mirror to a world powered by her imagination and desires. The magical landscape is filled with giant shoes, jewelry, perfume

Cover page of the score for *Irupé, Tango Brilliante,* by Argentinean composer Francisco Garcia.
LONGWOOD GARDENS LIBRARY AND ARCHIVES

404 VICTORIA: THE SEDUCTRESS

Del Sexto Concurso del Disco Nacional

A los Sres. VICTOR MERCANTE y CONSTANTINO GAITO autores del poema coreográfico "La Flor del Irupé" estrenado el corriente año en el Teatro Colón de Buenos Aires

IRUPE
(FLOR DE LA MESOPOTAMIA ARGENTINA)

TANGO BRILLANTE

MUSICA DE
FRANCISCO GARCIA

Queda hecho el depósito que marca la Ley
PROPIEDAD del AUTOR

Grabado en disco por la orquesta del Maestro ROBERTO FIRPO
De la Asociación Argentina de Editores de Música

Establecimiento Gráfico Musical
Julio Korn
CORRIENTES 931   BUENOS AIRES

PEDRO LUIS FUMAGALI

In this scene from The Wizard of Oz, *Dorothy, played by Judy Garland, stands on a bridge over a stream with artificial* Victoria *lily pads and flowers.*
TURNER ENTERTAINMENT CO., A WARNER BROS. ENTERTAINMENT COMPANY

bottles, and *Victoria* water lilies. A handsome male figure, played by Johnny Depp, enters this dreamy scene, jumping from one lily pad to the next. The two engage in a hypnotic tango on a *Victoria* leaf, which lifts them into the air and transports them deeper into nirvana. While all the elements of this scene are grossly exaggerated, the lily pads are not. Even at life size, they fittingly belong to the realm of fantasy.

A similar take on *Victoria* was employed in another movie seventy years earlier. Instead of an aging woman, there is a young girl played by Judy Garland, while the gallant tango partner is replaced by a benevolent witch portrayed by Billie Burke. The basic premise of the scene from 1939's *The Wizard of Oz,* however, is the same. Upon entering the dreamed-up world of fantasy, the girl is surrounded by supernatural flowers, magnified and colored beyond recognition, the kind that can exist only in a child's imagination. But floating in the stream that runs through this idyllic landscape are artificial *Victoria* lilies, faithfully reproduced and life size. Though the movie script called for lily pads "the size of barrel-tops," not the slightest exaggeration was required to make the aquatic nymph part of this phantasmagoria (Harmetz 1998). *Victoria*'s appearance in Oz demonstrates how the colossal lily often defies comprehension and is perceived as if she belongs to another world—one more attuned to dreams than reality.

While these cinematic blockbuster productions gave the lily only a minor role, Finnish video artist Salla Tykkä made the aquatic nymph the sole star of her short film *Victoria* in 2008. In her work, Tykkä often questions the established ideals of beauty in a world where nothing is as it seems. *Victoria* was created as part of a series of films that explored the meaning of beauty as it applied to four subjects: human, animal, plant, and stone. Filmed at the Botanical Garden of the University of Helsinki, *Victoria* depicts the opening of the nymph's flower at night. The scene is dark when the stark white lily begins her slow, sensuous ballet to the riveting music from Mahler's *Fifth Symphony*. Through lush and captivating cinematography, Tykkä reveals a disturbing side to the exquisite beauty of the nightly ballerina—her connection to the story of European colonialism that took *Victoria* from her faraway home. The irresistible flower embodies its desire for power and domination. Tykkä's point is that beauty can be both seductive and dangerous.

A similar attempt to reveal the giant lily's hidden nature appears in the work of American photographers Jim Wehtje and Jonathan Singer. Their still images show *Victoria* in a dramatic new light. Wehtje, like so many other artists before him, has been drawn to the striking appearance of the underside of *Victoria*'s leaves. Specializing in transmissive radiography, he explores our desire to see the unseen by applying x-ray technology to disparate images, plants among them. While x-rays of human and animal bodies are ubiquitous, similar imaging of botanical subjects is rare. Wehtje's 2010 radiograph of a trio of *Victoria* lily pads reveals with stunning clarity

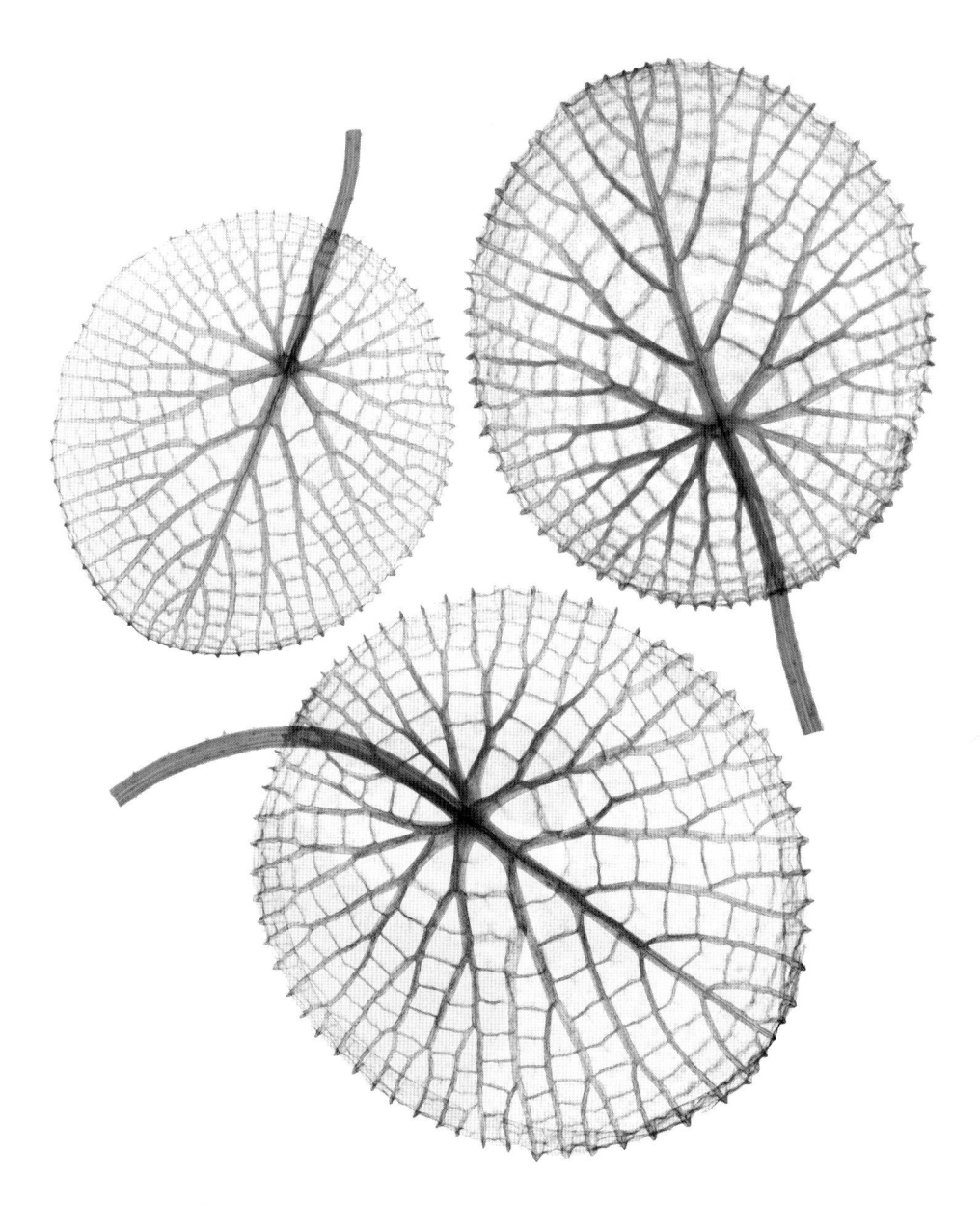

Victoria, a trio of lily pads, is an x-ray image created by Jim Wehtje, an American radiographer, in 2010.
JIM WEHTJE

and precision the dendritic pattern of primary and secondary veins radiating from the central point, which are interconnected by anastomosed concentric veins. This spiderweb of arteries that carry water, air, and nutrients through the nymph's body strongly suggests parallels with our own physical being.

Singer's studio photographs treat botanical subjects with the same precision and attention to visible light as portraits painted by old masters. His oversize images often shock viewers with their stunning details of floral structures that might otherwise escape notice. Bridging the world of science and art, Singer's botanical portraits have been featured in the pages of *Audubon* and *Vanity Fair*. For the opening page of his magnum opus—a collection of 250 images printed in double elephant folio and titled *Botanica Magnifica*—Singer chose the *Victoria* flower, subtly acknowledging her

Jonathan Singer with his *Victoria* triptych, featuring the flower and leaves photographed from above (left) and below (right).
JONATHAN SINGER AND HOWARD SCHATZ

supreme position in the Plant Kingdom. His painterly use of light and color evokes the glamour of the still lifes of the Dutch Golden Age, despite the fact that his images are unreservedly faithful to the living originals.

PORTRAITS IN PAINT AND POETRY

Victoria arrived in Europe too late to be a subject of the old masters, but she still inspired a slew of visually arresting botanical illustrations, many of them reproduced throughout this book. One nineteenth-century artist, however, made a name for herself by portraying floral subjects in lush and usually tropical surroundings. Marianne North, a self-taught English painter, spent thirteen years traveling the

INSPIRED ARTS 409

Victorias Regias, painted by Oswaldo Teixeira in Rio de Janeiro 1928.
Christie's Images / Corbis

world and produced hundreds of works that capture exotic flowers, birds, animals, and scenery in vivid color. She may be admired more for her scientific accuracy and the stamina required to conduct such extensive travels, however, than for her painterly genius. Among North's best-known works is a luxuriant interpretation of the Amazonian lily against a panoramic view of a river. This piece stands apart from the majority of North's works, which were painted in the field during her travels. Her *Victoria regia* was done in England, based on the illustrations Walter Fitch prepared for William Hooker at Kew, as well as on her own memories of traveling in Brazil.

Victoria's alienation from the indigenous landscape—as seen in North's experience with painting *Victoria* in London—may exemplify the fact that European painters could not easily relate to the South American colossus. This was contrary to their intimate relation to *Nymphaea* water lilies so frequently featured by them, with Claude Monet's roughly two hundred fifty paintings of water lilies being a convincing case. In Brazil, however, the nymph's homeland, her likeness can be found in paintings across the entire artistic spectrum—from the sophisticated works of Oswaldo Teixeira, one of South America's most celebrated twentieth-century painters, to the kitschy adornments of souvenir shops.

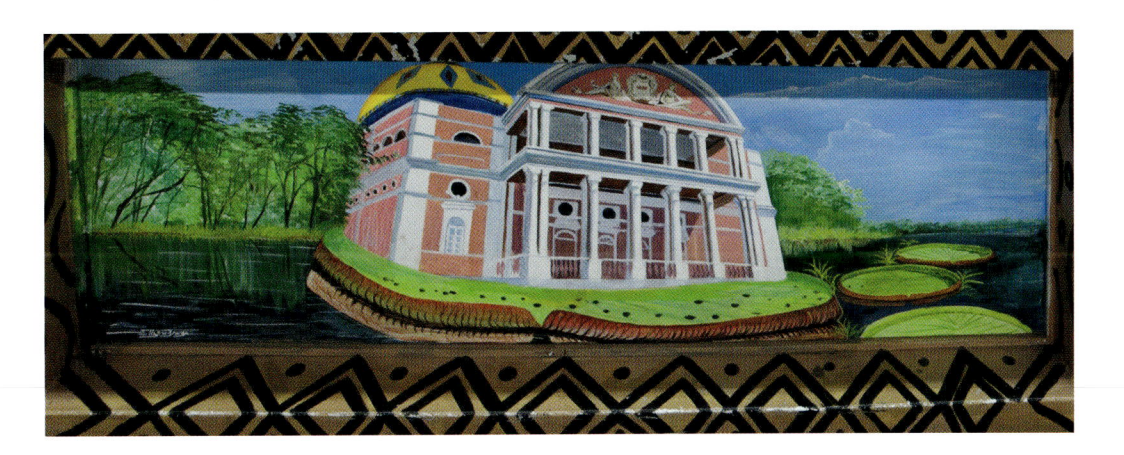

Victoria regia, by Marianne North, was composed and executed in London based on illustrations by Walter Fitch and North's own memories of her travels in Brazil.
ROYAL BOTANIC GARDENS, KEW

A painting decorating the front of one of the souvenir shops in Manaus, Brazil, depicts Teatro Amazonas, the city's famous opera house, floating on a *Victoria* leaf.
TOMASZ ANIŚKO / LONGWOOD GARDENS

INSPIRED ARTS   411

Thanks to *Victoria*'s seductive physical attributes, her allure is easily translated in the visual arts, but she has also frequently inspired literary works. For centuries in England, the rose, which "appeal'd to many a poet's page / to prove her right to reign," and the Madonna lily, "a fair imperial flow'r," vied for supremacy in the floral kingdom. But a half century before the Amazonian nymph's discovery, poet William Cowper prophesied that the two flowers can "each be deem'd a queen," but only "till a third surpasses" them (Cowper 1913).

Once *Victoria* arrived in England in 1849 to take the reign from the rose and the Madonna lily, she inspired poetic verses almost instantly. Perhaps the earliest were penned by Douglas W. Jerrold, who, after witnessing Joseph Paxton's daughter Annie bravely standing on a *Victoria* leaf at Chatsworth, hurried to write a short poem for *Punch* magazine. In it, Annie becomes a "little maid" in "fairy guise" floating on an "unbent leaf" of a water lily—an allusion to the folklore and mythology of many cultures that until then could only be imagined.

A dozen years later, at the height of Queen Victoria's rule, English poets no longer spoke of the South American nymph as a trivial vessel for a fairy. Instead, she was fully endowed with regal metaphors. *The Victoria Regia*, an 1861 volume of poetry and prose edited by Adelaide A. Procter, included a dedication to "Her Most Gracious Majesty" Queen Victoria, which exalted that "never happier name a flower, a woman, or a Queen could claim!" The patriotic euphoria of the author even transformed Robert Schomburgk into "an English traveler" who "sought a name whereby might be exprest the chiefest glory of this world of ours." Thankfully, he found it in the name

---

Douglas Jerrold, 1849:

On unbent leaf, in fairy guise
Reflected in the water,
Beloved, admired in hearts and eyes,
Stands Annie, Paxton's daughter.

Accept a wish, my little maid,
Begotten at the minute,
That scenes so bright may never fade,
You still the fairy in it.

That all your life, nor care, nor grief
May load the winged hours
With weight to bend a lily's leaf,
But all around be flowers.

Jerrold 1914

Adelaide Procter, *The Victoria Regia*, 1861:

When on the shining waters of the West
An English traveler saw the queen of flowers,
He sought a name whereby might be exprest
The chiefest glory of this world of ours.
Victoria Regia!—Never happier name
A flower, a woman, or a Queen could claim!

So we this title with due reverence chose
For this our flower, which we aspire to lay
At her dear feet round whose dominion flows
The perfect light of undeclining day.
Victoria Regia! May our blossom hold
In pure white leaves a loyal heart of gold.

Procter 1861

Francisco Galvão, *Victoria-Régia*, 1912:

Flor do Mysterío! a qual estranha flora
Pertences que sí mesmo Orpheu te vira
Morrería de espasmos em plethora!

Sombras n'agua... Livor...
Vejo, á procura
Do teu calice de ouro—cheio de ira,
A Amazonas, bramindo de amargura...

Galvão 1912

Francisco Galvão, *Mãe d'Agua*, 1912:

Perseguem-te, sensuaes, em graves rondas
Os tritões, côr do luar, as ardentias
Do amor, unindo ás lubricas e hediondas
Sensações do prazer, em vozerias.

Victoria Regia humana! ha no teu porte
A' deslumbrante perfeição da alvura,
O conforto suavissimo da Morte...

Galvão 1912

of the Queen around whose "dominion flows the perfect light of undeclining day" (Procter 1861).

A half century later in *Victoria*'s native Brazil, poet Francisco Galvão cultivated quite a different poetic association. In his 1912 volume of poetry, *Victoria-Régia*, Galvão struck a darker tone when he wrote of the aquatic nymph as the "Flor do Mysterio," who emerges like Orpheus from the shadowy underworld of dark waters while casting a mortal glance to those trailing behind. He also called her "Mãe d'Agua," uniting the breathtaking perfection of her purity with the sweetest delights found only in death brought about by all-consuming flames of love. The cover of Galvão's volume showed a chalky white female corpse floating in the green-and-violet waters under a similarly colored forest canopy.

Such intense emotions also surfaced in *Victoria-Régia,* written by another Brazilian poet, Humberto de Campos. In the trembling body of the *Victoria* flower, tenderly nurtured by the Amazon, Campos finds all the splendor and grandeur of this world. Before she flowers, *Victoria* is like a mournful nymph lost in her dreams in a quiet lagoon. But then her blossom appears above the surface of the water with the force of passionate love erupting from one's heart. She emerges white and nude and lies open on the placid waters at night to receive the courtship of her affectionate lover—the moon.

The erotically charged portraits of *Victoria* by Brazilian poets were far removed from the chaste, romantic naïveté of nineteenth-century British writers. The British rendered the lily as an innocent fairy or as a maternal sovereign of a dominion of "undeclining day." The twentieth-century poets, however, stripped the Amazonian nymph of her chastity. They saw in her the embodiment of self-destructive ecstasy brought about by passionate love.

Russian poet Igor Severyanin, a cult figure of the Ego-Futurist movement, filled his poems with bizarre and irrational subjects intended to shock his bourgeois audience, scandalize his emulators, and provoke outrage among critics and readers. Severyanin cast the aquatic nymph in a 1909 poem titled *Victoria Regia*. In it, the lily—which blooms all too rarely, as the poet tells us—becomes a metaphor for a rendezvous between two lovers. Before and after blossoming, the flower's existence is an elegy for what has passed and a hopeful anticipation for what is to come. When *Victoria* fully opens her flower, her trembling lover languishes with delight. One can only guess if Severyanin made his readers blush.

It would be premature to say that *Victoria* has already defined her place in culture. However, one idea appears to be consistent across the entire spectrum of the arts: The very few people who live where this nymph occurs in the wild consider her to be a common element in their environment. To them, *Victoria* is a part of their everyday experience with no particular meaning attached. To the rest of the world, however, who see the lily only occasionally and under highly contrived circumstances, *Victoria* is a creature beyond belief, a being from another world, alien yet fascinating. She comes from the world of our dreams, unconstrained, surreal, and imagined. In this fantasy land, utopian architecture attempts to save us from ourselves; one can travel like Orpheus between the underworld and the world of the living, exploring the depths of the human soul; and little girls are transformed into fairies and mermaids. In short, *Victoria* is a portal to our dreams.

Humberto de Campos, *Victoria-Régia***, 1917:**

E a flôr emerge, alva e nua,
No seu splendor extranho,
Sem vêr outra que possua
Seu perfume e seu tamanho!

E domina, em roda,
Tudo.
A imperar sobre a agua toda,
Aberto o seio alvo e mudo
A caricia maternal do luar,
Sabendo que, em si, resume
A patria onde floresce, enche com o seu perfume
As margens, a agua, a terra, a lua, as folhas, e ar . . .

Já vês que, na pompa egregia
Do teu porte alto e risonho,
Tu és a Victoria-Régia
Do lago azul do meu Sonho!

Campos 1917

Igor Severyanin, *Victoria Regia***, 1909:**

Наша встреча—Виктория Регия:
Редко, редко в цвету . . .
До и после нее жизнь—элегия
И надежда в мечту.

Ты придешь,—изнываю от неги я,
Трепещу на лету.
Наша встреча—Виктория Регия:
Редко, редко в цвету . . .

Severyanin 1995

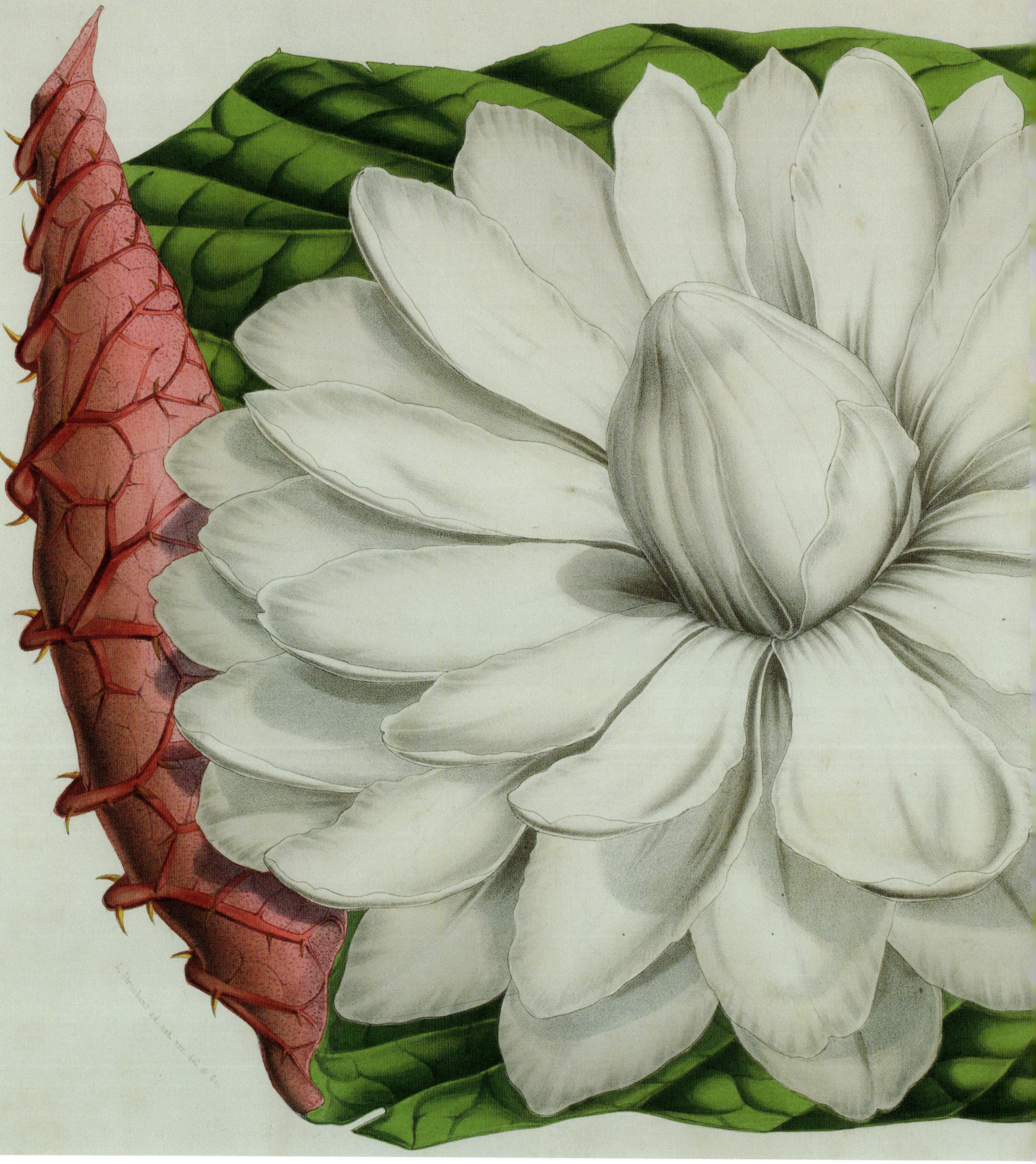

chapter 21

NYMPHS, GODDESSES, AND THE AMAZONS

EVERY DAY SOMEWHERE IN THE WORLD, a frightened child is probably being placed on a giant lily leaf to amuse eager onlookers. A photograph is taken to preserve this precious moment, as if out of a fairy tale. But how and when did this urge to have children pose on *Victoria* leaves begin?

Nineteenth-century travelers to South America noticed that when Indians were collecting the plant's seeds for food, they would "place their infant children upon the leaves, previously throwing a goat skin upon their surfaces, which, while equalizing the pressure, afford[ed] a dry and safe deposit" (Allen 1854). This, however, could hardly explain how the fad of placing children on *Victoria* leaves has spread so far and wide throughout the rest of the world.

It did not take long for Joseph Paxton, the cultivator of the first lily in Europe, to come up with the idea. When a "distinguished concourse of visitors of the nobility and literati" arrived at Chatsworth in 1849 to observe the queen lily's famed flower, Paxton dressed his eight-year-old daughter, Annie, as a fairy and stood her on a floating lily pad (Lockwood 1885). Taking at the same time precise measurements of the diameter of the leaf and the weight being borne by it, Paxton may have intended only to demonstrate the leaf's astonishing load-carrying capacity, but the scene he created resonated

First-night flower and a section of a leaf of *Victoria amazonica* from Jules Planchon and Louis Van Houtte's book *La Victoria Regia* (1850–51).
LONGWOOD GARDENS LIBRARY AND ARCHIVES

Yagua Indian child on a leaf of *Victoria amazonica*, photographed in 1977 near Leticia, Colombia.
LOREN MCINTYRE

Joseph Paxton, 1851:

Early in November [1849], the leaves being four feet eight inches [1 m] in diameter, and exhibiting every appearance of possessing great strength from the deep thick ribs, which form the foundation of the blade, I was desirous of ascertaining the weight which they would bear, and, accordingly, placed my youngest daughter, eight years of age, weighing forty-two pounds [19 kg], upon one of the leaves; a copper-lid, weighing fifteen pounds [7 kg], being the readiest thing that presented itself, was first placed upon it, in order to equalize the pressure, making together fifty-seven pounds [26 kg]. This weight the leaf bore extremely well, as did several others upon which the experiment was tried, their diameter being four feet two inches to four feet nine inches [1 m].

Hooker 1851

immediately with more profound cultural notions symbolized by a child floating on a lily pad. In Annie, spectators saw "a Naiad of the waters" presiding "as the fairy guardian of this beautiful floral queen"—an event that inspired at least one poet, Douglas Jerrold, to depict it in verse (Lockwood 1885).

When they were published, the announcements of the triumphant raising of the *Victoria* at Chatsworth were accompanied by a somewhat exaggerated illustration of eight-year-old Annie Paxton standing on a giant lily leaf. The copper lid that Paxton had placed beneath her feet to equalize the pressure was omitted.

It would be hard to overestimate the impact that this seemingly innocent juxtaposition—a young girl on a lily pad—had on the South American nymph's meteoric rise in popularity. Paxton's theatrical presentation was instantly emulated in every garden where the queen lily arrived.

In the meantime, Paxton wanted to test the limits of lily pad buoyancy with a different approach, one that would not risk Annie falling in the water. He had one leaf, about 1.5 m (5 feet) in diameter, removed from the plant and set it in a nearby brook. First, a light wooden trellis was placed on the leaf to distribute the pressure equally. Then weights were gradually added, totaling nearly 61 kg (135 pounds) before the leaf began to take up water.

416   VICTORIA: THE SEDUCTRESS

Would-be fairies posed on *Victoria* leaves, clockwise from top, in St. Paul, Minnesota; Clifton, New Jersey; Amsterdam, the Netherlands; Moscow, Russia; and Kennett Square, Pennsylvania.

Robert N. Dennis Collection of Stereoscopic Views, Miriam and Ira D. Wallach Division of Art, Prints and Photographs, The New York Public Library, Astor, Lenox and Tilden Foundations; Longwood Gardens; University of Amsterdam Library Special Collections; Moscow State University Botanical Garden; Author's Collection

Nymphs, Goddesses, and the Amazons 417

418 Victoria: The Seductress

Once the public had become accustomed to seeing a child floating on a leaf of the giant water lily, two or even three children were made to stand or sit together on the same leaf for greater effect. Shown here are photos taken in Tower Grove Park in St. Louis, left; Bonn, Germany, top; Kennett Square, Pennsylvania, center left; Missouri Botanical Garden in St. Louis, center right; and Dresden, Germany, bottom.
WILHELM BARTHLOTT, BOTANISCHE GARTEN DER UNIVERSITÄT BONN; AUTHOR'S COLLECTION; MISSOURI BOTANICAL GARDEN; LONGWOOD GARDENS LIBRARY AND ARCHIVES

NYMPHS, GODDESSES, AND THE AMAZONS 419

The old European folklore of storks bringing children to this world is widely known. Fewer people realize that—as these early twentieth-century German postcards demonstrate—these storks find the newborns on the leaves of water lilies.

LONGWOOD GARDENS LIBRARY AND ARCHIVES

420　VICTORIA: THE SEDUCTRESS

Following this test, the weights were removed. Next, a man upward of 63 kg (140 pounds) stood on the leaf. He was then replaced by another man weighing nearly 70 kg (154 pounds). Both men were able to stand on the leaf for two or three minutes, during which brief time they expressed a "feeling of perfect safety" (Hooker 1851).

Thus, Paxton demonstrated that the thrill of floating on a lily pad was not necessarily limited to children. Nevertheless, by staging Annie as a fairy, Paxton showed what Edgar Anderson called a "peculiar genius for transmitting his own enthusiasm to the general public" (Anderson 1965). His excitement soon caught on, not only in England but also across Europe and beyond, establishing a new horticultural tradition. Children posed wearing fancy costumes or plain clothes. The youngest ones were often nude. Soon, for greater effect, two or even three children stood or sat together on the same leaf (Wilke 1891, Elfving 1900).

In the 1890s, Englishman James Gurney brought Paxton's custom to the United States at the Missouri Botanical Garden in St. Louis. Since that time, countless books, newspapers, magazines, and postcards have reproduced images of children riding upon lily pads. "Many of us not native to St. Louis," Anderson confessed, "first heard about Mr. Shaw's fabulous botanical garden, when as children we saw one of these pictures."

EVOKING NYMPH MAGIC

In Europe, *Victoria* stepped into a role that for millennia had been played by her lesser cousins: the *Nymphaea* water lilies of the Old World. European folklore is rich with references to water lilies, or nymphs, and their association with the live-giving forces of Nature. In fact, according to both ancient legends and more recent birth announcement cards, the storks that deliver children into this world first find them on the leaves of water lilies.

But nymphs are not only floating flowers that emerge from the depths of water. Nymphs are also the beautiful maidens inhabiting ponds, lakes, or streams who conceal themselves in the form of water

Water lilies and nymphs have been closely associated with love magic in Europe since time immemorial. Once introduced into cultivation, *Victoria* often assumed the role long performed by *Nymphaea* water lilies, as in this picture by Fidus, a German symbolist artist of the late nineteenth and early twentieth century.
AUTHOR'S COLLECTION

lilies (De Cleene and Lejeune 2003). As maidens, nymphs exert seductive powers over the men who fall under their influence, while their floral incarnation, the water lily, has been used in love magic (Skinner 1911). The *Nymphaea* lily flower was worn as a love amulet by one wishing for love, but for it to be effective, it had to be collected under a full moon. Anyone desiring to gather such a flower had to plug his ears; otherwise, the enchanting songs of the nymphs, like those of the Greek Sirens, would lure the love-seeker under water (Rätsch 1992).

In a strange twist of meaning, the water lily was depicted in Christian iconography as the place of the Immaculate Conception. This may explain why it was deemed a symbol of chastity in medieval Europe and used to suppress "devilish desires" (Rätsch 1992, De Cleene and Lejeune 2003). The ancient Greeks also considered the water lily to be an anaphrodisiac, perhaps echoing earlier myths about the water lily arising from a nymph who died of unhappy love (Rätsch 1992). In one version, a nymph who was first seduced and then abandoned by Heracles so despaired over her loss that she threw herself into the water and drowned. As in so many other Greek myths, the gods took pity on the drowned girl and brought her back to life in the form of a water lily (Ward 1999, De Cleene and Lejeune 2003).

FERTILE GODDESS OF THE NILE

While water lilies do not feature prominently in either Greek myths or the Greek mountainous countryside, they were revered by another ancient Mediterranean civilization, this one founded in the delta of the Nile. Both the white and blue lotus of Egypt are in fact species of water lilies—*Nymphaea lotus* and *Nymphaea caerulea* respectively. In ancient Egyptian myths, Atum, the primordial god of creation, was depicted ascending from the lotus flower. Isis, the goddess of motherhood, was represented by a lotus bud rising from the water. Horus, the god of the morning sun and a son of Isis and Osiris, was reborn each dawn out of the lotus flower and died with it each evening. Ra, another permutation of the sun god, was also born from the floral womb of *Nymphaea* (De Cleene and Lejeune 2003, Manniche 2006). Egyptians believed that they too could be reborn from the lotus flower, often decorating the walls of their tombs with representations of the lotus flower. For instance, a wooden sculpture found in the tomb of Tutankhamun depicts the moment when the young pharaoh emerged from the flower of *Nymphaea caerulea* (Manniche 2006).

The ancient Egyptians' reverence for water lilies was inextricably linked to the Nile's cycle of life-giving floods. Their flowers appeared with the arrival of floodwaters and vanished in the dry season that followed. Each morning, the opening of the lily bud, which was shaped like an egg, suggested the beginning of new life—an act of creation from the fertile waters. To this day, Egyptians call *Nymphaea* the "bride of Nile" (De Cleene and Lejeune 2003).

In Egyptian wall decorations, water lilies were often portrayed in tandem with frogs, an association that may seem natural given that they inhabit the same aquatic environment. But this pairing also reflects an even older era of human thought.

Head of Tutankhamun, emerging from a flower of *Nymphaea caerulea*. This wood bust, covered with stucco and painted, was found at the entrance to the pharaoh's tomb.
BPK, BERLIN / EGYPTIAN MUSEUM, CAIRO, EGYPT / MARGARETE BÜSING / ART RESOURCE, NEW YORK

For Europe's Neolithic people, a life-giving goddess, whose name we may never know, assumed the form of a frog or toad (Gimbutas 1992). Archeological digs in the Balkans have unearthed figurines of a half-woman half-frog carved from stone or made of clay, dating to 5000–7000 B.C. Austrian archaeologist Alois Gulder theorized that Neolithic people, unaware of the real cause of conception, saw the human fetus as a frog that crawled into a woman's womb (Gulder 1960–62). The superficial similarity of a human embryo in the early months of pregnancy to a frog allowed the amphibians to take on a powerful regenerative symbolism that has lasted for millennia. Even today, in some churches in Europe, votive offerings in the form of frogs are intended to ward off barrenness and to bring pregnancy (Gimbutas 1992).

While Neolithic art presents a kaleidoscope of hybrid woman-and-frog forms, the Egyptians traditionally portrayed the deity as a woman with a frog's head. They gave her the name Heket and made her the goddess of fertility (Gimbutas 2001). As such, Heket breathed life into Horus as he emerged from the lotus flower each morning.

To the east, in India, images of the life-giving goddess Lajjā Gaurī can be found all over the subcontinent. Lajjā Gaurī is always presented crouching in a frog-like manner, often with her head replaced by a lotus flower. One of the figurines, identified as a fertility amulet, depicts the goddess conjoined with a frog. This figurine, which dates to the second century A.D., was found in Mathura in Uttar Pradesh and is now at the Victoria and Albert Museum in London (Bolon 1992).

As the examples from the Balkans, Egypt, and India illustrate, the symbolic association of a frog or toad with fecundity is not only ancient but also widespread in the Old World. Both frogs and water lilies possess the mysterious ability to reappear in response to floods or rain and to do so in huge numbers —a sure sign of the unbroken cycle of rebirth (Bolon 1992).

This primordial link between frogs, water lilies, and birth persisted intact in turn-of-the-twentieth-century birth announcements. Until the arrival of *Victoria* from South America, scenes of children on lily pads could only be dreamed up. When little Annie Paxton stood patiently on the leaf of the giant lily at Chatsworth in November 1849 while an artist sketched the scene for the *Illustrated London News*, little did she or anyone else present realize that it evoked one of the world's oldest beliefs regarding the origin of human life. As *Victoria* filled pools and ponds in Europe and beyond, the picture that for millennia had existed in people's imaginations was suddenly given a physical reality.

Since the goddesses of Old Europe had long been erased from memory, the crowds of admirers that flocked to witness this wonder of the plant world universally hailed her as the queen of flowers instead. It did not hurt that the nymph bore the name of beloved Queen Victoria, who had extended her motherly rule over the largest empire the world had ever seen. The South American nymph was proclaimed as the "royal plant," the "queen of all lilies" who emanated "more glory than even a Solomon" (Olcott 1861). All those who were privileged to see her, one of the "monarchs of the vegetable world," gave expressions of adoration and pledges of submission to "the foremost, the most beautiful, and the sweetest of all that dwell within the waters" (Anonymous 1851j).

FEMALE WARRIORS OF AMAZONIA

The fact that this regal creature came from Amazonia, the land named for the Amazons—mythical female warriors of antiquity who were ruled by a queen—only strengthened the public's perception that *Victoria* was an exceptional being from out of this world. While there is growing evidence that the Amazons did indeed once roam the coast of the Black Sea and perhaps came in contact with ancient Greece, the Greeks

Jules Planchon and Louis Van Houtte, 1850–51:

Nature does have her luxurious creations that seem destined for admiration, as models of grandeur, grace and beauty. Such is, above all, the noble plant which unanimous acclamation has hailed with the title of queen of the waters, a title that translates, with such rare fortuity of allusion, the name of Victoria regia. *Its majesty of bearing, grandiosity of proportions, its elegance of shape, richness of color, and sweetness of perfume; nothing is lacking that charms the imagination and the senses, that makes triumph of the artist and despair of humble prose.*

Planchon and Van Houtte 1850–51, translated by Adam Koppeser

Water Lilies: The Beginning of Life, 1900–1902, an aquatint print by František Kupka from the Musée National d'Art Moderne, Centre Georges Pompidou in Paris. Kupka painted a twentieth-century symbolist's vision of ancient beliefs that human life begins in a water lily flower, though he substituted *Victoria* for *Nymphaea.* CNAC / MNAM / Dist. Réunion des Musées Nationaux / Art Resource, New York / Artists Rights Society (ARS), New York / ADAGP, Paris

described them as existing outside the boundaries of the civilized world, even outside the boundaries of human experience.

Similarly, the purported Amazons of South America, mentioned by many early explorers, remained just as elusive, spurring legends and myths on par with their ancient Greek counterparts. The earliest report of the Amazons in South America was sent to Europe by Francisco de Orellana, a Spanish explorer, conquistador, and the first European to descend the length of the Amazon River. Coincidentally, Orellana placed the land of the warrior women in the same area where British explorers found *Victoria* water lilies three centuries later (Spruce 1908).

The reliability of Orellana's and other reports has been questioned, though; the historical existence of the Amazons in either South America or Europe may never be proven. However, the idea of a matriarchal society of warlike women ruled by a queen is firmly established in Western culture, aided by our inclination for mythmaking. Considering the scant evidence for the Amazons' existence in South America, Alexander von Humboldt remarked: "Such is the disposition of man's mind that, in the long succession of travelers discovering and writing about the marvels of the New World, each one readily declared that he had seen what earlier ones had announced" (Humboldt 1995).

Whether real or imagined, the Amazons helped the giant lily's reputation as a creature from another world. Her native land was beyond reach, inaccessible and incomprehensible. Her sightings were rare and often conflicting. Her local origin, as narrated by South American Indian legends, bore an astonishing similarity to Greek myths of a love-stricken nymph's accidental death and resurrection. While details vary between tribes, the tales all follow a similar plot.

Tupi legend tells of a girl who falls in love with the moon, whom she believes to be a great warrior. Seeing the moon's reflection on the lake, she follows it, throws herself in the water, and drowns. The moon god is so touched by the girl's fate that he brings her back to life in the form of a lily flower that opens every night (Perry 1963, Phillips 1999).

In the Guarani version, the moon is replaced by a young warrior who drowns while retrieving a bracelet thrown into the lake by a fickle girl. Attempting to rescue her lover, the girl drowns, too. A benevolent god intervenes, and the two are reincarnated as water lily flowers (Repún 2005).

Remarkably, the water lilies of both the New and the Old World trace their origin to similar tales of beautiful maidens falling in love with warrior deities. Both end with the drowning death of the grieving girl and her later resurrection as a flower. These myths inspired a plethora of artistic and poetic interpretations that unite the flower nymph with the maiden nymph as one creature.

Happy endings, however, are rarely, if ever, a part of nymph stories. Edgar Allan Poe in his *Dreamland* (1844) writes of a dreadful place, "Out of space—out of time," with "bottomless vales and boundless floods." In that land, lakes "endlessly outspread / Their lone waters," which are "still and chilly / With the snows of the lolling lily." Oliver Wendell Holmes in *The Star and the Water Lily* (1863) metamorphoses the classic theme and writes of the lily rather than a girl that falls for a star in the sky. The

Thomas Higginson, 1863:

After the strange flower-bud has reared its dark head from the placid tank, moving it a little, uneasily, like some imprisoned water-creature, it pauses for a moment in a sort of dumb despair. Then trembling again, and collecting all its powers, it thrusts open, with an indignant jerk, the rough calyx-leaves, and the beautiful disrobing begins. The firm, white, central cone, first so closely infolded, quivers a little, and swiftly, before your eyes, the first of the hundred petals detaches its delicate edges, and springs back, opening towards water, while its white reflection opens to meet it from below. Many moments of repose follow—you watch—another petal trembles, detaches, springs open, and is still. Then another, and another, and another. Each movement is so quiet, yet so decided, so living, so human, that the radiant creature seems a Musidora of the water, and you almost blush with a sense of guilt, in gazing on that peerless privacy.

Higginson 1863

Musidora, 1813–35, by Thomas Sully, is perhaps the finest of the many nudes inspired by the character from James Thomson's 1727 poem *Summer*.
THE METROPOLITAN MUSEUM OF ART / ART RESOURCE, NEW YORK

James Thomson, *Summer*, 1727:

...

Warm in her cheek the sultry season glow'd;
And, robed in loose array, she came to bathe
Her fervent limbs in the refreshing stream.

...

Meantime, this fairer nymph than ever bless'd
Arcadian stream, with timid eye around
The banks surveying, stripp'd her beauteous limbs
To taste the lucid coolness of the flood.

...

And fair-exposed she stood, shrunk from herself,
With fancy blushing, at the doubtful breeze
Alarm'd, and starting like the fearful fawn?
Then to the flood she rush'd: the parted flood
Its lovely quest with closing waves received;
And every beauty softening, every grace
Flushing anew, a mellow lustre shed:
As shines the lily through the crystal mild;

...

Thomson 1854

romance, characteristically, ends badly for the lily. As she "turned to the skies afar, / And bared her breast to the trembling ray," a cloud "darkened the sky" and brought "the beating rain," while the lily "sank in the stormy tide."

BEAUTIFUL TEMPTRESS MUSIDORA

There is, however, a less mournful side to the nymph. As an elusive, fleeting, and inaccessible creature—in both her floral and maiden forms—she hypnotized men with her physical beauty. In *Out-door Papers* (1863), Thomas Wentworth Higginson saw in the South American lily "Musidora of the water." For today's audiences, the name Musidora may not impart any particular meaning, but for nineteenth-century readers, she epitomized a woman who could be both chaste and erotic, modest and seductive. The idyllic portrayal of Musidora comes from *Summer* (1727), a widely popular poem by James Thomson that is part of his masterpiece *The Seasons*. In it, Musidora, a maiden of exquisite beauty, bathes in a forest stream without realizing her suitor is secretly watching. When Musidora immerses herself in the stream, Thomson compares her to a nymph of Arcadia and a lily, invoking classical associations.

The popularity of Thomson's works made Musidora the subject of several nude paintings of the Neoclassical and Romantic periods. Perhaps the most admired was created by Philadelphia artist Thomas Sully, who also painted portraits of Caleb

Cope and Queen Victoria. Sully finished his *Musidora* in 1835, two years before traveling to London to paint the young queen in her coronation year. Today, both paintings are at the Metropolitan Museum of Art in New York. In *Musidora*, Sully shows a maiden bathing in the stream at the moment she is surprised by her lover and shyly turns from the spectator. This rather unusual pose echoes the one he chose later for Queen Victoria's portrait. There, Victoria steps up to her throne while turning her head to look back at the viewer.

The precedence of Musidora marked the beginning of an artistic canon where secluded lakes and streams, often with water lilies, became important attributes of nude paintings and sculptures. Art critic Charles Caffin sarcastically fumed: "Here some nymph of antiquity for the thousandth time disposes of her maiden beauty to invite the approach of her divine or human lover" (Gerdts 1974).

When *Victoria* arrived in Europe, the cultural construct linking water lilies, nymphs, and sensual love was at the height of its popularity. The timing could not have been better. The giant lily of South America burst onto the stage as if the role were written for her. The aura of exoticism, rarity, and exclusivity that surrounded *Victoria* only heightened her desirability. Tales of bizarre fertilization rituals involving orgiastic conglomerations of beetles, stories of her flowers' sexual transformation, and even rumors that her plant juices were capable of suppressing erotic desires all inflamed the imagination of the nineteenth-century public (Parodi 1886).

Writers like Higginson who recognized *Victoria* as the new Musidora thrived on the metamorphosis of the nymph's flower after a turbulent night from "chaste loveliness" to "crimson passion" and from "virgin" to "voluptuous," going so far as to portray the Amazonian nymph as "Hebe turned to Magdalen"—Hebe being the Greek goddess of youth and patroness of young brides, and Magdalen being a poetic name of a prostitute (Higginson 1863).

Others were not as quick to equate the flower's overnight change with the loss of virginity. Instead, "the delicate pink" color was painted as "the most exquisitely beautiful" to be found in nature, comparable only to "the last fading glories of the evening sky" or "the blush of beauty," presumably on a cheek of a maiden (Anthon 1861). Some, moved by the sublime beauty of the "wonder of wonders," expressed reverence for the Almighty (Lawson 1851).

Whether infused with a metaphoric meaning of a writer's choosing or completely liberated from the burden of history and traditions, *Victoria* has never failed to seduce the senses and human emotions. One cannot pass the South American nymph without taking notice, then being tempted, and eventually becoming helplessly

Thomas Higginson, 1863:

As petal by petal slowly opens, there still stands the central cone of snow, a glacier, an alp, a jungfrau, while each avalanche of whiteness seems the last. Meanwhile a strange, rich odor fills the air, and nature seems to concentrate all fascination and claim all senses for this jubilee of her darling. So pass the enchanted moments of the evening, till the fair thing pauses at last and remains for hours unchanged. In the morning, one by one, those white petals close again, shutting all their beauty in, and you watch through the short sleep for the period of waking. Can this bright transfigured creature appear again, in the same chaste loveliness? Your fancy can scarcely trust it, fearing some disastrous change; and your fancy is too true a prophet.... Can this be the virgin Victoria—*this thing of crimson passion, this pile of pink and yellow, relaxed, expanded, voluptuous, lolling languidly upon the water, never to rise again? In this short time every tint of every petal is transformed; it is gorgeous in beauty, but it is "Hebe turned to Magdalen."*

Higginson 1863

Anonymous correspondent to George Lawson, 1851:

My pen fails me when I attempt to convey an idea of the magnificence of the Victoria. *Beautiful as is* Nymphaea alba, *unfolding her snowy petals on the bosom of our Scottish lakes, she sinks into mediocrity when compared with this monarch of the waters. Nothing can equal the beauty of this extraordinary plant.... You may think I express my admiration strongly, in speaking of this vegetable wonder; but these expressions do not even do it justice.*

Lawson 1851

Modern-era Venuses floating on *Victoria* pads instead of the giant sea shells of Botticelli's imagination were captured in Clifton, New Jersey (above); St. Louis, Missouri (top left); Moscow, Russia (top right); and Kennett Square, Pennsylvania (opposite).
ARCHIVES OF THE GRAY HERBARIUM, HARVARD UNIVERSITY; MOSCOW STATE UNIVERSITY BOTANICAL GARDEN; MISSOURI BOTANICAL GARDEN; LONGWOOD GARDENS

enamored with her. "Nothing in the world of vegetable existence has such a human interest," wrote Higginson, who hailed the lily as "a creature of vitality and motion" (Higginson 1863).

At a loss how to describe the magnificent nymph, writers looked to other established canons of beauty—especially those of the female body—for help. In the end, their language was filled with ambiguities blurring the distinction between the flower and a woman, not unlike the Balkan, Egyptian, and Indian images of frog-and-woman hybrids. When in 1486 Sandro Botticelli painted the divine *Birth of Venus* (on view at today's Uffizi Gallery in Florence), he made the goddess, the ideal of human beauty, float on a seashell of improbable dimensions. Nearly four centuries later, botanist George Lawson suggested replicating this feat, but with Venus riding the *Victoria* lily pad instead (Lawson 1851). Lawson's idea caught on, just as Paxton's earlier illustration did, and Annie the fairy grew up to become a beautiful maiden. A picture of a woman on the giant lily leaf, however odd and precarious it may seem, unites the eternal ideals of beauty, human and floral. *Victoria* and Venus meet at last.

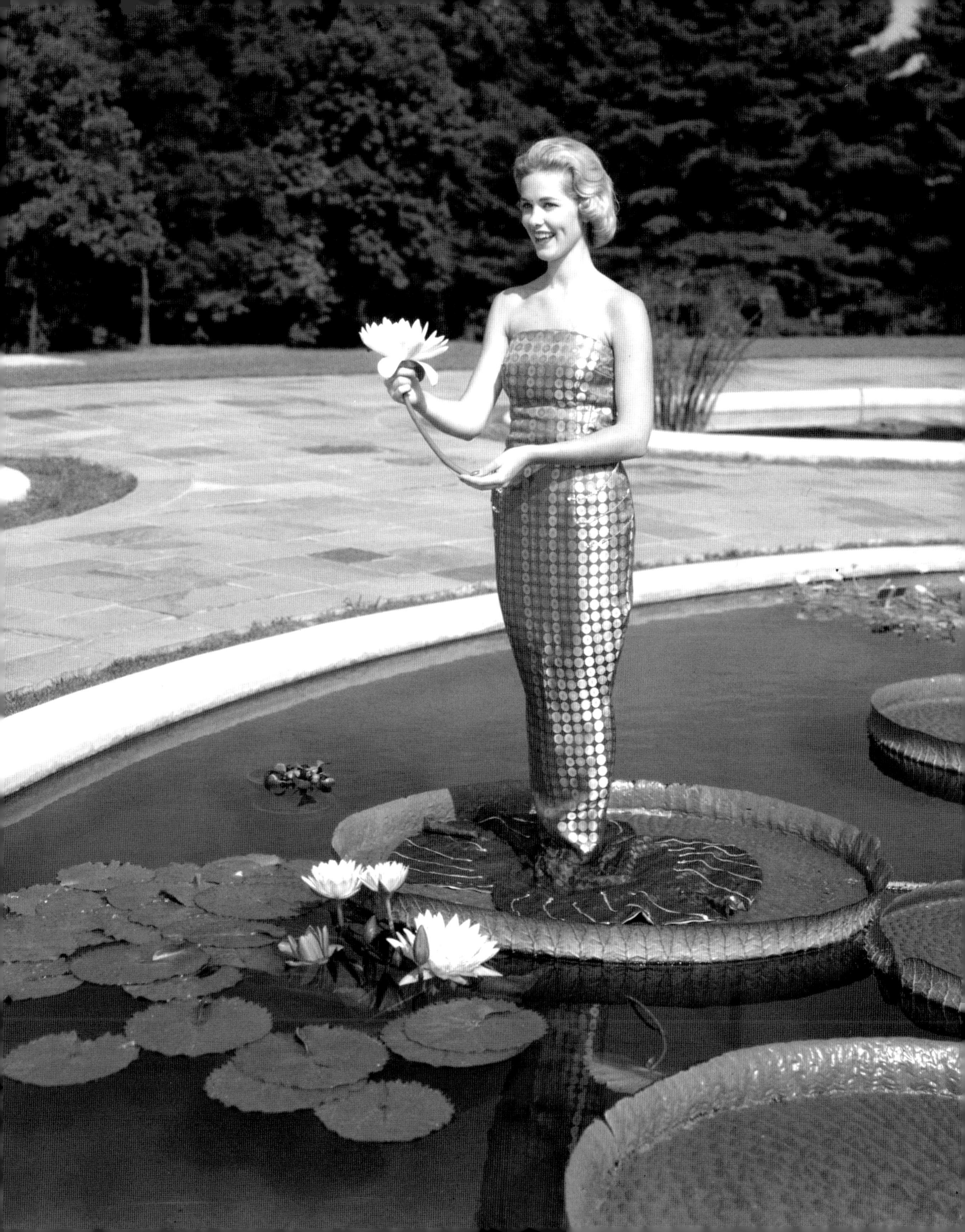

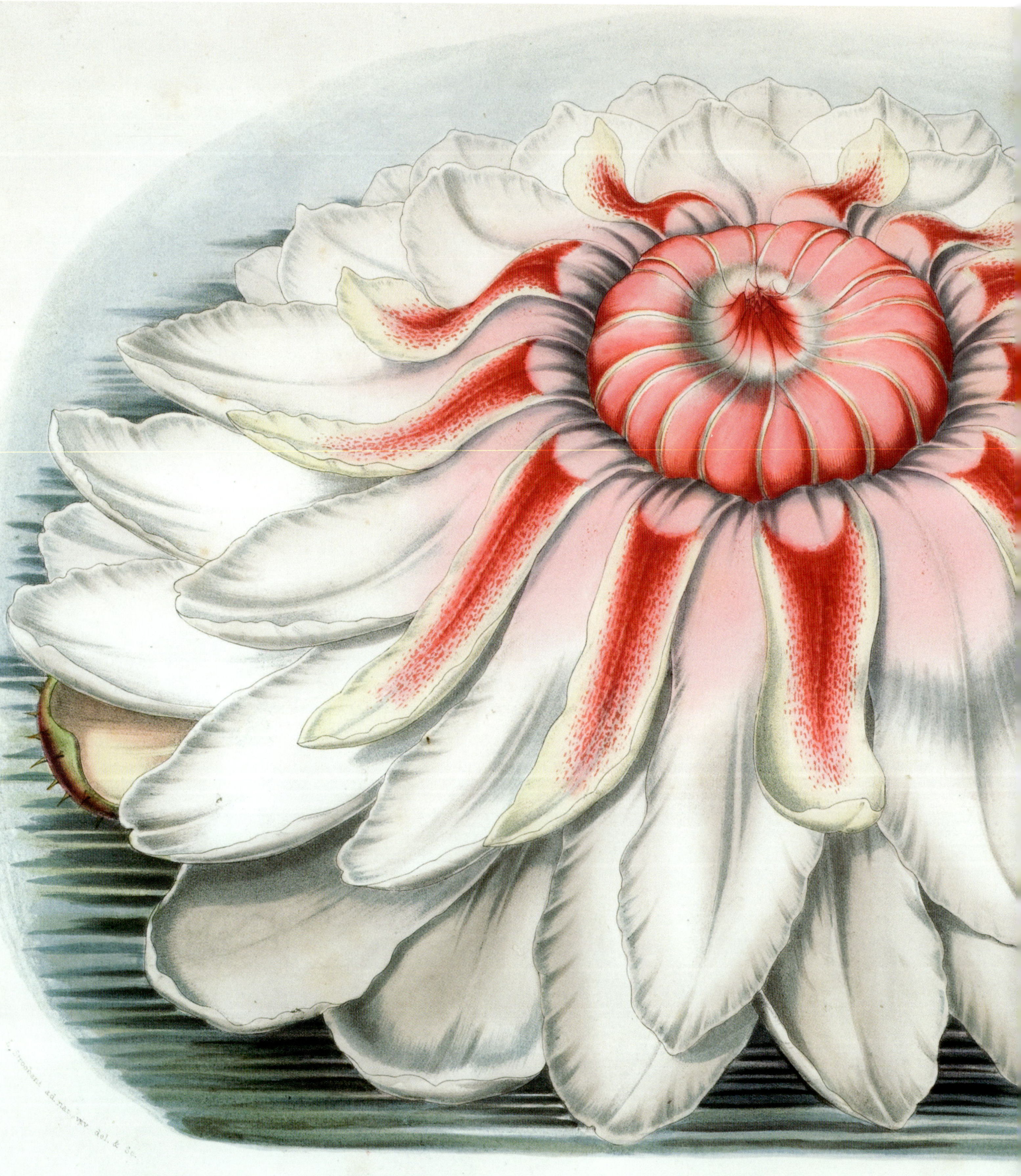
L. Stroobant ad. nat. viv. del.

chapter 22

PEOPLE'S CHOICE

VICTORIA'S EXQUISITE QUALITIES ARE immediately recognized by anyone coming face-to-face with her. As the embodiment of the floral canon of beauty and the Venus of the plant world, the South American nymph has shown over and over again her unfailing ability to seduce men to act irrationally, take great risks, and bear huge expenses to win her favors.

It took five such men from Europe—some of the most intrepid explorers of South America—nearly half a century to convince *Victoria* to leave the comforts of her primordial home and journey to other continents. In their travels to the New World, Thaddaeus Haenke, Aimé Bonpland, Alcide d'Orbigny, Eduard Pöppig, and Robert Schomburgk discovered more botanical treasures than any garden in Europe or elsewhere could hold. Yet each of these men was completely overwhelmed when seeing the nymph for the first time. A creature beyond comprehension, a being outside the realm of human experience, *Victoria* was universally received with admiration—by these men and the rest of the world. Even in the days when mail and news took weeks and months to travel, the water lily's fame spread rapidly: She became an instant celebrity, phenomenon, and obsession.

Second-night flower of *Victoria amazonica* grown in Ghent, Belgium, in 1850, pictured in *La Victoria Regia* (1850–51) by Jules Planchon and Louis Van Houtte.
LONGWOOD GARDENS LIBRARY AND ARCHIVES

William Hooker, the director of Royal Botanic Gardens, Kew, where the seeds of the giant lily germinated for the first time outside her native lands, proclaimed that "without any exception," *Victoria* was "the most beautiful plant yet known to Europeans" (Hooker 1851). And the nymph did not even have to present her "glorious" flowers because, as Hooker assured his readers, "the leaves alone would command our high admiration." Although written in 1851, these words could just as accurately express today's sentiment.

Across from Kew, on the opposite bank of the river Thames, visitors flocked to see the famed lily growing at Syon House and then told others about her. "You may think I express my admiration strongly, in speaking of this vegetable wonder," wrote an anonymous correspondent to Scottish botanist George Lawson, "but these expressions do not even do it justice. The plant at Syon House, which I have just left, with its noble flower and fifteen gigantic leaves, some of them sixteen and a half feet [5 m] in circumference, fills every beholder with admiration. To me, it is the wonder of wonders; and truly a befitting object to fill the mind with reverence and awe towards the Almighty" (Lawson 1851).

In Belgium, where *Victoria* made her first appearance on the European continent, she was acclaimed as one of Nature's "luxurious creations that seem destined for admiration" and as a model of "grandeur, grace and beauty" (Planchon and Van Houtte 1850–51, translated by Adam Koppeser). In Philadelphia, the lily's first port of call in the United States, her earliest cultivators were equally enamored. Caleb Cope of Philadelphia wrote to Andrew Downing, editor of the *Horticulturist*: "The *Victoria* is one of the few things that has not been exaggerated; nor is it possible to exaggerate it. It is truly a wonderful plant" (Cope 1851a). Cope's gardener, Thomas Meehan, wrote to Downing, echoing the praise of his superior: "It is not possible to select one property more than another, the which most to admire. It is everything to be wished for" (Allen 1854). Still another Philadelphia suitor of *Victoria* exalted the nymph "smiling ... sweetly in her beautiful blossom" (Anonymous 1859). Were all these men love struck upon first sight?

The spontaneous outburst of admiration helped place the nymph—a "truly superb floral Titan"—at the pinnacle of the Plant Kingdom, where she was hailed as its new queen (Flower 1860). Praised by the people for her sublime beauty, magnificent size, elegance of form, brilliant coloring, and delicious fragrance, the South American lily deserved the royal title, even if she had not been named for the queen of England. Just as Shakespeare's rose "by any other name would smell as sweet," so would *Victoria* by any other name remain as regal.

A group of schoolchildren learns about the queen lily in the greenhouse of Moscow State University Botanical Garden in the 1930s.
MOSCOW STATE UNIVERSITY BOTANICAL GARDEN

Victoria's grandeur is never diminished, even by fireworks lighting up the night sky or dramatically illuminated architecture.
LARRY ALBEE / LONGWOOD GARDENS

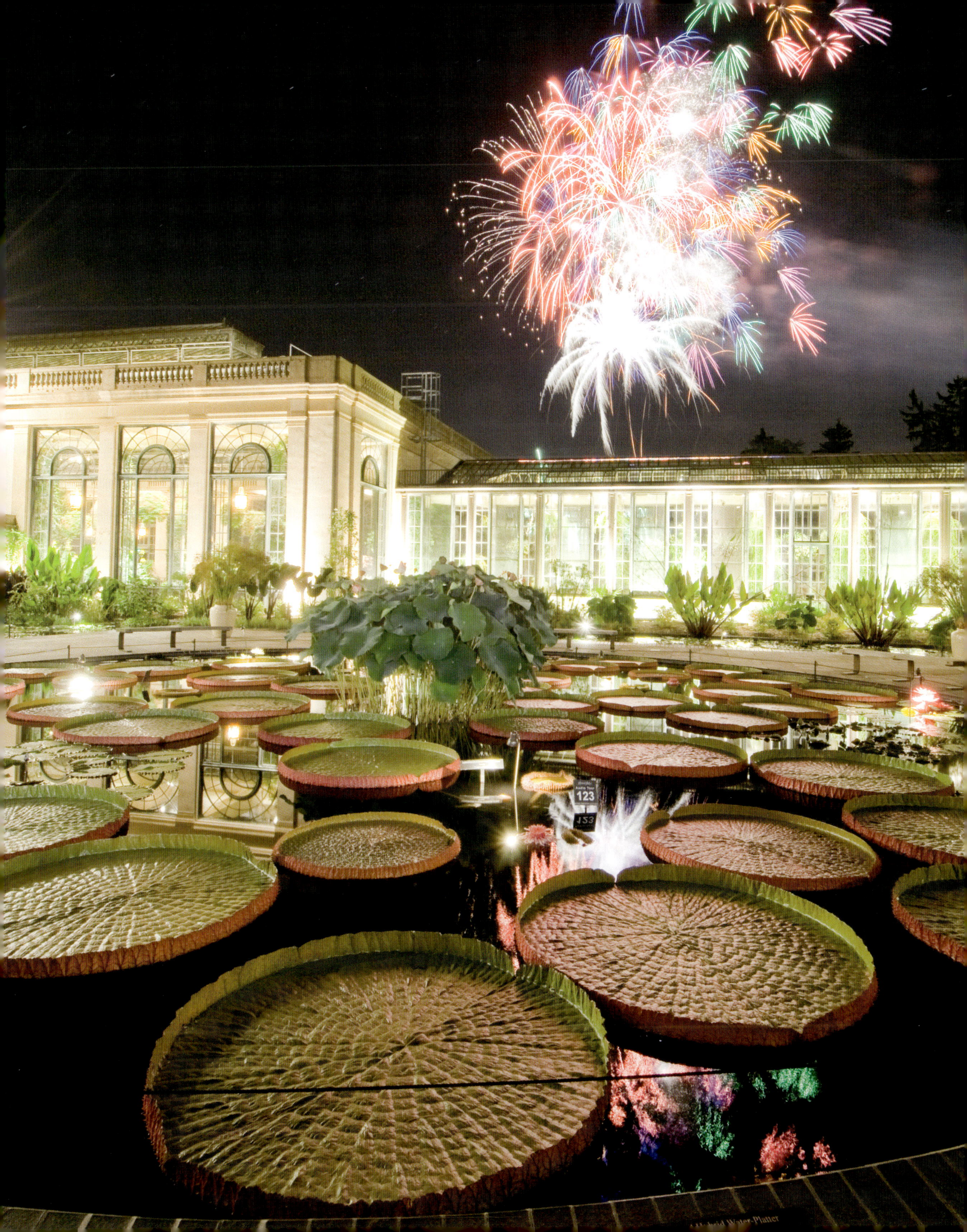

It is on the second night of flowering that *Victoria* displays many of her regal insignia.
Tomasz Aniśko / Longwood Gardens

William Paton, 1887:

I was driven three miles from town [Georgetown, Guiana] to one of the most extensive sugar-estates in Demerara—in fact, in the world, where, in harvest-time, there are nearly three thousand coolies employed. I saw at this place sugar-crushing, boiling, drying, refining apparatus and distilling machinery of enormous cost, remarkable size, and bewildering intricacy of construction. All these mechanical wonders, the stupendous engines, the whirling, roaring, and clanging machinery, were as nothing in comparison with the astonishing exhibition that was revealed to me when, prompted by listless curiosity, I wandered a short distance from the sugar-house to look over a low stone wall, and gazed down into an oozy ditch where the water was stagnant, covered with green weeds, and concealed by floating scum. There, in this unwholesome quagmire, I beheld a score, yes, full twenty score, of water-lilies in bloom. Never had I beheld so wonderful a show.

Paton 1887

QUEEN OF PLANTS

The South American nymph could have earned her crown on beauty alone. She was described as "exceedingly strange and fearfully pleasant," a spectacle that "could scarcely be comprehended" (Russell 1856). In addition, her remarkable rate of growth, expansion of leaves, and sheer scale was beyond belief. "Under favorable circumstances it comes forward with the rapidity of a sunflower," wrote John Fisk Allen (1853), revealing how helpless he was to find an adequate comparison. A visitor to a sugar refinery in Guiana, who marveled at the enormity and complexity of its "mechanical wonders," admitted that they were "as nothing" compared to a *Victoria* growing in a nearby ditch (Paton 1887).

The combination of the nymph's out-of-this-world beauty with her awe-inspiring grandeur gave *Victoria* an aura of superiority. "It would not be extravagant to call the beauties of this plant unsurpassable," declared Meehan, adding that the giant lily stood "among its class alone and unapproachable" (Allen 1854). John Ellis, Meehan's

434 Victoria: The Seductress

predecessor on Cope's estate, exalted *Victoria*'s beauties as "not to be equaled in any other plant known to the civilized world" (Cope 1851a). Her preeminence over lesser plants manifested itself in the "richest colours," "the structure of the most noble aspect," and even her "dimensions previously unheard of" (Lindley 1838b). All these extraordinary qualities, like a birthmark, predestined *Victoria* to assume her role as queen of other plants—all of which, according to George Lawson, "yield the palm of supremacy to their royal sister" (Lawson 1851).

When Reverend John Russell addressed members of the Essex Institute in Salem, Massachusetts, shortly before Christmas 1854, he could not contain his admiration for "the proud queen of the waters" (Allen 1854). His account of *Victoria*'s flower opening on two nights resembled more a mystic vision than a report of horticultural success. Russell described the nymph wearing "her robe of state," attired in "a drapery of Tyrian splendor," and crowned with "the royal diadem" of golden anthers.

The South American nymph's euphoric reception by the "civilized world" and her spectacular rise to a position of dominance were exploited in ways that may seem incomprehensible today. However improbable and naïve it may appear, even the presence of foraging beetles inside the flowers, for instance, was misconstrued to reflect views on the social order. One anonymous writer explained the scene as an allegory of inequalities among people, where *Victoria*, "the Queen of Flowers, like the royal potentates in the world of humanity, finds its peculiar parasites that feed on and nestle about it" (Anonymous 1860a).

Further, in the 1860s, when the United States was sharply divided over the questions of slavery and race, Hinton Rowan Helper of North Carolina, an opponent of slavery who nevertheless argued for the expulsion of former slaves, used *Victoria* and other white flowers in his writings to prove the supremacy of the white race (Helper 1867). Appointed by President Lincoln as a consul in Buenos Aires, Helper showed his gratitude by rebranding *Victoria* as the "Lincoln lily." This clumsy attempt to convert an anointed queen into an elected representative was, needless to say, unsuccessful.

What contributed to the perception that *Victoria* was a creature of great rarity, exclusive and elusive? Perhaps it was the fact that despite three centuries of Spanish and Portuguese exploration and exploitation in South America, no one in Europe had heard of the world's largest lily until the Bohemian, French, and German naturalists arrived in the early nineteenth century. The many traders and missionaries who settled in the continent's interior undoubtedly knew *Victoria*, so it was puzzling why such an extraordinary creature escaped mention by those returning to Europe. "It is not a little remarkable," noted Hooker, "that such a truly striking plant, now known to abound in the still quiet nooks, or *igaripés*, of most of the rivers in Tropical America, east of the Andes... should not appear to have attracted the attention of ordinary travelers, no one among them having, so far as we are aware, noticed it in a manner which would render it recognizable by the readers" (Hooker 1851).

Ironically, the people who live near the lilies have appeared indifferent to what outsiders perceive as *Victoria*'s most inspiring, almost divine qualities. This has continued to mystify those traveling to South America. The only places where William

John Russell, address before members of the Essex Institute in Salem, 1854:

[E]ach change showed something new and gorgeous. Here, on one portion, was the flower leaves (petals), no longer of ivory whiteness, but tinted with delicate rose; on another part were streaks and dashes and spots of rich carmine; and on others were pencil markings of the same color, and of a feathery outline; on others still, the crimson color was intense, and some petals were of that entire color, except at the very base, where a clear white obtained. Thus the regal lily had assumed her robe of state, and was attired in a drapery of Tyrian splendor, "such as Solomon in all his glory could never boast." Nor was this all. The proud attire of the queenly plant was not yet assumed. The plastic hands of the servitors of nature were yet to mould the royal diadem and crown their lovely monarch. The interior of the flower appeared like a large button carved out of delicate rose-colored carnelian, with its centre depressed. In a few minutes... [t]he depression rose visibly to the surface, and presently it became of a conical form. The rosy and narrow petals also, swelling at their curved portions, gradually became erect, and the points of each petal, standing close side by side, made an empalement of a circular outline.... At last, the golden anthers were visible, and the triple circle of their narrow laminae stood up around the precious disk of the flower, to minister to its future destiny and to complete its work.

Allen 1854

In contrast to the reverence surrounding *Victoria cruziana* outside her native lands, she shares a trash-filled pond with several swine on a farm near the city of Resistencia, Argentina.
Tomasz Aniśko / Longwood Gardens

Agnew Paton, a travel writer looking for the famed lilies in Guiana, caught sight of them were in a "filthy ditch" or a "fever-breeding slough" outside Georgetown, "so little were they prized by people accustomed to the daily view of them," he commented (Paton 1887).

Thus ignored or hidden from view, the nymph lived in seclusion "on the bosom of her native bays," as one writer put it, until men of science discovered her and "[took] her by the hand, and declared her loveliness to the world" (Anonymous 1851j). With characteristic zeal, Russell painted a compelling picture of the lonely tropical nymph, which, "for thousands of years on the marshy border of the great rivers," awaited "the time when it should elicit the spontaneous admiration of the first civilized man who beheld it, and the reverent heed of multitudes who look upon it as one of the wonders in horticultural art" (Russell 1856).

The perception of rarity was not just the result of her reclusive lifestyle and the remoteness of her native habitat. After all, these factors were quickly overcome once the queen lily arrived in the capitals of Europe. This reputation was also developed because of the expense associated with providing her an adequate environment; her requisite continuous care; and the difficulty in producing and then germinating her seeds combined with her lifespan of usually only one year. Even a century and a half later, these challenges remain unchanged.

Victoria's biological peculiarities and idiosyncrasies made her unsuitable for widespread cultivation, preventing her from becoming an ordinary garden plant of common folks—thus preserving her regal reputation. Notoriously ephemeral, *Victoria* remains elusive. She appears in ponds, pools, and basins in gardens and parks around the world, only to expire a few months or years later. No one can ever truly possess the nymph. At best, they can only host, accommodate, and care for her.

PILGRIM'S PROGRESS

With the reverence for the queen lily firmly established and the cult of *Victoria* spreading throughout Europe and the United States, pilgrims began to journey to South America to discover the object of their adoration in her native land. With the lily already in cultivation, the purpose of such escapades was not to collect seeds or to gain fame and recognition. It was to witness this wonder of Nature in her native glory and then share the experience with those less fortunate who could only see one or at best a few plants living in captivity.

One of the earliest such travelers was Sir Edward Sullivan, the fifth baronet of Thames Ditton. Arriving first in Georgetown, Sullivan mounted an expedition to the interior of Guiana to see the noble lily for himself. After ascending the Essequibo for two days, Sullivan's party made a landing along the shore and set out through the bush, carrying a dugout canoe. Soon, the men launched the canoe on a small creek, which took them through a "most painfully feverish-looking swamp" to a small lake completely covered with

Anonymous correspondent to the *Cottage Gardener*, 1851:

Not one of the least extraordinary facts connected with this sovereign of the water lilies is that, familiar to Europeans as have been the products of South America for some centuries, traversed as have been her rivers, ransacked as have been her mountains and streams for their natural productions, and though the seeds of this very plant were known in her markets, yet this, one of the monarchs of the vegetable world, was not even indistinctly known until the year 1837.

Anonymous 1851j

One summer night in 1959, visitors flocked to the greenhouses of the Botanical Garden in Amsterdam to witness the spectacle of *Victoria* opening her flowers.
UNIVERSITY OF AMSTERDAM SPECIAL COLLECTIONS

giant lilies in full bloom (Sullivan 1852). Sullivan survived his adventures in South America unscathed, despite the threat of "fevers, agues, &c.," and returned to England to write a book about them. Ever since, countless adventurers like Sullivan have repeated this routine all over South America.

As *Victoria*'s faithful devotees sought and found her, they carried back stories that nurtured the public's curiosity and excited even greater interest in the South American wilderness. Thomas Jefferson Page, a United States Navy officer who explored the Río Paraguay in 1852, painted the scene near Corrientes in Argentina: "Extensive shallow lagoons, pure and limpid, were gemmed with islands of the *Victoria regia*." Page considered himself "fortunate" to see the queen of lilies upon her native waters, "what alone would have repaid for a longer journey" (Page 1859).

No price was considered too high, in sweat or treasure, to pay for the thrill of spotting the giant lily in her primeval state. "The heat was intense, the air stagnant; clothes seemed insufferable, and my rifle increased in weight with every step," one correspondent to the *Gardener's Monthly* began his nerve-wracking account of an exhausting expedition to track *Victoria* near Obidos on the Amazon in 1872 (Anonymous 1872). "Eureka!" he exclaimed when the mythical queen lily materialized at last. "I did feel enthusiastic," the nymph hunter confessed, "in spite of heat, dirt, and fatigue."

Even in later years, when photographs of the colossal lily in her native surroundings accompanied the narratives of the travelers, the pictures did not diminish the public's desire to see *Victoria* in the wild. On the contrary, these images only heightened the awareness of the lilies living untamed in the Amazon and Paraguay-Paraná river systems, inspiring many more daring travelers to undertake such a pilgrimage.

In the twentieth century, as travel to South America became more affordable, many more naturalists followed in the footsteps of the previous century's great explorers to spot the legendary nymph. Among them was Russell Seibert, an American botanist collecting in South America for the United States Department of Agriculture. While exploring Peruvian Amazonia in search of rubber trees during World War II, he carefully recorded several sightings of *Victoria* and returned to them twenty years later. By that time Seibert was the director of Longwood Gardens and hoped to introduce a Peruvian strain of *Victoria amazonica* into cultivation. "It has not been adequately observed," he commented, "to see what differences might exist between this strain and that from the lower Amazon and Guianas from whence the cultivated species material has been derived" (Aniśko 2006).

Edward Sullivan, 1852:

After calling at Government-house [in Georgetown] to pay our respects to the Governor, we pursued our inquiries regarding the Victoria regia, *but could get no certain information as to the time and distance, and the amount of supplies necessary: some said it was nearly as far as the foot of the Andes, a thousand miles distant, and we ought to take supplies for three months at least; others said it was not more than one hundred miles, and that three days' provision would be abundant; but all agreed in strongly recommending us not to go at all, as the rainy season had commenced, and our chances of escaping fevers, agues, &c. were small indeed. However, being so near to our El Dorado, we determined not to be shaken in our plans by doubtful reports.... At length, after getting pretty well confused by the different advice and information that was vouchsafed to us, and not having a very clear idea whether the lily were one or five hundred miles [160 or 800 km] distant, we finished by laying in provisions that would have sufficed a party twice as numerous as ours in a trip to the Pacific.*

Sullivan 1852

Since the 1850s, travelers have come to South America for the sole purpose of seeing *Victoria* in her natural environment. Here, she reclines on placid waters along the Rupununi River in Guyana.

TOMASZ ANIŚKO / LONGWOOD GARDENS

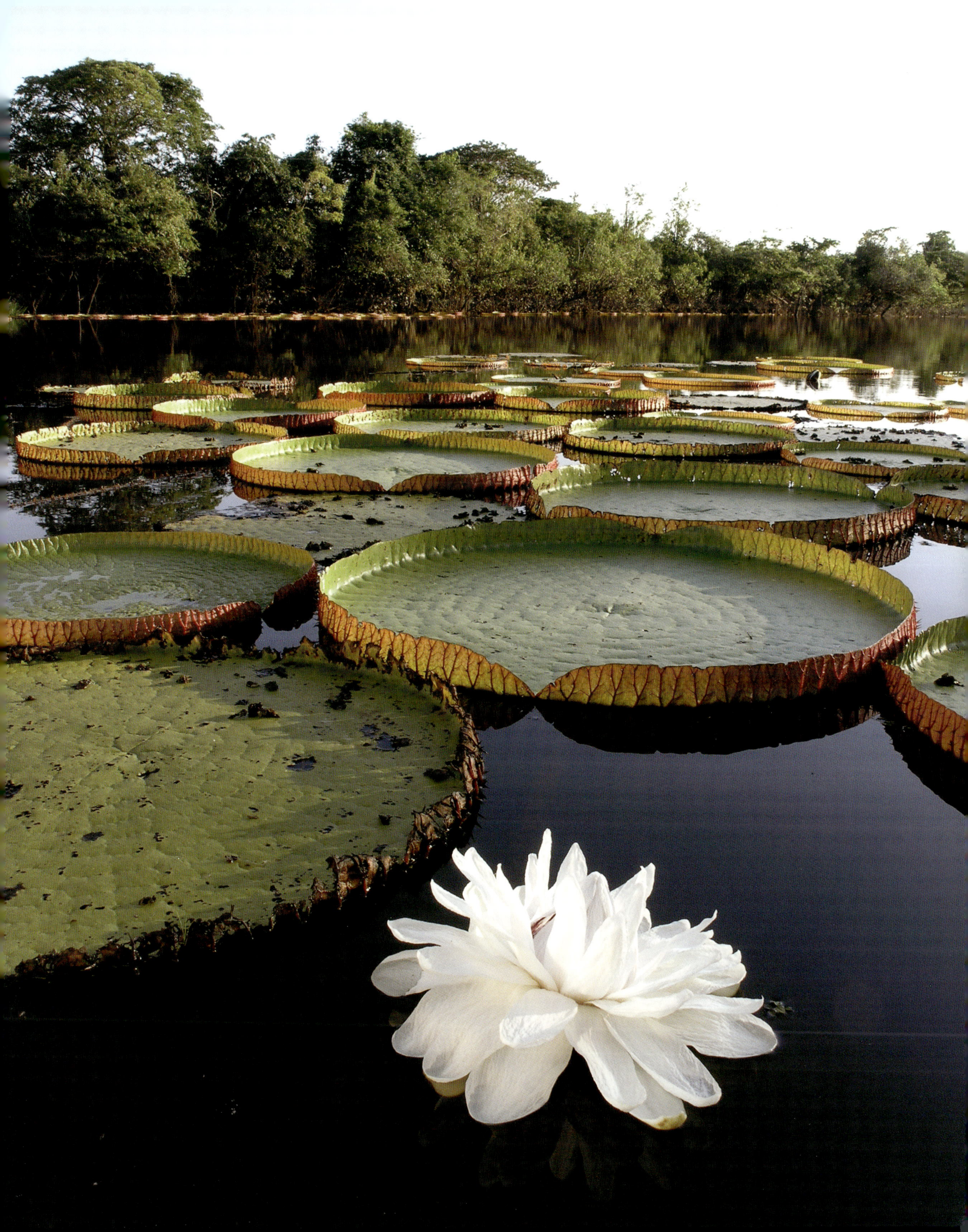

Louis Agassiz and Elizabeth Cabot Cary Agassiz, 1896:

We could not see it growing in its native waters—a type, as it were, of the luxuriance of tropical nature—without the deepest interest. Wonderful as it is when seen in the tank of a greenhouse, and perhaps even more impressive, in a certain sense, from its isolation, in its own home it has the charm of harmony with all that surrounds it—with the dense mass of forest, with palm and parasite, with birds of glowing plumage, with insects of all bright and wonderful tints, and with fishes which, though hidden in the water beneath it, are no less brilliant and varied than the world of life above.

Agassiz and Agassiz 1896

Toward the end of the twentieth century, as the Amazon morphed into a global tourist destination, the giant water lilies became one of the main attractions alongside indigenous dolphins and manatees. Tour boat operations sprang up in riverside towns throughout the Amazon and Paraguay-Paraná basins, promising the thrill of experiencing one of the last ecosystems that has not been subjugated by people, but without sacrificing any of the comforts of modern life.

Today, Brazil's old rubber capital of Manaus has become a veritable Mecca for this new breed of ecotourists. Moacir Fortes of Manaus, a veteran of Amazon navigation and owner of several large boats, has built a reputation as the foremost guide for *Victoria* devotees. Since the 1990s, Fortes, better known as Captain Mo, has ferried hundreds of would-be explorers—scientists, students, and avid gardeners—through the backwaters of the Amazon. His heavily built skiffs, which access the shallow lagoons typically inhabited by *Victoria,* have become to Captain Mo's expeditions what off-road vehicles are to African safaris. The colossal lily, the Amazon's ultimate trophy, stands in place of elephants and rhinos on these bloodless hunts.

But not all encounters with the queen lily, whether in cultivation or in the wild, were as exhilarating as *Victoria*'s admirers might have hoped. Some people suffered

Would-be explorers venture into the backwaters of great rivers of South America to come face-to-face with wild *Victoria* plants.
Tomasz Aniśko / Longwood Gardens

from expectations that were set unrealistically high by circulating rumors. One person who was disappointed by the lily's flower admitted that after seeing the gargantuan leaf, he "might have reasonably expected the *Victoria* to produce a flower as large as the top of a bushel basket" (Forsyth 1851). The flower's ephemeral nature did not please everyone, either. Critics pointed out that when the flower's second night of bloom passed, "the morrow dawns only upon its decline, its work finished, and the foot-prints of decay are stealing over its loveliness" (Forsyth 1851). Others who undertook a long and arduous journey to *Victoria*'s homeland sometimes felt less than adequately rewarded at the end. Sullivan, who endured all the hardships of traveling to the interior of Guiana, confessed: "Altogether, I don't think I was so much enchanted with the lily as I ought to have been; and although I think a trip up the Essequibo or any of the tropical rivers repays one very well, I don't think the lily itself is worth the trouble" (Sullivan 1852).

Further, the unpredictability of when exactly the lily flower would open often tormented cultivators who wanted to impress their guests coming to view *Victoria*'s evening performance. "This was an afternoon of great disappointment," wrote Edward Chitty of Kingston, Jamaica, when a flower in his garden did not open as he hoped. "To the grievous disappointment of some twenty or thirty friends who had come to enjoy a wonder, the petals lay withering and languishing upon and under the surface of the water. . . . It was a failure" (Chitty 1852).

THE CROWD-PLEASER

For most of her devotees, though, these were only minor imperfections that made the queen lily that much more interesting. Her charms attracted scores of spectators in every place she appeared. When Cope showed his lily in Philadelphia in 1851, he reported that "every evening, when the

Victoria never fails to attract attention and inspire wonder.
TOMASZ ANIŚKO / LONGWOOD GARDENS

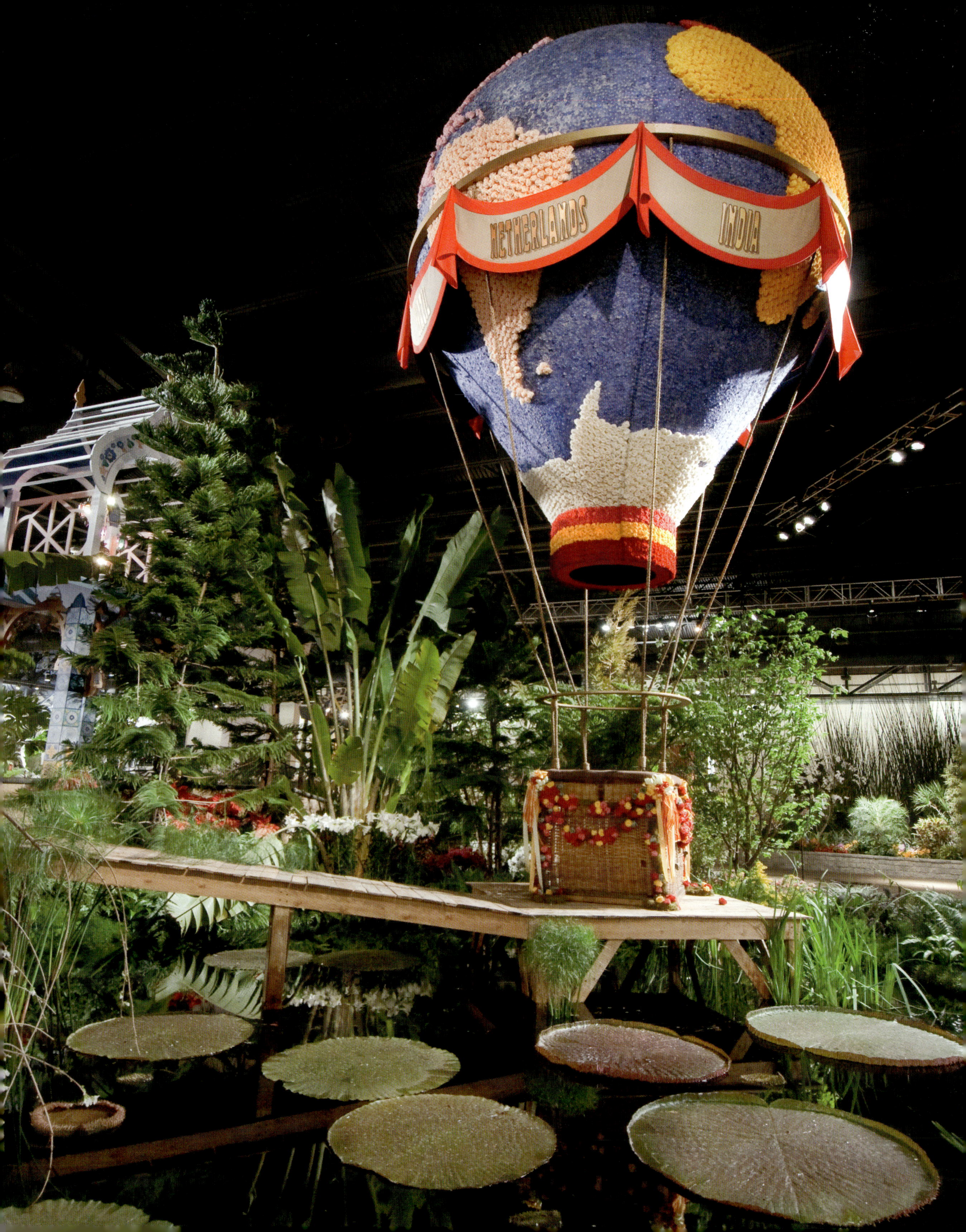
NETHERLANDS
INDIA

saloons were most crowded, an impenetrable cordon surrounded the tank gazing with admiration and surprise at the singular structure and immense proportions of this wonderful water lily" (Boyd 1929). Two years later, in Salem, Massachusetts, Allen threw open his house "to the admission of all who desire to see the *Victoria* in bloom," attracting crowds of visitors (Allen 1853). After *Victoria* was planted in outdoor pools in 1894, attendance at Tower Grove Park in St. Louis increased by one-third, reaching over thirty thousand on one Sunday afternoon (Grove 2005).

The South American nymph's admirers instantly recognized the seductive spell she cast over throngs of spectators, and she promptly became the ultimate crowd-pleaser. The giant lily made appearances at major exhibitions, from the Great Exhibition of 1851 in London, to the 1876 Centennial Exhibition in Philadelphia, to the 1934 Century of Progress Exposition in Chicago, where she was seen by millions of people. "It is hardly possible to conceive a more magnificent, novel, or interesting sight than this lily would present," wrote one correspondent to the *Gardeners' Chronicle,* suggesting *Victoria* receive a "noble" basin in the future Crystal Palace in Sydenham (Anonymous 1851g). After this project was realized, it was further proposed that a basin the size of the arena in the Roman Coliseum be built in London to allow the royal lily ample space and proper accommodations (Anonymous 1857).

The level of intense public interest in *Victoria*, bordering on hysteria, also sparked a wider interest in all sorts of water lilies and other aquatic plants. Large basins, pools, and ponds built and fitted for the queen lily usually afforded ample space for companion plants. These were always carefully selected because, as one writer put it, "dignity ought to be observed in the plants that are made to associate with this queenly flower"

In early March 2011, the giant water lily was a star of the Philadelphia International Flower Show.
LARRY ALBEE / LONGWOOD GARDENS

Thomas Higginson, 1863:

Nothing in the world of vegetable existence has such a human interest. The charm is not in the mere size of the plant, which disappoints everybody, as Niagara does, when tried by that sole standard.... But it is not the measurements of the Victoria, it is its life which fascinates. It is not a thing merely of dimensions, nor merely of beauty, but a creature of vitality and motion.

Higginson 1863

The Aquatunnel in the Climatron at the Missouri Botanical Garden in St. Louis offered visitors a rare underwater view of *Victoria* lilies.
MISSOURI BOTANICAL GARDEN

Victoria lilies without fail win over the public. In every garden, they become the highlights of the summer season.
LARRY ALBEE / LONGWOOD GARDENS

William Paton, 1887:

I had seen the flower but once before, when having read in a London newspaper of one rare specimen in full bloom at Sydenham I set out forthwith to see it; paid a shilling for a cab to the railway station, bought a first-class return ticket, for I was going in state to see the queen of flowers. I gave willingly (I would have paid double) the entrance-fee to the Crystal Palace, and struggled through a crowd of sight-seers surrounding a fountain where the wonderful lily was blooming in all its splendor. When I obtained a short peep of it, I beheld for the first time in my life the Victoria regia; to see which in full bloom, people flocked in crowds from London as they would have flocked to listen to the last-discovered and best advertised prima donna, or to stare at the Queen herself touch off the fireworks by electricity.

Paton 1887

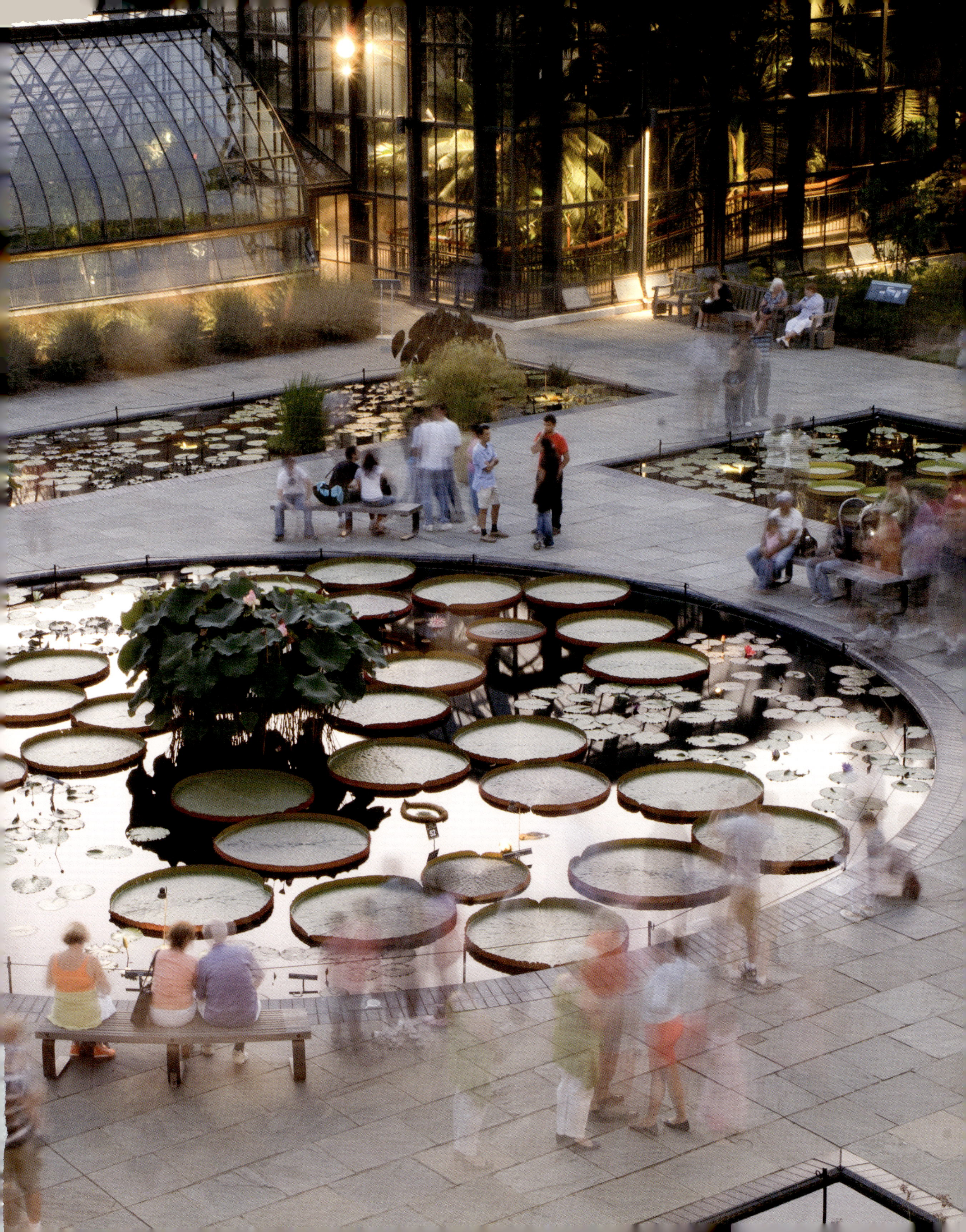

People living in the same environment as *Victoria* made the lily's seeds part of their diet and used the sap of the plant in various cosmetic and medicinal applications.

LOREN MCINTYRE

Alexander Forsyth, 1851:

The introduction of Victoria regia *into this country [United Kingdom] has been the commencement of a new era in the history of stove aquatics. The* Victoria *required a tank or basin of gigantic size, and would not be put off with an instalment [sic] of its demands; setting pots and tubs at defiance, it scorned all reasonable bounds, and could not be stowed into any kind of coopery, since a brewer's vat could scarcely float more than one of its splendid leaves. We have, therefore, to thank this noble plant for such a reformation in tanks, as never could have been anticipated by the warmest admirers of this tribe of plants; for if it would have behaved itself, and lived in a tub, two feet [60 cm] in diameter, and flowered, however shabbily, in a bushel [36 liters] of mud, and struggle as other aquatics heretofore had to be contented with, we should never have seen the splendid effect that Nymphaeas produce in an aquarium 30 feet [9 m] wide.*

Forsyth 1851

(Forsyth 1851). Once these special provisions were created for the queen lily, her sister *Nymphaea* water lilies were able to present themselves in a much better light, winning over many faithful followers and inspiring an entirely new form of gardening in water.

HOMEGROWN FAVORITE

The reverence afforded some plants in various cultures is usually grounded in the benefit they provide to a particular society, be it food, medicine, or a cosmetic, intoxicant, or hallucinogenic agent. Good looks and vanity are rarely enough to secure a place in the plant pantheon. *Victoria* has defied this principle: For all the veneration surrounding her, she gives nothing more than visual delight in return.

Yet in the nymph's home in South America, she has long had a number of practical uses. The most significant and widespread of these was the use of her seeds in cooking and baking. This was reflected in the names given to her by Spanish and Portuguese colonists: *maíz de agua* and *milho de água*, or "maize of the water."

Victoria's large and starchy seeds yielded flour of exceptional quality used for cakes and breads (Burkart et al. 1987).

Aimé Bonpland reported that in Corrientes at the confluence of the Paraná and Paraguay, the flour of *Victoria* was preferred to that of the finest wheat, and cakes made from it were considered a luxury (Hooker 1851). "Excellent and nutritious" bread was baked from this flour in Colombia (Bollaert 1861), whereas whole roasted seeds were consumed in Paraguay and the Brazilian Pantanal (Ragonese and Martinez-Crovetto 1947, Pott and Pott 2000). In the Chaco region of northern Argentina, *Victoria* seeds were pounded and mixed with corn flour or cassava starch to prepare baked treats for children (Schulz 1963).

Although the gathering of *Victoria* seeds has been largely given up today, it is clear that their nutritional value was appreciated by the people of South America as much as that provided by her sister water lilies in the Old World. There, Egyptians have collected seeds of *Nymphaea lotus* and *Nymphaea caerulea* since time immemorial. Pliny proclaimed that bread made with the flour of *Nymphaea* had no equal in the world as long as it was eaten hot (Irvine and Trickett 1953). In other parts of Africa and in India, *Nymphaea lotus* seeds were used similarly but also roasted, boiled, or made into a sauce. The Chinese have gathered and cultivated *Euryale ferox* for the same purpose for at least three thousand years (Sculthorpe 1967).

Another useful product of *Victoria* was the fresh sap pressed from the succulent parts of the plant, including the rhizomes, petioles, peduncles, leaves, and flowers. It found many cosmetic and medicinal applications in communities along the South American rivers. In Brazil, it was used to dye hair and give it a silky shine as well as to treat various skin conditions and dress wounds (Decker 1936, Pott and Pott 2000). In Argentina, in addition to dyeing hair, it was used to cure venomous snakebites

In Paraguay, dry *Victoria* leaves are sold as herbal tea to combat symptoms of colds, asthma, and bronchitis.
JORGE MONTEVERDE

Aimé Bonpland, letter to Robert Gore, 1850:

The mayz de l'eau *is so called because it bears fruits filled with an immense number of round seeds, containing an amylaceous substance of snowy whiteness, substituted occasionally for the grains of maize. The farina made from the* mayz de l'eau *is not only superior to that of the maize, on account of its quality, but it is even preferred to the finest wheat, and the flour of the white cassava, which yields the best farina of all the species of that genus and is considered better than sago. At the time when the fruits of the* mayz de l'eau *are fully ripe, the ladies of Corrientes hasten to obtain seeds, and to extract the flour, which they carefully preserve: with this substance they make many kinds of pastry, but particularly croquets, which are so superior to those manufactured of common flour, that it is considered a luxury in Corrientes to have cakes of the farina of the* Victoria regia.

Hooker 1851

Juan Valla, 1976:

In Esquina, in Corrientes Province, Mr. Basilio Marini, who knows the river very well, explained to me that seed collection is very difficult, since the maturity of the fruit coincides with the dropping of the water level of the river, and therefore places where the irupé *grow become barely accessible to the canoes. Also one needs to choose the opportune moment, before the seed pod opens and disseminates the seeds. In order to collect the seeds, long canes with an iron hook attached to the end are used. With this tool, one searches for fruit under the water, trying to detach them so that they float, or to spear them in order to haul them aboard the boat. Even though few people eat them, some grind the seeds and with the flour make cakes and breads or make popped seeds, the same way popcorn is made. Also when the harvest is abundant, they use the seeds to feed pigs.*

Valla 1976, translated by Kathleen Morgan

PEOPLE'S CHOICE

or to suppress libido (Parodi 1886, Valla 1976, Martinez-Crovetto 1981). To this day in Paraguay, one can purchase neatly packaged dried *Victoria* leaves to make a tea that purportedly alleviates coughing due to colds, asthma, or bronchitis (Monteverde 2010).

IN THE QUEEN'S IMAGE

While only a limited number of people can visit *Victoria* in one of the gardens where she resides, and even fewer can journey to see her in her native haunts, books and illustrations have played an important role in taking her places where she could not travel. When Schomburgk announced the wonder lily's existence to the world outside South America in 1837, there were only two other men in Europe who had actually seen her: Pöppig in Leipzig and d'Orbigny in Paris. Another twelve years would pass before a living plant appeared there. Fortunately, Schomburgk accompanied his announcement with an illustration he had prepared in Guiana. A promise of future bounty, this illustration was the only representation available to satisfy the public's curiosity about what this mystical *Victoria* was really like.

A lithographed frontispiece from Wilhelm Hochstetter's 1852 *Die Victoria Regia* was a mirror image of one of the plates in Jules Planchon and Louis Van Houtte's volume published a year earlier in Belgium.
LONGWOOD GARDENS LIBRARY AND ARCHIVES

Publishers did not hesitate to plagiarize, embellish, and transform Schomburgk's drawing, often with errors. It is difficult today, when images of everything we can think of are literally at our fingertips, to comprehend how important Schomburgk's sketch was. While his original drawing was sent to the London Botanical Society, another "splendid private delineation of the plant, of natural size," was placed on public view in the alcove of a greenhouse at Chiswick, the garden of the Horticultural Society of London (Hooker 1847). In the absence of an actual plant, its two-dimensional image, reconstructed under Schomburgk's supervision, served to answer the public's desire for a glimpse of the famed queen lily.

It was not until a decade later, when Thomas Bridges returned from his escapades in South America with preserved specimens of *Victoria*, that a new attempt was made in London to create a more accurate and complete picture of the majestic nymph. In 1847, Hooker published four plates prepared by Walter Fitch in *Curtis's Botanical Magazine*, which blended Schomburgk's drawings and descriptions with Bridges's specimens. "Of the *Victoria*," Hooker wrote, "we have the good fortune to possess flowering specimens, gathered by Sir Robert Schomburgk; and blossoms, both preserved in spirits and dried,

A charming scene featuring *Victoria* from George Lawson's book *The Royal Water-Lily of South America*, published in Scotland in 1852.
LONGWOOD GARDENS LIBRARY AND ARCHIVES

collected by Mr. Bridges. These, with coloured drawings executed on the spot by Sir Robert, enable us to present . . . all the more important analyses necessary to illustrate the genus and species of the plant" (Hooker 1847). Bridges also brought back *Victoria* seeds, which germinated at Kew. Although these seedlings died without yielding a single flower, Fitch's brilliant reconstructions reignited public interest in the nymph.

A couple of years later, when *Victoria* finally arrived in England, Fitch's 1847 illustrations were judged "more showy than correct" (Planchon and Van Houtte 1850–51, translated by John Luttrell). Soon they were replaced by a new set of magnificent plates from the Hooker-Fitch team—this time based on living plants raised at Syon House. Widely recognized as masterpieces, these four plates, published in Hooker's 1851 grand volume *Victoria Regia*, did more to promote the queen lily around the world than perhaps any other image of any other plant in history. To this day, they are frequently reproduced in books, including this volume, and as prints.

Others followed Hooker and Fitch's example, hoping to capitalize on the unprecedented level of interest in *Victoria* that had exploded in Europe. In Belgium, Jules Planchon and Louis Van Houtte produced a magnificent book titled *La Victoria Regia* (1850–51), which featured five color plates of the lily that were accompanied by many black-and-white line drawings of various anatomical and morphological details.

John Fisk Allen, 1854:

The heat and moist atmosphere of the lily house, caused by so large a body of tepid water, renders a long continuance in the house unpleasant, and, to an invalid, an unwarranted exposure. By the aid of this treatise and the accompanying illustrations, one may fully appreciate its beauty and wonderful growth. In the agreeable temperature of his parlor he may contemplate the changes of leaf, bud, and flower; to witness which, in its native or artificial waters, days of exposure to a tropical climate must be endured. It is always advisable, when convenient, to obtain a view of the living plant; but many cannot do this; to such, it is hoped, these descriptions and illustrations may afford instruction and gratification.

Allen 1854

Victoria Houses like this one in Brussels represented limitless possibilities offered by industrial and technological progress.
PAUL BORREMANS / COLLECTION OF THE NATIONAL BOTANIC GARDEN OF BELGIUM

Two smaller books were published in Germany in 1852: Wilhelm Hochstetter's *Die Victoria Regia* and Eduard Loescher's *Die königliche Wasserlilie Victoria Regia*, each with a single hand-colored lithographed frontispiece. Hochstetter had one of the plates from the Belgian book showing the second-night flower. It was reproduced as faithfully as possible, except it was reversed as a mirror image of the original. Loescher in turn combined the same flower with a leaf section that Planchon and Van Houtte's volume featured in the illustration of the first-night flower. Why this lack of originality? No doubt the high cost of creating and printing color plates in those days was a deciding factor.

In Scotland, George Lawson wrote *The Royal Water-Lily of South America*, which included a small color plate showing *Victoria* floating on the placid waters of presumably a river in Guiana. The last and the most impressive work in this short-lived eruption of literary and artistic creativity was John Fisk Allen's *Victoria Regia or the Great Water Lily of America*, published in the United States in 1854. It featured six splendid illustrations created by William Sharp, America's first chromolithographic printer. Although undeniably inspired by Fitch's, they were nevertheless based on plants growing in Allen's greenhouse in Salem. Sharp's spectacular plates were the earliest examples of large-scale color printing in the United States.

Forty years after Allen published his work on *Victoria*, Scotto Nash grew the queen lily in outdoor pools in Clifton, New Jersey, and used photography, a newer and far cheaper technique than lithography, to create images of the queen lily. Since his intention was to "[spread] the love of these plants by means of his pictures," Nash offered sets of twenty photographs of *Victoria* for four dollars (Anonymous 1895b, translated by Daniela Freitag). Several of the images featured a little girl or a woman as part of the scene, and some were accompanied by captions with quotes from Sir Walter Scott's hugely popular poem *The Lady of the Lake*.

POWERFUL PUBLIC ICON

As the nymph's fame and recognition grew beyond gardening circles, the intense public interest endowed her with varied symbolic meanings outside that of the queen of flowers. Most of them tinkered with the idea of power in its many permutations.

For Victorian society, the queen lily was a glorious symbol of Britain's imperial power, ever expanding its influence and control over the rest of the world (Scourse 1983). This sentiment was reflected in appellations that "aptly and correctly" described *Victoria* as "The Empress of the Waters of the New World" (Anonymous 1851f). It was, after all, the triumph of British colonial ventures in South America matched by the country's industrial supremacy in providing the glass and iron that built the palaces that enabled *Victoria* to flourish so far from her homeland.

PEOPLE'S CHOICE 451

James Gurney posing for a photograph on a lily pad in Tower Grove Park in St. Louis in the late nineteenth century. Was this a demonstration of human control over Nature or perhaps of the nymph's power to seduce men, making them go to extremes in order to provide for her needs?
TOWER GROVE PARK

Tamed and domesticated, the giant lily was viewed as a prime example of the limitlessness of Britannia's worldwide domination. Ordinary Victorians saw in her, more specifically, a symbol of their newest colony in the New World and its link to the dynasty ruling the empire, even after it was recognized that the lily was widespread in South America (Burnett 2000).

In the nineteenth century, *Victoria* became a compelling example of what Margaret Flanders Darby called "a triumphant domestication of nature's power by English technological culture" (Darby 2002). Outside the British Isles, however, the same plant was stripped of any nationalistic affiliations and renounced her allegiance to the empire. Instead, she provided testimony to human power and ability. "The patience and skill of man has borne this magnificent plant from its native home, and transplanted it in the gardens of these northern regions," John Russell observed to the members of the Essex Institute in the United States (Russell 1856). He told his audience that he was inspired by the lily to muse on "the ingenuity of man, who seizes the laws of Nature and with a bold hand and by patience, overcomes inequalities of climate and temperature."

One role assigned to *Victoria* in the endeavor to master Nature reflected what Darby described as man's inclination to choose "the feminine to express the mysteries of nature, including the vitality that escapes patriarchal control" (Darby 2002). The images of *Victoria* blissfully enjoying a warm bath in a glass palace inspired the metaphor of the "hothouse lily" as a model for the nineteenth-century woman—beautiful, tender, and entirely dependent on a man's ability and desire to protect and care for her (Darby 2002). Whether Queen Victoria, too, embodied the ideal "hothouse lily" is debatable, but her floral equivalent took on a number of monarchic functions—from becoming an iconic motif of the colony of British Guiana, featured on its stamps and coins, to assuming patronage of the Botanical Society of London for well over a century (Lousley 1951).

Victoria has been many things to many people. Meehan called her "a strange flower—so grand, yet so accommodating" (Allen 1854). On a friend's wedding day, he sent a box containing a closed flower bud as a gift. It was packed with damp moss to keep it moist and a heated brick to keep it warm. Upon reaching its destination, the box was opened, and a perfectly formed flower revealed itself to the bride and groom. "What can be more magical?" asked Meehan.

It is perhaps this tangle of meanings accorded *Victoria*—from hothouse lily to seductive nymph, divine birth-giver to goddess of sublime beauty, benevolent queen to Nature's magical wonder—that has fueled the public's insatiable fascination with her. It is perhaps our failure to categorically define what she is and what she is not, and what place in our culture and our lives should be assigned to her, that keeps our relationship with the lily vibrant and rewarding. The ambiguity surrounding her true character, her ever-changing personality, and her elusive material presence captivates our imagination today just as much as it did when Haenke fell to his knees in 1801 before the presence of a magnificent creation for which he had no name. In Salem in 1854, John Russell did not fall to his knees, but he might as well have, since as he described an evening spent watching the spectacle of a *Victoria* flower opening: "We stood as worshippers at its shrine; indeed! who could but feel that the August Presence was there in one of the many forms of mysterious wonder of this fair world" (Russell 1856).

A simpler and humbler, yet just as sincere, expression of our feelings for the nymph can be found in the 1903 appendix to *The Steward's Handbook* titled *How to Fold Napkins* (Whitehead 1903). One style presented is called *The Victoria Regia*. Once a flower of the queen lily is folded out of a "very stiff" napkin, it is set in the center of the plate. "The bread is not to be placed in or under it," the reader is told, "but a single flower, such as a rose, may very properly be slipped into the heart."

"What can be more magical?" asked Thomas Meehan of Philadelphia in the mid-nineteenth century. Here, visitors to Longwood Gardens experience a "magical" evening in the company of queen lily.

LARRY ALBEE / LONGWOOD GARDENS

REFERENCES

Abercrombie, J. 1857. The Gardener's Pocket Journal, and Daily Assistant in English Gardening. London: William Tegg and Co.

Agassiz, L. and Mrs. L. Agassiz. 1896. A Journey in Brazil. Boston: Houghton, Mifflin and Co.

Allan, M. 1967. The Hookers of Kew, 1785-1911. London: Michael Joseph.

Allen, J. F. 1853. Flowering of the *Victoria regia* in Salem, Mass. *Magazine of Horticulture, Botany, and All Useful Discoveries and Improvements in Rural Affairs* 19:367-372.

Allen, J. F. 1854. *Victoria Regia* or the Great Water Lily of America. Boston: Dutton and Wentworth.

Anderson, E. 1963. Why should *Victoria* leaves be stiff? *Missouri Botanical Garden Bulletin* 51 (9):10-12.

Anderson, E. 1965. *Victoria* water lilies: Plants which stir men's minds. *Missouri Botanical Garden Bulletin* 53 (5):1-18.

Anderson, W. H. 1993. Letter of 6 August to Patrick A. Nutt. Longwood Gardens Library and Archives.

Aniśko, T. 2006. Plant Exploration for Longwood Gardens. Portland, Oregon: Timber Press.

Anonymous. 1837. Report of the proceedings of the Botanical Society. *Athenaeum: Journal of Literature, Science, the Fine Arts, Music, and the Drama* (9 September):661.

Anonymous. 1840. The Guiana expedition. *Gardener's Gazette* 159 (January 18):45.

Anonymous. 1850a. Botanical information, *Victoria regia*. *Hooker's Journal of Botany and Kew Garden Miscellany* 2:218-219.

Anonymous. 1850b. Garden memoranda: Flowering of the *Victoria regia* at Sion House, Brentford. *Gardeners' Chronicle* (May 18):310-311.

Anonymous. 1850c. *Victoria regia*. *Gardener's Magazine of Botany, Horticulture, Floriculture, and Natural Science* 1:225-232.

Anonymous. 1851a. A trip to Syon-House and Gardens. *Visitor, or Monthly Instructor* (1851):354-357.

Anonymous. 1851b. Chiswick and Regent's Park exhibitions. *Florist and Garden Miscellany* (1850):166-168.

Anonymous. 1851c. Garden memoranda: Messrs. Veitch's Nursery, Exeter. *Gardeners' Chronicle* 11 (15 March):167.

Anonymous. 1851d. Garden memoranda: Messrs. Weeks and Co.'s Nursery, King's Road, Chelsea. *Gardeners' Chronicle* 13 (29 March):199, 21 (24 May):327, 28 (12 July):439.

Anonymous. 1851e. Home correspondence: Fragrance of the *Victoria regia*. *Gardeners' Chronicle* 35 (30 August):549.

Anonymous. 1851f. Home correspondence: London nurseries, *Victoria regia*, and the Crystal Palace. *Gardeners' Chronicle* 31 (2 August):485-486.

Anonymous. 1851g. Home correspondence: The Crystal Palace and the *Victoria regia*. *Gardeners' Chronicle* 32 (9 August):501.

Anonymous. 1851h. Miscellaneous: *Victoria regia*. *Gardeners' Chronicle* 46 (15 November):728.

Anonymous. 1851i. No title. *Gardeners' Chronicle* 2 (11 January):19.

Anonymous. 1851j. No title. *Cottage Gardener: Practical Guide in Every Department of Horticulture and Rural and Domestic Economy* 5:122-123.

Anonymous. 1851k. The *Victoria regia* in open ponds. *Horticulturist and Journal of Rural Art and Rural Taste* 6:359-360.

Anonymous. 1852. New-York Horticultural Exhibition. *The Plough, the Loom, and the Anvil* 5 (1):32-36.

Anonymous. 1853. Zur Kultur der *Victoria regia*. *Gartenflora Deutschlands und der Schweiz* (1853):28.

Anonymous. 1856. Dr. Robert Caspary. *Gardeners' Chronicle* (31 May):372.

Anonymous. 1857. History and cultivation of the *Victoria regia*. *Cottage Gardener and Country Gentleman* 19:82-86.

Anonymous. 1859. Things around Philadelphia. *Gardener's Monthly and Horticultural Advertiser* 1:119-120.

Anonymous. 1860a. Foreign intelligence. *Gardener's Monthly and Horticultural Advertiser* 2:252.

Anonymous. 1860b. National Botanic Garden and Conservatory, Washington, D. C. *Gardener's Monthly and Horticultural Advertiser* 2:174-176.

Anonymous. 1860c. Pennsylvania Horticultural Society. *Gardener's Monthly and Horticultural Advertiser* 2, 9:287.

Anonymous. 1860d. *Victoria regia* in the open air. *Gardener's Monthly and Horticultural Advertiser* 2:325.

Anonymous. 1862. Springbrook. *Horticulturist and Journal of Rural Art and Rural Taste* 17:325-326.

Anonymous. 1864. The *Victoria Regia*. *New York Times* (October 24).

Anonymous. 1872. Search for the *Victoria regia*. *Gardener's Monthly and Horticultural Advertiser* 14 (8):237-239.

Anonymous. 1878. The *Victoria* lily. *Gardener's Monthly and Horticulturist* 20:331-332.

Anonymous. 1879. The *Victoria* lily. *Gardener's Monthly and Horticulturist* 21:327.

Anonymous. 1885a. Science notes. *Student* 5:199.

Anonymous. 1885b. The *Victoria regia*. *Gardeners' Chronicle* (January 3):17.

Anonymous. 1886. Annual exhibition. September 14, 15, and 16. *Transactions of the Massachusetts Horticultural Society* (1886): 265-268.

Anonymous. 1887. Annual exhibition: September 13, 14, 15, and 16. *Transactions of the Massachusetts Horticultural Society* (1887):368.

Anonymous. 1888. The *Victoria regia*. *Garden and Forest* (August 22):309.

Anonymous. 1892. W. W. Lee's Aquatic Garden, Northampton. *Transactions of the Massachusetts Horticultural Society* (1892): 345-348.

Anonymous. 1895a. An amateur's walk around his garden – XXIX. *American Gardening* 16 (47):337-338.

Anonymous. 1895b. Der Wassergarten des Herrn S. C. Nash in Clifton, New-Jersey, Ver. Staaten. *Gartenflora Deutschlands, Russlands und der Schweiz* (1895):412-414.

Anonymous. 1895c. Water garden pictures. *American Gardening* 16 (32):126.

Anonymous. 1895d. Wm. Tricker and Co. advertisement. *American Gardening* 16 (32):40.

Anonymous. 1895e. The *Victoria regia* in New Jersey. *Scientific American* 72 (23):361.

Anonymous. 1910. Success crowns life work of St. Louis gardener. *St. Louis Star* (July 31).

Anonymous. 1915. Linnean House pools. *Missouri Botanical Garden Bulletin* 3 (7):103-106.

Anonymous. 1927. Amazon water-lilies as engineers. *Missouri Botanical Garden Bulletin* 15 (8):125-128.

Anonymous. 1995. No title. *Horticulture Week* (July 13):13.

Anonymous. 2007. Brynes find new *Victoria* spp. water lily in Brazil. *Florida Aquaculture* 60:1.

Anonymous. 2011. Record breaking: Giant Amazon water lily. http://www.livingrainforest.org/about-rainforests/record-breaking-giant-amazon-water-lily. Accessed 28 June 2011.

Anthon, W. H. 1861. Anniversary address before the American Institute, at Palace Garden, Oct. 6, 1860. *Transactions of the American Institute of the City of New York* (1860-61):71-81.

Arcangeli, G. 1908. Studi sulla *Victoria regia* Lindl. *Atte della Società Toscana di Scienze Naturali* 24:59-78.

Avé-Lallemant, R. 1859. Reise durch Süd-Brasilien in Jahre 1858. Leipzig: F. A. Brockhaus.

Bailey, L. H. 1953. The Standard Cyclopedia of Horticulture. New York: Macmillian Co.

Baker, H. G. and P. D. Hurd, Jr. 1968. Intrafloral ecology. *Annual Review of Entomology* 13:385-414.

Bannerman, M. 2008. Mamirauá: A Guide to the Natural History of the Amazon Flooded Forest. Rio de Janeiro: Instituto de Desenvolvimento Sustentável Mamirauá.

Barral, J. A. 1859. Chronique horticole. *Revue Horticole, Journal d'Horticulture Pratique* (1859):449-453.

Barry, P., J. Ritchie, H. Graham, M. P. Wilder, S. B. Parsons, J. S. Houghton. 1874. Report of the Committee of the Centennial Horticultural Society on horticultural buildings for the International Exhibition of 1876. *Gardener's Monthly* 16:95-96.

Bates, H. W. 1962. The Naturalist in the River Amazons. Berkeley: University of California Press (reprint of the 1864 edition by John Murray, London).

Bean, W. J. 1908. The Royal Botanic Gardens, Kew: Historical and Descriptive. London: Cassell and Co.

Beard, E. L. 1886. The progress of orchid culture in America. *Transactions of the Massachusetts Horticultural Society* (1886): 123-151.

Beidleman, R. G. 2006. California's Frontier Naturalists. Berkeley: University of California Press.

Beissner, L. 1893. Die *Victoria regia* im botanischen Garten zu Bonn. *Gartenflora Deutschlands, Russlands und der Schweiz* (1893): 206-208.

Bisset, P. 1929. The Book of Water Gardening. New York: A. T. De La Mare Co.

Bollaert, W. 1861. Products of New Granada. *Technologist: A Monthly Record of Science Applied to Art and Manufacture* 1:187-188.

Bolon, C. R. 1992. Forms of the Goddess Lajjā Gaurī in Indian Art. University Park, Pennsylvania: Pennsylvania State University Press.

Bornemann, G. 1886. Versuche über Erhaltung der Keimfähigkeit bei importirten Samen von Wasserpflanzen während des Transportes. *Gartenflora Deutschlands, Russlands und der Schweiz* (1886):532-534.

Borsch, T., C. Löhne, and J. Wiersema. 2008. Phylogeny and evolutionary patterns in Nymphaeales: Integrating genes, genomes and morphology. *Taxon* 57 (4):1052-1081.

Borsch, T., C. Löhne, M. S. Mbaye, and J. Wiersema. 2011. Towards a complete species tree of *Nymphaea*: shedding further light on subg. Brachyceras and its relationship to the Australian water-lilies. *Telopea* 13 (1-2):193-217.

Boussenard, L. 1901. Les merveilles de la nature: la *Victoria regia*. *Journal des Voyages* 252 (2nd series):278-280.

Boyd, J. 1929. A history of the Pennsylvania Horticultural Society. Philadelphia: Pennsylvania Horticultural Society.

Bruhns, K. (ed.) (transl. J. Lassell and C. Lassell). 1873. Life of Alexander von Humboldt. London: Longmans, Green, and Co.

Bryne, D. 2008. In search of the dwarf *Victoria*. *Water Garden Journal* 23 (3):11-14.

Burkart, A. 1957. Ojaeda sinóptica sobre la vegetación del Delta del Río Paraná. *Darwiniana* 11 (3):457-561.

Burkart, A., N. S. Troncoso de Burkart, and N. M. Bacigalupo. 1987. Flora Ilustrada de Entre Rios (Argentina). Buenos Aires: Coleccion Cientifica del I.N.T.A.

Burnett, D. G. 2000. Masters of All They Surveyed: Exploration, Geography, and a British El Dorado. Chicago: University of Chicago Press.

Campos, H. de. 1917. Poeira . . . : Segunda Série: 1911-1915. Porto: Emprêsa Literária e Typographica.

Caspary, R. 1855. Über Wärmeentwickelung in den Blüthen der *Victoria regia*, Lindl. *Bonplandia* 3 (13-14):178-199.

Caspary, R. 1865. Bericht über die in den Sitzungen. *Schriften der Königlichen Physicalisch-Ökonomischen Gesellschaft zu Königsberg* 6 (B):11-21.

Chitty, E. 1852. Account of the Cultivation of the *Victoria Regia*, in the Garden of the Hon. Edward Chitty. Kingston, Jamaica: Office of the Colonial Standard and Jamaica Despatch.

Clarke, P. 1855. Notice of the flowering of the *Victoria regia* in the Royal Botanic Garden, Glasgow. *Proceedings of the Botanical Society of Edinburgh* (1855):118-119.

Clifford, P. 2005. The cultivation of *Victoria amazonica* Sowerby in northern latitudes. *Sibbaldia* 3:59-65.

Clute, W. N. 1921. The *Victoria* water lily. *American Botanist* 27 (3):81-86.

Conard, H. S. 1953. Victoria. In: Bailey, L. H. The Standard Cyclopedia of Horticulture. Vol. 2. New York: Macmillian.

Conard, H. S. and H. Hus. 1907. Water-lilies and How to Grow Them. New York: Doubleday, Page and Co.

Console, M.A. 1857. Floraison en plein air de la *Victoria regia*. *Revue Horticole* (1857):602-604.

Cope, C. 1851a. First flowering of the *Victoria regia* in the U.S. *Horticulturist and Journal of Rural Art and Rural Taste* 6:459-463.

Cope, C. 1851b. Letter on the successful cultivation of the *Victoria Regia* in Philadelphia, U. S. A., addressed to Sir W. J. Hooker. *Hooker's Journal of Botany and Kew Garden Miscellany* 3:346-348.

Cope, C. 1851c. *Victoria Regia*. Manuscript. The McLean Library of the Pennsylvania Horticultural Society.

Cotter, H. 2008. Personal history, captured in plastic. *New York Times* (January 11).

Cowgill, U. M. and G. T. Prance. 1989. A comparison of the chemical composition of injured leaves in contrast to uninjured leaves of *Victoria amazonica* (Nymphaeaceae). *Annals of Botany* 64 (6):697-706.

Cowper, W. C. 1913. The lily and the rose. In: Milford, H. S. (ed.). The Complete Poetical Works of William Cowper. London: Oxford University Press.

Crookall, L. 1898. British Guiana or Work and Wanderings Among the Creoles and Coolies, the Africans and Indians of the Wild Country. London: T. Fisher Unwin.

Darby, M. F. 2002. Joseph Paxton's water lily. In: Conan, M. (ed.). 2002. Burgeois and Aristocratic Cultural Encounters in Garden Art, 1550-1850. Washington: Dumbarton Oaks.

Darwin, C. 1945. Charles Darwin and the Voyage of the Beagle (edited with an introduction by Nora Barlow). London: Pilot Press.

Darwin, C. 1876. The Effects of Cross and Self-fertilisation in the Vegetable Kingdom. London: John Murray.

Decker, J. S. 1936. Aspectos Biologicos da Flora Brasileira. São Leopoldo, Rio Grande do Sul: Rotermund.

De Cleene, M. and M. C. Lejeune. 2003. Compendium of Symbolic and Ritual Plants in Europe. Ghent, Belgium: Man and Culture Publishers.

Desmond, R. 2007. The History of the Royal Botanic Gardens Kew. Kew, Surrey: Kew Publishing.

Diagre-Vanderpelen, D. 2008. What shaped the Brussels Botanical Garden (1826-1912)? Botany and its numerous competitors duetting or dueling? *Studies in the History of Gardens and Designed Landscapes* 28 (3-4):400-413.

Díaz-Pérez, V. 1976. Espronceda en al "Revue Hispanique": Misceláneas Paraguayas. Palma de Mallorca.

DiMartino, C. 2005. The lily hunter: The historical and daredevil passion of Ken Landon. *Ponds Magazine* 5 (3):22-31.

Domning, D. P. 1982. Evolution of manatees: A speculative history. *Journal of Paleontology* 56, 3:599-619.

d'Orbigny, A. 1840. Note: sur les especes du genre *Victoria*. *Annales de Sciences Naturelles. Botanique* 13:53-57.

Downing, A. J. 1850. Magnificent water lily. *Horticulturist, and Journal of Rural Art and Rural Taste* 4:429-432.

Downs, A. (ed.). 2004. Peter Shepheard. London: Landscape Design Trust.

Eckardt, T. 1969. Letter of 19 December to Russell J. Seibert. Longwood Gardens Library and Archives.

Elfving, F. 1900. Die *Victoria regia* im botanischen Garten zu Helsingfors. *Gartenflora Deutschlands, Russlands und der Schweiz* (1900):12-13.

Elliott, C. 1996. Water lily fit for a queen. *Horticulture* 74 (1):20-24.

Emerson, G. 1851. Address Delivered Before the Delaware Horticultural Society, at Wilmington on the 24th of September, 1851. Philadelphia: T. K. and P. G. Collins, Printers.

Endress, P. K. and J. A. Doyle. 2009. Reconstructing the ancestral angiosperm flower and its initial specializations. *American Journal of Botany* 96 (1):22-66.

Ervik, F. and J. T. Knudsen. 2003. Water lilies and scarabs: faithful partners for 100 million years? *Biological Journal of the Linnean Society* 80:539-543.

Ettingshausen, C. 1879. Report on phyto-palaeontological investigations of the fossil flora of Sheppey. *Proceedings of the Royal Society of London* 29:388-396.

Fabian, A. and F. Micle. 1962. Din biologia nufărului *Victoria regia*. *Natura, Seria Biologie* 4:79-81.

Findon, B. 1996. Letter of 25 January to Patrick A. Nutt. Longwood Gardens Library and Archives.

Flower, T. B. 1860. The flora of Wiltshire. *Wiltshire Archeological and Natural History Magazine* 6:92-117.

Forsyth, A. 1851. The crimson *Nymphaea* and other water lilies. *Gardeners' Chronicle* 27 (5 July):420.

Fortune, R. 1852. A Journey to the Tea Countries of China; Including Sung-lo and the Bohea Hills; With a Short Notice of the East India Company Tea Plantations in the Himalaya Mountains. London: John Murray.

Frontaura Argandoña, M. 1971. Descubridores y Exploradores de Bolivia. La Paz: Los Amigos del Libro.

Gaerdt, H. 1894. Zur Geschichte des Borsig'schen Gartens in Berlin. *Gartenflora, Zeitschrift für Garten- und Blumenkunde* 43:6-12.

Galvão, F. 1912. Victoria-Regia. Rio de Janeiro: Livraria Schettino.

Gandolfo, M. A., K. C. Nixon, and W. L. Crepet. 2004. Cretaceous flowers of Nymphaeaceae and implications for complex insect entrapment pollination mechanisms in early Angiosperms. *Proceedings of the National Academy of Sciences of the United States of America* 101 (21):8056-8060.

Gawlak, P. 2009. Letter of 15 September 2009 to author. Longwood Gardens Library and Archives.

Gerdts, W. H. 1974. The Great American Nude: A History in Art. New York: Praeger Publishers.

Gessner, F. 1960. Die Blütenöffnung der *Victoria regia* in ihrer Beziehung zum Licht. *Planta* 54:453-465.

Gicklhorn, R. 1961. Streit und Politik um eine Wasserpflanze. *Südamerika* 11 (3):134-136.

Gimbutas, M. 1992. The Goddesses and Gods of Old Europe. Berkeley, California: University of California Press.

Gimbutas, M. 2001. The Living Goddesses. Berkeley, California: University of California Press.

Gladwyn, D. 1992. Leight Park: A 19th Century Pleasure Ground. Midhurst, West Sussex: Middleton Press.

Gicklhorn-Wien, R. 1966. Thaddäus Haenkes Reisen und Arbeiten in Südamerika nach Dokumentarforschungen in Spanischen Archiven. Wiesbaden: Franz Steiner Verlag.

Goodell, L. W. 1893. Aquatic plants and their culture. *Transactions of the Massachusetts Horticultural Society* (1893):144-157

Goodman, D. 1994. Letter of 25 October to Patrick A. Nutt. Longwood Gardens Library and Archives.

Goodman, D. 2008. Conversation of 3 October with author.

Graebener, L. 1891. Von unseren Wasserpflanzen. *Gartenflora Deutschlands, Russlands und der Schweiz* (1891):15-17.

Gray, J. E. 1837. Report of September 7th. *Proceedings of the Botanical Society of London* 1 (1):44-46.

Gray, J. E. 1850a. On the names of the *Victoria* water lily. *Annals and Magazine of Natural History, Including Zoology, Botany, and Geology* 6 (2nd series):146-147.

Gray, J. E. 1850b. On *Victoria regia*. *Annals and Magazine of Natural History, Including Zoology, Botany, and Geology* 6 (2nd series):491-494.

Grosse, W., H. B. Büchel, and H. Tiebel. 1991. Pressurized ventilation in wetland plants. *Aquatic Botany* 39:89-98.

Grove C. 2005. Henry Shaw's Victorian Landscapes: The Missouri Botanical Garden and Tower Grove Park. Amherst and Boston: University of Massachusetts Press.

Gulder, A. 1960-62. Die urnenfelderzeitliche "Frauenkröte" von Maissau in Niederösterreich und ihr geistesgeschichtlicher Hintergrund. *Mitteilungen der Prähistorischen Kommission der Österreichischen Akademie der Wissenschaften* 10:1-162.

Guillemin, M. 1840. Observations sur les genres *Euryale* et *Victoria*. *Annales de Sciences Naturelles* 13:50-52.

Guldmann, H. 1961. Letter of 9 January to Patrick A. Nutt. Longwood Gardens Archives.

Guldmann, H. 1965. Letter of 17 June to Patrick A. Nutt. Longwood Gardens Library and Archives.

Guttenberg, G. 1894. Botanical Guide through the Phipps Conservatories in Pittsburg and Allegheny. Pittsburg: Foster, Dick and Co.

Haage und Schmidt. 1922-23. Seedgrowers and Nurserymen: Trade Seed-Catalogue. Erfurt: Haage und Schmidt.

Haage und Schmidt. 1923. Gärtnerei, Samenbau, Samenhandlung: Haupt-Verzeichnis über Samen und Pflanzen mit Verkaufsbedingungen. Erfurt: Haage und Schmidt.

Hamy, E. T. 1906. Aimé Bonpland, Médecin et Naturaliste Explorateur de l'Amérique du Sud, Sa Vie, Son Oeuvre, Sa Correspondance. Paris: E. Guilmoto.

Harmetz, A. 1998. The Making of the Wizard of Oz. New York: Hyperion.

Heine, H. and D. J. Mabberley. 1986. An Oxford waterlily. *Kew Magazine* 3 (4):167-175.

Helper, H. R. 1867. Nojoque; A Question for a Continent. New York: George W. Carleton and Co.

Henderson, D. M. 1973. Letter of 14 February to Russell J. Seibert. Longwood Gardens Library and Archives.

Henfrey, A. 1852. On the anatomy of the stem of *Victoria regia*. *Philosophical Transactions of the Royal Society of London* 142:289-294.

Henfrey, A. 1859. On the anatomy of *Victoria regia*. – Part II. *Philosophical Transactions of the Royal Society of London* 149:479-492.

Henkel, F., F. Rehnelt, and L. Dittmann. 1907. Das Buch der Nymphaeaceen oder Seerosengewächse. Darmstadt: Friedrich Henkel.

Herkert, D. 2004. Botanisches Kleinod im Wandel der Jahreszeiten. *Wilhelma Magazine* 12 (2):8-10.

Heron-Allen, E. 1917. Presidential address, 1916-17: Alcide d'Orbigny, his life and his work. *Journal of the Royal Microscopical Society* (February):2-105.

Higginson, T. W. 1863. Out-door Papers. Boston: Ticknor and Fields.

Hochstetter, W. 1852. Die *Victoria Regia*: Ihre Geschichte, Natur, Benennung und Cultur. Tübingen: August Ludwig.

Hoffmann, F. 1889. Botanical gardens. *Popular Science Monthly* 35:105-111.

Hooker, W. J. 1847. *Victoria regia*. *Curtis's Botanical Magazine* 73:1-16.

Hooker, W. J. 1851. *Victoria Regia*; or, Illustrations of the Royal Water-lily, in a series of figures chiefly made from specimens flowering at Syon and at Kew by Walter Fitch; with descriptions by Sir. W. J. Hooker. London: Reeve and Benham.

Hornaday, W. T. 1885. Two Years in the Jungle. London: Kegan Paul, Trench and Co.

Hovey, C. M. 1838. Dicotyledonous, polypetalous, plants. *Magazine of Horticulture, Botany, and All Useful Discoveries and Improvements in Rural Affairs* 4:211-214.

Hudson, C. J. 1956. Water lilies in Georgia. *Popular Gardening* 7 (8):10.

Humboldt, A. von. 1804. Letter of 20 May to Zaccheus Collins. Academy of Natural Sciences, Philadelphia.

Humboldt, A. von. 1995. Personal Narrative of a Journey to the Equinoctial Regions of the New Continent. London: Penguin Books.

Huttleston, D. G. 1961. A hybrid *Victoria*. *American Horticultural Magazine* 40 (4):356.

Irvine, F. R. and R. S. Trickett. 1953. Waterlilies as food. *Kew Bulletin* 8:363-370.

James, T. P. 1851a. Pennsylvania Horticultural Society. *Horticulturist and Journal of Rural Art and Rural Taste* 9:438-439.

James, T. P. 1851b. Pennsylvania Hort. Society. *Horticulturist and Journal of Rural Art and Rural Taste* 11:528.

Jennings, T. 2011. Conversation of 8 September with author.

Jerrold, W. 1914. Douglas Jerrold: Dramatist and Wit. London: Hodder and Stoughton.

Johnson, M. W. 2005. *Victoria* waterlily species and hybrid chromosome count analyses to determine genetic background of "impossible" crosses. *Water Garden Journal* 20 (3):5-11.

Johnston, I. M. 1928. The botanical activities of Thomas Bridges. *Contributions from the Gray Herbarium of Harvard University* 81:98-106.

Jost, L. 1911. Das Victoriahaus des botanischen Gartens zu Strassburg. Strassburg: Strassburger Druckerei und Verlagsanstalt.

Junk, W. J. and M. T. F. Piedade. 1997. Plant life in the floodplain with special reference to herbaceous plants. In: Junk, W. J. (ed.). The Central Amazon Floodplain: Ecology of a Pulsing System. Berlin: Springer.

J. Weeks and Co. 1851. The Crystal Palace and the *Victoria regia*. *Illustrated London News* (August 9) (quoted in T. Carter. 1985. The Victorian Garden. Salem, New Hampshire: Salem House).

Kaiser, R. 2006. Meaningful Scents around the World: Olfactory, Chemical, Biological and Cultural Considerations. Zürich: Verlag Helvetica Chimica Acta.

Karr, A. 1853. Lettres Écrites de Mon Jardin. Paris: Michel Lévy Frères.

Kidder, D. P. and J. C. Fletcher. 1857. Brazil and the Brazilians, Portrayed in Historical and Descriptive Sketches. Philadelphia: Childs and Peterson.

Kite, G., T. Reynolds, and G. T. Prance. 1991. Potential pollinator-attracting chemicals from *Victoria* (Nymphaeaceae). *Biochemical Systematics and Ecology* 19 (7):535-539.

Klotzsch, J. F. 1847. Curtis's Botanical Magazine, January 1847. *Botanische Zeitung* 5 (14):244-245.

Klotzsch, J. F. 1852. No title. *Bericht über die zur Bekanntmachung geeigneten Verhandlungen der Königliche Preussische Akademie der Wissenschaften zu Berlin* (September-October):547-549.

Knoch, E. 1897. Untersuchungen über die Morphologie, Biologie und Physiologie der Blüte von *Victoria regia*. Ph.D. Dissertation. Universität Marburg.

Knotts, K. 2004. An adventure in Paradise: New developments in the raising of cultivars of the giant waterlily, *Victoria* Schomb. *Acta Horticulturae* 634:105-109.

Kohlmaier, G. and B. von Sartory. 1986. Houses of Glass. Cambridge, Massachusetts: MIT Press.

Krapovickas, A. 1970. Historia de la botanica en Corrientes. *Boletin de la Sociedad Argentina de Botanica* 11 (Supplement):229-276.

Krapovickas, A. 2008. Bonpland, sesquicentenario de su muerte. *Bonplandia* 17 (1):5-11.

Krieger, W. 1867. Ueber die Cultur der *Victoria regia* ohne Heizeinrichtung. *Gartenflora Deutschlands, Russlands und der Schweiz* (1867):166-167.

Kühnel, J. 1960. Thaddaeus Haenke: Leben und Wirken eines Forschers. Munich: Robert Lerche.

Kunii, H., S. Sunanisari, H. Fukuhara, T. Nakajima, and F. Widjaja. 2006. Leaf expansion rate and life span of floating leaves in *Victoria amazonica* (Poepp.) Sowerby growing in Kebun Raya, Bogor, Indonesia. *Tropics* 15 (4):429-433.

Lack, H. W. (ed.). 2004. *Victoria* and Co. in Berlin. Berlin: Botanisches Museum Berlin-Dahlem.

Lack, H. W. 2009. Alexander von Humboldt and the Botanical Exploration of the Americas. Munich: Prestel.

Lamarck, J.- B. 1778. Flore Françoise: Ou Description Succincte de Toutes les Plantes Qui Croissent Naturellement en France. Paris: H. Agasse.

Lamprecht, I., E. Schmolz, L. Blanco, and C. M. Romero. 2002a. Flower ovens: thermal investigations on heat producing plants. *Thermochimica Acta* 391:107-118.

Lamprecht, I., E. Schmolz, L. Blanco, and C. M. Romero. 2002b. Energy metabolism of the thermogenic tropical water lily, *Victoria cruziana*. *Thermochimica Acta* 394:191-204.

Lamprecht, I., E. Schmolz, S. Hilsberg, and S. Schlegel. 2002c. A tropical water lily with strong thermogenic behaviour – thermometric and thermographic investigations on *Victoria cruziana*. *Thermochimica Acta* 382:199-210.

Lamprecht, I. and E. Schmolz. 2004. Thermal investigation on whole plants and plant tissues. In: D. Lörinczy (ed.), The Nature of Biological Systems as Revealed by Thermal Methods. Dordrecht, the Netherlands: Kluwer Academic Publishers.

Langlet, O. and E. Söderberg. 1927. Über die Chromosomenzahlen einiger Nymphaeaceen. *Acta Horti Bergiani* 9 (4):85-104.

Larrañaga, D. A. 1922-30. Escritos de don Dámaso Antonio Larrañaga. Montevideo: Instituto Histórico y Geográfico.

Lawson, G. 1851. The Royal Water-Lily of South America, and the Water-Lilies of Our Own Land: Their History and Cultivation. Edinburgh: James Hogg.

Le Corbusier. 1937. A tribute: By Le Corbusier. *Architectural Review* 81:72.

Leppard, M. 1978. The Amazonian waterlily. *Garden* 103 (3):121-122.

Les, D. H., E. L. Schneider, and D. J. Padgett. 1997. Water lily relationships revisited: Lessons learned from anatomy, morphology and molecules. *Water Garden Journal* 13 (2-3):21-28.

Les, D. H., E. L. Schneider, D. J. Padgett, P. S. Soltis, D. E. Soltis, and M. Zanis. 1999. Phylogeny, classification and floral evolution of water lilies (Nymphaeaceae; Nymphaeales): A synthesis of non-molecular, rbcL, matK, and 18S rDNA data. *Systematic Botany* 24 (1):28-46.

Liang, L. 2009. Letter of 6 May to author. Longwood Gardens Library and Archives.

Lindley, J. 1838a. Note upon the plant named *Victoria regia*. *Magazine of Natural History* 2 (New Series):105-107.

Lindley, J. 1838b. *Victoria regia*. *Edwards' Botanical Register* 24:9-14.

Lindley, J. 1840. Note upon *Victoria regia*. *Edward's Botanical Register* 26:62-64.

Lindley, J. and J. Paxton. 1850-51. Paxton's Flower Garden. Vol. 1. London: Bradbury and Evans.

Lipman, J. 2003. Frank Lloyd Wright and the Johnson Wax Building. Mineola, New York: Dover Publications.

Lockwood, S. 1885. The *Victoria regia*, historical reminiscences. *Wisconsin State Horticultural Society* 15:143-146 (reprinted after *Canadian Horticulturist*).

Loescher, E. 1852. Die königliche Wasserlilie *Victoria Regia*, ihre Geschichte, ihr Wesen und ihre Kultur. Hamburg: Perthes-Besser & Mauke.

Löhne, C., M. Yoo, T. Borsch, J. Wiersema, V. Wilde, C. D. Bell, W. Barthlott, D. E. Soltis, and P. S. Soltis. 2008. Biogeography of Nymphaeales: extant patterns and historical events. *Taxon* 57 (4):1123-1146.

Lothian, T. R. N. 1960. Note from Botanic Gardens of Adelaide. Longwood Gardens Library and Archives.

Loudon, J. C. 1822. An Encyclopaedia of Gardening. London: Longman, Hurst, Rees, Orme, and Brown.

Lousley, J. E. 1951. "*Victoria regia*" – The Emblem of the Society. *Yearbook Botanical Society of the British Isles* (1951):89-95.

Lovejoy, T. E. 1978. Royal water lilies: truly Amazonian. *Smithsonian* 9 (1):78-83.

Malme, G. O. 1907. Några anteckningar om *Victoria* Lindl., särskildt om *Victoria cruziana* d'Orb. *Acta Horti Bergiani* 4, 5.

Manniche, L. 2006. An Ancient Egyptian Herbal. London: British Museum Press.

Marnier-Lapostolle, J. 1958. Ornamental and uncommon plants for gardens of the Côte D'Azur. *Journal of the Royal Horticultural Society* 83 (8):354-357.

Martinez-Crovetto, R. 1981. Las Plantas Utilizadas en Medicina Popular en al Noroeste de Corrientes (Republica Argentina). Tucuman, Argentina: Fundacion Miguel Lillo.

Maxwell, R. 1985. Letter of 5 February to Patrick A. Nutt. Longwood Gardens Library and Archives.

Meade, R. H. 2001. Depths of water in which *Victoria* grow. Manuscript. Longwood Gardens Library and Archives.

Meade, R. H. 2007. Transcontinental moving and storage: the Orinoco and Amazon rivers transfer the Andes to the Atlantic. In: Gupta, A. (ed), Large Rivers: Geomorphology and Management. Chichester, England: John Wiley and Sons.

Meade, R. H. 2009a. Letter of 25 May to author. Longwood Gardens Library and Archives.

Meade, R. H. 2009b. Letter of 10 June to author. Longwod Gardens Library and Archives.

Meade, R. H. and A. Pierce. 2000. *Victoria amazonica*: Propagation and perenniality. Manuscript. Longwood Gardens Library and Archives.

Meade, R. H., J. M. Rayol, S. C. Da Conceicão, and J. R. G. Natividade. 1991. Backwater effects in the Amazon River basin of Brazil. *Environmental Geology and Water Sciences* 18 (2):105-114.

Meehan, T. 1852. The *Victoria regia* at Mr. Cope's. *Horticulturist, and Journal of Rural Art and Rural Taste* 5:204-206.

Micle, F., A. Fabian, and N. Bodocan. 1969. Noi contributii experimentale la cunoasterea procesului de anteză la *Victoria regia* Lindl. *Studia Universitatis Babes-Bolyai, Series Biologia Fasciculus* 2:57-62.

Miller, L. E. 1918. In the Wilds of South America. New York: Charles Scribner's Sons.

Monteverde, J. 2009. Letter of 25 August to author. Longwood Gardens Library and Archives.

Monteverde, J. 2010. Letter of 23 January to author. Longwood Gardens Library and Archives.

Moore, F. W. 1903. *Victoria regia*. *Gardeners' Chronicle* (October 10):257.

Mori, S. A. 1995. NYBG study tour finds unusual Amazonian water lily. *Field Notes* (Fall-Winter):1.

Morton, T. G. 1897. The history of the Pennsylvania Hospital. Philadelphia: Times Printing House.

M. Thomas and Sons, Auctioneers. 1857. Catalog of Splendid and Rare Green and Hot-House Plants. Philadelphia: T. K. and P. G. Collins.

Müller, G. K. 1998. Eduard Pöppig – sein Leben. In: W. Morawetz and M. Röser (ed.), Eduard Friedrich Poeppig 1798-1868, Gelehrter und Naturforscher in Südamerica. Leipzig: Universität Leipzig.

Munich, A. 1996. Queen Victoria's Secret. New York: Columbia University Press.

Murray, A. M. 1856. Letters from the United States, Cuba and Canada. London: John W. Parker and Son.

Myster, R. W. 2009. Plant communities of western Amazonia. *Botanical Review* 75:271-291.

Naka, L. N., M. Cohn-Haft, A. Whittaker, J. Mazar Barnett, and M. de Fátima Torres. 2007. Avian biogeography of Amazonian flooded forests in the Rio Branco basin, Brazil. *Wilson Journal of Ornithology* 199 (3):439-449.

Nash, H. 1997. In the 'diehard' tradition: Patrick A. Nutt. *Water Gardening* (April):26-35.

Neiff, J. J. 1990. Aspects of primary productivity in the lower Parana and Paraguay riverine system. *Acta Limnologia Brasiliensia* 3:77-113.

Nielsen, D. 2010. *Victoria regia*'s bequest to modern architecture. In: C. A. Brebbia and A. (ed.), Design and Nature V. Southampton: WIT Press.

Nutt, P. A. n.d. *Victoria* Longwood Hybrid. Manuscript. Longwood Gardens Library and Archives.

Nutt, P. A. 1960. Letter of 10 December to George H. Pring. Longwood Gardens Library and Archives.

Nutt, P. A. 1961. Letter of 20 November to George H. Pring. Longwood Gardens Library and Archives.

Nutt, P. A. 1962. The *Victoria* waterlilies. *American Horticultural Magazine* 41, 3:132-138.

Nutt, P. A. 1994. Letter of 18 March to Ghillean T. Prance. Longwood Gardens Library and Archives.

Nutt, P. A. 1994. Letter of 26 September to Juan Jose Neiff. Longwood Gardens Library and Archives.

Nutt, P. A. 1996. *Victoria* . . . The pollination of the great water lily of America. *Pondkeeper* (March):20-23.

Nutt, P. A. 2006. Victorious Story. Manuscript. Longwood Gardens Library and Archives.

Olcott, H. S. 1861. Horticultural show of the American Institute, at Palace Garden. *Transactions of the American Institute of the City of New York* (1860-61):43-62.

Ossenbach, C. 2005. History of orchids in Central America. Part I: From prehispanic times to the independence of the new republics. *Harvard Papers in Botany* 10 (2):183-226.

Otto, E. 1851a. Das Aquarium für die *Victoria regia* und andere Wasserpflanzen im botanischen Garten zu Hamburg. *Neue allgemeine deutsche Garten- und Blumenzeitung* 7:292-293.

Otto, E. 1851b. Die erste Blüthenentwickelung der *Victoria regia* im botanischen Garten zu Hamburg. *Neue allgemeine deutsche Garten- und Blumenzeitung* 7:428-430.

Otto, E. 1851c. Ueber die erhöhte Temperatur in der Blume der *Victoria regia*. *Neue allgemeine deutsche Garten- und Blumenzeitung* 7:488-489.

Otto, E. 1852a. Ueber die erhöhte Temperatur in der Blume der *Victoria regia*. *Hamburger Garten- und Blumenzeitung* 8:459-460.

Otto, E. 1852b. On the increase of temperature in the flowers of *Victoria regia*. *Hooker's Journal of Botany and Kew Garden Miscellany* 4:62-63.

Oudemans, C. A. J. A. 1862. *Victoria regia* (De Koninklijke waterlelie). In: P. Harting, D. Lubach, and W. M. Logeman (ed.), Album der Natuur. Groningen: De Erven C. M. van Bolhuis Hoitsema.

Page, T. J. 1859. La Plata, the Argentine Confederation, and Paraguay. New York: Harper and Brothers.

Pagels, W. and L. B. Weaver. 1999. The search for irupé – the hardy *Victoria* waterlily of Argentina. *Water Garden Journal* 15 (2):10-17.

Parodi, D. 1886. Notas sobre algunas plantas usuales del Paraguay, de Corrientes y de Misiones. Buenos Aires: Pablo E. Coni é Hijos.

Parodi, L. R. 1964. Thaddaeus Peregrinus Haenke a dos siglos de su nacimiento. *Anales de la Academia Nacional de Ciencias Exactas, Físicas y Naturales de Buenos Aires* 17:9-28.

Paton, W. A. 1887. Down the Islands: A Voyage to the Caribbees. New York: Charles Scribner's Sons.

Paxton, J. 1849a. Letter of 2 November to Duke of Devonshire. Devonshire MSS., Chatsworth: 2nd series, 100.8.

Paxton, J. 1849b. Letter of 11 November to William Hooker. Director's Correspondence at Kew, vols. 28-30, pp. 149-51, 168-70.

Paxton, J. 1849c. Letter of 25 November to Sarah Paxton. Devonshire MSS., Chatsworth: Paxton Group, 541.

Paxton, J. 1850. Description of the *Victoria regia* house at Chatsworth. *Gardeners' Chronicle* (August 31):548-549.

Paxton, J. 1850-51. Lecture to the Royal Society of Arts on 13 November 1850. *Transactions of the Royal Society of Arts* 57:1-6.

Pellmyr, O. and L. B. Thien. 1986. Insect reproduction and floral fragrances: Keys to the evolution of the angiosperms? *Taxon* 35 (1):76-85.

Perry, R. 1963. Quest for the royal lily. *Gardeners Chronicle Gardening Illustrated* 154 (13):226-227.

Phillips, S. 1999. Amazon adventure. *Vero Beach* (November-December):82-90.

Planchon, J. E. and L. Van Houtte. 1850-51. La *Victoria Regia*, au point de vue horticole et botanique, avec des observations sur la structure et les affinités des Nymphéacées. Ghent: L. Van Houtte.

Pöppig, E. 1832. Doctor Pöppig's naturhistorische Reiseberichte. *Notizen aus dem Gebiete der Natur- und Heilkunde* 35 (9):129-136.

Pöppig, E. 1836a. Reise in Chile, Peru und auf dem Amazonenstrome, während der Jahre 1827-1832. Leipzig: Friedrich Fleischer.

Pöppig, E. 1836b. Reise in Chile, Peru und auf dem Amazonenstrome, während der Jahre 1827-1832. Von Edward Poeppig (Travels in Chili and Peru, and on the River Amazons, in the years 1827-1832). *Foreign Quarterly Review* 17:1-48.

Potonié, H. 1882. Der Königliche Botanische Garten und das Königliche Botanische Museum in Berlin. Erfurt: Verlag des deutschen Gärtner-Verbandes.

Pott, V. J. and A. Pott. 2000. Plantas aquáticas do Pantanal. Brasilia: Embrapa Comunicação para Transferência de Tecnologia.

Prance, G. T. 1991. Letter of 7 March to Patrick A. Nutt. Longwood Gardens Library and Archives.

Prance, G. T. 2002. Letter of 15 December to Patrick A. Nutt. Longwood Gardens Archives.

Prance, G. T. and J. R. Arias. 1975. A study of the floral biology of *Victoria amazonica* (Poepp.) Sowerby (Nymphaeaceae). *Acta Amazonica* 5 (2):109-139.

Prance, G. T. and A. E. Prance. 1976. The beetle and the waterlily. *Garden Journal* 26, 4:118-121.

Pring, G. H. 1949. Water-lilies. *Missouri Botanical Garden Bulletin* 37 (3):65-88.

Pring, G. H. 1952. Growing *Victoria cruziana* from seeds. *Missouri Botanical Garden Bulletin* 40 (5): 85-89.

Pring, G. H. 1960. Letter of 22 December to Patrick A. Nutt. Longwood Gardens Library and Archives.

Pring, G. H. 1961. Letter of 13 November to Patrick A. Nutt. Longwood Gardens Library and Archives.

Pring, G. H. 1963. Letter of 25 July to Russell J. Seibert. Longwood Gardens Library and Archives.

Procter, A. A. 1861. The *Victoria Regia*: A Volume of Original Contributions in Poetry and Prose. London: Emily Faithfull and Co.

Puchooa, D. and S. S. S. Khoyratty. 2004. Genomic DNA extraction from *Victoria amazonica*. *Plant Molecular Biology Reporter* 22:195a-195j.

Ragonese, A. E. and R. Martinez-Crovetto. 1947. Plantas indigenas de la Argentina con frutos o semillas comestibles. *Revista de Investigaciones Agrícolas* 1 (3):147-216.

Rätsch, C. 1992. The Dictionary of Sacred and Magical Plants. Santa Barbara, California: ABC-CLIO.

Regel, E. 1871. Des Herrn H. Wendland in Herrenhausen Verfahren, von der *Victoria regia* jährlich Samen zu erziehen, nebst Bemerkungen von E. Regel. *Gartenflora Deutschlands, Russlands und der Schweiz* (1871):117-119.

Regel, E. 1885. Neue und empfehlenswerthe Pflanzen: *Victoria regia* Lindl. *Gartenflora Deutschlands, Russlands und der Schweiz* (1885):339-340.

Repún, G. 2005. La Flor del Irupé: Leyenda Guaraní. http://www.folkloretradiciones.com.ar/_literatura/La-flor-del-irupe.pdf. Accessed 24 October 2011.

Ribero, T. 2006a. Expedition to investigate the Central Bolivian original collection site of La Rinconada victories. *Water Gardeners International Online Journal* 1, 1. http://www.victoria-adventure.org/victoria_images/2006_bolivian_cs/page1_wgi.html. Accessed 29 November 2007.

Ribero, T. 2006b. The largest Victoria pads ever recorded! La Rinconada, Santa Cruz, Bolivia. *Water Gardeners International Online Journal* 1, 1. http://www.victoria-adventure.org/victoria_images/2006_bolivian/page1.html. Accessed 29 November 2007.

Ribero, T. 2011. Conversation of 6 April with author.

Ring, M. 1883. Die deutsche Kaiserstadt Berlin und ihre Umgebung. Leipzig: Heinrich Schmidt and Carl Günther.

Rivière, P. 2006. The Guiana Travels of Robert Schomburgk 1835-1844. Vol. 1: Explorations on Behalf of the Royal Geographical Society 1835-1839. London: Hakluyt Society.

Ronse De Craene, L. P. 2010. Floral Diagrams. Cambridge: Cambridge University Press.

Roqué, J. R. and A. B. Romañach. 2006. El Paraguay en 1857. Un Viaje Inédito de Aimé Bonpland. Asunción: Universidad Nacional de Pilar.

Russell, J. L. 1856. Thursday, December 21, 1854. Evening meeting. *Proceedings of the Essex Institute* 1:81-88.

Sarton, G. 1943. Fifth preface to volume XXXIV: Aimé Bonpland (1773-1858). *Isis* 34 (5):385-399.

Saunders, W. 1853. Maryland horticultural. *Magazine of Horticulture, Botany, and All Useful Discoveries and Improvements in Rural Affairs* 19:512-513.

Scharf, J. T. and T. Westcott. 1884. History of Philadelphia 1609-1884. Philadelphia: L. H. Everts.

Schmid, M. 1997. Ein königliches Haus für eine Seerose. In: Anonymous, Das Victoria-Haus im Botanischen Garten der Universität Basel. Basel: Christoph Merian Verlag.

Schneider, E. L. 1976. The floral anatomy of *Victoria* Schomb. (Nymphaeaceae). *Botanical Journal of the Linnean Society* 72:115-148.

Schneider, E. L., S. C. Tucker, and P. S. Williamson. 2003. Floral development in the Nymphaeales. *International Journal of Plant Sciences* 164 (5, Supplement):S279-S292.

Schneider, E. L., P. S. Williamson, and D. C. Whitenberg. 1990. Hot sex in water lilies. *Water Garden Journal* 6 (4):41-51.

Schomburgk, R. 1873. Papers read before the Philosophical Society and the Chamber of Manufactures. Adelaide: W. C. Cox.

Schomburgk, R. H. 1840. A Description of British Guiana, Geographical and Statistical: Exhibiting Its Resources and Capabilities, Together With the Present and Future Condition and Prospects of the Colony. London: Simpkin, Marshall, and Co.

Schomburgk, R. H. 1865. The discovery of *Victoria regia*. *Magazine of Horticulture, Botany, and All Useful Discoveries and Improvements in Rural Affairs* 31 (1):148-151.

Schulz, A. G. 1963. Plantas y frutos comestibles de la region Chaqueña. *Revista Agronómica Noroeste Argentina* 4 (1):57-83.

Scourse, N. 1983. The Victorians and Their Flowers. Portland, Oregon: Timber Press.

Sculthorpe, C. D. 1967. The Biology of Aquatic Vascular Plants. London: Edward Arnold.

Seaman, W. H. 1892. The *Victoria regia*. *Proceedings of the American Society of Microscopists* 13:163-170.

Seibert, R. J. 1955. Report of Activities in Progress to Board of Trustees; 24 October. Longwood Gardens Library and Archives.

Seibert, R. J. 1956a. Letter of 27 September to Edgar S. Anderson. Longwood Gardens Library and Archives.

Seibert, R. J. 1956b. Memorandum of 2 April to Henry B. du Pont. Longwood Gardens Library and Archives.

Seibert, R. J. 1956c. Memorandum of 31 August to Henry B. du Pont. Longwood Gardens Library and Archives.

Seibert, R. J. 1957a. Letter of 12 April to George H. Pring. Longwood Gardens Library and Archives.

Seibert, R. J. 1957b. Letter of 1 July to George H. Pring. Longwood Gardens Library and Archives.

Seibert, R. J. 1959. Report of Activities in Progress to Board of Trustees; July 1, 1959 to September 30, 1959. Longwood Gardens Library and Archives.

Seibert, R. J. 1969. Letter of 24 December to Theo Eckardt. Longwood Gardens Library and Archives.

Seidel, C. F. 1869. Zur Entwickelungsgeschichte der *Victoria regia* Lindl. Dresden: E. Blochmann & Sohn.

Severianin, I. 1995. Sochinenia v piati tomakh. St. Petersburg: Izdatelstvo Logos.

Seymour, R. 2007. Hot plants: The physiology and behaviour of thermoregulatory flowers. *Comparative Biochemistry and Physiology, Part A, Molecular and Integrative Physiology* 146 (4):S273.

Seymour, R. S. and P. G. D. Matthews. 2006. The role of thermogenesis in the pollination biology of the Amazon waterlily *Victoria amazonica*. *Annals of Botany* 98:1129-1135.

Seymour, R. S. and P. Schultze-Motel. 1997. Heat-producing flowers. *Endeavour* 21 (3):125-129.

Skinner, C. M. 1911. Myths and legends of flowers, trees, fruits, and plants. Philadelphia: J. B. Lippincott.

Skubatz, H., P. S. Williamson, E. L. Schneider, and B. J. D. Meeuse. 1990. Cyanide-insensitive respiration in thermogenic flowers of *Victoria* and *Nelumbo*. *Journal of Experimental Botany* 41 (231):1335-1339.

Skvortzow, B. W. 1925. The Giant Water Lily of the Sungari Lakes. Harbin: Manchuria Research Society. Natural History Section. Miscellaneous Series.

Smith, K. G. E. 1961. The New Architecture of Europe. Cleveland and New York: World Publishing Co.

Sowerby, J. De C. 1850. On the names of the *Victoria* water lily. *Annals and Magazine of Natural History* 6:310.

Spencer, W. 1840-52. Diaries. Devonshire MSS., Chatsworth: The Sixth Duke Diaries, vol. 4, no. 1.150.

Spruce, R. 1908. Notes of a Botanist on the Amazon and Andes. London: Macmillan and Co.

Stafleu, F. A. 1969. Poeppig and Endlicher's Nova Genera. *Taxon* 18:321-323.

Stearn, W. T. 1973. An introduction of K. B. Presl's Reliquiae Haenkeanae (1825-1835). In: K. B. Presl. Reliquiae Haenkeanae. Amsterdam: A. Asher and Co.

Stearn, W. T. (ed.). 1999. John Lindley 1799-1865: Gardener – Botanist and Pioneer Orchidologist. Woodbridge, Suffolk: Antique Collector's Club in association with The Royal Horticultural Society.

Sternberg, H. O. 1975. The Amazon River of Brazil. Wiesbaden: Franz Steiner Verlag.

Storni, J. S. 1944. Hortus Guaranensis Flora. Tucuman: Universidad Nacional de Tucuman.

Stoverock, H. 2001. Der Poppelsdorfer Garten. Ph.D. Dissertation, Rheinische Friedrich-Wilhelms University.

Stransky, I. 1951. Zur Entdeckungsgeschichte der *Victoria regia*. Ph. D. Dissertation, University of Vienna.

Sturtevant, E. D. 1879. The *Victoria regia* and tropical nymphaeas in the open air. *Gardener's Monthly and Horticulturist* 21:140-142.

Sturtevant, E. D. 1883. *Victoria regia* in the open air. *Gardener's Monthly and Horticulturist* 25:66-67.

Sturtevant, E. D. 1895. The *Victoria regia*. *Land of Sunshine, A Southwestern Magazine* 3 (1):27-28.

Sullivan, E. 1852. Rambles and Scrambles in North and South America. London: Richard Bentley.

Takács, S., H. Bottomley, I. Andreller, T. Zaradnik, J. Schwarz, R. Bennett, W. Strong, and G. Gries. 2009. Infrared radiation from hot cones on cool conifers attracts seed-feeding insects. *Proceedings of the Royal Society B* 276:649-655.

Thien, L. B., P. Bernhardt, M. S. Devall, Z.-D. Chen, Y.-B. Luo, J.-H. Fan, L.-C. Yuan, and J. H. Williams. 2009. Pollination biology of basal angiosperms (ANITA grade). *American Journal of Botany* 96, 1:166-182.

Thomson, J. 1854. The Poetical Works of James Thomson. New York: D. Appleton.

Trelease, W. 1896. Seventh annual report of the director. *Missouri Botanical Garden Annual Report* (1896):12-24.

Trespe, G. 1925. Viktorija Regija: Eë Istorija i Kultura. Moscow. Published by author.

Tricker, W. 1897. The Water Garden. New York: A. T. de la Mare.

Tsinger, A. V. 1951. Zanimatelnaya Botanika. Moscow: Sovetskaya Nauka.

Urban, I. 1896. Biographische Skizzen. IV. 5. Eduard Poeppig (1798-1868). *Beiblatt zu den Botanischen Jahrbüchern* 21 (4):1-27.

Valla, J. J. 1976. El cultivo y los usos del irupe (*Victoria cruziana* D'Orb.) (Nympheaceae). *Boletin de la Sociedad Argentina de Botánica* 17 (3-4):315-322.

Valla, J. J. and D. R. Cirino. 1972. Biologia floral del irupé, *Victoria cruziana* D'Orb. (Nymphaeaceae). *Darwiniana* 17:477-500.

Valla, J. J. and M. E. Martin. 1976. La semilla y la plántula del irupé (*Victoria cruziana* D'Orb.) ("Nymphaeaceae"). *Darwiniana* 20 (3-4):391-407.

Vénec-Peyré, M.-T. 2004. Beyond frontiers and time: the scientific and cultural heritage of Alcide d'Orbigny (1802-1857). *Marine Micropaleontology* 50:149-159.

Vidal y Careta, F. 1920. Las producciones naturals de los diversos países. X. Algo mas acerca de la *Victoria regia*. *La Ciudad Lineal* 705:504-506.

Volkova, P. A., P. Trávníček, and C. Brochmann. 2010. Evolutionary dynamics across discontinuous freshwater systems: Rapid expansions and repeated allopolyploid origins in the Palearctic white water-lilies (*Nymphaea*). *Taxon* 59 (2):483-494.

Wagner, J. 1956. Die Königin der Seerosen. Wittenberg Lutherstadt: A. Ziemsen Verlag.

Wallace, A. R. 1889. A Narrative of Travels on the Amazon and Rio Negro, with an Account of the Native Tribes, and Observations on the Climate, Geology, and Natural History of the Amazon Valley. London: Ward, Lock and Co.

Walton, S. 2002. La Mortella: An Italian Garden Paradise. London: New Holland Publishers.

Ward, B. J. 1999. A Contemplation Upon Flowers. Portland, Oregon: Timber Press.

Weale, J. 1854. The Pictorial Handbook of London. London: Henry G. Bohn.

Weidlich, W. H. 1980. The organization of the vascular system in the stems of the Nymphaeaceae, III. *Victoria* and *Euryale*. *American Journal of Botany* 67 (5):790-803.

Weiss, M. 1995. Floral color change: A widespread functional convergence. *American Journal of Botany* 82 (2):167-185.

Whitehead, J. 1903. The Steward's Handbook. Part 1. Hotel Stewarding. Chicago: Jessup Whitehead and Co.

Wilke, J. F. 1891. Die *Victoria regia* im zoologischen Garten zu Rotterdam. *Gartenflora Deutschlands, Russlands und der Schweiz* (1891):339-340.

Witte, H. 1872. De *Victoria regia*. Leiden: Sijthoff.

Wood, J. G. 1877. Nature's Teachings: Human Invention Anticipated by Nature. London: Daldy, Isbister and Co.

INDEX OF PEOPLE AND PLACES

Note: Page numbers in italics indicate figures.

Abkhazia, 230, *231*
Åbom, Johan Fredrik, 360, *360*
Acapulco, 16
Adelaide, *166,* 166–167, 230–231, 317, 361–362, *361, 362,* 386, *386–387*
Africa, 167, 447
Agassiz, Elizabeth Cabot Cary, 440
Agassiz, Louis, 440
Alaska, 16, 19
Albert, Prince, 193, 194
Aleksandr III, Tsar, 156
Allen, John Fisk, 94, 95, *180–181,* 184–186, *185, 200–201,* 265–269, *280,* 281, *286–287,* 290, 306, *312–313,* 434, 443, 449, 450
Amazon, 16, 18–19, 21, 29, 52–53, 55, *61, 62,* 61–65, *65, 67,* 68–69, *69, 92,* 92–93, 105, 126, *127,* 128, *129,* 129–131, 136, 222, 243, 253, 255, *256,* 257, 259, *263, 263,* 289, 304, 306, 308, 316, 322, 329–353, *331*–332, *333, 334–335, 337, 339, 340, 342–343,* 425, 438, 440, *440*
Amazonas, 131
Amazonia, 267, 423
Amsterdam, 159, *159, 224,* 236, 298, 310, 363, 393, *394, 417, 437*
Andersen, Hans Christian, 177, 401
Anderson, Charles, 191–192
Anderson, Edgar S., 203, 213, 253–254, 263, 309, 421
Anderson, William H., 189
Andes, 15, 16, 18–19, 23, 50, 60–62, 126, 330, 332, 335, 343, 353
Anegada, 76
Antuco, 60
Apéré, 52, 343
Aptekarsky Island, 368
Argentina, 21, 32–34, 37, 42, *43,* 48, 53, 60, 126, 161, 187, 258, 263, *268–269, 285,* 290, *297,* 298, 302, *304–305,* 307, 317, 322, 329–330, 346–347, *350, 348–349,* 352, 352–353, *353, 436,* 447–448
Arredondo, Nicolás de, 15
Asunción, 40, 41, *41,* 330, *331,* 344, 346
Atlanta, 189
Auckland, 167
Australia, *166,* 166–167, 230–231, 361, *361,* 386, *386–387*
Austria, 14, 16, 18, 58, 105, 151–152, 352, 383
Avé-Lallemant, Robert, *35,* 42–43
Balat, Alphonse, 364–365, *364–365,* 367
Balfour, John, 343

Balkans, 423, 428
Baltimore, 59, 60, 188
Bangkok, 89
Banks, Joseph, 96
Barbados, 89
Barra, 131. *see also* Manaus
Barra do Quarai, *331,* 350
Bartholdi, Frédéric Auguste, 188–189, *189*
Basel, 96, 226, 261, 369, *370, 371,* 372, *372,* 373
Bates, Henry Walter, *127,* 128, 129, *129,* 131, 329
Bay of Biscay, 45
Bay of Finland, 367
Beamon, Bob, 292
Beauharnais, Eugène de, 32
Becar, Noel J., 169
Beijing, 383
Belém, 67, 254, 269. *see also* Pará
Belfast, 215
Belgium, 97, 143–146, *144, 145,* 155, 306, 309–310, 313–314, *354–355,* 356–358, 362–365, *363, 364–365,* 368, 379, *380, 430–431,* 432, 449–450, *450–451*
Belgrano, Manuel, *297*
Belzoni, Giovanni, 344
Beni, 292, *295,* 330
Benjamin Constant, *331,* 338
Berbice, 77, *78,* 78–82, *79, 80, 83, 87,* 95, 330, 340
Berlin, 43, 104, 146–151, *149,* 224, 261, 300, 314, 316–317, *317,* 319–320, 361, 362, 368–369, *369, 370,* 376, *378–379, 380,* 395
Bíobío, 60
Bogor, 207–208, 291
Bohemia, 12, 25, *25,* 105
Bolivia, *10–11,* 16, 17, *17, 20,* 21, 27, 50, 53, 55, 126, 127, 234, *243,* 257, *257,* 259, 292, *294–295,* 295, 329, 330, 340–341, *342–343,* 343–344, *345,* 346, *347*
Bonn, 146, *147,* 151, *362,* 363, 379, *380,* 419
Bonpland. *see* Santa Ana (Corrientes)
Bonpland, Aimé, 27–43, *28, 29, 30, 34, 35, 37, 38, 40, 41, 42, 43,* 45, 48, 53, 57–59, 86, 91–92, 93, 105, 158, 167, 252, 329, 346–347, *348–349,* 350, 431, 447
Bonpland, Juan, *39*
Bordentown, 186, 222, 254
Borsig, August, 149–150, 224, 362–363
Boston, 186
Botticelli, Sandro, 428, *428*
Bouché, Carl David, 150, 361, 363, 368
Bouché, Julius, *362,* 363
Boughton, E. G., 108, 126

Bourbon Island, 105, *105*
Boussenard, Louis Henri, 287–289, *288*
Braun, Alexander, 149–150
Brazil, 29, 34, 37, 40, 42, 47, 53, 62–64, *66,* 67–68, 73, 76, 78, *84,* 86, 125, 126, 128, 131, 136, 186, 217, 241, 254, 256–258, *263,* 269, 290, 317, 322, *327,* 330, 332, 338–340, *339,* 344, 346, *346,* 350, 396, 411, *410–411,* 413, 440, 447
Breslau (Wrocław), 151, 167
Brest, 47
Bridges, Thomas, *10–11, 99,* 107–108, 118–119, *126,* 126–128, 140, *257,* 259, 266, 271, 330, 338, 343–344, 448–449
British Empire. *see* Great Britain; *specific countries*
British Guiana. *see* Guiana
British Isles. *see* Great Britain
British Virgin Islands. *see* Virgin Islands
Bromfield, Louis, 204–205
Brongniart, Adolphe-Théodore, 53–54, *55,* 252
Brooklyn, 169, 184, *184,* 223
Brookshire, 317
Brunnsviken, 367
Brussels, 144, *145,* 147, 159, 364–365, *364, 368,* 380, *450–451*
Bryne, Donald W., 217, 256, *327*
Buchoz, Pierre-Joseph, 105, *105*
Budapest, 373, *375*
Buenos Aires, 15–16, 18, 21, 32–33, 47, 48, 91, 161, 298, 307, 317, 350, 352, 435
Buist, Robert, *176,* 177
Burkart, Arturo, 352, *353*
Burke, Billie, 406
Bustamante, José de, 15
Cádiz, 15, 23
Caffin, Charles, 427
Calcutta, 160
Calder, Alexander, 398, *398*
California, 16, 19, 23, 118, *119,* 191, 197–198, 381, 393, *394*
Callao, 16, 60–61
Callebaut, Vincent, 392–393
Cameron, Lewis, 79
Campana, Fernando, 396–397
Campana, Humberto, 396–397
Campbell, W. H., 343
Campos, Humberto de, 413
Cannstadt, 147
Cape Horn, 15, 48
Caribbean, 89, 160. *see also specific countries*
Carlos III, King, 14–15
Carlos IV, King, 28
Carpathians, 155
Casiquiare, 29, *84,* 86

Caspary, Robert, 235–236, 300, 314, *316, 317, 317,* 319, 320, 322, 344
Cassapi, 61
Cattley, William, 97
Cauper, Bernardino, 63
Cavendish, Edward, *122*
Cavendish, William Spencer, 97, 109, *109*
Cavendish family, 122, *123*
Ceylon (Sri Lanka), 160, 162
Chaco, 447
Chapare, 18–19
Charleston, 350
Chatsworth, 40, 109–117, *112–113, 114, 115, 117,* 121–123, *122, 123,* 131, *134,* 135, 139–140, *140,* 143, 145, 169–172, 176, 181, 192–193, 233, *234,* 236, 241, 266, 267, 302, 355–358, *358,* 360, *361,* 362, 381, 386, 412, 415–416, 423
Chelsea, 137, 138, *138,* 221
Cherkley Court, 136, *136, 137, 234,* 255, 290
Cheshire, 396–397, *397*
Chicago, 198, *198,* 443
Chihuly, Dale, *399*
Chile, 15, 50, 53, 60, 126, 127
China, 163, 251, 383
Chiswick Gardens, 109, 135, 448
Chitty, Edward, 160, 232–233, 240, 283, 441
Chřibská, 12, *12,* 18, 22, *23,* 25, *25*
Christmas Falls, *78,* 79, *82–83*
Cincinnati, 191, 192
Cirino, Donato Ricardo, 316, 317, 320, 322, 323, 326–327
Cisneros, Baltasar Hidalgo de, 21
Clarke, Peter, 307
Clement XIV, Pope, 12
Clifton, 186, *187,* 187–188, 222, *222,* 223, 256, *417, 428,* 450
Cluj-Napoca, 155, *368,* 374, *375*
Cochabamba, *16,* 17, *17,* 18, 21, 22, 23, 57, 126
Cocoa Beach, 191, *191, 233, 233,* 241, 261, *297*
Colares, 67
Collins, Zaccheus, 30
Cologne, 151, *393*
Colombia, 161, 330, *416,* 447
Colorado, 196
Conard, Henry, 206, 271
Congo, 167
Conyers, 189
Cope, Caleb, 9, 169–179, *170–172, 174,* 181–184, 226–227, 229, 281, *281,* 283, 290, 363–364, 426–427, 432, 435, 441, 443
Coral Gables, 191, 401, *401*
Cordier, Louis, 46
Corentyne, 78, 79, 82
Cornwall, 140
Corrientes, 32–34, 37–40, 42, 48, *49,* 50, 52–55, 92, 101, 187, *304–305,* 330, 346–350, *348–349,* 447

Corumbá, 257, *257,* 258, 259, 344, 346
Côte d'Azur, 230, *230*
Cotter, Holland, 396
Cowper, William, 412
Cuba, 59, 60
Cuchero, 61
Cumuná, 27
Cuvier, Georges, 46
Dahlem, *149,* 150, *150,* 261, 317, 319, 369, 376, *378–379, 379, 380*
Dalkeith, 109, 135
Dalton, Joseph, 133
Danish Virgin Islands. *see* Virgin Islands
Darby, Margaret Flanders, 452–453
Darmstadt, 224
Darwin, Charles, 30, 46, 236
Daubeny, Charles Giles Bridle, 139
Děčín, 25, *25. see also* Tetschen
de la Coste, Marguerite-Olive, 27
Delaware, 175, 283
Delaware (river), 30, 171, 186
Delessert, Benjamin, 98
Demerara, 77, 266, 434
Denver, 196
Depp, Johnny, 406
Desfontaines, René Louiche, 27–28, 47
Diamante, 347
Díaz-Pérez, Viriato, 243, 244
Disenchantment Bay. *see* Puerto del Desengano
Ditton, Thames, 437
Dixon, Abraham, 136, *136, 137,* 255
Dominican Republic, 89
d'Orbigny, Alcide, 19, 21, 34, 38, 42, 45–55, *47, 54,* 93, 98, 100–101, 104–105, 254, 329, *342–343, 343,* 347, 431, 448
d'Orbigny, Charles, 45–46
Downing, Andrew Jackson, 169, 170, 173, 226, 301, 432
Drake, Sarah Anne, 97
Dresden, 151, *237,* 290, 298, 363, *419*
Dublin, 139, 207, 215
Duddy, Steve, 386
Dundas, James, 182, *182,* 183, 192
du Pont, Henry B., 202, 204
du Pont, Pierre S., 9, 201
Dwight, 229
Edinburgh, 121, 135, 140, 266, 292
Edmier, Keith, 394, *395,* 396
Edward, King, 193
Ega, 63, *63,* 64, 67, 128, 131, 329, 338. *see also* Tefé (town)
Eggert, Georg Peter Hermann, 372
Egypt, 167, 422, *422,* 423, 428, 447
El Cerrito, 34
El Dorado, 77–78, 89, 289
Ellis, John, 170, 171, 283, 301, 434–435
El Recreo, 35, *38, 39,* 43
Emerson, Gouverneur, 176, 177
Encarnación. *see* Itapúa
England. *see* Great Britain
Erfurt, *258,* 259, 261

Esmeralda, *84,* 86
Esnandes, 45, *46*
Esquina, 317, 322, 326–327, *351, 447*
Essequibo, 77, 78, *84,* 86, 108, 126, 340, 343, 437
Ettingshausen, Constantin, 352
Falconer, Hugh, 160
Falkland Islands. *see* Islas Malvinas
Ferdinand I, Tsar, 155
Finland, 158, 367, 374, 407
Fitch, Walter, *11,* 44–45, 74–75, 98–99, 106–107, 124–125, 242–243, 328–329, 410–411, 448, 449
Fitzwilliam, Charles, 97
Flanders, 144
Florence, 428
Florida, 189–191, *190–191,* 217, 233, *233,* 241, 257, 261, 292, *293, 297,* 401, *401*
Forell, Philippe von, 28
Forrest, Edwin, 178
Forsyth, Alexander, 446
Fortes, Moacir (Captain Mo), 440, *440, 441*
Fortune, Robert, 160
Frampton, Kenneth, 390
France, 27, 30, 32, 33–34, 37, 38–39, 40, 45–47, 50, 55, 58, 77, 91, 92, 93, 96–98, 101–102, 105, 159, 230, *230,* 289, *363, 373,* 373–374, 448
Francia, José Gaspar de, 33, 34
Francis II, Emperor, 18
Frankford, 170–171
Frankfurt, *384*
Franz Joseph, Emperor, 152
French Guiana. *see* Guiana
Freyburg, 75
Füvészkert, 373, *375*
Gabekost, Christian, 156–157
Gainesville, 189–191, *190,* 217, 292–293
Gaito, Constantino, 404
Galvão, Francisco, 412, 413
Galveston, 199
Garcia, Francisco, 404, *405*
Garland, Judy, 406, *406*
Gentbrugge, 143, 144, *354–355,* 357, 358, 362, *363*
George III, King, 96
Georgetown, 77, 86, 108, 161–162, *162,* 206, 266, 434, 436–438
Georgia, 189
Germany, 58–60, 69, 75–76, 89, 96, 105, 144–151, *148–149, 152–153,* 156, 166, 224, 234–237, *237,* 251, 257–261, 298, 300, 314, 316–317, *317,* 319–320, 361–363, *362,* 368–369, *369–374, 372–373,* 376–377, *378–380, 379–381, 383–384, 393, 395, 419–420,* 435, 450
Ghent, 143, 145, 306, 309, 310, 313, 314, *430–431*
Gilliam, Terry, 404
Gippius, Karl, 157, 226
Glasgow, 139, 307, 358

INDEX OF PEOPLE AND PLACES 463

Glasnevin, 139, 207–208, 277
Goodell, Lafayette W., 226, 229
Goodman, Don, 217–218, 292
Gore, Robert, 32, 37, 39, 41, 92, 447
Gould, Jay, 198
Gould, John, *388–389*
Gowen, James Robert, 97
Gray, John Edward, 101, *101,* 102, 104, *125*
Graz, 352, 383, *385*
Great Britain, 9, 39, 40, 76–78, 82–86, 89, 93–94, 96–97, 101, 102, 104–105, 108–109, 115, 118–119, 122, *123,* 125–127, 131, *134,* 136–137, 139–141, 143, 145, 160, 169, 173, 193–194, 204–206, 266, 281, 290–292, 355, *361,* 362, 363, 394, *396–397,* 397, 401–402, 411, 421, 423, 432, 443, 448–449, 452–453
Greensburg, 169
Grimma, 57, 58
Guaiquiraró, 347, *351*
Guam, 16
Guaporé, 344
Guiana, 54, 76–82, *77, 82–84,* 86, *87–88,* 89, 94–95, 107–108, 125–126, 128, 131, 140, 161–162, *162,* 166, 206, 234, 254, 267, 290, 302, 317, *319,* 322, *328–329,* 329, *331,* 332, 340, 362, 434, 436–438, 441, 448, 450, 453. *see also* Guyana
Guillemin, Jean Baptiste Antoine, 100
Gulder, Alois, 423
Guldmann, Hans, 199, 238
Gurney, James, *193,* 193–194, 196, 204, 421, *452*
Guyana, 40, 263, 290, 317, *319,* 322, *331,* 340, 434, *438*
Haenke, Thaddaeus, *12,* 12–25, *13, 14, 16, 17, 20, 22, 23–25,* 27–28, 30, 50, 52–53, 57–59, 91–92, 95, 105, 126, 329, *342–343,* 343, 431, 453
Halle, *372,* 373
Hamburg, 59, 100, 145–147, 149–152, 314, 316, 361
Hampshire, 136
Hampstead Norris, 290
Hanover, 145, 151, 238
Hartweg, Karl Theodore, 97
Havana, 59
Havant, 135–136
Helper, Hinton Rowan, 435
Helsinki, 158, *158,* 374, *376–377,* 407
Hendon, 204
Henfrey, Arthur, 270–271
Herrenhausen, 145, 146, 147, 238
Higginson, Thomas Wentworth, 425, 426, 427, 428
Hirt, Stephen, 393, *394*

Hochstetter, Wilhelm, 146, 147, 226, *448,* 450
Hodge, Walter H., 205, 207
Hollywood, 197–198
Holmes, Oliver Wendell, 425–426
Holmesburg, 170–171, 178, *179*
Hoo Ah Kay, 162, *163*
Hooker, Joseph Dalton, 112, 128, 133
Hooker, William, 101–102, 104–105, 107–110, 118–119, 126–127, 130–131, 133–134, 140, 160, 172, *172,* 175, 181–182, 186, 241, 254, 310–311, *328–329,* 330, 338, 344, 411, 432, 435, 448–449
Hopkins, Mark, 197
Hovey, Charles Mason, 181, 185
Huallaga, 16, *61,* 62
Huánuco, 61
Humboldt, Alexander von, 27–31, *29–30,* 30, 34, 38, 41, 43, 46, 47, 57, 59, 71, 73, 86, 425
Hungary, 58, 152, 373, *375*
Huttleson, Donald G., 213
Hyde Park, 115–116, *116–117,* 117
Ilha Grande, 130
Illinois, 198, *198,* 443
India, 160, *160,* 162, 251, 423, 428, 447
Indiana, 192, *192*
Indonesia, 291, 298
Iquitos, 63, 332, 338
Ireland, 97, 207, 277
Iribicuá, 48
Ischia, 385, *386,* 402, *402–403,* 404, *404*
Islas Malvinas, 15
Isle of Sheppey, 352
Isle of Wight, 133
Itacoatiara, 338, 339
Italy, 160, *229,* 230, 385, *386,* 391, *391,* 402, *402–403,* 404, *404*
Itapúa, 34
Itatí, 48
Iveson, 133, 134, 135, 355
Izera (mountains), 11. *see also* Krkonoše
Izera (river), 11, 12, *13*
Jackson, John Wayne, 393, 394
Jacquin, Nicolaus Joseph von, 13, 15
Jamaica, 160, 161, *161,* 232–233, 240, 283, 441
Japan, 163, 164, *164,* 251
Japurá, 338
Jardine, William, 102
Jefferson, Thomas, 30
Jena, 381
Jerrold, Douglas, 412
Jibou, 385, *385*
Johnson, Matthew, 262
Joseph II, Emperor, 14, 18
Joséphine, Empress, 31–32
Josst, Franz, 151
Juanjuí, 62
Jussieu, Antonie Laurent de, 27
Kachoen, *164–165,* 165–166
Kaiser, Roman, 283
Kakegawa City, *164–165,* 165–166
Kaliningrad. *see* Königsberg
Kansas, 196, *196*
Karkonosze. *see* Krkonoše

Karlsruhe, 151
Karr, Alphonse, 100, 158, 159
Kennett Square, *417, 419,* 428–429
Kenya, 167
Kew, 96, 101–102, 107–110, 126–127, 130–131, *132–133,* 135, 136, 139–140, *140–141,* 145, 160, 161, 172, 176–177, 181, 186, 194, 204–206, 208, 215, 232–233, 236, 239, 241, 283, 292, 310, 355, 358, *358,* 361, *361,* 362, *401,* 401–402, 411, 432, 449
Kimball, William S., 198
Kingston, 232–233, 283, 441
Klotzsch, Johan Friedrich, 104, 105, 314, 316–317
Knoch, Eduard, 314, 316, 323, 324
Knotts, Ben, 191, 233, *233,* 241, *296*
Knotts, Kit, 191, 233, *233,* 241, 261, *296*
Koerner, Alfred, 150, 376, 379
Königsberg, 73, 235–236
Korea, 163
Kramer, Hein, 393, *394*
Krkonoše, 12
Künneke, Eduard, 404
Kunze, Gustav, 59
Kyoto, 164
La Condamine, Charles Marie de, 62
La Coruña, 17, 28
La Cueva, Father Luis, 18–19, 21, 50, 52
Ladario, 344
Laeken, 365
Laguna Saladeiro, 350
Laja, 60
Lake City, 256
Lalanne, Claude, 401, *401*
Lamarck, Jean-Baptiste, 313, 314, 319
La Mortella, 160, 385, *386,* 402, *402–403,* 404, *404*
Lamprecht, Ingolf, 317, 319, 320, 323, 324, 325
Landon, Ken, 199
La Paz, 16, 50
La Rinconada, 234, 292, *294–295,* 295
La Rochelle, 27, 45, *46*
Larrañaga, Dámaso Antonio, 91–92
Latvia, 155
Lawson, George, 109, 126, 138, 144, 266, 427, 428, 432, 435, *449,* 450
Leatherhead, 136, 255, 290
Le Corbusier, 123
Lee, William W., 186, 223
Leguan Island, 108, 126
Le Havre, 32
Lehmann, Johann Georg Christian, 314
Leicester, 128
Leiden, *362,* 363, 381, *383*
Leigh, 135–136
Leipzig, 57, 58, *58,* 59–60, 65, 69, 71, 73, *73,* 75, 76, 95, 373, *374,* 448
Leningrad, 368. *see also* St. Petersburg
Leppard, Martin, 269
Leticia, 338, *416*

Liang, Lei, 404, *404*
Liberec, 381, *383*
Lighty, Richard W., 208, 210
Lima, 16, 23
Lincoln, Abraham, 435
Lincoln, D. Waldo, 186
Lindley, John, 54, 55, *90–91, 96,* 96–98, 100, 101, 102, 104, *104,* 105, 107, 118–119, 252
Linnaeus, Carl, 15, 30, 95, 97, 108
Lockwood, Samuel, 309, 310
Loescher, Eduard, 100, *142–143,* 145–146, 147, 149, 152, 280, 314, 450
London, 76, 78, 79, 82, 85, *85,* 86, 95, 96, 97, 100, *101,* 102, 109, 111, 115–119, *116–117, 125,* 126, *135,* 137–139, *138,* 164, 193, 204, 309, 355–356, 358, *358,* 394, 397, 404, 411, *411,* 423, 427, 443, 444, 448, 453
Longwood, 6, 7, 9, 196, 201–219, *202–203, 207–212, 214, 215, 216, 217, 219, 223, 235,* 239, 241, 261, *261, 262, 266,* 292, *292, 317,* 319–320, *319–320, 327,* 393, *438, 444–445*
Longworth, Nicholas, 191, 192, 198–199, 226
Los Angeles, 197–198
Loudon, John Claudius, 97, 356, *356,* 357
Louisiana, 198–199
Lucas, 204–205
Luco, 129, 131
Lyon, 159, *363, 372, 373,* 374
Maconochie, Alexander, 76
Madeira, 332, 338, 340, 343
Madison, James, 30
Madre de Dios, 343
Madrid, 14, 21, 22, 25, 28, 91, 160
Malaspina, Alessandro, 14–15, 16–17, 22, 25, 28, 92
Malmaison, 31, 32
Malme, Gustav O., 256, *257,* 257–259, 344, *346*
Mamiraú Reserve, *68–69,* 335
Mamoré, *16,* 18, 19, *19,* 21, *21,* 23, 25, 30, 50, 52, 54, 126, 330, 340, *342–343,* 343
Manaus, 131, 217, *256, 262,* 322, 332, 337–339, *339, 411,* 440. *see also* Barra
Manchuria, 251
Manhattan, 184. *see also* New York
Marañon, 16, 62, *62,* 63, 70, 330, 332
Marburg, 314
Marini, Basilio, 447
Marnier-Lapostolle, Julien, 230
Marnock, 270–271
Martin, Maria Elena, 298, 300, 302, 307
Martinsville, 192, *192*
Maryland, 188
Massachusetts, 95, 184–186, *186,* 187, 223, 229, 265, *280,* 435, 443
Matanzas, 59
Mathura, 423

Mato Grosso, 257, 258, 259, 344
Matthews, Albert, 189, 323
Matthews, Philip, 317
Mauritius, 167
Maxwell, R., 215
McClure, George E., *194*
McConnellsburg, 59–60
McNab, Gilbert, 160, 161
McNab, James, 161
Meade, Robert H., 196, 332, 337, 338
Meehan, Thomas, *175,* 177, 182, 204, 282, 432, 434–435, 453
Meise, *364–365,* 365, 373, 379, *380*
Mendoza, 60
Messam, Steve, *396–397,* 397
Mexico, 16
Mikan, Joseph Gottfied, 12
Miller, Leo Edward, 161–162
Milles, Carl, 398, *399*
Mimiraúa Reserve, *66–67*
Minnesota, 198, *199, 417*
Mirbel, Charles-François Brisseau de, 38–39, 40
Mirbel, M., 37, 41
Mirime. *see* Miriñai
Miriñai, 39, 350, *353*
Misiones, 32, 33, *33,* 34
Mississippi, 198–199
Missouri, 192, *193, 194,* 194–196, *195,* 201, 203, 204, 205–206, 218, *227,* 229, 253, 261, 291, 297, 311, 383, *384,* 397–398, *398–399, 418–419,* 421, *428, 443,* 452
Mohl, Hugo von, 146
Monet, Claude, 411
Monte Alegre, 128, 129, 130, 329, 340
Montevideo, 15, 16, 37, 41, 47, 48, 91
Moore, Frederick W., 277
Moore, Merle M., 196
Mori, Scott A., 256
Morris, William, 118
Moscow, 156–158, *156, 157,* 226, *232, 417, 428, 432*
Moxos, 18, *19,* 22, 50, 52, 55, 126, 259, 261, 263, *342–343,* 343, 344
Muir, John, 118
Munich, 96, 379
Munich, Adrienne, 105
Münster, 376, *380*
Naples, 191, *191*
Napoleon I, Emperor, 17, 18, 31, 77
Napoleon III, Emperor, 139, 193, 194
Nash, Scotto C., *187, 222,* 222–223, 450
Nashville, 198
Naumberg, 76
Née, Louis, 14
Nervi, Pier Luigi, 391, *391,* 392
Netherlands, 159, *159,* 251, 362, *362,* 363, *363,* 381, *417*
Neva, 368
New Amsterdam, 79, 82
New Granada, 28, *30*

New Jersey, 171, 186–188, 187, *188,* 197, 206, *222,* 222–223, 229, 243–244, *245,* 254, *251, 255, 256, 417, 428,* 450
New Orleans, 198–199
New Spain, 28
New York, 118, 161, *162,* 182–184, *184, 185, 197,* 198, 223, *234,* 317
New Zealand, 16, 167, *167*
Nicaragua, 127–128
Nielsen, David, 393
Nietner, Eduard, 149
Nigeria, 167
Nile, 422
North, Marianne, 409, *410–411,* 411
Northampton, 186, 223
North Carolina, 435
Northern Ireland, 215. *see also* Great Britain
Northwest Passage, 16
Nutt, Patrick A., *204,* 204–206, *205,* 206, 208–209, 210, 212–213, 215, 217–218, *218,* 238, 239, 241
Nymphenburg, 379
Óbidos, 129, 131, 340, 438
O'Connell, John, 385, 402
Oddos, 373
Ohio (river), 198
Ohio (state), 191, 192, 204–205
Olcott, Henry, 183
Orellana, Francisco de, 62, 425
Orinoco, 29, 30, *30, 84,* 86
Örtendahl, Ivar, Anders, *366–367,* 367
Ortgies, Eduard, 143–144
Osaka, 164, *164*
Osborne House, 133
Oscar II, King, 155, 360, *360*
Otto, Eduard, 314, 316, 322
Oudemans, Corneille, 298–299, 310
Oxford, 139, 358, *358–359, 361*
Padua, 160, *229,* 230
Page, Thomas Jefferson, 347, *348–349, 349,* 438
Pagels, Walter, 290, 291, 298, 302
Palermo, 230
Pampas, 15, 19, 23
Pampayaco, 60, 61, 62
Pantanal, 257, 259, 261, 263, 344, *346,* 447
Pará, 67, 68, 70, 76, *127,* 128, 129, 130, 131, 186, 254. *see also* Belém
Paraguay (country), 33, 34–35, *37,* 38, 40–41, 42, 48, 53, 93, 258, *262,* 330, 344, 346–347, *447,* 448
Paraguay (river), 32, *41,* 92, 234, 253, 257, 298, 329, 344, 346, 347, 438, 440, 447
Paraná River, *31,* 32–34, *33,* 48, 55, 92, 93, 234, 241, 253, 257, 259, 263, *268–269, 285,* 290, 298, 306, 326–327, 329, 330, *330–331,* 344, 346–347, *347, 348–349,* 349–350, *351,* 352–353, *352,* 440, 447
Parintins. *see* Villa Nova

Paris, 27, 28, 31, 33, 37, 38, 41, 46–47, *47,* 48, *53,* 54, *54,* 55, 57, 85, 91, 98, 100, 104, 158, 159, 448
Parodi, Domingo, 93
Paso de los Libres. *see* Restauración
Passaic County, 186
Patagonia, 48
Paton, William Agnew, 434, 435–436, 444
Paxton, Annie, 111, *111,* 415–416, 421, 423, 428
Paxton, Joseph, 40, 97, *108,* 109, *110,* 110–118, *111, 114, 117, 118,* 121–123, *121,* 127, 133, 139, 140, 143, 169, 171, 181, 193, 205, 233, 241, 267, 302, 308, 355–360, *358,* 390–392, 397, 412, 415–416, 421, 428
Paxton, Sarah, 111, *114*
Pearce, George, 121, *123*
Pedro I, King, 64
Peirce, Joshua, 9
Peirce, Samuel, 9
Pellegrini, Carlos, *28, 43*
Pennsylvania, 9, 59–60, 169–179, 191–192, 196, 198, 201, 215, 226–227, 229, 283, 290, 381, *417, 419, 429*
Pensiero, José Francisco, 350
Perry, Roger, 338
Peru, 16, 17, 21, 23, 28, 53, 60–62, 70, 330, 338, 343, 438
Perucho-Verne, 352, *353*
Pfeffer, Wilhelm, 284
Philadelphia, 9, 30, 59–60, 169–172, 174–179, *176, 179,* 181–186, *183,* 188, 192, 198, 223, *223,* 226–227, 229, *281,* 283, 290, 432, 441–443, *442, 443,* 453
Philippines, 16
Pierrefitte-sur-Seine, 55
Piešťany, *154–155,* 155
Pineda, Antonio, 14, 15
Piper, John, 402, *402–403*
Pirara, 125
Pittsburgh, 191, 381
Planchon, Jules, *56–57*
Planchon, Jules Émile, 98, 209, *264–265,* 306–307, 311, 313, 316, *414–415,* 423, *430–431,* 432, *448,* 449, 450
Plauen, 57
Poe, Edgar Allan, 425
Poland, *267*
Pollock, John, 182
Pontremoli, 17
Popp, Wilhelm, 404
Poppelsdorfer, *147, 362,* 363
Pöppig, Christian Gottfried, 57
Pöppig, Eduard, 52–53, 57–73, *58, 71–73,* 75–76, 93, 95, 100, 104, 105, 127, 145, 252, 329, 338, 431, 448
Port-Louis, 167
Portugal, 29
Prague, 11, 12, 16, 25
Prance, Ghillean T., 215, 218, 317

Pring, George H., 194, *194,* 195–196, 199, 201, 203–206, *204, 205,* 208, 212–213, 291, 297
Procter, Adelaide A., 412
Prussia, 73, 150, 379
Puerto del Desengano, 16
Pujol, Juan, 41, 42
Pyrenees, 130
Racine, 390, *390*
Raleigh, Walter, 77, 85
Rand, Edward S., 136, 186, 254, *255*
Regel, Eduard August von, 156, 240
Reiss, Charles, 79, 82
Repton, Humphry, 397
Restauración, 37, *42,* 43, 350
Rhine, 58, 144–145
Riachuelo, *31,* 33, *33, 35, 347, 348–349,* 349
Ribero, Tonchi, 292, 295, *295*
Richmond, 75
Riesengebirge. *see* Krkonoše
Riga, 155
Rio Arapiuns, 339
Rio Arrapixuna, 340
Rio Branco, *84,* 86, 256, *256,* 257, 262–263, 339, 340, *340*
Rio de Janeiro, 47, 241
Río de la Plata, 15, 47, 350
Río de Madeiras, 52
Rio Grande do Sul, 37
Río Magdalena, 161
Rio Negro, 29, 62, *84,* 86, 131, 256, *256,* 330, 332, 338, 339, 340
Rio Pardo, 37, 40
Rio Trombétes, 340
Rivadavia, Bernardino, 32
Riverton, *188,* 229
Rochester, 198
Rockies, 191
Rodie, Hugh, 108
Romania, 155, *368, 374, 375,* 385
Römisch, František Zachariás, 11–12, 25
Rosendal, 155, *155,* 360, 360–361, 367
Rosenhöhe, 224
Rothschild, Lionel de, 213
Rotterdam, 159, 237, 257–258, 290, 344, 362
Rupununi, *84,* 86, *87–88,* 89, 290, 291, *319,* 322, 340, *340–341, 438–439*
Ruskin, John, 118
Russell, John Lewis, 185, 435, 436, 452, 453
Russia, 155–158, *157,* 230, *231, 232,* 251, 368, *368,* 373, *417, 428, 432*
Saint-Maurice, 27
Salem, 95, 185, 265, *280,* 290, 435, 443, 450, 453
Salisbury, Richard A., 95, 248
San Angelo, 199
San Antón, 17, 28
San Carlos, 29
San Francisco, 128, 197, 381, 393, *394*
San José, 48, 50, 53
San Rafael, 344
Santa Ana (Corrientes), *35,* 37, 38, 39, 42, 43

Santa Ana (Misiones), 32, 33, *33*
Santa Ana (Moxos), 126, *257,* 343, 344, *344–345,* 346
Santa Bárbara, 344
Santa Cruz, Andrés de, 50, *52,* 54
Santa Cruz de Helicona, 18, 22–23
Santa Cruz de la Sierra, 234, 292, *294–295,* 295, 330
Santa Fé, 33, 350, *351*
Santa Lucia, *285,* 347, *347*
Santa María, 34
Santarém, 67, 128, 129, 130–131, 289, 290, 339, 340
Santa Rosa, 34
Santiago de Chile, 15
São Borja, 34, *34,* 37, 38
São Paulo, 396
Sarton, George, 31
Saxony, 57, 75
Sayreville, 243–244
Scharf, John, 182
Schirmer, Friedrich Gottlob, 57
Schneider, Edward, 323
Schomburgk, Heinrich Wilhelm, 76
Schomburgk, Richard, 86, 89, *90–91,* 125–126, 166–167, 290, 291, 340, *340–341,* 362
Schomburgk, Robert Hermann, 75–89, *76, 78, 80, 81, 82, 83, 84, 85,* 94–95, 97–98, 101–102, 104, 107, 118–119, 125, 130–131, 140, 145, 166–167, 181, 234–235, 252, 267, 290–291, 302, 316, 326, *328–329,* 340, *340–341,* 362, 431, 448–449
Schönbrunn, *152–153,* 155
Schöneberg, 89, 149–150, 300, 314, 361–362, *363,* 368–376, *369, 371,* 376
Schott, Heinrich Wilhelm, 152
Schulze, Friedrich, 150, 368, 369
Schwägrichen, Christian Friedrich, 58
Schwäringen, Christian, 76
Scotland, 135, 139. *see also* Great Britain
Scott, Walter, 450
Scottsdale, 393
Seibert, Russell J., 196, 201, 202, 203, 204, *205,* 206–207, 213, 438
Senebier, Jean, 313
Senna Gastal, Cláudio Vinícius de, 350, *353*
Seume, Johann Gottfied, 58
Severyanin, Igor, 413
Seymour, Roger, 317, 323
Sharp, William, *168–169, 180–181, 200–201, 286–287, 312–313,* 450
Shaw, Henry, 192–193, 194
Sheffield, 192
Shepheard, Peter, *214,* 215, *215, 217*
Siam, 89
Sicily, 159, 160, 230
Sierra Nevada, 118
Silves, 338
Simpkins, John, 186, *186,* 229
Singapore, 162, *163*

Singer, Jonathan, *9, 407,* 408–409, *408–409*
Sitwell, Edith, 402
Slocum, Peter D., 217
Slovakia, *154–155,* 155
Smith, John, 232, 233, 236, 239
Smith, Kidder, *390,* 391, 392
Smith, William R., 188
Smyth, James Carmichael, 78
Solimões, *62,* 68, 330. *see also* Amazon
Sorata, 17
South Africa, 167
South Carolina, 350
Sowerby, James De Carle, *104,* 104–105
Spain, 13, 14–15, 16–17, 18, 21, 22, 28, 91–93, 95, 105, 160
Spree, 362
Springbrook, 170–173, *171, 173,* 174–179, *179,* 184, 363
Spruce, Richard, *127,* 128, 129–131, *130,* 267, 289, 290, 302, 329, 339, 340
Sri Lanka. *see* Ceylon
Staunton, George Thomas, 135–136, 140
Stearn, William T., 96–97
Steed, Maggie, 404
St. John, 76
St. Louis, 192–196, *193–195,* 199, 201, 205–206, 229, 261, 297, *311,* 383, *384, 397–398, 398–399, 418–419,* 421, *428,* 443, *443,* 452
Stockholm, 155, *155,* 257, 258, 261, 344, *360, 366–367,* 367, *368,* 373
Stóg Izerski, 11
Storni, Julio S., 93
St. Paul, 198, *199, 417*
St. Petersburg, 155, 156, 240, 367, 368, *368,* 373
Strasbourg. *see* Strassburg
Strassburg, 151, 372, *372,* 373, *373*
St. Thomas, 75, 76
Stuart, George, 178, 179, 183, 184
Sturtevant, Edmund D., 186–187, 188, 197–198, 222, 229, 254, 255, 301
Stuttgart, 146, 147, *148–149,* 224, *225,* 234
Styler, Nancy, 196
Sukhumi, 230, *231*
Sullivan, Edward, 437, 438, 441
Sully, Thomas, *94, 170, 426,* 426–427
Surinam, 78, 86
Susquehanna, 59
Sweden, 155, *155,* 257–261, 344, *360,* 360–361, *366–367,* 367, *368,* 373
Switzerland, 58, 226, *372*
Sydenham, 117, 118, *120,* 121, 123, 443, 444
Syon House, 109, *124–125,* 133, *134,* 135, *135,* 145, 176, *234,* 355, 356, 432, 449
Tabatinga, 338
Tacutu, *84, 86,* 340
Talcahuano, 60
Tapajós, 128, 130, 332, 339, 340
Tapiruari, 130–131, 340
Tarapacá, 21
Tarata, 23, *24–25*
Tarrytown, *197,* 198
Tatton, *396,* 397
Tatton Mere, 397
Taut, Bruno, 393, *393*
Tefé (town), *63,* 64, *67,* 128, 329, *335, 336,* 338. *see also* Ega
Tefé River, 63, *63,* 64, 65, 68, *68*
Teixeira, Oswaldo, *410,* 411
Téllez-Girón y Beaufort-Spontin, Mariano, 160
Tennessee, 198
Tête d'Or Park, 159
Tetschen, *151,* 151–152. *see also* Děčín
Texas, 199, 317, 323
Thailand, 89
Thames, 145
Thomaston, 189
Thomson, James, *426, 426*
Thun-Hohensteins, 151
Tijamuchi, 52, *342–343,* 343
Tomocik, Joseph V., 196
Topeka, 196, *196*
Toulon, 28
Trespe, Georgy, *156,* 158
Tricker, William M., *187,* 187–188, 198, 206, 223, 227, 231, 239, *255,* 256
Trinidad (island), 161, 343
Trinidad (town), 292
Tropenhaus, 383, *385*
Tsinger, Aleksandr, 156
Tübingen, 146, 147, 149, 151, 226, 284
Tula, 156
Turin, 391, *391*
Turner, Richard, *358, 358,* 360, 361
Tuscany, 17
Tutankhamun, Pharoah, 422, *422*
Tykkä, Salla, 407
Ucayali, *62,* 63, 93, 330
United States, 59–60, 93, 96, 168–179, 180–199, *188, 189,* 221–241, 254–255, 256, 261, 290, 338, 347, 349, *349,* 350, 390, 393, 432, 437, 438, 441, 443, 450. *see also specific states and cities*
Unstrut, 75
Uruguay (country), 41, 53, 350
Uruguay (river), 32, 34, *35,* 37, 43, 352, *353*
Valla, Juan Jose, 298, 300, 302, 307, 316, 317, 320, 322, 323, 326–327, 447, 448
Valparaíso, 15, 50, 60, 67, 126, 127
Van Houtte, Louis, *56–57,* 98, 100, 143–145, *144,* 209, 236, 238–239, *264–265,* 290, 306, 307, 310, 313, 316, *354–355,* 356–358, *357,* 362–363, 372, *414–415,* 423, *430–431,* 432, *448,* 449–450
Venezuela, 78, *84,* 86
Ventenat, Étienne Pierre, 31
Verity, Simon, 385, 402, *402–403*
Vero Beach, 189, *191*
Victoria (town), *268–269,* 290, 350, 352, *352*
Victoria, Empress, 362
Victoria, Queen, 54, *81,* 82–84, 89, *94,* 94–98, 100, 102, *103,* 104–105, 107, 110–111, 117–118, 125, 130, 133, 139–140, 144, 155, 193–194, 265, 362, 412–413, 423, 426–427, 453
Vidal y Careta, Francisco, 243, 389
Vienna, 13, 15, 16, 22
Vieth, William, 79
Villa Bricherasio, 160
Villa Nova, 131
Villa San José, 352, *353*
Villa Taranto, 160
Vilmorin, Philippe-André de, 39, 41
Virginia, 75
Virgin Islands, 75, 76, 95
Vranov, 11, 12
Wallace, Alfred Russel, *127,* 128, 129, 130, 131, 329, 340
Walla Walla, 401
Walsh, Thomas J., 207
Walton, Susana, 402, 404
Walton, William, 385, 402, *402–403*
Washington (state), 401
Washington, D.C., 188–189, *189,* 229, 230, 290–291, 292
Waterloo, 161
Weaver, Lindsay, 290, 291, 298, 302
Weddell, Hugh Algernon, 330, 344
Weeks, J., 119
Weeks, Messrs., 221–222, 224, 226
Wehtje, Jim, *407,* 407–408
Weidlich, Wayne D., 271, 277
Wellington, 118, 167, *167*
Wendland, Heinrich Ludolph, 145–146, 238
Westcott, Thompson, 182
West Indies, 75–76
Westphalia, 376
Whampoa. *see* Hoo Ah Kay
White, Ross, *400,* 401
Willdenow, Carl, 31
Wilhelma, 147, *148–149,* 224, *225,* 234
Wilke, Johann F., 231, 237
William IV, King, 76, 78, 82, 84
Wilmington, 175, 283
Windsor, 111
Wisconsin, 390, *390*
Wisley, 204
Witte, Henrick, 283
Woburn, 109, 135, 193
Wolstenholme, George E., 206
Wood, John George, 116–117, 118
Worcester, 186
Wright, Frank Lloyd, 390, *390,* 391, 392
Württemberg, 146, 147, 224, *224–225*
Xingu, 332
Yacuma, 126, 343, 344
Yakutat Bay, 16
Yarmouth, 186, *186,* 229
Youde, Thomas, 125–126
Yucay, 37
Yurimaguas, 62
Zambia, 167
Zarate, José María, 126
Zurich, 144

LONGWOOD GARDENS

Victoria: The Seductress was developed by Longwood Gardens to fill a gap in literary works dedicated to the subject of this giant lily, *Victoria*. Longwood Gardens was founded in 1906 by Pierre S. du Pont. Today, it encompasses 1,077 acres of display gardens, meadows, fountains, and a 4-acre conservatory.

1001 Longwood Road
Kennett Square, PA 19348
610.388.1000
www.longwoodgardens.org

Copyright © 2013 Longwood Gardens
All rights reserved. No part of this book may be reproduced or transmitted in any form or by any means, electronic or mechanical, including photocopying or recording, or by any information retrieval system, without the written permission of the copyright holder.

Requests for permissions to reproduce any part of this work should be sent to the following email address: marketing@longwoodgardens.org

Library of Congress Control Number: 2012955715
ISBN: 978-1-935442-22-6
Printed in Canada
10 9 8 7 6 5 4 3 2 1

FSC MIX Paper from responsible sources FSC® C016245

BECKON BOOKS

Victoria: The Seductress was produced by Beckon Books. Beckon develops and publishes custom books for leading cultural attractions, corporations, and nonprofit organizations. Beckon Books is an imprint of Southwestern Publishing Group, Inc., 2451 Atrium Way, Nashville, TN 37214. Southwestern Publishing Group, Inc., is a wholly owned subsidiary of Southwestern, Inc., Nashville, Tennessee.

Christopher G. Capen, *President, Beckon Books*
Monika Stout, *Design/Production*
Betsy Holt, *Editor*
Powell Ropp, *Production Manager*

www.beckonbooks.com
877-311-0155